Educating About Social Issues in the 20th and 21st Centuries

Critical Pedagogues and Their Pedagogical Theories
Volume Four

A volume in
Research in Curriculum and Instruction
O. L. Davis, Jr., *Series Editor*

Educating About Social Issues in the 20th and 21st Centuries

Critical Pedagogues and Their Pedagogical Theories
Volume Four

edited by

Samuel Totten
University of Arkansas at Fayetteville

Jon E. Pedersen
University of Nebraska–Lincoln

INFORMATION AGE PUBLISHING, INC.
Charlotte, NC • www.infoagepub.com

Library of Congress Cataloging-in-Publication Data

A CIP record for this book is available from the Library of Congress
http://www.loc.gov

ISBN: 978-1-62396-628-7 (Paperback)
       978-1-62396-629-4 (Hardcover)
       978-1-62396-630-0 (ebook)

Printed in the United States of America

CONTENTS

INTRODUCTION

Samuel Totten

This volume is the fourth, and last, volume in the series entitled *Educating About Social Issues in the 20th and 21st Centuries: An Annotated Bibliography*. Volumes I and Volume 2 focused on (a) the lives and work of notable scholars dedicated to addressing why and how social issues should become an integral component of the public school curriculum, and (b) various topics/approaches vis-à-vis addressing social issues in the classroom. Volume 3 addressed approaches to incorporating social issues into the extant curricula that were not addressed in the first two volumes. This volume, Volume Four, focuses solely on critical pedagogy: both the lives and work of major critical pedagogues and the different strains of critical pedagogy the latter pursued (e.g., critical theory in education, critical feminism in education, critical race theory).

I firmly believe that this series of annotated bibliographies (*Educating About Social Issues in the 20th and 21st Centuries: A Critical Annotated Bibliography, Volume I–IV*) would have been incomplete had we not dedicated a volume to the work of those critical pedagogues who vigorously confront the systemic problems facing our society and schools *and* call into question the status quo, which, more often than not, results in the marginalization and disenfranchisement of entire groups of people. There is, of course, no single definition of critical theory or for that matter a common umbrella under which all critical pedagogues reside. Be that as it may, broadly speaking, critical pedagogues critique the systemic flaws of

Educating About Social Issues in the 20th and 21st Centuries, pages ix–xiii
Copyright © 2014 by Information Age Publishing
All rights of reproduction in any form reserved.

society and the educational system and are committed to changing society through the empowerment and liberation of individuals to act on their own and others' behalf.

I strongly believe that it is imperative that teachers, administrators, school board members, professors of education, and the general public become conversant with the theory and practical realities of critical pedagogy in order to, at least, begin to understand and appreciate what it is, what it pushes against, what it works toward and what it means to live in a society and teach in schools that accept the status quo as a given despite the rash of systemic issues that create marginalized populations and contribute to unconscionable conditions and injustices in our society and schools.

In part, the inclusion of this volume evolved out of my own experiences in both the public schools (as a former English and social studies teacher and principal, and later as a professor who provided inservice to school faculty) and at the university where I served as a professor (the University of Arkansas, Fayetteville) for the past 25 years. More specifically, over that long haul, I continued to discover that large numbers of teachers, school administrators, and university faculty were barely conversant with, let alone steeped in or dedicated to, critical pedagogy. More often than not, I also found that those immersed in critical pedagogy are far and few between and basically, if you will, outliers.[1]

More than a few students and professors have complained (both in my classes and in published articles) about the difficulty of reading and understanding the writings of various critical pedagogues, arguing that "they" are "too dense" and/or laden with jargon. Others have asserted that being unfamiliar with critical pedagogy in the first place put them at a disadvantage in their attempt to understand what an author was talking about in a specific article or chapter in a book.

Anyone who has even a modicum of interest in critical pedagogy knows that criticism has been levied against critical theorists for their lack of impact on changing schools and society (Heilman, 2003), and for their writing being far too heavy on theory and far too light when it comes to addressing practical matters. As a result, many students *and* professors of education are not sure how to "take it."

While I agree that certain critical theorists do, in fact, have a tendency to write jargon-laden sentences that, at times, seem overly dense and not a little convoluted, it is also true that with patience, one can and will adjust over time to such writing and get something of real value from it. At one and the same time, to assert that all critical theorists are prone to writing convoluted-like sentences is simply not true.

Too many, I believe, throw their hands in the air and simply give up before really giving the authors, the theories, and the field, a chance, and thus "write off" critical pedagogy as being "beyond them." My suggestion is that such individuals need to get serious about education and about the injustices in our society and knuckle down and put in some serious effort to overcome their own intellectual laziness.

As far as the complaints that critical pedagogues are not practical enough and generally fail to explain how their theories are applicable to actual school business and classroom instruction, I believe that this is where educators who share the deep concerns of critical pedagogues need to come together and work towards the implementation of generally agreed upon criticism/ideals/ suggestions in an effort to make our society and schools more just places and not ones that are complacent with the status quo. In other words, to complain about something and not attempt to be part of the solution is, again, laziness or a sign of a real lack of care in the first place.

There are also those, of course, who assert that critical educators are "too radical"—too radical in their beliefs, too radical in what they stand for, and too radical in their goals. That, of course, is a judgment call that each and every individual must make for him/herself. At one and the same time, though, I believe it would behoove each and every educator/reader to seriously examine his/her own lived life, his/her own beliefs and why such beliefs are held, whether or not he/she *truly* attempts to understand why people in society are marginalized and/or disenfranchised, *and why most in the world seemingly accept the world as it is and then and merrily go on their way as if all is well with the world*—and, I might add, mindlessly assume that "none of that has anything to do with me or my beliefs and actions as a human being and/or educator."

There is also the problem, at least for some, if not a vast number of, educators (both at the secondary and college levels) that many of their students seem incapable of reading and/or understanding the works of the critical theorists in education. That, alone, it seems, scares many educators away from using such works in the classroom.

To bring a critical focus to the classroom, teachers and professors do not necessarily need to have their students read the work of the critical pedagogues. (This is not to say that there is no merit in doing so or that there are not pieces that would be invaluable for students to read and discuss.) So, for teachers and professors to assert that they have given up on attempting to create, with their students, a critical approach to education due to the difficulty their students have in reading the critical theorists is nothing short of a cop out.

As for those professors of education who wish to teach a course on critical pedagogy but have been leery of doing so in light of the difficulty they may have had when reading certain critical theorists, it is my sense that there are at least a few, if not many, works (articles, chapters, and even books) about each and every one of the critical approaches to education that are highly readable, extremely engaging and highly informative. A requisite task of any conscientious educator is to put in the time and effort to locate those works that are likely to speak to their students and to include them in the curriculum. (Here the annotated bibliographies that accompany each chapter in the volume should come in handy.)

Essentially, this volume in the series constitutes an introduction to both major critical theorists and critical pedagogy. That said, in order to become *thoroughly* conversant with the many theories, issues, concerns, ideas, and controversies addressed in this volume, it is imperative go to the primary sources and read, study and wrestle with the writings of the critical pedagogues themselves.

I strongly encourage all readers (and their students, particularly those in colleges of education) to be resilient and tenacious in their study of the critical theorists and to think deeply about what it means to avoid engaging in a radical critique of education and society (in other words, to remain on a superficial level versus digging down to the roots of the matter).

In closing, I wish to extend a hearty and sincere thank you to all of the contributors to this volume for the hard work they put into writing their chapters and compiling the accompanying annotated bibliographies. Many wrote and revised their essays two, three, and more times, and I greatly appreciate the fact that they hung in there with us (the editors) and persevered throughout the process.

I also wish to offer a special thank you to Gail Russell-Buffalo who, at the last minute, after two earlier attempts by two other authors were found sorely lacking, graciously accepted the challenge of writing the chapter on Henry Giroux. Not only did she do so after already having co-authored another chapter for the book but she put in long hours conducting research and writing in the days, literally, leading up to her wedding!

Jon Pedersen and I also extend a heartfelt thank you to Dr. Ronald Evans of San Diego State University for writing the preface to this volume. We believe that Ron is one of the best and deepest thinkers in the field of education today, and are honored that he accepted our invitation to write the Preface. For the past couple of decades Ron has been a leader of the long and illustrious movement to incorporate social issues into the extant curriculum and in that role he has written intelligently and passionately about the value of critical pedagogy. He has also, over the years, become a valued colleague. Thank you, Ron.

Last but not least, we, Jon Pedersen and I, wish to offer a hearty thank you to all of the contributors to this series. Many of the contributors are among the most noted educators across some three generations dedicated to developing pedagogically sound, effective and highly engaging means for incorporating social issues into the extant curriculum. Indeed, many of the contributors constitute a Who's Who in the field of social issues and education, both past and present.

NOTES

1. Granted, my sample is small but it does range over my interactions with literally thousands of teachers and scores of professors. While it is impossible to generalize from such a small sample, I'd be willing to bet that if a national survey were conducted to attempt to ascertain just how many college of education faculty members are *extremely* conversant with (or *well versed in*) critical pedagogy that the number would be relatively small. Likewise, I believe that if the same survey attempted to ascertain how many faculty members taught a course on critical theory, the number would even be smaller. And, if it queried those taking the survey as to whether one considered him/herself a critical pedagogue, I believe that the number would be the smallest of all. And this is not, obviously, even taking into consideration teachers and administrators in the public schools.

   Anyone who wishes to incorporate critical theory readings into the classroom, and/or is having difficulty doing so, should read the following fascinating and thought-provoking piece by a former high school history teacher: "Adventures in Critical Pedagogy: A Lesson in U.S. History" by Deborah Seltzer-Kelly. *Teacher Education Quarterly*, Winter 2009, 36(1): n.p.

PREFACE

REFLECTIONS ON CRITICAL THEORY IN EDUCATION

Ronald W. Evans

Critical theorists have made important contributions that help us better understand the nature of human society in the modern and postmodern eras. This much-needed volume—*Educating About Social Issues in the 20th and 21st Centuries: Critical Pedagogues and Their Pedagogical Theories. Volume 4* edited by Samuel Totten and Jon E. Pedersen—provides a helpful introduction to numerous key critical theorists in education. Critical theorists in a variety of fields have contributed enlightening frameworks, perspectives, concepts, and analyses that provide key insights without which our knowledge of the current state of our society and its origins through the vagaries of capitalism, militarism, neo-colonialism, racism, sexism, ageism, and other forms of difference would not be so clear or unvarnished. Without critical theory we might not be as aware of the domination of the common people by an elite, of the historic and continuing oppression of persons of color, women, and of those with alternative sexual identities or lifestyles. We might accept the 1950s stereotypical social life portrayed in the sitcom world of "Leave it to Beaver," "Father Knows Best," or a host of more recent entries, as the norm. We might not question the hegemony of dominant interests over economic

Educating About Social Issues in the 20th and 21st Centuries, pages xv–xxi
Copyright © 2014 by Information Age Publishing
All rights of reproduction in any form reserved.

structures and other issues and concerns that matter in determining the context in which we live.

Without critical theorists in education, we might not understand the ways that schools function to reproduce oppression through tracking, the savage inequalities of school funding, and the pigeonholing of student performance via so-called "standards," the textbook regime, and testing machine. We might not understand the ideological implications of pedagogical choices, and that how we teach can liberate or oppress. We might not comprehend the ways that mainstream ideologies are transmitted through our socializing institutions, customs, and culture. We might not fully grasp the fact that we are living in the heart of a vast military and economic empire, and that we too often view other nations through a distorted lens. And, we might be deluded into believing that the wonderful world of consumer and entertainment culture is, for most of us, little more than a temporary palliative to help us escape the harsh realities of human society.

A critical perspective is warranted. The evidence and the literature supporting a critical perspective are well established (Domhoff, 2013). Its contours are broad and deep, rooted in concepts of injustice, exploitation, and oppression. These are not just empty concepts, but are a reflection of the social realities faced by a majority of humans on the planet. Critical theorists have added a conceptual richness to our language that has, sometimes, moved outside the realm of the academy. Empowerment, oppression, marginalization, resistance, hegemony, agency, praxis, and possibility are useful concepts that have seeped into common parlance, to varying degrees. Driven, for some, by utopian visions, by deep dreams of social justice and fair play, or by a general commitment to social melioration, critical theorists have made important contributions to both the rhetoric and realities of our world. As Harold Rugg once wrote, "The world is on fire, and the youth of the world must be equipped to combat the conflagration" (Rugg, 1932, p. 11).

CHALLENGES OR OPPORTUNITIES?

As a project aimed at making our social world more humane and compassionate, critical theorists face several important challenges and constraints. The ongoing struggle among competing interest groups to define and enact the curriculum in U.S. schools means that critical theory is not without opposition. Critical perspectives are frequently challenged as politically biased, Marxist, socialist, or extremist. For example, during the heyday of social reconstructionism, a forerunner of more recent critical theory, school administrators complained about its limited prospects for success, and/or charged that it was a visionary romanticism that "wouldn't work"

(Krug, 1972, pp. 238–239). One superintendent reportedly said that the Teachers College, Columbia University oligarchy "should be put in rear seats and muzzled" (Krug, 1972, p. 251). Over the past century and longer, competing interest groups have struggled over the direction of schools and the content of the curriculum, projecting differing visions of the future and of the core purposes of the American school (Kliebard, 1986; Evans, 2004). Such struggles among competing interest groups reflect the broader ideological struggles among political parties and their supporters over the future of U.S. society and the globe, a reflection of differing beliefs and value orientations. Within this context, the critical project in education faces several difficulties or obstacles that have served to limit its influence and impact. Among these are: conceptual density and perceptions of irrelevance; limited influence in schools due, in part, to the persistence of recitation style teaching; the difficulties inherent in translating critical pedagogy into thoughtful classroom practice; and the inevitable controversies that arise when pedagogy stems from a particular ideological base rooted in critique. In what follows I shall briefly address each of these concerns.

First, critical theory is rooted in the rhetoric and language of the academy and includes many difficult and slippery terms. How many teachers or teacher educators have taken the time and energy needed to understand them? Take for example the terms postmodernism, poststructuralism, deconstructionism, neo-liberalism—each of these concepts can be difficult to understand and most teachers, indeed, most teacher educators, have a limited grasp of them, if they are even familiar with them at all. We have had some work on helping with this—from Joan Wink, Antonia Darder, Bill Bigelow and others at *Rethinking Schools*—but it has probably made only a little difference.

Second, critical theory has had only limited influence on schools and classrooms. Instead, classroom practice is dominated by the persistence of the recitation and the grammar of schooling, which frequently constrains teacher choices and leads to pedantic approaches focused on textbooks, workbooks, test prep, and other low-level approaches. Frank Ryan's 1970's description of students sitting in rows, responding to low-level teacher questions focused on textbook content still rings true (Ryan, 1973; Tyack and Cuban, 1995; Evans, 2011). Also, we must accept the fact that a significant number of teachers will not be ideologically supportive of a critical perspective, or will choose another curricular path.

Moreover, the present climate in educational policy is not particularly supportive of the critical project. The current school reform movement is rooted in corporate values and culture, and is reconstructing schools as training grounds for worker-citizens, with the emphasis on worker productivity. The Business Roundtable, the most active group initiating a business-driven approach to school reform, was created in the early 1970s largely as an answer to a memo from Lewis Powell Jr., then a corporate lawyer and later a Supreme Court justice, in which he called for business to organize and fight for greater control in American politics and institutional life. Powell's 1971 memo, which was entitled "Attack on American Free Enterprise System," outlined a broad approach by which corporate America could organize for greater policy influence, touching a variety of institutions (Powell, 1971; Hacker & Pierson, 2011). The resulting impact on schools has been devastating, and explicitly anti-progressive in orientation. It has, for the most part, led to teaching to the test and policies that reinforce low-level approaches to learning and that restrict the freedom of teachers and students that is necessary for critical inquiry to blossom. In the schools I visit, I observe a focus on recitation, almost without interruption. As I help my children with their homework, I witness nearly continual use of textbook focused worksheets. In recent years, critical pedagogy has lost ground in the struggle over school curricula. It is no coincidence that policy moves favoring corporate influence over education and a host of other institutions parallel a striking rise in the micromanagement of workers to raise productivity (Semuels, 2013), an alarming rise in measures of social isolation (Mohan, 2013; Putnam, 1995), and the burgeoning threat of environmental catastrophe in a society built largely on the foundation of rugged individualism, greed, and ambition.

Third, critical teaching, all of teaching for that matter, is subject to difficult conundrums on questions of theory into practice, centered on the question, "What is the role of a teacher's beliefs in her or his teaching?" Critical pedagogy is especially prone to the danger of the dogmatic teacher clumsily imposing his or her beliefs on unsuspecting or resistant students. How do those of us who are in agreement with critical perspectives introduce our perspectives to others? We are in agreement that students must confront the critical issues and must be challenged with "critical perspectives." But there are certain dangers inherent within this project: (a) the teacher who lectures students, providing only his or her preferred critical interpretation with little time devoted to discussion of alternatives, student beliefs, or competing views; (b) the teacher who raises critical issues, questions, and topics, but then provides a biased set of materials for students to read or view, omitting the rich balance of resources, competing viewpoints, and dissonant primary sources that can inspire deep student inquiry, investigation, and reflection.

For an effective critical dialogue to occur, students and their teachers should confront critical issues within the framework of an open and supportive classroom climate guided by compassion and the unrelenting search for truth, driven by a steely determination to get to the bottom of the matter, to consider evidence, alternatives, value implications, and consequences (Engle & Ochoa, 1988; Evans & Saxe, 1996). This implies putting students on center stage as much as possible, with teacher guidance, and encouraging them to find their own answers to some of the most persistent and troubling questions faced by human societies. There is a fine line that teachers must be careful not to cross, which can lead to students feeling that the teacher is trying to impose her or his perspective on them. With few exceptions, the teacher's point of view should be minimized, or withheld, except, perhaps as an example tracing how the teacher arrived at her or his beliefs. Or, as Michael Harrington once confided, "I tell students what I think, but I bend over backward to include other perspectives" (Personal communication, 1980).

Fourth, controversies spawned by teaching innovations and ideas, especially when rooted in a critical framework, illustrate another constraint on teaching for social justice. Let us consider a few examples. In January, 2012, the Tucson, Arizona school board voted to suspend its Mexican American studies program to avoid losing $14 million in state funds. This was in response to a state law that banned classes primarily designed for a particular ethnic group or that "promote resentment toward a race or class of people." The incident followed a long and highly politicized period of controversy over the program, which corresponded with a move to limit immigrant rights (Cesar, 2012).

The more distant past is littered with controversies spawned by attempts at innovative and critical teaching, such as the early 1940s controversy over the innovative Rugg social science textbooks, leading to the removal of his books from the schools (Rugg, 2007); the 1970s turmoil over MACOS (Man: A Course of Study) and the broad reaction against new wave humanist/progressive school reforms and materials. Among the local controversies of the 1970s, a seedtime for the conservative restoration and accountability reform, were: the textbook war in Kanawha County, West Virginia; the burning of *Values Clarification* materials in Warsaw, Indiana; and, the controversy over MACOS in multiple cities and towns across the nation (Dow, 1991; Evans, 2011). In each case, these controversies garnered national attention and led to reversals for critical teaching. The list could go on. To one degree or another, teaching innovations that were perceived as challenging mainstream values and traditional approaches to teaching stirred opposition and censure. In more than a few cases, teachers were literally put on trial.

WHAT TO DO?

Though the obstacles may seem overwhelming, we have the opportunity to make a difference. Teacher educators can continue to pursue a vision of the teacher as a transformative intellectual and creative designer of curriculum, rather than simply serving as a gatekeeper or, even worse, a script reader. Though increasingly threatened by de-professionalization, our aim should be to help each teacher develop and learn to thoughtfully enact a purposeful pedagogic creed. Many of our brightest and most committed students will pursue a critical approach and implement their own versions of teaching for social justice. We can support robust pedagogical choices for K–12 teachers. Though in many states, it is a struggle to implement any thoughtful or in-depth approach to learning in the current test-driven framework, we can still support teachers in the effort to become thoughtful practitioners who will create an open and supportive classroom environment and facilitate critical thought and consideration of alternative perspectives within a framework of open inquiry.

If we are to make progress, we must maintain eternal vigilance in the fight for academic freedom. Basic intellectual freedom, the freedom for teachers to teach and students to learn, is threatened by the current regime of corporate control of schools, by the lock-step standards, textbook and testing regime, and by privatization. It is threatened by the commodification of curriculum materials, by which student learning is packaged, sanitized, and controlled from above, then imposed on teachers and students. As seen from a distance, current school reform is a case of education for social efficiency taken to a new and dangerous extreme. In this context, for critical perspectives to flourish, academic freedom is a prerequisite.

Despite the dangers and constraints I have discussed, the future offers possibility. We must continue the effort to educate teachers, introducing them to critical pedagogy and its many useful issues-centered variations. This is important work and it can and has made a difference. One teacher who thoughtfully implements a critical, issues-centered perspective in the classroom can touch thousands of lives, and that should be all the motivation we need.

REFERENCES

Cesar, S. (2012). "Tucson Students Confront Loss of Their Chicano Studies Class." Los Angeles Times, January 11, 2012. (Accessed April 10, 2013 at http://articles.latimes.com/2012/jan/11/nation/la-na-ethnic-studies-20120112).

Domhoff, G. W. (2013). "Wealth, Income, and Power." (Accessed April 10, 2013 at http://www2.ucsc.edu/whorulesamerica/power/wealth.html).

Dow, Peter F. (1991). *Schoolhouse Politics: Lessons from the Sputnik Era.* Cambridge, MA: Harvard University Press.

Evans, R. W. (2004). The Social Studies Wars: What Should We Teach the Children? New York, NY: Teachers College Press.

Evans, R. W. (2007). This Happened in America: Harold Rugg and the Censure of Social Studies. Charlotte, NC: Information Age.

Evans, R. W. (2011). *The Tragedy of American School Reform: How Curriculum Politics and Entrenched Dilemmas Have Diverted Us from Democracy.* New York, NY: Palgrave Macmillan.

Evans, R. W. and Saxe, D. W. (1996). *Handbook on Teaching Social Issues.* Washington, DC: National Council for the Social Studies.

Engle, S. H., and Ochoa, A. S. (1988). *Teaching for Democratic Citizenship: Decision-making in the Social Studies.* New York, NY: Teachers College Press.

Hacker, J. S., and Pierson, P. (2011). *Winner-take-all-politics: How Washington Made the Rich Richer and Turned Its Back on the Rest of Us.* New York, NY: Simon and Schuster.

Kliebard, H. M. (1986). *The Struggle for the American Curriculum, 1893–1958.* Boston, MA: Routledge and Keegan Paul.

Krug, E. A. (1972). *The shaping of the American high school, 1920–1941.* Madison: University of Wisconsin Press.

Mohan, G., (2013). "Social Isolation Increases Risk of Early Death, Study Finds." *Los Angeles Times*, March 26, 2013, p. A9.

Powell, L. F. (1971). *Lewis F. Powell to Eugene B. Snydor, "Confidential Memorandum: Attack on American Free Enterprise System." August 23, 1971.* (Accessed April 10, 2013 at http://billmoyers.com/content/the-powell-memo-a-call-to-arms-for-corporations/2/).

Putnam, R. (1995). "Bowling Alone: America's Declining Social Capital." *Journal of Democracy, 6*(1), 65–78.

Rugg, H. O. (1932). "Social Reconstruction through Education." *Progressive Education, 9*(8), 11–18.

Ryan, F. (1973). "Implementing the Hidden Curriculum of the Social Studies." *Social Education 37*(7), 679–680.

Semuels, A. (2013). "How the Relationship Between Employers and Workers Changed." *Los Angeles Times*, April 7, 2013, p. A1.

Tyack, D., & Cuban, L. (1995). *Tinkering toward utopia: A century of public school reform.* Cambridge, MA: Harvard University Press.

CHAPTER 1

CRITICAL THEORY IN EDUCATION

Tabitha Dell'Angelo, Gregory Seaton, and Nathaniel Smith

A theory is critical to the extent that it seeks human emancipation,
to liberate human beings from the circumstances that enslave them.
—*Horkheimer, 1982, p. 244)*

AN INTRODUCTION TO CRITICAL THEORY

What is Critical Theory? The question is difficult to answer definitively, as the field of critical theory includes disparate ideas and theorists, each of which have contributed to an evolving historical dialogue. Perhaps Horkheimer's words, quoted in the epigraph to this chapter, provide the best starting place for understanding critical theory. Certainly all critical theorists are concerned with issues of inequality and oppression, and beyond theorizing oppression, critical theorists struggle toward social change and the creation of a more fair and just world (or what they deem "praxis"). This generality, however, offers only a vague outline of a theoretical body that is historically important, highly varied in implications and methods, and continually evolving. In this chapter, we provide a historical overview and delineate key ideas and approaches that, together, constitute the central elements of critical theory.

CRITICAL THEORY IN HISTORY

The historical beginnings of critical theory can be found in the philosophy of The Frankfurt School. Critical theory emerged as a reaction against the materialism of Hegelian philosophy. Hegel was a brilliant philosopher, who dwelled heavily in theoretical thought. Karl Marx, a foundational theorist in the history of Critical theory, saw an opportunity to make philosophy *work* by making it more practical. To achieve that end, people, societies, and communities needed to both understand and reflect upon their ideals and then act upon them, ultimately creating an ideological, political, and social revolution. Thus, in order to create real change, dialogue, while valuable, could not itself be the end goal. Instead, Marx posited, dialogue must serve as an empowering tool for evaluating, refining, and actuating tangible change.

As indicated in the introduction, the defining aspect of critical theory is that it has social justice through empowerment as a central objective. Stated differently, the goal of critical theory is to identify factors that limit human freedom and then to carry out a plan of action to overcome such factors. Furthermore, this goal is realized through collaboration between all stakeholders (a striking contrast to the notion that academics or other "experts" must be called in to generate solutions for others). For critical theorists, then, dialogue is a valuable initial step, but insufficient for creating real change. Dialogue must lead to action that "...liberates human beings from the circumstances that enslave them." (Horkheimer, 1982, p. 244). The question of how best to achieve that liberation is probably the greatest point of contention within the field. According to Horkheimer (1993), critical theorists themselves contribute to the struggle for emancipation in three main ways: their work is explanatory, practical, and normative (p. 21). Each of these approaches to critical theory supports the realization of change in our current social reality. For oppression to be addressed, it must first be explained and understood. There must also be practical changes instituted that interrupt the process of social reproduction, or the recreation of existing inequalities across time. Finally, the work must be normative—it accepts that we do not need to "prove" that equality and freedom are somehow more "natural" or "pragmatic" ways to configure a society. This last point is perhaps the most philosophically complex. Essentially, it accepts that the endeavor to create a more open society, one in which individuals of all walks have the greatest possibility of achieving self-actualization, is not a goal that needs to be "proven." Thus, arguments that often justify the existence of social inequality based on examples in nature or problematic historical examples can never sway the critical theorist's commitment and certainty that a just and participatory society *is the norm* to which we must compare ourselves.

As the solutions are not simple and the results of one's efforts difficult to fully evaluate, a critical perspective requires constant mindfulness concerning one's practice. In its explanatory mode, critical theory seeks to understand how extant power imbalances are created, reified, and reproduced across time. Through thorough and dialogic examination of power imbalance, critical theorists attempt to identify new practices that promote consciousness and understanding of where and how one is located within a given social system, and ultimately how individuals of various positions in that system might create change. This constant attention and critique of practice has the potential to be the antidote for the problem of reproducing the very structures that are oppressive. Many more educators than not, though, continue to reproduce the very circumstances and results that critical theorists have highlighted as inimical to justice and fairness for all. The work and efforts of Jean Anyon provide a classic case of the latter. Anyon's work (1980) on social class and the hidden curriculum, both of which are inherent in the type of work students are engaged in "contrasting school communities"[1] (p. 1), provide a sobering reminder of how little progress has been made over the years.

The problems tackled by Anyon some 33 years ago still plague our society. Certainly U.S. society is not the same—but oppressive mechanisms are resilient and capable of adaptation, which confirms the critical theorist's commitment to ongoing reevaluation and critique. In the present era, the critical theorist must recognize the importance of the United States' first African-American president as a milestone of racial progress. At the same time, it would be foolhardy to accept, based on this one significant historical event, that the structures of racism and white supremacy have been dismantled, for nothing could be further from the truth.

Critical theorists believe tangible progress is achievable through interdisciplinary collaborative work. Consideration of social reality from multiple theoretical (i.e., historical, psychological, sociological, cultural, and institutional) perspectives, as well as from multiple individual perspectives (i.e., various individual stakeholders occupying different locations in society), provides a strong basis for the development of initiatives to create meaningful change. Additionally, facing a problem from multiple dimensions provides a framework for forecasting criticism and pre-emptively solving problems associated with strategies employed. Habermas (1984), a founding father of critical theory, used his concept of "communicative rationality" as a tool to "cope with the emergence of problems within a context of intersubjectivity" (p. 312). In other words, communication and collaboration as described above can serve to explore and explicate issues related to the problems at hand. Beyond this intellectual discourse, it can, through inter-subjectivity (a concept that stresses that shared thinking and consensus is integral to shaping ideas and relationships) help to counter one dimensional or simplistic approaches vis-à-vis efforts toward bettering social conditions within society and individuals' lives.

White (2004) writes that "two commitments are minimally necessary" to characterize an approach as critical. These include Ricoeur's idea of the "hermeneutics of suspicion" (essentially all understandings should be regarded with suspicion as we make meaning of texts and experiences through the biased lens of prior experience and prior meanings) and that suspicion must constantly call structures of power into question (p. 310).

Two concepts that are integral to Critical Theory and related to the latter are alienation and reification. Alienation refers to the psychological impact of oppression and exploitation suffered as a result of reification (people being treated as and viewing themselves as *things* or commodities). Thus, when in feminist theory, queer theory, or multicultural theory, theorists propose challenges to the ways in which identities are defined, portrayed, categorized, essentialized, they are enacting a form of critical theory.

Returning to the importance of inter-subjectivity, Critical Theory also demands a balance between emic (native cultural participant) and etic (outside observer) perspectives. The relationships that an observer or participant within a situation has a profound impact on the way that situation is assigned meaning. Looking at a social reality from the outside/in has the potential downside of not fully understanding the situation, a point ethnographers have made since the time of Margaret Mead and Bronislaw Malinowski. Indeed, the anthropologists' practice of participant observation and the development of ethnography as a field represent attempts to access the emic perspective in cultures and societies. The emic perspective is not to be mistaken for a superior understanding or "truth," however. Participants who are often fully invested in meaningful ways often have too little distance between themselves and their reality to be critically reflective, and certainly their perspectives are imbued with different but equally problematic biases when evaluating and understanding the world. Therefore, both perspectives at once have the potential to be both problematic *and* valuable. We see this tension in the ways in which qualitative and quantitative research is received.

Quantitative researchers frequently claim that their work is observable, measurable, generalizable and objective and therefore more valid than other methodologies. By focusing on issues such as precision in measurement, statistical significance of sampling, and repeatability of results, quantitative research looks to escape problems of researcher bias and what may be idiosyncratic anecdotal evidence. Critics of quantitative research, on the other hand, question whether this work is too far removed from the realities to capture the nuances that help to explain the nature of the issue. That is, the fine detail of individual experience must be understood as hugely significant to understanding any social phenomena. Some might also argue that the mere notion of objectivity is problematic; it may not in fact offer any superior position over subjectivity, and it may not even be attainable through any method. It is possible that within subjectivity one may glimpse realities that cannot be quantified, and these realities cannot be ignored without compromising one's understanding. By implication, quantitative data is necessarily biased and blind to these matters, incapable of accounting for the meaning of social phenomena. It is worth noting that both quantitative and qualitative research have the same goal—to produce the most effective analyses and discover the most promising solutions to social problems. Likewise, the schism between the two should not be thought of as a 'battle' (though it is often perceived as such), as many mixed methods researchers integrate both approaches effectively. Investigating and interrogating the immense intricacy of social inequality is, therefore, a central pragmatic concern for contemporary critical theorists.

A pragmatic approach to Critical Theory recognizes the complex nature of our society and the reality that determining who is responsible for the unequal distribution of power is not easily accomplished. It is too simplistic to imagine that we might at last identify the "puppet masters" responsible, get rid of them, and end oppression once and for all. Rather, we must accept that we are all located within and influenced by oppressive societies. This kind of pragmatism is found in the work of philosophers like Pierre Bourdieu and Michel Foucault. In the case of Foucault, the focus is on the ways in which discipline, punishment, and observation are used to control thought and behavior. He examines the history and technologies of imprisonment, punishment, and surveillance to understand how oppressive ideologies are inculcated in the oppressed so that they will monitor, control, and ultimately repress their own instinct to rebel and seize control of life and circumstance. This concept is most famously illustrated in his exploration of the "panopticon" prison in his work Discipline and Punish (1975).

In the case of Bordieu, however, his seminal work *Distinction: A Social Critique of the Judgment of Taste* (1984) reveals how cultural capital and habitus, among other aspects of our cultural and economic locations in societies of unequal power and resource distribution, can be clearly understood and mapped—ideally so we might understand and dismantle the less overt but equally powerful barriers to self-actualization. In both cases, these theorists elucidate the ways in which we ourselves are complicit in the reproduction of oppressive structures, often acting as agents in the continuation of problems we seek to resolve.

Extending the relationship between Critical Theory and pragmatism, White (2004) reminds us of John Dewey's contention that a healthy society requires deliberative equality, not just majority rule. Further, White (2004) critiques Dewey's reliance on quantity with regard to deliberation as insufficient. In fact, he argues that

> in cases of conflict in which the processes or structures have helped to constitute the problem situation...his simple recommendation of "more deliberation" is not an adequate response; in fact, it may function so as to mask phenomena about which one should be rightly suspicious. (p. 310)

CRITICAL THEORY AND EDUCATION

In the application of Critical Theory proper, offshoots have been born that seek to shed light on how various aspects of culture function. In that regard, there are various "cross-pollinations" between critical theory and other theoretical arenas. These include education and pedagogy, contemporary feminism, and critical race theory, among others. In this section, we will offer an explanation of some of these areas and how they fit into the larger tradition of Critical Theory more generally. Each of these theories is legitimately linked to Marx's original conception of Critical Theory as they each seek to analyze and create change within various aspects of culture where oppression exists. In terms of Critical Theory in Education, Marx would evaluate the ways in which education, curriculum, and classroom interactions are socially constructed and to what degree these interactions are based on what the participants truly believe is right. Though much of his philosophy is tinged with a kind of determinism, an idea that societal structure can define and limit human thought, a central tenant of Critical Theory is the belief that change is possible, no matter how great the obstacles to that change. As Paulo Freire (1970) spells out in *Pedagogy of the Oppressed*, if the examination of oppression is conducted without hope for change, it is a sterile enterprise, inculcating hopelessness in students, which, in turn, can only further discourage individuals from seeking emancipation and change. In his eyes, the only reason to spend time and energy understanding oppression is so that it can be ultimately dismantled.

Critical theories of education recognize that (a) educational systems are at least complicit in oppression (though many would go farther and state that these systems are the most powerful mechanism for the reproduction of social inequality), and (b) there must be a corresponding plan for emancipatory action through education. The mechanisms of oppression and the opportunities to create change exist simultaneously in two important aspects of education—the nature of curriculum and the pedagogies teachers enact. Thus, teachers must explore their roles and ideologies to avoid perpetuating negative constructions of their students, and they must also struggle against overly proscribed and often misleading curricular content that envisions poor and minority students as deficient while overtly or covertly teaching the lesson that in contemporary society everything is fair and just as it should be. Thus, in education as in other arenas, Critical Theory explores the dialectic between consciousness and self-reflection on the one hand, and the external social reality on the other (Turner, 1986).

Both of these elements, the self and the external social reality, are situated historically, geographically, and culturally. Thus, Critical Theory eschews the notion that there can be a single "fix" for oppression. Instead, Critical Theory provides a way to examine one's situatedness and sense of self in the broader social structure and history, as well as in the local context over which the individual can arguably have the greatest impact. As an illustration, consider the feminist perspective in Critical Theory and education. Including a discussion of Feminism is historically important because it has become an important part of [big C] Critical Theory as well as a [little c] critical theory all on its own. Just as Critical Theory considers oppressive factors and those who are oppressed, feminism interrogates and interrupts the ways in which male oppression has shaped the lived experience of women and men alike. Given that the work force of teachers has long been dominated by females and that the majority of our public and private schools are co-educational settings, the consideration of how gender factors into the young's development is essential. According to the National Center for Educational Information, women represented 84% of public school teachers in 2011. This was an increase from 69% in 1986. Furthermore, the work of Myra and David Sadker (2000) illustrates with quantitative and qualitative data the systematic disenfranchisement and alienation of young women in public education. The distribution of gender within the teaching force, coupled with the unequal educational attainment between men and women, demands consideration if one is to interrogate social reproduction within the educational system. In doing so, we must consider how the nature and mechanisms of male oppression function differently at home, in the community, or in schools. How do these multiple social worlds occupied by teachers and students come together to perpetuate patriarchy? How do essentializing notions about teachers translate into the teacher's own essentializing notions about the male and female students in their classrooms? Further, if Marx's notion of consciousness is correct, then what are the implications for teachers who are critically reflective? This perspective might suggest that teachers engaged in critical reflection and dialogue will understand that they can change their reality, and create mechanisms for doing so. But will they? Perhaps the increasingly centralized curricula and bureaucratization of the work of teaching is an endeavor to prevent teachers from reaching this critical consciousness or enacting pedagogies and curricula that might threaten the status quo. Perhaps teachers will be unwilling or unable to let go of their own notion that student gender largely determines student aptitudes and identities—in which case, can they in any way help students to emancipate themselves from patriarchy? These questions and ideas provide examples of the kinds of concerns stakeholders in schools must collaboratively explore and address if tangible change for the better is to be realized.

CRITICAL THEORY AND PEDAGOGY

Critical theory and pedagogy are a logical pairing when one considers how schools historically, and currently, function to maintain social and political realities that support the oppression of certain groups of people. Looking at education from a critical perspective requires awareness that schools function to reproduce the same power structures and economic conditions that have existed over time, despite our tendency to think of education, as Horace Mann (1940) framed it in the late 19th century, "the great equalizer." In contrast to this idealistic vision of education, Freire describes *banking pedagogy* as the predominant mode of educational instruction, and one that inevitably functions to maintain oppression. He describes the relationship between teachers and students as one in which information is "deposited" into the students. The student receives this information passively and is required to memorize it, so that it might be "withdrawn" on the day of a test. This pedagogy is inevitably oppressive because, regardless of the information taught, it also teaches students that what they know of their worlds is unimportant, that they should accept that there is an unquestionable authority who can hand them "truth," and that this individual/institution not only knows everything, but is rightfully entitled to dictate what is right and wrong in terms of personal conduct and ideology. Freire exposes this hidden curriculum of banking pedagogies, urging us to imagine the relationship between teachers and students differently. In Freire's model, teachers share in knowledge building with their students, valuing their extant knowledge of the world, and sharing with students the power to determine curriculum as well as rules of conduct. In other words—if the school system, school and/or classroom look like a dictatorship, it accustoms students to accepting dictatorial subjugation. If, on the other hand, the school system, school and/or classroom are structured more like a democracy, it teaches students how to participate in their own governance. In schools and classrooms, educators are challenged to use the power that they have to help students be critically reflective, advocates for themselves, and agents of change in their own contexts.

Freire also articulated the concept of *praxis*, the unification of pedagogical theory and practice. All classroom practice reflects a theory of education, whether explicit or not. The critical educator's praxis includes five steps; problem identification, problem analysis, creation of a plan of action to address the problem, implementation of the plan, and analysis and evaluation of the action. This model fits perfectly with the call for teacher research by contemporary scholars (Shor, 1992, Cochrane-Smith & Lytle, 1999), and parallels the fundamental tenets of critical theory described above. When teachers apply the habits of mind of a researcher, they create a cycle of awareness, action, and reflection that defies any kind of "one size fits all" curriculum. Building on Freire's work in this area, Antonia Darder (2004), argues against standardized curricula and in favor of classroom pedagogy that meets students where they are. Darder advocates for considering context in the development of curricula and incorporating the cultural diversity of students into classroom practice. Darder sees love as central to critical pedagogy and the act of designing classroom practice in a critical way is a demonstration of love for one's students and one's practice. Obviously, discussing education in these terms represents a radical departure from the dominant contemporary dialogue concerning education reform in the United States, and that is perhaps reflective of the potential to interrupt the continuation of the inequalities to which the current educational system contributes.

As mentioned above, stretching all the way back to the work of Horace Mann and the origins of public education as an institution, many have argued that education is an entrée to a better life and economic mobility. This is what David Labaree (1999) describes as the "social mobility" goal for education, in which education is seen as a commodity for students, the primary value of which is not to make a better society but to allow the individual student to compete and prosper within society as it stands. However, if one examines historically underperforming schools it is easy to see the statistically consistent correlation between poverty and student success. Some deficit theorists claim that this reality is inevitable because of intellectual inferiority of certain groups (e.g., Blacks and Latinos). This theory became most recently popular in the mid-1990s when Hernstein and Murray published *The Bell Curve: Intelligence and Class Structure in American Life* in 1994. The fact that U.S. school districts suffer greatly from de facto segregation, well documented in the work of Massey and Denton (1993), makes it all too easy for entire communities to be written off as failing and deficient. Putting the burden of failure on the people in a community—alienating them and reifing their status as appropriate—has allowed the public discourse to accept this failure with very little questioning about underlying causes that could be changed. For instance, referring once more to Anyon's (1980) study, we see that there is a strong relationship between socio-economics and the quality of education that a student receives. Anyon finds a system in which students from lower socio-economic backgrounds receive the exact kind of educational experience that Freire denounces, while students with greater means receive an experience more like what Freire advocated. However, the broader conversation about these issues largely ignores the economic disparities that drive failure and success school by school, allowing the myth of meritocracy to continue. The meritocratic ideal, in turn, further reinforces the perception that society is just. More specifically, those adhering to a meritocratic ideal argue, and seeming believe, that if there are whole communities failing to prosper, it must be because they do not merit it. They lack either the talent or the industry to realize success, and thus there is nothing unjust about it.

CRITICAL THEORY AND CURRICULUM

Curriculum is often defined as a set of coherent practices and exercises that are strategically designed to bring about particular educational ends. Mastery of a particular content area (e.g., mathematics or science) is the traditional objective of curriculum.

Curricular design is hugely significant in its impact—it not only declares what facts, perspectives, and skills are important enough to address in the classroom, but also what educational methods and pedagogical designs are the most effective and appropriate for teaching those skills and information. Much of the debate characterizing the multiculturalist movement, from the 1960's through to today, has centered on exactly this issue, and theorists and educators of all political stripes have, in their arguments, indicated that the design and implementation of curriculum is central to achieving educational equity, creating an American national identity, and securing America's place as an economic and military leader of the world. With such high stakes, it is no wonder that, increasingly, the desired outcomes are set by a department of education (state or national) and professional content area organizations (e.g., National Council for Teachers of English), as opposed to individual teachers creating their own curricular designs for their own courses and students.

Since the implementation of the No Child Left Behind (NCLB) Act of 2001, increased emphasis has been placed on curriculum standardization and standardized testing as a means of minimizing national risk—specifically the risk of America losing global economic dominance. Additionally, NCLB was a monumental policy acknowledgement that the nation was indeed "at risk" if it did not provide a quality education for all disadvantaged groups. Ironically, although the rhetoric of NCLB claims to ensure a quality education for disenfranchised groups (economic and racial minorities), the implementation of NCLB has only further alienated the same students and those who teach them from authentic educational experiences.

As education reformers seek to standardize the classroom experiences of youth, teachers and curriculum have become increasingly scripted and mechanized. That is to say, less emphasis has been placed on the professionalism and expertise of teachers while more emphasis has been placed on developing curricula that is "teacher proof" while tying school funding, faculty salaries, and teacher retention to student test scores. Thus, the curriculum is generated outside of the local context, as are the recommended instructional strategies and assessments. This type of alienation is in direct contradiction to Dewey's notion (1943) of naturalistic interest:

> Abandon the notion of the subject matter as something fixed and ready made in itself, outside of the child's experience; cease thinking of the child's experience as also something hard and fast; see it as something fluent, embryonic, vital, and we realize that the child and the curriculum are simply two limits which define the same process. Just as two points define a straight line, so the present standpoint of the child and the facts and truths of the studies define instruction. It is continuous reconstruction, moving from the child's present experience out into that represented by the organized bodies of truth that we call studies. (p. 11)

Accordingly, critical theory, clearly, opposes such top-down standardization of curriculum for a host of reasons. Peter McLaren (2009) unpacks these critiques particularly well in his typology of knowledge, in which he divides knowledge into three types: technical, practical, and emancipatory. Curriculum that takes on a critical orientation would strive to collaboratively create *emancipatory knowledge*—that which "creates the foundation for social justice, equality, and empowerment" (p. 86). As discussed above with regard to the work of Paulo Freire, it would be impossible for a state-generated curriculum, produced far from the actual classroom, to offer emancipatory knowledge to students, for no matter what facts and skills are targeted, it is necessarily grounded in the notion that it is the government, not the students, who determine truth and legitimacy. The current testing and standards' emphasis now reigning in U.S. public education systems have a clear preference for *technical knowledge*. The preference for technical knowledge is demonstrated by the emphasis on only those types of knowledge that can be generated far from the classroom and, in turn, measured quantitatively via standardized test scores.

This conception of curriculum serves to divorce teacher and student from creating their own meanings, understandings, and knowledge. In short, teachers are divorced from their professional autonomy and agency as they must follow the script and "teach to the test." Similarly, students are constrained in how they can explore and understand course content in relation to the material world, as learning is relegated to experiences that do not maximize meaning making or reflection. As noted previously, meaning making and reflection are as fundamental to critical consciousness as critical consciousness is to attaining social justice. A critical theory perspective would argue that the contemporary movement toward standardization brings with it not just a conception of what constitutes the best curriculum, but also an implicit set of goals for education itself—a statement as to why our public education system should exist in the first place.

In the Table 1.1, Sowell (2004) provides a quick starting point for considering the relationship between curriculum and the purpose of education writ large.

Note that with each conception of curriculum is an implied (and usually unspoken) rationale for education itself. For another example of critical examination of the goals for education, consider David Labaree's (1999) work, which articulates three often conflicting goals for education. There are those who, as stated above, believe public education should serve to preserve U.S. dominance in the global economy, and also to facilitate the continuation of the ways in which U.S. society is currently organized. Labaree (1999) calls this the "social efficiency" goal for education, as it allows our society, just or unjust, to efficiently continue without disruption. Then there are those who advocate for the "social mobility" goal for education—wherein education is seen as a consumer good, something that should provide students with the necessary tools for their own personal economic advancement. While this goal might arguably favor the creation of a meritocracy, allowing social mobility for oppressed populations, it is significant to note that it does not encourage any critique or restructuring of society—rather, it is a type of education that merely facilitates the economic advancement of individuals within the existing socioeconomic structure.

TABLE 1.1 Curriculum Conceptions, Purposes of Education, and Content Sources

Curriculum Conception	Purpose of Education	Primary Source of Content
Cumulative tradition of organized knowledge	To cultivate cognitive achievement and the intellect	Academic disciplines, subject matter
Social Relevance Reconstruction	To prepare people for living in an unstable, changing world; to reform society	Needs of society and culture
Self Actualization	To develop individuals to their fullest	Needs and interests of learners
Development of cognitive processes	To develop intellectual processes[a]	Any source, but usually subject matter
Technology	To make learning systematic and efficient[a]	Any source, but usually subject matter

[a] This purpose is a process goal that does not state an educational end.
Source: Sowell (2004)

Finally, there is the "democratic equality" goal for education, which seeks to prepare all citizens for informed, critical participation in a democracy. The last of these three objectives is closest to the heart of critical theory, as it targets the development of critical consciousness in all citizens, so that they might be equipped to participate in their own governance—in other words, to be *empowered*. Labaree's work is an excellent illustration of modern critical theory in curriculum, particularly because it is primarily concerned with spurring the reader to make explicit the hidden agendas of these educational goals and the curricula that serve them, so that we might more carefully evaluate educational initiatives in terms of their potential to create a more just society.

REFLECTIVE PRACTICES AS SOCIAL JUSTICE

Toward Action

As noted previously, critical theory consists of both the critique and emancipatory action, the latter of which demands pragmatic and tangible changes to the existing modus operandi. This section will explore some examples of emancipatory actions that create spaces (social and psychic) for critical consciousness. Critical theory, when applied to public education, critiques the ways in which current educational practices fail both teachers and students by attacking, and even eliminating, such spaces.

Consider, for example, the concept of professional development for teachers. Ongoing professional development is widely regarded as a must for teachers. Be that as it may, the definition of professional development is contentious. A great deal of contemporary professional development parallels the national curriculum, with its emphasis on technical knowledge created by outside experts that teachers are expected to adapt and implement. In contrast, in their work regarding "Inquiry as Stance," Susan Lytle and Marilyn Cochran Smith (2009) argue that teachers' knowledge and skill is best honed by teachers themselves, through collaborative exploration and research. In their work they focus on dissolving the imaginary divide between theory and practice, providing a theoretical framework for empowering teachers to value their hard won expertise and to take charge of their own professional development. They also point out that the academic tradition of manufacturing "expertise" and then marketing it to schools as professional development or "teacher proofed" materials, what they term "research for practice," is delegitimizing to teachers and, ultimately, oppressive to them and their students. Lytle and Cochran-Smith's (2009) focus on empowering teachers, challenging the authority of institutional academic knowledge, and encouraging teachers to value and publish their own expertise is clearly one modern outgrowth of critical studies and Freirean pedagogy, and remains a highly relevant and powerful pedagogical perspective. Their idea of inquiry as "stance" is predicated on the notion that all teachers should look critically at their work, investigate their own classrooms, and methodically develop an expertise that is culturally relevant and highly contextualized—one that offers a situated pedagogy, more powerful and relevant to the students than anything created in the far removed realm of academia. It also creates the aforementioned space for critical consciousness—a space in which teachers can critically evaluate their own curricula and pedagogical efforts, so that more effective and relevant teaching may be enacted. Obviously, this perspectives professionalizes teachers, granting them power and expertise over their own classrooms that is discouraged and undercut by the national standards movement. To be clear, the point is not that there should be no standards or benchmarks, but rather that teachers should be involved in the development of those standards, and they should, together with their students, the latter of whom should be engaged in questioning and exploring their world en route to educational achievement versus simply drilling and memorizing their way to a higher test score.

A situated pedagogy connects the curriculum to the everyday lives of students and is interested in identity and self-formation, but also social-formation and the relationships between the two, and asks students to pay attention to their environment and to listen to what places have to tell us. It also asks students to read the world and to decode it politically, socially, historically, and aesthetically. A situated pedagogy attends to place, not only as the focus of student inquiry or academic study, but as the spaces for performative action, intervention, and perhaps transformation. As such, education moves beyond schools to their communities as students participate in remapping their material and curricular landscapes (Kitchens, 2009).

CONCLUSION

The scope and importance of critical theory warrants volumes of history, commentary, and practice. Herein, we have attempted to introduce the historical beginnings of critical theory in order to illustrate its significance and enduring relevance over time. We have also introduced the relationship between critical theory and pedagogy, curriculum and educational policy. In the pages that follow we offer suggestions for reading that offer more detailed views of classic Critical Theory and of the offshoots that apply more directly to the field of education.

NOTES

1. The work and efforts of Jean Anyon provide a classic case of "contrasting school communities." Anyon's work (1980) on social class and the hidden curriculum, both of which are inherent in the type of work students are engaged in "contrasting school communities" (p. 1), provide a sobering reminder of how little progress has been made over the years. The "contrasting school communities" described in Anyon's work included four types of schools ranging from working class to elite and primarily based on socio-economic resources. More specifically, the problems tackled by Anyon some 33 years ago remain solidly in place.

REFERENCES

Anyon, J. (1980). Social class and the hidden curriculum of work. *Journal of Education*, Fall, 162(1), 67–92.

Bordieu, P. (1984) *Distinction: A social critique of the judgment of taste*. Cambridge, MA: Harvard University Press.

Cochran-Smith, M., & Lytle, S. (1999). Relationships of knowledge and practice: Teacher learning in communities. In P. Pearson & A. Iran-Nejad (Eds.), *Review of Research in Education, 24*, (pp. 249–307). Washington, D.C.: American Educational Research Association.

Darder, A. & Torres, R. D. (2004). After *race: Racism after multiculturalism*. New York, NY: New York University Press.

Dewey, J. (1943). *The school and society*. Chicago, IL: The University of Chicago Press.

Foucault, M. (1977). *Discipline and punish: The birth of the prison*. New York: Pantheon.

Freire, P. (1970). *Pedagogy of the oppressed*. New York, NY: Continuum International Publishing Group.

Habermas, J. (1984). *The theory of communicative action*, Boston, MA: Beacon Press.

Hernstein, R. & Murray, C. (1994). *The bell curve: Intelligence and class structure in American life*. New York, NY: The Free Press.

Horkheimer, M. (1982). *Critical theory*. New York, NY: Seabury Press.

Horkheimer, M. (1993). *Between philosophy and social science*. Cambridge, MA: MIT Press.

Kitchens, J. (2009). Situated pedagogy and the situationist international: Countering a pedagogy of placelessness. *Educational Studies, 45*(3), 240–261.

Labaree, D. (1999). *How to succeed in school (without really learning anything)*. New Haven, CT: Yale University Press.

Lytle, S. & Cochran Smith, M. (2009). *Inquiry as stance: Practitioner research for the next generation*. New York, NY: Teacher's College Press.

Horace M. (2010). "Means and objects of common school education." In A.J. Milson, C. Haeussler Bohan, & P.L. Glanzer, (Eds.), *American educational thought: Essays from 1640–1940* (pp. 133–176). Charlotte, NC: Information Age Publishing.

Marx, K. & Engels, F. (1969). *The communist manifesto*. Baltimore, MD: Penguin. (Original work published in 1848).

Massey, D. S., & Denton, N. A. (1993). *American apartheid: Segregation and the making of the underclass*. Cambridge, Mass: Harvard University Press.

Mead, M. & Malinowski, B. (2001). Coming *of age in Samoa*. New York, NY: Harper Collins.

McLaren, P. (2009). Critical pedagogy: A Look at the major concepts. In A. Darder, M. P. P. Baltodano & R. D. Torres (Eds.) (2009) *The Critical pedagogy reader* (pp. 3–83). Second Edition. New York, NY: Routledge.

The National Center for Educational Information. (2011). *The condition of education 2011.* Retrieved from http://nces.ed.gov/pubsearch/pubsinfo.asp?pubid=2011033

Sadker, M. & Sadker, D. (2000). *Failing at fairness: How our schools cheat girls.* New York, NY: Scribner.

Shor, I. (1992). *Empowering education: Critical teaching for social change.* Chicago, IL: University of Chicago Press.

Sowell, E. (2004). *Curriculum: An integrative introduction (3rd ed.).* New York, NY: Pearson.

Turner, J. (1991). *The Structure of sociological theory.* Belmont, Wadsworth Publishing.

U.S. Department of Education (2001). *The Elementary and secondary education act of 2001.* Alternate Title: *No child left behind (NCLB) Act of 2001,* Washington, D.C.: U.S. Department of Education. Accessed at: http://www2.ed.gov/policy/elsec/leg/esea02/index.html.

White, S. K. (2004). The very idea of a critical social science. In F. Rush (Ed.), *The Cambridge Companion to Critical Theory.* Cambridge, UK: Cambridge University Press.

ANNOTATED BIBLIOGRAPHY

Anyon, J. (1997). Ghetto *schooling: a political economy of urban educational reform.* New York, NY: Teacher's College Press.

Though not Anyon's most current work, this text is surely her most influential. In it she details her personal experience working for educational reform in inner city New York. The book in many ways models the end goals of critical theory—she moves from personal firsthand accounts of the trial of reform to a broader critique of education, business, and government. Ultimately, she locates the fault for the deplorable state of urban education not in the schools and their administrations, but in the conduct of business and especially government at the level of policy and law. In other words, she refutes the standards movement's tendency to use test scores to attach student achievement levels strictly to teacher performance, instead pointing out that the racist and classist ideologies predominating in governmental and economic institutions have created a structure within which no urban school, teacher, students are likely to succeed. This critical perspective is precisely the kind of social justice orientation that critical pedagogy seeks to instill in students, one in which the problems at hand are understood in connection to the greater shape and structure of society.

Anyon, J. (2005). Radical *possibilities: Public policy, urban education, and a new social movement.* New York, NY: Routledge.

A natural extension of Anyon's earliest work, here she outlines how historical and modern public policies have shaped the educational injustices of present day urban education. Her text offers compelling evidence that civic engagement and the application of political pressure on representatives in government have historically brought about more just law and policy. She explores a vast coalescence of policies from housing to minimum wage to taxation and more, revealing how these have come together to determine the shape of the public education system as we now know it. Perhaps most interesting, she arrives at the optimistic conclusion that new social movements geared toward the correction of these injustices could feasibly bring about a more effective and just educational system. Hence, the title of the book, "radical possibilities," suggests a complete reimagining of the existing economic, political, and educational policies that have brought the current system into being.

Anyon, J. (1980). Social class and the hidden curriculum of work. *Journal of Education, 162*(1), 67–92.

Decades after this article was first written and published, it still has resonance in the public school system in the US. Herein, Anyon looks closely at different types of schools which are basically categorized on the socio-economic conditions of the students who attended each school. Her findings suggest that in schools with children from the most under resourced families, expectations of students are heavily rule-based and reward students based on their ability to follow directions in lieu of encouraging them to think creatively. As she moves through her four types of schools the reliance on control of student's decreases and the support of problem solving skills, critical thinking, and freedom to explore and learn increase. The most freedom is found in the schools with children from the most privileged backgrounds. This reality from 1980 sheds light on how little the public school system in the United States has changed in the last three decades.

Anzaldúa, G. (1987). *Borderlands/La Frontera: The new mestiza.* San Francisco, CA: Aunt Lute Books.

This book captures the essence of Anzaldúa—multilingual, multi-cultural, and multi-national. The text combines very personal prose and theory to explore the difficulties and triumphs of existing within and moving across language, cultural, and national borders. Anzaldúa describes the tensions and triumphs associated with challenging the status quo while not replacing it with a new form of oppression. The book is an essential read as the work of critical theorists exists in the borderlands. Anzaldúa, G. & Keating, A. (Eds.) (2002). *This bridge we call home: radical visions for transformation.* New York: NY. Routledge.

This book showcases the work of over eighty contributors, seeking to challenge existing definitions of identity. It is feminist and critical in orientation, providing autobiographical and theoretical explorations of experiences of classism, racism, homophobia, and other forms of discrimination. Though it is hard to generalize about such a diverse collection of voices, it is clear that Anzaldúa and Keating intend to challenge simplistic categories of identity and the oppression that has historically been exercised across those lines of division. It captures the element of critical theory which is deeply connected to postmodernism—the idea that there is no such thing as a unified or neatly bounded identity. If one explodes seemingly solid identity categories and the associated stereotypes and preconceptions linked to them, the exertion of prejudice around those categories becomes not just unjust or absurd, but impossible.

Apple, M. (2009). Can critical education interrupt the right? *Discourse: Studies in the Cultural Politics of Education,* 30(3), pp. 239–251.

Apple argues that "one of the most important tasks of critical education is an empirical one." Staying true to his focus on understanding the stance of the right and why it resonates with so many and how to counter that, he argues that educators (and others) need to communicate a more progressive and critical agenda for education just as effectively as the right argues its position. One of the methods he suggests is sharing the available research that demonstrates the negative impact of conservative movements in education. He also provides examples of where these movements are being successfully interrupted. Last, he suggests some creative, perhaps some would say radical, ways in which it is possible to respond to the neo-liberal and neo-conservative movements.

Apple, M. (1996). *Cultural politics and education.* New York, NY: Teachers College Press.

In this book Michael Apple seems to see the future. He takes a critical look at how the conservative social and political movements are attempting to restructure education. And, indeed, much of what he forecasted became reality over the decade and a half after this book was published. Even if you have read this book previously, it is worth another look as it helps the reader imagine the roads not taken and perhaps think about where to go from here. For instance, Apple cautions his readers to carefully examine and respond to the motives behind the conservative agenda and to respond in kind, rather than with theoretical jargon that is often disregarded. This work implores readers to take seriously and understand the larger macro social and political realities and competing philosophies that are part of the discussion about how to move schools in a positive direction.

Apple, M. (2006). Educating *the right way.* New York, NY: Routledge.

Here Apple analyzes political discourse around education, with particular attention to the ways in which those on the left alienate and misunderstand the true nature and power of the right. He examines the rise of the influence of the right in education, but also explores political discourse to reveal that the liberal vision of the right is reductive and damning to any chance of reconciliation and progressive cooperation. He reveals that the right can be conceived of as a fractured group, differentiated into various types of demographics within the right (e.g., the religious right as distinct from neoconservatives or neoliberals). He reveals that the tendency of the left to homogenize and demonize the right only strengthens the unity of the groups. He also undertakes a powerful analysis of how the right effectively couches ineffective pedagogies and educational systems as based in "common sense."

Apple, M. (2011). Global Crisis, Social Justice, and Teacher Education. *Journal of Teacher Education*, 62(2), pp. 222–234.

> In this article, Apple argues that globalization has profound impacts on teachers and teacher education and that understanding its effects is imperative. In doing so, he discusses what he sees as an assumption that "one can comprehend global realities through the use of a single lens" (i.e., class, gender, and race). Instead, he urges educators to see the world "relationally" so that schooling is viewed in relation to its social and political context. In that regard, he point out that many educators rely on very general stereotypes about what children and parents are like based on generalizations about their background, and that that is counterproductive and unjust. Additionally, Apples, suggests other key works that he believes should be read by all educators.

Apple, M. (2004). Ideology *and curriculum.* 3rd ed. New York, NY: Routledge.

> In this updated third edition, Michael Apple rewrote one of his earliest books articulating the relationship between ideology and the shaping of curriculum. Originally published in 1979, this book has long been heralded as a seminal work in the development of critical dialogue around education. In it, he critically analyzes the relationship between curriculum, politics, economic forces, and educational policy in the United States. This updated version examines many of the same issues in their present day manifestations, particularly following the resurgence of the power of the right in shaping education (a phenomenon he analyzes at length in other works).

Apple, M. (1999) *Official knowledge: Democratic education in a conservative age.* New York, NY: Routledge.

> This work offers a powerful critique of conservative educational politics, as well as a compelling bit of autobiographical material. Apple looks at his son's educational experiences as well as his own, in light of a then growing conservative takeover of educational practice. He also focuses heavily on the process of textbook composition and selection as a politically driven process. Though he examines many examples and issues in American education, his treatment of the government's contract with Whittle Communications is particularly powerful. He looks at Whittle's development of a school system-wide television channel, a project which teachers and students resisted and ultimately proved a failure. The critique is especially informative now, a decade later, when Whittle has most recently been involved in privatization of schools in urban districts. Taken as an historical perspective, Apple's insightful work reveals the roots of the present day discourse in educational politics, as well as ongoing conservative projects in educational curriculum and bureaucracy.

Apple, M. (2002). Power, *Meaning, and Identity.* New York, NY: Peter Lang Publishing.

> This volume of collected essays represents an excellent introduction to a range of Michael Apple's writings. Topics include politics, identity, sociology of curriculum, discourse analysis, and more. These essays, written between 1983 and 1998,

provide an outline of the state of critical education studies writ large. It also provides further insight into the range of issues at play in the politics of education and the development of curriculum, assessment, and educational evaluation.

Berlak, A. & Moyenda, S. (2001). *Taking it personally: Racism in the classroom from kindergarten to college.* Philadelphia, PA: Temple University Press.

A case study of what happens when an African-American elementary school teacher is invited to speak in a graduate level education class by one of her former professors. What seemed like a simple presentation from a seasoned teacher turned into an emotional, sometime angry, exercise in self-reflection. Reactions from the class forced deep reflection about how each person thought about race, class, and their role as a teacher. There is no way to read this book and not have a strong reaction.

Boal, A. (1979). *Theatre of the oppressed.* London, UK: Pluto.

This book draws from classical critical theory and shows how theatre can be used to reflect the realities and subjectivity in society. Boal suggests a way to use theatre as a transformative process to assist in reflection and the creation of change.

Bonner, S. E. (2011). Critical theory: A very short introduction. Oxford, UK: Oxford University Press.

Part of a series of "Very Short Introductions," this volume offers basic historical underpinnings of Critical Theory, beginning with Marx and following through to the Frankford School.

Clark, K. B. & Clark, K. (1939). The development of consciousness of self and the emergence of racial identification in Negro preschool children, *Psychological Bulletin*, 10, 591–599.

In this early study, Ken and Mamie Clark begin the important conversation about when children begin to develop consciousness about their own race. This empirical study describes a study involving 150 "Negro" children who attend segregated schools and explores how children become more self-aware with respect to race at about five years old. The Clark's work was integral in the Brown vs. Board of Education Supreme Court case because they were able to show that segregation causes psychological harm to children.

Cochran-Smith, M. & Lytle, S. (2009). *Inquiry as stance: Practitioner research for the next generation.* New York, NY: Teachers College Press.

In this seminal work, Lytle and Cochran-Smith lay out the theoretical and practical foundations for positioning teachers as researchers, not simply "practitioners" without theory or expertise of their own. The latter portions of the book include a host of excellent examples of teacher research and publications. It is a must read for any teacher seeking to inform classroom practice through qualitative research in their own classroom.

Campano, G. (2007). *Immigrant students and literacy: Reading, writing, and remembering.* New York, NY: Teacher's College Press.

Campano's writing follows in the tradition of practitioner inquiry research. In essence, it represents a current example of critical educational thought in several dimensions. For one, the text challenges the academic ownership of pedagogical expertise, locating it instead in classroom practice. Secondly, Campano's research proffers a critical perspective on high stakes testing and standardized curricula, instead positing an inquiry-based pedagogy for the empowerment of urban student. Finally, Campano challenges the dominant, deficit-based discourse regarding urban student identity. The text positions urban students as young as Campano's own fifth grade student population not as "deprived children in need," but instead as "cosmopolitan intellectuals" with the capacity to inquire, investigate, and generate new knowledge of their own.

Darder, A., Baltodano, M. P., & Torres, R. D. (Eds.) (2003). *The Critical Pedagogy Reader.* Second Edition. New York, NY: Routledge.

This volume contains essays from many great thinkers relating critical studies to pedagogy in a meaningful way. Among the issues examined are those of race, gender, language and literacy, among various practical classroom concerns. While this is a solid academic resource, it also does a nice job of connecting theory and practice in a usable way for classroom teachers, administrators, and other stakeholders in the education community.

Darling-Hammond, L. (2010). The *flat earth and education: How America's commitment to equity will determine our future.* New York, NY: Teacher's College Press.

In this impressive piece of research, Darling-Hammond uses extensive factual information regarding educational history and global educational movements to explore how a genuine commitment to equity is an absolute requirement for the betterment of the American educational system. Though arguably less radical in tone and less theoretical in perspective than many of the other works in this bibliography, Darling-Hammond's grounding of her argument in educational research is unparalleled and provides an unanswerable argument in favor of a critical rethinking of educational practice and policy. A well informed critical theory perspective should take into account such a comprehensive review of educational history and global perspectives on educational advancement, in order to remain grounded in the historical and contemporary realities of educational policy and achievement.

Dewey, J. (1943). *The child and the curriculum.* Chicago, IL: The University of Chicago Press.

John Dewey is the father of progressive education. Although many of his writings are from the early 1900's, he remains relevant to today's world. In this short text, Dewey argues for a curriculum that integrates student interest and experiences. While, at least to some extent, some of the ideas seem overly idealistic, Dewey does provide extremely thoughtful insights into both the developmental nature of children and the societal benefits of a highly engaging curriculum. Essentially, Dewey argues that curricula based on student interest is the foundation of student growth and democracy.

Duncan-Andrade, J. M. & Morrel, E. (2008). The *art of critical pedagogy: Possibilities for moving from theory to practice in urban schools.* New York, NY: Peter Lang Publishers.

In the true spirit of Critical Theory, Duncan-Andrade and Morrel address how to create meaningful change within institutional structures that are seemingly set up to oppress. They begin with a discussion of how they view critical pedagogy and then offer practical applications of critical pedagogy. This book is explicitly focused on urban contexts, but the content is relevant across contexts.

Freire, P. (1998). Pedagogy *of freedom: Ethics, democracy, and civil courage.* Lanham, MD: Rowman and Littlefield Publishers.

In the *Pedagogy of Freedom,* Freire offers a vision of freedom that includes more equity, cultural freedom, and a civil society where everyone fully participates. This book advocates for teachers in their ability to make decisions that help to combat discrimination in all forms. In addition, in the traditional sense of critical theory, Freire reminds us that education cannot stop with dialogue. Teachers must engage in both the exposition and explanation of the socio-economic realities that impact the educational process. The importance of critical reflection for teachers is emphasized as Freire reminds the reader that teachers are learners as well and cannot see themselves as independent of the social process.

Freire, P. (2000). *Pedagogy of the oppressed.* New York, NY: Continuum Press.

First published in 1970, this is the seminal work of Brazilian educational philosopher Paulo Freire. Required reading in most graduate education programs, herein Freire lays out the philosophical foundations for a pedagogy of liberation and emancipation. More specifically, he explains and critiques the "banking" model of education, and proposes an alternative model stressing student engagement and democratic participation.

Freire, P. (1985). The *politics of education: Culture, power, and liberation.* South Hadley, MA: Bergin & Garvey.

In this collection of essays, Freire argues that education serves one of two purposes—to domesticate or liberate. From Freire's perspective there is no neutral ground in the educational endeavor. He believes that critical awareness and the development of intellectual curiosity are achieved through reading and studying. And, reading and studying are required elements in the creation of new ideas as readers must be active participants in the creation of knowledge, not just passively memorizing literal meanings [banking] what is read. From this perspective, literacy is presented as a core political issue.

Freire also presents competing philosophies related to illiteracy. Illiteracy can be seen as a disease or as social inequity. If illiteracy is viewed as a disease,

Freire argues, we will likely see the "cure" as some kind of mechanistic approach that ultimately stifles learners' ability to be creative and analyze what they are reading. The end result is that we stifle liberation. Instead, literacy must be seen not as a disease but as social inequity. And, the "cure" is supporting readers' ability to not only understand but also critically consider what is being read—as well as being empowered to create new knowledge.

Gadotti, M., & Torres, C. (2009). Paulo Freire: Education for development. *Development & Change, 40*(6), 1255–1267.

For those looking for a historical perspective on both the life and works of Paulo Frieire, this article is a must read. Gadotti and Torres provide a detailed overview of the social and political climate in Brazil that served to shape Frieire's thinking around critical theory and education. Further, the article highlights the connection between critical theory and corresponding educational practices. Essential terms germane to critical theory—such as "banking" and "citizen schools"—are discussed. The authors conclude with a critique of how critical theory has been applied in Brazil and Africa.

Giroux, H. A. (2009). Critical theory and educational practice, (pp. 27–51), In Darder, A., Baltodano, M. P., & Torres, R. D. (Eds.), *The critical pedagogy reader* (2nd ed.). New York, NY: Routledge.

In this chapter, Giroux uses the foundational work of critical theorists such as Adorno, Horkheimer and Marcuse in order to frame a discussion about how a critical theory of education can be developed. He argues that we must revisit the central tenets of critical theory in light of the current contexts in which we live. Giroux challenges his readers to maintain "the emancipatory spirit" that generated critical theory and then creatively apply it in a meaningful way today.

Giroux, H. A. (1981). *Ideology, culture, and the process of schooling.* Philadelphia, PA: Temple University Press.

This book represents the true spirit of critical theory in that the discourse does not stop at the discussion of the problem, but rather tries to create a pathway through which curriculum can be transformed in order to be transformative. Giroux begins by discussing the theoretical underpinnings of educational research in the United States and connecting what we know about schools, classrooms, and curriculum to that base. Giroux offers a framework for educators to begin to question their own assumptions about what kinds of knowledge are valued in schools and classrooms, what achievement really means, and the nature of the relationships between teachers and students, and teachers and administrators.

Giroux, H. A. (2009). Teacher education and democratic schooling, (pp. 438–459), In Darder, A., Baltodano, M. P., & Torres, R. D. (Eds.), *The critical pedagogy reader.* Second Edition. New York, NY: Routledge.

In this chapter, Giroux offers a comprehensive look at how teacher education has been shaped by current educational reforms that focus less on seeing schools as places for equity and justice and more about blaming schools for a wide range of societal failures. He reminds his readers of the roots of democracy in education and calls for a critical view of teachers' work that is more consistent with democratic values. Giroux's call is for pedagogical empowerment and resistance against oppression fueled by the democratic tradition of Dewey.

Gore, J. (2001). Beyond our differences: A reassembling of what matters in teacher education. *Education Journal of Teacher Education.* 52 (2), 124–135.

In this article, Gore presents a four-pronged framework for the evaluation of teacher education programs. Her basic premise is that teacher educators have embraced critical theory but not critical practices. Her model urges teacher educators to focus on achievement outcomes through critical practices. For Gore, student learning is what matters most in teaching and teacher education.

Gore, J. (1992). *The struggle for pedagogies.* New York, NY: Routledge.

Gore explores a fierce struggle between theorists for dominance within the educational world, a struggle which, according to Gore, has in many ways prevented the advancement of either body of theory vis-à-vis critical pedagogy and feminist pedagogy, and in turn, of educational practice and thinking, generally. Gore's examination of the conflict between feminist pedagogy and critical pedagogy reveals the elitism and territorialism of the academic world itself, ultimately pointing out that the greatest conflict is one of egos and validation as opposed to the promise of either body of theory. After reviewing this history throughout the body of the text, she proposes a fusion of the two orientations toward pedagogy and social justice, revealing that the aims and practice of both are not so terribly irreconcilable. Indeed, each tradition has much to offer in the struggle to educate effectively for social justices and democratic participation in society.

Henrickson, B. & Morgan, T. E. (Eds.). (1990). Reorientations: *Critical theories and pedagogies.* Chicago, IL: University of Illinois Press.

Reorientations explicitly links classical critical theory with educational practice. This book contains four main parts: Shifting Canons, Rethinking Texts, Reading and Writing Otherwise, and Teaching Reorientations. In Part One, readers are challenged to consider what is being taught in schools and how to shift away from the traditional canon to something more critical and reflective in nature. In Parts Two and Three more practical applications of critical theory are offered. In Part Four, readers are challenged to think about the preparation of teachers. Each of these parts works together to build a complete framework to take readers from the ground level of what is happening in schools to the critical analysis of what it might take to create lasting and worthwhile change.

hooks, b. (2000). Feminism is for Everybody: Passionate Politics. South End Press.

Simple and straightforward, readers will get a clear idea of how feminism is easily accessible and part of a critical perspective. hooks deals with many issues related to feminism including race, class, reproductive rights, and violence against women. This book encourages its readers to engage in critical reflection about discourse in our society and how we [do or don't] fit in to that discourse. And, in true critical fashion, hooks encourages action to create change in structures that serve to oppress.

hooks, b. (1994). *Teaching to transgress: Education as the practice of freedom.* New York, NY: Routledge.

hooks encourages her readers to challenge the status quo and resist racial, class, and gender boundaries. Specifically meant for teachers, hooks makes an argument that teachers truly have a great deal of power to affect change if they see their role as one of "practicing freedom." She provides very practical advice with clear theoretical grounding.

hooks, b. (2012). *Writing beyond race: Living theory and practice.* New York, NY: Routledge.

Herein, hook focuses on the persistence of race in a seemingly postracial era. hooks argues that white supremacist capitalist patriarchy has always been and continues to be deeply intertwined in the American discourse regarding class and power. She furthers suggests that those who have gained status in the class structure (including affluent blacks) have become less concerned with changing an oppressive class structure. She argues that class serves as a relatively new border for blacks within the black community, while race and gender inequities persist across all racial groups. Overall, the book examines how white supremacist ideology shapes, complicates, and limits collective and shared identities, particularly among the most oppressed. hooks identifies ways in which critical theory can be practiced to overcome the boundaries imposed by white supremacist capitalist patriarchy.

hooks, b. (1990). *Yearning: Race, gender, and cultural politics.* Cambridge, MA: South End Press.

In this book, bell hooks presents a collection of essays that challenge existing conceptual frameworks that view race, gender and cultural politics as three separate conceptual strands. For hooks, all of these are dynamically interrelated. She argues that current frameworks of racial and gender boundaries and the cultural politics that surrounds them work to subjugate various social groups namely black women. hooks proclaims that the fixations on the discourse of difference (racial and gendered) allows one to easily disengage from the struggle for social justice. The primary point of hook herein is that the struggle for social justice must go beyond mere acknowledgement and analysis of differences.

How, A. (2003). Critical *theory.* Hampshire, UK: Palgrave MacMillan.

A clear and thorough handling of critical theory that is organized chronologically beginning with Horkheimer's work in the early 20th century on through to postmodernism and critical theory today.

Johnson, A. (2005). Privilege, *power, and difference.* New York, NY: McGraw-Hill.

This is a very accessible book that intends to challenge its readers to reflect on their own privilege. Johnson writes in a relatively conversational tone and shares his personal journey toward recognizing his own cultural identity development as well as grounding his ideas with evidence and theoretical connections.

Kanpol, B. (1998). Confession as strength: A necessary condition for critical Pedagogy. *Educational Foundations,* 12(2), 63–75.

In this article Kanpol argues for "confession" as a pedagogical tool. He grounds the concept of *confession* in the work of Cornell West, bell hooks, as well as others, and clearly links *individual* and *institutional confession* to the work of critical pedagogy. He argues that while critical pedagogy is extremely important in the effort to create change in schooling, it has been misunderstood and underutilized. The concept of *bearing witness* to and *owning up to* injustices and oppressive social structures is the step beyond mere awareness that will create opportunities for pre and in-service teachers to be prepared to deal with and challenge the oppression and alienation that are part of our schools. Kanpol leaves teacher educators with a call to "add weight" to current practices in teacher education in order to support the development of teachers as critical agents for change.

Kanpol, B. (1998). Identity politics: The dialectics of cynicism and joy and the movement to talking back and breaking bread. *Journal of Educational Thought,* 32(1), pp. 57–74.

Building on the works of bell hooks and Cornel West *(Talking Back* by hooks and *Breaking Bread* by hooks and West), Kanpol continues to argue for the importance of personal and collective testimony as a form of reflective practice. He points out that our identities related to spirituality and religion impact how we teach and should be acknowledged. And, he asks the question, "to what end do we do what we do?" In this piece, Kanpol advocates for an openness to find emancipatory knowledge via spirituality and religion.

Kanpol, B. (1995). Multiculturalism and empathy: A border pedagogy of solidarity. In Kanpol, B. & McLaren, P. (Eds.), *Critical Multiculturalism* (pp. 177–195). Westport, CT: Bergin & Garvey.

In this chapter, Kanpol calls on educators to engage in critical reflection to find commonalities with "the other." He writes that although our experiences may be different in many ways, it is within the spaces where we can find similar "oppression, pain, and feelings" that we may share feelings of empathy. Empathy, in this sense, allows for a border pedagogy that considers multiculturalism as a key piece of the puzzle in achieving equity in classrooms.

Kincheloe, J. (2008). *Critical pedagogy primer.* New York, NY: Peter Lang.

In this book, Kincheloe introduces the overall concept of critical pedagogy with attention to how it can be sustainable over time. He presents a comprehensive image of the traditional understandings and practical implications of critical theory in a highly accessible way.

Kincheloe, J. (1991). Teachers *as researchers: Qualitative inquiry as a path to empowerment.* Philadelphia, PA: Falmer Press.

Kincheloe advocates for teachers to own their place in education as experts and producers of knowledge rather than only being consumers of knowledge. This book encourages teachers to think of the classroom as the research site and view themselves as researchers in order to truly understand classroom dynamics. He argues that through the process of looking closely at one's own classroom and using what is learned to improve practice, teachers are able to empower themselves and their students in creating positive change.

Labaree, D. (1999). *How to succeed in school (without really learning anything).* New Haven, CT: Yale University Press.

In this insightful analysis, David Labaree explores the function of public education in U.S. society. Specifically, he articulates three often conflicting goals for the public education system, arguing that these three goals are often invoked, without explicit explanation, to compel students to study harder, to justify the status quo, and to support educational reforms. The conflicting objectives that coexist within the system and within our public dialogue about the system hampers educational progress and certainly limits the possibilities for achieving social justice.

Ladson-Billings, G. (2001). Crossing *over to Canaan: The journey of new teachers in diverse classrooms.* San Francisco, CA: Jossey-Bass.

The central metaphor of this book, the biblical reference to crossing over to the promised land, reflects Ladson-Billings motivation to see teachers, individually, and the education system, as a whole, "cross over" to delivering well educated, well prepared, civically engaged citizens for the future. While she does not draw out a road map to get there, she argues that improvements in pedagogy, teacher education, and professional development could provide the means for reaching such a goal.

She explores case studies of eight novice teachers as they evolve in their pedagogies, becoming what she terms, here and in other works, "culturally relevant teachers." For Ladson-Billings, cultural relevance is an indispensable quality of effective teachers, which clearly indicates her rejection of the "banking" mode of education, in which knowledge and skill sets, irrespective of student identity, are the chief focus of pedagogical practice.

Herein, Ladson-Billings also extensively outlines her own teacher education initiative, Teachers for Diversity, as a potential model for teacher education. Perhaps what is most instructive in this work is the combination of theoretical discussions of culturally responsive teaching with more tangible examples from her teacher education program.

Ladson-Billings, G. (1997). *The dreamkeepers: Successful teachers of African-American children.* San Francisco, CA: Jossey-Bass.

The most important part of this work is that Ladson-Billings highlights the importance of culturally relevant teaching as a key ingredient in supporting the success of children. By following the challenges and successes of eight teachers, she shows that teachers who see African-Americans as a distinct cultural group and use that knowledge as a way to hone in on children's strengths find success in schools where success has not been the norm.

Ladson-Billings, G. (1998). Just what is critical race theory and what's it doing in a nice field like education? *Qualitative Studies in Education,* 11(1), 7–24.

In this article, Ladson-Billings lays out a clear definition of Critical Race Theory (CRT) and how it relates to American society. She draws comparisons between CRT and the discourse about race and citizenship in U.S. society and encourages educators to look critically at the civil rights movement and its legacy.

Lather, P. (1992). Critical Frames in Educational Research: Feminist and Post-structural Perspectives. *Theory Into Practice,* 31(2), 87–99.

Staying true to her feminist lens on qualitative research, Lather advocates for post-structuralism and against the "one best way" approach to research. Her goal is to encourage researchers to approach inquiry from a variety of different perspectives in the hope that more creative and interesting epistemology will emerge.

Lather, P. (1998). Critical pedagogy and its complicities: A Praxis of stuck places. *Educational Theory,* 48(4), 487–497.

In this piece, Lather attempts to analyze two important perspectives in critical pedagogy, that of McLaren and Ze'ev. Both McLaren and Ze'ev believe their perspective is the "right story." Instead of playing into either interpretation, Lather embraces the counter-narratives and then attempts to frame them using Derrida's "ordeal of the undecidable." She argues that there is a "praxis of not being so sure" that enables one to accept a lack of clear definition and thus grow amidst the challenge inherent in the ideas.

Lather, P. (1986). Research as praxis. *Harvard Educational Review,* 56(3), 257–277.

In this classic article, Lather argues that "a more collaborative approach to critical inquiry is needed to empower the researched, to build emancipatory theory, and to move toward the establishment of data credibility within praxis-oriented, advocacy research." Drawing from classic critical theorists like Gramsci, Lather encourages readers to view social science as a way to achieve equity. To this end, researchers must consider subjectivity as part of the research process, not as necessarily problematic. That said, research must strive for the delicate balance that does not stray too far into "hyper-objectivity" or "rampant subjectivity." Through her discussion of negotiation, reciprocity and empowerment, readers begin to see how research can be used as new ideas and emancipatory knowledge.

Lather, P. (2004). Scientific research in education: A critical perspective. *British Educational Research Journal,* 30(6), 759–772.

This article confronts and critiques the movement toward "evidence based policy and practice." Lather argues that this movement oversimplifies the problems faced by American schools and that the current research paradigm adhered to by the federal government is narrow minded and ultimately insufficient to capture what is really going on in schools. Essentially, Lather calls for a "critical qualitative presence" in educational program and policy evaluations.

Luke, C. (Ed.) (1996). *Feminism and pedagogies in everyday life.* Albany, NY: State University of New York Press.

The title of the text is somewhat misleading. At first glance one may correctly assume that the book is about classroom practices and equality for females. It is indeed about those things, yet the text covers so much more. Luke broadens the notion of pedagogy by exploring how pedagogy goes beyond the classroom and permeates every aspect of our social and cultural lives. There are structured social curricula that teach us to think about gender, sexuality, and class in very specific ways. These curricula include media, games, and the social scripts that guide gender roles. As a society, we are at once teaching and learning about race, class, ender and power. Given the ubiquitous nature of pedagogy in our everyday lives, the authors argue for a deliberate use of a feminist perspective as an ideal critical perspective, as they seek the inclusion of multiple voices and highlight the multidimensional nature of identity (e.g., gender, race, class, motherhood, and sexual preference). The text provides an excellent critique of existing pedagogies and thoughtful insights on how to create and enact more feminist pedagogies.

McLaren, P. (2009). Critical pedagogy: A Look at the major concepts. In Darder, A., Baltodano, M. P., & Torres, R. D. (Eds.) The *Critical pedagogy reader* (pp. 61–83). *Second Edition.* New York, NY: Routledge.

In this chapter, McLaren explains the big ideas driving critical pedagogy and attempts to provide an overarching theoretical framework. He introduces the idea that critical theorists endorse theories that recognize that the problems of society are inextricably linked to the problems of individuals. It is this interactive context that forms dialectical theory—an attempt to look closely at the relationships between contexts, appearances, and accepted meanings. The ways in which we view knowledge are also handled in this chapter as McLaren discusses knowledge as social construction, along with the impact of culture, curriculum and the hidden curriculum, and critical pedagogy and social reproduction. The chapter outlines important issues, links them with theory and theorists, and provides practical examples of how these concepts are acted out in school settings.

McLaren, P. (2002). Life *in schools: An introduction to critical pedagogy in the foundations of education.* Boston, MA: Allyn & Bacon.

This book takes an interdisciplinary approach in its examination of factors that inform decisions in schools. It takes a critical approach by both providing a theoretical framework with which to consider schools and classrooms and encouraging action. In doing so, McLaren suggests ways in which educators, students and members of the public can impact change.

McLaren, P. (2002). *Life in schools*. Boston, MA: Allyn and Bacon.

This book is divided into two parts. The first is a text focused on McLaren's own experience as an urban teacher in Canada, and reads much more like a teacher's journal or early practitioner research. The second half is far more densely theoretical, explaining the foundations of Freirean critical pedagogy and using that theory as a lens for interpreting the experiences chronicled in the first half of the book.

McLaren, P. & Giarelli, J. M. (Eds.). (1995). *Critical theory and educational research*. Albany, NY: State University of New York Press.

This book addresses a wide range of topics related to critical pedagogy and education. It includes essays on curriculum theory, urban schools, action research, and ethnography, among others. Essentially, the editors and authors challenges researchers in education to explore how critical theory can inform their work.

Morago, C. & Anzaldúa, G. (Eds.) (2002). *This bridge called my back: Writings of radical women of color*. Berkeley, CA: Third Woman Press.

Unlike other books referenced in this chapter, *this bridge called my back* is not about critical education, per se. It does not deal with school structure or schooling. Rather, it highlights the critical perspectives of women in general and women of color in particular. Those who read this book of essays will encounter the very personal voices of women of color as they grapple with topics that range from managing the competing social demands of womanhood, the tensions of being member of multiple disenfranchised groups (e.g., black, female, and lesbian), and reconciling building bridges within and across identity groups. All of the works in this edited book deals with the impact of inequities and how women recognize and respond to them. Given that white females comprise the majority of the teaching force and that the student body is becoming increasingly more brown, this text offers important insights that may improve a teacher's understanding his/her own positioning regarding privilege, equity, and change. This understanding is fundamental to enacting a critical pedagogy.

Sadker, D., Sadker, M. and Zittleman, K. (2009). *Still failing at fairness: How gender bias cheats boys and girls in school and what we can do about it*. New York, NY: Scribners.

In this follow up to Sadker and Sadker's work of the 1990's, extensive qualitative and quantitative data demonstrate the ways in which education socializes young men and women into different identities and social positions. Ultimately, the authors argue that public education as an institution circumscribes gender roles in society and limits the potential of young women and men.

Shor, I. (2009). What is critical literacy? In A. Darder, M. Baltodano, P., & R. D. Torres, R. D. (Eds.) The *Critical pedagogy reader* (2nd ed.) (pp. 282–304). New York, NY: Routledge.

In this chapter, Shor provides an in-depth description of critical literacy from many different angles. He begins by offering some overarching definitions of the concept: "critical literacy as a language that questions the social construction of the self" and critical literacy as that which "challenges the status quo in an effort to discover alternative paths for self and social development." Once the stage is set, Shor applies critical literacy frames to pedagogical choices. He questions the premise of pedagogical neutrality and creates deep and meaningful connections between the foundational work of John Dewey and the transformational needs of today's schools. In the end, he offers examples of how this is being done successfully and offers possibilities for moving toward an effort for critical literacy to become part of the development of democratic education and a just society.

Shor, I. (1992). *Empowering education: Critical teaching for social change.* Chicago, IL: University of Chicago Press.

Shor offers a practical application of critical theory that is relevant across all grade levels. He argues that critical pedagogy should be student-centered, democratic, and support students' ability to advocate for themselves and have a sense of agency to create social change. While acknowledging the challenges that schools and teachers face, Shor explores ways in which teachers can approach their curriculum in order to create learners who are skillfully learning the content, becoming critical thinkers, and developing an understanding about what it means to be a citizen.

Sleeter, C. E. (2002). State curriculum standards and the shaping of student consciousness. *Social Justice,* 29(4), 8–25.

In this article, Sleeter uses the History-Social Science Framework for California Public Schools as a case study to explore the dialectic between curricular frameworks and multicultural perspectives in education. According to Sleeter, curricular frameworks not only promote standardization of teaching, but also perpetuate market driven ideologies by shaping what is taught. Dominant ideologies are reinforced as student (and teacher) efficacy is increasingly proscribed and evaluated by standardized testing. Multicultural education, on the other hand, seeks to broaden the discourse by including the perspective(s) of the disenfranchised and by making power imbalance a central theme to teaching and learning of content. The article concludes that it is possible for teachers to integrate frameworks into the pedagogy and still maintain a commitment to critical educational practices.

Sleeter, C. & Cornbleuth, C. (Eds.) (2011). *Teaching with vision: Culturally responsive teaching in standards-based classrooms.* New York, NY: Teachers College Press.

In this volume, Sleeter's most recent work at the time of this writing, Sleeter, along with Cornbleuth, bring together contributions from teachers working in public education settings, primarily in diverse urban environments. Each of the chapters offers reflections and lessons from the field as accounted for by teachers of varying levels of experience. Sleeter's critical position toward current educational policy and discourse is perhaps best seen in the book's orientation towards high stakes testing and standardized practices, and those chapters that focus specifically on teachers who either manage to successfully sidestep the demands of such an approach, or find ways to make those standards and tests function in the service of their own vision of education, namely, one that strives to effect social justice rather than simply cultivate skill sets in students.

Steele, C. M. (1997). A threat in the air: How stereotype shapes intellectual identity and performance. *American Psychologist, 52* (6), 613–629.

In this groundbreaking article, Steele describes how identifying with a particular cultural group can sometimes increase anxiety and inhibit academic success. Since its publication, much has been written about *stereotype threat*, but this article remains a very clear and powerful description of a concept that is now understood to be a reality for many members of oppressed groups.

Torres, C. (1998). Democracy, *education, and multiculturalism: Dilemmas of citizenship in a global world.* New York, NY: Rowman and Littlefield.

Though Torres has produced numerous works since the late nineties, this book offers a particularly profound contribution to critical theory. Torres deftly synthesizes historical writings regarding citizenship and governance, as well as economics, in order to examine the role of politics in education, and vice versa. The book manages to integrate thinkers like Locke, Hobbes, Hegel, and Marx with modern theorists working in multicultural and global education. He pushes educators to consider the value of political discourse in education, pointing out that there is no politically neutral position from which to practice pedagogy. This work serves as an excellent complement to other works grounded more strictly in modern pedagogical and sociocultural theory by drawing on philosophical and intellectual history writ large. This in turn lends a different theoretical lens to the analysis of the politics of education.

Torres, C. & Noguera, P. (2008). (Eds.) *Social justice education for teachers: Paulo Freire and the possible dream.* Rotterdam, NL: Sense Publishing.

This edited books examines both the history and future possibilities of the work of Paulo Freire. What is particularly fascinating about the book is its deep theoretical rigor but equally deep practical applications to education. For example, some chapters are devoted to exploring the theoretical linkages between the work of Freire, Rousseau and Gramsci, while other chapters address the application of Freire's work in urban settings across the globe. Each chapter has a strong commitment to clearly presenting Freire's ideas and connecting them to social justice efforts across a variety of contexts. This book provides thorough coverage of social justice education and is a must read for teacher educators.

Young, R. (1990). A *Critical theory of education: Habermas and our children.* New York, NY: Teachers College Press.

This book is intended to provide a clear portrait of Habermas' critical theory of education and show how it is relevant today. While Young does not go into great detail regarding educational practices or solutions informed by critical theory for that matter, the text does provide a general idea of the goals of education and how education limits the potential of society. Critical reasoning is presented as the missing ingredient vis-à-vis public education and true economic reform.

CHAPTER 2

CRITICAL FEMINISM IN EDUCATION

Desiree R. Lindbom-Cho, Kirsten T. Edwards, Kenneth J. Fasching-Varner, and Roland W. Mitchell

WHAT IS CRITICAL FEMINISM?

In order to answer the question, "What is critical feminism?" and further, "What has been its impact in education?" we have found it helpful to first consider the individual components that encompass this topic—feminism and critical theory. With that being said, we begin by asking, "What is Feminism?" followed by "What is Critical Theory?" We hope through this individualized method we will be able to more thoughtfully traverse the nuances of critical feminism in education and consider its aims, intentions, manifestations, and responses in holistic and particular ways.

Feminism

Not many theoretical and philosophical traditions or activist movements can claim as vibrant, complicated, and contested a history and community as feminism. Feminist action, and to a lesser extent theorizing, is traditionally organized within three temporal settings or "waves" (Hewitt, 2012).

Educating About Social Issues in the 20th and 21st Centuries, pages 35–52

First-wave feminism is generally acknowledged as having occurred during the late 1800s and early 1900s, with second-wave feminism beginning in the mid- to late 1960s, and third-wave feminism describing the efforts of the early 1990s to the present (Hewitt, 2012). With these traditionally organized waves, feminism has found its commitments increasingly challenged and its deployment more diverse with each succeeding iteration.

The term "feminism" is a fairly recent term, with its genesis harkening back to the late nineteenth century (Freedman, 2007; LeGates, 2001). It has been defined as an "organized movement for women's rights and interests" (LeGates, 2001, p. 8), or simply, "the belief that women have the same human capacities as men" (Freedman, 2007, p. xi). What distinguishes feminism or the feminist movement from the vast array of woman-centered consciousness evidenced throughout history is its focus on an organized and collective thought and response against sexism (Alexander-Floyd & Simien, 2006; Hill-Collins, 1996; Walker, 1967). Feminist theory identifies patriarchy as a pervasively cross-cultural mechanism for the control of women. Patriarchy's ubiquity manifests in its ability to exist beyond the bounds of the familial and within the foundation of the public. In its public dimensions, according to Kate Millett, patriarchal dominance is revealed throughout society: "The military, industry, technology, universities, science, political office, and finance—in short, every avenue of power within the society, including the coercive force of the police... [rests] in male hands" (cited in LeGates, 2001, p. 12). Feminism asserts that patriarchy is not simply a value-free family structure but instead is a systemic organizing ideology, privileging men in every arena that produces and employs power. Feminist theory as a project seeks to address the historical and contemporary physical, psychic, economic, intellectual, political, cultural, and social subordination of women in its manifold expressions (Aisenberg & Harrington, 1988; Austin, 1995; Barnes, 2006; Baskin, 2008; Berry & Mizelle, 2006; Branyon, 2005; Charlesworth, 1996; Cuomo & Bailey, 2008; Dillard, 2000; Eagleton, 2011; Epstein, 2002; Freedman, 2007; Fuss, 1989; Hawkesworth, 2006; Hill-Collins, 1990, 1996; hooks, 1981; LeGates, 2001; Lorde, 1984; Ropers-Huilman & Shackelford, 2003; Rupp, 1997; Schmidt, 2006; Williams, 1985).

Beyond definitions, at the core of the feminist project is a moral imperative (Cuomo & Bailey, 2008; Hawkesworth, 2006). It is the indictment, typically by women, in recognition of their status as a subjugated class, that the systemic oppression of females globally, locally, historically, and contemporarily is not simply a women's rights issue, but a threat to humanity (Cuomo & Bailey, 2008). Feminism contends that the epistemological and ontological dehumanization of women is a reflection of a collective defective human existence and that conversely, the liberation of women will also denote greater progress towards the development of the human condition (hooks, 2000). As such, a feminist endeavor is not simply concerned with the well being of women but the well being of women as central to the production of a healthy humanity (hooks, 2001).

Feminism's influence, consequently, is not limited to the esoteric or abstract. The insight that arises from gendered domination often manifests in the methodological, as well as conceptual and theoretical work of feminist (Cuomo & Bailey, 2008). Within the feminist tradition, notions and efforts at pluralism, interdependence, democracy, self-reflexivity, and compassion are exhibited. As with many other intellectual endeavors, however, the experiences of middle to upper-class white women have been foundational to the vast majority of the field, often causing oppression to be obvious components of feminists' practices (hooks, 1981; Lorde, 1984, 2008; Rupp, 1997). Nevertheless, an ethic of care (Noddings, 1984, 2005), collective emancipation (Lorde, 2008; Perkins, 1983; Simon-Kumar, 2004), and solidarity (Mohanty, 2003) have served as the ideal vision of feminism, albeit sometimes in the midst of recurring polemics.

As is evident in the work and writing of several scholars and activists (Baskin, 2008; Baszile, 2006; Berry & Mizelle, 2006; Epstein, 2002; Hill-Collins, 1996; hooks, 2000b, 2000c; hooks, 2001), feminism has struggled to adequately recognize many of its multiple dimensions. That much of early feminist theorizing and critiques focus on the lives and struggles of white women is unsurprising since the first reflections of an established feminist discourse are attributed to the written work and efforts of European and American women of a certain social class (Alexander-Floyd & Simien, 2006; Hill-Collins, 1996; Walker, 1967). Because the waves of feminism have conceptualized feminism's origins as occurring in nineteenth century Europe and North America (Hewitt, 2012), this lens not only effectively delegitimizes earlier manifestations of a woman-centered consciousness in Europe, but it also undermines the genesis of action and response on the part of women in other parts of the world. Like their male counterparts who conflated male existence with human existence, these early feminist theorists perpetually identified their life-experiences as a totalizing truth for all women (LeGates, 2001). This totalizing belief is reflected in the words of early twentieth century reformer Anne Kenney when she stated, "No nationality, no political creed, no class distinction, no difference of any sort divides us as women" (LeGates, 2001, p. 3). Kenney's ability—like many of her contemporaries—to see gender as a singularly unifying identity perpetuated a belief that women have more in common with each other than with other members of their same social, racial, or ethnic identity. The privileged perception of "self as woman" silenced (and potentially continues to silence) the voices of differently situated women for years.

In response to the exclusionary description of womanhood that early white feminist often supported since feminism's inception, some women have chosen, as a political move, not to identify as feminist (LeGates, 2001). For instance, womanists and womanist theologians developed a completely different term in an effort to appreciate the distinctions in the experiences of Black women apart from white women, and to also incorporate deeper analyses of religion and spirituality as significant to the lives of Black people and other women of color (Beauboeuf-Lafontant, 2005; Cannon, 1995; Floyd-Thomas, 2006; Phillips, 2006; Walker, 1983). In other instances, women activists have found their energies better spent in community with specific movements, such as socialism, the labor movement, and/or the Black Power movement, believing that feminism did not adequately address the multiple disenfranchisements of women's different communities (LeGates, 2001). While women activists who do not associate with feminism, nor refer to themselves as feminists, often recognize the gendered oppression they too experience, these women nevertheless see themselves apart from feminists and, instead, often identify as socialists or affiliates of other political and social movements (LeGates, 2001). Many women activists have gone so far as to regard the feminist movement as one of their greatest enemies, as these women contend feminism has, at times, distracted from the more pressing issues of class and poverty within capitalism (Alexander-Floyd & Simiens, 2006).

Feminism most notably began to experience collective efforts to address the raced, classed, and cultural deficiencies in its foundation through the work of scholars, activists, and writers associated with third-wave feminism. Cultural and social lacunae, however, remain. Many current academic texts on generalist feminist theory and philosophy are compelled to regularly make clear their focus on works originating in Europe and North America (Aisenberg & Harrington, 1988; Eagleton, 2011; Freedman, 2007; LeGates, 2001; Rupp, 1997). Feminist text working within a particularly Eurocentric frame, consistently include some of the earliest articulations of a woman-centered consciousness in Europe. However, these same feminist texts often do not include a parallel expression of organized women's struggle or individual conceptualization prior to the nineteenth century outside of a white cultural lens (Eagleton, 2011; Freedman, 2007; LeGates, 2001; Rupp, 1997). For instance, these text may include works by Mary Wollstonecraft and Sappho—women who worked and wrote prior to the development of feminism or the feminist movement—but do not include their African, Asian, Latina, or indigenous contemporaries. Feminism's continued dependence on a white cultural origin narrative necessarily influences the tenor of its contemporary ideals, which supports many of its divisions (hooks, 1981; Phillips, 2006). So while exteriorly there may be a cohesive terminology describing the work that has formed what we now label the "feminist movement," the interior can be described as quite pluralistic (Eagleton, 2011). Feminist work is done by individuals who choose to address patriarchy and the devaluation of women as a systematic, collective, and explicit endeavor. This is where the relationship ends. The paths to resistance and renewal have at times been amicably divergent and at other times bitterly divergent.

CRITICAL THEORY

Mapping the influence, trajectory, and diversity within the field of critical theory can be a daunting task, particularly in light of its contemporary manifestations. Engaging research from a "critical" perspective can include the use of theoretical lens such as postcolonial studies (Said, 1979), feminism (Campbell, 1992), critical race theory (Ladson-Billings & Tate, 1995), queer studies (Harding, 1998) or any combination of the latter. While a critical scholar in the 21st Century can find her scholarly home in a multitude of theoretical traditions, critical theory maintains a very particular history identified with the Institute for Social Research at the Frankfurt am Main in the mid-20th Century (Held, 1980). The collection of scholars most closely associated with the early days of the Frankford School and ultimately the emergence of critical theory include Max Horkheimer, Theodor W. Adorno, Herbert Marcuse, and Jürgen Habermas.

As Rasmussen (1996a) posits, "Critical Theory is a metaphor for a certain kind of theoretical orientation which owes its origin to Kant, Hegel, and Marx, its systematization to Horkheimer and his associates at the Institute for Social Research in Frankfurt, and its development to successors, particularly to the group led by Jurgen Habermas, who have sustained it under various redefinitions to the present day" (p. 11). Through its German descent at the Frankfurt School and the localized concerns evident in that space, a broad conception of what it means to theorize critically emerged, essentially the philosophical work of emancipation (Adorno, 1991; Bertonneau, 2010; Marx & Engels, 2005; Rasmussen, 1996b). The original philosophers credited with the development of critical theory saw their work as an intellectual pursuit to fundamentally transform an oppressive social order.

For early critical theorists, capitalism and social class was the primary lens through which critiques of power and privilege were taken up (Walsh, 2012). An early manifestation of this theoretical position is Marxism. Developed by Marx in dialogue with Engels, Marxism is a critique of capitalism and the ways capitalism as an economics system affords power to the small wealthy segment of the population, the bourgeoisie. The bourgeoisie, with this power, is then allowed the ability to subjugate the poor working class, or proletariat. For Marx and Engels, it was imperative to consider ways to disrupt this uneven and unjust power relationship through philosophical critique. Furthermore, critical theorists such as Marx and Engels argued that these systemic oppressions persisted primarily because of a flawed ideology. For Marx, ideology represented, "the expression of a false and freedom-limiting conscious-ness that impedes progress" (Bertonneau, 2010, p. 420).

Through Marxism and other early by-products of critical theory, a connection is revealed between oppression, emancipation, and social assumptions. Critical Theory introduced the idea that the normal, everyday accepted reality camouflages the control of human lives; that is, the belief that the very things that seem liberating, reserved for the free, or "high culture," are actually the systems that maintain an oppressive reality (Adorno, 1991). Critical theory encourages individuals to question their taken-for-granted assumptions and the systems in place around them that appear natural and appropriate (Apple, Au, & Gandin, 2009). Critical theory, further, is a theoretical tradition that provides a window by which to analyze the ways hierarchies of humanity and unjust realities exist because of these uninterrogated beliefs (Geuss, 1981). Critical theory provides the platform to begin disrupting the façade of absolute truth. As such, critical theory engages multiple realities, particularly those relevant to the needs of the oppressed, and lends itself to powerful application among many other more specific theoretical traditions aimed at the liberation of particular populations.

CRITICAL FEMINISM—A HARD CONVERSATION

Given the fact that feminist and critical scholars alike are varied in their ideologies, yet unified in their desire to disrupt societal hegemonies, critical feminism as a term is not often used (see Angelique, 2012 and McCluskey, 2011). With the history and goals of feminism in mind, the term "critical feminism" appears at first glance to be redundant. Feminism, by definition, is critical of taken-for-granted notions of gender (Atkinson, 2012). Feminist theory is critical theory. In many respects, and for many communities of people, feminist theory has not, unfortunately, fulfilled its own emancipatory goals (LeGates, 2001). Critical feminism exists, therefore, as a space for oppressed groups whose narratives cannot be fully told through feminism alone as noted by Singh (1997): "If critical feminist theory is to achieve its objective of democratizing literacy and schooling practices, then it is imperative that we hear and not suppress the voices of all women" (p. 91). Focus on the transformational nature of both critical theory and feminist theory is key to understanding what critical feminism in education entails. We must, consequently, look at what critical feminism seeks to do rather than limiting it to a definition that claims to explain what it is.

CRITICAL FEMINISM IN EDUCATION

Critical feminism in education manifests in a variety of ways that range from abstractions of educational philosophies (Hill-Collins, 1990/1991; Ladson-Billings & Tate, 1995; Marshall, 1997) to classroom pedagogy and practice (hooks, 1989; Lott & Bullock, 2010). Critical feminism in education is not simply a concern for those in higher education. Critical feminism is, in fact significant to educators from preprimary through postsecondary settings, both at the level of discussions and activism traced back to critical feminist lenses (Davis, 1994; Guy-Sheftall, 1992; Ladson-Billings & Tate, 1995; Lather, 1991; Yelland, 1998).

We wish to be clear, however, that the term critical feminism is not actually used by many scholars to describe their own work. Scholars, such as hooks (1991, 2000a, 2000b, 2000c, 2000d, 2001a, 2001b), have cautioned that language is an important consideration in how one constructs his/her identity; given this caution, there appears to be some resistance to naming one's work "critical feminism," even when the work engages the ideas, tenets, and philosophies of critical feminism. We are cognizant of the fact that our overview of critical feminism in education, both within the main body of the chapter and in the annotated bibliography, is not comprehensive vis-à-vis all of the discussions of critical feminism in education. By its very nature, such a chapter would be nearly impossible to write, and critical feminism will continue to transform the ways in which educators consider the importance of emancipatory as well as liberation ideologies.

While she herself did not identify as a critical feminist educator, the importance of Sojourner Truth's "Ain't I a Woman" speech cannot be overlooked as a key point in critical feminism. Truth's words deconstructed society's very ideas about the definition of a woman and even an intellectual (St. Pierre, 2000): "I could work as much and eat as much as a man, when I could get it, and bear de lash as well! And ain't I a woman?" (quoted on Sojourner Truth Institute, n. d.). The question Truth originally posited to listeners at the 1851 Women's Rights Convention in Akron, Ohio, endures through the ages, and still challenges how educators think about gender and its operation within society and schooling. Truth's landmark speech, furthermore, displayed a need for more than just the first-wave feminism of her time, in essence exposing that the discussion on women's right to vote at the time did not have to be reserved only for white females of a certain class.

While little scholarship appears to look at critical feminism in education between Truth's revolutionary speech and more recent years, the fact remains that those who have spoken and continue to speak against hegemony are often overlooked, unacknowledged, and/or deliberately silenced (St. Pierre, 2000; Walker, 1967). In an attempt to change this injustice, the United States responded with the Civil Rights' Movement, glorifying cases that attempted to establish equity in America's public schools (Brown v. Board of Education, 1954; Mendez v. Westminster, 1946). Yet, more recently, scholars have done much to reveal that inequities in all realms of education still persist. The field of Critical Race Theory (CRT), for instance, as brought to the forefront of education by Ladson-Billings and Tate (1995) and Ladson-Billings (1998), is especially important in featuring the complexity of the individuals educators teach through attention to intersectionality. Intersectionality of identity features such as race, gender, class, sexuality, etc. existing in one person emphasizes the fact that (s) he cannot merely be defined by any single identity aspect alone. Other CRT scholars also note that cases to desegregate schools and legislation upheld as equalizing forces upon students, faculty, and staff have actually served to further oppress people of color (Bell, 1995; Crenshaw, Gotanda, Peller, & Thomas, 1995). Delgado (1991), specifically, notes that affirmative action legislation, created as a response to years of inequity for people of color and women, most often benefits only white women despite the popular perception that affirmative action solely benefits persons of color.

Movements in multicultural education have likewise served as a philosophical basis for teachers who embrace the complexities of their students' genders, races, classes, and sexual orientations (Gay, 2000; Ladson-Billings, 1995; Dixson & Rousseau, 2006; Fasching-Varner and Dodo-Seriki, 2012). Critics note, however, that actual classroom praxis related to multicultural education becomes more concerned with designating one day to "celebrate" a given culture's heritage by merely sampling foods or making arts and crafts (Ladson-Billings & Tate, 1995). Critical feminism as a transformative field, on the other hand, upholds multiculturalism and diversity in education as foundations for philosophies of education that seek seamless integration of diversity into everyday classroom practice through teacher awareness (King, 1991) and culturally relevant materials such as accurate portrayals of diversity within children's literature (Knowles & Smith, 2007; Ladson-Billing, 1995; Ladson-Billings, 2000; Dixson and Fasching-Varner, 2008).

Race and class are not the only intersections of identity that have been overlooked by traditional feminist critiques. Current conversations in education about Lesbian, Gay, Bisexual, Trangendered, Questioning/Queer, Intersex, and Ally (LGBTQIA) populations have been brought to the forefront by students themselves and popular media (Butler, 2006; Loutzenheiser, 1996; Schullman, 2013). As more and more individuals question the binary labels and roles of gender that have previously been set forth by societal norms, students have demanded and founded groups that address spectrums of individuality at colleges across the nation (Schullman, 2013). Scholars recognize the importance of addressing these concerns and facts of life within the lives of even preprimary to secondary level students, and go so far as to link this conversation to basic considerations of citizenship and participation within a free democracy of, for, and by the people (Loutzenheiser, 1996). Ongoing calls for teachers to recognize their own prejudices in gender stereotyping and to become more open to supporting students of all orientations (hooks, 1981; Loutzenheiser, 1996; Johnson, 2005) are indicative of the need for critical feminism in the field of education.

Firsthand accounts of education through the eyes of those schooled in oppressive circumstances are especially revelatory in the conversation of critical feminism in education. hooks (1989) notes the following of a be-loved teacher:

> Miss Moore knew that if we were to be fully self-realized, then her work, and the work of all our progressive teachers, was not to teach us solely the knowl-edge in books, but to teach us an oppositional world view—different from that of our exploiters and oppressors, a world view that would enable us to see ourselves not through the lends of racism or racist stereotypes but one that would enable us to focus clearly and succinctly, to look at ourselves, at the world around us, critically—analytically—to see ourselves first and foremost as striving for wholeness, for unity of heart, mind, body, and spirit. (p. 49)

hooks (1989) further notes how these teachers like Ms. Moore became models upon whom she would draw to develop her own teaching pedagogy. Such narratives must be included as part of the discussion on critical femi-nism in education, for they display the need for critical analysis of feminist perspectives in academia and in the preparation of teachers.

CONCLUSION

Critical feminism, as an enterprise, draws from critical theory roots and a challenge to traditional (white) feminist movements, and calls into ques-tion not only the nature of patriarchial orientations (hooks, 2000b, 2000c), but also the ways in which intersections of difference within feminism (class, race, ethnicity, religion, etc.) have create microhegemony and micro privi-lege within umbrella ideas of feminism. In 21st Century education, critical feminism creates an opportunity to re-evaluate our historical relationship with feminism to create expanded vistas into the ways in which educators across the K–20 spectrum might better engage the realities of student iden-tities at the same time they interrupt traditionally hegemonic systems of privilege. The challenge, as presented in this chapter, is not to be lost in the process of naming any particular action or approach as "critically feminist" so that the focus remains on the acts of critical feminism in challenging and dismantling patriarchal dominance.

REFERENCES

Adorno, T. W. (1991). *The culture of industry: Selected essays on mass culture.* London: Routledge.

Aisenberg, N., & Harrington, M. (1988). *Women of academe: Outsiders in the sacred grove.* Amherst, MA: The University of Massachusetts Press.

Alexander-Floyd, N. G., & Simien, E. M. (2006). Revisiting "What's in a name?" Exploring the contours of Africana womanist thought. *Frontiers, 27*(1), 67–89.

Apple, M. W., Au, W., & Gandin, L. A. (Eds.). (2009). *The Routledge international handbook of critical education.* New York, NY: Routledge.

Atkinson, B. (2012). Apple jumper, teacher babe and bland uniformer teachers: Fashioning the female teacher body, pp. 93–104. In E. Meiners and T. Quinn, (Eds.), *Sexualities in education: A reader.* New York, NY: Peter Lang. (Invited reprint).

Austin, R. (1995). Sapphire Bound! In K. Crenshaw, N. Gotanda, G. Peller, & K. Thomas (Eds.), *Critical Race Theory: The key writings that formed the movement* (pp. 426–437). New York, NY: The New Press.

Barnes, S. L. (2006). Whosoever will let her come: Social activism and gender inclusivity in the Black Church. *Journal of the Scientific Study of Religion, 45*(3), 371–387.

Baskin, C. (2008). "I don't know what hurts more—to shut up or speak up": Aboriginal female leaders learners in the academy. In A. Wagner, S. Acker, & K. Mayuzumi (Eds.), *Whose university is it, anyway? Power and privilege on gendered terrain* (pp. 27–43). Toronto, ON: Sumach Press.

Baszile, D. T. (2006). In this place where I don't quite belong: Claiming the onto-epistemological in-between. In T. R. Berry & N. D. Mizelle (Eds.), *From oppression to grace: Women of color and their dilemmas within the academy* (pp. 195–208). Sterling, VA: Stylus Publishing, LLC.

Beauboeuf-Lafontant, T. (2005). Womanist lessons for reinventing teaching. *Journal of Teacher Education, 56*(5), 436–445.

Bell, D. A. (1995). Serving two masters: Integration ideals and client interests in school desegregation litigation. In K. Crenshaw, N. Gotanda, G. Peller, & K. Thomas (Eds.), *Critical Race Theory: The key writings that formed the movement* (pp. 5–19). New York, NY: New Press.

Berry, T. R., & Mizelle, N. D. (Eds.). (2006). *From oppression to grace: Women of color and their dilemmas within the academy.* Sterling, VA: Stylus Publishing.

Bertonneau, T. F. (2010). A counter-curriculum for the pop culture classroom. *Academic Questions, 23,* 420–434.

Branyon, J. B. (2005). Education for All: Gender equity in Kenya. *Delta Kappa Gamma Bulletin, 71*(2), 8–11.

Brown v. Board of Education, 347 U. S. 483.

Butler, J. (2006). *Gender Trouble: Feminism and the Subversion of Identity.* New York, NY: Routledge.

Cannon, K. G. (1995). *Katie's canon: Womanism and the soul of the Black community.* New York, NY: The Continuum International Publishing Group Inc.

Campbell, K. (1992). *Critical feminism: Argument in the disciplines.* Berkshire, UK: Open University Press.

Charlesworth, H. (1996). Women as sherpas: Are global summits useful for women? *Feminist Studies 22*(3), 537–547.

Collins, P. H. (1996). What's in a name? Womanism, black feminism, and beyond. *The Black Scholar, 26*(1), 9–17.

Crenshaw, K., Gotanda, N., Peller, G., & Thomas, K. (1995). Introduction. In K. Crenshaw, N Gotanda, G. Peller, & K. Thomas (Eds.), *Critical Race Theory: The key writings that formed the movement* (pp. xiii–xxxii). New York, NY: New Press.

Cuomo, C., & Bailey, A. (2008). A feminist turn in philosophy. In C. Cuomo & A. Bailey (Eds.), *The feminist philosophy reader* (pp. 1–8). Boston, MA: McGraw-Hill.

Delgado, R. (1991). Affirmative action as a majoritarian device: Or, do you really want to be a role model? *Michigan Law Review, 89,* 1222–1231.

Dillard, C. B. (2000). The substance of things hoped for, the evidence of things not seen: Examining an endarkened feminist epistemology in educational research and leadership. *Qualitative Studies in Education, 13*(6), 661–681.

Dixson, A. D., & Fasching-Varner, K. J. (2008). This is how we do it: Helping teachers understand culturally relevant pedagogy in diverse classrooms. In C. Compton-Lilly (Ed.), *Breaking the silence: Recognizing the social and cultural resources students bring to the classroom* (pp. 109–124). Newark, DE: International Reading Association.

Dixson, A. D., & Rousseau, C. K. (Eds.). (2006). *All God's children got a song.* New York, NY: Routledge.

Eagleton, M. (Ed.). (2011). *Feminist literary theory: A reader (Third ed.).* West Sussex, UK: Blackwell Publishing

Epstein, B. (2002). The successes and failures of feminism. *Journal of Women's History, 14*(2), 118–125.

Fasching-Varner, K., & Dodo-Seriki, V. (2012). Moving beyond seeing with our eyes wide shut: A response to "There is no culturally responsive teaching spoken here." *Democracy and Education, 20*(1), 1–6.

Floyd-Thomas, S. M. (Ed.). (2006). *Deeper shades of purple: Womanism in religion and society.* New York and London: New York University Press.

Freedman, E. (Ed.). (2007). *The essential feminist reader.* New York: Modern Library.

Fuss, D. (1989). *Essentially speaking: Feminism, nature, & Difference.* New York, NY: Routledge.

Gay, G. (2000). *Culturally responsive teaching: Theory, research, and practice.* New York, NY: Teachers College Press.

Geuss, R. (1981). *The idea of a critical theory: Habermas and the Frankfurt school.* Cambridge, UK: Cambridge University Press.

Harding, J. (1998). *Sex Acts: Practices of femininity and masculinity.* London: Sage.

Hawkesworth, M. E. (2006). *Globalization and feminist activism.* Lanham, MA: Rowman & Littlefield Publishers, Inc.

Held, D. (1980). *Introduction to critical theory: Horkheimer to Habermas.* Berkeley, CA: University of California Press.

Hewitt, N. A. (2012). Feminist frequencies: Regenerating the wave metaphor. *Feminist Studies, 38,* 658–680.

Hill-Collins, P. (1990). *Black feminist thought: Knowledge, conciousness, and the politics of empowerment.* Boston, MA: Unwin Hyman, Inc.

Hill-Collins, P. (1996). What's in a name? Womanism, black feminism, and beyond. *The Black Scholar, 26*(1).

hooks, b. (1981). *Ain't I a woman: Black women and feminism.* Boston, MA: South End Press.

hooks, b. (1989). *Talking back: thinking feminist, thinking black.* Boston, MA: South End Press.

hooks, b. (1991). Theory as liberatory practice. *Yale Journal of Law and Feminism, 4*(1), 1–12.

hooks, b. (2000a). *All about love: New visions.* New York, NY: William Morrow.

hooks, b. (2000b). *Feminism is for everybody: Passionate politics.* Cambridge, MA: South End Press.

hooks, b. (2000c). *Where we stand: Class matters.* New York, NY: Routledge.

hooks, b. (2001a). *Salvation: Black people and love.* New York, NY: William Morrow.

hooks, b. (2001b). Sustained by love: A call for spiritual practice that restores community. Witness, 84, 19–21.

Johnson, E. (2005). "Back to the backlash?" Primary practitioner discourses of resistance to gender-inclusive policies. *Discourse: Studies in the Cultural Politics of Education, 26,* 225–246.

King, J. E. (1991). Dysconscious racism: Ideology, identity, and the miseducation of teachers. *The Journal of Negro Education, 60,* 133–146.

Knowles, E., & Smith, M. (2007). *Understanding diversity through novels and picture books.* Westport, CT: Libraries Unlimited.

Ladson-Billings, G., & Tate, W. F., IV. (1995). Toward a Critical Race Theory of education. *Teachers College Record, 97,* 47–68.

Ladson-Billings, G. (1998). Just what is critical race theory and what's it doing in a nice field like education? *Qualitative Studies in Education, 11,* 7–24.

Ladson-Billings, G. (2000). Fighting for our lives: Preparing teachers to teach African American students. *Journal of Teacher Education, 51,* 206–214.

Ladson-Billings, G., & Tate, W. F., IV. (1995). Toward a Critical Race Theory of education. *Teachers College Record, 97,* 47–68.

LeGates, M. (2001). *In their time: A history of feminism in western society.* New York, NY: Routledge.

Lorde, A. (1984). *Sister outsider.* Freedom, CA: Crossing Press.

Lorde, A. (2008). The master's tools will never dismantle the master's house. In A. Bailey & C. Cuomo (Eds.), *The feminist philosophy reader* (pp. 49–51). New York, NY: McGraw-Hill.

Lott, B., & Bullock, H. (2010). Teaching briefs. *Psychology of Women Quarterly, 34,* 418–424.

Loutzenheiser, L. W. (1996). How schools play "smear the queer." *Feminist Teacher, 10*(2), 59–64.

Marshall, C. (1997). Dismantling and reconstructing policy analysis. In C. Marshall (Ed.), *Feminist critical policy analysis: A perspective from primary and secondary schooling* (pp. 1–39). Washington, DC: The Falmer Press.

Marx, K., & Engels, F. (2005). *The communist manifesto.* Minneapolis, MN: Filiquarian Publishing.

McCluskey, M. T. (2011). Defending and developing critical feminist theory as law leans rightward. In M. A. Fineman (Ed.). *Transcending the boundaries of law: Generations of feminism and legal theory* (pp. 352–366). New York, NY: Routledge.

Mendez v. Westminster School District. (1946). 64 F. Supp. 544.

Mohanty, C. T. (2003). "Under Western eyes" Revisited: Feminist solidarity through anticapitalist struggles. *Signs, 28*(2), 499–535.

Noddings, N. (1984). *Caring: A feminine approach to ethics and moral education.* Berkeley, CA: University of Cambridge Press.

Noddings, N. (2005). Identifying and responding to needs in education. Cambridge *Journal of Education*, *35*, 147–159.

Perkins, L. M. (1983). The impact of the cult of true womanhood on the education of Black women. *Journal of Social Issues*, *39*(3), 183–190.

Phillips, L. (2006). Womanism: On its own. In L. Phillips (Ed.), *The womanist reader* (pp. xix–lv). New York, NY: Routledge.

Rasmussen, D. M. (1996a). Critical theory and philosophy. In D. M. Rasmussen (Ed.), *The handbook of critical theory* (pp. 11–38). Oxford and Cambridge: Blackwell Publishers.

Rasmussen, D. M. (Ed.). (1996b). *Handbook of critical theory*. Oxford and Cambridge: Blackwell Publishers.

Ropers-Huilman, B., & Shackelford, M. (2003). Negotiating identities and making change: Feminist faculty in higher education. In B. Ropers-Huilman (Ed.), *Gendered futures in higher education: Critical perspectives for change* (pp. 135–147). Albany, NY: State University of New York Press.

Rupp, L. J. (1997). *Worlds of women: The making of an international women's movement*. Princeton, NJ: Princeton University Press.

Schmidt, P. (2006). Flaps and false starts in enforcing gender equity. *Chronicle of Higher Education*, *52*(37), 30–31.

Schullman, M. (2013, January 9). Generation LGBTQIA. *The New York Times*. Retrieved from http://www.nytimes.com/2013/01/10/fashion/generation-lgbtqia.html?pagewanted=all&_r=0

Said, E. (1979). *Orientalism*. New York, NY: Vintage Books.

Simon-Kumar, R. (2004). Negotiating emancipation. *International Feminist Journal of Politics*, *6*(3), 485–506.

Singh, P. (1997). Reading the silences within critical feminist theory. In S. Muspratt, A. Luke, & P. Freebody (Eds.), *Constructing critical literacies: Teaching and learning textual practice* (pp. 77–94). New York, NY: Hampton Press.

Sojourner Truth Institute. (n. d.). *Ain't I a woman?* Retrieved from http://www.sojournertruth.org/Default.htm

St. Pierre, E. A. (2000). Poststructural feminism in education: An overview. *Qualitative Studies in Education*, *13*, 477–515.

Walker, A. (1967). *In search of our mothers' gardens*. Orlando, FL: Harcourt, Inc.

Walsh, A. (2012). *Criminology: The essentials*. Los Angeles, CA: Sage Publications.

Williams, D. S. (1985). The color of feminism: Or speaking the Black woman's tongue. *Christianity and Crisis*, *45*(7), 164–165.

Yelland, N. (Ed.). (1998). *Gender in early childhood*. New York, NY: Routledge.

ANNOTATED BIBLIOGRAPHY

Ali, S., Mirza, H., Pheonix, A., & Ringrose, J. (2009). Intersectionality, Black British feminism and resistance in education: A roundtable discussion. *Gender and Education*, *22*(6), 647–661.

The roundtable discussion at the center of this essay reflects the inherently cosmopolitan nature of Black feminism. Epistemologically speaking, the authors illustrate that a feminism that is not intersectional is ill equipped to address the pervasive type of oppression that plagues women today. The essay provides an illustration of how women of color and white women across academic disciplines and continents can use their scholarly and geographical locations as starting points for meaningful academic inquiry and subsequent political action.

Allen, E., Iverson, S., & Ropers-Huilman, R. (2009). *Reconstructing policy in higher education: Feminist postructural perspectives.* New York, NY: Routledge.

Reconstructing Policy in Higher Education takes head on longstanding critiques of academia in general, and philosophies like feminism as being abstracted from the work of policy makers, analysts, and practitioners in particular. The authors explore issues such as administrative leadership, athletics, diversity, student activism, and the history of women in postsecondary institutions in a manner that represents the utility of both feminists and poststructuralist thought to the work of policy makers and educators.

Butler, J. (1999). Gender trouble: *Feminism and the subversion of identity.* New York, NY: Routledge.

This text is among the most influential books in the field of gender studies and has attracted significant praise and critique inside and outside academia. Influenced by the work of French poststructuralists like Foucault, Lacan, and Sartre, Butler argues that orthodox feminisms' focus on sex/gender distinctions are themselves produced by relations of power.

Butler, O. (2000). *Parable of the sower.* New York, NY: Grand Central Publishing.

In this near-future dystopia Butler, appropriately titled *The Grand Dame of Sci-Fi*, tells the story of her Black female protagonists' survival amidst environmental decline, massive unemployment, gang warfare and corporate greed that risk destroying society in general and her Southern California neighborhood in particular.

Cook, L. (2001). Feminist pedagogies and resistance. *Feminists Media Studies, 1*(3), 380–38.

Feminist pedagogies and resistance examines feminist ideas in the actual practice of teachers. It takes up difficult epistemological questions concerning what knowledge counts, whose knowledge counts, and, ultimately, how dialogues that promote democratic classrooms challenge teachers and students about their positions and agendas in classrooms.

Davis, A. (1983). *Women, race, and class.* New York: Vintage Books.

Prominent activist, scholar, and political figure, Angela Davis historicizes the Women's Movement in order to highlight tensions associated with class and race during the Suffrage Movement. It is particularly noteworthy that the tensions that Davis highlights between working class women and women and of color when compared to their upper middle class white counterparts is at the heart of the current call for a more critical approach to feminism.

Dixson, A. D., & Dingus, J. E. (2008). In search of our mothers' gardens: Black women teachers and professional socialization. *Teachers College Record, 110*(4), 805–807.

Extending the work in culturally relevant approaches to education, Dixson and Dingus explore how Black women teachers are socialized to the education profession, situating their discussion within the metaphorical garden of intergenerational feminism described by Alice Walker. The article draws from narrative accounts of Black women educators from throughout the United States, and the authors suggest that all educators, regardless of race, gender, class, have much to learn from the narratives of Black women. Ultimately, Dixson and Dingus argue for careful attention to be paid to Black women teachers, and the accompanying Black feminism, as a mechanism to improve educational experiences for underrepresented student populations.

Griffiths, M. (2006). The feminization of teaching and the practice of teaching: Threat or opportunity? *Educational Theory, 56*(4), 387–405.

In this essay, Griffiths considers the effect that epistemologies that arise from feminism have on the practices of educators and the broader community's perception of teaching as a profession. Consequently, Griffiths challenges hegemonic notions of teaching as devalued "women's work." Griffiths argues to the contrary, that the influence of feminist thought within education actually affords increased diversity and decreased social stratification of the profession.

Guy-Sheftall, B. (1995). *Words of fire: An anthology of African-American feminist thought.* New York, NY: The New Press.

In this comprehensive volume, critical feminist scholar Beverly Guy-Sheftall assembles, presents, and speaks analytically to the leading work of African-American feminist writers from the 1830's (i.e., Maria Miller Stewart, Sojourner Truth, and Anna Julia Cooper) through contemporary thinkers such as Alice Walker, bell hooks, and Patricia Hill-Collins. While the naming of feminism is a modern notion constructed within the last 40 years, Guy-Sheftall illustrates that African American, or Black, feminism has had a long and complex history. In that regard, Guy-Sheftall writes that "black women's liberation... is a continuation of both intellectual and activist traditions whose seeds were sown during slavery and flowered during the antislavery fervor of the 1830's" (p. 1).

hooks, b. (2000). *Feminist theory: From margin to center, 2nd edition.* Boston, MA: South End Press.

Herein, hooks, a leading scholar in Black feminism, explores the location of feminism, patriarchy, hegemony, and liberation, suggesting that the particular nature of the discourse we use, the language, has a powerful means of identifying and defining how movements, such as feminism, are located politically. hooks argues that "to be in the margin is to be part of the whole but outside the main body," exploring how feminism in general and Black feminism more specifically have been marginalized (p. xvi). At the same time they seek to move out from the margins.

hooks, b. (2000). *Feminism is for everybody: Passionate politics.* Boston, MA: South End Press.

In this nineteen chapter volume of short essays, hooks explores feminism from myriad perspectives, including feminism's intersections with parenting, violence, sexual politics, class, beauty, and education. hooks challenges the patriarchal orientation of much modern thinking, suggesting that "whenever domination is present love is lacking," encouraging readers to understand the role of love in moving beyond hegemony within critical feminist approaches (p. 77).

Hill-Collins, P. (1990). *Black feminist thought: Knowledge, consciousness, and the politics of empowerment.* New York, NY: Routledge.

This now classic text represents a canonical presentation of African American woman intellectuals whose work formed the foundation of Black feminist thought. These thinkers include prominent Black feminist intellectuals, writers, and luminary individuals like Angela Davis, bell hooks, Alice Walker, and Audre Lorde. The interpretive framework that Hill-Collins develops explores the intersecting issues associated with racial, gender, and epistemological discrimination experienced by Black women.

Jipson, J., Jones, K., Munro, P., Rowland, G., & Victor, S. (1995). *Repositioning feminism & education: Perspectives on educating for social change.* New York, NY: Praeger.

The collection of chapters in this book explores issues associated with exactly what it means to be a feminist in education in the contemporary world. The ongoing tensions associated with this exploration cause the authors to describe the book as a testimony of feminism in process.

Ladson-Billings, G. J. (1994). *The dreamkeepers: Successful teachers of African American children.* San Francisco, CA: Jossey Bass.

The Dreamkeepers was one of the first book-length works to explore what has come to be known as "culturally relevant pedagogy." Culturally relevant approaches place a significant value on having high expectations for student achievement, being culturally competent, and socio-politically committed. Ladson-Billings draws from Black feminism as a lived ethic of caring, saying that caring has a "centrality to black women's lives and scholarship," and was in fact exhibited by all of the participants she identifies as culturally relevant (p. 156). Ladson-Billings further draws from ideas of personal accountability, a basis in experience unique to Black women, and a committed use of dialogue as being a part of "Afrocentric feminist epistemology," consistent with critical feminism (p. 156).

Lather, P.A. (1991). *Getting smart: Feminist research and pedagogy within/in the postmodern.* New York, NY: Routledge.

In this groundbreaking work, Lather explores feminism and feminist educational research within a postmodern context. According to Lather, writing in the postmodern ". . . is to simultaneously use and call into question a discourse, to both challenge and inscribe dominant meaning systems in ways that . . . [are] contingent, positioned and partial" (p. 1). Important in this text is Lather's use of poststructuralism which "refuses both individual/social dualisms and reductionist views...," which has, in the case of critical feminism, allowed scholars "...to explore the meanings of difference and the possibilities for struggling against multiple oppressive formations simultaneously."

Lawrence-Lightfoot, S. (2004). *The essential conversation: What parents and teachers can learn from each other.* New York, NY: Ballantine Books.

Sociologist Sara Lawrence-Lightfoot explores the nature of the relationship between teachers and parents as it plays out within the setting of parent–teacher conferences. Lawrence-Lightfoot argues that teaching as a predominately female centered profession should pay attention to feelings, emotions, and experiences brought to the table at parent-teacher conferences. This text draws from critical feminism to the extent that it honors and gives attention to intersections of difference, consistent with critical feminisms attention to intersectionality.

Lorde, A. (2007). *Sister outsider: Essays and speeches.* New York, NY: Crossing Press.

Sister Outsider provides a collection of speeches that Lorde delivered over the course of her career. As a self-described Black lesbian, poet, feminist, mother, and cancer survivor, Lorde lived at the cross-section of communities that are individually marginalized and often conflicted amongst their on parts. However, the essays in the text illustrate the powerful possibilities that come from embracing each of these identities as a means to challenge sexism, racism, ageism, homophobia, and class and to ultimately develop numerous vehicles for action and change.

Loutzenheiser, L. W. & MacIntosh, L. B. (2004). Citizenships, sexualities, and education. *Theory into Practice, 43*(2), 151–158.

Loutzsenheiser and MacIntosh connect traditions of queer theory and critical race theory to ponder the relationship between sexuality, systems of education, and constructs of sexuality in Canadian and U.S. contexts. Making a parallel argument to critical feminism, the authors' state that queer theory "...offers the ability to look locally and contextually, using theories of fluidity and intersectionality to make sense of, take action, name, or refuse naming" (p. 155). Though the authors do not situate the piece or name the piece within feminism, this text makes an important contribution to the larger enterprise of critical feminism as it works through the concept of intersectionality, considering the relationships between race, class, gender, and sexuality.

Singh, P. (1997). Reading the silences within critical feminist theory. In P. Freebody, S. Muspratt, A. Luke, & Freebody, P. (Eds.). *Constructing critical literacies* (pp. 77–94). New York: Hampton.

This meta-review of literature is situated within critical feminism and literacy curriculum in its examination of the state of literature as it relates to what is meant by women's work. Singh's aim was "opening up, rather than closing off, the issues within feminism and education in Australia" (p. 78). As such, this piece provides a global balance to the larger conversation of feminism. The paper is critical of "discursive practices which have produced a particular set of critical feminist texts" to the exclusion of others (p. 78).

St. Pierre, E., & Pillow, W. (1999). *Working the ruins: Feminist poststructural theory and methods in education.* New York: Routledge.

This text merges theory to practice by illustrating the utility of feminist's post-structualism when applied to a wide range of topics to include theory in every-day life, ethnography, writing the body, emotions in the classroom, qualitative research, and "gossip" as a counter-discourse.

CHAPTER 3

CRITICAL RACE THEORY IN EDUCATION

Laura Quaynor and Timothy Lintner

WHAT IS CRITICAL RACE THEORY?

Critical race theory (CRT) is premised on the notion that select machinations of American society—the legal and educational systems in particular—foster political benefits for whites and assuage the racial underpinnings of a predominantly racist white America (Chandler, 2010). Though there is no patent doctrine to which all scholars of CRT adhere, there are some common definitional parameters that have come to shape both theory and practice. Five of the most significant parameters shall be delineated here.

First, racism and racial inequality are endemic to American society (Delgado, 1995). Such racial inequalities can be found in, amongst others, interpersonal relationships sought (or avoided), neighborhoods inhabited, and schools attended (Zamudio, Russell, Rios, & Bridgeman, 2011). These, and other "racial choices," have created a natural, subliminal acceptance of race and racial spaces. The role of CRT is to unravel and ultimately unmask the various permutations of racism.

Second, CRT challenges notions of neutrality, objectivity, and color blindness. Hartlep (2009) argues that such constructs serve to minimize white responsibility for the struggles of people of color. In doing so, opinions and assumptions are made devoid of the social context in which they reside.

Third, CRT is historically based. Contemporary manifestations of race cannot be understood unless they are situated in historical contexts. Racism did not "just appear." From the Three-Fifths Compromise to Jim Crow, a read of the historical record reveals systemic and sustained examples of social, economic, and educational inequalities.

Fourth, the experiential knowledge of people of color is both recognized and prized. Credence is given to the voices—the storytelling—of people who have experienced discrimination. Such voices serve, not as an appendage to the meta-narrative, but as the guiding narrative itself (Chandler, 2010).

Lastly, CRT challenges the tenets of liberalism which often viewed racial equality as "a long, slow, but always upward pull" (Crenshaw, 1988, p. 1334). CRT advocates a more expedient pace and sweeping vision of racial equality. In this view, equality cannot wait for the slow but steady wheels of change to turn. Racial progress should not be bound by notions of incrementalism, but rather defined by swiftness and permanence of thought and action (Delgado, 1995).

At its core, critical race theory works to eliminate "racial oppression as part of the broader goal of ending all forms of oppression" (Matsuda, Lawrence, Delgado, & Crenshaw, 1993, p. 6). To do so, CRT focuses on ways to transform the entities that both embody and perpetuate inequality. By challenging the hierarchical paradigms and practices that enable racism to continue, CRT offers a new vocabulary and a new vision in the fight against racial inequality.

THE ORIGINS OF CRITICAL RACE THEORY

Though there is no precise date of origin for CRT, its theoretical beginnings are rooted in the work of legal scholars who, in the late 1970s, argued that the Civil Rights movement of the previous decade was hemorrhaging and the gains made during that period were being compromised. What became clear to those working in the civil rights field was that the "conceptions of race, racism, and equality were increasingly incapable of providing any meaningful quantum of legal justice" (Matsuda, et al., 1993, p. 3). In response to such legal and perceptual recalcitrance, individual legal scholars and small groups of students met to conceive ways of challenging the dominant institutional and societal ideologies that perpetuated racial inequalities with the goal of dislodging racial discrimination (Bell, 1995; Delgado, 1995; Matsuda, et al., 1993).

This fledgling movement was spurred by a student protest at Harvard Law School calling for an increase of tenured professors of color within the faculty ranks. In particular, students desired that a professor of color teach a course called "Race, Racism, and American Law." When the Harvard administration balked, students organized an alternate course for which they invited guest scholars to campus to lead discussions premised on Derrick Bell's groundbreaking 1987 book, *We Are Not Saved: The Elusive Quest for Racial Justice*. At its core, the course brought together a small but passionate and potent group of students and scholars focused on a common outcome.

With a burgeoning body of scholarship in hand, CRT expanded into other fields of study, most notably education (Ladson-Billings & Tate, 1995; Parker, Deyhle, Villenas, & Crosland Nebeker, 1998; Solorzano, 1997; Tate, 1997). Significantly, the constructs of critical race theory can be found in contemporary research focusing on Chicana/o, Latina/o, African American, Asian American/Asian Pacific Islander, and Native American educational experiences.

CRITICAL RACE THEORY AND EDUCATION

As we have outlined above, critical race theory originated from Critical Legal Studies, continuing a long line of links between legal and education scholars (Lynn & Parker, 2006). Critical race theory began appearing in the educational literature in the mid-1990s, as researchers employed this theory as a lens to understand educational inequalities. Specifically, Gloria Ladson-Billings and William Tate (1995) introduced a critical race theory of education, originating from an analysis of the failure of the implementation of *Brown vs. the Board of Education* to provide for educational equality.

Subsequently, scholars in the field of education have utilized critical race theory in a variety of ways, including its application as a unique lens for policy studies, qualitative methodology, teacher education, literacy education, mathematics education, and curriculum inquiry. In this section, we provide a brief overview of the work of seminal scholars in each of these areas, pointing to the key ways CRT has influenced the development of such fields. The works highlighted herein, as well as others, are described more fully in the annotated bibliography at the end of this chapter.

CRT and Policy Studies

In a foundational article, Ladson-Billings and Tate (1995) suggested that CRT could be a critical lens through which scholars might interpret the connections between policy, race, class and U.S.-based education. By using race and property as the center of analysis, the concept of "whiteness" as property helped to explain educational inequalities between children of different races and classes. As an example of such scholarship, Tate and others (Tate, Ladson-Billings, & Grant, 1993) used CRT to criticize the Supreme Court's specifications in the *Brown vs. Board of Education* decision, claiming the Supreme Court was guilty of attempting to create a mathematical formula to determine equality. Essentially, they argued that the type of equality specified by the court does not provide for an equitable education for African American students.

This idea of using CRT to reinterpret the execution of the *Brown vs. Board of Education* ruling was later taken up by Love (2004), who used a CRT framework to collect and weave counter stories to the narrative that this Supreme Court decision led to increased educational equality and integration for students of color in the United States. In complementary work, Morris (2001) examined the ways school desegregation affected African-American teachers and discussed the lives and perspectives of educators who had their own critical views on school desegregation.

CRT and Qualitative Methodology

Scholars using critical race theory have made significant contributions to the field of qualitative methodology. In the early 2000s, a special issue of the journal *Qualitative Inquiry* was dedicated to developing the links between CRT and educational research (Lynn, Yosso, Solorzano, & Parker, 2002). This helped to bring about the birth of critical race methodology: a methodology that required foregrounding race and racism; challenged traditional research paradigms explaining the experiences of youth of color; created transformative solutions to inequities; and focused on the intersecting raced, gendered, and classed experiences of students (Solorzano & Yosso, 2002). More specifically, in critical race methodology, scholars draw on ethnic studies, sociology, anthropology, and other fields of study to understand student experiences. Scholars using critical race methodology can employ narratives that challenge dominant modes of thought in a process named "counter storytelling" (Solorzano & Yosso, 2002).

Building on this seminal work, other scholars have widened the scope of critical race theory as a methodological tool. In particular, Gloria Ladson-Billings (1999) discusses using CRT to challenge scholarship that dehumanizes students of color. In a special issue of the *International Journal of Qualitative Studies in Education*, Marx (2004) expanded the contexts of CRT by discussing the ways white educational researchers could use CRT and be a part of creating a more equitable society.

Researchers from a variety of backgrounds continue to adapt CRT for their specific needs. For example, Jones Brayboy (2005) writes about tribal CRT, which combines the use of narrative by tribal nation groups with CRT's legal critiques of racism in order to create a tool with which to challenge racism against native peoples. Other adaptations, including the combination of CRT with Chicana/o studies and Asian American/Asian Pacific Islander studies, are discussed in the annotated bibliography that accompanies this narrative.

CRT and Student Lives

One of the most common uses of CRT in education is as a rationale and theory for studying the lives of students. For example, Duncan (2002) used CRT to discuss the inherent contradictions in schooling for African-American males, framing the ideas of both cultural wealth and resiliency among his participants through CRT. In another illustrative case, DeCuir and Dixson (2004) utilized the concept of whiteness as property to discuss the impact of racism on the lives of Black students at a White private school. That is, they considered how the concept of whiteness as property manifested itself in the everyday events at the school. CRT continues to call for scholars to focus on telling such (counter) stories of students' lives in educational research.

CRT and Teacher Education

An important initial application of CRT was in the field of teacher education. As early as 1997, Solorzano called for teacher educators to contest the ways K–12 students of color could be stereotyped within teacher education classrooms. Ladson-Billings (1999, 2005) built on this work in two ways. First, she provided a critique of literature about teaching for diversity that did not hold race at the forefront; second, she researched and told the stories of teacher educators who did present race and racism in meaningful ways to preservice teachers. As the use of CRT in education grows, it continues to have a meaningful impact on teacher education research and practice.

CRITICAL RACE THEORY IN THE CLASSROOM

Aligning with other work in education described above, K–12 teachers can utilize CRT in their own classrooms to change the way they teach. The concept of critical race pedagogy (Lynn, 1999) is used to denote antiracist, anticlassist, and antisexist pedagogies. Teachers of literacy, social studies, mathematics, and even science have begun to use CRT to center the idea of race within their disciplines. Across content areas, scholars use CRT to question the concept of a multicultural curriculum, suggesting that schooling has a hidden racial curriculum not yet engaged by multiculturalism (Jay, 2009; Yosso, 2005).

The field of social studies has an especially rich cadre of scholars advocating for the use of CRT in the classroom. In Ladson-Billings' (2003) book about CRT and social studies, she provides a theoretical backdrop by arguing that race should in fact be a centerpiece for understanding social studies. As an example of how social studies teachers can use CRT, Haynes Writer (2002) describes ways that CRT can help students to be critical of media representations of Native Americans. In the same vein, Lintner (2004) suggests that teachers of U.S. history can interrogate common stereotypical representations of African-Americans and Native Americans. In a different but similar manner, Iseke-Barnes (2000) has promoted the use of *ethnomathematics* (a term describing the teaching of mathematics while considering race, culture, and language), as a means to help math educators address racial biases in math.

FRONTIERS IN THE USE OF CRITICAL RACE THEORY

As CRT research continues to grow and change, scholars such as Lynn and Parker (2006) suggest that researchers examine race as contextualized within the field of sociology (Bonilla-Silva, 2001; Lewis, 2003) to help understand the intersection between race and schooling. In their reflections on a decade of research on CRT in education, both Lynn and Parker (2006) and Dixson and Rousseau (2005) focus on the possibility for praxis: that is, ways in which CRT can bring about greater equity in education, so that students no longer have to ask "how come we here?" (Lynn & Parker, 2006, p. 283). Lynn and Parker (2006) also highlight how such fields as area studies and anthropology can be used as tools to continue a CRT-based analysis of education.

REFERENCES

Bell, D. (1987). *And we are not saved: The elusive quest for racial justice.* New York, NY: Basic Books.

Bell, D. (1995). Who's afraid of critical race theory? *University of Illinois Law Review, 1995,* 893–910.

Bonilla-Silva, E. (2001). *White supremacy and racism in the post-Civil Rights era.* Boulder, CO: Lynne Rienner Publishers.

Chandler, P. T. (2010). Critical race theory and social studies: Centering the Native American experience. *The Journal of Social Studies Research, 34*(1), 29–58.

Crenshaw, K. (1988). Race, reform, and retrenchment: Transformation and legitimation in antidiscrimination law. *Harvard Law Review, 101,* 1331–1387.

DeCuir, J. T., & Dixson, A. D. (2004). "So when it comes out, they aren't that surprised that it is there": Using critical race theory as a tool of analysis of race and racism in education. *Educational Researcher, 33*(5), 26–31.

Delgado, R. (Ed.). (1995). Critical race theory: The cutting edge. Philadelphia, PA: Temple University Press.

Dixson, A. D., & Rousseau, C. K. (2005). And we are still not saved: Critical race theory in education ten years later. *Race Ethnicity and Education, 8*(1), 7–27.

Duncan, G. A. (2002). Beyond love: A critical race ethnography of the schooling of adolescent Black males. *Equity & Excellence in Education, 35*(2), 131–143.

Hartlep, N. D. (2009). *Critical race theory: An examination of its past, present, and future implications.* (ERIC Document Reproduction Service No. ED 506 735)

Haynes Writer, J. (2002). Terrorism in Native America: Interrogating the past, examining the present, and constructing a liberatory future. *Anthropology & Education Quarterly, 33,* 317–330.

Iseke-Barnes, J. (2000). Ethnomathematics and language in decolonizing mathematics. *Race, Gender & Class, 7*(3), 133–149.

Jay, M. (2009). Race-ing through the school day: African American educators' experiences with race and racism in Schools. *International Journal of Qualitative Studies in Education (QSE), 22,* 671–685.

Jones Brayboy, B. M. (2005). Toward a tribal critical race theory in education. *Urban Review: Issues and Ideas in Public Education, 37,* 425–446.

Ladson-Billings, G. (1999). Preparing teachers for diverse student populations: A critical race theory perspective. *Review of Research in Education, 24,* 211–247.

Ladson-Billings, G. (2003). *Critical race theory perspectives for social studies.* Charlotte, NC: Information Age Publishing.

Ladson-Billings, G. (2005). *Beyond the big house: African American educators on teacher education.* New York, NY: Teachers College Press.

Ladson-Billings, G., & Tate, W. F. (1995). Toward a critical race theory of education. *Teachers College Record, 97*(1), 47–68.

Lewis, A. E. (2003). *Race in the schoolyard: Negotiating the color line in classrooms and communities.* New Brunswick, NJ: Rutgers University Press.

Lintner, T. (2004). The savage and the slave: Critical race theory, racial stereotyping, and the teaching of American history. *The Journal of Social Studies Research, 28*(1), 27–32.

Love, B. J. (2004). "Brown" plus 50 counter-storytelling: A critical race theory analysis of the "Majoritarian Achievement Gap" story. *Equity and Excellence in Education, 37,* 227–246.

Lynn, M. (1999). Toward a critical race pedagogy: A research note. *Urban Education, 33,* 606–626.

Lynn, M., & Parker, L. (2006). Critical race studies in education: Examining a decade of research on U.S. schools. *Urban Review: Issues and Ideas in Public Education, 38,* 257–290.

Lynn, M., Yosso, T. J., Solorzano, D. G., & Parker, L. (2002). Critical race theory and education: Qualitative research in the new millennium. *Qualitative Inquiry, 8*(1), 3–6.

Marx, S. (2004). Regarding whiteness: Exploring and intervening in the effects of white racism in teacher education. *Equity and Excellence in Education, 37*(1), 31–43.

Matsuda, M. J., Lawrence III, C. R., Delgado, R., & Crenshaw, K. W. (1993). *Words that wound: Critical race theory, assaultive speech, and the first amendment.* Boulder, CO: Westview Press.

Morris, J. (2001). Forgotten voices of Black educators: Critical race perspectives on the implementation of a desegregation plan. *Educational Policy, 15,* 575–600.

Parker, L., Deyhle, D., Villenas, S., & Crosland Nebeker, K. (Eds.). (1998). Critical race theory in education [Special Issue]. *International Journal of Qualitative Studies in Education, 11*(1).

Solorzano, D. G. (1997). Images and words that wound: Critical race theory, racial stereotyping, and teacher education. *Teacher Education Quarterly, 24*(3), 5–19.

Solorzano, D. G., & Yosso, T. J. (2002). Critical race methodology: Counter story-telling as an analytical framework for education research. *Qualitative Inquiry, 8*(1), 23–44.

Tate, W. F., Ladson-Billings, G., & Grant, C. A. (1993). The *Brown* decision revisited: Mathematizing social problems. *Educational Policy, 7,* 255–275.

Tate, W. F. (1997). Critical race theory and education: History, theory, and implications. In M. W. Apple & D. Cooper (Eds.), *Review of research in education: Vol 22* (pp. 195–247). Washington, DC: American Educational Research Association.

Yosso, T. J. (2005). Whose culture has capital? A critical race theory discussion of community cultural wealth. *Race, Ethnicity, and Education, 8*(1), 69–91.

Zamudio, M. M., Russell, C., Rios, F. A., & Bridgeman, J. L. (2011). *Critical race theory matters: Education and ideology.* New York, NY: Routledge.

ANNOTATED BIBLIOGRAPHY

Aleman, E. (2009). Through the prism of critical race theory: "Niceness" and Latina/o leadership in the politics of education. *Journal of Latinos and Education, 8*(4), 290–311.

This article outlines a study of Latina/o educational and political leaders in Utah who advocate closing the achievement gap for Latina/o students. Based in CRT, this discourse analysis isolates the themes of "niceness," "respect," and "decorum," which shape the political rhetoric of the participants. Aleman argues that these concepts serve to regulate the speech and lived experiences of Latina/o students, as well as silence their voices. If these leaders can be armed with theories such as CRT, Aleman holds that they and other educational advocates will be able to participate more significantly in political debates around education.

Apple, M. W. (2009). Is racism in education an accident? *Educational Policy, 23*(4), 651–659.

In this opinion paper, a leading leftist educational theorist critiques the text *Racism and Education* by David Gillborn. Overall, Apple contends that Gillborn provides a clear explanation of CRT, and agrees that "one cannot adequately understand this society, its history, or how it functions today without placing the dynamics of racial exploitation and domination and their accompanying logics and power relations at the heart of one's analysis" (p. 652). Drawing on his own work, Apple discusses the ways that CRT disrupts the common sense rhetoric that normalcy and property are white in color. Apple praises Gillborn's use of storytelling in arguing for the importance of CRT, as well as his honest treatment of the dangers inherent in centering a white scholar's voice on CRT. In closing, Apple suggests ways in which Gillborn could strengthen his work by drawing on Gramsci, Lipsitz, Pedroni, and other scholars who have treated questions of whiteness, race, and power in educational policy.

Chandler, P. T. (2010). Critical race theory and social studies: Centering the Native American experience. *The Journal of Social Studies Research, 34*(1), 29–58.

Chandler posits that race, racism, and the political machinations behind them are entwined in understandings of American history. Specifically, this article examines how the topic of race has been addressed in social studies classrooms. The author contends that social studies classrooms fail to adequately address the issue of race. Out of fear of offending groups of students and the controversy that may ensue, or devoid of empathetic experiences regarding race and racism, teachers often (overtly or covertly) avoid race-based discussions in social studies classrooms. Students thus perceive race as neutral, benign, and noncontentious. By using critical race theory as the theoretical and pedagogical instructional cornerstone, students will gain a critical, comprehensive understanding of social studies, heretofore absent from many classrooms. Ultimately, the author supports the use of CRT in social studies classrooms by offering specific examples of its application within the realm of Native American history.

Cole, M. (2009). *Critical race theory and education: A Marxist response.* New York, NY: Palgrave MacMillan.

Critical Race Theory and Education is the first book to examine critical race theory from a Marxist perspective. The premise of the work is not to position Marxism as the pragmatic, programmatic panacea to the underlying subversive tenets of critical race theory; rather the goal is, simply (yet profoundly), to offer yet another insightful perspective in how to situate critical race theory within a more broad and diverse conversation. In doing so, the author provides examples of how classroom teachers can present critical race theory from a Marxist framework.

Crenshaw, K., Gotanda, N., Peller, G., & Thomas, K. (Eds.). (1995). *Critical race theory: The key writings that formed the movement.* New York, NY: The New Press.

This reader, edited by the principal founders and leading theoreticians of the critical race theory movement, gathers together the movement's most important essays as of the mid–1990s. The book chronicles the intellectual genesis of critical race theory as well as maps the various methodological directions taken since inception. The first section presents a chronological compilation of seminal (legal) articles that served to both define and contextualize the core tenets of critical race theory. The second half of the book examines critical race theory via individual methodological strands, with a particular emphasis placed on gender.

Delgado, R. (Ed.). (1995). *Critical race theory: The cutting edge.* Philadelphia, PA: Temple University Press.

In this seminal work, Delgado offers a sweeping compilation of the multiple contexts of critical race theory. Issues such as the social construction of race, the influence of class and gender on access and equity, and the impact a shifting legal system has on poverty, serves to formulate—and formalize—how race is constructed and perceived. In doing so, this volume examines racial constructions, challenges such orthodoxies, and offers alternate ways to envision the potentialities of race and racial understandings. Divided into twelve sections, the book contains 50 chapters by leading scholars in the field of critical race theory and legal studies. Each chapter is succinct and accessible. The sections regarding Critical Race Feminism and Critical White Studies are of particular import and they push the proverbial envelope of critical race theory into new directions.

Delgado, R., & Stefanic, J. (2001). *Critical race theory: An introduction.* New York, NY: New York University Press.

This volume is arguably the most concise and accessible book regarding the basic tenets and underlying principles vis-à-vis critical race theory. Penned by two of the most influential figures in the early origins of the movement, this work offers a broad breadth of information, including definitions and descriptions, the legalistic foundations of CRT, the notion of hegemony and disparate power, and a brief (but seminal) exposé of the sociocultural manifestations and implications of CRT. Most interesting is the chapter that examines the path of CRT through the 1990s and muses about where the movement may head at the turn of the twenty-first century. This is truly a must read for anyone interested in understanding the broad expanse of CRT.

Dixson, A. D., & Rousseau, C. K. (2005). And we are still not saved: Critical race theory in education ten years later. *Race Ethnicity and Education, 8*(1), 7–27.

In the title of this article, Dixson and Rousseau repeat a segment of the title of Derrick Bell's 1987 text suggesting that *Brown vs. Board of Education* has not yet led to educational equity in the United States. The authors present an in-depth discussion regarding the "unfulfilled promise of CRT in education." Although they point to the many ways CRT has failed to move educational policies and practices towards equity, Dixson and Rousseau also provide a broad review of literature published on CRT in education in the ten years since Ladson-Billings and Tate's (1995) seminal article on CRT. By grouping studies by concepts commonly used in CRT such as voice, restrictive views of equality, and the problem with colorblindness, they bridge CRT work in legal studies with CRT work in education. These connections are strengthened in the second section of the article, in which the authors examine legal cases that have impacted educational policies throughout the years. The authors argue that CRT scholarship in education should draw from legal scholarship on the same topic, maintaining that legal studies both formed the field of CRT and will continue to be central to efforts to advocate for equality in education.

Dixson, A., & Dingus, J. (2007). Tyranny of the majority: Re-enfranchisement of African-American teacher educators teaching for democracy. *International Journal of Qualitative Studies in Education (QSE)*, *20*, 639–654.

In this work, Dixson and Dingus reflect on their own experiences as teacher educators of color who practiced Black feminist pedagogy during their teaching about multicultural education in predominantly white institutions (PWIs). They tell counter stories and use the CRT tenet of whiteness as property to examine the presence of teacher educators of color, the existence of Black female professors as symbols rather than individuals, and the ways multicultural teacher education can silence professors of color. They point out that the work of multicultural education is as a whole ineffective if courses are focused on proving to white preservice teachers that race and racism are real. Using Lani Gunier's work on the rule of the majority in U.S. democracy, Dixson and Dingus draw an analogy to the way power functions within multicultural teacher education, whereby the majority opinion (i.e., White, Eurocentric, hegemonic) is taken for fact. The recognition of such unchallenged discourses is the first step in promoting and practicing the ideals of multicultural education, which contest the structures that support dominant discourses. The goal for teacher educators is to ultimately create diverse and egalitarian classrooms that question both the story and the storytellers.

Jay, M. (2009). Race-ing through the school day: African American educators' experiences with race and racism in schools. *International Journal of Qualitative Studies in Education (QSE)*, *22*, 671–685.

Attempting to make visible the often invisible discourses of race and racism in schools, the author of this article conducted phenomenological interviews with five African American educators. Through these interviews, seven major themes became clear: (1) hyper-visibility/invisibility; (2) intersecting identities; (3) challenging assumptions; (4) challenges to authority; (5) pigeonholing; (6) presumptions of failure, and (7) "coping fatigue" (as in, fatigue with coping). Based on the results of this study, the author concludes that the central facet of CRT is upheld: racism is present and powerful in both U.S. schools and society. Tying in with CRT's focus on praxis, Jay posits that school administrators are the individuals most able to challenge discourses of racism within public schools.

Jones Brayboy, B. M. (2005). Toward a tribal critical race theory in education. *Urban Review: Issues and Ideas in Public Education*, *37*, 425–446.

As CRT grows and widens in use, scholars such as the author of this work are adapting critical race theory for new purposes and populations. After outlining the origins of CRT, Jones Brayboy describes how he used critical race theory, anthropology, political/legal theory, political science, American Indian literatures, education, and American Indian studies to create a new tribal critical race theory (TribalCrit). TribalCrit focuses on the relationship between U.S. indigenous peoples and the U.S. government. There are nine basic principles of TribalCrit: colonization is endemic to society; U.S. policies towards indigenous peoples are based in imperialism, White supremacy, and a desire for material gain; indigenous peoples' identities are politicized and racialized in a liminal space; indigenous peoples desire tribal sovereignty and autonomy; an indigenous lens provides the concepts of culture, knowledge, and power with meaning; governmental and educational policies for Indigenous peoples are associated with assimilation; understanding the realities of indigenous peoples requires looking at tribal philosophies, beliefs, customs, traditions, and visions for the future; stories are intimately related to theory; and theory and practice are linked.

Ladson-Billings, G. (Ed.). (2003). *Critical race theory perspectives on the social studies: The profession, policies, and curriculum.* Greenwich, CT: Information Age Publishing.

In this definitive book linking critical race theory to the field of social studies, Ladson-Billings examines how race is both perceived and practiced within the broad scope of social studies education. The relationship between critical race theory and social studies is presented through four contexts: Professional, political, curricular, and technological. Ultimately, the editor hopes to see race and racial understandings inserted squarely within the context of social studies policy and practice, bridging what she perceives to be a disconnect between the culture of the classroom and culture writ large. For this work, Ladson-Billings culled scholars who work both inside and outside of the field of social studies education. The "outsider's view" is particularly refreshing as it adds unique and important insights into the relationship at hand.

Ladson-Billings, G., & Tate, W. F. (1995). Toward a critical race theory of education. *Teachers College Record, 97*(1), 47–68.

In this historic work, Ladson-Billings and Tate focus on the need to understand school inequities, and the possibility for using race as both a theory and tool for this purpose. They use CRT to critique both the contemporary use of multiculturalism in schools as simply a study of differences (rather than an examination of the differential distribution of power in U.S. history and society) and the status quo of segregated and unequal schools for African-American children and other children of color—how inequities in the United States continue to be significantly tied to race; how both U.S. schooling and society are centered around property rights; and how the intersection of race and property provides a lens for understanding inequalities in U.S. schools. The authors propose that when using CRT in educational studies, both race and property must be at the center of the effort.

Lipman, P. (2003). Chicago school policy: Regulating Black and Latino youth in the global city. *Race Ethnicity and Education, 6*(4), 331–355.

Through a qualitative study of four schools in Chicago and the gathering of quantitative data from Chicago Public Schools, Lipman created a case study of school policy around accountability in Chicago. Because school reformers have hailed the case of Chicago as an exemplar of successful school reform, Lipman points to the importance of understanding the implication of these policies for African-American and Latino youth. Rather than providing access to equal education, African-American and Latino youth are sorted and disciplined by policies to prepare them for specific service roles within the global knowledge economy. Critical race theory is used to center race as a lens of analysis, challenging the colorblind rhetoric around education policies in Chicago.

Love, B. J. (2004). "Brown" plus 50 counter-storytelling: A critical race theory analysis of the "Majoritarian Achievement Gap" story. *Equity and Excellence in Education, 37*(3), 227–246.

Herein, Barbara Love uses CRT to critique the popular understanding of an "Achievement Gap" in the context of *Brown vs. Board of Education*. In doing so, she discusses the achievement gap as a continuation of the narrative of African-American intellectual inferiority in the United States. Challenging this untruth, Love tells the counter story of African-Americans' struggle for equal education before and after *Brown*, and uses CRT to analyze the path of integration for African-American students. Specifically, she promotes the idea that the implementation of *Brown vs. Board of Education* was undermined and did not lead to an equal education for African-American students. In this counter narrative, the achievement gap is, as Gloria Ladson-Billings called it in her 2004 AERA Presidential Address, an "education debt."

Lynn, M., & Parker, L. (2006). Critical race studies in education: Examining a decade of research on U.S. schools. *The Urban Review, 38*(4), 257–290.

This article provides a comprehensive review of the use of critical race theory in a variety of fields within K–12 educational research. After grounding CRT within the history of critical legal studies and clarifying the themes that unite work in CRT, the authors provide an overview of the direction of the use of CRT in fields other than education, specifically law and economics. This article traces the ways that CRT made inroads into educational studies, elucidating seminal articles, books, and journals vis-à-vis this journey. Furthermore, a summary of the use of CRT in subfields of education research is provided, including qualitative research, educational policy, educational history, teacher education, and critical race pedagogy. The authors conclude by suggesting future directions for the use of CRT in education, both by looking to sociological research on race and suggesting the need for praxis—the uniting of theory and action.

Marx, S. (2004). Regarding whiteness: Exploring and intervening in the effects of white racism in teacher education. *Equity and Excellence in Education, 37*(1), 31–43.

In this study, the author used critical race theory and critical white studies to frame understandings of preservice white teachers' conceptions of students and race. During one semester, nine white English-only speaking preservice teachers engaged in tutoring students of Mexican origin who were also English language learners. This research drew on tutoring observations and analysis of learning journals to investigate the beliefs of these preservice teachers about race, teaching, and the children with whom they were working. Embodying the CRT call for praxis, after the researcher found that racism and whiteness were impeding the enactment of participants' noble intentions, she shared this information with the participants with the goal of disrupting the invisible discourses of whiteness at work in their professional lives.

Matsuda, M. J., Lawrence III, C. R., Delgado, R., & Crenshaw, K. W. (1993). *Words that wound: Critical race theory, assaultive speech, and the First Amendment.* Boulder, CO: Westview Press.

In this seminal book, four legal scholars bridge the intersection between critical race theory and racially tinged hate speech, framing the discourse within the boundaries of the First Amendment. At its core, this book argues that race is the underlying factor in the contradictory means by which the First Amendment alternately exempts and ignores free speech. This reading is essential, particularly for students, faculty, and administrators who navigate the murky waters of free speech on colleges and universities. Though laced with legal terminology, the chapters included are nonetheless accessible and succinctly written, each offering the reader important—and timeless—insights into the racially backed construction of words and how such words inevitably wound.

Parker, L., Dehyle, D., & Villenas, S. (Eds.). (1999). *Race is . . . race isn't: Critical race theory and qualitative studies in education.* Boulder, CO: Westview Press.

The sweeping focus of this book is to both examine and illustrate the way(s) that critical race theory is manifest in the personal, professional, and educational aspirations and outcomes of students of color. The premise here is that critical race theory is more than a theory: manifestations have alternatingly liberating and dire consequences in the lives of everyday people. Compiling a rich and diverse array of perspectives and practices, the editors never stray from the assertion that critical race theory impacts lives. The focus of the articles range from educational equity for Navajo, Chicana/o and Latina/o students, to identity formation for second-generation Korean women to the ways gender and class impact classroom discourse.

Rashid, K. (2011). "To break asunder along the lesions of race." The critical race theory of W.E.B. Du Bois. *Race Ethnicity and Education, 14,* 585–602.

This article adds to the CRT literature by examining the writings of W. E. B. Du Bois and positioning them within a framework of coupling African American education and CRT. Though Du Bois wrote extensively about Pan-Africanism, class and sex inequality, and the indelible blight of entrenched and intractable racism, it is his writing on education that often gains the most interest. The author argues that many of the contemporary derivations on and conversations about CRT may, in fact, have their roots in Du Boisian thought. The article pays close attention to the intersection between race and education (with a noted emphasis on the imperative of the classroom teacher to transform individual and collective consciousness), and asserts that Du Bois remains relevant as a (unwitting) pioneer of CRT.

Smith-Maddox, R., & Solorzano, D. G. (2002). Using critical race theory, Paulo Freire's problem-posing method, and case study research to confront race and racism in education. *Qualitative Inquiry, 8*(1), 66–85.

Central to critical race theory is the opposition to social and institutional paradigms that subordinate and, ultimately, marginalize. The authors of this article link the tenets of CRT with Freirian thought that asserts that schools are conduits for personal and/or group liberation. To move towards such liberation through the challenging of educational inequities, Freire poses a three-step process that involves analyzing the problem (injustice) at hand, understanding its cause(s), and finding a solution. The authors fuse CRT and Freire's model of problem-posing methodology through the use of case study development and analysis. This model of theory into practice offers students alternate ways of both confronting and reshaping their own concepts of race and shows how such newfound concepts can ultimately shape classroom practice.

Solorzano, D. G., & Ornelas, A. (2004). A critical race analysis of Latina/o and African American advanced placement enrollment in public high schools. *High School Journal, 87*(3), 15–26.

In this article, the authors demonstrate the use of critical race theory as a framework for policy studies. Through an investigation of the availability of AP courses in a school district in California serving a large percentage of both African-American and Latina/o students, the authors demonstrate how race and educational access intersect. Overall, the study showed that schools serving low-income Latina/o and African-American communities enrolled fewer students in AP courses than schools in other communities. In addition, across the district, Latina/o students were underrepresented in AP courses, even when attending schools with a large proportion of students enrolled in such courses. These findings support the authors' criticism of the ways schools preserve racial and ethnic discrimination vis-à-vis student access to AP courses. In line with the tenets of CRT, the responses of Latina/o and African-American students and parents to these realities are discussed. The authors suggest reforms to end such differentiation in access among students from different racial backgrounds.

Solorzano, D. G., & Yosso, T. J. (2002). Critical race methodology: Counterstory-telling as an analytical framework for education research. *Qualitative Inquiry*, *8*(1), 23–44.

Herein, Solorzano and Yosso propose a critical race methodology that can be used to perform the work of CRT in education. The central facets of this methodology are the foregrounding of race and racism; challenging traditional research paradigms explaining the experiences of youth of color; creating transformative solutions to inequities; and focusing on the raced, gendered, and classed experiences of students. They highlight how the use of ethnic studies, sociology, anthropology, and other fields of study for understanding student experiences are an integral part of critical race methodology. They also discuss how scholars using critical race methodology can employ narratives that challenge dominant modes of thought in a process named "counter storytelling," or telling the stories of individuals who are marginalized by racism, classism, and sexism.

Stovall, D. (2005). A challenge to traditional theory: Critical race theory, African-American community organizers, and education. *Discourse: Studies in the Cultural Politics of Education*, *26*(1), 95–108.

In line with a call for praxis—or the joining of theory and practice—by critical race theorists, this article explores the work of three African-American community organizers in Chicago, IL. Through interviews, the organizers' understandings of relationships between communities and schools are highlighted. Such relationships are posited as crucial for the success of students of color in public education, as these connections allow both the examination and transformation of the world around them. Essentially, critical race theory is used as an impetus for this praxis.

Tate, W. F. (1997). Critical race theory and education: History, theory, and implications. *Review of Research in Education*, *22*, 195–247.

William Tate is often considered, along with Gloria Ladson-Billings, to be the founder of CRT in education. In this influential article, he discusses the tenets of CRT that are useful in the field of education. He does so by first describing the parallels between educational research and legal work in the United States, outlining the ways that both help to create belief systems and provide evidence for policies (i.e., such as local funding of education, single-test entry systems for magnet schools, tracked high school courses and limited funding for early childhood education) that contribute to educational inequities for students of color. Next, he reviews the history of the CRT worldview, explaining its roots in the legal studies that stemmed from the 1960s social justice movement. Finally, he provides a clear distinction between the paradigms of CRT and critical legal studies (CLS). CLS, while focusing on civil rights, does not explicitly center race. Scholars who subscribe to the CRT worldview hold that the experiences of people of color in the United States are not sufficiently explained by CLS.

Vaught, S. E., & Castagno, A. E. (2008). "I don't think I'm a racist": Critical race theory, teacher attitudes, and structural racism. *Race Ethnicity and Education, 11*(2), 95–113.

This article examines teacher attitudes towards concepts of race and racial privilege in response to district-supported in-service sessions. Such sessions at two culturally diverse "underperforming" schools were designed to raise racial and cultural awareness of teachers in hopes of ultimately alleviating the achievement gap evident in the district. Through a series of interviews, the authors sought to understand what teachers "took away" from the in-service sessions, with particular reference to the concept of white property or the expectation of entitled privilege evidenced through the color of one's skin. The authors conclude that awareness did not lead to a corresponding empathy among teachers towards the academic/social/racial/economic struggles many of their students face. Raising individual awareness (which was the premise of the in-service sessions), is presented as ultimately futile unless there is a collective rally to combat the entrenched structural beliefs and practices that perpetuate inequality and inequity. Using critical race theory and its push for the de-legitimation of White hegemony, the authors hold that teachers (and school districts) can begin to meaningfully address the achievement gap through a transformation of both priority and purpose.

Yosso, T. (2002). Toward a critical race curriculum. *Equity and Excellence in Education, 35*(2), 93–107.

This important article bridges theory and practice as Yosso moves the tenets of CRT into the classroom. She argues that educators should use CRT as a means to confront racism and discrimination found in the structures (the offering of specific classes), processes (the placement of certain students in certain classes, thus acquiring a certain knowledge base), and discourses (the justification of why some students have access to a certain knowledge based and others do not) surrounding the design and delivery of school-based content. The sweeping goal here is to challenge the dominant curricular structures that codify and limit educational access and equity particularly for students of color.

Yosso, T., Smigh, W., Ceja, M., & Solorzano, D. (2009). Critical race theory, racial micro aggressions, and campus racial climate for Latina/o undergraduates. *Harvard Educational Review, 79,* 659–690.

The authors of this piece explore how racial micro aggressions—defined as interpersonal, racial, and institutional acts—are experienced by Latina/o students on select college campuses and the degree by which such forms of racial micro aggressions affect Latina/o students. The various overt and alternately subtle ways by which Latina/o students ultimately respond to such micro aggressions are explored. The authors contend that by fostering a sense of community (shared vision, shared experiences) and developing a set of critical navigational skills (questioning, advocating), Latina/o students are able to become both self and collectively empowered.

Zamudio, M. M., Russell, C., Rios, F. A., & Bridgeman, J. L. (2011). *Critical race theory matters: Education and ideology.* New York, NY: Routledge.

Critical Race Theory Matters provides a comprehensive overview of critical race theory writ large, yet pays particular attention to its influence upon the field of education. The authors initially provide an accessible and succinct theoretical overview of CRT. This is followed by a discussion on how CRT influences the design and delivery of education. Topics range from macro-policies such as bilingual education and affirmative action to micro-policies such as classroom management and the curriculum. The book concludes by offering Native American, Chicano/a, Latino/a, and African American counter-narratives as a means of challenging and refuting racial and cultural assumptions. Moving beyond the identification of problems into the realm of problem solving, *Critical Race Theory Matters* is a call to action to put into praxis a radical new vision of education in support of equality and social justice

CHAPTER 4

PEDAGOGY OF REINVENTION

Paulo Freire in 20th and 21st Century Education

Gail Russell-Buffalo and Nichole Stanford

INTRODUCTION

Born in 1921 in Recife, Brazil, Paulo Freire came to theorize education as an intrinsically political act as a result of reflecting on his own experiences growing up in a variety of socio-economic and political conditions. His family was forced to move from urban Recife to a cheaper, rural area in 1931 when the effects of the Great Depression reached Brazil. Hungry and distracted with poverty, Freire's concentration level and scholastic abilities dropped so markedly that his teachers were concerned he had developmental delays, as he was testing two years behind his grade. Ultimately, Freire came to see this academic failure as a result of the gross inequalities of Brazil's feudal-like socio-economy. Reflecting later, he wrote:

Educating About Social Issues in the 20th and 21st Centuries, pages 71–93

I wanted very much to study, but I couldn't as our economic conditions didn't allow me to. I tried to read or pay attention in the classroom, but I didn't understand anything because of my hunger. I wasn't dumb. It wasn't lack of interest. My social condition didn't allow me to have an education. Experience showed me once again the relationship between social class and knowledge... When I began to eat better, I began understanding better what I was reading." (Gadotti, 1994, p. 5)

Observing his rural community, particularly the children of farmers and laborers, Freire realized that, like him, they weren't uninterested or incapable of learning; they were simply distracted by social conditions such as hunger and cold. Before Freire and the other children could excel academically, it was imperative to meet their physical needs.

Though his family eventually returned to their former middle-class status when the economy improved, Freire never forgot the lessons he learned from playing and going to school with the poorer children of the community. Social class and social conditions came to dominate his theories of education and pedagogy.

Freire studied law and philosophy at the University of Pernambuco and was admitted to the legal bar but chose to pursue teaching shortly after marrying Elza Maia Costa de Oliveira, a teacher of elementary school literacy with whom he had five children, in 1944. Completing his doctoral work on adult illiteracy in 1959, Freire took a position at the University of Recife as a professor of history and philosophy. He was appointed director of the Department of Education and Culture of the Social Service in Pernambuco in 1946, and subsequently, in 1961, director of the Department of Cultural Extension of Recife University. During these years, he further developed, along with his wife Elza, his class-informed theory of education, focusing on the poor illiterates who were banned from voting.

Freire is most known for criticizing the "banking model" of education, a pedagogical arrangement that rewards students for rote memorization by treating them as empty receptacles for "depositing" information (which is "withdrawn" for the test). He pushed instead for a "problem-posing" model that invites "critical thinking," a way of "reading the world" (not just "reading words") that leads to both alphabetic and political literacy. His education model based on "culture circles" (which we describe later) was so successful that in one instance 300 sugarcane workers learned to read and write in 45 days. Eventually, he was recognized nationally for his work. Freire's commitment to radicalizing Brazilian peasants in his adult literacy classes, however, ultimately resulted in his political imprisonment and exile during a military coup in 1964, leading him to transfer his theory and work outside Brazil. After being imprisoned in Brazil for 70 days, ended up residing and working in several different countries, including Bolivia, Chile, the United States, and Switzerland.

Freire is generally recognized as a radical pedagogue who applied his understanding of class inequality to educational models and initiated the critical pedagogy movement with his foundational book *Pedagogy of the Oppressed,* first published in 1968. He returned to Brazil in 1980 after his exile was rescinded, where he served again in educational capacities. He died in 1997 in São Paulo, Brazil.

Freire's radical philosophy and practice of education were *dialectical* in that they were designed to be negotiated between the teacher and students in ways that would suit each classroom, not universally defined and instituted across time and space. He never aimed to be replicated (Roberts, 2000; Mayo, 2004). He wanted his work, if used, to be reinvented. As the introduction to *Mentoring the Mentor* puts it, "Since the early 1970s Freire himself has been calling for a process of reinventing Paulo Freire in the North American context, or in any other context where he himself has not worked or is not currently working" (Freire, P., Fraser, J., Macedo, D., McKinnon, T., and Stokes, W. T., 1997, p. xiv). Pedagogy was to be "situated," specific to its context. To that end, Freire intentionally left his theory open for interpretation, and as a result critical pedagogy today is a dynamic collaboration of Freire's and other influential theorists' work.

Because of Freire's preference for collaboration and reinterpretation, this chapter examines Freire's pedagogical theory in light of his own writings as much as how he has been translated and reinvented for other contexts. After providing an overview of his theory and terms, we look at some of his most important collaborations translating his pedagogy from adult literacy courses among Brazilian peasants to North American and other "first-world" classrooms. Then we move on to examples of Freirean theorists who have reinvented his theory in interesting contexts throughout the world. This chapter is written from our mostly "first-world" perspective and based on literature that has been translated into English.

FREIRE'S PEDAGOGY

Freire once commented, "God led me to the people [...] and the people led me to [...] Marx" (MacKie, 1981, p. 126). While Freire never committed wholesale to liberation theology, his Catholic faith and radical politics were intimately entwined, leading him to advocate passionately for social justice and what he called the "humanization" of people who had been dehumanized by oppression.

Freire argued that people are lowered to the level of animals when they are denied the ability to think and make decisions for themselves, and he blamed educational systems in large part for encouraging students to memorize platitudes and political slogans or rely on "magical thinking" (myths, folklore, religion) instead of critical thinking. He believed that people wind up "internalizing the oppressor" and effectively monitoring their own actions to maintain unequal political conditions that hurt themselves.

The process of humanization involves coming to a critical consciousness (*conscientização*) of the sociopolitical context (for example, Brazilian peasants in Freire's literacy classes did the bulk of the national work, yet three percent of the population controlled half the land) and initiating a process of *praxis*, a combination of action and reflection building on and informing further action and reflecti, to achieve social change. Because of Freire's passion to see people democratically govern themselves, key Freirean concepts and terms derive from the new relationship he proposes for classrooms, in which the purpose of education is to teach that social conditions are not something to which the people must adapt but something that can and should be adapted to the people.

1. Dialogue

One of the most important ideas underlying Freirean pedagogy is the interdependence of the dialectic and dialogue in education. Based on the Hegelian dialectic model of thesis/antithesis/synthesis, Freire sees dialogue as a negotiation between humans that leads to social change, and he seeks to create the same kind of encounter between teachers and students in classrooms. In this regard, he writes, "Education must begin with the solution of the teacher-student contradiction, by reconciling the poles of the contradiction so that both are simultaneously teachers and students" (1970/1993, p. 53). In Freire's critical pedagogy, therefore, the centerpiece of liberating pedagogy is dialogue; teachers and students engage in dialogic encounters instead of unilateral transfers of information (as in the banking model); thus, discussions, not lectures, are at the heart of the process. Essentially, Freire seeks to eliminate the hierarchy between teachers (whom he renames "teacher-student" to stress the fact that teachers also learn from their students) and students (or "students-teachers") by demanding that critical educators be humble and respectful of students' prior knowledge, not just paternalistically tolerant. This kind of approach shifts education from an act of memorization to an act of investigation: "The students—no longer docile listeners—are now critical coinvestigators in dialogue with the teacher" (Freire, 1970/1993, p. 62). Student-teacher dialogue that honors students' knowledge enables the ongoing dialectical process of engagement of learners with their learning. To further level the hierarchy within the classroom, Freire suggests the need for creating a *culture circle*, which is to be led by a facilitator who helps *literants* to learn to the read "the world" and "the word" through dialogical encounters.

2. Generative Themes

Another tenet of Freirean pedagogy is that of "generative themes," in which teachers invite students to collaborate on course content decisions rather than requiring them to submit unthinkingly to a predetermined curriculum. In this regard, Freire (1973/1990) writes, "The starting point for organizing the program content of education or political action must be the present, existential, concrete situation, reflecting the aspirations of the people" (p. 76). Using generative themes helps accomplish the connection Freire often makes between "reading the world" and "reading the word": students who are invested in the topics will be more invested in learning to write about them. Not only does he favor this approach because he wants to involve the natural curiosity and inquisitiveness of people in learning, but Freire also maintains that it is fundamentally wrong to leave students out of the decision making process. Like other postcolonial critics of "center" (a postcolonial term for the empire or ruling class) policies and reforms done *to* the periphery (colonies or savages who are "inferior" and "incapable" of ruling themselves), Freire argues that teachers shouldn't make decisions *about* or *for* students, but *with* them. Finally, beginning with the "present, existential, concrete situation" helps literants in Freire's culture circles understand that any social circumstance can be challenged, including social changes that they decide to initiate themselves, not just the lofty ideas of politicians or "great men."

3. Problem Posing/Codification

The role of the teacher is not to "deposit" information in the students' brains (as in the banking model) but to engage in dialogue with them. Because most students have been taught in traditional classrooms *not* to think for themselves, Freire suggests that critical educators may need to take extra steps to provoke authentic dialogue. First, a problem-posing approach invites students to think of everyday situations (which are introduced by the students themselves in generative themes) as problems to be solved instead of facts to be memorized.[1] To invite students to think for themselves, Freire developed a process he called codification: educators select an everyday negative situation (which students may generally accept as normal, unchangeable, or even deserved) and "codify" it into an unfamiliar scenario so that the students can discuss the situation without the influence of emotions or memorized platitudes. The students then "decode" the scenario and continue the discussion, which is newly informed by each codification and decoding of the scenario. Shor (1992) gives an example of a teacher who "steals" a student's purse, claiming that he "discovered" it, as Columbus discovered America (Shor, 1992, pp. 118–126). Souto-Manning (2010) gives more examples. The teacher "re-presents" situations to students in an unfamiliar way, stressing the changeable nature of their conditions.

The entire process is designed to teach people how to engage in class struggle and win better sociopolitical conditions. Freire advocated problem-posing pedagogy to help students distinguish between the hegemonic beliefs they memorize (the "oppressor consciousness" they internalize) and what they really think about the world. He called this a process of humanization: rising from the level of beasts to humans. That accomplished, he then urges students to use the dialoguing skills they learn in their dialectical encounters with teachers (who have traditionally represented authority) to negotiate a new reality for themselves beyond classrooms. Freire provided the most comprehensive description of his radical approach to teaching in *Pedagogy of the Oppressed,* but he developed and nuanced these ideas in numerous writings until his death in 1997.

In his later work, Freire extended his pedagogies to national educational systems, including the United States, arguing that the democratization of schools will lead to the democratization of society. Though critical pedagogy (as well as other left teaching practices) has been criticized in the United States for its explicit "political agenda," Freire maintained that education is never neutral and is always fundamentally political, whether it is explicit or concealed (Shor and Freire, 1987). Meanwhile, he demanded that practitioners of critical pedagogy be loving, humble, and respectful of their students, and that they engage in deep reflection on the appropriateness of their teaching methods and learners' engagement. Other critics argued that, unlike Freire's home country, Brazil, the United States is a classless nation, so students do not need conscientization. Yet Freire pointed out that levels of student resistance and rebellion in U.S. classrooms reveal a sense of inequality even in the United States (Shor and Freire, 1987). He maintained, along with other education theorists such as Michael Apple, Jean Anyon, Henry Giroux, Stanley Aronowitz, Elspeth Stuckey, and Ira Shor, that the notion of the United States as a classless society is a deeply misguided one. He also later responded to criticisms of his being sexist in his writings (for ignoring the differences that men and women face) by apologizing, conscientiously altering his pronoun usage, and extending his social justice arguments to gender equality.

TRANSLATING FREIRE
FOR A NORTH AMERICAN CONTEXT

In this section we focus more on the translation of Freire's "worlds" than on the literal, or "word for word" translations of his texts into English. Given the privilege of North American (especially the English-speaking United States and Canadian) educational contexts relative to the poverty in locations of Freire's work, it is important that North American educators aptly apply Freire's peda-gogical theories. Thus, this section describes how two of Freire's North American colleagues and his English-speaking second wife, Nita, "translate" Freire's particular context. We also explain the need to translate Freire's works beyond the literal level, as specific to the urgency, passion, love, and humility intended by Freire and the particular gaps created in translation from Portuguese into English. (For more on this topic, consult Borg and Mayo, 2000a.)

In its original conception, problem-posing education was meant for third world, adult education contexts. However, due to Freire's rising popularity across the globe, it became necessary to imagine Freire's pedagogy in first-world and North American contexts. In response, Freire has been translated in a number of ways. Several scholars have devoted their work to further-ing critical pedagogy and have been central to translating Freire's work from his language and settings in Brazil to classrooms in North America and else-where. Donaldo Macedo, Freire's "chief translator and interpreter into Eng-lish" (The Freire Project, n.d., para. 1) has greatly contributed by literally translating several of Freire's texts from the original Portuguese to English. He and three coeditors, along with Freire, produced *Mentoring the Mentor: A Critical Dialogue with Paulo Freire*, (Freire, Fraser, Macedo, McKinnon, & Stokes, 1997), an edited volume that traces how Freire has been translated for the North American context since 1991. Macedo also importantly coau-thored one of Freire's first and most seminal talking books, *Literacy, Reading the Word and the World* (Freire & Macedo, 1987). Macedo focuses on the im-portance of always reinventing methods for Freire's pedagogy, reporting that Freire once said, "'Donaldo, I don't want to be imported or exported. It is impossible to export pedagogical practices without reinventing them. Please, tell your fellow American educators not to import me. Ask them to recreate and rewrite my ideas'" (quoted in Macedo, 1997, p. 3). Accordingly, Macedo insisted that North American educators remember that we cannot reproduce Freire's methods, because context demands different approaches/methods.

In 1992, Ira Shor authored *Empowering Education: Critical Teaching for So-cial Change*, a book other critical pedagogy proponents have referred to as the "bible of critical pedagogy," to provide practical applications of Freire's theory in U.S. classrooms. In this comprehensive book, Shor provides hands-on descriptions and illustrations to apply some of the main features of Freire's critical pedagogy—for example, how to conduct a democratic classroom, how to foster dialogue (rather than solely engage in teacher talk), how to use problem-posing teaching methods that lead to activism, and how to create what he calls "desocializing" experiences to raise critical consciousness (such as the Columbus example mentioned above). In *When Students Have Power: Negotiating Authority in a Critical Pedagogy* (1997), Shor examines issues of student resistance in U.S. college classrooms, from the special layout of classrooms (panopticon-like and with a special desk for the teacher) that reifies student-teacher inequality to possibilities for students' steering the curriculum in after-class meetings. Drawing on a theme of utopia throughout the book and his experiences with one particularly challenging class, Shor translates Freire's theories for use in the United States, a context radically different from that of Freire's adult classes in Brazil.

Ana Maria Araújo Freire, Freire's second wife (his first wife died in 1986), translates Freire's work into English by means of exhaustive expository footnotes through what is often called "free translation" (M. Souto-Manning, personal communication, November 1, 2012), because she provides details and clarity to the literal translations of Freire's work. Essentially, a free translation provides the contextual and expressive nuances of a particular language. As the contrastive rhetoric branch of applied linguistics has shown (Kaplan, 1966; Connor, 2004), languages are comprised of more than just vocabulary and grammar; second-language users may not pick up on the conventions for things like argument, humor, hints, and politeness through particulars like sentence structure and register of vocabulary. With Portuguese translations into English, it is even more important, because Portuguese has greater expressive capacities than English forms. Freire wrote in depth about dispositional qualities of teachers, such as love, humility, and passion. In Portuguese, his meaning is crystal clear; in English, the words translate into complicated sentence structures that are not particularly clear (M. Souto-Manning, personal communication, 2012). Ana Maria Araujo Freire, popularly known as Nita, fills in the gaps in Freire's English translations so that the spirit of his Portuguese writing comes through along with the letter meaning.

Beyond the literal complications of translating Freire's Portuguese writing, there is a significant concern for translating the ethos, or being true to the content, of Freire's writing. In an interview with Peter Mayo, published in 2000, Nita explains that Portuguese is more expressive than English; as such, it offers much more range in terms of expression (as cited in Mayo, 2004; see Borg and Mayo, 2000a). Also, very significant to the work of Freire is the ability to express thought and emotion simultaneously. English is more influenced by Cartesian thinking, Nita explains, where thought and emotion are separated.

Indeed, Freire insisted that pedagogical work be contextualized. In the now famous quote to Donaldo Macedo, cited above, Freire exhorted his friend, "Please, tell your fellow American educators not to import me. Ask them to recreate and rewrite my ideas" (cited in Macedo, 1997, p. 3). In order to reinvent Freire in new contexts, one needs to know the details of Freire's belief in the critical need to "educate in context." Nita's footnotes provide many ways for educators to connect to Freire's life and works, so that they can make it relevant to their own work without "importing" Freire. In fact, Nita describes Freire's political context in exhaustive detail. In a footnote for *Letters to Cristina* (Freire, 1996), she explains political corruption in the election of General Dantas Barreto as governor of Pernambuco and his effect on the population in the following way:

> In fact, he was elected with the intervention of the federal government in Pernambuco using the local army—today the seventh military regiment—for electoral fraud. . . . The person whom the forces in power had decided should take power (see note of the fourteenth letter), Dantas Barreto, instilled terror after taking office,. [sic] His mission was to replace the oligarchy of Rosa e Silva and to frighten the news reporters and the most daring colonels, thereby establishing a stronger military government. (p. 211)

This footnote continues for another one and one half pages. Tellingly, Nita's footnotes to *Letters to Cristina* are 61 pages in length. For Nita's part, translating Freire's sociopolitical context for English-speaking audiences is a labor of love, which resembles Freire's investment in political action and passionate writing. Nita's provision of deep knowledge and details of Freire's context in the form of English explanations enhance for North American readers the necessary backdrop of social and political conflicts that surrounded Freire's work in action. Nita was a passionate but careful free translator and editor of Freire's Portuguese writing for English-speaking audiences. She also coedited *The Paulo Freire Reader* with Donaldo Macedo (A. M. A. Freire & Macedo, 1998), gave lucid interviews (Borg and Mayo, 2000a), and cofounded The Freire Project with Shirley Steinberg.

Given the criticism that Freire's work excludes women (Roberts, 2000; Mayo, 2004), whether it is through the use of the masculine form to talk about humankind or the overwhelming majority of male scholars contributing to the English conversation about Freire, Nita's work is especially important. A former student of Freire's and Brazilian, she provides informed exposition that is humble, passionate, and accessible. Like Freire (2005), Nita assumes, "We all know something; we are all ignorant of something" (p. 71). Ultimately, she provides an incredible amount of information for the informed and the uninformed, which ultimately grants a wide range of access to Freire's theory in the English language.

Similarly, her notes to *Pedagogy of Hope* (Freire, 1994) provide an intimate and immediate portrait of Freire's life behind his work. Freire insisted that context determines human subjectivity, and Nita's notes provide us with additional context vis-à-vis Freire's life, which is needed in order to fully understand what he was attempting to do and why and under what circumstances. Steinberg (2005) has criticized researchers' lack of attention to Nita's scholarship on Freire's life and work. As explained herein, Nita's contribution is important, not only in providing the details of Freire's context, but also because not enough scholarship on Freire comes from women. Establishing Nita's reputation as a Freirean scholar will likely enable more women to publish about how Freire can be rein-vented to support the concientization of women who are marginalized. See, for example, Souto-Manning (2005).

Macedo, Shor, and Nita Freire provide important translation of Freire, par-ticularly for North American contexts. Besides being known for their own work, Macedo and Shor are among Freire's most important collaborators (Roberts, 2000, p. 25). Nita offered cultural and historical context for much of Freire's writing, while Macedo and Shor helped to usher in Freire's "talking book" for-mat he used in the last decade of his writing. In the final decade of his life, Freire invested in writing for multiple audiences and writing in forms that reflected his dialectical values. This is how his "talking books" (Freire & Macedo, 1987; Freire & Shor, 1987) and his more conversational texts were born. The talking books transition Freire's "teaching," or expository, form of earlier texts such as *Pedagogy of the Oppressed* into a conversational style. In these books, Freire struggles with his own ideas, asks rhetorical questions, and allows his interviewer (the coauthor) to cross-examine him on controversial topics, such as his inter-ventionist tactics and his work as Secretary of Education in São Paulo. In Freire's single-author writings of the last decade of his life, he continues with the dia-lectical tone and style of the "talking book" in such works as *Teachers as Cultural Workers: Letters to Those Who Dare Teach* (1998/2005). Freire's conversationally-toned books demonstrate Freire's dialectical approach to thinking, his open-ness to being wrong or being corrected, and his desire to make his writing more accessible. The publication of Freire's thinking in this format is very important, because it brings him "full circle" as an author whose form follows his purpose and function.

Due to the efforts of Freire's North American colleagues and his second wife, Nita Freire, there are many enhancements to translations of Freire's work into the English language. Yet, in the rich tradition of Portuguese expression and the context of Freire's educational specialization, more translation is need-ed. Indeed, not enough of the immense amount of Freire's Portuguese writ-ings are translated into English. Additionally, we need continued variety in the types of translations available. Thus far, we have literal renderings of Freire's writings into English. That means that the writing is more complex than nec-essary for the English structure. More free translation of the Portuguese into English would provide a broader range of English readers greater access to Freire's texts. Perhaps, educators should take up this task. Souto-Manning (personal communication, November 1, 2012) insists that educator-translators could render the nuances in Freire's original writing about teaching in ways that would make us better readers of Freire's emphases on education and the passion necessary to living this action in our teaching praxis.

REINVENTING FREIRE FOR THE TWENTY-FIRST CENTURY

In addition to the work of the theorists mentioned above who wrote with Freire and translated his pedagogy for North American contexts in the 1980s and 1990s—some of whom might be called "first-generation" Freireans—there have been important reinventions of Freire for twenty-first century contexts. The following "second-generation" Freireans are university-based researchers and scholars who have applied (and in various cases, still apply) Freire's principles to new contexts.

Henry Giroux (2012) has contributed significantly to reinventing Freire for educational theory in the realms of policymaking and administrative decisions. Giroux, who could just as well be considered a first-generation Freirean because of his close work with Freire, is a noted critical educator in his own right (see the chapter on Giroux, this volume; and, see Riley in Volume 1 of this series by Totten and Pedersen); Freire cites Giroux significantly in several of his works (Freire, 1996; Freire and Macedo, 1987); and, notably, Giroux is the author of the introduction to Freire and Macedo's 1987 talking book. Giroux's focus has been on critiques of so-called educational reform (ultimately a return to the banking model via standardized testing) and the deprofessionalization of teaching (which destroys the possibility for critical dialogue [Freire, 1997b]). Giroux also offers a radical critique of the contemporary charter school movement and the dehumanization of students and teachers in contemporary U.S. public schools. He historicizes this situation within the longer process of neoliberal values infiltrating the ideologies of public education. Giroux argues that these ideologies conceal the private sector's attack on public schools, particularly in the United States, as venture capitalists see K–12 education as an up-and-coming opportunity for investments (Simon, 2012).

In a recent book Giroux (2012) points out that his predictions about privatization across two decades (Giroux, 1988, 2000) have become reality. In delineating the most recent trends in the politics of education, Giroux argues that extreme reinvention in public schools is essential to countering the neoliberal politics that will eventually devastate what remains of U.S. public education. In his final chapter, "Paulo Freire and the Pedagogy of Bearing Witness," Giroux explains how Freire's "pedagogy of witness" should play a key role in countering the foreclosure of public education by the private sector. He explains that the military-industrial (corporate) complex is subversively erasing the memory of people's—educators', students', and citizens'—experiences by depleting the agency available to them with regard to public education. This happens variously through the move towards privatization and increases in standardized testing in order to "prove" student, teacher, and school success. Experience is important for promoting thought and action in a Freirean-inspired pedagogy. In fact, the codification process, the bedrock of Freire's methods in Brazil, depends on individual experience. By simultaneously deskilling teachers and lulling students to sleep vis-à-vis the practice of rote memorization and test-taking, military-industrial-like inspired schools promote thoughtlessness, and, as a result, students disengage with the curriculum while teachers lose interest in reinventing a democratic curriculum for their students. In order to provide critical education, teachers must implement a pedagogy of remembering of experience and bearing critical witness to it.

Teacher educator Mariana Souto-Manning (2010) shows how she has used Freirean principles across three contexts in North America: with children, with preservice teachers, and with in-service teachers. Her research with early elementary learners focuses on problem-posing education in Freire's "culture circles," showing how she uses them to help students "read their world" and act upon it. In her study, the students raised questions about why they and their peers were being "tracked" through the school day and asked if they could eliminate tracking in their classroom. Souto-Manning, a teacher researcher at the time, worked with the students, principal, and parents to "untrack" the students for the following year. The work draws from her earlier research as a teacher using Freirean culture circles (Souto-Manning, 2004, 2005). She continues the theme of culture circles and problem posing outside of the childhood classroom as she re-invents these principles in teacher education (preservice) and professional development (in-service) contexts. Souto-Manning's work is important in a classroom in which social issues are the focus of study. Her work is inspirational in that she maintains Freire's demands for humility and respect for students' prior knowledge and their concrete situations through ongoing dialogue and problem posing.

Like Souto-Manning, Mayo (2004), a Maltese professor of education, maintains the Freirean spirit of reinvention across contexts. Deeply influenced by a series of conferences organized by the Instituto Paulo Freire, Mayo reads Freire and reinvents his work in the southern Mediterranean region. This includes national curriculum reform, research on educational partnerships with parents, and work on decolonizing museum education in Malta, where issues of difference and social class determine educational outcomes and positions of social class. Besides applying Freire to his first-world-yet-oppressed Mediterranean context, Mayo emphasizes the spiritual rigor of Freire's work. Mayo's (2004) book-length treatment of Freire begins with a discussion of the emotional draw of Freirean theory. Most Freire-influenced writers use Freire, he writes, because they feel a personal connection to his work. Then he reiterates Freire's demands that educators incorporate love into their work (something Ana Maria Araújo Freire also emphasizes).

In addition to his 2004 book-length text, Mayo has written substantially about decolonizing museum education, and he has coauthored several articles with Carmel Borg (2000b), a colleague at the University of Malta.

Mayo's reinvention of Freire for the southern Mediterranean context and even in museum education serves as another model of how Freire's values are dialectically applicable in different situations.

While Giroux, Souto-Manning, and Mayo offer examples of how we might interpret Freire and reinvent his work across physical contexts and educational specializations, Peter Roberts (1996, 2000) focuses on reinventing Freirean theory for twenty-first-century ideological contexts. Roberts (2000) provides an exhaustive overview of old and new critiques of Freire, with an emphasis on the disconnect between Freire's theory and postmodernism and poststructuralism. His ideological recontextualization of Freire is especially relevant today, since so many researchers are currently working out of postmodern and poststructuralist schools of thought, and since such schools are the most likely to condemn critical pedagogy. Postmodernist and poststructuralist deconstructions of language, thought, and identities undermine many projects of critical theorizing. In order to "name" an oppressor, one must have a critical realists' view of reality. This is in conflict with the postmodernist "death of the self" and the poststructuralists' claim that "reality" is constituted in language, socially constructed, and under erasure. Freire did not believe that reality is fixed, but he believed in a "self" and a reality that is changing, rather than one that is always subjective or under erasure. He called for the oppressed to name and act on their reality; this dialectical mode of being differs from a view of reality in which language alone produces subjectivity. In Freire's view, language, action, and reflection produce subjectivity, but his "subject" is an agentive person who can and should work to improve her or his reality.

Where postmodern and poststructuralist renderings of human subjectivities reject notions of a single unified "self," Roberts reminds us, "The importance of collectivity for Freire cannot be overemphasized" (p. 149). Along the same lines, Freire always emphasized the dynamic nature of human subjectivity, and actually began to adopt more postmodern conceptions of subjectivity later in his career. Roberts reminds readers of Freire's fundamental interest in dialectics and social interaction in *Pedagogy of the Oppressed*, demonstrating the very dynamism and possibility for reinvention available for second- (and third-) generation Freireans, as we reinvent him in the twenty-first century. In the spirit of Freire's request never to be "imported" unchanged for new educational encounters, this cross-section of authors working from and in notably different contexts illustrate just some of the many possibilities for successful reinventions of Freire in the twenty-first century. Since this is not intended to be a comprehensive list, please also consult the annotated bibliography below for elaboration on this work and that of additional second-generation Freirean scholars.

POSSIBILITIES AND LIMITATIONS
OF FREIRE'S DIALECTICAL APPROACH

Because of the dialectical nature of Freire's educational philosophy and practice, his theories can be situated in any context and applied to any content to teach students to think critically about and participate in negotiating their learning conditions and, later, their labor conditions. Each of the Freirean theorists we examine above demonstrate the possibilities for reinventing Freire's basic appeal to create dialogue between students and teachers in an effort to model the dialogues he hoped would happen one day between those who make political decisions and those who are required to obey political decisions.

The open-endedness with which pedagogues can reinvent Freire, however, can also lead to confusion in applying his theory; there are limits to how Freire can be reinterpreted. As his life and primary work become more widely circulated, there is a risk of his work being misunderstood by twenty-first century educators. At what point is reinvention of Freire no longer critical pedagogy? For example, the term *critical thinking* is ubiquitous in pedagogical conversations today, used even by advocates of standardized testing and the sociopolitical "reproductive" function of schools, aspects of schooling that Freire deeply opposed. These curriculum designers and policy makers are probably unaware of the revolutionary ideas underlying the term, but they have appropriated it to mean something altogether different from Freire's intention. It is possible to continue to reinvent Freire's work for the twenty-first century, but only by thoroughly appreciating and fully understanding his contributions as a radical and deeply spiritual educator who was committed to hope, social justice, and humanizing people who have been taught not to think for themselves.

NOTES

1. Freire does not take credit for the term *problem-posing* but reports that he borrowed it from a colleague while theorizing *Pedagogy of the Oppressed* (Roberts, 2000).

REFERENCES

Borg, C. & Mayo, P. (2000a). Reflections from a third age marriage. A pedagogy of hope, reason, and passion. An interview with Ana Maria (Nita) Araújo Freire. *McGill Journal of Education*, 35(2), 105–120.

Borg, C., & Mayo, P. (2000b). Maltese museums, adult education and cultural politics. *Education & Society*, 18(3), 77–97.

Connor, U. (2004). Intercultural rhetoric research: Beyond texts. *Journal of English for Academic Purposes, 3*(4), 291–304

The Freire Project. (n.d.). Donaldo Macedo. Retrieved from The Paulo and Nita Freire International Project for Critical Pedagogy website: http://www.freire-project.org/content/donaldo-macedo

Freire, P. (1970/1993). *Pedagogy of the oppressed.* New York: Continuum.

Freire, P. (1973/1990). *Pedagogy of the oppressed.* New York: Continuum.

Freire, P. (1994). *Pedagogy of hope: Reliving pedagogy of the oppressed.* New York, NY: Continuum.

Freire, P. (1996). Letters to Cristina: Reflections on my life and work. London: Routledge. Freire, P. (1997). *Pedagogy of the heart.* New York, NY: Continuum.

Freire, P. (1998/2005). *Teachers as cultural workers: Letters to those who dare teach.* New York, NY: Perseus Books Group.

Freire, P., Fraser, J. W., Macedo, D., McKinnon, T., & Stokes, W. T. (1997). *Mentoring the mentor: A critical dialogue with Paulo Freire.* New York, NY: Peter Lang.

Freire, P., & Macedo, D. (1987). *Literacy: Reading the word and the world.* London, UK: Routledge & Kegan Paul.

Freire, A. M. A. & Macedo, D. (1998). *The Paulo Freire Reader.* New York, NY: Continuum.

Gadotti, M. (1994). Reading Paulo Freire: His life and work. Albany: State University of New York (SUNY) Press. Giroux, H. (1988). *Teachers as intellectuals.* Westport, CT: Bergin & Garvey.

Giroux, H. A. (1988). *Teachers as intellectuals.* Granby, MA: Bergin & Garvey.

Giroux, H. A. (2000). *Stealing innocence: Corporate culture's war on children.* New York, NY: Palgrave.

Giroux, H. A. (2012). *Education and the crisis of public values: Challenging the assault on teachers, students, & public education.* New York, NY: Peter Lang.

Kaplan, R. (1966). Cultural thought patterns in intercultural education. *Language Learning, 16*(1), 1–20.

Macedo, D. (1997). An anti-method pedagogy: A Freirean perspective. In P. Freire, J. W. Fraser, D. Macedo, T. McKinnon, & W.T. Stokes (Eds.), *Mentoring the mentor: A critical dialogue with Paulo Freire* (pp. 1–9). New York: Peter Lang.

MacKie, R. (Ed.). (1981). *Literacy and revolution: The pedagogy of Paulo Freire.* New York, NY: Continuum.

Mayo, P. (2004). *Liberating praxis: Paulo Freire's legacy for radical education and politics.* Westport, CT: Praeger.

Riley, K. (2012). Touching the sacred garment: Paulo Freire, The Frankfurt School, and beyond. In S. Totten & J. E. Pedersen (Eds.), *Educating about social issues in the 20th and 21st Centuries: A critical annotated bibliography* (Vol. 1, pp. 479–507). Charlotte, NC: Information Age Publishing.

Roberts, P. (2000). *Education, literacy, and humanization: Exploring the work of Paulo Freire.* Westport, CT: Bergin & Garvey.

Shor, I. (1992). *Empowering education: Critical teaching for social change.* Chicago, IL: University of Chicago Press.

Shor, I. (1997). *When students have power: Negotiating authority in a critical pedagogy.* Chicago, IL: University of Chicago Press.

Shor, I., & Freire, P. (1987). *A pedagogy for liberation: Dialogues on transforming education*. London, UK: Macmillan.

Simon, S. (2012, August 1). Privatizing public schools: Big firms eyeing profits from U.S. K–12 market. *Huffington Post Education*. Retrieved from http://www. huffingtonpost.com/2012/08/02/private-firms-eyeing-prof_n_1732856. html?utm_hp_ref=fb&src=sp&comm_ref=false

Souto-Manning, M. (2004). Circles of culture: Literacy as a process for social inclusion. *Colombian Applied Linguistics Journal*, 6, 23–41.

Souto-Manning, M. V. (2005). Critical narrative analysis of Brazilian women's schooling discourses: Negotiating agency and identity through participation in Freirean culture circles (Unpublished dissertation). The University of Georgia: Athens, GA.

Souto-Manning, M. (2010). *Freire, teaching, and learning: Culture circles across contexts*. New York, NY: Peter Lang Publishing.

Steinberg, S. (2005). Afterword. In *Teachers as cultural workers* (pp. 173–177). Cambridge, MA: Perseus Books.

ANNOTATED BIBLIOGRAPHY

For readers new to Freire's writing, we recommend starting with *Pedagogy of the Oppressed*. As Freire's seminal text, it provides the foundation for Freire's oeuvre. *Pedagogy of the Oppressed* is the most "modern" of Freire's major writings. Freire complicated his explanation of human subjectivity throughout his career, which enabled more complex interpretations of humanization, emancipation, dialogue, etc. If further guidance is needed, we recommend *Letters to Cristina* as an accessible text into the world of Freirean pedagogy. This book shows Freire's thoughtfulness in every project and provides detailed notes (added by Nita Freire) that contextualize Freire's work in Brazil. As a reflection on Freire's life and career, it will guide readers into subsequent studies.

Pedagogical Works by Freire

Freire, P. (1970/1993). *Pedagogy of the oppressed*. New York, NY: Continuum.

> *Pedagogy of the Oppressed*, Freire's seminal text establishes Freire's primary principles. He begins with a discussion of the conditions and mechanics of oppression, similar to the theory of postcolonial scholars like Franz Fanon, Aimé Césaire, and Ngũgĩ wa Thiongo. Next, in Chapter Three, he moves to the pedagogical implications of his theory, critiquing the problems of traditional classroom arrangements. In Chapter Three, he paints a picture of a dialogic classroom, including approaches such as generative themes, problem posing, and encoding situations for conscientization. Chapter Four returns to the themes of Chapter One with further critiques of the methods of domination, as well as

critiques of efforts out of oppression that only recreate similar conditions. This book is recognized as a revolutionary text throughout the world and a classic in education theory.

Freire, P. (1974). *Education for critical consciousness.* New York, NY: Crossroad Publishing Company.

Originally written for educators in Brazil, this book mirrors many of the themes in *Pedagogy of the Oppressed,* but also includes assignments for adult literacy classes. Freire begins with a nuanced discussion of equality and the dangers of "false" forms of liberation (paternalism and "aid" programs), then looks at conditions in Brazil through a Marxist lens. Next, he contrasts education as propaganda and education as conscientization, focusing on the careful and respectful role of the educator in a critical classroom, before appending a series of sample assignments for critical educators. While the pedagogy is not especially helpful for non-Brazilian educators, the theorization of society and education is balanced and thought-provoking.

Freire, P. (1998). *Pedagogy of freedom: Ethics, democracy, and civic courage.* Lanham, MD: Rowman and Littlefield.

Again, Freire returns to the theme of humanizing, this time focusing explicitly on the role of the teacher instead of primarily on the students. He emphasizes a connection between theory and life practice, asking teachers to respect themselves and respect their colleagues. He also returns to the idea of the dialectical classroom by stressing that teachers should be sharing their knowledge but also learning from students. Similarly, he writes that education is not just a "transfer of information" but a relationship that requires mutual respect, hope, and serious dialogue. Freire concludes by emphasizing that teaching is a "human act." *Pedagogy of Freedom* is an encouraging read for educators who are looking more for a mindset from which to make pedagogical decisions than for specific ideas or assignments.

Freire's Talking Books and Books of Letters

Freire (1998/2005) *Teachers as cultural workers: Letters to those who dare teach.* New York, NY: Perseus Books Group.

Teachers as Cultural Workers addresses a number of issues regarding the critical consciousness of teachers. Here, Freire distinguishes professionalization as critical consciousness from professionalization that serves neo-liberal demands for standardizing teaching. He devotes a great deal of attention to how teachers (addressed as mostly women) are positioned to be mother-types to their students. Freire critiques such deprofessionalization of women through maternalizing the teacher's role. The voice of this book, written directly to teachers, welcomes readers into the openness of Freire's later writings. Practical questions such as how to conduct the first day of school and how to have authority without being authoritarian are addressed.

Freire, P. & Macedo, D. (1987). *Literacy: Reading the word and the world.* London, UK: Routledge and Kegan Paul.

Most of this text is presented as what Freire called a talking book interview (book-length, multi-topic dialogues written with coauthors). It provides a chapter-length description of and reflection on Freire's educational programming in Chile, including excerpts from the workbook texts that were used and explanation of how they were used. Freire discusses his enduring concerns about neo-liberalism, responds to critiques of his work in Guinea-Bissau, and critiques U.S. literacy education. The book opens with two essays by Freire. "The Importance of the Act of Reading" (cited below), was originally published in 1983. In the second essay, "Adult Literacy and Popular Libraries," Freire lays out a vision for the popular public library.

Shor, I. & Freire, P. (1987). *A pedagogy for liberation: Dialogues on transforming education.* London, UK: Macmillan.

With the same strong focus on pedagogy as found in his other books, Freire documents his conversations with Shor on a collection of questions from teachers interested in transformative education. After touching on a few typical classroom practices they reject and mistakes they have made, Shor and Freire stress that teachers of critical pedagogy must begin by examining their own ideologies about class inequalities and idealism about liberatory education. They argue that critical pedagogy cannot change the world, but it can (and does) equip students to recognize and address inequalities. Next, they discuss the risks teachers face when dropping their authoritarian stance in the classroom (e.g., awkwardness and student resistance), and concerns about the scholastic rigor of the critical pedagogy approach. After explaining practical ways to implement the "dialogical method" and "situated pedagogy," Shor and Freire move on to questions about using liberatory pedagogy in first-world classrooms, overcoming language difference with students, and finally what to do the first day of class. Freire's sometimes heavy-handed focus only on teachers' attitudes combines well with Shor's hands-on interpretations to offer teachers a well-rounded approach to using critical pedagogy.

Intimate Freire: Semi-Autobiographical Texts

Freire, P. (1983). The importance of the act of reading. *Journal of Education,* 165(1), 5–11.

This brief essay is part memoir, part summary of the codification process, and part defense of why Freire chose his world-word reading methods for teaching adults to read.

Freire, P. (1994) *Pedagogy of hope: Reliving pedagogy of the oppressed.* New York, NY: Continuum.

More autobiographical than theoretical, *Pedagogy of Hope* is a reflection on Freire's work in Brazil and abroad. Nita Freire provides the notes, as she does in *Letters to Cristina* (see below). The translation (by Robert R. Barr) conveys the deep sentiment of Paulo Freire's merger of emotion and logic. It explains why and how Freire left his law practice, after having only one client, and describes the spiritual-emotional background of his transformation into education of the poor.

Freire, P. (1996). *Letters to Cristina: Reflections on my life and work*. London, UK: Routledge.

The emphasis here is a semi-linear progression of Freire's life and thought. His niece, Cristina, originally asked for a reflection of how Freire became a great educator; Freire did not respond until years later, when Cristina was an adult in college. Freire made the book an occasion for critical reflection on his life as it had been lived. Freire describes the relationship of social class to education as he directly engages his family's progression into poverty, including the impact of the untimely death of Freire's father. *Letters to Cristina* provides an accessible point of entry into Freirean thought that is accompanied by comprehensive background on Freire's context via the footnotes provided by Nita Freire. Like the talking books, these letters prove that Freire is accessible to audiences outside of the Academy. Additionally, the poetic and figurative dimensions of Freire's style are both emotionally and logically engaging.

Comprehensive Books and Edited Collections

Darder, Antonia. (2002). *Reinventing Paulo Freire: A pedagogy of love*. Boulder, CO: Westview Press.

Darder enacts what Giroux calls "pedagogy of bearing witness" in this volume that praises Freire, theorizes his work in personal ways, and presents the voices of teachers in order to highlight examples of excellence in critical teaching. The book is divided into three theoretical chapters and one chapter that is a collection of eight elegant, personal essays written by critical (mostly public) educators. Though Darder's theoretical language in the beginning of the text is difficult to read, the sense she makes of Freire's work is unmistakable. Particularly useful in her theoretical introduction are her clear definitions of how Freire uses "love" (p. 34) and "empowerment" (p. 65). Furthermore, Darder uses the initial theorizing to emphasize the gravitas of the teachers' essays. The teachers' testimonials of politicizing teaching through everyday praxis is important, because, according to Freire, teaching is a political act."

These teachers see their teaching as a political act, and they understand the empowering significance of their work across grade levels (early childhood, high school, and teacher education) and disciplines (special education, math, and cross-disciplinary studies). Examples include one teacher's provision of bilingual access to parent resources to increase parent involvement and another teacher's reflection on fighting the link between school discipline and prison pedagogy.

Darder comes close to romanticizing Freire and critical pedagogy, but her vulnerable reflection and emphasis on the political necessity of critical teaching more than compensates for her borderline worship of Freire. This book should be useful to a wide range of audiences, because it is somewhat accessible as a practice-inflected book. It especially complements Freire's original text *Pedagogy of the Oppressed* and *Teachers as Cultural Workers*.

Mayo, P. (2004). *Liberating praxis: Paulo Freire's legacy for radical education and politics.* Westport, CT: Praeger.

Relevant to our discussion on the translation of Freire in North American contexts, Mayo shows how Freire is translated in European first world contexts in the twentieth-century. His chapter, "Reinventing Freire in a Southern Context: The Mediterranean," deals specifically with the relationship between the politics of representation and dialogue across difference. Mayo's final chapter is a review of his research across contexts in Malta, and addresses such issues as national curricular reform and museum education.

Roberts, P. (2000). *Education, literacy, and humanization: Exploring the work of Paulo Freire.* Westport: CT, Bergin & Garvey.

This book articulates the strengths and limitations of Freire's philosophies. It includes nuanced explanations of the prominent criticisms of Freire's work but also defends Freire's interventionist strategies. Chapter two is particularly helpful, because it gives a clear explanation of Freire's dialectic of consciousness, something that helps explain Freire's use of the Portuguese word *conscientização*, a word that does not translate into English. This discussion is necessary for understanding Freire's ontology. Roberts writes that, for Freire, to make inquiries and to question knowledge is to shake up the assumed reality and decide if and how it can be acted upon in order to be changed. This is important to Freire's work, because he argues that humanization depends on the dialectic between reality and individual power to transform the world. Roberts cites Freire's later texts, such as *Teachers as Cultural Workers* (Freire, 1998/2005) in order to demonstrate the centrality of dialectic of consciousness to all of Freire's writing.

Souto-Manning, M. (2010). *Freire, teaching, and learning: Culture circles across contexts.* New York, NY: Peter Lang Publishing.

This book presents a short history of Freirean "cultural circles," an original theoretical framework for culture circles, and examples of Souto-Manning's reinvention of culture circles across three United States contexts. These contexts include one early childhood classroom, early childhood preservice teacher education, and an early childhood education professional development group. Freire, Teaching, and Learning is written mostly for teacher educators, but facilitators and adult educators across fields will benefit from the author's reflective method for generating culture circles. Chapter three, "Culture Circles in an American First-grade Classroom," shows how Souto-Manning formed one culture circle with young children; it can be used as a stand-alone chapter with preservice or practicing teachers. In addition to these contributions, a few examples of Theatre of the Oppressed, á la Francis Boal, are also provided.

Torres, C. A. & Noguera, P. (Eds.) (2008). *Social justice education for teachers: Paulo Freire and the possible dream.* Rotterdam: Sense Publishers.

This text provides clear evidence of the range of ways in which twenty first-century scholars are looking at and using Freire. This includes fresh takes on Freire by Mayo and Roberts (see above). Mayo looks at comparisons between Freire and Gramsci and Roberts defends Freire as a scholar who valued emotions. Freirean scholar and volume lead editor, Carlos Alberto Torres, provides an introduction to Freire in terms of social justice. Chapters from this book reveal the wide-ranging relevance of Freire in twenty-first century classrooms and scholarship. Several scholars—Torres, Mayo, Roberts, and Gadotti—have a strong reputation for the ways in which they historicize Freire. The juxtaposition of their work alongside younger scholars is an effective way to validate the newer scholarship in the book. Though the book is very useful in terms of Freirean breadth and knowledge, it is poorly edited.

Articles and Book Chapters

Giroux, H. (2012). Paulo Freire and the pedagogy of bearing witness. In *Education and the crisis of public values: Challenging the assault on teachers, students, & public education* (pp. 116–124). New York, NY: Peter Lang.

In the last chapter of this crushing description of the decline in American public values, Giroux argues that Freire's ideals are essential to reinventing reform in the twenty first-century. He focuses on similarities between privatization and tracking, which serve to stratify the social structure and perpetuate the mis-education of poor and minority students. To prevent corporate dehumanization, he argues, educators must implement a pedagogy of bearing witness, in which experience is remembered and critiqued, so that individuals can enact social change in the context of policy that favors privatization over democratic education, which includes an emphasis on literacy and dialogue. A pedagogy of bearing witness requires that individuals speak up about past and current injustices, such as tracking poor and minority students into vocational education, so that previous outcomes are not repeated. The chapter places Freire in the context of twenty first-century educational disparities and provides a current example of how Freire can and should be reinvented.

This book is a continuation of Giroux's larger project to show how poor white and minority students are denied the tools of a humanities education and critical pedagogy, which are necessary to help name and struggle against their social condition.

Ladson-Billings, G. (1997). I know why this doesn't feel empowering: A critical race analysis of critical pedagogy. In P. Freire (with J. W. Fraser, D. Macedo, T. McKinnon, & W. T. Stokes (Eds.), *Mentoring the mentor: A critical dialogue with Paulo Freire*, (pp. 127–141). New York, NY: Peter Lang.

Ladson-Billings uses the title of Elizabeth Ellsworth's (1989) seminal critique of critical pedagogy (see Ellsworth below) in order to recommend a framework for explicitly anti-racist education. Using vignettes from research on teachers who adopt culturally relevant methods for teaching about race, Ladson-Billings shows how critical race theory and culturally relevant pedagogy can be combined with critical pedagogy in order to address the limitations in critical pedagogy's inexplicitness. This short chapter is useful because it demonstrates the saliency of critical pedagogy, when it is teamed with agendas that name problematic realities.

Critiques of Paulo Freire and/or Critical Pedagogy

Ellsworth, E. (1989). Why doesn't this feel empowering? Working through the repressive myths of critical pedagogy. *Harvard Education Review*, 59, 297–324.

This essay is one of the first to problematize critical pedagogy. Ellsworth traces her own creation of a course in anti-racist education at the University of Wisconsin-Madison. She critiques the use of the word "critical" and other critical pedagogy jargon, because, she argues, it is too abstract to be effective in challenging oppression in education, and presumably, because the abstraction "critical" leads to the essentialization of students whom critical pedagogy purports to champion. Ellsworth recommends that teachers and researchers *name* the oppressions they fight. "Antiracist education" is presented as one example of naming critical pedagogy's purposes. This article is important to students of critical pedagogy, because it presents clearly and seminally one of the limitations of critical pedagogy, as recognized by the field. See Roberts (2000), Mayo (2004), and Ladson-Billings (1997) for responses to this seminal text.

Torres, C.A. (1994). Paulo Freire as secretary of education in the municipality of Sao Paulo. *Comparative Education Review*, 38(2), 181–214.

In this article, Torres contextualizes Freire's curriculum reform work as Secretary of Education in São Paulo, Brazil, suggesting that Freire didn't accomplish much in the way of social improvements. Torres frames the article with a theory of the state and the role of class in the implementation of state policy in education, and he examines the role of social movements in changing and implementing new education policy. Torres often notes a general theme of tension between government power and the various social movements' desire for autonomy, whenever social movements and government make partnerships. In terms of Freire's "outcomes" while serving as secretary, there was an increase in teacher salaries and student retention rates. However, the question remained as to whether the quality of education and the amount of discrimination had changed during Freire's tenure.

Online Resources

The Freire Project. (n.d.). *The Paulo and Nita Freire International Project for Critical Pedagogy*. Retrieved from: www.freireproject.org.

The Freire Project, cofounded by Nita Freire and Shirley Steinberg, is a comprehensive site that provides links to current projects in critical pedagogy. The site includes biographies, blogs, and interviews with major Freirean scholars, as well as a full-length documentary that is just one of several examples of the types of free resources available from this site on Freire's work. Frequently updated, The Freire Project offers Freire in context as reinvented by scholars and practitioners around the world. The Freire Project is also a useful resource for teachers interested in making their classrooms more critical, offering classroom ideas and opportunities for teacher development. www.freireproject.org

CHAPTER 5

STANLEY ARONOWITZ

Reproaching Labor, the Political Left, and the Self-Imposed Limits of Public Education

Shaun Johnson

INTRODUCTION

The historical significance of Dr. Stanley Aronowitz is still being written. As a sociologist and labor scholar, Aronowitz's work warrants very careful attention because of the current political climate in the United States. Members of the conservative right, with strong allies in the business community, persist in their opposition to organized labor and the general social safety net protecting the poor. In certain cases, capital interests have sought (and continue to seek) to roll back hard-won gains won by labor unions for all workers across decades of struggle, drastically reducing the social welfare protections, and privatizing public services like education and health care. As a matter of fact, Aronowitz presaged many of these contemporary concerns. He has been warning us for at least forty years.

As a labor scholar and sympathetic critic of leftist political movements, Aronowitz's theoretical contributions come directly from working the

Educating About Social Issues in the 20th and 21st Centuries, pages 95–110
Copyright © 2014 by Information Age Publishing
All rights of reproduction in any form reserved.

factory floor with subsequent transition to union organizing. He parlayed these life experiences towards his scholarly development, eventually becoming an extraordinarily prolific author, cultural commentator, and long-time faculty member in sociology and urban education at the City University of New York. Teaching union workers, high school students, and graduate engineers "piqued" his interest in education. Consequently, dovetailing with his leftist social beliefs and politics, Aronowitz has written several major texts that are critical of the current system of education, in particular *The Knowledge Factory: Dismantling the Corporate University and Creating Higher Learning* (2000); *Against Schooling: For an Education that Matters* (2008); and, with colleague Henry Giroux, *Education Under Siege: The Conservative, Liberal, and Radical Debate Over Schooling* (1985) and *Postmodern Education: Politics, Culture, & Social Criticism* (1991).

We are repeatedly reminded of the most salient critique from Aronowitz: Leftist political and social organizations, labor unions and professional educational organizations included, have been all too willing to capitulate and negotiate away their influence. Aronowitz strongly indicts the reticence of liberals at nearly every written turn. He has questioned throughout the many decades of his written work the Left and Labor's confounding alliances with the Democrats, a political party differing very little from the conservative opposition. Essentially, liberals and leftists reconciled with Democrats out of some marriage of convenience. (Why they have done so is addressed later in this chapter.) They eschewed the creation of a truly transformative social and intellectual culture, which would have, at the very least, offered an alternative hope for those disenchanted with the limitations of a two-party political system. Ultimately, liberal and labor groups abandoned their radical roots in favor of a conciliatory approach towards capital and business. The ascendance of a relevant and influential progressive political organization, relative to recent accomplishments of movement conservatives, has not been very successful. Aronowitz's vehemently argues that as a result, we have less democracy overall.

Several of his works document the siege laid against public education in America. Business leaders, technocrats, and bureaucrats of all kinds, he argues, have diminished (and continue to diminish) the professionalism of educators in order to take control of an institution responsible for inducting future citizens into our theoretically democratic society. Not surprisingly, Aronowitz is staunchly critical of this corporate takeover of schooling. Rather than prepare young persons for critical and participatory citizenship, schools and curricula are being reformed as a rehearsal space for the workforce. This is evidenced by single-minded focus on standardized metrics, high-stakes testing, accountability, and choice at the expense of educating the whole person.

Concomitant to shifting the focus of schooling from education to job training, conservatives attack teachers' unions in the interest of eroding educators' professional autonomy over curriculum and pedagogy. Aronowitz, however, also accuses the large national unions, namely the National Education Association (NEA) and the American Federation of Teachers (AFT), of being partly responsible for their own demise, which he repeatedly notes is true of other labor unions as well. In regard to teachers' unions, Aronowitz notes that "in the early 1980s, the teachers' unions abandoned their militant class posture and reverted to professionalism and to a center-right political strategy" (2008, p. 47). Neither of these postures serves the teachers' unions well within the current education reform climate.

At one point, Aronowitz (1998) excoriates labor unions for stepping away from confrontations with corporate power, following with: "the answer to the question, 'Can and will labor rise to the task?' will determine the future not only of the United States, but of the world" (p. 213). A relatively heady appeal, but so far, more than a decade beyond this question, labor has not risen to the task and neither have the national teachers' unions, as starkly evidenced by their failure to step up and protect public education from facets of privatization.

Aronowitz pleads continually for resurgence of a "radical democracy" that directly defies corporate power. Within educational institutions, mainly K–12 public schools, democratic dialogue and participation, if present at all, ends at the main office. It is simply not visible elsewhere in the schools. Aronowitz provides ample advice on how to proceed towards a dynamic social and political culture for progressives. For instance, analogous to the aforementioned shirking of a transformative sociopolitical culture, it is absolutely essential that the Left muster the courage to identify fundamental and specific goals for a socially just curriculum and pedagogy in public schools. There must be an alternative to job or career training, which is the current mission of public education.

ON THE CONDITIONS FOR SOCIAL ISSUES

Proposing theories is not necessarily Aronowitz's mission. His work is heavily invested in presenting a list of grievances to leftist and labor movements that have in recent decades been knocked off balance by persistent barrages from conservatives and the business community. Accusations read in some cases like calls to action, or perhaps even a dare, prodding left wing social and political movements to rise into a cohesive and unified resistance to corporate power. The underscoring of failures of contemporary leftist organizations is meant to motivate, or to light a fire beneath, a new generation of radical activism. It is almost as if Aronowitz is the ghost of democracy's past, present, and future, playing out in succession for a stunned liberal reader what was, is, and could be if a worthwhile forbearance fails to materialize.

There is a sense of three overlapping challenges issued by Aronowitz, all premised upon a meticulous recollection of historical events. These ideas map the decline of liberal sociopolitical movements throughout the latter half of the twentieth century: the submission of liberal movements to capital and an alignment-of-convenience with a none-too-sympathetic Democratic Party; the abandonment by organized labor of independent radical and social movements; and a relatively recent strain in his work on schooling as an engine of cultural reproduction rather than social change.

The fading strength of the left is addressed frequently by Aronowitz (1996) in a reproachful manner, redolent of a disappointed, albeit loving, parent whose child consistently fails to measure up to expectations: "the once ideological left—social democratic and communist groups, the anarchists, and the independent radicals—has virtually disappeared from public view. Its ranks are depleted and its minions are demoralized" (p. 3). Almost incredulously, Aronowitz (2006) asks, "Why do liberals and a considerable fraction of the left cling to the Democrats?" (p. 9). Political expedience, basic survival instincts, and the dearth of viable third parties are glib explanations for an unseemly alliance with a political party just as interested in demolishing social and economic justice as the conservatives are. The only consolation is that they do so at a slower pace than conservatives.

Unions and organized labor have fallen the farthest. The history of organized labor in the United States includes several obvious signposts contributing to the decline of union power; more recently and frequently noted, President Reagan's bust of the air-traffic controller's union, uncompromising technological innovations that eliminate or de-skill specific jobs, and the inability of labor to adjust to global economic capital. But these are largely external circumstances. Aronowitz (1992) casts heavy aspersions towards union leadership itself as the reason for its demise: "First is organized labor's failure of nerve in the wake of direct challenges of its traditional economic power; second is the inability of the unions to 'smell the coffee' and take on the characteristics of a social movement rather than clinging to the fiction—after the global changes that induced the state's and capital's anti-labor offensive—that it is still part of the Establishment" (pp. 405–406).

Aronowitz frequently argues that unions never established an independent political and social culture: neither an ideology separate from the fundamentally center-right Democrats, nor progress towards social justice goals that link the struggles of other marginalized identity groups. If labor unions are going to succeed, they must develop a sovereign strategy "rooted equally in new social relations and in the development of a conscious opposition culture generated by the workers themselves" (Aronowitz, 1992, pp. 15–16).

Aronowitz demands a system of schooling in the United States that is transformative rather than socially and politically reticent. His work is not the first to underscore the takeover of public education, in addition to other public services, by neoliberal and conservative entities. Michael Apple and Henry Giroux are important reads in this regard. Nonetheless, schooling in America is currently absorbed with preparing new generations for the world of work, thereby closing the gap divisions between the needs of capital and everyday workers. Laws and regulations are passed by corporate-controlled legislators, which mandate high-stakes standardized testing, a national set of core standards, and the abrupt erosion of teacher judgment and autonomy. For managers, "teacher-proofing" the classroom is a form of quality control in order to guarantee consistent instruction in "conformity to the social, cultural, and occupational hierarchy" in lieu of "independence of thought and action" (Aronowitz, 2008, p. 19).

Historical analysis of working class movements offers us a much clearer picture of how schooling in America solidifies class divisions. For instance, one would expect professional educators to be democracy's frontline intellectuals; instead, management culture reduces teachers "to the status of low-level employees or civil servants whose main function is to implement reforms decided by experts in the upper levels of state and educational bureaucracies" (Aronowitz & Giroux, 1985, p. 23). Similar to the Left when it comes to larger political and social movements, Aronowitz further chastises liberalism for its failed defense of public education from assault by capital interests. But the Left also stands accused of the failure to develop substantial intellectual and curricular alternatives to the business conservatives' new marketing strategy of "college and career readiness." To their detriment, liberals are still blinded by strict egalitarianism of educational opportunities without simultaneously devising a radical approach to schooling to captivate the imagination.

ON THE SOCIAL ISSUES TO TEACH

Upon the recognition of the necessity for a new social revolution from the left, Aronowitz has formulated the following curricular objectives: redirecting liberals and labor away from capitulation and compromise and ushering in a new epoch of counter-hegemonic rejuvenation. This will, he asserts, ultimately renew the efforts of traditionally liberal outposts, namely labor unions, educational organizations, and other social movements, seeking to improve the lives of identity groups based on race, gender, and sexual orientation. One principal way to achieve these goals would be for liberal organizations, especially labor unions, to increase their distance from state and party politics, thus creating an independent political and social reform machine, which Aronowitz calls "a new doctrine of democratic syndicalism" (1998, p. 209).

In reading a broad swath of Aronowitz's work, one gets a feel for the goals and objectives of an alternative educational program. More specifically, he advocates for an education that is "postmodern." In other words, one that takes empowerment to the extreme, giving students and groups the freedom "to transform knowledge in accordance with their own plans" (Aronowitz, 1991, p. 23). Postmodern or critical education emerges from an alliance between a radically democratic K–12 education system, a cadre of teachers-as-organic-intellectuals, and a renewal of activist union education programs. At the height of union membership and power, oppositional political parties, from socialists to communists, "established adult schools that not only offered courses pertaining to political and ideological knowledge but were also vehicles for many working and middle-class students to gain a general education" (Aronowitz, 2008, p. 39). A new unionism, would, he argues, therefore reaffirm a commitment to educational services, in addition to its extensive efforts to preserve collective bargaining, legal aid and social welfare programs (Aronowitz, 1983, p. 169). Thus, any new educational program based on radical principles would need to be open to expanding opportunities for schooling beyond traditional brick-and-mortar institutions.

Teaching social issues would not necessarily occur in just conventional public schools for school-age students. It would include individuals and groups from all walks of life in a variety of formal and informal settings, but would be especially accommodate working and middling classes. While Aronowitz (1998) rarely discusses an actual vision of a school curriculum he has made a significant suggestion vis-à-vis the need for a more holistic approach to education: "school curricula, for example, could concentrate on broadening students' cultural purview: music, athletics, art and science would assume a more central place in the curriculum and there would be a renewed emphasis on the aesthetic as well as the vocational aspects of traditional crafts" (p. 68).

Perhaps the simplest way to characterize an Aronowitz curriculum would be democracy, a lot of it, and very radical. But how radical? Potential students would learn how to "change relations of power, allowing entrance to those who are partially or entirely excluded from participation in civil society under representative forms and are unable to influence, let alone share, power over key decisions affecting their lives" (Aronowitz, 2003, p. 222). Alternative institutions would be created to "share decision-making within the economy, allocation of resources, and determination of what should be produced" (Aronowitz, 2006, p. 214). The curriculum would also discourage "patriarchy, heterosexism, and racism, for these doctrines and their practices overtly assert the superiority of white men over all others" (Aronowitz, 1996, p. 181).

Aronowitz is actually rather thorough when describing a proposed core postsecondary curriculum, which is more than can be said of many authors who theorize curriculum without offering much in the way of content or method. In his benchmark text on the corporatization of colleges and universities (The Knowledge Factory: Dismantling the Corporate University and Creating True Higher Learning), Aronowitz calls for a "higher learning," where "[t]he point of the core is to find articulations between economic, political, and social currents, social and cultural movements, and knowledge orientations and, perhaps, to discover unexpected relationships with other cultures and contexts" (Aronowitz, 2001 p. 177). This, he writes, is achieved via analysis of the theoretical and philosophical underpinnings of humanity's big ideas across historical time periods, chunked into roughly yearlong core courses of intense study. The goals (and methods) for this kind of learning are transformative relative to what essentially passes for postsecondary education at present: job or career training. Faculty and students engage with the curriculum in less formal arrangements and free from the boundaries of classroom walls. "Rolling seminars" and "working study groups" are examples, and this curriculum would also require extensive "faculty development institutes" to prepare for instruction.

Education programs are fundamentally paralyzed by corporate assault and an imposition of a market-oriented ideology. This mentality deskills and de-professionalizes educators, who become civil servants rather than change agents. As such, faculties, or those with the most expertise to understand academic programs, are stifled by an administrative bureaucracy more invested in the smooth operation of the machine rather than intellectual life (Aronowitz, 2000, p. 159).

Aronowitz is very clear that a radically democratic education program, which aligns with justice-minded social movements, is only possible if a coalition of parents, students, teachers, and labor are "armed with a political program directed toward forcing legislatures to adequately fund schooling at the federal, state, and local levels and boards of education to de-authorize the high-stakes standardized tests that currently drive the curriculum and pedagogy" (Aronowitz, 2008, p. 50). Freeing knowledge from the bonds of capital would mean a rejection of the recently mandated Common Core State Standards (CCSS) and preservation of the autonomies of professional educators. Curricular standardization, of which the CCSS is a prime example, is clearly a victory for those who maintain economic and corporate control over society that for now postpones the "struggle between dominant and subordinate discourses" in favor of those who seek to recede the role of educators as "public intellectuals" (Aronowitz, 1991, p. 92). Furthermore, the CCSS is suspiciously absent from private school curricula. For many public school students, this means a substandard mass curriculum that prepares them for the "secondary labor market: industries in highly competitive markets, with low technological development, and offering nonunion wages and working conditions" (Aronowitz, 1991, p. 9). Perhaps with the continued publication, discussion, and dissemination of Aronowitz's catalogue of writings, an ideal counter-culture of and by the working class will be created to successfully defy capital and a suppressive corporate culture.

CONCLUSION

Provocative is certainly a fitting term to describe Aronowitz's extensive catalogue of writings. To wit, "people no longer imagine the possibility of the end of work" (Aronowitz, 1998, p. 64). We work ourselves to death with barely enough time and energy to spend doing whatever makes us feel whole. With work demands, we can devote only very little of ourselves to the democratic system which sustains us, and with the exception of our courtship during the Presidential Olympiad, democratic participation does not reach far beyond voting. It is oftentimes all the people have left to give. That is, if they can get off of work on Election Day.

Notwithstanding Aronowitz's broad, if friendly, condemnation of labor unions and liberals, especially the Democratic Party, for collaborating with capital, the corrosion of participation in democracy is both explicitly and implicitly present in all of Aronowitz's major works. The abandonment of democratic institutions by everyday persons and the disappearance of funds for public services like education or antipoverty measures create a vacuum. And working folks do not stand much of a chance to eliminate it, thus corporate influence fills the void. Aronowitz quotes extensively from the political scientist Francis Fukuyama on his declaration of the "end of history" (1992). This end comes with the abolition of alternative political and economic systems, relegated to the annals of history. As a result, globalization homogenizes the ways in which we live and work. So-called liberal capitalist-democracies, apparently the least-worst arrangement available, will become the only structure of economic prosperity and governance. This will regulate culture as well. Our ability to customize everything, from our smart phone covers to embroidered shirt logos, is all a fantastic illusion to oblige our reterritorialization as well-behaved consumers.

A postwork society would, for Aronowitz, include dramatic reforms such as guaranteed income, reduction of working hours, full funding of the arts, and universal public service, among others (Aronowitz & Cutler, 1998). They are dramatic insofar as the unimaginable shift in our thinking that these ideas would require if implementation would ever be possible. In a more recent work, Aronowitz (2009) argues: "Mass democracy and its concomitant creation of a self-valorized oligarchy is the result of the ability of capital and the state to impose a labor regimen that, with the exception of a few hours a week, gobbles up all or most of the time available to workers, professionals and almost everybody else (p. 125).

Suppose democracy came first, before work and other obligations, perhaps the exception being care for loved ones. Imagine the elimination of most distractions, especially those that result in our accumulation of more "stuff" and the enrichment of corporate coffers. There is no single vision of what that world might look like; Aronowitz nearly gives one, but demurs. It would be a world of our collective creation.

REFERENCES

Aronowitz, S. (1983). *Working class hero.* New York, NY: Pilgrim Press.

Aronowitz, S. (1992). *False promises: The shaping of American working class consciousness* (2nd ed.). Durham, NC: Duke University Press.

Aronowitz, S. (1996). *The death and rebirth of American radicalism.* New York, NY: Routledge.

Aronowitz, S. (1998). *From the ashes of the old: American labor and America's future.* New York, NY: Houghton Mifflin Company.

Aronowitz, S. (2000). *The knowledge factory: Dismantling the corporate university and creating true higher learning.* Boston, MA: Beacon Press.

Aronowitz, S. (2001). *The last good job in America: Work and education in the new global technoculture.* New York: Rowman & Littlefield.

Aronowitz, S. (2003). *How class works.* New Haven, CN: Yale University Press.

Aronowitz, S. (2006). *Left turn: Forging a new political future.* Boulder, CO: Paradigm Publishers.

Aronowitz, S. (2008). *Against schooling: For an education that matters.* Boulder, CO: Paradigm Publishers.

Aronowitz, S. & Cutler, J. (Eds.). (1998). *Post-work: The wages of cybernation.* New York, NY: Routledge.

Aronowitz, S., & Giroux, H.A. (1985). *Education under siege: The conservative, liberal, and radical debate over schooling.* South Hadley, MA: Bergin & Garvey Publishers.

Aronowitz, S., & Giroux, H.A. (1991). *Postmodern education: Politics, culture, & social criticism.* Minneapolis, MN: University of Minnesota Press.

Fukuyama, F. (1992). *The end of history and the last man.* New York, NY: Free Press.

ANNOTATED BIBLIOGRAPHY

Aronowitz, S. (1974). *Food, shelter, and the American dream.* New York, NY: The Seabury Press.

An early work by Aronowitz, this relatively short and accessible text focuses very narrowly on the political, social, and economic crises of an approximate two-year time frame around which these words were written. The reader can, however, recognize the prominent foundational ideas on which the author's later works are built. "In short, the United States is losing its privileged position in the world economy" due to various crises in energy, ecology, and the proliferation of global capital (p. 102). Of course, all of these issues are still with us. At that time, educational institutions were also failing "to provide the tools of mobility" (p. 132), alternatively focusing on the receipt of "training rather than education to prepare them for the job market" (p. 133). Ultimately, Aronowitz calls for a new radical politics to resist, among other items, "regimentation, military discipline in the work place and in the neighborhood [including the school, of course] and the ultimate danger of war as the only resolution of the crisis" (p. 168). Essentially, he argues, new forms of management and democratic control of resources are necessary to improve our social lives.

Aronowitz, S. (1983). *Working class hero.* New York, NY: Pilgrim Press.

The American labor movement has undergone numerous shifts and transitions throughout its history; however, recent changes to social and political conditions threaten the influence of unionism unless more responsive, independent, and activist stances are taken. Aronowitz calls this at one point "self-management": "a framework that contains the fundamental ideological banner of redistributive justice, not only of economic resources but also of social and political power" (p. 199). Set against a detailed account of the historical rise of trade and labor unions in the United States, Aronowitz laments their recent collaboration of convenience with capital and the state, undermining the motivations of membership and of its original character as a social movement. Current union activities fail to establish independent political organizations to challenge dominant parties; they are unresponsive to emerging technologies and computer mediated work; and unions are finally, according to Aronowitz, shedding their democratic functions. Solutions to this crisis in labor organization include increased workplace democracy, voluntary rather than contract-based membership, and "a new program of political and ideological independence" (p. 208).

Aronowitz, S., & Giroux, H.A. (1985). *Education under siege: The conservative, liberal, and radical debate over schooling.* South Hadley, MA: Bergin & Garvey Publishers.

The authors argue chiefly that formal schooling in the United States has abandoned its emancipatory and revolutionary potentials in favor of a management mentality, preparing students for the labor market rather than educating them. "Education conservatives," or the neoliberal-minded, drives this shift, simultaneously advocating for reductions in "federal aid to education" and insisting that schools "upgrade themselves through changed curriculum and new management systems rather than massive financial inputs" (p. 4). It is suggested that, alternative to reinforcing dominant, market-based ideologies, schools should engage in a Gramscian project of establishing a counter-hegemonic movement with its own oppositional "common sense." Difficulties arise, the authors argue, when prevailing education reformers attenuate the autonomy of teachers in preparing critical citizens and of teacher education programs that embrace management over educating "students to be teacher-scholars" with a focus on "the immediacy of school problems" (p. 27). Various intellectuals must, according to the authors, unite to form a critical opposition to what they term "business pragmatism." Instead, the critical mission of schools requires a rebirth with the development of a defiant "language of possibility" (p. 214).

Aronowitz, S. and Giroux, H. A. (1991). *Postmodern education: Politics, culture, & social criticism.* Minneapolis, MN: University of Minnesota Press.

This text is a collection of essays, both singularly and co-authored, written in modified form for other publications. They are gathered here to underscore the influence of postmodernism on various aspects of education. Perhaps the most fundamental argument within this volume is the struggle between what counts as knowledge in the formal school environment and the kinds of knowledge students and educators bring to the table. The authors proffer answers to questions in regard to who should get to choose what knowledge is most important and what gets included in the traditional curriculum. Postmodern educators invite local deliberations on what is taught, and that goes even in regard to the most sacred concepts of our established school traditions. "In short, schools may be arenas for contesting increasing regimentation, according to which all public institutions are obliged to subordinate themselves to centralized authority" (p. 23).

Aronowitz, S. (1992a). *False promises: The shaping of American working class consciousness* (2nd ed.). Durham, NC: Duke University Press.

Originally published in 1973 as a detailed history of the rise and fall of union organization in the United States throughout the 20th century, this could be considered one of Aronowitz's seminal works as a labor scholar. The author seeks to answer one fundamental question, "Why [does] the working class in America remain a dependent force in society and what [are] the conditions that may reverse this situation?" (p. 6). Workers as a class in the United States, Aronowitz argues, are fractured and are consistently removed from any control over the what and how of production. "The contemporary crisis of labor is manifested in membership losses, a veritable avalanche of give-backs at the bargaining table, [and] organizing defeats" (p. 395). Labor, according to Aronowitz, ultimately failed in its opposition as it tried to cling to whatever attachments it could find to the Establishment in order to save itself. In later works, Aronowitz details this transition further, but does begin here to flush out the necessary transition to a radical democracy. The labor movement undercuts itself by not including "democracy and human rights" in its mission, thus restricting membership to a largely white male population, which has resulted over the decades in a "rightward shift" (p. 436). Center-right politics do not typically favor progressive arrangements with respect to capital and production; thus, it behooves union organizing to embody a "new social relations and in the development of a conscious opposition culture generated by workers themselves" (pp. 15–16).

Aronowitz, S. (1992b). *The politics of identity: Class, culture, and social movements.* New York, NY: Routledge

The central thesis of this text is summed up by the author as follows: ignorance of intersectional identities like race, gender, and other qualitative issues "has narrowed the political base of labor and socialist movements which, as often as not, perceived class politics as inimical to their aims" (p. 67). Labor scholarship has largely ignored the complexities of other identities and how they influence the manifestation of class. Unions have also narrowed their foci on economic terms, turning them into "the repository of social welfare for union members and their families" (p. 33). Ignoring race and gender, according to Aronowitz, limits the potential base of union rank-and-file, which is crucial during a period where labor organizations have lost considerable influence. To increase activism and participation, social and labor movements should expand their operations beyond economic justice since "the most oppressed of the working class are, indeed, likely candidates for membership, if the unions fuse struggles for social justice with those of racial and gender dignity" (p. 70). The key is to extend the mission of unions and other social organizations from just economic progress so that cooperation with management becomes tertiary to active resistance.

Aronowitz, S. (1996). *The death and rebirth of American radicalism.* New York, NY: Routledge.

Herein, Aronowitz presents a highly critical view of the failures of the political left to establish a worthy opposition to conservative and capitalist worldviews. Generally remiss in re-evaluating their own political strategies, liberal activist and theorists instead willingly participate in the regulatory state responsible for assailing them. As stalwarts of Democratic and liberal-seeming goals, "labor and most popular movements have offered only token resistance to the corporate and right-wing onslaught against the welfare state," a once-crowning achievement of the left movement (p. 16). Liberal political theorists continue to resist "the idea that we have a common 'good' based on an agreement on what constitutes the truth" (p. 153). This prevents the development of an oppositional political culture. Moreover, society appears reluctant to affiliate with "radical and revolutionary ideas, including those that originated in our own history" (p. 156).

After a detailed historical recollection of the rise and fall of the political left, particularly of organized labor, Aronowitz calls for an immediate implementation of a "radical democracy." This would include "limiting the power of representatives by requiring shorter terms and a simple system of recall" (p. 181); refuting hierarchies and power based on economic privilege; possessing clear social justice goals including anti-racism, sexism, and homophobia; and "directing popular participation in crucial decisions affecting our economic life, political and social institutions as well as everyday life" (p. 197).

Aronowitz, S. (1998). *From the ashes of the old: American labor and America's future.* Boston, MA: Houghton Mifflin Company.

This is perhaps one of the most accessible and mainstream texts available from Aronowitz on the labor movement. It focuses on the decline of labor power throughout the 20th century, motivated principally by a massive assault from conservatives and an inconvenient alliance with center-right Democrats, which sealed a new era of compromise and accommodation. Aronowitz underscores another prominent cause of labor's decline: union involvement in politics. An early tradition "was to be independent of both major political parties and concern itself with legislation" only if the bargaining table failed (p. 194). Unions bargained away their independence in pursuit of an ally against corporate influence, which it saw in a neutral government. It is perhaps unions' unction to be part of the middle class and preserve its own leadership that perpetuates its problems. Additionally, labor abandoned its mission of social change in favor of strict economic bargaining. Increasing its distance from the state is, per Aronowitz, one of labor's best hopes.

Aronowitz, S. & Cutler, J. (Eds.). (1998). *Post-work: The wages of cybernation.* New York, NY: Routledge.

This edited volume emphasizes arguments similar to those found in Aronowitz's other works, namely that leftist labor and other social movements are rapidly declining in membership and influence. But rather than detailing their historical decline, he shares the pulpit with authors focusing other contemporary issues in relation to labor, such as the effects of technology, the absence of the working poor, and a defense of welfare. Together, the chapters extol a future where without "compulsory labor and where human freedom is the measure of social life" (Aronowitz, et al., p. 75). This includes, among other reforms, a guaranteed income, reduction in working hours, and universal public service. Chapters specifically written by or with the assistance of Aronowitz define some facts of a "jobless future" whereby the collective populace is obliged to share work rather than compete for survival. Rather than seeking gratification from our labors, we are alternatively less secure than ever, more pressed and stressed to meet unreasonable demands, and must do more with less. As Aronowitz argues in many of his other works, these conditions lead to less democracy and less time for participation from citizens. This political situation is ultimately responsible for the demise of workers in a world predominantly defined by work, without a balance vis-à-vis other aspects of our identities.

Aronowitz, S. (2000). *The knowledge factory: Dismantling the corporate university and creating true higher learning.* Boston, MA: Beacon Press.

This book paints a rather dispiriting picture of postsecondary education in the United States. Aronowitz details a highly stratified system based on social class, the derogation of intellectualism for its own sake, the narrowed focus of colleges and universities on job training, and the success or failure of which is dependent on outcomes-based metrics that do not value intellectual growth.

Aronowitz mourns the lost potential of "higher learning" and of intellectual curiosity at the university level. Alternatively, the near compulsory nature of college attendance is justified simply by job market anxieties and the soft promise that a degree "provides the minimum qualification to enter the market for a large variety of jobs" (p. 9). Both graduates and undergraduates, consequently, learn very little of value from a harried faculty whose own work has been diminished by the market-driven motivations of administration. Dismantling the corporate university requires revisiting what is approximately a canonical, trans-disciplinary core curriculum available to all students, not just the privileged. Additionally, Aronowitz recommends a reconfiguration of pedagogy to include less structured methods, thus suggesting such approaches as rolling seminars, student-driven scheduling, faculty tutorials with limited lecturing, and frequent study groups.

Aronowitz, S. (2003). *How class works*. New Haven, CT: Yale University Press.

Aronowitz defends class as an essential analytical category of social and political life despite consistent claims by Americans that they are exempt from class divisions. Class is an elusive category in the United States because of its historicity; that is, class comes "into existence under specific conditions that, almost invariably, are superseded by new conditions and new social formations" (p. 11). Class divisions may not always be visible by income alone and can be rooted in other social categories, forming alliances across economic boundaries. Within whatever cultural referents connote class at a given moment in history, divisions are prevalent: "Professionals and managers do not mingle much with service or industrial workers, and none of the above socialize with the poor, working or not" (p. 31). Aronowitz complicates the definition of class throughout this text, settling mainly on power as a clear dividing line. Prior victories by social movements and organized labor have ushered in a new "culture of subordination" (p. 216). This culture can be undone by shifting power relations so that those who have been excluded can influence key decisions. Aronowitz argues that if traditionally progressive organizations are dragging their feet, then new caucuses or organized movements must be created to counteract liberal malaise and capitulation to the interests of capital.

Aronowitz, S. (2004). Against schooling: Education and social class. *Social Text, 79*(22:2), pp. 13–35.

In this relatively recent essay, Aronowitz discusses many of his most visible ideas about education, namely that conservatives forced schools to abandon progressive goals in favor of methods and curriculum focused on career training. Additionally, he argues that the educational left offers few alternatives, eschews the promotion of intellectual content, and focuses too heavily on egalitarianism, or equal educational access, at the expense of a "genuine education" (p. 14). The remainder of the essay concentrates on the latter point. The left, in opposition to market-driven education policies, is distracted by equal opportunity as the sole measure of democracy in education, at least with regard to social class. There is an element of quality missing; that is, even if access is equitable, the quality of the educational experiences is still far from equal and thus diminishes the potential for marginalized groups, namely persons of color and low-income populations, to enjoy all the benefits of education as some kind of cultural and economic equalizer. The educational priorities of the left fall short relative to corporate opposition of their goals. Among other things, Aronowitz insists on disbanding corporate ties to our system of education.

Aronowitz, S. (2006). *Left turn: Forging a new political future.* Boulder, CO: Paradigm Publishers.

One basic question appears early in the text: "Why do liberals and a considerable fraction of the left cling to the Democrats?" (p. 9). According to Aronowitz, liberals and their political organizations, namely labor unions, fight within the constraints and oppressions of current political and economic systems rather than suggesting any worthwhile radical alternatives. Social-democratic organizations have been present during the gradual decline of the welfare state and, cloistered within its own identity "sectarianism," the left "lost contact with the everyday life of the population" (p. 123–124). Perhaps it is a failure to offer a coherent and consistent message to those seeking an alternative to the conservative and neoliberal positions and approaches. This could be solved by what Aronowitz calls a "centralization" of efforts; that is, "create organs of communication and analysis that become the embodiment" of social democratic theory and practice (p. 171). Radical and bold detachments from institutions within the prevailing capitalist system are necessary to forge a new left. Concluding sections of the text cover a few "utopian" political and social alternatives that might be championed by a new left: establishing a "pluralist commonwealth" of shared wealth and power; creating a "cooperative commonwealth" that organizes social and economic life around workers' and consumers' councils; and finally a fundamental transition to an ethos of self-management and democracy in the workplace.

Aronowitz, S. (2008). *Against schooling: For an education that matters.* Boulder, CO: Paradigm Publishers.

Schools and education itself, according to Aronowitz, are inextricably appended to corporate interests, "worshipful" rather than "critical" of their own traditions, and beholden to legislators that defund education and impose grueling programs of high-stakes standardized testing. Teachers' unions, expected to defend public education from corporate assault, have "abandoned their militant class posture and reverted to professionalism and to a center-right political strategy" (p. 47). This has further destabilized the political Left, since labor unions, especially those affiliated with education, are failing to provide "an alternative education for its activists, let alone its potential constituents" (p. 13). Schools are now too interested in career readiness to produce active and critical future citizens; moreover, the teachers are viewed as technicians rather than intellectuals. Thus, according to Aronowitz, we must once again advocate for a school system that forms the backbone of new social movements and challenges prevailing common sense. For now, the radical objective is quite simple: "say no, not so fast, never mind, whether or not you have any degree of an alternative" (p. 56).

Aronowitz, S. (2010). Education reconsidered: Beyond the death of critical education. *Truth-out*. Retrieved from http://truth-out.org/opinion/item/72-education-reconsidered-beyond-the-death-of-critical-education

There is definitely a pattern to the condemnations Aronowitz levels against the political left, even though he has always been a major supporter of progressive ideas in education. This recent essay follows this design, calling the left out for trotting out the same old reform ideas: "more money for schools, wider access of poor and working-class students of color to higher education, the end to privatization" (p. 2). He also chastises the lack of passion and radicalism in the left's proposals for education. But there is also a newer call here for a dramatic reformation of teacher education so that novice teachers are prepared to teach critical thinking and big ideas that Aronowitz proposed in many of his previous works on education. Student teachers should focus less on methods and more on the philosophy and history of education. Faculty should be developed to the extent that they can foster this new culture of intellectualism. Rather than waxing poetic about critical pedagogy, "education activists need to begin to explore what an education reveille for radicals... would look like" (p. 6).

CHAPTER 6

IRA SHOR

Cathy Leogrande

This democratic disturbance of the teacher-centered classroom confirms a primary goal of shared authority: to restructure education into something done by and with students rather than by the teacher for and over them.

—Ira Shor

INTRODUCTION

Ira Shor, whose work is grounded in Freirean principles, has sought, throughout his career, to help teachers and students smash the status quo in terms of power relationships, and reform the realm of education in ways that are democratic rather than indoctrinatory. Concomitantly, Shor, like Freire, has helped educators the world over apply the concepts and skills of critical pedagogy in their own classrooms.

Shor's life events retain their power through the power of his writing. More specifically, his voice is strong and readers are able to look back in time with him to see how his life events troubled and transformed him.

Educating About Social Issues in the 20th and 21st Centuries, pages 111–131
Copyright © 2014 by Information Age Publishing
All rights of reproduction in any form reserved.

BIOGRAPHICAL EXPERIENCES

Ira Shor grew up in a Jewish working class family in post-World War II-South Bronx in New York City. In the 1950s, his urban, working class neighborhood was primarily populated with white families in which both parents worked in factories or shops. He frequently describes that neighborhood in his writing and the pivotal role it had in shaping his beliefs.

At an early age, Shor became aware at of difference and status; he describes memorable situations in elementary school through which he came to realize that those who wore suits to work had power over others, and those who did not, like his father, were "less than." More specifically, when his third-grade teacher asked how many students had fathers who went to work in a suit and tie, only a few hands went up. As Shor explains, "The teacher's question that morning invited me to be ashamed of my family and our clothes which, like our thick urban accents and bad table manners, marked us as socially inferior (Shor, 1999, p. 3). He began to see that this concept of being substandard expanded to all aspects of life. Some people had were better by virtue of clothes, skin color, and proper English, and they held the power over others. For example, when the elementary principal banned a small school newspaper begun by Shor and his friend, he realized that young people in a purported democracy did not have real freedom. He explained the lesson he learned: "The suit's word was power and law (Shor, 1999, p. 3). It is not surprising that he has asserted that "neighborhood life and schooling are two formidable sites where the local and global converge" (Shor, 1999, p. 3).

Ultimately, he was selected for Admission to t he Bronx High School of Science, one of the best schools in the United States. That led him to realize that internal tracking in the New York City public school system that the smartest and whitest students were systematically selected based on intelligence scores and thus removed from the chaos of the public school system in order that they be prepared for an elite type of education usually reserved for students from higher social classes and betters schools. Essentially, they became part of the chosen. Shor neither provides his readers with a sense of his journey through this part of his life nor the eventual impact this practice had on his peers, but he does tell us how he was shepherded towards higher education, first, at the University of Michigan and then, at the University of Wisconsin. Using Freire's term that refers to those who divest themselves of the trappings of the social class into which they were born, he refers to this as "class suicide."

Ultimately, Shor earned a BA in English at the University of Michigan in 1966, a MA in English at the University of Wisconsin at Madison in 1968, and his PhD in English at the University of Wisconsin at Madison in 1971.

Subsequently, in 1983, Shor was a Guggenheim Fellow, and in 1985 he received the CUNY Chancellor's Scholarship in Residence Award.

While it is a fact that Shor used his special treatment within the public school system to become an academic and intellectual, it is also true that after earning his doctorate in 1971, Shor returned to the people and place from whence he got his start. In that regard, he chose to return to Staten Island Community College, then a two-year institution within the City College of New York (CUNY) system, where he taught composition and basic writing. Unlike professors at many other institutions who taught well prepared and academically strong students, Shor began his career immediately after the Open Admissions Policy was instituted in response to protests by Black and Hispanic students. Remedial classes were available to support students who needed additional skills, along with free tuition. Shor was educating the very type of working class individuals he had left behind during his higher education journey. He has continued to work within the CUNY system for over 40 years, although free tuition ended in 1976 and the Open Admission policy ended in 1999 (Tsao, 2005). The CUNY system still has a diverse student body of working class individuals seeking affordable higher education.

Any reading of Shor's work demonstrates the ways he used, and continues to use, his life situations to shape his practice. For example, his early writing reflects the work he did when he began his teaching career at CUNY immediately after earning his dissertation in 1971, i.e., his interaction with working class students and his successes as well as challenges attempting to implement critical pedagogy (Shor, 1972; Shor 1974; Shor, 1977a; Shor, 1977b; Shor, 1977c). He has also written and spoken about how to continue to challenge the status quo as it relates to the attacks on the World Trade Centers, how to foster activism in conservative times, and how to use methods with millennial students (Shor, 2006; Shor, 2007a; Shor, 2007b).

He has been a professor of English at the College of Staten Island (CSI) since 1971. He has, in fact, a dual appointment, and has been a professor of English at City University of New York (CUNY) Graduate School since 1992. As a member of the English faculty at CSI, Shor teaches courses in writing, literature, and mass media as well as graduate classes for classroom teachers. In 1993, he began a new doctoral program in Rhetoric/Composition at the CUNY Graduate Center. There, his work includes directing dissertations and offering seminars in literacy, writing theory, critical pedagogy, whiteness studies, the rhetoric of space and place, and working-class culture.

Shor has noted that a great deal of his passion vis-à-vis his experimentation and revising/reworking of various educational philosophies resulted from his teaching at a number of urban community colleges in along the east coast of the United States. It was in such settings, Shor says, that he began to ponder the lives and education of his students and the lives and working conditions of his fellow faculty members that he gleaned invaluable insights and began to develop various ideas and themes in relation what a liberatory classroom would look like, one that would be focused on the relationships between society and school and culture. Furthermore, having learned about the lives of his students, many of whom were from lower socioeconomic classes, and witnessed that they were led to attend vocational schools and thus, overtly or inadvertently, discouraged from seeking degrees in higher education, Shor began to gravitate to and craft an educational philosophy imbued with the concept of critical thought and an educational program where the student and the teacher learn together and from one another.

BRINGING FREIRE TO NORTH AMERICAN CLASSROOMS

When Shor discovered the work of Paolo Freire, it provided him with the basis for his understanding of the power of education to mitigate discrimination. Shor was already forging his own identity as a teacher in the late 1970s when he became fascinated with the work of Paolo Freire. Shor worked to integrate his own ideas related to social critique with Friere's pedagogical techniques. Together, the combination result in a democratic style of teaching that engages students and challenges the norm of social class structures found in most educational institutions (The Friere Project, n.d.).

In 1980, Shor wrote *Critical Teaching and Everyday Life*. It was the first book to describe how and why teachers outside Freire's home base of Brazil and South America could take concepts (i.e., critical theory) developed in a vastly different culture and apply them within their own classrooms. Freire developed his methods within an oppressed society, and the rationale for their implementation was to create citizens who would question and subvert the social structures that maintained a subordinate class. Some felt that the United States as a democracy did not require such radical methods, but Shor disagreed. He believed that public education in most places in the United States resulted in a preservation of an unequal status quo and that that needed to change. Having witnessed the results of the pervasive banking model as perpetuation of existing values (respect authority, don't make waves), knowledge (traditional canon), and skills (those necessary for workers in an industrial society) in the nation's schools, Shor was critical of the message that education provided a means to a better life.

Essentially, then, Shor was among those who recognized the façade of democracy in the United States, and the public schools' agenda: that is, to inculcate future citizens into existing values in ways that will not only preserve the status quo, but result in those who are being subordinated to virtually become co-opted as champions of a society in which they are oppressed.

After his book was published, Shor received a handwritten note from Freire that resulted in their first meeting at a restaurant in Massachusetts (Shor, 1998). The subsequent relationship between the two became one of mutual understanding, affection, but above all else, learning. Shor describes the experience of writing their "talking book" (Shor & Freire, 1986), along with the hundreds of hours spent in dialogue with Freire, as "the most intense education I ever had" (Shor, 1998, p. 75). In a happy convergence of time and place, Shor found in Freire a mentor who was committed to the belief that education that employs a vastly different pedagogy than the traditional banking model found in most schools can liberate oppressed people. Freire found in Shor an impatient disciple who would show how the façade of American schooling helped keep poor and working class students subordinate.

Together, Shor and Freire spread the notion that critical pedagogy was as relevant in seemingly democratic North American schools as the schools in obviously troubled South American countries. The radical nature of their writings and lectures often made them targets of those in authority, from school administrators to elected officials. By demonstrating that language, writing and education are never neutral and always political, their work amply demonstrated that public education was a powerful means for questioning existing social and political norms.

As Shor pursued his efforts as a vocal advocate of change through critical pedagogy, others, such as E. D. Hirsch Jr., often championed the very opposite, a curriculum that evoked images of the very banking model that Freire denounced. Incensed by those who called for increased improvement in poor schools via more accountability and high stakes testing such as that seen during the era of the No Child Left Behind mandate, Shor claimed such efforts resulted in a disconnect between poor children and the means to improve their lives. Rather than an authentic and meaningful education grounded in their own personal lives and experiences, these students became marginalized by homogenized and irrelevant curriculum. The result were failing scores, a lack of real learning, and an alarming dropout rate.

Shor and Freire strongly believed that curricula should be relevant to all students. In fact, that constituted a basic belief of their philosophy. They argued that using such an approach in a thoughtful and systematic manner would, hopefully, illustrate the pointlessness and vacuity of those who attempted to make their classrooms more "diverse" and "multicultural" by conducting superficial lessons. Well-meaning teachers may unwittingly perpetuate inequality and difference when, for example, they study people of color only at specific times of the year (such as Black History in February, Hispanic Heritage during September, or on holidays such as Chinese

New Year or Cinco de Mayo), and engage their students in perfunctory study due to a lack of deep knowledge or severe time constraints. Instead, through critical pedagogy, all students would have the opportunity, and take the responsibility, to share their beliefs, experiences, and questions.

Rather, they argued, students would have the opportunity, and take the responsibility, to share their beliefs, experiences, and questions vis-à-vis such issues. Every student, no matter his/her race, gender, class or other socially constructed distinction, should be encouraged and assisted in making each lesson his/her own through dialogical pedagogy. Shor and Freire strongly argued that when the teacher begins with the student's experience(s) and makes it a critical component of every lesson, students begin to see themselves as partners in the construction of knowledge. They are not only welcome but urged and required to become active constructors of knowledge. The end result is a mutual effort by students and teachers to question the status quo and use their knowledge and skills to effect change. This, of course, is a radically different vision from that of inculcation. And because it is radically different, it often proved (and continues to do so to this day) to be controversial.

THE CRITICAL PEDAGOGY CLASSROOM

There are many principles that serve as the foundation of classrooms in which critical pedagogy is at work. Three that are paramount are subversion versus reproduction, literacy as skill and practice, and participation.

Subversion is a word that carries pejorative connotations in the post-9/11 world. Fear has been used in subtle ways to shift public discourse away from change that threatens the status quo. Within this context, Shor has continued to stress the value of critical questioning at a time when such behavior is often labeled as constituting treason and/or being unpatriotic. More often than not, those in positions of power see critical pedagogy as a threat. Teachers who encourage students to actually examine their world know that real inquiry will lead to emotions, such as anger and frustration. These emotions may make the far from the docile rooms where passive students take seemingly endless notes.

One of the goals of critical pedagogy is to empower students. One of the first areas for this is curriculum. Students often question the value and relevance of what is taught, especially when it is supposedly politically neutral. Shor recognizes that expecting students to absorb material in a passive way discourages their development as critical thinkers. Before long students become socialized to a school society that mirrors the larger one, and expects docile obedience. Shor and others believe many students express their frustration with the system through misbehavior and apathy. Through critical pedagogy, teachers are able to channel rather than stifle the habits of thinking and debating that are necessary in a meaningful society. The nurturing of such habits is, for the most part, far from the goal of those who see schools as places for the reproduction of existing knowledge. Indeed, the latter are, for the most part, not truly supportive of classrooms and schools as places where creativity and inquisitive minds forge new knowledge through active learning.

As a teacher, Shor agreed with Freire regarding the significance of literacy in the battle for social change. His work has often taken the precepts of critical pedagogy and applied them to basic writing classes at the City University of New York. Some experts in the field of writing recommend that the best way to help students who lack basic skills in the dominant language is to use formulaic instruction in remedial classes to increase and standardize their competency. Shore decries such an approach. He starts with the notion that all students despite their diverse backgrounds enter the classroom with valuable knowledge and skills. Although many of them have been silenced long before they enter college, basic writing and freshman composition classes, in thoughtfully, developed are capable of providing an opportunity for them to make the world meaningful. There is no need for special readings or prompts to encourage diversity; if a teacher is using critical methods, he notes, everyone will reflect on his or her identity and such individuality will include real diversity.

When Freire stressed the importance of basic literacy through his work with the poor in Brazil, he also recognized the political nature of the skills the students were learning. He asserted that those in a subordinate group must at once celebrate their own unique language while also acknowledging, and accepting, the fact that expertise in the dominant language is critical for the struggle to advance. Shor has taken these lessons from illiterate sugar cane workers in South America and demonstrated that they are essential in contemporary America. He has questioned canon and core curricula in terms of their implicit celebration of existing class relationships, gender roles and other socially constructed categories. In the latter regard, he has weighed in on the intense debates over ESL instruction and English only mandates and has demonstrated the ways those in control use the smoke screen of education and assimilation to maintain their authority. However, he provides examples such as slam poetry, hip hop, rap, reggae, salsa and tejano songs to demonstrate how those who feel oppressed in traditional spaces find avenues for authentic expression. Shor recognized long ago that literacy is a battleground by which those with influence maintain the existing hierarchy, and he demonstrates and articulates how teachers and students can change this through critical literacy practices. He uses the writing class as a place where all members work together to make the world meaningful. He asserts that there is no need for special readings or prompts to encourage diversity; if a teacher is using critical methods, everyone will reflect on his or her identity and individuality will include real diversity.

Participation is a hallmark of Shor's work. Oppressed people often become complicit in their own oppression through apathy. In the days of AIDS activism, the motto "Silence = Death" drew attention to the fact, and with it the awareness that disrupting the status quo was a matter of survival (Goldstein, 1997). This is the same sense of urgency that Shor brings to his classroom and to his writings on critical pedagogy. The lived world of the classroom must be one in which all members engage, not through coercion or bribery but as active agents in shaping their world. In such a classroom, there is no need of definitions such as teacher-driven or student-centered. All members join in mutual work of meaning making. Ira Shor has often been credited with providing comprehensive explanations of the theoretical foundations of critical pedagogy along with practical skills that assist teachers in selecting and adapting strategies to fit the realities they face.

The Role of the Teacher

Essential to Shor's conception of critical pedagogy is the concept of mutual benefit (see Shor, 1999). In this regard, he states that "critical literacy is an activity that reconstructs and develops ALL parties involved, pulling teachers forward as well as students" (Shor, 1999, p. 21). Shor makes a distinction between teachers who practice critical pedagogy and others who may act in similar ways because they believe it will help student learning. Although such teacher behaviors may appear similar, one set of actions are founded on assumptions that the teacher is behaving this way in order to best help students learn, while the other set of assumptions is founded on the belief that the teacher as well as the students gain from the process. In this regard, Shor traces the connections from Dewey to Vygotsky to Freire, showing how critical pedagogy has its roots in a problem-based constructivist approach to education.

Shor reminds teachers to begin with the belief that their students are capable of critical thought, speech and writing. This is not a call to throw out structure in classrooms and allow a laissez faire atmosphere; rather, it speaks to the sort of climate that seeks to eliminate the status quo where students are rewarded for passively absorbing teacher-directed instruction. Shor would have all teachers not just engage their students, but engage *with* their students in dialogue.

Difficulties in Putting Critical Theory Into Practice

The beginning of the 21st Century has been a volatile time for teachers. More than ever, educators in schools across the nation are being forced to teach in ways that perpetuate the banking style of knowledge transmission. Student test results, primarily on standardized tests that emphasize rote memory and regurgitation of lower level facts in a one size fits all pattern, largely constitute a main component vis-à-vis the basis for what students have learned, as well as public evaluations of teachers. The latter is especially true of teachers in low-performing schools in urban settings with populations of children without advantage or wealth. Like a beauty contest, teachers are rated and ranked in an attempt to identify winners and losers. Unlike a fair contest, educators have no control over the funding, curricula, and assessments. It is this type of system that makes it difficult for brave teachers to look to Ira Shor for advice on how to breathe life into their classrooms.

Indeed, current economic and political strife may cause teachers to be afraid to take the seemingly high risks that are part and parcel of adhering to and putting into practice critical pedagogy. Teachers may find themselves being defensive as they attempt to put into practice what they believe within a system that seeks to force hegemony and standardization on an America that is more diverse than ever before. Students and parents may not only fail to join in questioning inequalities, they may even balk at the very notion of doing so, hence aiding their oppressors by falling into expected passive roles. Shor understands why many teachers give up on their beliefs in the value of critical pedagogy. In this regard, he says:

> Disturbing the socialization of students and teachers into the system is certainly not easy, transparent, or risk-free (try questioning Nike's use of sweatshop labor to students who are Nike'd from head to toe and for whom Michael Jordan is an airborne god; try questioning such ventures as the Gulf War of 1991 among students with military relatives ordered to the front in Iraq). Coming to critical literacy is a rather unpredictable and even contentious process filled with surprises, resistances, breakthroughs, and reversals. It's no easy or open road for a number of reasons I've been defining in various books. The forces that need questioning are very old, deeply entrenched, and remarkably complex.... (Shor, 1999, p. 18)

Above all, critical pedagogy means dialogue. Even for teachers who are comfortable with the verbal give-and-take of discussions, there is a balance that is difficult to navigate. Conversation that challenges authority may be difficult for students who are seeking to gain approval by giving the teacher the response that they think he or she wants. And some teachers may, in fact, find such conversation extremely uncomfortable and unsettling.

Shor's strength comes from his own practice. The volumes he has penned are full of examples of his attempts, and failures, vis-à-vis the very skills for which others seek his wisdom. Through anecdotes from his classes, particularly those focused on composition, Shor becomes a true hero to those who seek to rattle the existing power structure. He refuses to allow his students to remain passive, but he shows that he must first learn from them before he can move forward. In Shor's world, teachers do not help students; they are partners on an uncomfortable but fantastic adventure.

While Shor has provided many examples of the difficulties in fostering such a culture, he has also given hope to those who would risk aiming for it. He writes of students who shift from passive receivers to individuals who care deeply about their own learning and the environment in which it happens. Students who may have appeared subservient to authority, whether lethargic or studious, frequently end up demonstrating a range of emotions, from humor and curiosity to respect and openness (Shor, 1992). As Shor (1992) states, "The goals of this pedagogy are to relate personal growth to public life by developing strong skills, academic knowledge, habits of inquiry, and critical curiosity about society, power, inequality, and change" (p. 15). Instead of resisting education, Shor asserts, students will come to see it as a right and a step towards greater sense of self. Indeed, they will embrace participation, and demand it at various levels.

In light of the difficulties and controversial nature of implementing critical theory in the classroom, why would any teacher interested in maintaining his or her employment attempt critical pedagogy? Since 1980 Shor has provided many answers to that very question. In doing so, he has reminded us that public school classrooms are hallowed ground, and that teachers can and do make amazing change happen. Ever the realist, though, he does not paint a simple or cheerful picture of the journey. *The journey, however, is the reward, because teachers practicing true critical pedagogy are on that journey with their students, to the mutual benefit of all parties.* As Shor states, "The mutual-development ethic constructs students as authorities, agents, and unofficial teachers who educate the official teacher while also getting educated by each other and by the teacher" (Shor, 1999, p. 13). So the struggle brings its own reward, in growth and change for teacher and students.

SHOR IN THE 21ST CENTURY

Ira Shor continues to provide a voice for alternative viewpoints vis-à-vis the demonization of public schools, teachers, and teacher unions. One can find his remarks in a variety of places from letters to the editor in journals to comments on blogs. His recent response to the documentary *Waiting for Superman* (Shor, 2010) painted a dismal portrait of the ways that people such as filmmaker Davis Guggenheim provide fodder to those who would privatize public education. Shor explains how the film painfully manipulates viewers and undermines public confidence. In doing so, he put to the test Guggenheim's painting of charter schools as being the only home for desperate parents and students, as well as Guggenheim's cavalier and blatant disregard of the many and positive gains in local public schools made by grassroots activists.

Shor has also weighed in on topics such as the corruption of academia as seen in situations like the sexual abuse scandal at Penn State, and the unrealistic expectation that traditional freshman composition classes will build writing competence in sixteen weeks. He joined with others, such as Professor Mark Naison of Fordham University, to start "99% Clubs" affiliated with the Occupy movement.

While Shor's place within the field will forever be linked with Freire, he has provided his own American understanding and impatience to this effort. Many teachers who adhere to the practice of critical theory look to Shor for ways to keep the faith in these troubled times. Undoubtedly, future teachers will do so as well.

Shor's grand vision of education as a powerful force for social change begins with critical pedagogy. When teachers and students create and experience democratic sharing of authority, the results are "cooperativeness, curiosity, humor, hope, responsibility, respect, attentiveness, openness, and concerns about society" (Shor, 1987). These characteristics of citizen-activists are the qualities necessary for the global world of this century. Shor's applications of critical pedagogy are roadmaps for this important journey.

REFERENCES

College of Staten Island. (n.d.). Ira Shor. Retrieved from http://www.csi.cuny.edu/faculty/SHOR_IRA.html

Gallagher, K. (2010). Teaching Freire and CUNY open admissions. *The Radical Teacher, 87*(1), 55–67.

Shor, I. (1972). Questions Marxists ask about literature. *College English, 34*(2), 178–179.

Shor, I. (1974). Reading and writing at Staten Island Community College. *College English, 35*(8), 945–996.

Shor, I. (1977a). Learning how to learn: Conceptual teaching in a course called "Utopia." *College English, 38*(7), 502–506.

Shor, I. (1977b). Reinventing daily life: Self-study and the theme of "work." *College English, 39*(4), 640–647.

Shor, I. (1977c). Writing about "work": A sequential syllabus. *The Radical Teacher, 4*, 21–24.

Shor, I. (Ed.). (1987). *Friere for the classroom: A sourcebook for liberatory freedom.* Portsmouth, NH: Heinemann.

Shor, I. (1992) *Empowering education: Critical teaching for social change.* Chicago: University of Chicago Press.

Shor, I. (1998). The centrality of beans: Remembering Paulo. *Convergence, 31*(1–2), 75–80.

Shor, I. (1999). What is critical literacy? In I. Shor. I. & C. Pari, C. (Eds.), *Critical literacy in action: Writing words, changing worlds* (pp. 1–30). Portsmouth, NH: Heinemann.

Shor, I. (2006). War, lies, and pedagogy: Teaching in fearful times. *The Radical Teacher, 77,* 30–35.

Shor, I. (2007a). A disruptive student. *The Radical Teacher, 80,* 44–45.

Shor, I. (2007b). Can critical teaching foster activism in this time of repression? *The Radical Teacher, 79,* p. 39.

Shor, I. (2010). Ira Shor is not "Waiting for Superman." Retrieved from http://www.notwaitingforsuperman.org/Articles/20101004-IraShor

Shor, I., & Friere, P. (1986). *A pedagogy for liberation: Dialogues on transforming education.* Westport, CT: Praeger.

The Friere Project. (n.d.). Ira Shor. Retrieved from http://www.freireproject.org/content/ira-shor

Tsao, T. M. (2005). Open admissions, controversy, and CUNY: Digging into social history through first year composition course. *History Teacher, 38*(4), 469–482.

ANNOTATED BIBLIOGRAPHY

Shor, I. (1980). *Critical teaching and everyday life.* Boston, MA: South End Press.

In this, Shor's first book, Paulo Friere's thinking vis-à-vis liberatory education is discussed in relation to the educational context in the United States (purposes, teacher's role, student's role, school's role, et al) in the United States. Friere had used his radical ideas of democratic education in the troubled country of Brazil, with revolution and military coup as the daily reality. Shor risked controversy with this book as he opened with a scathing comparison of the need for such techniques in the ostensibly democratic society of the United States. The books first section, Problematic Schooling, contains two chapters. The first details assumptions upon which much of public education in the United States was founded, the notion of socializing citizen workers through the façade of education (including affordable college opportunities in the 1950s and 1960s). The second demonstrates how the mechanism of traditional schooling has creates unconscious acceptance of status quo by both students and citizens. The remaining chapters are a detailed description of Shor's work as a teacher committed to bringing critical thought and action to his students. His description of the daily struggle and magnificent rewards of this work were an early call for change in American schooling. While the book provides foundational theory for such efforts, it is also a deeply personal portrait of a teacher's struggle.

Shor, I. (1986). *Culture wars: School and society in the conservative restoration 1969–1991.* Chicago, IL: University of Chicago Press.

In this text, Shor sets down a liberal account of the political swing back to conservatism after the revolutionary ideas and actions various movements (i.e., students, civil rights, black power, and women's liberation) of the 1960s.

Beginning with the election of Richard Nixon in 1968, Shor describes the seemingly slow but steady and seemingly innocuous elimination of student empowerment that occurred on college campuses partially as a result of open admissions. Shor explains how the insidious use of fear for the future derailed critical pedagogy in favor of career education and technical education. Through the Literacy Wars of the 1970s and early 1980s, those in authority learned to master public relations and re-place education at the political center of an agenda designed to maintain their power. The underlying goals, Shor argues, were to de-activate thinking students and teachers and re-activate them as purveyors of the sanctioned curricula in the name of excellence. Educators and students became unwitting agents in weakening their own impact. Highlighting the work of John Goodlad, Theodore Sizer and Ernest Boyer, Shor demonstrates how various cracks in the corporate and military juggernaut allowed openings for those citizens who hoped to return to and create more democratic methods of education. Shor's belief that the inauthenticity of the conservative agenda would be exposed in time through misuses of power has not been realized fully. Some signs do exist that the change he called for did occur in pockets of the country, but what Arthur G. Wirth called the unacceptable domination of the dominant in his review of Shor's book (1986) seems much more obvious.

Shor, I. (1992) *Empowering education: Critical teaching for social change.* Chicago, IL: University of Chicago Press.

This book is one that is very often used in preservice teacher education programs due to its brief but fairly comprehensive overview of critical pedagogy. From the introduction ("The First Day of Class: Passing the Test") and opening chapter ("Education is Politics: An Agenda for Empowerment") to chapters on activist research and working for change within the system, it is a timeless compilation of key ideas for teachers who hope to move themselves and their students beyond the traditional transfer of knowledge approach (in Freire's terms, the banking approach) to education. As with any of Shor's writing, he situates key educational issues within their political and historical context. The book still resonates as it did in 1992 due to the even more diverse nature of the American population and the overt gap between the elite and minorities and working class citizens. One of the most important chapters discusses the reasons why student play dumb, and the challenge to teachers who seek to use dialogic and problem-posing methods. Walk down almost any high school or college hallway, and Shor's description of docile and apathetic students silently waiting for the teacher to give them the requisite information comes to life. Drawing from Dewey and Vygotsky as well as Friere, Shor's passion and belief in teachers' abilities to bring about change rather than passively accept the status quo makes the possibility of a better future seem an attainable goal. This is a book that continues to provide even the most cautious educators tangible and practical strategies for risk-taking within classrooms from elementary to college levels.

Shor, I. (1996). *When students have power: Negotiating authority in critical pedagogy.* Chicago, IL: The University of Chicago Press.

This is Shor's most personal narrative. He allows the reader to sit in during a class in which he continues to practice critical pedagogy, but where a lack of student cooperation verging on rebellion causes him to reshape his teaching. The text resembles a fascinating scrapbook or travelogue to a distant land; in fact, Shor refers to the class as Siberia for many reasons, including those related the physical setting (a crowded basement cinderblock room) and the culture of the school (some students seek a return to their traditional passive roles). After twenty years of practice and study of critical pedagogy, Shor found his beliefs tested in new ways. Each class session is described in depth, and what some teachers may view as rebellion becomes, for Shor, a powerful learning opportunity. He watched and reflected as democratic dialog created citizen activism in some students. Tellingly, the class of City University students in Staten Island bore more than a passing resemblance to the Brazilian adults of Friere's Popular Culture Movement. The resistance of some students to an examination of their realities, the development of student learning contracts, and the creation of an After-Class Group reminded Shor that critical teaching is messy, fraught with failure and mistakes, *and* a means to transform the world through individual action. More than any of his other books, this text allows readers to get up close to Ira Shor, and see the power of critical pedagogy through his eyes.

Shor, I. (1997). Our apartheid: Writing instruction and inequality. *Journal of Basic Writing*, Spring, 16(1), 91–104.

Like his mentor Friere, Ira Shor has always believed that literacy is a primary battleground for critical pedagogy. In this essay, he provides a scathing analysis of the ways college composition classes have worked in concert with economic forces to place and keep working class students in a subordinate position. He revisits the birth of freshman composition classes at Harvard in the 19th century, and describes its spread within higher education as a gate-keeper for upward mobility. Shor has written on this issue before, and he summarizes the complaints and crises that used the "correct usage gate" as the well-protected opening to upper-level courses that lead to upper level jobs. Shor calls this policy, "comp for containment, control, and capital growth" (p. 92)." With testing for writing competence came noncredit basic writing courses, taught most often by poorly paid adjuncts or unpaid student tutors with little supervision or professional development. Shor sees the entry and exit exams so prevalent in such courses, along with the basic writing remedial courses, as extra sorting mechanisms designed to shape each new generation of students into existing societal inequalities. Nonwriting tests like the SAT or timed impromptu essays graded on a 1–6 scale are used to supposedly help provide students with the skills necessary to be successful yet, he argues, they lower the output of graduates while also keeping a group of instructors, primarily female, underpaid and low in status. He describes tracking and testing as the "Twin Towers of the Unequal City in which BW (basic writing) resides" (p. 97). Shor sees the overall arrangement as undemocratic and immoral. At the same time, he offers ideas for change along with admiration and praise for those writing teachers in the trenches who make remarkable changes in the lives of students and themselves through inspired pedagogy.

Shor, I. (Ed.). (1987). *Friere for the classroom: A sourcebook for liberatory freedom.* Portsmouth, NH: Heinemann.

This work is a compilation of articles that appeared in other venues, such as *Radical Teacher* and the *Harvard Educational Review* during the 1980s. That period was a time in which Paulo Friere was unable to return to Brazil for political reasons. He spent those years traveling and teaching in various countries, including the United States. During those years, American public school and university teachers began to infuse critical pedagogy into their practice. This volume provides the personal stories of their struggle to move from traditional teaching to democratic practice.

Several of the authors supply readers with information that is practical, but at the same time revisit the theoretical basis for Friere's methods and situate that theory in the context of American education. Shor includes his own revised essay on infusing Frierean approaches into teacher education in order to shape pedagogy in multitudes of future classrooms.

The book closes with a short description of Friere's work with Brazilian adults, *Literacy in 30 Hours: Paulo Friere's Process in Northeast Brazil,* which revisits the power of teaching and literacy. Friere's *Letter to North American Teachers,* especially written for this volume, links practices that began in a Third World setting to the alienation and passivity present in First World schools.

In the end, this book is a call to arms as well as a roadmap for teachers dissatisfied with the status quo. It remains a seminal sourcebook for critical pedagogy.

Shor, I., & Friere, P. (1986). *A pedagogy for liberation: Dialogues on transforming education.* Westport, CT: Praeger.

Described by many, including the authors, as a "talking book," this book is, in a sense, a manual of how to transform teaching through dialogic pedagogy. Responding to the key questions that teachers often asked about such an approach/methodology, Shor and Friere present their thoughts in a dialogic manner rather than a narrative. The essence of the book is its faith in the transformative and liberatory power of discourse. There is a distinction between dialogue and communications, dialogue and conversation.

Shor poses questions and responses as one who has struggled with the method in his own classrooms. Friere raises as series of risks and tensions associated with the strategies. Readers are privy to the power of dialogic teaching through the skillful application of these two colleagues who demonstrate the messy yet empowering nature of critical pedagogy. Both Shor and Friere freely discuss the risks and uncertainty associated with letting go of the authoritarian or helping roles that teachers slip into as comfortable as a pair of old shoes.

The two authors remind readers of the place of teacher competency and creativity in framing the educational space in which structure and rigor remain important. They also help those within the system see possibilities for change from within, in ways that work in daily classroom life. They also focus on language as a tool for empowering students and helping teachers themselves learn from their students' realities.

A deeper discussion of the need for bringing such strategies for resistance to the seemingly well-off first world students helps reveal the dangers of classroom instruction based on conformity and silence. Finally, the two enthusiastically summarize the possibilities and benefits of the method for remaking a participatory future.

Shor. I. & Pari, C. (Eds.). (1999a). *Critical literacy in action: Writing words, changing worlds.* Portsmouth, NH: Heinemann.

After Paulo Friere's death in 1997, Ira Shor and Caroline Pari produced three volumes as a tribute to his life and work. This first text begins with a lengthy chapter ("What is Critical Literacy?") that systematically describes the rationale and specifics of Friere's critical pedagogy and its relationship to empowering change through literacy. Shor details his own and others' experiences using strategies and problem posing to create democratic classrooms where literacy is at the center. He continues to remind readers that Friere built his theory on progressive ideas, from Dewey to Vygotsky, that are celebrated and honored at a conceptual level but find little practical application vis-à-vis traditional schooling. The remaining essays provide diverse examples of how critical pedagogy can be applied especially well in programs for populations that are marginalized in most cultures, including students for whom English is not their primary language, students with disabilities, workers, prisoners, and females. Through such a wide range of accounts of teachers struggling to create democratic community in places where individuals have become almost comfortable with their subservient status, all educators can find strategies and assignments that resonate. The final essay on the use of cultural studies as an opportunity to engage students in topics that are famously public (such as welfare, charter schools, or gun control), yet allow them to reflect, speak and write from the personal experiences. The text is comprehensive, thought provoking and practical and will likely serve as a real help to teachers who seek ideas and support for critical pedagogy.

Shor. I. & Pari, C. (Eds.). (1999b). *Education is politics: Critical teaching across differences, K–12.* Portsmouth, NH: Heinemann.

The core of this book is celebration. With so many threats today to teachers' jobs and autonomy (and so many factors working against creativity in classrooms), the authors of these essays provide stories of hope and change in public schools in ways that make us confident that dedicated teachers can still perform acts of magic and transformation with artistry and commitment. Friere urged critical educators not to be deterred by the top-down mandates designed to produce and maintain standardization, and the educators whose work is represented in these pages have taken on that challenge. In doing so, they tell the tales of their bottom-up endeavors, teachers who work alongside their students to pull back the curtains hung by those in power in hierarchical systems, and expose the myths that pass as educational reform.

Teachers from the primary grades through high school help their students actively examine their education and make connections between personal learning and larger social issues. These teachers are risk-takers, but they are also believers and survivors. They are generous in sharing their stories of change, warts and all. This volume is a fitting tribute to Friere, with its honest descriptions of the resistance and unexpected results of helping students question topics such as Nike sweatshops, AIDS education, and Christopher Columbus. The individuals and settings differ, but the dedication to the practice of critical pedagogy shines throughout.

Shor. I. & Pari, C. (Eds.). (2000). *Education is politics: Critical teaching across differences, Postsecondary.* Portsmouth, NH: Heinemann.

Shor begins his introduction to this work with a comparison of Elie Wiesel (a Holocaust survivor and noted novelist) and Paulo Friere, both of whom exhort everyone to avoid neutrality and to work to make beliefs reality in the face of top-down oppression. This call to action is the theme of the book. Shor recognizes that it is important to have allies within the struggle for change, and he is aware of the points of disagreement within various "sects" of critical pedagogy. While he describes conflicts that exist between Friere's ideas, feminist pedagogy, and Deweyan education, he also identifies points of convergence. This sets the tone for the essays that follow.

The contributors to the book relate their experiences at various universities where critical pedagogy is practiced in various and eclectic ways (e.g., within courses on music and social movements, through the use of lesbian and gay language in word problems in statistics and literature, and through an examination of the importance of mass media on the social construction of student identities). They also discuss the successes and failures of classroom interaction and assignments. None of the authors pretend that the work is easy, but also describe the mutual impact on themselves and their students, and, at times, their institutions and colleagues.

These educators all find ways to help students read the cultural curricula that act as informal "teachers" in the form of commercials, television shows, and more. One of the most important themes of this volume is the ramification of those who attempt to remain neutral; each chapter demonstrates that ignoring the status quo is tantamount to supporting it. Readers are reminded that Friere urged university teachers to remember that the façade of concepts and subject matter disciplines serve to make education opaque and removed from realities. When teachers discover that education is politics, they can make conscious choices about how they will use their skills and for whom. And when they do, neutrality is no longer an option.

Shor, I. (2009, June). *Can critical teaching change the world?* Keynote address presented at Alternative Education Resource Organization Conference, Albany, NY. Retrieved from http://educationrevolution.wordpress.com/2010/02/20/can-critical-teaching-change-the-world-ira-shor-keynote-address-video/

In 2009, the Alternative Education Resource Organization (AERO) celebrated 20 years as an organization dedicated to helping parents and educators provide students with alternatives to the traditional banking model of knowledge transmission that serves as the basis for curriculum, instruction and assessment in most schools. A highlight of their 6th Annual Conference in Albany, New York, was a keynote address by Ira Shor entitled, "Can critical teaching change the world?" This video of his talk reminds those interested in critical pedagogy that Ira Shor is still one of the most powerful voices encouraging courageous educators to engage their students in a shared questioning the status quo. Speaking to a roomful of individuals already dissatisfied with traditional public education, Shor steps comfortably in and out of his presenter role to annotate his method, the theory behind it, the difficulties associated with it in practice and the desperate need for others to employ similar strategies. His demonstration of snippets of his own teaching strategies serves as reminders that the critical teacher is always looking for ways to connect with his or her students. He is unabashedly honest in his articulation of his own mistakes and flaws as he struggles to improve and stay true to the ideals of critical teaching in what he calls the worst of times. For those who have read Shor but not seen him, this video provides a glimpse of someone who is not only a great theorist and writer, but a person who continues to fight and live his ideals in small spaces as well as grand stages.

Commentary on Shor's Work and/or Critical Theory

Collins, T. G. (1997). A response to Ira Shor's "Our Apartheid: Writing Instruction and Inequality. *Journal of Basic Writing, 16*(2), 95–100.

Collins takes issue with Shor on two separate topics. In his essay, Shor used the basic writing and composition classes at the University of Minnesota as an example of a "cash cow"—programs that generate revenue for the institution by requiring students to pay full tuition while classes are staffed with low-paid adjunct instructors. Collins was instrumental in designing and coordinating basic writing programs at Minnesota, and he carefully explains the factual distinctions and fallacy in Shor's example. He then proceeds to examine Shor's broader points about the overall nature of basic writing programs, and provides other examples that dispute the generic nature of Shor's arguments. Collins' essay is thoughtful, and well balanced, providing agreement with Shor's criticism of exclusionist practices in higher education, but he challenges Shor's criticism of basic writing programs as the home of this cynical agenda. Collins provides examples of programs and institutions he believes use basic writing courses to empower students, as Shor advocates. He ends with a cautionary worry that while reformists argue with each other, conservatives move their own agenda forward.

Ellsworth, E. (1989). Why doesn't this feel empowering? Working through the repressive myths of critical pedagogy. *Harvard Education Review, 59*(3), 297–324.

With this article, Elizabeth Ellsworth became one of the most cited critics of critical pedagogy. She, along with colleagues such as Susan Gabel, Jennifer Gore, Carmen Luke, and Kathleen Weiler, challenged many of the basic assumptions of critical pedagogy within the constructs of feminist pedagogy as an ideology that perpetuates the repressive nature of education in its domination over certain groups while it claims to empower the oppressed. Her main argument against critical pedagogy is that, when left unchallenged, practices of critical pedagogy in classrooms situated within existing university structures, merely give voice and credibility to student experiences, many of which replicate existing authoritarian power structures. Like Shor, Ellsworth uses her own experience as a White middle class female professor teaching a university class designed to provide students with space for critical examination of race, class, and gender. However, her encounters and reflections led her to contest the assumptions of critical pedagogy as something that was, beneath the surface, more homogenizing and restrictive than it seemed.

Gabel, S. (2002). Some conceptual problems with critical pedagogy. *Curriculum Inquiry, 32*(2), 177–201.

Susan Gabel courageously used her own life circumstances and the power of auto ethnography as a research methodology to gently chide proponents of critical pedagogy to consider how the theory seemingly excludes the concept of "ability diversity." The author, a practitioner who espouses the power of critical pedagogy, found critical theory lacking when she attempted to empower her daughter, Tiffany, a person with some developmental and cognitive challenges. Gabel describes in detail her inner thoughts and decisions, weighing the various costs and benefits not only for herself and Tiffany but all family members as well as individuals in schools and community. When Gabel seeks examples of liberatory pedagogy applied to this specific marginalized population in the literature, she finds that a theory she embraced for its inclusivity is strangely silent in this area. Her search makes her aware of the gap in the field; neither Freire, Shor nor others document specific cases involving diversity of ability. Individuals involved in the bureaucratic maze that is attached to evaluations and adaptations of school settings and services for students with disabilities are no less in need of the respect and voice that critical pedagogy promises than any other group. Gabel also finds critical pedagogy problematic when its seemingly inclusive nature is at odds with a person's sense of self and identity. Diverse abilities make it difficult to listen and accommodate the individual's concept of self and needs, and Gabel finds herself wondering if the parental assessment and decision-making is "just another form of blatant, unexamined coercion" (p. 194). She comes to a place that tests her beliefs regarding the nature of liberatory practice: the recognition that the negotiation of choice is critical. As she says, "The first question is not whether a student is in an ability diverse inclusive classroom. The first question is whether the student (and his or her family, when age requires it) wants to be where they are and whether that classroom is a place where students and teachers are free to struggle to become new people and to live self-constructed lives as much as possible" (p. 194). Susan Gabel bravely challenges what critical pedagogy means for all individuals, and shows the difficulties involved in making one's actions congruent with one's beliefs.

Gur-Ze'ev, I. (1998). Toward a non-repressive critical pedagogy. *Educational Theory*, *48*(4), 463–486.

Gur-Ze'ev makes the case that the wide varieties of critical pedagogies make it difficult to offer critiques of the field. He posits that the utopian view held by most practitioners of critical pedagogy is limiting, even normalizing. Counter-education includes negative views, something that is not part of the sought after utopia that forms the basis of critical pedagogy. In counter education, there is no promise of what he calls "collective emancipation" (p. 463). He contrasts the concept of reason in Critical Pedagogy (found in the work of Friere, Habermas, Shor, and Giroux) with Critical Theory (found in the work of Heidegger, Michel Foucault, and Lyotard). He chastises Shor and others for being naïve and not recognizing that the consensus reached through dialogue is, in itself, hegemonic. He cites Shor's description (in *Critical Theory and Everyday Life*, 1980) of the experience of trying to criticize students' knowledge about that seemingly most American of foods, the hamburger, as an example of a situation that ultimately becomes part of the current order of the way things work in a college class. He views this limitation of critical pedagogy as repressive, and puts forth Critical Theory as a more open, if negative, option.

Greenberg, K. L. (1997). A response to Ira Shor's "Our Apartheid: Writing instruction and inequality. *Journal of Basic Writing*, *16*(2), 90–94.

Greenberg is harsh in her criticism of Shor's attack on basic writing classes. She argues that he speaks of students and courses as stereotypes, while in reality they are much more diverse across and within universities. She makes a distinction between students' need for academic literacy skills and political enlightenment, while Shor see these as combined in critical pedagogy. Her assertion is that without basic writing courses, the very students Shor champions would fail within the constraints of college. She argues that the wholesale changes and conditions Shor describes are improbable, so it is better to provide quality basic writing courses taught by knowledgeable and proficient teachers.

Harris, J. (2003). Opinion: Revision as critical practice. *College English*, *65*(6), 577–592.

Harris posits a fundamental question: Can we separate the practice of teaching writing skills from the politics of teaching? He uses Shor's book *When Students Have Power* (1996) as a way to discuss specific examples of what he means by the labor of writing. He does not so much disagree with Shor as pose additional questions. He thoughtfully presents different points of view vis-à-vis several of the aspects of Shor's course. Ultimately, Harris argues for a greater use of the revision process as a way to help students see how their choices matter. In this way, revision becomes the means to achieve the critical practice and student empowerment that serve as Shor's aims. Harris is also concerned with student consciousness; however, he makes distinctions between the degree and methods of practice that he sees as small but important.

Wardekker, W. L., & Miedema, S. (1997). Critical pedagogy: An evaluation and direction for reformulation. *Curriculum Inquiry, 27*(1), 45–61.

Wardekker and Miedema provide a historical context for variations within the evolution of critical pedagogy, but do so with limited mention of Friere and no reference to Shor. Nevertheless, this article provides a strong evaluation of the theory in its various forms, and possible reasons it remains less than widespread. The authors spend time on two main points in their criticism. First, they discuss the lack of practical consequences that have resulted from this theory. They describe the lack of a specific vision or project that will allow the theory to move from mere hoped-for utopian change to actual democratization of society. Wardekker and Miedema find a key flaw in most articulated theories of critical pedagogy: the absence of the concept of identity formations as a crucial part of education. They value above all this internalization of dialogue between the individual and society; in their view, this dialogue describes the activities of thinking as much, if not more, than that between teacher and student. In addition, they reject a notion of a "free and self-aware humanity" (p. 56) as a function of a view that posits becoming human as more universal and less political. They call for a reformulated view of critical pedagogy that speaks to "the relationship between the private and the public sphere, between the development of the person and that of society" (p. 59). These authors find that the original theory of critical pedagogy, while plausible in concept and capable of producing some change in individuals as a result of criticism, does not provide, enough of a roadmap for action to assist and guide practitioners in the schools. Based on these missing components, Wardekker and Mieldma characterize critical pedagogy as a conservative theory, something one can imagine would offend Shor.

CHAPTER 7

MICHAEL APPLE

Neo-Marxist Analyst of Schooling, the Curriculum, and Education Policy

Miguel Zavala

INTRODUCTION

This chapter is centered on the scholarship of Michael Apple, who has made significant contributions to the critical study of schooling processes, schooling systems, and education policy, investigating how these operate within a broader nexus of social relations of power. Developing an analytic rather than exhaustive overview of Michael Apple's works, this review traces two intersecting trajectories to his analysis of education. The first is a strategic one, marked by a shift from the study of curricular processes themselves (1970s–1980s) to studying-up (a type of scholarship that shifts that gaze to groups occupying higher echelons of power in a given society) the actors and interests shaping public education policy more generally (1990s–present). The second is a theoretical one, evident in the transition from a structural, reproductive framework grounded in the neo-Marxist tradition to a "nonsynchronous parallelist" position that views class, race, and gender as interlocking social relations and processes (see McCarthy & Apple, 1988).

Educating About Social Issues in the 20th and 21st Centuries, pages 133–151
133

While key works are identified and discussed in relation to each other, this review includes a brief biographical sketch of his life, an intellectual biography that outlines the major traditions informing Michael Apple's scholarship, and an annotated bibliography of key works (major books, articles, and chapters).

A LIFE OF POLITICAL ACTIVISM AND SCHOLARSHIP

Michael W. Apple (1942–) is John Bascom Professor of Curriculum & Instruction and Educational Policy Studies at the University of Wisconsin-Madison. Prior to his university appointment in 1970, he completed his doctoral studies in the Philosophy of Education at Teachers College, Columbia University. In his dissertation (Apple, 1970), titled "Relevance and Curriculum: A Study in the Phenomenological Sociology of Knowledge," are traces of an emerging, critical scholar rooted in his working class background and history of political activism.

Michael W. Apple grew up in a working class family setting and, after struggling to complete his undergraduate studies, enlisted in the army in the late 1950s, ending his term in 1962. He taught for five yours in a poor neighborhood in Paterson, New Jersey. In an interview (Morrow & Torres, 1990) and his own reflections (Apple, 2006d; Apple, 2009c), Michael Apple identifies his experience growing up in a family with a history of political activism as formative in his development as a scholar-activist. During his early teaching years he was one of the founding members of the Congress of Racial Equality in Paterson, which organized around desegregation and literacy campaigns for African-Americans. He also became president of a teachers union and lead local efforts in Paterson against city politics that did not represent the interests of the poor. Since the 1970s, he has continued his activism with teachers unions, educators, and governments, giving talks throughout the world and providing keen insights on the social forces shaping public education. A prolific writer, Michael Apple has made significant contributions to the sociology of education and thus renewing neo-Marxist scholarship in the United States.

INTELLECTUAL TRADITIONS

It is an understatement to say that Michael Apple's work has contributed greatly to neo-Marxist scholarship in the United States. While departing from critical theory, in particular Jürgen Habermas's contributions (see Morrow & Torres, 1990), Michael Apple's earlier work grappled with the problem of school knowledge and its relation to the social relations of economic production. Along these lines, he commented as follows: "I had left [critical theory] for particular conceptual and political reasons, in part because I think that there are traditions (e.g., the neo-Gramscian and the radical democratic) that say it better and clearer and offer a different and more democratic kind of politics as well" (quoted in Morrow & Torres, 1990, p. 288).

His engagement with scholars from Britain and neo-Marxist scholarship lead him to the production of, perhaps, the most widely read publication in the field of critical curriculum studies, *Ideology and Curriculum*. Published in 1979, this seminal text drew heavily from two major neo-Marxist scholars: Raymond Williams in Britain and Antonio Gramsci in Italy. A common thread found in the book and in Apple's approach to the question of the relation of school knowledge and the reproduction of social class relations was the importance of ideological and cultural mediations, often missing in structuralist approaches or under-theorized in phenomenological studies of school knowledge. Apple's analysis of ideology and culture draws from and expands on major concepts that have become fundamental to neo-Marxist analysis: *selective tradition* (Raymond Williams), *hegemony* (Antonio Gramsci), and *common sense* (Antonio Gramsci).

EARLIER WORKS: CONTRIBUTIONS
TO THE SOCIOLOGY OF SCHOOL KNOWLEDGE

Whitty (1985), a well-known scholar of the sociology of school knowledge, has argued, along the lines of neo-Marxists critiques, that the overemphasis in studying the social construction of knowledge within the classroom has led to a neglect of the greater "macro" economic and political processes. Indeed, many of the studies that deployed a social constructionist lens afforded new insights into *how* knowledge was processed in the classroom, but lacked analyses of *why* such knowledge forms were constructed in the first place. A danger with social construction or phenomenological conceptualizations of school knowledge, that Michael Apple clearly lays out in his *Ideology and Curriculum* and in other published pieces (see Apple, 1976a), is that they presume ideology to be a mere "sense-making" or "system of interacting symbols" (Apple, 1979, p. 20). It is this tension, between phenomenological accounts of ideological transmission in the classroom and relational analyses, which situate the construction of knowledge within systems of economic and cultural reproduction, that informs Apple's (1979) analysis in *Ideology and Curriculum*. The distinction between a relational critique of the curriculum and a social-interactionist analysis of socialization is crucial: the former necessarily embodies a conception of ideology that is intimately tied to the systematic distribution of power relations.

The theoretical work on role socialization in school settings by Dreeben (1967) illustrates the weaknesses in functionalist approaches that Michael Apple identified early in his work (see Apple, 1978a; Apple, 1982). Dreeben looked at schooling processes and focused not so much on the explicit outcomes of schools (i.e., the technical transmission of knowledge) but on the "unintended" learning that exists in educational settings. In particular, he found that students in industrialized nations, through public schooling, acquire the norms of "independence," "achievement," "universalism," and "specificity"—all conducive to political and economic "participation" in the greater industrial society. Although seemingly a critique of the socialization that occurs within industrial capitalism, his work is presented as nothing more than a theoretical survey of the schooling process within a functionalist framework: ". . . the main purpose of this analysis was to present a formulation, hypothetical in nature, of how schooling contributes to the emergence of certain psychological outcomes, not to provide an apology or justification for those outcomes on ideological grounds," (p. 49). Clearly, his project is not about the contradictions in how schooling norms reproduce social-property relations and economic inequities.

Apple's critique in *Ideology and Curriculum* attempts to move beyond Dreeben's functionalist analysis of socialization. In his discussion of the kindergarten classroom, Apple (1979) argues that it is a place where students are "initiated" into the "experience of being a worker," where the value of conformity is stressed, and normality/deviance is learned (p. 57). Further, he contends that this is a necessary part of the process by which schools serve to reproduce "normative and communicative structures of industrial life" (Apple, 1979, p. 58). Although not explicitly resolving the question he raises (i.e., "in whose interests does the school function?"), he does suggest that schooling serves to preserve existing cultural/class relations (p. 64). Again, the key distinction between his approach and functionalist ones, such as Dreeben's, is that Apple attempts to situate classroom processes within larger socio-cultural-political structures—but attempts to do so using a relational rather functional mode of inquiry. That is, he seeks to explain the reasons why "norms/values" are reproduced in the classroom and how "ideology" mediates the linkage between classroom life and economic reproduction.

In searching for theorizations on cultural mediation in the process of social reproduction, Apple resorted to the work of Raymond Williams and Antonio Gramsci. Later, the works of Basil Bernstein and Paul Willis within the sociology of school knowledge in Europe played a fundamental role in reconceptualization of what seemed like a structuralist account of schooling in *Ideology and Curriculum* (see Apple, 1979a; Apple, 1982; Apple, 1992a; Apple, 2002a). Published in 1982, *Education and Power* introduces a more nuanced understanding of social reproduction and represents a more developed stage in his theorizations on schooling and social reproduction. "Schools are not 'merely' institutions of reproduction, institutions where the overt and covert knowledge that is taught inexorably molds students into passive beings," they are contradictory sites of cultural production and contestation as well (Apple, 1982, p. 14). Laying out a sophisticated argument grounded in research studies on labor processes and school life, in *Education and Power* Apple (1982) argues that we cannot, at a fundamental level, reduce culture and ideology to the reproduction of economic processes: "At the very least, the search for such an understanding requires us to take much more seriously the idea that the cultural sphere is not totally reducible to the economic" (p. 86). In many ways, *Education and Power* marks his critical break from structural Marxism and an expansion of his earlier theorizations found in *Ideology and Curriculum*, taking a new cultural Marxist approach to understanding cultural production as contradictory, as relatively autonomous, yet never losing site of schooling and school knowledge as dialectically linked and determined by macro- structural forces (see Apple, 1980a; Apple, 1986b).

TOWARDS A PARALLELIST, NONSYNCHRONOUS POSITION

The correspondence of structural determinations of reproduction in the school, such as a tiered educational system that reproduces a working class (Bowles & Gintis, 1976), and an emphasis on the reproductive capacities of an institutionalized credentialing system (Bourdieu & Passeron, 1977) were superseded by a new cultural reproduction analysis which stipulates a micro-analytic reformulation of these earlier theories of reproduction. According to this new analysis, schools are conceptualized as "places for the formation of subjectivities, identities, and subcultures," where systems of domination are constituted along racial, ethnic, and class lines (McCarthy & Apple, 1988; Morrow & Torres, 1990). This contemporary analysis has been described as a "parallelist, nonsynchronous" position because it posits that patriarchy and racism, as well as other forms of domination, are not reducible to capitalism (McCarthy & Apple, 1988). In one of his earliest articulations of the ways in which patriarchy, racism and capitalism interlock, Apple (1986b) iterates, "In the preceding discussion, I have taken what is commonly known as the parallelist position. That is, I have argued that we should not automatically assume the primacy of class relations over those of gender and race. These latter two dynamics must be given equal weight in the analysis of any concrete situation," (p. 411).

This parallelist framework is most evident in *Teachers and Texts*, where Apple (1986) documents the control of curriculum and teaching by drawing from historical analysis and empirical studies on women's work. Apple's central argument is that the management of curriculum and teaching is a historically gendered practice and that teaching, especially in the elementary grades, has been readily controlled and exploited given the patriarchal discourses that shape management ideologies and how these intersect with material conditions of women teachers who also work at home. What sets *Teachers and Texts* apart from his earlier work, such as *Ideology and Curriculum* or *Education and Power,* is the explicit attempt to theorize education processes in more complex ways. That is, not only does Apple center culture and ideology in his analysis, but he grounds these in relation to interlocking, yet parallel, forms of power more broadly, all of which are not reducible to social class relations.

While a parallelist position informs more contemporary studies on gender and race and their relation to education policymaking (see Apple, 1994a; Apple, 1999a), the corpus of Apple's published work as a whole, post the publication of *Teachers and Texts,* does not explore the interlocking aspects of race, class, and gender; his work is predominantly centered on social class interests and represents a project of mapping the actors vying for education since the early 1990s. While this trend in his scholarship may signal the challenges in undertaking parallelist analysis, I argue that his emphasis on social class relations is due to the material conditions impacting public education: Since the late 1980s and clearly into the 1990s what we see at the fore are *social class* interests converging and colliding in the struggle for public education.

LATTER WORKS: STUDYING-UP AND "MAPPING" THE RIGHT

Michael Apple's latter works, post 1990, can be characterized as studying-up scholarship that attempts to "map" the actors and interests shaping public education in the United States. Building from Gramsci's (1971) categories such as *common sense* and *hegemonic bloc,* Apple's latter work combines both cultural-ideological analysis of the formation of *common sense* and political-economic analysis of the convergence of group interests in formulating a nuanced argument of how the Right has been shaped and has managed to co-opt popular consent over society. His earliest articulation (see Apple, 1990a; Apple, 1993a) of this kind of studying-up or "mapping" strategy, documents the conservative set of policies, such as the standardization of curricula and shifts to privatize public education, in a systematic fashion.

Grounded in the concrete political, institutional, and cultural landscape of public education, Apple's attempts at "mapping" the Right had been laid out in several articles (see Apple, 1997a; Apple, 1998a; Apple, 1998b), yet his most developed arguments take form in two published books: *Cultural Politics and Education* and *Educating the "Right" Way*. In *Cultural Politics and Education* Apple (1996) outlines the ways in which neoconservatives and neoliberals have played a fundamental role in controlling education vis-à-vis a tendency towards a national curriculum and the institutionalization of standardized testing. Subsequently, the most insightful contribution to our understanding of how the Right has won increasing power over education policy is made in Apple's analysis of how conservative movements materialize. Based on a case study of a local community, Apple documents how individuals who did not consider themselves a part of the Right experience a shift as they voice their interests as they respond to a growing bureaucratic state. The essence of his argument is that we must analyze these cultural shifts while being mindful of the contradictory and contested ways in which they take form, not with simplistic notions that render "the Right" a unitary set of ideologies and interests.

Outlined in *Cultural Politics and Education* is the macro-context of conservative discourses that set parameters on how people make sense of education and the solutions to education problems. Building on his prior work, *Educating the "Right" Way* represents Apple's (2006) most developed integration of cultural-ideological analysis and political-economy. Delineating the convergence of key interests in shaping what he terms "conservative modernization," Apple identifies four major groups: neoliberals, neoconservatives, authoritarian populists, and the new managerial middle class as pivotal in the current shift to standardize, control, and privatize public education. Tied to this mapping project is the analysis of how conservative education policies are more than expressions of these group interests. Conservative education policy-making is made possible by shifts in our common sense. Our notions of "freedom" and "choice" have been altered by market logics and discourses, to the point that popular conceptions of what schools are about and how they should be "reformed" are constricted within the rhetoric of "competition," "efficiency," and "standardization."

CONCLUSION

As a whole, Michael Apple's works over the last three decades have left a lasting impact on the sociology of education. Although neo-Marxist frameworks still remain marginal given the non critical and applied-policy character of most published scholarship in the field, most impressive is the role his scholarship has played in integrating a neo-Marxist analysis of schools and schooling systems, which was generally absent prior to 1980. Nevertheless, we see in his work the development of a scholar whose earlier studies on the hidden curriculum have taken us from the micro-spaces of the classroom to the macro-cultural, political, and economic contexts that are currently shaping public education at all levels, from the curriculum to teaching to its transformation as a sector. That said, in providing an overview of Michael Apple's scholarship, it's important to conclude with a general assessment of the theory and method in the corpus of his published work.

While the privatization of education, standardization, etc. are processes that have been underway since the 1980s, what limits do we see in projects that "map" the Right within a predominantly social class lens and politics? This question grows out of Apple's own admonition for the need to develop parallelist analyses that do not reduce gender and race to class. A rich tradition, albeit marginal, can be found in perspectives from Latin America and in the field of postcolonial studies that have, at the very core, reconceptualized race and class as inseparable. Much of this scholarship has been framed within an anticolonial standpoint that names white supremacy as an operating historical and political force in "post" colonial contexts such as the United States. Indeed, one wonders how Apple's analyses in *Ideology and Curriculum* and *Educating the "Right" Way* would be enriched, challenged, and substantiated by rethinking schooling, school knowledge, and political-economic relations within this stretched dialectic of race-class (see Fanon, 1961). Taking these frameworks seriously, works like *Ideology and Curriculum* and *Educating the "Right" Way* may need to be reinvented in the context of Arizona and other states where primarily *racist* cultural politics are playing out in such policies as SB1070, which outlawed ethnic studies programs and ethnic-based curricula throughout the state.

Moreover, while Michael Apple has been mindful of the problems with theoretical and conceptual work that is largely disconnected from the realities of the teacher, students, parents and other groups deeply affected by social forces—a critique he and other raise against functionalist and structuralist readings of how school knowledge is interconnected with the reproduction of social class structure—his work would be enriched by engaging that very strategy in his own methodology. His writing and scholarship are largely theoretical, with scant conceptual pieces grounded in empirical modes of inquiry. The recommendation here is not for Apple to empirically verify his claims or to substantiate his arguments, but to engage in a renewed scholarship and mode of inquiry that, at the same time, concretizes theory and theorizes the concrete. Moving from investigation as a form of "reading" to investigation as a political strategy driven by community struggle and self-determination, decolonizing methodological strategies have been employed by well-known indigenous scholars in New Zealand (see Smith, 1999) and participatory action research in Latin America (see Orlando Fals-Borda, 1985). This last point is significant, because it implies a radical transformation of scholars (and their scholarship), as they become co-producers of critical scholarship alongside working class and other subaltern groups. One can only imagine the possibility of a particular kind of grassroots research that grows out of the spaces that Michael Apple knows well, of teachers unions, activist circles, and other spaces that he has been a part of for the last four decades.

REFERENCES

Apple, M. W. (1970). *Relevance and curriculum: A study in phenomenological sociology of knowledge.* (Doctoral Dissertation, Columbia University). Retrieved from http://www.proquest.com/en-US/catalogs/databases/detail/pqdt.shtml

Apple, M. W. (1976a). Curriculum as ideological selection. *Comparative Education Review, 20*(2), 209–215.

Apple, M. W. (1978a). Ideology, reproduction, and educational reform. *Comparative Education Review, 22*(3), 367–387.

Apple, M. W. (1979). *Ideology and curriculum.* New York, NY: Routledge & Kegan Paul.

Apple, M. W. (1979a). Curriculum and reproduction. *Curriculum Inquiry, 9*(3), 251–257.

Apple, M. W. (1980a). Analyzing determinations: Understanding and evaluating the production of social outcomes in schools. *Curriculum Inquiry, 10*(1), 55–76.

Apple, M. W. (1982). *Education and power.* Boston: Routledge & Kegan Paul.

Apple, M. W. (1986). *Teachers and texts: A political economy of class and gender relations in education.* New York, NY: Routledge & Kegan Paul.

Apple, M. W. (1986b). Review Article—Bringing the economy back into educational theory. *Educational theory, 36*(4), 403–415.

Apple, M. W. (1990a). Ideology, equality, and the new right. *Phenomenology + Pedagogy, 8,* 293–314.

Apple, M. W. (1992a). Education, culture, and class power: Basil Bernstein and the neo-Marxist sociology of education. *Educational Theory, 42*(2), 127–145.

Apple, M. W. (1993a). The politics of official knowledge: Does a national curriculum make sense? *Teachers College Record, 95*(2), 222–241.

Apple, M. W. (1994a). Text and contexts: The state and gender in educational policy. *Curriculum Inquiry, 24*(3), 349–359.

Apple, M. (1996). *Cultural politics and education.* New York, NY: Teachers College Press.

Apple, M. (1997a). Justifying the conservative restoration: Morals, genes, and educational policy. *Educational Policy, 11*(2), 167–182.

Apple, M. (1998a). Education and the new hegemonic blocs: Doing policy the "right" way. *International Studies in the Sociology of Education, 8*(2), 181–202.

Apple, M. (1998b). How the conservative restoration is justified: Leadership and subordination in educational policy. *International Journal of Leadership in Education: Theory and Practice, 1*(1), 3–17.

Apple, M. W. (1999a). The absent presence of race in educational reform. *Race Ethnicity and Education, 2*(1), 9–16.

Apple, M. W. (2002a). Does education have independent power? Basil Bernstein and the question of relative autonomy. *British Journal of Sociology of Education, 23*(4), 607–616.

Apple, M. (2006). *Educating the "right" way: Markets, standards, god, and inequality.* New York, NY: Routledge.

Apple, M. W. (2006d). Education, politics, and social transformation. In Samuel Totten and Jon E. Pederson, *Researching and teaching social issues: The personal stories and pedagogical efforts of professors of education* (7–28). Oxford, UK: Lexington books.

Apple, M. W. (2009c). On being a scholar/activist in education. In Edmund C. Short and Leonard J. Waks (Eds.), *Leaders in curriculum studies: Intellectual self-portraits* (1–14). Boston, MA: Sense Publishers.

Bourdieu, P. & Passeron, J. (1977). *Reproduction in education, society and culture.* London, UK: Sage Publications.

Bowles, S. & Gintis, H. (1976). *Schooling in capitalist America.* New York, NY: Basic Books.

Dreeben, R. (1967). The contribution of schooling to the learning of norms. *Harvard Educational Review, 37*(2), 211–237.

Fals-Borda, O. (1985). *Conocimiento y poder popular: lecciónes con campesinos de Nicaragua, Mexico y Colombia.* Mexico City, MX: Siglo Veintiuno Editores.

Fanon, F. (1961). *Le damnés de la terre.* Paris: Présence Africaine.

Gramsci, A. (1971). *Selections from the prison notebooks.* Translated and edited by Quintin Hoare and Geoffrey Nowell-Smith. New York, NY: International Publishers.

McCarthy, C. & Apple, M. W. (1988). Race, class, and gender in American educational research: Towards a nonsynchronous parallelist position. In Lois Weis (Ed.), *Class, race, and gender in American education,* (9–42). New York, NY: SUNY Press.

Morrow, R. A. & Torres, C. A. (1990). Education, power, and personal biography: An interview with Michael Apple. *Phenomenology + Pedagogy, 8* (1), 273–290.

Smith, L. T. (1999). *Decolonizing methodologies: Research and indigenous peoples.* New York, NY: Zed Books.

Whitty, G. (1985). *Sociology and school knowledge: Curriculum theory, research and politics.* London, UK: Routledge.

ANNOTATED BIBLIOGRAPHY

Apple, M. (1979). *Ideology and curriculum.* New York, NY: Routledge & Kegan Paul.

In this seminal text Michael Apple presents a theoretical framework and model for critically analyzing the content, form, and exchange of social relations that constitute the lived curriculum. Drawing from the works of Antonio Gramsci and Raymond Williams, Apple terms his approach a *relational analysis* that makes ideology central to the reproduction of social relations of economic production. The book includes a model for engaging with ideological critique and the analysis of hegemony. Two chapters concretize this strategy by presenting a contextual analysis of classroom life and a historical account of curriculum production and its control in the United States. Apple's analysis is timely and still echoes in the present. While grappling with the problem of determinism in social reproduction theory, his work at points represents classroom life solely within the lens of cultural and social reproduction. What else may be happening in classrooms besides the socialization to worker ideologies?

Apple, M. (1982). *Education and power.* New York, NY: Routledge & Kegan Paul.

An expansion of his earlier treatise, *Ideology and Curriculum,* Apple develops a relational, critical framework for understanding school knowledge as cultural production and how it is tied to the social reproduction of macro- structurations of power in our society. The core chapters of the book center on the commodification of culture manifest in the development of technical knowledge and the concept of "culture as lived." Situated within the growing body of neo-Marxist studies in the sociology of school knowledge, *Education and Power* provides a balanced analysis of the contradictions and contestations under theorized in social reproduction models of schooling. Yet, Apple's analysis remains largely theoretical and relies on theorizing and abstraction as modes of inquiry. A key question is: What happens when his theorizations are enriched with empirical investigations of contestation, resistance, and cultural production?

Apple, M. (1986). *Teachers and texts.* New York, NY: Routledge & Kegan Paul.

Deploying a parallelist, nonsynchronous framework that does not reduce race and gender dynamics to social class relations, Michael Apple studies in great detail the deskilling and "proletarianization" of teachers. Building from prior studies on workplace processes and the history of women's work, he argues that the intensification teachers experience today, along with the standardization and control of teaching, has come about through the re-inscription of managerial discourse as it intersects with patriarchal ideologies. The other subject analyzed in less detail is the political economy of texts and the curriculum. Apple discusses the need for engaging in a relational analysis of the curriculum that involves an analysis of the actors and interests producing curricula and the curriculum itself, yet notes the limitations in approaches that do not theorize the ways in which curricula are take up by teachers and students.

Apple, M. (1996). *Cultural politics and education.* New York, NY: Teachers College Press.

With the ascendance of the Right in the United States, Michael Apple brings a cogent analysis of the present economic situation and ideological shifts that enable the Right to win consent over subordinate groups. In this book, Apple "maps" the groups that have been instrumental in forming what he terms as the present condition of conservative modernization. His analysis of the politics of a national curriculum brings to light how neoconservative and neoliberal interests and ideologies have enabled standardized testing and a push for a "common" curriculum." But perhaps the heart of the book rests in the analysis of how conservative movements are forged. This is accomplished via a case study of a local, emerging campaign led by parents and later joined by other groups challenging textbook adoption. The case study teases out the nuances in building conservative alliances. Apple argues that, while these alliances are not forged overnight nor are they automatic, what the Right has managed to do at a local level is to change our common sense and language about education problems, society, and how to address these changes. The book ends with a somber note on the possibilities of social change and how progressive pedagogical, curricular, and community strategies need to be re-evaluated given the Right's control over education today.

Apple, M. (2006). *Educating the "right" way: Markets, standards, god, and inequality.* New York, NY: Routledge.

In this book Michael Apple brings together previously published arguments into a rather comprehensive framework for understanding conservative modernization and the impact the Right has had on public education and society more generally. Apple argues that public education today is steered by four major groups: neoliberals, neoconservatives, authoritarian populists, and the professional and new managerial middle class. While these groups do not form a cohesive ideological front and represent vying social class interests, their convergence has impacted education in profound ways, leading to such reforms as standardized testing and the push for a national curriculum. Apple's most significant contribution lies in his poignant analysis of how our common sense, language, and general ideology have shifted to the Right. His discussion of audit cultures, for instance, while mapping how the new professional middle class is invested in promoting state control of education via testing and curricula, presents the reader with a concrete analysis of how market logics have been accompanied by increasing surveillance and control of teaching and the curriculum.

Articles

Apple, M. (1976a). Curriculum as ideological selection. *Comparative Education Review, 20*(2), 209–215.

In this review essay, Apple highlights contributions from the sociology of school knowledge in Britain and points to a fundamental limitation: the dangers in social constructionist approaches that disconnect the production of school knowledge from political, economic, and social forces. Apple's review essay is timely, as it introduces developments in the sociology of school knowledge in Britain to a U.S. audience. His assessment of the field is balanced, noting the merits and limitations of such scholarship within the sociology of school knowledge.

Apple, M. (1977a). Power and school knowledge. *The Review of Education, 3*(1), 26–49.

In this review essay, Apple summarizes the major contributions from the sociology of school knowledge in Britain, highlighting the centrality of power and how knowledge is distributed within schools. Apple argues that undertaking this kind of analysis, which links school knowledge to social relations of power in society, requires a nonneutral, political posture on behalf of researchers. While he specifies the kinds of questions and frameworks *critical* researchers are to assume, little discussion is made about contributions from traditions outside the United States that were already grappling with the question of politics, power, and research knowledge.

Apple, M. (1978a). Ideology, reproduction, and education reform. *Comparative Educational Review, 22*(3), 367–387.

The author develops a methodological analysis of how the question of school knowledge is analyzed in relation to ideology and economic reproduction. In doing so, he notes and discusses the conceptual limitations of the achievement tradition, which posits school knowledge as technical and neutral, and socialization studies, which under theorize the social construction of knowledge within macro- social and economic relations. Apple highlights the strengths of the "critical tradition" emerging in Britain, grounded in neo-Marxist analysis, and locates the reproduction of high status knowledge within schools as tied to the reproduction of the social division of labor. While Apple's analysis of high status knowledge represents an early articulation of social and cultural reproduction theories, it also carries with it many of the limits within that tradition. Apple's assessment of the "socialization" tradition is bound to the field of sociology, yet lacks a critical assessment of socialization within the anthropology of education, which has made significant inroads in understanding cultural mediation and the production of knowledge.

Apple, M. W. (1980b). The other side of the hidden curriculum: Correspondence theories and the labor process. *Interchange, 11*(3), 5–22.

Apple's critical assessment of correspondence theories, in particular that articulated by Bowles & Gintis in *Schooling and Capitalist America*, leads to a critique of the mechanistic notion of socialization as transmission embedded in correspondence theories. Rather than socialize students to workplace norms in a totalizing fashion, Apple invokes studies of workplace settings that document how workers resist, transform, and challenge workplace norms. His essay ends with a word of caution not to romanticize resistance and oppositional behavior, as it may lead to the reproduction of the economic social order.

Apple, M. W. (1984a). The political economy of text publishing. *Educational Theory, 34*(4), 307–319.

In this essay Apple develops a framework for studying the political economy of text publishing. Building on the growing body of work in the sociology of school knowledge, Apple develops an argument for analyzing textbooks as primary carriers of ideology. His analysis points to the production of texts, noting how publishers are predominantly male, trained in managerial work, and work to publish texts that were the purpose of profit. The reproduction of "official knowledge" is circumscribed by a market logic; text selection, Apple argues, will also re-inscribe patriarchal values, as it is mostly men who select textbooks. Despite Apple's stipulation that textbook production and selection is not fully determined, what is missing is the analysis of how textbooks are "consumed" and taken up by teachers in students. This kind of political economic analysis (as conducted by Apple herein) can be one-sided, thus minimizing the role teachers and students play in interpreting and implementing "official knowledge" vis-à-vis textbooks.

Apple, M. W. (1990a). Ideology, equality and the new right. *Phenomenology + Pedagogy, 8,* 293–314.

In this initial mapping of the Right, Apple demonstrates the shift towards the Right and how this has circumscribed and framed education issues. Some of the major policy changes impacted by this shift to the Right include voucher plans that subject schools to the rules of the market, the movement to "raise standards" and "teacher performance," and the conservative critiques of the curriculum for not being Western-centered, etc. Major ideological shifts can be traced, Apple argues, to group interests vying for power and whose effects lead to cultural change. He argues that the rise of *authoritarian populism* since the 1980s is part of a conservative restoration and a backlash against progressive social movements by Blacks and the LGBTQ community during the 1960s. Apple's analysis is visionary and sets a roadmap that can be quite useful in understanding the rise of conservatism today.

Apple, M. W. (1992d). Channel One and the political economy of the text. *Educational Researchers, 21*(4), 4–19.

Apple builds from his earlier analysis of the political economy of text publishing in his analysis of Channel One, a broadcast network used by public schools that presents international news and commercial propaganda to students. The adoption of Channel One, argues Apple, must be seen within the context of a conservative restoration. Pressed with tight fiscal budgets, districts feel compelled to adopt such resources as Channel One. Apple then deconstructs the way Channel One news, as an extension of mainstream media, legitimates conservative ideologies and simplifies problems worldwide. Apple's analysis of the cultural, ideological, and social forces leading to the adoption of Channel One is vital in critically understanding the interests shaping "texts" such as Channel One. That said, his analysis of Channel One content, accomplished by referencing media culture more generally, is lacking an empirical dimension that would lead to a clearer understanding of what is shown and how teachers and students receive Channel One propaganda.

Apple, M. W. (1993a). The politics of official knowledge: Does a national curriculum make sense? *Teachers College Record, 95*(2), 222–241.

Herein, Apple author argues that a national curriculum, while seemingly contradicting the conservative move to decentralize government functions, would legitimate the national system of standardized testing and thus subject schools to market ideologies that scrutinize students and schools. Apple's analysis leads him to the conclusion that nationalizing the curriculum vis-à-vis standardized tests will enable the political and social control of school knowledge. His insights and predictions have been verified by the recent operative to standardize school knowledge across the United States.

Apple, M. W. (1998a). Education and the new hegemonic bloc: Doing policy the 'Right' way. *International Studies in Sociology of Education, 8*(2), 181–202.

Apple "maps" the key forces and social groups that, in his words, have formed a "conservative restoration." These are neo-liberals, neo-conservatives, authoritarian populists, and the professional new middle class. Outlining the ideological tendencies within each group, Apple charts the ways in which these ideologies intersect and contradict each other. He argues that this new conservative restoration project is shaping public education in fundamental ways: by winning over peoples' "common sense" conservatives are thus able to frame education problems and their purported solutions within the discourse of the Right.

Apple, M. W. (1999a). The absent presence of race in educational reform. *Race Ethnicity and Education, 2*(1), 9–16.

Perhaps the only publication where Apple explicitly articulates a nonsynchronous parallelist position that leads him to theorize race and race relations as fundamental to understanding power and culture in the United States, Apple argues that race has been rendered invisible in the discourse of privatization and markets. Building from the works of critical race scholars, Apple identifies ways in which race has been used to rationalize neoconservative education policy. Reconstructed as fear of the "other," race either functions to build consensus among Whites and conservative groups or it is absent as a category within neo-liberal discourse of privatization. Apple's subsequent discussion of whiteness and how it is contested and strategically used to build a conservative movement in Britain and the United States is limited by the theory of race and race relations that Apple develops. The issue is not so much that race is absent in conservative rhetoric (or that it reappears as a mobilizing signifier) but that neo-liberal and neo-conservative alliances might be understood within a theory of white supremacy.

Apple, M. W. (1999d). Freire, neo liberalism and education. *Discourse: Studies in the Cultural Politics of Education, 20*(1), 5–20.

Writing after Paulo Freire's death, Apple raises questions about the role of progressive, critical analysis and reflection given the current expansion of neo-liberal privatization in the United States. Apple argues that the challenges Paulo Freire set for progressive social change are inverted in a world where conservative groups have been instrumental in winning the active consent of people. His essay ends with a discussion of activist and progressive pedagogies that are challenging, however locally, neo-liberal policies and discourses, thus living out the legacy of Paulo Freire's work.

Apple, M. W. (2000a). Can critical pedagogies interrupt rightist policies? *Educational Theory, 50*(2), 229–254.

In this conceptual essay, Apple provides a critical re-framing of critical pedagogy as a field and its possibilities in forming a counter-movement to the growing conservative restoration project that has been underway since the 1980s. Charting the global expansion of neo-liberal privatization of education in England, New Zealand, and the United States, Apple documents the extent of this expansion and how all facets of education, from policy to testing and teaching, have been fundamentally altered. Apple's main criticisms of critical pedagogy as articulated by scholars is that its language is often too confusing and disconnected from on the ground education projects and it tends to under theorize the structural realities that condition and limit progressive social change.

Apple, M. W. (2001b). Markets, standards, teaching, and teacher education. *Journal of Teacher Education, 52*(3), 182–196.

Apple provides a critical analysis of teacher education within the context of conservative modernization, which is the convergence of neo-liberal privatization, neo-conservatism, and managerial ideologies. These forces have shaped education and have set the current landscape to standardize and control teaching and learning in England, New Zealand, and the United States. Apple cautions that teacher education is subject to these forces and points to the limits of education reforms today.

Apple, M. W. (2001f). Creating profits be creating failures: Standards, markets, and inequality in education. *International Journal of Inclusive Education, 5*(2/3), 103–118.

In this essay Apple reworks his previous articulations of conservative modernization and its impact on education reforms and the standardization and control of public education in England and the United States. He argues that current reforms are limited by the very discourse and strategy promulgated by the Right and points to research that documents the deleterious effects of market-based reforms. He concludes that in order to rupture the discourse of the Right, an emphasis needs to be placed on alternative progressive policies that require a different language and set of concepts.

Apple, M. W. (2005a). Education, markets, and audit cultures. *Critical Quarterly, 47*(1/2), 11–29.

Building from his analysis of the forces leading to a conservative modernization and its impact on public education, Apple situates the formation of audit cultures within higher education. He goes into a detailed historical and political analysis of the convergence of managerial ideologies and the interests of the new professional middle class that are the carriers of audit, "accountability" practices. While providing a nuanced and complex reading of the central role the new professional middle class has in the cultural diffusion of audit, accountability education systems, Apple's analysis emphasizes ideological mediations that could be strengthened by an economic analysis that situates cultural shifts within economic restructuring more broadly, thus the role of the new professional middle class may be overestimated in his analysis.

Apple, M. W. (2007a). Ideological success, educational failure? On the politics of No Child Left Behind. *Journal of Teacher Education, 58*(2), 108–116.

In this review essay, Apple problematizes the discourses that ultimately shape the arguments made by scholars who assume such policies as No Child Left

Behind (NCLB) in unproblematic ways. Apple argues that NCLB is the effect of conservative modernization and an expression of a growing audit culture that attempts to control public education. More devastating, the author argues, is the ideological shift that comes with policies such as NCLB. This shift is visible in the lexicon of "standards," "excellence," and "performance," all of which set parameters of how we now frame school reform.

Apple, M. W. (2009a). Some ideas on interrupting the Right: On doing critical educational work in conservative times. *Education, Citizenship, and Social Justice,* *4*(2), 87–101.

The first part of the essay is dedicated to an analysis of the social forces converging in what Apple terms conservative modernization, a hegemonic bloc responsible for conservative discourse and the neo-liberal impetus to subject public education to market logics. The second part outlines possible strategies and tactics on how to interrupt and challenge the Right. These include counter-media and research by activist organizations, democratic funding strategies in Brazil, etc. The most important, Apple argues, is providing real, concrete alternatives that serve as models for progressive social change.

Apple, M. W. (2009b). Can critical education interrupt the Right? *Discourse: Studies in the Cultural Politics of Education, 30*(3), 239–251.

Apple expands on his analysis in *Educating the "Right" Way* and develops a set of strategies for challenging the Right's control of education reform, discourse, and policies. His essay is a re-articulation of a previously published piece titled, "Some Ideas on Interrupting the Right: On Doing Critical Educational Work In Conservative Times."

Apple, M. W. (2011a). Global crises, social justice, and teacher education. *Journal of Teacher Education, 62*(2), 222–234.

This exploratory essay provides a working definition of globalization, which the author argues is vital to a critical understanding of teacher education locally and nationally. Globalization is theorized as an intra- and trans- national phenomenon not reducible to class relations but to intersectional processes. Apple argues that a critical understanding of globalization can be attained by thinking relationally, repositioning one's work as a scholar-activist. The essay ends with a set of working "tasks" scholar-activists can fulfill in developing a progressive social movement that challenges globalization. This essay provides a fresh angle in Apple's work, signaling an orientation towards praxis beyond critical social analysis.

Apple, M. W. (2011c). Democratic education in neoliberal and neoconservative times. *International Studies in Sociology of Education, 21*(1), 21–31.

The author provides a critique of critical pedagogy scholarship and scholars who are often disconnected from actual schools and the practice of democratic, progressive alternatives to the dominance of neoliberal and neoconservative education. The author explores the possibilities of transformation in education and argues that scholars have much to learn from social movements and projects in the global South (for example, in places like Brazil). Apple highlights the lessons learned from the Citizen School in Porto Allegre, Brazil, which involved grassroots participation and governance as well as the implementation of a curriculum grounded in the lives of students and their representative communities.

Book Chapters

Apple, M. W. (1980). Curricular form and the logic of technical control: building the possessive individual. In L. Barton, R. Meighan, and S. Walker (Eds.), *Schooling, ideology, and the curriculum* (11–28). Sussex, UK: The Falmer Press.

Applying a political-economic analysis of the curriculum, Apple analyzes how managerial discourse borrowed from the industrial sector has transformed how the curriculum is organized. Using the example of a prepackaged curriculum targeting elementary students, he demonstrates such processes as the de-skilling of teachers and the construction of the teacher as manager of content knowledge. Although he concludes with a discussion of teacher resistance, the study leaves many unanswered questions regarding the tension between socialization and re-appropriation by teachers and students of technocratic and controlling models of curriculum design.

Apple, M. W. (1993). Constructing the "other": Rightist reconstructions of common sense. In C. McCarthy and W. Crichlow (Eds.), *Race, identity, and representation in education* (24–39). New York, NY: Routledge.

In this chapter the author delineates a situated theory of ideology as a process that people construct in their everyday actions, yet is tied to the reproduction of macro- relations of power. Using this theory of ideology, he unpacks the ways in which conservative groups have mustered support by re-framing progressive gains made by minority groups and building alliances in opposition to these racialized and gendered "others." Thus, progressive policies that expand rights and resources to people of color, gays, and women, are seen as attacks on nonminority groups and counter to the presumed logic of meritocracy. The chapter ends with an assessment of the Right's expansion, noting internal contradictions and external progressive forces that may interrupt its expansion.

Apple, M. W. (2000). Standards, markets, and curriculum. In B. M. Franklin (Ed.), *Curriculum and consequence: Herbert M. Kliebard and the promise of schooling* (55–74). New York, NY: Teachers College Press.

In this chapter Apple documents how neoliberal ideologies and policies, such as free markets and control of education, although seemingly contradictory, are part of a conservative restoration project that has been underway since the 1980s. These ideologies converge and have lead to national standards and testing. He reviews research that debunks the "successes" in market driven reforms in Britain. The present wave of reforms, Apples argues, are an expression not of the voices of broad sectors of the society but a conservative coalition steering education policy in the United States.

Apple, M. W. (2004). Between good sense and bad sense: Race, class, and learning from *Learning to Labor*. In N. Dolby & G. Dimitriadis (Eds.), *Learning to labor in new times* (52–70). New York, NY: Routledge- Falmer.

This chapter presents a more complex elaboration of Apple's theory of conservative modernization. Herein, Apple outlines the complex process by which vying interests that may historically be in opposition to each other coalesce through a process of consent. In the case of policies such as vouchers, which are imbued with neo-liberal rhetoric and neo-conservative interests, how disparate racial groups, i.e., Blacks and Whites, come together is analyzed. This case highlights the problematic in seeing "conservative" movements as homogeneous.

Apple, M. W. (2007). Schooling, markets, race, and an audit culture. In D. Carlson & C. P. Gaus (Eds.), *Keeping the promise: essays on leadership, democracy, and education* (27–44). New York, NY: Peter Lang.

In this essay the author unpacks one of the central components to the privatization of public education, namely the constitution of an audit culture. Apple argues that, contrary to what neo-liberal privatization promotes, such as the decentralization of public services and institutions, the pressure to subject education to the rules of the market by instituting standards and tests has lead to the centralization and control of public education. Moreover, he asserts that little work has been done with respect to how the privatization of public education has impacted people of color and how their consent is won by dominant, conservative groups.

Apple, M. W. (2010). Global Crises, social justice, and education. In M. W. Apple (Ed.), *Global Crises, Social Justice, and Education* (1–24). New York, NY: Routledge.

This introductory chapter lays the groundwork for understanding education processes and reforms within an increasingly globalized world. The author argues that thinking relationally leads to seeing the interconnectedness of developments in the industrialized world as dependent on crises in third world regions. In the latter half of the chapter Apple outlines principles and "tasks" for scholar-activists, which includes, for example, engaging in critical analysis, transforming knowledge and skills so that they are in the service of progressive social change, reinventing research, etc. While the call to action is grounded in a critical, yet realistic, understanding of resistance movement throughout the world, Apple's recommendations for action are limited in that they speak of tactics without the articulation of a political ideology that is to bring the multiple forms of resistance into a social movement.

CHAPTER 8

JEAN ANYON

Social Theory and Education

**Jessica Nina Lester, Todd Cherner,
and Rachael Gabriel**

INTRODUCTION

Herein, we introduce the life and scholarship of Jean Anyon, a well-known voice in social theory. She is currently a professor of Educational and Social Policy in the Doctoral Program in Urban Education at City University of New York. Across her work, Anyon critiques the ways in which public policies shape core educational practices, urban development and structures, and economic social structures. Much of her work occurs at the intersection of race, class, and education.

We begin with a brief biography, and then transition to highlight some of the major themes across Anyon's work. We conclude by presenting an annotated bibliography that highlights some of her most seminal work.

Educating About Social Issues in the 20th and 21st Centuries, pages 153–167
Copyright © 2014 by Information Age Publishing
153

A SHORT BIOGRAPHY

Jean Anyon (2005) was born in the 1940s to parents who she described as being "active in the radical social movements of the 1930s" (p. 1). Her parents were labor organizers throughout her childhood. During the mid-1950s, Anyon's father, a tenured faculty member at a university,[1] was charged with being a member of the Communist Party[2] by Senator Joseph McCarthy. As a result of this charge, his passport was revoked. Her parent's commitment to social movements and willingness to stand against the norm shaped who she was and where she was willing to spend her time.

Anyon (2005) stated that early on in her life she "imbibed the family passion for social justice" (p. 1). During high school and college, she was actively involved in the Congress of Racial Equality, resulting in her picketing and marching for racial equality. She also actively raised money for the movement in Mississippi in 1964, eventually opening a store in New York City where she sold leather goods and cotton made by African American women in South Carolina. The money earned in this venture was sent to the South to support the Civil Rights Movement.

Prior to teaching, she received her bachelor's degree from the University of Pennsylvania in 1963, where she was an All-University Scholar.[3] She received her Master's degree in education in 1965, also from the University of Pennsylvania.

In the 1960s and early part of the 1970s, Anyon taught elementary grades within inner-city schools in Washington D. C. and Brooklyn, New York. She was also an active protestor against the Vietnam War.

Following seven years of teaching, Anyon left the elementary classroom to pursue her doctorate degree in education and psycholinguistics at New York University. Following the completion of her degree in 1976, Anyon took an academic position at Rutgers University and taught there from 1976 through 2000.

During her time at Rutgers, Anyon published several seminal books and articles, including *Ghetto Schooling: A Political Economy of Urban Educational Reform*. This text was central to much of Anyon's work, highlighting how the failure of Newark public schools was not based on the increasing numbers of Black Southern families, as some would have it, but rather the structural and economic histories that sustained the inequities faced by the local populace.

In 2000 Anyon eventually began working at City University of New York, where she is Professor of Urban Education.

COMMENTARY ON ANYON'S WORKS

In this section, we discuss the major themes across Anyon's work. First, though, we begin by examining the ways in which Anyon speaks to how public policy impacts education.

The Impact of Public Policy on Education

The concept that public policy and education are intimately intertwined is a central component in Anyon's work. From her point of view, putting effort towards education reform without creating a social context that includes community-building measures does not constitute meaningful reform. Rather, education and public policies must complement and build off one another if meaningful reform is to happen. In her two most influential texts—*Radical Possibilities* and *Ghetto Schooling*—Anyon did not focus solely on the staggeringly poor conditions of inner-city schools and what educational reforms need to be implemented in order to improve them, but also provided large-scale, quantifiable data from numerous sources—including U.S. census data, reports authored by state and city investigators, independent reports from auditors, and scholarly research among others. She illustrated how enormous poverty's influence is and how public policy cannot be divorced from education policy. One example Anyon used to draw on how these two sets of policies cannot be disconnected relates directly to student motivation. For example, Anyon argued that students who attend urban schools in low-income neighborhoods where employment opportunities are very limited and low paying do not have the same motivation for education as students who attend affluent, suburban schools where employment opportunities are abundant and pay considerably higher salaries.

In various articles and books Anyon has authored, she describes how the relocation of jobs from cities to suburban communities impacted students who attended inner-city schools. From a historical perspective, Anyon pointed out how cities during the 19th century on into the early 20th century used to be home to factories, which provided large quantities of jobs that paid middle-class salaries. Moreover, she notes, to be qualified to work in these factories a person did not have to attain a high level of schooling. In fact, Anyon points out that some school-aged children actually preferred working in factories over attending schools because the factories did not physically abuse them. However, as Southern Blacks began migrating north starting in the late 1800s, they were no longer needed to tend the land because of the invention of mechanized farming equipment. Large numbers of White families concurrently left cities and moved to newly formed suburban communities. As they relocated, the Whites took their political, economic, and educational advantages with them.

One of the debilitating results of this White migration was that factories and companies also left the cities and were relocated to suburban hubs, which meant that people living in inner-cities did not have access to such jobs because of geographical reasons. Additionally, even if an inner-city person was able to land a job, he or she was not likely able to afford the daily transportation costs. Moreover, following World War II, the jobs that were left in the city became increasingly polarized. For instance, while increasing numbers of high-level, professional jobs required an advanced education and low-level, labor-based jobs did not require a formal education existed in the cities, manufacturing jobs that middle class citizens once sought out, became increasingly scarce. As the jobs left cities, it threw a metaphorical economic rock that created a ripple effect, which impacted politics and education.

As Whites left the cities and jobs were relocated to the suburbs, the urban populations remaining in the cities had limited prospects for employment. In turn, this joblessness resulted in an epidemic of poverty in inner-city communities. Even though the government attempted to assist these communities in various ways (e.g., via the Food Stamp Act of 1964 and the Elementary and Secondary Education Act's Title I Program of 1965), the programs only allowed low-income families to continue to exist; they did not create a path for families to lift themselves out of poverty, let alone provide them with a political voice. Additionally, decades of political corruption in the schools, unfunded educational initiatives, inappropriate curriculum, and the gaming of tax codes resulted in inner-city children who attended urban schools being poorly educated and having to suffer verbal and physical abuse in school, attend schools in desperate need of renovations, and receive instruction from unqualified teachers. Students in suburban schools experienced inverse advantages, including: learning appropriate curricula from qualified and supportive teachers, newly constructed schools, and a host of other benefits from favorable tax policies that helped to fund their schools. When stepping back to take a holistic view of the context Anyon has, described, it begins to become clear why public policy cannot be divorced from educational policy.

When public policy is separated from education policy, it creates a situation that supports the status quo and does not consider innovative policies to improve the living situations for all people. From the perspective of an inner-city student who sees her parents and neighbors living on government assistance because there is a lack of jobs, and who is being consistently put down by her teachers who are supposed to support her, and sees her life chances as limited because of the poverty-stricken culture in which she exists, what and where does hope exist? What is her motivation to get up each morning in order to attain an education? Arguing alongside Anyon, it is clear that this child's hope may not exist—or if it does, such hope may be both rare and fragile. She likely has few, if any, role models of individuals who were able to lift themselves out of poverty-stricken neighborhoods. However, as Anyon has pointed out using the Moving to Opportunity and New Hope for Families and Children programs as examples, if we improve the neighborhoods where families live and provide both more and better job opportunities for parents, children perform better academically, their positive behaviors increase significantly, and they are better prepared for the work force. As such, to isolte school reforms from public policy is equivalent to putting new tires on a car that needs a new motor and transmission. To implement school reforms, then, addresses only part of the challenge. We need comprehensive policy packages to simultaneously address the myriad of challenges facing poverty-stricken communities of which school reform is only one. Simply but profoundly, public policy cannot be isolated from education policy.

Neo-Marxism

Anyon's interest in the impact of public policies on education and the possibility of reform is grounded in a Marxist approach to social theory, one which privileges issues of class in seeking to understand social issues. In her American Educational Research Association lifetime achievement award acceptance speech, Anyon explained that her use of Marx's social theory flowed from three of Marx's basic concepts:

1. Capitalism is a primary source of systemic social, economic and educational inequality;
2. Social class is an explanatory social and educational heuristic; and
3. An analysis of the culture that accompanies the capitalist system can be a source of neo-Marxist practice—in this regard vis-à-vis education, critical classroom pedagogy.

These three basic concepts underlie Anyon's ethnographic research, which investigates the impact of social class as an explanatory heuristic within as well as outside of schools. It further serves as an example of Neo-Marxist praxis, that is, actions that actualize Marx's social theory by working to deconstruct and make visible the invisible hegemony that creates and sustains inequality. Her largest contribution on this front, as described above, is an empirical basis for the oft-quoted need to attend to educational equity within a larger social setting, as well as clear documentation of the differences between the schooling that is possible in different social settings.

The ethnographic study in Newark Public Schools that provided the inspiration for two of her books was an example of how Anyon developed an empirical foundation for the importance of social factors in studies of educational equity and reform. As described above, data from these comparative studies made the differences in schools for students of varying classes explicit. They also drew concrete connections between class and opportunity, curriculum, access to learning and status. Anyon is among a handful of scholars (e.g., Bowles & Gintis, 1976; Apple, 1979) who not only described, but demonstrated the presence and impact of social struggles inside and outside education.

CRITIQUES OF ANYON'S APPROACH

One critique of Anyon's use of Marxist social theory is that her application of it is more Weberian (grounded in the word of the theorist Max Weber) than Marxist. According to Malott (2011), this distinction has to do with her focus on social class preventing upward mobility without directly outlining a theory against class or capitalism. In a review of her recent book, *Marx and Education*, Malott (2011) notes the following: "Focusing on categories of social class is to examine the consequences of capitalism without ever delving into the root causes of capitalism and the labor/capital relationship" (p. 4). Her focus on seeking opportunity within a capitalist system rather than wanting its dismantlement through a "revolutionary pedagogy against capitalism" (Malott, 2011) arguably separates her work from Marx. Her "Neo-Marxism," then, is aimed at reform, rather than revolution, and is therefore criticized by leftist Marxists as a weakened, liberal interpretation of Marx's work. On the other hand, this approach could be preferred, at least by some, for its pragmatism.

Malott (2011) has also argued that Anyon's idea of opportunity evokes an uncritical use of the term "the American Dream," such that questions of access, power and social mobility are addressed without considering the possibility that not all people define the "American Dream" or "success in terms of rugged individualism or upward class mobility."

Still, even those who critique her application of Marx to education acknowledge that her earlier work was eye opening when it came to the ways in which class distinctions are reproduced by the structures of schooling and the stark differences in public education between the classes.

This research, though, is not without strident critics. For example, Ramsay (1985) engaged in a series of responses and rejoinders to Anyon's research as reported in the journal of *Curriculum Inquiry*. His critiques were more methodological than theoretical, replete with questions about the selection and characterization of sites for research. Ramsay emphasized the need to make methodological and interpretive decisions transparent in order to demonstrate that theory guided the work, but did not determine the findings. The general thrust of Ramsay's suspicion of Anyon's work as reported hinges on the neatly packaged ways in which her data elaborated her theory of social reproduction. Rather than acknowledging variation within and across schools, or within and across teachers in schools, Anyon, Ramsay said, suggested that class structures and general hegemony dictated what teachers in given schools said and did in their classrooms without accounting for individual agency or resistance. Moreover, he pointed out that Anyon's conclusions were framed as identified causalities rather than suggested relationships between class, education and opportunity.

Despite such criticisms and questions, the contributions of Anyon's empirical and theoretical work are undeniable. Excerpts of entire versions of her chapters and articles have been reprinted repeatedly. She has been invited to deliver keynote addresses at more than 40 colleges and universities, and was the recipient of the American Educational Research Association's Lifetime Achievement award from Division G: Social Contexts of Education.

NOTES

1. We could not locate the name of the university.
2 We could not verify whether he was a member or not.
3 The University of Pennsylvania reports that "The University Scholars program provides an unusual academic environment for intellectually dynamic students who have already demonstrated their commitment and dedication to research. Through mentoring, research funding and scholarly events the program encourages and supports students to make the most of their undergraduate years, not only with in-depth research, but also by making an early start in graduate and professional courses, ranging widely or in some cases focusing narrowly on their curricular choices.

"The University Scholars meet weekly for lunches at which they present and discuss their research. Because University Scholars attend all four undergraduate schools, the presentations come from a range of disciplines, and they illustrate a variety of research techniques. University Scholars learn how to approach and conduct effective research projects by participating in the greater community of researchers."

REFERENCES

Apple, M. W. (1979). *Ideology and curriculum.* London, UK: Routledge.

Bowles, S., & Gintis, S. (1976) *Schooling in capitalist America: Education reform and the contradictions of economic life.* New York, NY: Basic Books Inc.

Anyon, J. (2005). *Radical possibilities: Public policy, urban education, and a new social movement.* New York: Taylor & Francis.

Ellsworth, E. (1989). Why doesn't this feel empowering? Working through the repressive mythos of critical pedagogy. *Harvard Educational Review, 59*(3), 297–324.

Malott, C. S. (2011). Pseudo-Marxism and the reformist retreat from revolution: A critical essay review of Marx and education by Jean Anyon (2011). *Journal for Critical Education Policy, 9*(1), 1–6.

Ramsay, P. (1985). Social class and school knowledge: A rejoinder to Jean Anyon. *Curriculum Inquiry, 15*(2), 215–222.

ANNOTATED BIBLIOGRAPHY

The following annotated bibliography includes some of Jean Anyon's most seminal works. In developing it, we aimed to include articles and books that capture particular segments of Anyon's life's work, relate to the themes described above, and were most commonly cited. Admittedly, our description is partial and positional.

Anyon, J. (1978). Elementary social studies books and legitimizing knowledge. *Theory and Research in Social Education, 7*(3), 40–55.

> Where some individuals may see schools as unbiased, objective elements of American society, Anyon argued that schools have a large influence over how individuals perceive and understand their government and economy. Anyon argued that uncritical individuals blindly accept how young students are socialized and knowledge is legitimized in elementary schools. To build her argument, Anyon focused on the uncontested content found in social studies textbooks commonly used in elementary schools throughout the United States. In her analysis, Anyon specifically investigated how the government and the economy were depicted. In doing so, she found that the textbooks largely supported keeping the empowered individuals in a position of influence and downplayed actions that disenfranchised people could take to increase their societal position. For example, Anyon identified that the textbooks supported the idea that individuals could dissent from their leaders by voting them out of office, voice their disagreement by writing letters, or through peaceful demonstration. While all such actions are certainly legitimate, the textbooks omitted historical examples of people taking stronger actions such as burning draft cards, participating in sit-ins, or taking other actions that might be considered as violent or threatening. These ideas are also reflected in textbooks supporting individuals who have made use of generally acceptable behaviors to change society versus omitting those who made use of what might be deemed more "questionable" methods (e.g., textbooks including the story of Dr. Martin Luther King but avoiding that of Malcolm X). In these ways, Anyon argued that social studies textbooks used in elementary schools actually teach (actually, indoctrinate) students to acquiesce to making use of already established social structures versus those that are not, thereby teaching children to accept their place in society.

Anyon, J. (1980). Social class and the hidden curriculum. *Journal of Education, 162*(1), 67–92.

> Using ethnographic data, Anyon analyzed the relationship between the hidden curriculum and socioeconomic status (SES) in five New Jersey elementary schools. To do so, Anyon first classified each school based on its students' SES and then used empirical examples to explain how each school conceptualized "work." Anyon found that as students' SES increases, so does the expectation for students' learning. For example, students who attended either of the "working class schools" (schools that served students from the poorest

households with annual incomes of $12,000 or less) were instructed to follow procedures to complete a task. Next, students who attended the "middle-class school" (a school that served students from a mix of social classes with the majority of household incomes ranging from $13,000–$25,000 annually) were taught to make simple decisions to find a correct answer. At the "affluent professional school" (a school that served students from upper-middle class families with average household incomes ranging from $40,000–$80,000 annually), students were viewed as being capable of expressing themselves clearly and thinking creatively and independently. Finally, students who attended the "executive elite school" (a school that served students from upper class families with average incomes over $100,000 annually) were taught to analyze data in order to make decisions. In her conclusion, Anyon identified the hidden curriculum, as schools have differing expectations for students based on SES contexts, which works to perpetuate a cycle that privileges students from the wealthiest families while limiting opportunities for students from the poorest households.

Anyon, J. (1981). Social class and school knowledge. *Curriculum Inquiry*, 11(1), 3–42.

To develop a critical awareness of how different social classes view knowledge, Anyon evaluated how students and teachers from five New Jersey elementary schools conceptualized knowledge. In her article, Anyon first introduced and described each school based largely on its socioeconomic status (SES) and physical and historical contexts. Next, Anyon reported specific comments made by teachers and students about knowledge, which she coupled with empirical evidence she observed. Overall, Anyon found that students' SES does impact teachers' and students' view of knowledge, and she concluded by connecting how embodying certain perspectives of knowledge work as "reproducive" or "nonreproducive" agents. Reproducive knowledge works to continue already established societal ideologies, economic structures, and policies that privilege certain groups of people, while the nonreproducive aims to transform society. Therefore, students at the "working-class" and "middle-class" schools (schools that served students from households with incomes ranging from under $12,000–$25,000 annually) were largely taught knowledge that Anyon considered reproducive and that did not equip students with the ability to critically analyze and improve the contexts in which they exist. Students who attended the "affluent professional school" (a school that served students from households with annual incomes ranging from $40,000–$80,000) were taught that knowledge resided in experience, and this guiding principle paved the way for contradictions between their education and society to exist, which may allow for them to engage in nonreproducive actions. At the "executive elite school" (a school that served students from households with annual incomes over $100,000), students were taught logic and reasoning skills, and Anyon pointed out that although these skills would equip students to engage in nonreproducive actions, their already privileged social status might deter them from doing so. Essentially, Anyon used this study to illustrate how deeply class and education are intertwined and result in societal inequalities.

Anyon, J., (1982). Adequate social science, curriculum investigation, and theory. *Theory Into Practice, 21*(1), 34–38.

In this article, Anyon compared two books of curriculum investigations published in 1979 (Frances Fitzgerald's *America Revised*, and Anyon's own *Ideology and US History Textbooks*) in order to highlight elements of "more adequate curriculum theorizing." Anyon used each book as artifacts of different approaches to social science inquiry/critiques. She identified two theoretical flaws: naive empiricism (in which researchers collect and process data with the assumption that data is objective and theory-free); and grand theory (the withdrawal to systematic work on concepts without empirical data). These mark two ends of a spectrum of trends in social science research that are each incomplete. She argued instead for work that is "empirically grounded, theoretically explanatory and socially critical" (p. 35). This means, at a minimum, that one collects data to build a case, situates social data in some theory of society, and that claims go beyond dominant ideology/ies to "challenge social legitimations and fundamental structures" (p. 36).

Regarding studies of curriculum specifically, Anyon argued that curriculum theory should include a unified field theory, which specifies the "interconnections between school knowledge, school process, contemporary society and historical change" (p. 37) in ways that explicate and seek to eliminate what she describes as "structurally induced exploitation and pain" (p. 37). Within this call for a unified field theory is the resonance of her primary assumption, that schools (re)produce structures of oppression, in and through curriculum (broadly defined), thus curriculum is a potential site of social change.

Anyon, J. (1983). Intersections of gender and class: accommodation and resistance by working-class and affluent females to contradictory sex role ideologies. In S. Walker and L. Barton (Eds.), *Gender, class, & education* (p. 1–18), Sussex, UK: The Falmer Press.

Here, Anyon argued that for women to gain equality, they must take collective action; however, in doing so, it would require women to engage in traditionally unfeminine behavior. To make her argument, Anyon first recognized that socialized gender roles do exist, and women do subscribe actively to them. Furthermore, she noted, contradictions between society's view of self-esteem and expected behaviors for women also exist. For example, a girl from an affluent family may be expected to complete college and graduate school and begin a career; yet, that same family may also expect her to quit her career to have children and raise a family when the time comes. In this example, if the girl acquiesced to her family's expectation, she engaged in "accommodation and resistance" behavior, which Anyon traced back to the paternalistic relationship between slaves and slaveholders. When engaging this behavior, the person with less power may openly accommodate certain authorial expectations while internally resisting others. Two examples of this behavior are (1) a slave intentionally misunderstanding her slaveholder's instructions in order to slow production and, therefore, resist her slaveholder, and (2) a professional female being outwardly submissive to her male boss while internally resisting him by plotting her own dreams for an improved life in the future. While Anyon recognized these acts as personal resistance, she stressed that collective action is needed to make structural changes to society; thus arguing that personal resistance is not enough. Be that as it may, according to Anyon, collective action may be unlikely because it is an unfeminine behavior.

Anyon, J. (1994). The retreat of Marxism and socialist feminism: Postmodern and post structural theories in education. *Curriculum Inquiry*, 24(2), 115–133.

In her critique of postmodernism and post structuralism, Anyon identified contradictions made by theorists working in these fields before suggesting ideas to minimize them. To begin, Anyon discussed the relationship that exists between theory and practice. Where the mainstream perspective separates theory from practice—theory being based in science or philosophy and practice as a behavior—postmodernists and poststructuralists see the two as connected, with one informing the other. However, the problem of contradiction arises when postmodernists and poststructuralists allow their particular theory's tenets to blind them. One powerful example Anyon used was her critique of Henry Giroux's work. Whereas Giroux's works have argued passionately for the inclusion of Others' voices, no voices of minorities were actually included in his work (Ellsworth, 1989). Anyon commented for a criticalist to give up pages in an article to allow an Other to have a direct voice (not one that has been washed in the author's language, but a true, authentic voice), it would mean that the criticalist had given up authority, which Giroux neglected to do and thus constitutes a serious contradiction in Critical Theory. To reduce such contradictions, Anyon suggested that future theories make connections between theories and individuals' lived experiences, create "middle-range" theories that connect the micro to the macro, and that theories be grounded in direct actions so they may be enacted.

Anyon, J. (1994). Teacher development and reform in an inner city school. *Teachers College Record, 96*(1), 14–31.

This article describes a teacher development project used as a case study of the impact of social marginalization and poverty on educational outcomes. Anyon suggested that education reform cannot make good inner city schools until/unless more fundamental social changes take place.

Anyon, J. (1995) Inner city school reform: Toward useful theory. *Urban Education, 30*(1), 56–70.

Anyon argued that the traditional factors to which researchers attribute failures of school reform efforts always assume that these factors can be changed. Characteristics of districts, schools, personnel, and reform plans and policies are assumed to be malleable and thus are implicated in attributions of failure or success. Instead, she suggested that schools are constructed within an already unequal system that perpetuates social inequality. Thus, neither schools nor reforms of school systems themselves can ever be expected to change the larger social constraints within which children, teachers and administrators already operate.

Anyon, J. (1995). Race, social class, and educational reform in an inner city school. *Teacher College Record, 97*(1), 70–95.

Set in Newark, New Jersey, this 1989 case study explored Marcy elementary school's experiences with school reform. To create a context for why school reform was needed, Anyon first outlined the school's history to highlight its record of low student achievement. Anyon pointed to the migration of poor, under-educated Blacks to Newark from 1917 through the 1960s, which resulted in the middle class leaving the area, as a catalyst for the low levels of student achievement. In fact, Anyon reported that Newark was identified by the state in 1940 as a place with "low [student] achievement and dilapidated schools" (p. 70). Be that as it may, it was not until 1989 when the Newark School District initiated a school reform plan.

In her work, Anyon identified three reasons why the reforms faltered. First, Anyon pointed to the sociocultural differences between education reform stakeholders—parents, school personnel, and retired business people—as for why collaboration that may have resulted in school reform did not happen. Second, cultural differences between students and their teachers, learning materials, and language impeding student learning were noted. Third, the treatment of students by teachers, which at times was verbally and physically abusive, likely contributed to students not wanting to comply with their teachers. Moreover, as a backdrop to these three instances was low standardized test scores, which Anyon predicted would not increase in this context. Moreover, Anyon concluded by stating that the only remedy to eradicate low student achievement in inner city schools is to eliminate poverty and racial inequalities.

Anyon, J. (1997). *Ghetto schooling: A political economy of urban educational reform.* New York, NY: Teachers College Press.

In this, her seminal, text, Anyon used the Newark Public School System and Marcy Elementary School to exemplify how historical, political, and economic trends have resulted in inequitable opportunities for low-income individuals living in cities, as compared to their more affluent, suburban peers. Moreover, this thesis is central not only to this book, but also to many of her other works. To create her comparison, Anyon analyzed how the enormous influx of immigrants and migrants who moved to Newark from the early 1800s through 1940 affected the city. Major components of Anyon's analysis included where different groups of people lived in Newark—whether they resided in suburbs, downtown areas, or ghettoized neighborhoods; who held political power, which was largely held first by rural elites and then suburbanites; how Newark's economy transitioned from manufacturing jobs in the 1800s to more professional "white collar" jobs following World War II; and the impact of these moving variables on Newark's public school system in general and Marcy Elementary School specifically. Overall, Anyon found that almost 100 years of political corruption, relocation of manufacturing jobs, White Flight, unequal educational funding, and lack of investment in urban centers has resulted in low-income minorities not having a realistic opportunity to earn a high school diploma, graduate from college, and begin a professional career. As such, Anyon concluded her book by offering ideas aimed at increasing taxes for businesses to support social programs to eliminate poverty, which in turn will motivate low-income students by offering opportunities to them that their parents never had.

Anyon, J. (2005). *Radical possibilities: Public policy, urban education, and a new social movement.* New York, NY: Taylor & Francis.

In this book, Anyon built upon her work in *Ghetto schooling: A political economy of urban educational reform*. She aimed to address injustices within schools by examining the ways in which macroeconomic policies shape how schooling and living conditions are generated and sustained. Anyon showed how policies that determine minimum wage, affordable housing, and transportation within particular cities result in institutionalized practices and everyday conditions within schools that make equitable practice challenging within urban schools. She argued that many of the policies make it impossible for urban education reform to push beyond that which becomes institutionally legalized. She concluded by calling for a social movement that speaks back to the social and political policies that make urban education reform difficult. In doing so, she plainly laid out four benefits to engaging students in civic activism: 1. Activities generally foster positive personal development and a deeper involvement in academics, which generally improves academic achievement; 2. Activities embed a student in positive social activism, which often continues after they've concluded their schooling; 3. Students are asked to perform concrete lessons which can impact them long after their school career is completed; and 4. Because students and teachers are working together toward a common goal it can increase the trust between the two groups, which can have a positive affect on a student's academic success.

Anyon, J. (2005). What "counts" as educational policy? Notes towards a new paradigm. *Harvard Educational Review, 75*(1), 65–88.

In this article, Anyon took a critical perspective to analyze the relationship between economics and education. To do so, Anyon first provided a historical context of American educational policies to highlight how they focus on changing schools, not on ending poverty. This distinction is paramount, she argued, because it is the culture of poverty that has resulted in substandard educational attainment by low-income students. For example, Anyon questioned why poor, inner-city students would be motivated to earn the necessary education for higher paying jobs when the latter have been moved to suburban communities, which make the jobs geographically inaccessible for the impoverished who frequently do not even have the financial wherewithal to cover the costs for local transportation on a daily basis. As such, policies to improve the education of inner-city students do not address larger issues, such as relocating higher paying jobs from the suburbs back to urban communities. Moreover, Anyon reported statistics about the staggering number of families and school children who live in poverty and then explained how poverty affects them. For instance, people living in poverty have less access to community and educational resources, are at an increased risk for stress and other health problems, and poverty-stricken children engage in higher levels of delinquent behavior. Anyon argued that if we change our policies to reduce poverty, it would most likely increase student educational achievement, with the Moving to Opportunity and New Hope for Families and Children programs demonstrating this phenomenon. Ultimately, Anyon concluded that if we are to improve inner-city schools, we first need to implement policies that will alleviate poverty.

Anyon, J. (Ed.) (2009). *Theory and educational research: Toward critical social explanation.* New York, NY: Routledge.

In her introductory chapter, Anyon argues that theory must not be separated from the research process, but educational researchers—with the exception of a few—have tended largely to avoid theory in their work. Moreover, she argued that, the political climate following the passage of the No Child Left Behind Act of 2001 emphasized quantitative studies, which further removed theory from educational research. In response, Anyon claimed that "no fact is theory-free" and using theory enriches work.

Anyon went on to discuss her experience of using Marxism as a guide when she authored *Ghetto Schooling*, noting that as a result she was only able to analyze her data on a macroeconomic level. Anyon reflected that if she were able to use theory to connect her macro analysis to the micro experiences she observed when analyzing her data, it would have resulted in stronger, more substantiated work. In this way, she argued that, theory is something that must be "kneaded" into all parts of the research process. Following her introduction are six chapters—each authored by one of Anyon's doctorate students—that exemplify the theoretical work Anyon described in her opening. The book closes with an epilogue by Michelle Fine in which she reflects on how theory was used by the different authors and praises them for being part of the next generation of critical scholars.

Anyon, J. (2011). *Marx & education.* New York, NY: Routledge.

In this book, Anyon described Marx's social theory and its application to three periods of education in the United States, noting the differences in organization and impact of the economic and school policy climates of the 1970s and 1980s versus the 1990s and early 2000s. The book has, as its introduction, the text of Anyon's acceptance speech for the American Educational Research Association's lifetime achievement award. It begins with a description of what Anyon believed that Marx himself had to say about social theory and how it relates to educational endeavors. She distinguished this from the many forms of Marxism that have existed in literature on education, beginning with the period when Marx himself was writing. Her understanding of Marx marks a sort of middle ground between the structuralism or existentialism that can sometimes be attributed to his theories. For example, she argued that Marx would say people have some agency and self-determination, but this agency is within a preexisting system, a system that is, in part, constructed and sustained by systems of education. Educational systems are constructed by and benefit those with the greatest economic capital. Thus, notions of educational meritocracy, or education as a democratic, social equalizer, are called into question. Instead, Anyon argued that schools are not neutral, but always ideological, tightly bound to the political economy, and likely serve the goals and processes of mainstream ideas.

CHAPTER 9

HENRY GIROUX

The "Crisis" of 21st Century Education

Gail Russell-Buffalo

INTRODUCTION

Henry Giroux is recognized as a key and founding scholar of critical pedagogy (Besley, 2012; Kincheloe, 2008; Pinar, Reynolds, Slatterly, & Taubman,
1995; Riley, 2012; Robbins, 2006; Sandlin, O'Malley, & Burdick, 2011). Despite his reception as a critical scholar and his impressive impact on critical
education, his writing often elicits mixed reactions. His work is philosophical, innovative, and vision-oriented, but it is difficult for some readers to
overlook problems with his scholarship, and at the least, what Pinar et al.
(1995) describe as his "doses of inspiration and guilt" (p. 311), or melo-
drama. Many have also complained about the style of his writing, calling it
jargonistic and at times turgid. Even his endorsers, in their various introductions to collections of his essays, hedge their praise with statements such
as, "While Giroux's writings disclose a deep theoretical erudition, there are
grounds upon which they can and should be challenged and contested as
part of an ongoing dialogue" (McLaren, 1988, x–xi). If not for Giroux's
grave and evocative poetics, persistence about current issues such as the

Educating About Social Issues in the 20th and 21st Centuries, pages 169–192
Copyright © 2014 by Information Age Publishing
All rights of reproduction in any form reserved.

169

privatization of public goods, and the visibility of his work in the field, one might more quickly dismiss the writing of Giroux. Henry Giroux's 38-year career is formidable, and I propose that we carefully read or re-read his key works and entertain his newest writing. Henry Giroux has made a significant impact and should not be ignored as a scholar and public intellectual in the twentieth and twenty-first centuries.

The title of this chapter is a partial critique of Giroux's overuse of the word "crisis" combined with the unfortunate paradox that some of Giroux's alarmist language is alarmingly on point. For example, Giroux's *On Critical Pedagogy* (2011a) starts with a chapter titled "Youth and the Crisis of the Future." On one hand, Giroux has overused "crisis" to the point that readers are left to wonder if his discussion will really reveal an imminent crisis; on the other hand, it is becoming clear that students are not being thoroughly prepared to become democratic citizens, that they are misrepresented and misled in the media, and that, as Giroux so poignantly describes, the social contract has eroded to the point that youth are not being supported through public welfare and education. Perhaps we do have a crisis in the immediate future. For this reason, and others, it is important for readers to re-evaluate Giroux's work in the context of recent developments in social and educational history. Over the years, Giroux has produced an impressive framework for neoliberalism, provided intellectuals with a formidable critique of positivism in educational research, and created theoretical imagery that is passionate and moving. In this chapter, I describe the strengths and weakness in Giroux's oeuvre.

BIOGRAPHICAL OVERVIEW

Henry Giroux was born to working class parents in Providence, Rhode Island. He started his undergraduate career on a basketball scholarship at the University of Southern Maine at Gorham, a small teacher training college (Giroux, 2012a). This "historical accident" (McLaren, 1988, p. xii) launched Giroux into a teaching career. After graduation, Giroux was a high school social studies teacher and grass roots organizer for seven years (McLaren 1988). Giroux's publishing career began in 1975 while he was a PhD student at Carnegie Mellon University, working with Professor Tony Penna, who distinctly shaped Giroux's life and work (Giroux, 2012c).

Giroux has held numerous positions since he wrote his dissertation about curriculum and earned his doctorate at Carnegie Mellon in 1977. Following graduation, he began teaching and conducting research at Boston University but was denied tenure. The politics surrounding this event, described personally and powerfully in *Disposable Youth* (2012a), helped to shape Giroux's then nascent conceptualization of the university as neoliberal, and it presented him with one of his first opportunities to resist oppression in a politically hostile environment. Giroux resisted the university president's—the notoriously confrontational John Silber—opposition and continued to publish in the new field of critical pedagogy. This led to his first move in 1984 to Miami University in Oxford, Ohio. Giroux held a prestigious position at Pennsylvania State University from 1992 until 2004, when, feeling oppressed by the political climate in the United States, he moved to McMaster University in Ontario, Canada and now holds the Global Network and Television Chair at that institution.

SUMMARY OF HIS CAREER

It is important to note that Giroux is both a cultural critic and an educational theorist. He does not claim that education is more important than his interest in cultural studies but that education became an essential part of his study of culture and the circulation of power (i.e., the role of representation and identity politics in the production of what Giroux calls "market identities") (see Giroux, 2004). Giroux's work in cultural studies and education essentially complement each other. Giroux chose to do his research on education, because he had been a teacher and wanted to make a larger impact (Giroux, 1992). Because of this inter-disciplinarity, Giroux, along with critical pedagogue Michael Apple, was able to borrow the notion of reproduction from the Frankfurt School and apply it to reproduction in education—as it applied to curriculum issues such as textbook selection and teaching issues such as the de-professionalization of teaching. After establishing the reproductive consequences of certain educational models, Giroux moved towards a more hopeful pedagogy, which he believed was needed to counter a defeated attitude towards education and youth. Giroux's early career reflects his foundational understanding of reproduction theory; however, Giroux quickly evolved to framing a broader, more empowering study of resistance. This allowed Giroux to model how to employ a Marxian analysis without having his writing dictated to or depressed by it.

Early Career

It is well established that Giroux began his career as a critical pedagogue as a reproduction theorist (see Pinar et al., 1995 for a full description and further references). Reproduction theory in education argues and explains how curriculum and instruction socializes students into the market economy and functions to make students workers and consumers. In the reproduction phase of his career, (from the late 1970s until 1980), Giroux and colleague Michael Apple (Professor of Curriculum and Instruction at the University of Wisconsin, Madison) founded reproduction theory in education and, in doing so, drew specifically from the Marxist-inspired Frankfurt School. As mentioned previously, Giroux and Apple argued that schools, in their socialization of students, reproduced in students the needs and values of a market economy (Kincheloe, 2008). After a few short years of evaluating reproduction as it applies to curriculum, Giroux began to theorize reproduction in less deterministic, more dialectical terms, and this led to the work he is most well known for, resistance theory (see below). Giroux and most of his colleagues eventually dismissed his/their earlier emphasis on reproduction theory, because it was too deterministic and nondialectical in nature (Giroux, 1992; Pinar et al., 1995).

Resistance Theory

Using metaphors for hope, borrowing from the language of Maxine Greene (Professor of Philosophy at Teachers College, Columbia University) and the language of "not yet," and invoking an imagery of possibility, Giroux began to acknowledge the limitations of reproduction theory in his writing. In the beginning of this period, Giroux completed books such as *Border Crossings: Cultural Workers and the Politics of Education* (1992). Giroux was essentially developing a theory of how the agency of individuals could produce positive, progressive change. In an interview in *Border Crossing*, Giroux defines radical pedagogy as at once synonymous with critical pedagogy and at the same time more hopeful. The dream for hope in the midst of political opposition remains important in the writing of Giroux.

Giroux's resistance theories translated easily to his work on youth and teacher education and professionalization. In an introduction to *Teachers as Intellectuals*, McLaren (1988) noted that Giroux had moved into the wider field of social theory and cultural studies as they relate to empowering students and democracy: "The overarching project of Giroux's work... can be summarized as an attempt to formulate a critical pedagogy committed to the imperatives of empowering students and transforming the larger social order in the interests of a more just and equitable democracy" (p. xi).

Giroux's foray into cultural studies was, however, problematic for Pinar, et al. (1995). Such criticism was later dismissed. According to Kincheloe (2008), Giroux is responsible for re-establishing cultural studies as important to education. In fact, at McMaster University, Giroux's position as Global Network and Television Chair allows him to operate within a larger field of curriculum, which includes the curriculum of culture.

As shown below, in addition to his role in resistance theory and reestablishing cultural studies within education, Giroux's contribution to public pedagogy is fierce, and for purposes of this book edited by Totten and Pedersen, provides readers a way to think about teaching about social issues in the twenty-first century.

Frameworks for Neoliberalism and Public Pedagogy

Giroux's writing in the 1990s and on into the beginning of the twenty-first century focused on developing a theory of neoliberalism to describe the emergence of a strong Right-winged politic, which included Reaganomics and the erosions of the welfare state. Stated simply, neoliberalism is a new form of liberalism that on a large scale minimizes federal regulation of the market and corporations. On an individual level, it socializes people to believe that taxes should be reduced to accommodate their spending within the market. Neoliberalism feeds off of meritocracy ideologies. According to Giroux (2011a), "The neoliberal state no longer invests in solving social problems; it now punishes those who are caught in the downward spiral of its economic policies" (p. 111).

Giroux's critiques of neoliberalism parlayed well with his work on resistance, and in that regard he established himself as a scholar of public pedagogy and neoliberalism. Giroux's critique of the allocation of public goods for private purposes demonstrated, early on, Giroux's foresight into what he would eventually call the "crisis in public values." It also provides a window into the fact that Giroux, though sometimes heavy on "doses of inspiration and guilt" (Pinar et al, 1995, p. 311) is often ahead of what eventually become trends. What seems like hyperbole in Giroux's writing today may be part of tomorrow's headlines in the news. Just as Besley (2012) has argued that "Giroux's predictions in the 1980s are uncomfortably accurate" (p. 598), Giroux's writings in the 1990s and in the first decade of the twenty-first century are also often accurate. For example, Giroux's critiques of how privatization would erode the social contract long predate the financial crisis that unfolded in 2008.

A framework for neoliberalism and examples of public pedagogy for resistance emerged at about the same time in Giroux's mid-career writing. Sandlin et al. (2011), who reviewed scholarship in the field of public pedagogy in order to establish the term *public pedagogy* within a theoretical context, found that Giroux had contributed fifteen percent of the established scholarship on public pedagogy and noted that before Giroux's contributions, the term did not even exist in the literature. In fact, Giroux, himself, started working with the concept of public pedagogy before actually employing it as an explicit term (which he did not invent). In the same article, Sandlin et al. (2011) found that the majority of writers today use versions of Giroux's specific framework for neoliberalism. Giroux essentially gave currency and meaning to both *public pedagogy* and *neoliberalism.* Researchers are understandably indebted to Giroux for making this language and theory exportable to education scholarship.

Giroux and Teacher Education

Some of Giroux's best work (1988; 1992; 2012b) focuses on the de-professionalization of teaching and a passion for teacher resistance. Occasionally borrowing from the work of Freire, but primarily focusing on how the de-professionalization of teaching is part of the larger neoliberal project, Giroux aptly describes how the charter school movement and the No Child Left Behind testing climate accelerated the public's devaluing of the teaching profession. Giroux shows this as part of a cycle in which traditional public school teacher turnover rates are high because of the onerous imposition of testing (which, more often than not, results in forcing teachers to "teach to the test") and poor conditions. He argues that as experienced teachers leave, new teachers enter schools and frequently under perform. He also notes that as a result of the departure of the more experienced teachers, mentorship of the new teachers is often dropped by the wayside, and test scores continue to drop. In this environment, he notes, the establishment of charter schools is frequently presented as *the* solution, but, often, once in place, the charter schools also frequently end up failing. As student performance plummets, private schools are then conveniently offered as *the* solution. After providing initial support and low-cost initial leases, Giroux asserts, corporate "sponsors" raise rents on charter school spaces, and the schools are bankrupted. In typical "zombie"-like fashion, corporate interests purchase the schools and profit tremendously from this vacuum of public spending (see Giroux, 2012b).

Giroux's interest in the teaching profession extends beyond this expansive explanation for neoliberalism within U.S. education and is tied to his earlier work on resistance, teacher education, and democracy (Giroux, 1992). Even if the devaluing of the profession were not tied to the larger insidious process of neoliberalism, he argues, when teaching is de-politicized, it cannot effectively engage students as part of the democracy. Drawing on his work vis-à-vis resistance, Giroux (2012b) reminds teachers and teacher educators of the important role we play in shaping a democratic future.

Giroux's (2012b) argument for teacher education and development also overlaps with his work in cultural studies. He insists that teachers must teach about social issues in a way that engages the media, culture, and a wide range of modalities, "The literacies of the 21st century are electronic, aural, and image-based; and it is precisely within the diverse terrain of popular culture that pedagogical practices must be established as part of a broader politics of public life" (p. xvii).

In an interview in *America on the Edge* (2006), Giroux specifically describes the role he believes teachers should have in teaching and using literacy. He believes that the teaching of literacy should include multiple literacies (it should not consist of teaching discrete sets of skills in isolation), and new literacy instruction should be included in adult education. Giroux (2006) views literacy as, "part of a broader critical discourse grounded in a politics of representation in which students and others learn how to analyze the cultural and ideological codes in various forms of signification" (p. 4).

Emerging Developments in the Twenty-First Century

Giroux uses metaphor to punctuate major themes in his writing. A major metaphor he is making use of in early in the twenty-first century is that of corporate, neoliberal thieves robbing children of the social-contractual right to education, justified by the urgency of U.S. global policing and war. With the beginning of this century, Giroux has focused more and more on issues of representation as they relate to the neoliberal project. For example, Giroux (2013) examines how post-9/11 rhetoric has, according to this perspective, overemphasized terrorist threats and bred fear in the general public in order to promote neoliberal agendas.

Giroux has also turned his attention to the fallout after the 2008 U.S. financial crisis, the worst such crisis since the Great Depression of the late 1920s and 1930s. After 2008, Giroux began to use his neoliberal frameworks to examine the specific corruption of Wall Street and the irony that private investors and venture capitalists would be allowed to invest in public school charters (Giroux, 2012b). More recently, Giroux has written about events such as the Occupy Movement of 2011–2012 and the Chicago teachers' union strikes of 2012. These events showcase human agency, resistance, and will, all themes in Giroux's writing, which were mostly explained as ideals prior to these waves of protest. Quite often, interested readers can find his most up-to-date commentary and analysis in Giroux's Truth-out blogs (www.truth-out.org), where Giroux locates his most passionate critiques of trends in social movements.

In the late 1990s, Giroux began to write about youth and the implications as to how they are represented in the media. In one 1996 *Educational Researcher* article, Giroux deconstructs the film *Kids* (Woods, 1995) to show how youth are construed as hedonistic, irresponsible, and socially burdensome. This article is just one example of Giroux's passion for youth, whose role in society he reframes as politically important, reminding readers that the resistance of youth, "has a long and dignified legacy in the United States" (Giroux, 2012a, p. xviii).

Giroux has warned that negative representations of youth could drive the politics of disposability in which older citizens justify the disinvestment in youth through the defunding of social welfare and education. In his short book *Disposable Youth*, Giroux (2012a) effectively links the representation of youth in the media to the disinvestment in youth through the politics of neoliberals. If youth are disposable, the line of reasoning goes, it is okay not to support them with social welfare and education. It is okay to burden them with debt on over-priced postsecondary education, and it is okay to relegate them to life-long working class status. This work is an important resource for teaching about social issues in the twenty-first century, because it has immediate relevance to a critical population in education. To date, *Disposable Youth* is some of Giroux's most effective work on youth, possibly because he takes up parts of his own autobiography in order to build his arguments. For commentary on Giroux's work on youth, see Hatch (1996) for criticism and Besley (2012) for praise.

Giroux's Poetics and Metaphors

Giroux's writing style, because of its poetics, is yet another important reason his public pedagogy writing is relevant and necessary to read in the twenty-first century. Across Giroux's career, he has created an image-filled landscape using metaphors such as corporate zombies and thieves. This landscape is one of the most effective vehicles for teaching that Giroux consistently uses. Yet, missing from most reviews of Giroux's work is an evaluation of his poetic persuasion. Giroux has taken risks in his writing style that other scholars would be unwilling to take (Aronowitz, 2001; McLaren 1998), and he locates in writing a place to search for and find critical solutions to problems. Sometimes this alterative approach has cost Giroux a larger audience. Giroux's poetics infuses his theory with power, expression, and emotion, which stand in stark contrast to the eviscerated, technically rational writing of most of his social science colleagues in education. In this regard, Aronowitz (2001) notes, "[Giroux] is still among the few engaged intellectuals, as opposed to the researchers and academics, in the field of education" (p. xv). Giroux's humanities-based imagery makes his writing especially important in the twenty-first century, because the erasure of the humanities is part of the neoliberal project.

Notably, because of his own passionate writing style and powerful theory, one of the few academics to even mention Giroux's poetics is beloved educator, Paulo Freire. In his introduction to Giroux's *Teachers as Intellectuals*, Freire (1988) writes, "What characterizes [Giroux] as a superb writer is his esthetically pleasing style, which keeps the reader attentive by the many brilliant metaphors that capture the essence of the context and the content of the themes about which he writes" (p. xxvii). In his foreword to Giroux's *Theory and Resistance in Education,* Freire (2001) describes Giroux's thought as "restless" (p. xiii), a feeling that reminds the reader that critical pedagogy is unfinished. Freire also notes that Giroux's works demand a response, "His thought does not allow those who approach him to remain indifferent" (p. xiv). Giroux's emotional persuasion is established through literary elements such as metaphor, entendre, and imagery. Such elements give Giroux's writing the signature (and important) restless feel that Freire describes.

To accomplish his poetics, Giroux has invoked a range of metaphors across his writing, including the metaphor that corporations are zombies. For example, in discussing "neoliberalism," he writes as follows: "Neoliberalism—reinvigorated by the passing of tax cuts for the ultra-rich, the right-wing Republican Party taking over the House of Representatives, and an on-going successful attack on the welfare state—proceeds once again in zombie-like fashion to impose its values, social relations, and forms of social death upon all aspects of civic life" (Giroux, 2011b, p. 118). This is one of the most powerful metaphors that Giroux has used as of late. It shows up across several of his works and demonstrates how Giroux "deploys" metaphor as a powerful response to neoliberal discourses. Through his use of metaphor, Giroux infuses discourses with persuasive, memorable imagery that far exceeds traditional uses of logic that are typically used in educational literature.

CRITICISM

In a review of *Education Under Siege* (Aronowitz and Giroux, 1986), literacy researcher David Hamilton (1987) argued, from a critical pedagogy "outsider" perspective, what he perceived to be a major problem with Giroux's writing, "To penetrate Aronowitz & Giroux's prose style the reader needs so much prior knowledge that the 'message' of their book becomes redundant. In short, to know what they are saying you already need to know what they are saying" (p. 90). Additionally, Hamilton (1987) claimed that the work of Giroux and Aronowitz "speaks to the already-converted, not the unpersuaded" (p. 90), which, he argues, has impacted the sense that criticism of Giroux is generally lacking; that is, either one ignores the work of Giroux as much as possible, or one adopts it wholesale. In fact, most reviews of Giroux's work are decidedly uncritical, especially in recent years.

The most well-known critique of Giroux as the figurehead for critical pedagogy is Elizabeth Ellsworth's (1989) seminal, "Why Doesn't this Feel Empowering? Working through the Repressive Myths of Critical Pedagogy?" Ellsworth's article generated so much debate that scholars continue to reference it; one scholar specifically critiqued the chain of dialogue that ensued following Ellsworth's initial article, ironically framing the discussion as " 'Lather's critique of Giroux's critique of Ellsworth's critique of Giroux' " (Carlson, quoted in Lather, 2001, p. 184). Like Hamilton, Ellsworth criticized the abstraction of power relationships within the discourse of critical pedagogy; further, she argued that the discourse perpetuated dominant power structure ways of knowing, essentially making critical pedagogy a "'boy thing'" (Lather, 2001, p. 184), and at the very least, a pedagogy that reifies the construction of the teacher as the one with authority, the one who knows, and ironically, the arbiter of empowerment. In this social dynamic, Ellsworth argued (1989) "student empowerment has been defined in the broadest possible humanist terms, and becomes a 'capacity to act effectively' in a way that fails to challenge any identifiable social or political position, institution, or group" (p. 307), and so the discourse not only makes students dependent upon the paternalistic wisdom of the teacher: it also denies them the opportunity to name specific oppressions. Ten years later, Lather (2001) continued to see the same problems within critical pedagogy, which, she argued, confirms the unresponsiveness of Giroux and his male colleagues to the critique: "Now almost ten years later, my interest is in how critical pedagogy in the contemporary moment is still very much a boy thing. This is due not so much to the dominance of male authors in the field as it is to the masculinist voice of abstraction, universalization, and the rhetorical position of the 'one who knows'" (p. 184). To this day, this abstraction and the taking for granted of male privilege continues to be a problem.

Hatch (1996) has raised an issue in regard to Giroux's problematic representation of youth when he voices advocacy for the disenfranchised. Like Ellsworth and Lather, Hatch's argument centers on the paternalism inherent in Giroux's advocacy. Hatch further explains the implications for this paternalism within the context of Giroux's pedagogies of hope. In spite of his theoretical narratives of hope and possibility, Hatch (1996) argues, Giroux frequently denies the subjects of his writings possible agency within their social environment.

Similarly, Giroux cannot claim to write from the perspective of the working classes, as if he is still a working class person. Stated most simply in relation to Spivak's (1988) well-rehearsed rhetorical question, "Can the subaltern also speak?" Giroux-as-subaltern cannot speak, because he is no longer subaltern, illustrated by the fact that he has esteemed presence in the Academy. There are alternate interpretations of Spivak's question, and some of them do not fit with my analysis of Giroux as no longer subaltern. However, it is worth noting that Giroux fails to effectively establish his middle class positionality when he attempts to speak for the disenfranchised. While he may reluctantly admit his privilege, he could emphasize more how his positioning negates his immediate identification with subaltern others.

Pinar et al. (1995) were more concerned with Giroux's wide theoretical net than with the concerns raised above, and they warned that perhaps Giroux had spread his theory too thin by combining it with cultural studies. The authors suggested that it was possible for critical pedagogy to implode as it moved into the twenty-first century as a result of this diffusion of theory. However, we now know that critical pedagogy continues to thrive well past the first decade of the twenty-first century, and new scholars are engaging its principles. Furthermore, Giroux's inter-disiciplinarity in cultural studies is now one of his greatest strengths (Kincheloe, 2008; Trend, 2012). Yet, it remains true that sometimes Giroux sometimes tries to do too much. In the accompanying annotated bibliography, one will see that in various collections of his own work, the final product lacks coherence in book form and that is largely because he addresses too many topics in one volume.

Several criticisms of Giroux have been addressed in this section, but some critiques have only been touched upon. Pinar et al. (1995) do a superb job of covering theoretical weaknesses in Giroux's writing from 1977 through 1994. The authors address problems with Giroux's appropriation of Gramsci's theory of *hegemony*, his overly orthodox application of Marxism (a critique that Giroux eventually responded to), and his problematic appropriations of feminism in his writing. Many fewer well thought out critiques of Giroux have been published in the twenty-first century, perhaps because he is addressing an audience who largely agrees with his claims.

LASTING CONTRIBUTIONS

Giroux continues to write about resistance theory, but he applies it to current examples and contexts, which demonstrates the applicability and integrity of his frameworks across more than 30 years. In 1995, Pinar et al. criticized Giroux for abandoning critical education for a more nebulous specialization of cultural studies. However, this was an essential turn (Kincheloe, 2008; Trend, 2012), since critical education alone would not satisfy his imperative for equity through public and critical pedagogy. For Giroux, education is ubiquitous and educators must be cultural workers engaging with the public at large as part of their influence in the classroom.

As his endorsers have acknowledged, Henry Giroux is relentless. McLaren writes, "There is a passion and indignation in Giroux's writings—one could also say a militant hope—which betray little of the detachment and academic smoothness of conventional scholarly work" (McLaren, 1988 p. xi).

Though at times he is repetitive, the overall impression Giroux gives is that he will repeat his messages until he drives them home. This is critical to his formidable career. For Giroux, the way to teach about social issues is to be a public intellectual, whether you are a classroom teacher, teacher educator, or engaged citizen. As public intellectuals, educators must find multiple means for resisting mainstream discourses, which create the social structures that determine student learning, representations, and how people consume in an era of hyper-capitalism.

Giroux has supplied his readers with a foundation for critical pedagogy that has been used across a range of writings in the field. As mentioned above, Giroux's writing accounts for a large percentage of what Sandlin, et al. (2011) called *public pedagogy scholarship*. Giroux remains active in writing about current issues as they impact education. Though hypercritical of Giroux in many ways, Pinar et al. (1995) make him the main focus in their chapter on political scholarship, indicating that while one can resist Giroux's scholarship, it cannot be ignored.

Giroux stands out as a public intellectual through op-ed columns in newspapers and for blogs such as The Freire Project and Truth-out. To understand Giroux's oeuvre it is especially important to read his open-source material, including blogs, op-eds, and open access journals (see "Websites" below for a short list of links where Giroux most frequently publishes). Giroux believes in alternative media outlets as a way to resist excessive neoliberal censorship of radical pedagogies; therefore, his use of alternative media outlets constitutes an extension of his personal resistance to neoliberalism. Additionally, Giroux treats his public scholarship and public intellectualism as integral to his career and responsibility as an academic. Similarly, as former student of Giroux's, Christopher Robbins (2006), points out, in a time where the value for teaching is under attack, Giroux continues to invest ample time, energy, and thoughtfulness into his pedagogical efforts. Like his public pedagogy, Giroux's classroom teaching plays a key role in his scholarship and his ethic. Giroux's deep-seated commitment to teaching should not be ignored.

To echo Riley (2012) from Volume One *of Educating about Social Issues in the 20th and 21st Centuries: A Critical Annotated Bibliography,* the same could be said for Giroux that Maxine Greene says about herself: "I am not yet" (quoted in Riley, pp. 488). As a public intellectual, Henry Giroux lives the dialectic between citizen-educator and, located in a cultural reality, scholar. We are indebted to Giroux for his patient and relentless work on building a framework that goes beyond describing neoliberalism: it offers up possible and hopeful responses for resisting the real crisis that neoliberalism is.

CONCLUSION

Though it is problematic that Giroux has overlooked some very coherent and consistent criticism of his work, it is important to read and reread Henry Giroux's writing, especially in the twenty-first century. When all is said and done, Giroux's theories are foundational to critical pedagogy and often prescient in regard to the oppressive forces at work in our schools, society, and individual lived experiences.

It should be duly noted that this chapter has notable limitations. First, I have only skimmed the surface of Giroux's work on youth, his corporate critiques that focus on Disney, his attempt to write feminist-sensitive scholarship, and his engagement with the arts and the politics of representation. Giroux has written so broadly that it is impossible to fully capture the breadth of his writing in one chapter. As stated and reverberated throughout the chapter, it is important to let this chapter serve as a starting place for reading and re-reading of Giroux.

NOTE

The chapter was written with support from editor Samuel Totten. I thank him for his time, patience and editorial expertise.

REFERENCES

Aronowitz, S. (2001). Preface. In H.A. Giroux, *Theory and resistance in education* (pp. xv–xviii). Granby, MA: Bergin & Garvey.

Aronowitz, S. A. & Giroux, H. A. (1986). *Education under siege: The conservative, liberal, and radical debate over schooling.* London: Routledge & Kegan Paul.

Besley, T. (2012). Why read Giroux? *Policy Futures in Education, 10*(6), 594–600.

Ellsworth, E. (1989). Why doesn't this feel empowering? Working through the repressive myths of critical pedagogy. *Harvard Education Review, 59*(3), 297–324.

Freire, P. (1988). Editor's introduction. In H. A. Giroux, *Teachers as Intellectuals* (pp. xxvii–xxviii). Westport, CT: Bergin & Garvey.

Freire, P. (2001). Foreword. In H. A. Giroux, *Theory and resistance in education* (pp. xv–xviii). Granby, MA: Bergin & Garvey.

Giroux, H. A. (1988). *Teachers as intellectuals.* Granby, MA: Bergin & Garvey.

Giroux, H. A. (1992). *Border crossings: Cultural workers and the politics of education.* New York, NY: Routledge.

Giroux, H. A. (1996). Hollywood, race, and the demonization of youth: The "kids" are not "alright." [Review of the motion picture *Kids*, produced by Woods, 1995]. *Educational Researcher, 25*(2), 31–35.

Giroux, H. A. (2004). Cultural studies and the politics of public pedagogy: Making the political more pedagogical. *Parallax, 10*(2), 73–89.

Giroux, H. A. (2006). *America on the edge.* New York, NY: Palgrave Macmillan

Giroux, H. A. (2011a). *On critical pedagogy.* New York, NY: Continuum.

Giroux, H. A. (2011b). Once more, with conviction: Defending higher education as a public good, *Qui parle, 20*(1), 117–135.

Giroux, H. A. (2012a). *Disposable youth: Racialized memories and the culture of cruelty.* New York, NY: Routledge.

Giroux, H. A. (2012b). *Education and the crisis of public values: Challenging the assault on teachers, students, & public education.* New York, NY: Peter Lang.

Giroux, H. A. (2012c, November 19). Interview with Henry Giroux/Interviewer: Angelo Letizia. Figure/Ground Communication. Retrieved from http://figureground.org/interview-with-henry-giroux/

Giroux, H. A. (2013). Militarizing higher education, neoliberalism's culture of depravity, and democracy's demise after 9/11. In *Neoliberalism, education, and terrorism: Contemporary dialogues* (pp. 36–66). Boulder, CO: Paradigm.

Hatch, T. (1996). If the "kids" are not "alright" I'm "clueless": Response to a review by Henry Giroux of the movie *Kids. Educational Researcher, 25*(7), 40–43.

Hamilton, D. (1987). Education under siege: The conservative, liberal, and radical debate over schooling by Stanley L. Aronowitz and Henry A. Giroux [Review of the book]. *British Educational Research Journal, 13*(1), 89–91.

Kincheloe, J. (2008). *Critical pedagogy primer.* New York, NY: Peter Lang.

Lather, P. (2001). Ten years later, yet again: Critical pedagogy and its complicities. In K. Weiler (Ed.), *Feminist engagements: Reading, resisting, and revisioning male theorists in education and cultural studies* (pp. 183–195). New York, NY: Routledge.

McLaren, P. (1988). Foreword: Critical theory and the meaning of hope. In H. A. Giroux (Ed.), *Teachers as Intellectuals* (pp. ix–xxi). Westport, CT: Bergin & Garvey.

Pinar, W. F., Reynolds, W. M., Slatterly, P., & Taubman, P. M. (1995). Understanding curriculum as political text. In W. F. Pinar, W. M. Reynolds, P. Slatterly, & P. M. Taubman (Eds.), *Understanding curriculum: An introduction to the study of historical and contemporary curriculum discourses* (pp. 243–314). New York: Peter Lang.

Riley, K. L. (2012). Touching the sacred garment: Paulo Freire, The Frankfurt School, and beyond. In S. Totten & J. E. Pedersen (Eds.), *Educating about social issues in the 20th and 21st centuries: A Critical annotated bibliography, Volume 1* (pp. 479–507). Charlotte, NC: Information Age Publishers.

Robbins, C. (Ed.). (2006). *The Giroux reader.* Boulder, CO: Paradigm Publishers.

Sandlin, J. A., O'Malley, M. P., & Burdick, J. (2011). Mapping the Complexity of Public Pedagogy Scholarship: 1894–2010. *Review of Educational Research, 38*(5), 338–375.

Spivak, G. C. (1988). Can the subaltern speak? In C. Nelson & L. Grossberg (Eds.), *Marxism and the interpretation of culture* (pp. 271–313). Urbana, IL: University of Illinois Press.

Trend, D. (2012). Henry Giroux and the arts. *Policy Futures in Education, 10*(6), 616–621.

Woods, C. (Producer), & Clark, L. (Director). (1995). *Kids.* [Film.] Shining Excalibur.

ANNOTATED BIBLIOGRAPHY

Recent Work

Giroux, H. A. (2012). *Disposable youth: Racialized memories and the culture of cruelty.* New York, NY: Routledge.

> *Disposable Youth* distills Giroux's work on "the war on youth" and the representations of youth in the media. In this very short text (I read it in two sittings),

Giroux mixes autobiography and theory to connect his experiences of growing up as a working class white teenager in a predominately African American neighborhood with his being denied tenure at Boston University. Giroux extends this combination of "theoretical resources and autobiographical memories" (p. xvii) to explain the implications for representations of youth in popular culture and their educational prospects. He also positions his situation at Boston University in relationship to university politics. Giroux claims, "At stake here is not just the future of a new generation of young people but democracy itself" (p. xviii). Due to its explicit narrative and its connections to Giroux's autobiography, the book is a worthwhile read.

Giroux, H. A. (2012). *Education and the crisis of public values: Challenging the assault on teachers, students, & public education.* New York, NY: Peter Lang.

Herein, Giroux argues that if the government fails to provide an education to each student, and corporations control the curriculum, then poor white and minority students will be vocationally trained instead of equipped with the tools of a humanities-based education and critical pedagogy, the latter of which is crucial in helping them understand their social conditions better. Giroux graphically describes the charter school movement's relationship to hedge fund management, venture capitalists, and politicians, and he links the relationship of private corporations to public charter schools to the "crisis in public values," where current governments are shirking their responsibility of providing each citizen with a democratic education. Giroux argues that if the private sector controls curriculum, then U.S. education will become increasingly inequitable, and it will track poor and working class students into deskilled labor. In the last chapter, Giroux argues that Freire's ideals are essential to reinventing reform in education in the twenty first-century. To prevent further corporate dehumanization, educators must implement a pedagogy of bearing witness, in which experience is remembered and critiqued so that individuals enact social change to counter policies that favor privatization over truly democratic education.

Other Book-Length Works

Giroux, H. A. (1992). *Border crossings: Cultural workers and the politics of education.* New York, NY: Routledge.

Border Crossings is an anthology of Giroux's best early writing and includes two interviews with him. By mixing critical issues with public intellectualism (i.e., clearly and consistently defining and/or using terms such as *social* and *critique*), Giroux makes plain some of his most important theories: a theory of discourse as a way to differentiate, a baseline theory for pedagogy, and a theory of teaching as political, intellectual, and social work. Giroux highlights the strengths of modernism and identifies how the overlaps between postcolonial theory and critical pedagogy can help generate fresh resistant discourses. He also emphasizes his "post-" leanings, which successfully moved his resistance theory beyond a critique of reproduction. By this point, Giroux has explicitly accepted the criticism that critical educators cannot appropriate Marxism wholesale.

Border Crossings produces a transformative, interdisciplinary, working theory of education. Most of the chapters of this book were published elsewhere, but Giroux claims that most of them have been revised substantially. *Border Crossings* is now in its third edition.

Giroux, H. A. (2001). *Theory and resistance in education: Towards a pedagogy for the opposition.* Westport, CT: Bergin & Garvey.

While some of Giroux's books seem more like an eclectic mix of essays, this work presents a cogent discussion of Giroux's enduring themes. In synthesizing his critique of positivism, Giroux argues that "behind traditional theory's insistence on a definition of truth, one that appears to be synonymous with objective methodological inquiry and empirical verification, there is a structured silence around how normative interests provide the grounding for theory and social inquiry" (p. 74), with implications for social structures and schooling. Giroux claims that traditional social research does not question its own logic and misses the "deep grammar" (p. 74) of social relations. As the title suggests, Giroux applies his critique by recommending a resistance-based pedagogy that questions the social structures of education and the claims of educational logic.

Giroux, H. A. (2011). *On critical pedagogy.* New York, NY: Continuum.

At first glance, *On Critical Pedagogy* appears to be a primer of critical education, but the book, in fact, is a collection of essays that address a host of issues that Giroux has written about for years and thus there is nothing new here. At least three of the chapters have been printed elsewhere: "Schooling and the Culture of Positivism" was originally published in *Education Theory* 29(4); "Rethinking Cultural Politics and Radical Pedagogy" was originally published in *Education Theory* 49(1); the highly interesting interview by Manuela Guillermo was originally published in *Language and Intercultural Communication* 6(2) and is also included in *The Giroux Reader.* The remaining essays seem redundant.

Robbins, C. (Ed.). (2006). *The Giroux reader.* Boulder, CO: Paradigm Publishers.

Unique from the rest of the titles in this bibliography because Giroux did not edit it, *The Giroux Reader* is a labor of love by Christopher Robbins, a former student of Giroux's who holds his mentor in high esteem. Robbins' incisive understanding of Giroux's oeuvre is clear in both his introduction and the editorial selections. The interview, "Is There a Role for Critical Pedagogy in Cultural Studies?" is one of the best interviews of Giroux that is readily available.

Journal Articles and Book Chapters

Several recommended articles are from *Policy Futures in Education,* a good journal for thinking about public pedagogy within formal educational contexts.

The journal is not typically available through many institutions, but a 60 USD one-year subscription gives unlimited access to all of the journal's archives. Giroux is also widely published in *JAC* (*Journal of Advanced Composition*), a rigorous, partially open-sourced (archives are available through 2007), and peer-reviewed journal. Available online at http://www.jaconlinejournal.com.

Giroux, H.A. (1980/1999). Dialectics and the development of curriculum theory. In W. F. Pinar (Ed.), *Contemporary curriculum discourses: Twenty years of JCT* (pp. 7–23). New York, NY: Peter Lang.

This article/chapter served as the beginning of Giroux's reinvention of curriculum theory after his initial "reproduction" phase of writing. The framework he establishes here, which begins with the question, "Whose interests does [curriculum] serve?" (p.18) is still employed by critical educators today.

Giroux, H. A. (1996). Hollywood, race, and the demonization of youth: The "kids" are not "alright." [Review of the motion picture Kids, produced by Woods, 1995]. *Educational Researcher, 25*(2), 31–35.

In this piece, Giroux reacts to the movie *Kids*, which portrays young people as out of control and reckless.

Giroux, H. A. (2004). Cultural studies and the politics of public pedagogy: Making the political more pedagogical. *Parallax, 10*(2), 73–89.

This article explains how corporate culture has permeated every facet of American culture to the point of establishing what Giroux calls *neoliberal public pedagogy*, which uses the media and other public discourses to develop a neoliberal common sense and "market identities" (p. 74) unfamiliar with the language of critique. In this new corporate culture, private interests gain governmental contracts for everything from weapons and education to hospital care. As a result, public dollars are siphoned off into the coffers of corporate wealth and public needs are subordinated to private interests. Rather than see this turn of culture as a negative, Giroux focuses on the possibilities of new media to counter neoliberal public pedagogy with critical discourse and teaching. This is another article that feels prophetic, given its 2004 date and the later 2008 federal bail out of Wall Street.

Giroux, H. A. (2011). Once more, with conviction: Defending higher education as a public good. *Qui parle, 20*(1), 117–135.

One of Giroux's many articles about the neoliberal take over of higher education, this article illustrates how liberal arts education and democracy are linked. Giroux further explains how privileging market demands over higher education erodes the social fabric, "Market-driven rewards cancel out the ethical imagination, social responsibility, and the pedagogical imperative of truth telling in favor of pandering to the predatory instincts of narrow-minded individual awards and satisfactions" (p. 121).

This article also includes a list of "symptoms" of the corporatization of the university. In elaborating further on how the university is not just reproducing students to participate in the corporate structure, he discusses how the university is taking on corporate-like characteristics, perceiving students as customers and using federal loans, which students are indebted to repay, to satisfy the demands of escalating tuition prices. He ties this phenomenon to the larger crisis in public values, "The current assault threatening higher education, and the humanities in particular, cannot be understood outside of the crisis of public values, ethics, youth, and democracy itself" (p. 124). What is perhaps even more important for Giroux if this trend continues is that the neoliberal state will have no humanities-educated, democratic thinkers to call into question its practices.

Giroux, H. A. (2013). Militarizing higher education, neoliberalism's culture of depravity, and democracy's demise after 9/11. In J. R. Di Leo, H. A. Giroux, S. A. McClennen, K. J. Saltman (Eds.), *Neoliberalism, education, and terrorism: Contemporary dialogues*, pp. 36–66.

Giroux describes the new role of higher education: conducting research for private interests and on war technologies. He reframes the familiar "military-industrial complex" to include the new neoliberal "military-industrial-*academic*" complex [emphasis added]. He recommends student and professor resistance to the militarism of higher education by engaging in traditional critical pedagogies.

Giroux casts a vision for higher education in which students and professors collaborate to raise awareness and resist the barrage of images that normalize the politics, the finance, and the violence of war. Giroux brings in the elements of his standard neoliberal framework, but he adds new analyses that include the potentially destructive long-term implications of a higher education affiliation with the military.

This chapter is within Giroux's interdisciplinary sweet spot, offering critiques of popular media and film imagery that connect to his deep understanding of neoliberal frameworks and the relations of power that sustain neoliberalism within the context of higher education.

Criticism and Praise

Aronowitz, S. & Giroux, H. (1991). *Postmodern education: Politics, culture, and social criticism.* Minneapolis, MN: University of Minnesota Press.

Included in chapter five of this text (pp. 132–133), Giroux's brief response to/critique of Elizabeth Ellsworth's "Why Doesn't this Feel Empowering?" is included (see the annotation of Ellsworth article below). Though this is one of a few versions of the article/chapter, this is the version that is most frequently cited. Here, Giroux clearly argues for the possibility of using students' differences as an asset to critical pedagogy rather than treating difference as exclusively problematic. While an interesting response, it is quite clear Giroux skirts Ellsworth's main critique of critical pedagogy, which is the problem with universalism and abstraction so characteristic of Giroux and other critical pedagogues' writing.

Besley, T. (2012). Why read Giroux? *Policy Futures in Education, 10*(6), 594–600.

Besley employs her breadth of reading on Giroux to write a helpful summary of Giroux's writing about youth. Her main argument is that Giroux offers a thorough exploration of how youth are misrepresented in the media, and emphasizes the important point that he does so with a focus on hope and staying positive. Significantly, Besley also shows, as this author has tried to argue, that Giroux's predictions as a theorist are frequently and alarmingly on target. Giroux may not be the last and most authoritative word on such issues, but he very well might be the first, which is a trend in a lot of his writing. The article is limited by the author's lack of criticism. Like so many of Giroux-enthusiasts, Besley is seemingly hesitant to discuss how Giroux could engage a wider readership.

Besley, T. (Ed.). (2012). Henry Giroux on youth cultural studies and critical pedagogy [Special issue]. *Policy Futures in Education. 10*(6).

This special issue on Giroux is important because it provides a good sense of the breadth of issues Giroux has addressed (and continues to address) by some key and emerging scholars whose own work in education has been influenced by Giroux's. The contributors include Kenneth Saltman, Peter Mayo, and Giroux's former student, Christopher Robbins. Notably, the special issue includes a piece on Giroux's aesthetics, something that I argued in the essay accompanying this annotated bibliography that is largely missing from evaluations of his work.

Bowers, C. (1980). Orthodoxy in Marxist educational theory. *Discourse, 1*(2), 54–63.

Bowers' early criticism that critical pedagogy scholars should not be overly orthodox in their attachment to Marxism is one of the few critiques that Giroux integrates into his dialectical theory of resistance. This is an important work, because it shows an emerging critique that would help define the field of critical pedagogy.

Bowers' (1991) later work, "Some Questions about the Anachronistic Elements in the Giroux-McLaren Theory of a Critical Pedagogy" (*Curriculum Inquiry*, 21(2), 239–252), a book review of Giroux's *Teachers as Intellectuals* and McLaren's *Life in Schools: An Introduction to a Critical Pedagogy in the Foundations of Education*, criticized Giroux and McLaren's failure to write coherent scholarship. They published articles in book chapters piecemeal and often failed to differentiate, in McLaren's case, his scholarship from Giroux's, and in Giroux's case, his scholarship from Freire's and Dewey's. The effect is a scholarship that is in the moment and convenient, based on the particular need in a particular argumentative moment. Bowers combined his review of the two books, because the two scholars, at the time, had the same problems and as a result, their theories were indecipherable from one another.

Ellsworth, E. (1989). Why doesn't this feel empowering? The repressive myths of critical pedagogy. *Harvard Educational Review, 59*(3), 297–324.

Though not limited solely to criticism of Giroux and McLaren, this oft-cited text about the abstraction of critical pedagogy discourse is best understood as a direct critique of Giroux and McLaren. Ellsworth's criticism is multi-layered in that beyond the exclusivity that "universalist" discourse creates, it has the further effect of disenfranchising students from participating in their own "empowerment," which critical pedagogues claim to be their *raison d'etre*. Ellsworth's initial article is important, but the ensuing dialogue that spans several years provides even greater context for the ruptures in theory among researchers who are interested in empowerment. Giroux responded to Ellsworth in 1991.

Kincheloe, J. (2008). *The critical pedagogy primer.* New York, NY: Peter Lang.

In the second chapter, "The Foundations of Critical Pedagogy," Kincheloe, unlike many other Giroux reviewers, provides a thoughtful, balanced, and sympathetic criticism of Giroux. Given that Giroux polarizes most of his readers, Kincheloe's informed reading of Giroux's body of work is very important.

Overall, *The Primer* provides helpful additional context regarding the history and connections vis-à-vis critical pedagogy. For example, Kincheloe includes a discussion of Lev Vygotsky and W. E. B. Du Bois in his review of the work of various critical theorists and discusses their relationship to the field (i.e., Du Bois's influence on Cornel West and so forth).

Pinar, W. F., Reynolds, W. M., Slatterly, P., & Taubman, P. M. (1995). Understanding curriculum as political text. In W. F. Pinar, W. M. Reynolds, P. Slatterly, & P. M. Taubman (Eds.), *Understanding curriculum: An introduction to the study of historical and contemporary curriculum discourses* (pp. 243–314). New York, NY: Peter Lang.

A good way to ascertain the placement of various issues and publications across Giroux's career is to think in terms of before and after Pinar, et al's 1995 edition of *Understanding Curriculum.* Not only did the field change dramatically following this publication, but Pinar, et al's book provides the most exhaustive look at the field up to that point, and therefore, it provides a contextual and fine-grained analysis of Giroux's strongest contributions—as well as his most significant weaknesses. Indeed, this is where to go for an overview of the first fifteen years of Giroux's career. It provides readers a mostly balanced (even if harshly critical in places) and foundational understanding of Giroux's early works and the major concerns in the field at that time.

This is an essential read for anyone who wishes to understand Giroux within the broader context of politically based pedagogies. Pinar et al. use the generalization *political* so that within the chapter they can separate those from the Frankfurt school (namely McLaren, Giroux, and Apple) from other scholars doing political criticism in education (such as Patti Lather and Elizabeth Ellsworth).

Something not addressed in the chapter by this author (Russell-Buffalo), but worth considering is the authors' criticism that Giroux and Apple have been known to use theory piecemeal—in a way that works for their particular argument in the moment. The chapter is quite dense, which combined with its 72-page length, makes it equivalent to a short book rather than a book chapter.

Riley, K. L. (2012). Touching the sacred garment: Paulo Freire, the Frankfurt School, and beyond. In S. Totten & J. E. Pedersen (Eds.), *Educating about social issues in the 20th and 21st centuries: A Critical annotated bibliography, Volume 1* (pp. 479–507). Charlotte, NC: Information Age Publishers.

This is a brief introduction to the influence of Paulo Freire and the Frankfurt School on Michael Apple, Henry Giroux, and Peter McLaren. Riley quotes Giroux saying that he would not want to be called a student of Freire, since this would be antithetical to all that Freire cared about. This is an important issue, since, as Kincheloe (2008) argues, that there is not a single, unified critical pedagogy, because over-defining the field would undermine the project of naming and rewriting the world. Riley does not address Giroux's move from reproduction to resistance pedagogy but focuses instead on Giroux in terms of his moves within resistance theory—from talking about "schooling" to focusing on students.

Sandlin, J. A., O'Malley, M. P., & Burdick, J. (2011). Mapping the complexity of public pedagogy scholarship: 1894–2010. *Review of Educational Research, 81*(3), 338–375.

This is the first full literature review of the term *public pedagogy* in education. The authors pay significant attention to Giroux and his role in establishing *public pedagogy* scholarship. They give him credit for establishing the conceptual framework of neoliberalism that most education scholars use today. With the exception of Pinar, et al's Understanding *Curriculum*, nothing is as exhaustive as this text in explaining Giroux's key contributions to education.

Overall, this is an excellent review of theory in research related to public pedagogy since the late 1800s.

For Further Reading

Interviews

Due to the volume and variation in Giroux's writing, the best primers for reading Giroux include his interviews. The interviews in the short annotated list below are readily available. Additional interviews can be found online through basic Internet searching.

Giroux, H. A. (1992). Interview: The hope of radical education. In H. A. Giroux (Ed.), *Border crossings: Cultural workers and the politics of education* (pp. 9–18). New York, NY: Routledge.

In this interview, Giroux asks, "What are the necessary conditions to educate teachers to be intellectuals so they can engage critically the relationship between culture and learning and change the conditions under which they work?" (p. 15). This type of work and theory are important for Giroux, who places emphasis on the specific potential power of teachers and critical education in schools to counter what he perceived as an assault on public values. Also important herein is Giroux's discussion of his dissertation on curriculum and the value of experience as a valid social proof, which is part of his larger project to deconstruct positivism.

Giroux, H. A. (2006). Henry Giroux on critical pedagogy and the responsibilities of public intellectuals/Interviewers: Marcia Morales, Mike Pozo, and Sina Rahmani. In H. A. Giroux (Ed.), *America on the Edge: Henry Giroux on politics, culture, and education* (pp. 3–20). New York, NY: Palgrave Macmillan.

In this interview Giroux reframes what critical pedagogy is—a discourse "for asserting the primacy of the political and the ethical as a central feature of educational theory and practice" (p. 4). Because of the involvement of multiple interviewers, this is a vivid conversation that both recasts what critical pedagogy is and further develops common understandings, such as the popular critical pedagogy question, "Whose future, story, and interests does the school represent?" (p. 5). In terms of recasting the focus of critical pedagogy, Giroux emphasizes the inter-disciplinarity of critical pedagogy: "Another major task of critical pedagogy is to link the language of critique to the language of possibility" (p. 5). The interview evolves into raising questions about Giroux's relation to the United States, following his move to McMaster University, and his strategies for resisting the continued educational investment in positivism.

Giroux, H. A. (2012, January 30). Henry Giroux: The necessity of critical pedagogy in dark times/Interviewer J.M.B. Tristan. *Global Education Magazine.* Retrieved from *http://www.globaleducationmagazine.com/critical-interview-henry-giroux/*

This interview uniquely gives Giroux the opportunity to establish, as Joe Kincheloe also argues, that critical pedagogy prides itself on not being overly codified. Giroux cites Roger Simon, the Canada-based critical pedagogue, who said, "the attempt to define a set of 'founding fathers' for critical pedagogy suggests that 'an authentic version could somehow be found in a patriarchal vanishing point.'"

Giroux, H. A. (2012, November 19). Interview with Henry Giroux/Interviewer: A. Letizia. Figure/Ground Communication. Retrieved from http://figureground.org/interview-with-henry-giroux/

This interview is important for exploring Giroux's biographical context. Included is a brief description of Giroux's relationship to his Carnegie Mellon advisor, Dr. Tony Penna. Giroux credits Penna with providing him with the historical backdrop of critical education. In addition to this context, Letizia's questions interrogate the center of Giroux's theory for neoliberalism. Questions range from whether or not tenure protects academic freedom to what makes a good teacher.

Recommended Short Articles

Below is a list of recommended short articles (usually under 10 pp.) printed in reliable journals. Due to the length of this chapter already, it was not possible to provide annotations of these works.

Giroux, H. A. (1997). Race, pedagogy, and whiteness. *Dangerous Minds. Cineaste, 22*(4), 46–49.

Giroux, H. A. (1998). Education incorporated?: Corporate culture and the challenge of public schooling. *Educational Leadership, 56*(2), 12–17.

Giroux, H. A. (with Giroux, S. S.). (1999). Making the pedagogical more political: Reading Homi Bhabha. *Journal of Advanced Composition, 19*(2), pp. 139–147.

Giroux, H. A. (2003, May–June). Neoliberalism's war against youth: Where are children in the debate on politics? *Against the Current*, 20–23.

Giroux, H. A. (with Searls-Giroux, S.). (2003). Take back higher education: A task for intellectuals in a time of crisis, *Tikkun, 8*(6), 28–32.

Giroux, H. A. (2003). Zero tolerance, domestic militarization, and the war against youth. *Social Justice, 30*(2), 59–65.

Giroux, H. A. (2004). When hope is subversive. *Tikkun, 19*(6), 62–64.

Giroux, H. A. & Searls-Giroux, S. (2006). Challenging neoliberalism's new world order: The promise of critical pedagogy. *Cultural Studies/Critical Methodologies, 6*(1), 21–32.

Giroux, H. A. (2006, September 1). The politics of disposability. *Dissident Voice*. Retrieved from http://www.dissidentvoice.org/Sept06/Giroux01.htm

Giroux, H. A. (2007). Educated hope in dark times: Critical pedagogy for social justice. *Our Schools/Our Selves, 17*(1), 195–202.

Giroux, H. A. (2008). Education and the crisis of democracy: Confronting authoritarianism in a post 9/11 America. *Journal of Educational Controversy, 3*(1), 1–6.

Giroux, H. A. & Giroux, S. S. (2009). Beyond bailouts: Education after neoliberalism. *Policy Futures in Education, 7*(1), 1–4.

Giroux, H. A. (2009). Beyond the audacity of educated hope: The promise of an educated citizenry. *Policy Futures in Education, 7*(2), 271–274.

Giroux, H. A. (2009). Educating Obama: A task to make democracy matter. *Policy Futures in Education, 7*(4), 450–454.

Giroux, H. A. (2009). Ten years after the Columbine: The tragedy of youth deepens. *Policy Futures in Education, 7*(3), 356–361.

Giroux, H. A. (2009). Youth and the myth of post-racial society under Barack Obama. *Policy Futures in Education, 7*(5), 574–577.

Giroux, H. A. & Saltman, K. (2009). Obama's betrayal of public education? Arne Duncan and the corporate model of schooling. *Cultural Studies/Critical Methodologies, 9*(6), 772–779.

Giroux, H. A. (2010). Stealing of childhood innocence–Disney and the politics of casino capitalism: A tribute to Joe Kincheloe. *Cultural Studies/Critical Methodologies, 10*(5), 413–416.

Giroux, H. A. (2010). Zombie politics and other late modern monstrosities in the age of disposability. *Policy Futures in Education, 8*(1), 1–7.

Giroux, H. A. (2010, October). Learning from Paulo Freire. *The Chronicle of Higher Education,* B15–B16.

Giroux, H. A. (2010, Spring). Public intellectuals, the politics of clarity, and the crisis of language. *State of Nature.* Retrieved from http://www.stateofnature.org/publicIntellectualsThePolitics.html

Giroux, H. A. (2011). Memories of hope and the politics of disposability. *Journal of Advanced Composition, 31*(1–2), 102–121.

Giroux, H. A. (2012). Formative culture in the age of imposed forgetting. *Tikkun 26*(1), p. 41.

Websites

Giroux's online contributions are ubiquitous. Below are links to a few of the websites to which he most frequently contributes.

www.henryagiroux.com

> One of the best ways to get a sense of Giroux's public pedagogy is to go to his website and read/peruse the plethora of articles (online and in established journals) and range of topics that Giroux addresses from year to year. At this writing, the articles extend from the year of his very first publications through 2011. Anything later is indicated as *in press.*

http://truth-out.org/index.php?option=com_k2&view=item&id=4327:the-public-intellectual-henry-a-giroux

> *Truth-out* is where one will most likely find Giroux's criticism regarding current issues that abound in society. He frequently uses this website as a platform for timely discussions. For example *Truth-out* is where Giroux first published his commentary on the Chicago Teachers' Strikes in 2012. The articles here are passionate and interesting, but they tend to exacerbate pitfalls in Giroux's scholarship, leaning towards the overly dramatized and lacking self-critique.

CHAPTER 10

TRANSFORMATIVE PRAXIS

Barry Kanpol and the Quest
for a Public Identity

Karen Ragoonaden

Through the course of his extensive career as an educator and a university administrator, Barry Kanpol has been a strong advocate of critical pedagogy as a form of intellectual and cultural resistance, posited as a reaction against the *savage inequalities* (Kozol, 1991) of mainstream ideology and schooling. In his quest to democratize the reproduction of social and cultural capital within educational contexts, Kanpol has been adamant about using accessible, transparent language to redefine a collective, inclusive conceptualization of educational structures. In order to speak to the multiplicity of societal voices and to promote the possibility of hope as a foil to the existing postmodern cynicism, Kanpol has striven to develop a critical pedagogy for the Other. He has decried the fact that the de-contextualized, liberatory, dense pedagogies of critical theory do not often translate *back to the rough ground* (Dunne, 1993) of public schools. In order to address this paradox, his nascent productivity early in his career focused on Altenbaugh (1987) and Carlson's (1987) conceptualization of the distinction between

Educating About Social Issues in the 20th and 21st Centuries, pages 193–215
Copyright © 2014 by Information Age Publishing
All rights of reproduction in any form reserved.

institutional and cultural politics of resistance. Coupled with Aronowitz and Giroux's (1985) vision of a *transformative intellectual*, these seminal episte-mologies provided a foundation for discussions that promoted an applied resistance to the mainstream ideologies in contemporary educational prac-tice. Based on Mead's (1934) concept of self and community, which negates the inherent individualism and negative competitive educational practices, Kanpol's writing has promoted the emergence and the development of counter-hegemonic frameworks, which mobilize the self, the community, and complex issues related to race, religion, culture, gender, and class. In keeping with this engaged and committed approach to teaching and learn-ing, Kanpol has emphasized that curriculum must be reconceptualized as a platform for active negotiation and for knowledge mobilization and knowl-edge construction.

As with much of his writing, Kanpol's numerous articles and books, many of them infused with critical narratives, serve as a call to action, pos-iting that contemporary educational practice and curriculum should be transformative and led by *reskilled* teachers (Kanpol, 1999) promoting the *democratic imaginary* (Laclau and Mouffe, 1985). An intrinsic theme of his work is the deconstruction of assumptions about linearality, competition and mainstream cultural paradigms contrasted with the best of postmoder-nity, community, justice and freedom.

It is important to note that as a theorist Kanpol has contributed to the intellectual critical pedagogy debate by introducing the concept of the spiritual and the moral within the epistemology of postmodern thought. Kanpol reiterates, in a consistent manner, his strong belief that the critical pedagogy movement must come to terms with the existence of profound theological possibilities and its implications in the development of transfor-mative educational paradigms imbued with hope, possibility and joy.

The impact of his graduate work in urban middle schools made him aware of the rampant inequalities present in the public school system. This professional and academic awareness led to the moral, spiritual and ethical implications of examining the great divide between lofty ideological tenets of university and the harsh realities of the streets in urban America. In an attempt to address in a hopeful manner the hopelessness and desperation emerging from dark realties portrayed by critical pedagogy, Kanpol moved towards Liberation Theology, a conceptualization of the relationship be-tween spirituality and the social order. Liberation Theology finds its roots in Latin America, during a period when priests mobilized religious com-munities to overcome the suffering endured at the hands of Central and South American dictators.

Based on spirituality in action, Liberation Theology provides a trans-formative framework upon which to challenge societies breeding alien-ation, subordination and oppression. Liberation Theology first appeared in Kanpol's article entitled "Critical Pedagogy and Liberation Theology: Borders for a Transformative Agenda" (1996), and since then elements of applied Liberation Theology have been present in the majority of his work. For example, in order for praxis-infused action to occur, he encouraged preservice teachers and service teachers to respond to constraints in ways that create opportunities for democratic hope and critical citizenry (p. 182 of "Critical Pedagogy and Liberation Theology: Borders for a Transformative Agenda"). In keeping with a faith-based approach to change and transformation, Kanpol posited that teacher education must create the practical possibility for "confession" (p. 184 of "Critical Pedagogy and Liberation Theology: Borders for a Transformative Agenda"). In this case, "confession" is interpreted as an awareness of the dissonance between mandates established by governing educational structures and the diverse socio-economic and cultural realities of modern society and schooling. By confronting this dichotomy, Kanpol argues, preservice and in-service teachers can be directed toward challenging the set curriculum, abolishing stereotypes, promoting fair competition and redefining authority between the principal, the teacher and the students. Cases studies conducted in middle schools when Kanpol was in graduate school and done during his first academic postings at Chapman University in Orange, California and at Penn State University, Harrisburg demonstrate the progression of his theoretical formulations towards a faith-based prophetic approach to education and focus on glimpses of the democratic possibilities in public schools. (See *Critical Pedagogy 2nd ed.* 1999; *Teachers Talking Back and Breaking Bread,* 1998.)

As Kanpol's academic career evolved from assistant professor at Chapman University to associate professor at both Penn State Harrisburg and Saint-Joseph's University and finally to full professor at Indiana University-Purdue, Fort Wayne, he remained true to his progressive action bound, praxis-oriented proactive initiatives meant to galvanize faculty and students. For example, he provided integral leadership by editing seven faculty books (the most recent ones at Penn-State Harrisburg, *Teacher Education and Urban Education: The Move from the Traditional to the Pragmatic* (2002) and at St. Joseph's University, *The Politics of Inclusion: Preparing Education Majors for Urban Realities* (2005)). Both volumes provide orientations and parameters necessary to preparing education majors for urban realities and, most importantly, provide the means for faculty to foster and promote intellectually cohesive communities of thought and action. To this day, the examination of the relationship between spirituality in action and urban education remains a priority for Kanpol.

During the course of the last twelve years (2000–2012), Kanpol has been actively working on developing a Public Identity for those educators in higher education. He has championed an action-oriented approach for professors, beseeching them to retreat from their hallowed halls and to enter into the fray of the real world and to actively seek democratic and universal strategies for teaching and learning.

The abiding influence of Liberation Theology on Kanpol's thinking culminated with the belief that faith is unconsciously embedded into schooling. The presence of this liberation spiritualism in contemporary education has been referred to as "prophetic education" (Kanpol, 1998). In *Teachers Talking Back and Breaking Bread* (1998), Kanpol embraces the concept of prophetic education and expounds on this ideological alternative as a counterpoint to the educational Right and Left's notions of pedagogy and society. It is within this ideological context that Kanpol develops his epistemology relating to transformative intellectual and teacher as prophet. According to traditional critical pedagogy, the transformative intellectual is a teacher who is considered to be a political agent of social change. This educator is committed to incorporating all aspects of democracy into teaching activities, helping students understand and question historical constructs of schools and cultural systems and negotiating the realities of race, class and gender in the classroom. While retaining elements of critique, the new conception of the transformative teacher as prophet promotes an empathetic representation of educational hope, joy and enlightenment. This approach borrows lessons from religion vis-à-vis cultural transformation and applies them selectively to the classroom. Through this language of possibility and by way of understanding one's own voice, teachers and students progress through an agency of change that seeks to alter oppressive, social, cultural and institutional paradigms that shape and restrain different/other voices.

In Kanpol's article, "Reflective Critical Inquiry on Critical Inquiry: A Critical Ethnographic Dilemma Continued" (1997), Kanpol revisits his early experiences with discrimination at school, aimed at his religion and as his status as an immigrant, first in Australia and then in Israel. He basically recognizes that his academic output has been (and continues to be), in many ways, a reflection of his own personal experiences with marginalization. These lived experiences, he writes, provided him with the necessary foundations to observe and to examine the subordination of students and teachers in educational contexts. Observations made during case studies focused on how students and teachers' reactions exemplified forms of institutional and cultural political resistance. Within the scope of the same article, Kanpol eventually came to the understanding that school change and liberation can only occur when the educator and the student attain a level of intersubjective compromise, where personal voice and relationship to institutional and societal structure is negotiated within fair and democratic parameters.

As an example where intersubjectivity was not attained, he recounts an anecdote that took place at Tel Aviv University in Ramat-Aviv, Israel, where he, as a student teacher enrolled in the teacher education program, became embroiled in an ideological battle with a female professor and to a certain extent his female classmates. Despite his attempts to engage his professor and classmates in conversations on conflict and the feminization of teaching, he was refuted for being different and for being too passionate. The women were focused on a rational technocratic approach to education and were not interested in debating critical thought. As Kanpol (1999) recalls, any attempt to discuss criticality was smothered by the following superficial comments, "they said my posture wasn't correct, my tone was off and that I should have dressed differently" (p. 11).

He also recounts his struggle as a young teacher at the Gymnasia Realit High School in Rishon Le Zion, Israel, to establish his authority as a new teacher in a senior high classroom and as a recently hired teacher with an autocratic principal. In this instance, Kanpol learned about the challenges of dealing with the contradictory qualities of authority and autonomy in the schools. Just as the young student he was dealing with had to acquiesce to his authority, he, in turn, had to acquiesce to the principal's authority. This experience helped him understand the moral and ethical importance of developing a democratic vision of education based on compassion, hope and spirituality. Essentially, he came to believe that life can be better, more joyful and filled with hope and possibility.

Kanpol's numerous books reflect this personal journey, as he became a teacher prophet. In the course of them, he confesses to many of the contradictions and stereotypes inherent in his practice. For example, in *Critical Pedagogy* (1999, 2 ed.), anecdotes abound about his witnessing discriminatory and highly questionable pedagogical practices during his early years of teaching. More specifically, he writes about having witnessed sexism, patriarchal control, mechanistic teaching processes and learning activities. He also discusses his own quest for survival. *Breading Bread and Talking Back* (1998), for example, reflects his prophetic journey seeking empathetic and humanistic connections while seeking the promised land of democracy, fairness and inclusiveness for all students regardless of their race, class and gender.

As a professor of education and as a dean of education, Kanpol did his utmost to personify the qualities of a supportive, empathetic leader whose goal was to bring hope and joy into the academic context. Often working with tenure-track colleagues as well as tenured faculty, he instigated faculty-wide and community-wide initiatives that focused on creating positive change. At Penn State Harrisburg (now Pennsylvania State University–Capital College) and at Saint Joseph's University in Philadelphia, he challenged faculty to consider the moral implications of exploring liberal and critical perspectives of urbanity. He organized book clubs for faculty and introduced them to forms of cultural resistance, encouraging them to abandon academic competition, to build community around who they were rather than what they had achieved, and taught them how to approach democratic negotiation of collective writing. Unwittingly the faculty became involved in the process breaking bread; that, is, sitting down and discussing through open dialogue critical issues surrounding teacher preparation and urban education. At Indiana-Purdue Fort Wayne, he made forays into the community and for five years organized a Cabinet of the Fort Wayne Community Schools composed of superintendents, principals and lawyers whose aim was to discuss and analyze critical issues related to the curriculum and urban and rural schooling.

As an introduction to Kanpol's work, this short chapter deviates from a traditional presentation and integrates elements of a Skype interview conducted with Dr. Barry Kanpol during the 2012 Fall semester. By then, Dr. Kanpol's Deanship of the College of Education and Public Policy at Indiana University-Purdue University, Fort Wayne (IPFW) had been terminated. Reflecting the struggles that this transformative scholar-practitioner has grappled with, the question *"To what end do we do what we do?"* seems to be at the crux of his work as a critical theorist and as educational leader promoting a *Public Identity*. During the course of the on-line interview, the responses to the questions posed reflect Kanpol's personal, professional and academic journey and the development of his critical stance towards contemporary education. The accompanying annotated bibliography reflects this trajectory and the emergent philosophy that has characterized Kanpol's scholastic work.

THE EARLY YEARS: PERSONAL HISTORY, INSTITUTIONAL, AND CULTURAL RESISTANCE

An exploration of Barry Kanpol's formative years demonstrates how his personal history with alienation, oppression and marginalization impacted his academic work. Kanpol, like many other critical theorists such as Michael Apple, Henry Giroux, Maxine Greene, bell hooks, and Gloria Ladson-Billings, has been deeply affected by life history and significant experiences which have nourished his interest in critical educational theory (Heilman, 2003). The intersection of his early experiences with cultural and religious marginalization, his reoccurring conflicts with established educational institutions and his nontraditional career path have shaped his postmodern sensibilities relating to freedom and social justice. Like many critical theorists before him, Freire's (1974) emancipatory vision provided him with a solid direction, thus facilitating his examination of oppressive educational structures that undermine cultural and religious validity. For example, in his seminal work *Critical Pedagogy: An Introduction* (2nd ed., 1999) Kanpol discusses his personal experiences growing up in middle-class suburban neighborhoods in Melbourne, Australia and in Israel. His schooling experiences in Melbourne as a Jewish boy and, later on, as a sixteen-year-old professional Australian Rules football player with the St. Kilda team, were tarnished by the stereotypical views that other students and neighbors had about Judaism. More specifically, he notes that a defining moment during his childhood was the brunt of discrimination and prejudice he experienced:

> I have written about being Jewish. I have heard many racial and cultural epithets. Being in Australia, even though I grew up in privilege and went to a private school, I was often sanctioned because of my differences. I mean, they did not come to our house, we didn't go to theirs. Another example: I was an athlete. In the change room, the other men would leave me alone—they would not come in with me. Despite my talents, I was alienated because of my background. (B. Kanpol, personal communication October 30, 2012)

Despite his future scholastic abilities, he dropped out of high school in Australia:

> I dropped out of high school in grade 11. I did not like the way kids were educated. The emphasis was on achievement not who you were. I was very critical of the culture I was growing up in. That was difficult, critiquing my own Jewish culture and yet trying to find the positive in it. (B. Kanpol, personal communication, October 30, 2012)

Due to the diligence of his parents, he eventually graduated from the Walworth Barbour American International School in Kfar Shmaryahu, Israel. An accomplished athlete, he became the starting center of the school's basketball team and eventually received a partial scholarship to enter Tel Aviv University. He also played for the Israeli national rugby and cricket teams over an eight-year span from 1974 to 1982. Due to his sportsmanship, his school and university experiences in Israel were mostly positive.

Outside of school, though, his experiences in Israeli society were similar to the oppressive, defamatory experiences that characterized his time in Australia. In Israel, despite being part of the majority Jewish culture, he was treated as the Other and marginalized because of his accent. He recounts how a taxi driver told him that he could never be fully accepted in Israeli society because of his anglicized Hebrew accent.

After completing Teacher College in Israel, he moved to The Ohio State University in the United States to pursue a graduate degree. As a result of marginalized school experiences in Australia and in Israel, Kanpol (1999), through a critical reflective practice, identified five problematic elements in his school experience: the authoritarian stance adopted by teachers and the administration, issues relating to gender, the constant fear and temptation to cheat, the ever-present competition and omniscient presence of stereotyping anyone who was different (p. 3).

As a graduate student at Ohio State University, Kanpol was introduced to Paul Willis' Learning to Labour (1977), a standard text in sociology focusing on the class system in Great Britain, and Richard Bernstein's Restructuring of Political Theory (1978), a noted philosopher who engaged in cross-disciplinary analysis of philosophy. These books introduced a young Kanpol to a critical philosophy of education, which interrogated cultural reproduction and dominant ideology. These seminal readings provided him with the foundations to begin to understand and to legitimize his early personal experiences with discrimination and use the academic discourse of critical pedagogy to examine inequalities in education and in society.

In keeping with his childhood experiences with discrimination, Dr. Kanpol's early academic output dating from 1980s through to the 1990s explored institutional and cultural resistance as a means of empowering and validating nondominant worldviews. These writings also served as a platform for his future ruminations in the area of critical pedagogy, critical multiculturalism and spirituality. The articles and books produced during this time frame demonstrate a solid theoretical framework based on Freire (1974), Aronowitz and Giroux (1985), Laclau and Mouffe's (1985) and Mead's (1934) epistemologies. These philosophical foundations formed an integral component of his emergent critical multiculturalism focusing on similarities within differences, transformative intellectuals, and the possibility of hope and joy within the context of a historical legacy of enlightenment and progressive educational thought. Through the lens of the above epistemologies, the five problematic elements identified during his school years evolved into the following theoretical oppositions representing the nexus of his approach to critical pedagogy: schooling vs. education; control vs. democracy; authoritarianism vs. authority; individualism vs. individuality; deskilling vs. reskilling; and traditional literacy vs. critical literacy.

Kanpol's numerous articles, books and edited publications reflect the above dichotomies and critique the issues of race, class and gender as found within school systems. Despite the pressures he felt to conform to what was considered "normal" or "standard" within both secondary school and academia and in spite of the professional upheavals he experienced over the years, Kanpol was committed to airing his concerns about how society fails and oppresses children. Likewise, he was intent on advocating for and working towards the establishment of democracy, diversity and social justice in educational contexts.

MOVING FROM A POSITION OF CRITICALITY TO A POSITION ON CYNICISM AND JOY

As Kanpol's career as an educator progressed, he began moving beyond a position of criticality. In this regard, he was profoundly impacted by the works, positions and insights of Cornel West, bell hooks and David Purpel. West (1993) posited that the need for change is propelled by the democratic and ethical implications of a spiritual conception of what it is to be human. Frustrated over the crises within the political Left, decrying the loss of democracy and equity in the educational mainstream and Right, Kanpol embraced West's conception of the *human quest* (p. xi); that is, the spiritual conception of what it means to be human (p. xi). In hooks and West's book *Breaking Bread* (1991), the authors allude to sitting down, sharing bread and having a critical discussion about difference. For Kanpol, this was and is reminiscent of the Jewish Festival of Passover where breaking the traditional Passover Bread represents the hard-earned freedom of a nation bound to slavery. Kanpol reconceptualizes this political quagmire into a context of hope as it relates to the moral and the spiritual dimensions of one's life. This reframing has been redefined as *prophetic education.* Speaking of such, he said:

> When I moved from a position of cynicism to a position of joy, I was influenced by Cornel West and other kinds of writers, other theologians that moved into traditions that looked at faith-based issues or religious-based issues in different kinds of ways. And so the possibility of moving from cynicism to a position of joy and faith was used as an element for that. So that is what I mean by prophetic education. That's what I mean in using the class as a holy place. It's a place not only of criticism but of moving ahead to possibility, the possibility of hope. (B. Kanpol, personal communication, October 30, 2012)

Kanpol was also impacted significantly by David Purpel's (1989) book *The Moral and the Spiritual Crisis in Public Education* in his quest to determine moral and spiritual agency within the critical education tradition:

> I knew David well. We spent one year as postdocs with Svi Shapiro in North Carolina. David introduced me to spiritual education. You can see how this was important to me after my earlier experiences being a conflicted Jewish kid in Australia. He looked at one element of the biblical perspective and at the possibility, the need for spirituality. I wanted teachers to travel beyond the mundane. It is a complex issue, critiquing your own culture while at the same time accepting the positive in it. (B. Kanpol, personal communication, October 30, 2012)

In numerous publications during this time span (1988 to 1999), Kanpol pondered why only the Right claimed spirituality as their guide to right and wrong. Why, he wondered, did the educational Left ignore for the most part matters concerning spirituality? Ultimately, in *Teachers Talking Back and Breaking Bread,* Kanpol (1998) invites readers to explore a spiritual orientation to moral and just action in an effort to challenge, despite political orientation, institutional oppression, alienation and subordination.

As a critical theorist, Kanpol was able to analyze the patterns of alienation, oppression and discrimination experienced in professional contexts.

He asked difficult questions, challenging the administration at Saint Joseph's University, Penn State, and Indiana University-Purdue in Fort Wayne about mainstream decisions, posing the essential question, *"To what end do we do what we do?"* In his enlightened quest to support human agency and to engender knowledge mobilization, he recognized the established positions of the educational Left, the educational mainstream and the educational Right. A multitude of urban critiques (that is, the examination of political, social, economic and historical societal constructs) based on Marxian, Neo-Marxian, Post-Modern, Feminist, and Critical Multicultural analyses have all reached the conclusion that schools transmit and reproduce mainstream ideology to the detriment of the vast social, cultural, economic and political diversity present in contemporary society. Despite this conclusion, though, there is no established consensus regarding recommendations to challenge these institutionally constructed inequities. Despite the fact that the educational Left recognizes that schools are places of oppression, alienation, and subordination and that they must rectify historically constructed conceptions of race, class, and gender disparities, there is no clear stance on how to construct an inclusive vision of difference. Kanpol attributes this dilemma to academic competition and in-fighting over obscure philosophical texts that undermine a call to action. His more recent writing, as a dean, at Indiana University-Purdue, at Fort Wayne calls for a reform in higher education emphasizing an educational Public Identity infused with a moral imperative towards developing just, inclusive democratic paradigms for teaching and learning. Essentially, "to create a Public Identity is to challenge stagnant forms of essentialist university thinking (such as an essential neo-liberal logic) versus using the university as a collective public space. A Public Identity has an ethical component that builds on a collectivism of the future where universities/schools of education and the public coconstruct knowledge and where university people are not the "lone" authorities of knowledge. (Kanpol, personal communication November 27th 2012).

Speaking of his own experience in this regard, Kanpol (2012) writes:

> Being in a leadership position and having a critical background, I was able to ask difficult questions about the university Tenure and Promotion process. Why is there so much focus on publishing and grants? What about service and civic responsibility? What about the educator who is actively engaged in the community, doing good and improving peoples' lives? But the system will only tolerate you for so long. In fact, I just lost my job nine months ago as a Dean. A lot of that had to do with me really challenging the Administration on *"to what end do we do what we do?"* I was trying to link other issues they said they were dealing with to the reality of what went on with students in order to create what I call a Public Identity. Creating an identity within your college, of moving beyond a critique of accountability, of challenging that critique and moving beyond it. (B. Kanpol, personal communication, October 30, 2012)

THE IMPACT OF BARRY KANPOL'S WORK

Speaking about what he perceives as his greatest impact in education, Kanpol asserts the following, which is reflective of what critical theorists refer to as praxis:

> Working on group solidarity over issues, rising together in cooperation despite our differences and to build a faculty culture—that's the possibility of joy. In Fort Wayne, I instituted a principal advisory board so that faculty and school principals can join in working together towards fundamental change. That, to me, is putting critical theory into action. My other biggest impact has been the mentoring that I have done with junior faculty in various institutions. It is part of a reconceptualization, a philosophy of dealing with Public Identity, of challenging the critique and moving beyond the discourse. So, you translate that and put faculty into positions where they can make public statements about reforms. That to me is joy—a faculty that can be used as a mouthpiece for leadership, and building on that culture, the culture possibility and of moving away from the technocratic view of teacher education. At issue in Teacher Education is the dialectic between technocratic rationality and critical inquiry. Moving out into the public arena and creating your identity around that is a university issue not just a teacher education issue. If you take that to university—that becomes the possibility of joy. And that's where I want to go. Why are we doing what we are doing? Where is the place of democratic and civic engagement in society, in higher education? How do we create with one another and not impose on another. My strength is in educational leadership. I want to create and to question what it is that we do and why do we do it. (B. Kanpol, personal communication, October 30, 2012)

The above example of transformative praxis is reflective of Kanpol's impassioned commitment to moving beyond educational critique and embracing action-oriented strategies aimed at creating inclusive, democratic communities of learning.

The on-going debate over which way to disrupt and interrupt the structure of public schooling and, by proxy, higher education, has prompted Kanpol to voice a passionate plea for reform. His astute approach to praxis-oriented policies provides teacher educators with a depth and dimension that allows for intellectual exploration. Through his educational leadership, he has called for a critical democratic philosophy in which preservice teachers, teachers and teacher educator's dialogue over concepts of knowledge, power, experience and identity. His coedited books such as *Teacher Education and Urban Education: The Move from the Traditional to the Pragmatic* (2000) and *The Politics of Inclusion: Preparing Education Majors for Urban Realities* (2005) with his university colleagues demonstrate how praxis-oriented strategies connecting theory to field experiences, to self-reflection and self-inquiry are necessary to understand difference and reactions to difference. Of great importance is connecting curriculum to experience and identity through a metamorphosis of the traditional curriculum and the hidden curriculum with movement towards a pragmatic curriculum, which provides a venue for all voices to be validated and recognized. The aforementioned volumes attest to the importance of unifying the voices of like-minded colleagues in Teacher Education, and of searching for the similarities within differences in order to develop cohesive faculty-wide epistemologies focusing on libratory practices infused with the possibility of hope.

Kanpol's journal articles, reports and editorials are representative of a number of studies advocating a pragmatic praxis-oriented approach to critical educational theory. His collection of academic publications offers educators a discourse that encourages them to re-conceptualize pedagogy and its relationship to contemporary society. Through the inclusion of praxis-oriented cases studies, Kanpol proposes valuable strategies that have aimed to destabilize the impact of the neoconservative direction on the U.S. educational system over the course of the last generation. The development of critical pedagogical skills in teachers and students, tantamount to an intellectual reskilling, can inform these educators' progression to transformative scholar-practitioners weaving between research and practice, constantly working within communities to foster learning and a just, democratic society. Using a strong foundation of knowledge of content, methodologies, exemplary practices and diverse worldviews, these transformative educators can develop the necessary tools to critically reflect upon the ills of modern society and contemporary education. By being aware of inequities created by neo-conservatism corporatism and unabashed mercantilism which fosters intense competition, educators can launch into an engaged quest for a public voice and a Public Identity. As committed agents of change, teachers can begin to advocate for public policies and practices that benefit the students they serve, their local community, and their profession while striving to build a more just, inclusive, democratic community. Schools, Kanpol argues, should become forums where teachers practice institutional, cultural and political resistance by teaching students to deconstruct the reproduction of meanings such as individual success, competitiveness, egotistic desires, sexism, and racism, which emerge out of dominant ideology and worldviews. The aim of Kanpol's critical reflection is to empower educators through knowledge mobility (that is, providing accessible knowledge to communities in order to facilitate progressive, democratic change) to become autonomous agents, able to emancipate themselves from contemporary forms of domination and able to become more active citizens, eager and competent to engage in processes of social transformation. Kanpol offers educators and students a praxis-oriented, hope-infused, contemplative approach to conceiving, developing and acting upon critical pedagogy in the 21st century. His focus is to prepare future leaders who thoroughly understand, consciously apply, and intentionally use democracy, community, habits of mind, and advocacy in their professional lives.

The interview conducted with Dr. Kanpol provided a forum in which the main tenets of his epistemology, dispersed in his many writings, were brought to the forefront of the discussion. It is evident that his life history and many of his life experiences have impacted his academic output and cemented his interest in critical theory in the educational sphere. However, what distinguishes Kanpol from many other critical theorists is the attention paid to transformation framed by spiritual issues and notions of possibility and joy. Within this framework arises the concept of a Public Identity emphasizing the importance of accountability in Teacher Education. In his own words, what this means is as follows:

> It is all about critical ethics, joyous metaphors and working with community to create public hope. Let's make changes with society, not impose changes on society. Let's develop a public educational identity that is accountable, create leaders that are engaged in an agenda who can move beyond critique to the possibility of hope and joy. I am so much more than a critical theorist. (B. Kanpol, personal communication, October 30, 2012)

REFERENCES

Altenbough, R. (1987). Teachers and workplace. *Urban Education, 21*(4), 365–389.

Aronowitz, S., & Giroux, H. (19851992). *Education under siege.* West Port, CT: Bergin & Garvey.

Bernstein, R. (1978). *The restructuring social and political theory.* Pennsylvania: University of Pennsylvania Press.

Carlson, D. (1987). Teachers as political actors. *Harvard Educational Review, 57*(3), 283–306.

Dunne, J. (1993). *Back to the rough ground: Practical judgment and the lure of technique.* Notre Dame: University of Notre Dame Press.

Freire, P. (1974). *Pedagogy of the oppressed.* New York, NY: Seabury Press.

Heilman, E. (2003). Critical theory as a personal project: From early idealism to academic realism. *Educational Theory, 53*(3), 247–274.

hooks, b., & West, C. (1991). *Breaking bread.* Boston, MA: South End Press.

Kanpol, B. (1996). Critical pedagogy and liberation theology: Borders for transformative agenda. *Educational Reform. 46*(1), 105–117.

Kanpol, B. (1997). Reflective critical inquiry on critical inquiry: A Critical ethnographic dilemma continued. *The Qualitative Report, 3*(4). Retrieved from http://www.nova.edu/ssss/QR/QR3-4/kanpol.html

Kanpol, B. (1998). *Teachers talking back and breaking bread.* Cresskill, N.J: Hampton Press.

Kanpol, B. (1999). *Critical pedagogy. An Introduction (2nd ed.)* Westport, CT: Bergin & Garvey.

Kanpol, B. (Ed.). (2002). *Teacher education and urban education: The move from the traditional to the pragmatic.* Hampton Press.

Kanpol, B. (Ed.). (2005). *The politics of inclusion: Preparing education majors for urban realities.* Cresskill, NJ: Hampton Press.

Kozol, J. (1991). *Savage inequalities.* New York, NY: Crown.

Laclau, E. & Mouffe, C. (1985). Hegemony and the socialist strategy. London, UK: Verso).

Mead, G. (1934). *Mind, self and society.* Chicago, IL: The University Press of Chicago.

Purpel, D. (1989). *The moral and spiritual crisis in education.* West Port, CT: Bergin & Garvey.

West, C. (1993) *Prophetic thought in postmodern times.* Monroe, ME: Common Courage Press.

Willis, P. (1977). *Learning to labor: How working class kids get working class jobs.* New York: Columbia University Press.

ANNOTATED BIBLIOGRAPHY

Selected Books

Kanpol, B. (1992). *Towards a theory and practice of teacher cultural politics: Continuing the postmodern debate.* Norwood, NJ: Ablex Publishing.

This volume reignites the postmodern debate about education envisioned as an emancipatory practice imbued with a sense of hope and possibility. Based on the concept of similarity within difference, Kanpol attempts to move educational praxis towards a conception of a just, democratic, and compassionate society. Within this paradigm exists a healthy respect for cultural, linguistic, and historical distinctiveness juxtaposed with the vitality and viability of the common human struggle for freedom and social justice.

Kanpol, B. (1998). *Teachers talking back and breaking bread.* Cresskill, NJ: Hampton Press, Inc.

Kanpol situates the language and practice of critical pedagogy within the framework of moral and spiritual ruminations. This book serves as a connection between spirituality and the critical education tradition. As a counterreaction to the cynicism and criticality of the educational Left, Kanpol posits that Liberation Theology provides the parameters for a transformative, inclusive agenda bereft of the dense, abstract language of educational theory. Kanpol argues that re-democratization of social and educational paradigms can only occur through a synthesis of critical theory, postmodernism and Liberation Theology.

Kanpol, B. (1999). *Critical pedagogy: An introduction.* (2nd Ed). Westport, CT: Bergin & Garvey.

Written in a concise manner, this book serves as an introduction to the concept of critical social theory, its epistemology and its practice within an educational context. Taking its roots from Western Marxist and Postmodern epistemologies and their emancipatory themes, educators are called upon to question and to reflect on the inequities present within the categories of social class, race and gender and to contest the reproduction of traditional, dominant ideologies in institutionalized school settings. Through a praxis-oriented lens, Kanpol combines personal narratives, case studies and classroom experience to demonstrate the importance of developing a critical stance in contemporary schooling. An important discussion surrounds the practice of deskilling and reskilling teachers. By providing clear, concise definitions of abstract concepts, this volume promotes the use of critical pedagogy and recognizes the educational challenges of dealing with identity, race, culture and gender within contemporary educational paradigms.

Kanpol, B. (Ed.) (2002). *Teacher education and urban education: The move from the traditional to the pragmatic.* New York, NY: Hampton Press.

This edited volume was written as a departmental project when Kanpol was a member of Penn State University Harrisburg Education Faculty. As head of the education department, Kanpol galvanized the faculty to respond to concerns relating to teacher education, urban education and social change. Recognizing that the technocratic rational approach to teacher education does not prepare future teachers for urban education, each author re-conceptualized his/her own epistemology to better reflect the challenges afforded by the urban diversity of the 21st century. Within this critical reframing, faculty examined their own personal histories, course curricula, and their reproduction of economic, social and cultural capital. Bearing witness to the importance of progressive, enlightened thinking, this collective endeavour allowed for the development of institutional resistance whereby academics abandoned excessive and personal competition and committed to building a shared community imbued with democratic accountability and leadership.

Kanpol, B. (Ed.). (2005). *The politics of inclusion: Preparing education majors for urban realities.* Cresskill, NJ: Hampton Press, Inc.

Written during Kanpol's tenure at Saint Joseph's University in Philadelphia, this collective faculty volume explores the politics of inclusion and the inherent contradictions relating to social justice, inclusion and democracy in an urban university. At the crux of the discussion are the internal tensions and the marginalization experienced by the education faculty. Serving as a political and social treatise, the various chapters provide the platform upon which faculty members delineate disparities vis-à-vis race, class and gender at the university, in schools and in society. At a micro level the arguments focus on a preservice teacher education program, and at the macro level discussions emphasize the oppression and the alienation of the education department by the university system. Divided into two sections, Curriculum Integration and Educational Reform, this book provides a praxis-oriented framework necessary to preparing education majors for urban realities while fostering and promoting ideological cohesiveness for faculty.

Kanpol, B., & McLaren, P. (Eds.) (1995). *Critical multiculturalism: Uncommon voices in a common struggle.* Westport, CT: Bergin & Garvey.

Published in the Critical Studies in Education and Culture Series, this edited volume introduces the voices of fourteen educators who discuss their struggle towards achieving equity and democracy in schools and in public forums. As editors, Kanpol and McLaren establish parameters for new conceptualizations and new frameworks that promote educational and social emancipation.

The various contributors emphasize the ongoing social, cultural, and political reproduction that takes place in schools; contest the myth of the ongoing assertion of democracy present in the United States; and promote transformative critical multicultural pedagogy for all. The primary thesis of the book is that social justice is not evenly distributed and that a radical and profound change in educational and social structures is required to address this inequity. Within the framework of historical agency and a praxis of possibility, the authors espouse a critical or resistance multiculturalism led by transformative intellectuals grounded in critical pedagogy.

Batagiannis, S., Kanpol, B., & Wilson, A. (2012). (Eds.). *The hope for audacity: From cynicism to hope in educational leadership and policy.* New York, NY: Peter Lang.

This edited volume, part of a trilogy of books examining the educational conditions of the United States, addresses the absence of progressive educational reforms promised by President Barack Obama in 2010. In particular, the neoliberal, market-logic ideology of the Obama administration is critiqued via the lens of postmodern interrogations. The contributors to this book engage in critical, theoretical and practical discussions focusing on the disconnect between the president's former rhetoric and his present actions. In particular, his 2010 discourse based on reform, change and action is juxtaposed with his more recent regressive educational initiatives emphasizing competitive economic efficacy. Within this framework, the book challenges Obama to re-examine and to reaffirm his vision of hope and audacity. Despite being directive in nature, the authors move beyond critique to express their commitment and engagement towards working with President Obama's vision of *Yes, we can* within the context of educational reform.

Select Articles

Kanpol, B. (1988). Teacher work tasks as forms of resistance and accommodation to structural factors of schooling. *Urban Education, 23*(2), 173–187.

This article reviews research on the emergence of teacher movements that parallel the experience of industrial trade unions. In particular, references made to Carlson (1987) and Altenbaugh (1987) provide examples of how in industries and in schools workers both resist and accommodate the workplace. Most critical theorists agree that teacher resistance has to do with transformative awareness, a reflexive stance towards the dominant ideology and actions that subvert the ideology. Kanpol presents the conclusions of a case study in which he explored examples of teachers' subtle but subversive resistance to institutional, cultural and political disparities. Four teachers in an urbanized, unionized middle school context were observed and interviewed over a four month period. The article concludes with suggestions about the collection and interpretation of data relating to resistance and accommodation and the importance of promoting an emancipatory agenda.

Kanpol, B. (1989). Institutional and cultural politics resistance: Necessary conditions for the transformative intellectual. *The Urban Review, 21* (3), 163–179.

This article reviews the literature related to the nature of teacher resistance, the nature of cultural production and the nature of the transformative intellectual. Teacher resistance involves interrogating dominant ideology and disrupting established paradigms. Since teachers are at the forefront of the educational experience, their ability to act as transformative intellectuals is acknowledged and recognized. Distinctions are made between institutional political resistance, whereby structural facets of schooling are questioned, and cultural political resistance, whereby emancipatory critique provides opportunities to reflect, to act, to interrogate and to reconstruct cultural reproduction of dominant ideology. Within the scope of a case study conducted in a public school examples of institutional political resistance and cultural political resistance are delineated. The article concludes with a discussion of Aronowitz and Giroux's (1985) concept of transformative intellectuals and questions whether teachers are able to use critical language that is both political and pedagogical.

Kanpol, B. (1989). Incentives to alleviate teacher frustrations: Inroads to better work production for teachers and administrators. *Education, 109*(4), 469–474.

Referring to previous publications, which focus on teacher collective trade union movements as well as teacher transformative thinking, this article examines teachers' schoolwork as problematic and subject to analysis and critique. In particular, administrative ineptness and stagnancy is at the forefront of this discussion. A distinction is made between official teacher and pragmatic work zones. It suggests that teacher autonomy can be achieved through completing administrative duties within the pragmatic zone. Conclusions proffer suggestions to both administrators and teachers about conceptualizing work zones based on a unified democratic vision.

Kanpol, B. (1990). Self and community in a fourth-grade global education project: Necessary conditions for the emancipatory agenda. *The Urban Review, 22*(4), 267–282.

This article provides empirical evidence that the development of self and community in a marginalized school context is attainable. Mead's (1934) concepts of self and community form the basis of discussions which negate the inherent individualism and ever present negative competitive practices of contemporary educational practice. As a classic participant–observer, Kanpol observed a grade 4 classroom at Parkview Elementary School in Orange, California, during the 1988–1989 school year. This case study demonstrates the viability of counter-hegemonic platforms, which facilitate pathways between the self and community thus ensuring success for students. The concept of critical pedagogy becomes paramount in the development of intellectual resistance to a collective reinterpretation of the world.

Kanpol, B. (1991). The principal's "voice": A bundle of contradictions. *The Clearing House, 65*(1), 19–22.

Within the scope of two branches of critical social education theory (i.e., correspondence theory and cultural theory), Kanpol expounds on the impact of the principal's voice in an educational environment. He examines the messages conveyed to teachers and students by the voice of the principal and demonstrates how these messages affect relationships in the school. Of particular interest is the newness of the concept of voice within academic literature. In this instance, voice refers to meaningful dialogue reflecting meanings and interpretations of cultural history as well as shared visions of historically constructed relationships and practices of power. For example, the principal's voice can be posited within the framework of numerous interpretations: authority figure, humanist, coercion/power figure, moralist, worker and boss. Despite the contradictory interpretations of the role of the principal, it is recognized that respect for each individual's voice in the school is critical on all levels of the institutional hierarchy. By acting as a moral agent, the principal's voice can provide teachers and students with the hope that a just, inclusive, school culture is possible.

Kanpol, B. (1991). The politics of similarity within a pedagogy for the other. *The Urban Review, 24*(2), 105–131.

In this article, Kanpol focuses on similarities within differences in order to gain a more empathetic understanding of the Other. Recognizing Laclau and Mouffe's (1984) concept of the *democratic imaginary*, Kanpol refers back to teachers' histories and their relationship to race, class and gender. According to Kanpol, a focus on similarities within differences can be advanced as emancipatory possibilities for urban schools. Within the scope of a naturalistic study, the author discusses five ESL teachers and their struggles to democratize a traditional curriculum. The personal histories of these teachers denote that they have felt isolated and alienated within the school setting. Discussions surrounding the democratic imaginary, the intersubjectivity of teachers' lives as well as the tradition of resistance against traditional approaches abound.

Kanpol, B. (1992). Postmodernism in education revisited: Similarities within differences and the democratic imaginary. *Educational Theory, 42*(2), 217–229.

Herein, Kanpol argues that the deconstruction of difference by some postmodernists in education has not considered the exploration of *similarities* as exemplars of affirmations of community, dialogue, and identity. Here, Kanpol is referencing Laclau and Mouffe's (1985) concept of the *Democratic Imaginary*—shared democratic resistances and discourses in different places, forms and times. Kanpol situates the dominant theoretical theme of this article, similarity, within difference in the context of the democratic imaginary. Within the scope of a naturalistic study of five ESL classes, he draws parallels between critical pedagogical strategies that focus on the celebration of community, similarity and difference. Conclusions attest to the importance of exploring the cultural history of teachers and administrators in order to deconstruct the similarities within differences as part of an inter-subjective, counter-hegemonic, and postmodern political project.

Kanpol, B. (1993). The pragmatic curriculum: Teacher reskilling as cultural Politics. *Journal of Educational Thought, 27*(2), 200–215.

In this article, Kanpol discusses how teachers can become reskilled practitioners by questioning the hegemony of standardized curricula. Within the scope of cultural politics, this reskilling can facilitate the progression towards becoming transformative intellectuals. The notion of teacher cultural politics married to the concept of the pragmatic curriculum allows teachers to question and to become accountable for curricular choices. Three case studies illustrate how teachers create pragmatic curricula, develop their own critical skills and, most importantly, provide a voice for underrepresented populations. The themes of voice, similarity and difference emerge as important concepts central to the notion of cultural politics. Conclusions indicate that teachers who transform themselves from deskilled technicians to reskilled practitioners can examine and critique the socio-political environment in which curricula function.

Kanpol, B. (1995). Outcome-based education and democratic commitment: Hopes and possibilities. *Educational Policy, 9*(4), 359–374.

Kanpol analyzes outcome-based education (OBE) within a context of democratic hope and possibilities. Kanpol builds on Capper and Jamieson's (1993) position that OBE merely reproduces dominant ideology and power structures. The problematic struggle of postmodernist difference within a multiethnic society is at the forefront of this discussion. Basically, he asks: How can educational reform respect a multiplicity of narratives, identity and voices? He argues that if viewed through a critical pedagogical lens, liberating structures reinforcing success for minorities can be implemented into educational policy. In order to do this, Kanpol proposes twelve guiding principles based on critical, postmodern teaching processes. Praxis-oriented strategies connecting theory to field experiences, to self-reflection and self-inquiry are necessary to understand difference and reactions to difference. Of great importance is connecting curriculum to experience and identity through a metamorphosis of the traditional curriculum and the hidden curriculum to provide a venue for all voices to be recognized and validated.

Kanpol, B. (1995). Critical literacy. *Educational Studies, 26*, 76–84.

Kanpol reviews four single authored, coauthored and edited books by Peter McLaren. McLaren's books examine questions of difference and identity, analyze educational policies and comment on Freire's social revolutionary work. Recognizing that McLaren is a leader in critical education theory, this discussion focuses on his essential epistemology: the transformative postmodernism of difference, the development of critical pedagogy and the subsequent impact on contemporary educational practice. Kanpol adds to this discussion by introducing the concept of the spiritual and the moral within the tradition of postmodern thought. Through his commentary, Kanpol attempts to transcend the political impact of McLaren's work by exploring the relationship between spirituality and the various forms of oppression, subordination and alienation.

Kanpol, B. (1995). Inner-City realities: Democracy within difference, theory and practice. *The Urban Review, 27*(1), 77–91.

Within the lens of a critical ethnography based on Kozol's (1991) concept of savage inequalities, Kanpol discusses the necessity of creating democratic educational platforms in inner-city schools—and, in particular, the attempt to support democratic possibilities within the context of despair and disillusion. A study conducted by Kanpol in the notorious Watts neighbourhood of Los Angeles, California provides the context to discuss teaching experiences in an inner-city school and the emancipatory paradigm of hope and possibility. Holistic-Constructive principles juxtaposed with critical-democratic positions are posited as possible, though not exhaustive, guidelines for teacher education programs that specialize in urban education. The crux of this article lies in the critical need to address the undoing of oppressive, alienating and subordinating educational conditions by a process of re-conceptualizing the curriculum through socially negotiated value frameworks related to race, class and gender.

Kanpol, B. (1996). Critical pedagogy and Liberation Theology: Borders For a transformative agenda. *Educational Theory, 46*(1), 105–117. doi:10.1111/j.1741–5446 .1996.00105.x

Herein, Kanpol emphasizes the profound theological possibilities and implications of the critical pedagogy movement. Based on Kozol's (1991) analysis of inner-city schools in the United States, critical pedagogues have re-conceptualized structural school issues around race, class, and gender, much of it within a framework of hopelessness and despair. As a consequence of this analysis, the question *to* what *end* emerges as a central tenet in the discussion. The salient points of this article offer alternative ways to reflect upon what an emergent social transformation for schools would look like. Explorations of James Cone (1986) and Sharon Welsh's (1990) views of emancipation through the spiritual reality of joy and hope for transformation are posited as challenges against oppression, alienation, and subordination.

Kanpol, B. (1998). Identity politics: The dialectics of cynicism and joy and the movement to talking back and breaking bread. *Journal of Educational Thought, 32*(1), 57–74.

To what end do we do what we do? As the central tenet of this article, this question allows Kanpol to explore postmodern cynicism within a prophetic framework of possibility, hope and joy. Referring to bell hooks (1986) and Cornell West's (1991) analogy of breaking bread, Kanpol suggests that Teacher Education should be immersed in identity politics contextualized within theological traditions. By exploring personal narrative and reflection as a form of pedagogical reflection and interrogation, imminent changes to oppressive institutional and cultural structures can be implemented. Kanpol views Teacher

Education as having a messianic vision, where teaching can be transformative, innovative and creative. He invites students to connect with both cynicism and joy in their quest to achieve human emancipation.

Kanpol, B. (2002). Critical educational leadership: Put up or shut up. *Educational Foundations, 16*(1), 5.

In this narrative account, Kanpol asserts that critical pedagogy has failed to seriously challenge institutional structures of oppression, alienation, and subordination found in Teacher Education and in Higher Education. In order to do rectify this, Kanpol suggests that a redefinition of educational leadership using concepts derived from the recent work of Chantal Mouffe around the development of counter-hegemonic communities of *Antagonism vs. Agonism* and *Enemy vs. Adversary*. According to Mouffe, political engagement should be viewed as agonistic and adversarial rather than antagonistic and enemy-centric. In this manner, the development of adversarial relationships allows a democratic discourse in which the primary focus is to progressively challenge forms of institutional subjugation in order to create socially just structures. A critical narrative based on Kanpol's professional experiences as a university administrator provides the framework upon which the theoretical concepts are analyzed and discussed.

Kanpol, Barry (2010) True to self and the institutionalization of a new Public Identity: It's NOT only up to Barack Obama! *scholarlypartnershipsedu: 5*(1) 23–30. Retrieved from: http://opus.ipfw.edu/spe/vol5/iss1/3

Kanpol draws upon similarities between his own life history and that of Barack Obama's life history, educational philosophies and practices, and does so in order to discuss the contradiction of democratic hope within institutional educational practices. Kanpol states that educational leaders share one common trait with the U.S. president: personal commitment in the face of harsh institutional realities. By providing an analysis of the current educational reforms in the United States, Kanpol delves into the tension between democratic spaces and market driven forces and their impact on public schooling. Within the context of Giroux's (1988) concept of *transformative intellectuals* and Obama's electoral motto, *Yes, we can*, Kanpol calls for a renewal of the Public Identity of education by challenging oppressive school structures through action and critical understanding. Referring back to Cornell West's (1993) concept of prophetic education, he transposes the original title of Obama's book (*The Hope of Audacity*) and provides a framework for a renewed educational Public Identity based on integrity and democratic values. Underlying this treatise is a veiled criticism of the university promotion and tenure system based on publications and grant funding to the detriment of service work focusing on community initiatives and actions for the betterment of all. Within this perspective, Kanpol strongly urges the educational community to move away from academic criticism and to launch into engaged action.

Brady, J. & Kanpol B. (2000). The Role of critical multicultural education and feminist critical thought in teacher education: Putting theory into practice. *Educational Foundations, 14*(3), 39–50.

Within the scope of the postmodern lens, this article focuses on reform in Teacher Education. Transformative praxis focusing on critical reflection is posited as a progression away from the technocratic and limited approach adopted by most professors in higher education. The authors advocate for personal and institutional responsibility for social change. Stemming from this critical stance is the importance of personal and collective disclosures which are central to change and evolution. Further discussions emphasize the role of critical multiculturalism, critical feminist theory, and critical personal narrative in preservice and in-service teachers' conceptions of identity, public lives and civic responsibilities. At issue is the ethical awareness and practice of teacher education programs and their ability and inability to engage in issues relating to race, class and gender. The alignment of critical multiculturalism and critical feminism can provide teacher education with the parameters necessary to interrogate the assumptions propelled by dominant worldviews of a capitalistic society entrenched in individuality and competition.

Jenks, C., Lee, J. O., & Kanpol, B. (2001). Approaches to multicultural education in preservice teacher education: Philosophical frameworks and models for teaching. *Urban Review, 33*(2), 87–105.

The authors argue that minimal progress has been made in developing teaching practices and reconceptualising curricula to be more representative of the multiple voices and diverse realities of school cultures in the United States. Despite calls for reform, schools are still ill equipped to achieve the goals of equitable multicultural education. Since the majority of teachers are white, middle-class and monolingual, an important consideration is the development of cross-cultural competency for preservice teachers. Banks' models of multicultural curriculum and pedagogy and Grant and Sleeter's concepts of cultural pluralism demonstrate how schools can progress towards curriculums characterized by equity and excellence. In order to develop the skills, the knowledge and the attributes necessary for a socially, just, pedagogical environment, the authors posit that teacher education programs must focus on nurturing transformative practitioners with a commitment to critical multiculturalism.

Weisz, E., & Kanpol, B. (1990). Classrooms as socialization agents: The three R's and beyond. *Education, 111*(1), 100–114.

This article addresses the idea that curriculum should be conceptualized as a platform for active negotiation and for construction of knowledge. Based on data collected from two studies, the authors explore different types of curriculum within two instructional contexts: two elementary classes and a group of grade eight teachers. The authors present an alternative to the overt curriculum that is the specific, academic material that teachers transmit to students, which the authors refer to as the enacted curriculum. The enacted curriculum is defined as a document that facilitates knowledge construction through social processes. The authors discuss the social process curriculum as well as other types of enacted curriculum: pragmatic, unofficial, masked, social, and hidden. Conclusions indicate that an enacted curriculum, composed of the above interconnected elements, serves as a social process which conveys norms, behaviors, and values to students and to teachers. In order for change to occur, research in the area of curriculum implementation and the social process of teaching and learning need to be undertaken.

Articles About Barry Kanpol

Heilman, E. (2003). Critical theory as a personal project: From early idealism to academic realism. *Educational Theory, 53*(3), 247–274.

This article examines the life stories and significant experiences of critical educational theorists and explores the connection between their life history and emergent educational theory. Framed within the epistemological traditions of existentialist philosophy, phenomenology and hermeneutics, the author examines how belief systems, school contexts and power structures impact on race, identity and gender. In the section entitled *Early Idealism: The Making of Critical Theorists,* stories of marginalization and alienation abound. In particular, Heilman refers to Kanpol's statements relating to discriminatory remarks aimed at his Jewish culture made by friends, teachers and administrators during his school years. The author relates these discriminatory experiences to Kanpol's academic output which has focused on the oppressive power of school coupled with themes of marginalization and otherness. However, despite such troubling experiences, Kanpol, like many of his contemporaries, has been committed to establishing democracy, diversity and social justice within educational settings.

Pennycook, A. (1991). A reply to Kanpol. *Issues in Applied Linguistics. (2)*2, 305–312.

The author responds to Kanpol's analysis of principled postmodernism (the counter-hegemonic characteristics of political and critical applied linguistics) by revisiting salient elements of political and critical applied linguistics. Kanpol critiqued the notion of principled postmodernism stating that the absence of critical practice failed to generate a practical agenda for teaching. He had suggested that an approach based on the similarity of difference would support a critical practice of applied linguistics. However, Pennycook notes that his explorations of global English and applied linguistics reflect the discourses of colonialism and imperialism and their role in reproducing global inequalities. He provides solid, empirical arguments that support previous and present interpretations of principled postmodernism. In conclusion, the author recognizes the additive nature of Kanpol's deliberations and the fact that the discussion will provide direction for future examinations of critical applied linguistics.

CHAPTER 11

EVOLVING CRITICAL PEDAGOGY

Contributions From Joe Kincheloe

Todd Cherner, Rachael Gabriel, and Jessica Nina Lester

INTRODUCTION

Joe Kincheloe is a significant voice in the field of critical pedagogy in education. His work transcends traditional research boundaries and forges interdisciplinary approaches to conducting research. Herein, a brief summary of Kincheole's life is presented, followed by a discussion of some of the major themes that cut across his work. An annotated bibliography, which concludes the chapter, highlights some of his most cited works.

A SHORT BIOGRAPHY

Scholars around the globe have been captivated by Kincheloe as a writer, a speaker, and a human being who routinely pushed the boundaries of academic thought (Smyth & Brown, 2010). A number of tributes

Educating About Social Issues in the 20th and 21st Centuries, pages 217–236
Copyright © 2014 by Information Age Publishing
All rights of reproduction in any form reserved.

217

to Kincheloe, who died in 2008, are available online and in print. Many of which include personal anecdotes and biographic information about him, as it seems to have been difficult for those who knew him well to separate the remarkable man from his remarkable writing. As a leader in several fields of inquiry, his body of work is itself an example of the "bricolage" he advocated for within qualitative research. In this way, he provided an important example of the integration of life, inquiry, and scholarship. Biographical sketches that appear on his own Freire Center webpage (http://www.freireproject.org/content/joe-kincheloe-0), as well as a website designed in his honor by his longtime partner, Shirley Steinberg (http://joekincheloe.com/about), are summarized here in an attempt to outline the roots and inspirations of his work.

Biographical Information

Joe Lyons Kincheloe, Jr. was born in 1950 in Kingsport, TN, a small town in the Smokey Mountains region of East Tennessee. Raised in Sullivan County, a rural county that borders Kentucky, Kincheloe was the only child of two educators. His father was a principal and his mother a third grade teacher in the local school system. His parents were among the few Democrats in the region, and held strong commitments to issues of social justice related to race and class, though they were often in the minority. From an early age, Kincheloe, himself, was outspoken about his political views and dislike of segregation in schools. A combination of his outspokenness and mediocre grades led one teacher to tell him he would "never be more than a piano tuner," and encouraged him to go to vocational school. Kincheloe later wrote (in books and articles) critiques of, and new visions for, vocational education.

Up to the age of twelve, Kincheloe was his uncle's apprentice who was a traveling Methodist preacher. Though Kincheloe's reputation for powerful public speaking may have had its roots in this apprenticeship, he also learned that this path was not for him, and thus sought other ways to, in his words, "bring people together and move them." All accounts of his lectures and presentations indicate that he was able to do this with words in academia, but also had the power to do so with music.

At the age of 16, Kincheloe formed a four-piece blues band, named the VIPs that played regularly at school dances. This was the first of many bands he would play with throughout his life. The prolific writing he was known for as a scholar was matched by his equally prolific songwriting. When he died, Kincheloe had written more than 600 songs.

His pattern of writing for publication and his visionary leadership can also be traced back to the eighth grade, when he and a few friends started publishing and circulating a satirical newspaper. They published it under the name "DRUT" (turd spelled backwards), an early indication of his mastery of wit and humor as rhetorical strategies, as well as his ability to question and craft critique.

Kincheloe attended Emory & Henry College for his undergraduate studies, a small Methodist college in neighboring Virginia. While an undergraduate student, Kincheloe's rock 'n roll tendencies and political commitments reportedly got him put on probation for his long hair and propensity to take part in anti-war rallies (Steinberg, 2010). Still, he graduated with a degree in History and moved west towards the Knoxville, Tennessee area to work as a teacher and pursue graduate training.

Kincheloe worked as a middle school language arts teacher for four years, and a high school history teacher for two years, as he completed two master's degrees (in History and Social Studies Education) and a doctorate degree (in Curriculum and Instruction), all at the University of Tennessee. His master's thesis was entitled "The Camp Meeting and the Political Rally," while his doctoral dissertation investigated the evangelical camp meetings of fundamentalist Christians in the 1800s. Essentially, in his earliest academic writing, Kincheloe united his youth and undergraduate experiences with the Methodist Church, various teaching experiences, and his training as a historian. The combination of his degrees also foreshadowed how Kincheloe would write across disciplines and fields of inquiry throughout his career. His training as a historian aligned with the characteristic breadth of his arguments and depth of his analyses, as his work could rarely be contained in a single area of inquiry.

Kincheloe's first academic job was at Sinte Gelska College, a small school on the Rosebud Sioux Reservation in South Dakota. While there he began to research and publish about the disenfranchisement of Native Americans. He would continue to develop methods and ideas around subjugated/indigenous ways of knowing with his postformal theory of cognition (a postformal theory of cognition is one that challenges reductionist notions of intelligence that undergird much of cognitive development. This theory moves the conversation regarding cognition to include a post-Piagetian understanding of intelligence that takes up feminist and postmodern ideas.). Far from attempting to be an objective observer, Kincheloe embraced the opportunity to engage with the community. He worked to privilege the knowledge and perspectives of those he studied and to learn from and with them, arguing that other researchers to do the same.

Upon becoming a department chair at LSU, Kincheloe was charged with creating a doctoral program in curriculum studies. While at LSU he wrote two books: *Understanding the New Right and Its Impact on Education* (1983), and *Getting Beyond the Facts: Teaching Social Studies in the Late Twentieth Century* (1989). In the former book, he focused on the ways in which the conservative right threatened the future of public education, in this case in the 1980s. Tellingly, these are conversations still being had today.

After spending seven years (1982–1989) at LSU, he moved to Clemson University in South Carolina. While at Clemson (1989–1992), he met his life partner, Shirley Steinberg, at the Bergamo Conference, a radical Marxist feminist conference in Ohio. Ultimately, Steinberg and Kincheloe had a legendary partnership in life and work. They coedited a book series that includes over 400 volumes, and coauthored several books, and dozens of chapters and articles, while also raising four children.

After meeting in Ohio, Steinberg, and her four children moved to live with Kincheloe in South Carolina. As one academic position after another drew Kincheloe up and down the Eastern Seaboard to Florida International University (1992–1994), Pennsylvania State University (1994–1998), Brooklyn College (1998–2000), and the CUNY graduate center in New York (2000–2005), where he started a doctoral program in Urban Education, he and Steinberg made the moves together. In 2006 they moved to Canada, where Kincheloe held the Canada Research Chair in Education at McGill University in Montreal.

With his experience founding doctoral programs at two universities (Curriculum Studies at Louisiana State University, and the Urban Education Program at the City University of New York (CUNY)), and serving as department chair at two other universities (at the Sinte Gleska College on the Rosebud Sioux Reservation in South Dakota, and at Brooklyn College), Kincheloe founded the Paulo and Nita Freire International project for Critical Pedagogy at McGill in 2008. As the first and only project of its kind, the Freire Project (www.freireproject.org) is both a physical and virtual archive of global initiatives in critical pedagogy. Though Kincheloe had long been committed to ideals related to social justice and education, he was first introduced to Paolo Freire's *Pedagogy of the Oppressed* while completing his doctoral studies in Tennessee. Freire's ideas would inform Kincheloe's work throughout his career, as he too became a leading thinker in the area of critical pedagogy.

At the time of his death in 2008, Kincheloe was working on five books (his 56th through 60th books), editing more than eight books with Steinberg for the *Critical Counterpoints* series with Peter Lang publishers, and serving as the founding, senior editor of the *International Journal of Critical Pedagogy*. He had supervised more than 50 doctoral students and continued to teach graduate courses. His work continues to be published posthumously as collaborators see the latest in his enormous body of work through to publication.

MAJOR THEMES

Many credit Kincheloe with bringing critical theory to educational research and carrying forward the work of Paulo Freire. Yet, his work does not rest only at the intersection of critical pedagogy and educational research. Rather, Kincheloe broadened and extended the breadth of his work by underpinning each publication with major ideas drawn from the fields of psychology, sociology, history, political science, cultural studies, media studies, and economics.

Among some of the many approaches and themes that demand attention, and constitute some of his major contributions to the field, are as follows: (a) an ever-evolving criticality across areas of inquiry; and (b) a postformal theory of cognition; and (c) bricolage as an approach to qualitative research methodologies. Within these three broad themes are nested a range of topics and entire domains of inquiry for which Kincheloe is well known (the use of bricolage and interdisciplinary research methods, critiquing education and neoliberalism with a critical lens, rejecting positivism, and privileging nonwestern cultures' ways of knowing).

Indeed, it was his ability to write across fields, never narrowly within one, that makes his body of work unique and, arguably, so powerful and lasting. There are few, if any, scholars in the world who can so consistently write as bricoleurs to such astounding effect. No volume or essay of Kincheloe's is only about curriculum or methodology. Instead, he wrote about education via an historical, political, and critical lens. In turn, he wrote about early childhood education and media by providing an economic, social, and cultural analyses. Furthermore, he wrote about qualitative methodologies and argued that they should not be separate from critical theories, human rights, and social justice. He was a bricloeur par excellence.

An Ever-Evolving Criticality

In the context of Post-World War I Germany, scholars at the Frankfurt School—notably Max Horkheimer, Theodor Adorno, Walter Benjamin, and Herbert Marcuse—at the University of Frankfurt began discussing topics that analyzed the ways power and capitalism shaped the world. Their legacy is the development of critical theories that have been interpreted and developed across fields of inquiry. Kincheloe explained that pinpointing the exact definition of Critical Theory is not possible because of the multiple critical theories that exist—such as Critical Race Theory, Queer Theory, and LatCrit (Critical Latino Theory)—and that although each subgroup has its central tenets related to power, the lens used to understand those power dimensions is unique to its own stakeholders. As such, one specific way of seeing power is not suitable; indeed, it would provide a sorely limited, incomplete and mistaken view. Instead, Kincheloe (2008) described Critical Theory as being concerned "with transforming oppressive relations of power in a variety of domains that lead to human oppression" (p. 45).

In this way, Kincheloe did not see critical theory as an academic theory to be taught or used in isolation; rather, he saw it as a way of living, as a way of identifying human suffering and working to stop it. It is the notion then that critical theory can be used to make the world a better place for all peoples and cultures that is central to Kincheloe's work, and it is reflected in his work about a critical pedagogy.

A CRITICAL PEDAGOGY OF EDUCATION

In education, Kincheloe pioneered a critical pedagogy as a way of teaching that sought to inform students about power. Kincheloe saw the current education systems in the United States that use technical standards, which dictate what content and skills students must learn during their years of compulsory education (for example, The No Child Left Behind Act's reliance on state standards, the granting of waivers from the Elementary and Secondary Education Act for states that adopt the Common Core State Standards, and professional standards from sanctioned organizations such as the National Council of Teachers of English and the National Council of Teachers of Math, all constitute technical standards) as being used by dominant powers to only tighten their grip on society, not to create a more egalitarian society. With these critiques in mind, Kincheloe traced the roots of the current educational system in the United States back through the Industrial Revolution to its origins in European Enlightenment.

Kincheloe noted, as many have, that positivism was first developed as the European Enlightenment transitioned the world into an age defined by logic, rationalism, and scientific reasoning. In doing so, it created a belief that scientific methods used to study natural phenomenon could also be used to study social issues. Kincheloe critiqued positivism on the grounds that it did not consider how history, politics, and contexts influenced social phenomenon. Instead, he argued, positivism sought to remove all phenomena—whether social, natural industrial, etc.—from their natural environment and transplant them into a laboratory setting where they could be studied. In this way, positivism allowed scientists of the European Enlightenment to study all phenomena using a specific set of methods (such as Newtonian, Cartesian, and single-disciplinary perspectives). This system of inquiry did not value any methods outside of those used by European scientists and, subsequently, did not value knowledge that was created using alternative methods (including Eastern or tribal treatments for illnesses, religions, and gender roles). Kincheloe has also argued that any standards-based approach to education is built on a positivistic foundation.

In a standards-based educational system, the curriculum standards students are required to learn are consistent with the knowledge positivists have decided students must know. The use of standardized tests to evaluate student learning is seen by critical theorists as a decontextualized method for assessing the content students are asked to learn. The problem is that individuals who do not share the same racial, ethnic, or linguistic background or the same cultural knowledge, as the developers of the standards and tests are at a disadvantage. However, because positivism uses only empirical data to make decisions to assess students' cognitive abilities, such as test scores in this instance, differences between the developers' culture and that of the students are not considered. This lack of consideration is harmful to minority students as they are routed into lower academic tracks in school, such as remedial classes or courses that have lowered expectations based on their test scores. This tracking of low-performing students (typically minority students) does not allow them to engage with a rich curriculum, which then leaves them inadequately prepared for college or career success. Moreover, these same tests privilege high-performing students (typically majority students), which then further cements in place the current dominant ideology. In response, Kincheloe put forth ideas about teaching a critical pedagogy where teachers engage in reflection to understand the forces and influences that worked to shape their identity, recognize how the current educational system hurts massive numbers of minority students, use multiple perspectives when engaging knowledge with students, and become producers of educational research as one form of activism. By enacting a critical pedagogy, Kincheloe sees teachers as the agents who have the ability to make systemic changes vis-à-vis educational equity.

POSTFORMAL THEORIES
OF COGNITION AND DEVELOPMENT

Kincheloe envisioned an educational system with a wider view of learning and development than that implied by sets of standards and standardized tests. Informed by John Dewey, Lev Vygotsky, Kenneth Gergen, Jean Piaget and others steeped in constructivism and enactivism, Kincheloe proposed postformalism as a means of making sense of cognition at the intersection of cultural studies, critical pedagogy and cognitive science. Presenting a critique of fields such as educational psychology that have functioned to reduce the human mind to appear as ahistorical and acultural, postformal theory incorporates and attends to the historical, cultural, political, and economic nature of thinking and acting. Kincheloe wrote extensively about the ways in which empirical inquiry in fields informed by psychology often proceeded without conceptual and/or theoretical analysis, resulting in claims that presumed universal evidence and applications. For instance, he wrote about the construction of intelligence testing and the ways in which it has been framed as a neutral, ahistorical tool. Kincheloe argued that much of the research within the field of educational psychology (and the related cognitive sciences) constructs a mono-cultural value system, ultimately situated within Western modernist empiricism. Such an epistemological orientation, he argued, is one that fails to acknowledge the culturally embedded nature of cognition and of ways of being and doing in the world. This failure is evident in the assumptions and biases inherent in intelligence testing. The very construct of intelligence can therefore be used as a tool of oppression because it asserts a mono-cultural value system in the evaluation of people from different cultures.

Kincheloe's postformalism was part of his call for a reconceptualization of psychology; one in which feminist theory, indigenous ways of knowing and critical theories were embraced and served to ground a more interpretivist orientation to cognition. This particular perspective has provided practitioners and scholars with a framework by which to make sense of cognition as a culturally, historically, economically, and socially embedded construct produced, always already, in relation to power. As such, much like his other work, postformal theory of cognition takes up a critical approach and works against universal claims about selfhood and mental functioning. Ultimately, such a perspective invites scholars and practitioners to reframe their understandings of cognition, as Kincheloe sought to reveal and critique the very assumptions about cognition that sustain inequitable educational practices (e.g., assumptions related to intelligence). With new conceptions of the mind, Kincheloe called for an orientation to cognition that was democratic in scope. This democratic approach, spanning across disciplinary knowledge and methodological approaches to understanding and research, was one that served to critique the testing and curricular practices that serve to target and denigrate the everyday knowledge of students and teachers.

Critical Bricolage

Much of Kincheloe's work is a prime example of bricolage, as he exemplified the value in embracing multiple theories, disciplines and methodologies. Informed by the work of Jacques Derrida, Claude Levi-Straus, Norman Denzin, and many others, Kincheloe wrote extensively about the researcher as a bricoleur, with the research process conceptualized as a multi-methodological, multidisciplinary, and multitheoretical process. He proposed that educational researchers should engage in this multi-disciplinarity as they seek to make sense of the very structures and processes within which they are situated, never denying that knowledge is always already produced within a social, political, economic, and cultural context. Viewing the research process as inherently laced with power, the bricoleur recognizes their own positionality within the research process, and acknowledges the ways in which they shape and inform the interpretations proffered. According to Kincheloe, the researcher-bricoleur, then, must locate him/herself within the complex web of everyday life, and work to tease out the ways in which power is at play in the research process, as well as within the structures and institutions under examination.

Within this perspective, Kincheloe positioned research as an active process; one in which the researcher was part of the construction of knowledge, not simply an objective observer reporting some purported "truth." Adopting a critical bricolage approach allows educational researchers to reorient to how they engage in research, pushing them to engage with multiple methods, theories, and understandings. Kincheloe suggested that checklists and a priori guidelines, most often crafted in decontextualized ways, are not particularly useful as they are detached from local ways of knowing and navigating the everyday complexities of human life. Rather, he suggested that a researcher-bricoleur must seek to generate understandings in situated and layered ways. Ultimately, Kincheloe proposed that in order to engage in rigorous, sound and honest research, the researcher must be familiar with and capable of employing multiple methods and diverse theoretical frameworks that are responsive to varied contexts and local knowledge. Concomitantly, he argued, a researcher then often turns toward indigenous ways of knowing.

INDIGENOUS KNOWLEDGE AND RESEARCH APPROACHES

Shirley Steinberg (1999) noted that Kincheloe's first job in higher education, as a department chair for a small college on a Native American reservation, was perhaps his most important one as it had a formative influence on his research, writing, and ideas about indigenous knowledge and related methods for indigenous research. Part of Kincheloe's sociopolitical theory of cognition was the recognition that an individual's view of him/herself and others is influenced by social and sociohistorical forces. This, he argued, has implications both for the study and education of indigenous populations for numerous reasons, including differences in the idea of self and knowledge. According to Steinberg (1999), Kincheloe was concerned with developing a critical theory that worked, not to explain the world, but to guide the kinds of questions needed to explore it. The acknowledgement of indigenous knowledge allows teachers and researchers to attend to the issues of power and justice that shape the identity, experience, role and history of a subjugated group, as well as to explore the implications for multicultural education.

In many ways, Freire's notion that the oppressed required a specific pedagogy, one that explicitly identifies forces and systems of oppression and intentionally teaches skills, strategies and ways of knowing that lead to liberation, transformation and freedom, was applied to indigenous people and other subjugated groups by Kincheloe and those who took up his theories. Similarly, the notion that teachers must question, inquire and construct new knowledge (learn) is evidence of how Kincheloe privileged the knowledge of those presumed to be unknowing: workers, widgets in a factory-style system. Just as he noted that education for work would not change unless the workplace did, he pointed out that teaching would not change unless teachers were allowed to practice pedagogies of freedom: that is, to become researchers and scholars in their own right. Kincheloe's efforts sparked a body of research and publications around theories and methods for teachers to act as researchers and scholars in order to transform education. In his writings on standardized testing, multiple-choice indicators of achievement, and the re-emphasis on rigor and standards in the 1980s, 1990s and 2000s, Kincheloe called for teachers to demand and embrace the professional culture of researchers, rather than being ravaged or colonized by outside experts who ignore their practical knowledge, thereby beginning cycles of institutionalized oppression.

Along with critical teacher scholars, truly progressive teacher scholars would be incapable of stooping to a one-size-fits-all curriculum, or bowing to the decontextualized micro-information so often available as "student data" or test results, rather they would understand how and why curriculum should be responsive to students, and would know how to ensure this responsiveness in everyday interactions with students. Ideally, they would research their own professional practice and engage with research conducted by professional researchers, not because it was better or more rigorous, but because it offered perspectives on the forces shaping education that might not be within their current view. Again, ideally, they would understand the contributions they could make to the field and reject the idea that an outside expert "staff developer" could come with no understanding of their particular knowledge and experiences, and teach them something. Like workers in Kincheloe's re-envisioned workforce, teachers would know, embrace and use their own power and expertise in ways that transform students' experiences and opportunities, as well as their (teachers') relationships to those currently viewed as "experts" and "authorities" on the educational systems they live in each day.

A CRITICAL PEDAGOGY OF WORK

One of the core principles of Kincheloe's approach critical theory involved questioning the idea that North American and European societies were free or democratic. In that regard, during the 1990s, Kincheloe explored the current and possible roles of vocational education in a democratic society. He argued that vocational education as we know it in the United States is part of a system of inequality that sorts students based on class, race, and narrow measures of academic achievement into different tracks with different opportunities. He further analyzed the ways in which the vocational curriculum privileges reproduces the qualities and behaviors of menial workers, those that could be managed and would be loyal, punctual, and unquestioning. Rather than engaging the market economy version of vocational education, Kincheloe questioned the rationality of the entire concept of "human capital" and the need for a skilled workforce to carry out the ideas of an enlightened upper class of engineers, politicians and business owners. Indeed, he suggested that workers themselves (and in other work of his, this extended to teachers and students) be researchers and scholars in their own right—that they should have a choice in what they learn and how they learn it, and that their ways of knowing and practical experience should be integrated into academic pursuits.

Drawing on some of the same principles he highlighted in his explorations of indigenous knowledge, Kincheloe suggested that the knowledge and ways of knowing associated with "work" in a democratic society should not be limited to workers, nor should workers be limited to an impoverished curriculum designed to subjugate versus liberate them. His argument stretched from analyses of workplace routines to vocational curricula to case studies of factories where workers manage themselves and are part of the leadership structure of the company they support.

Above all, Kincheloe warned that schooling is not and never can be value-free and politically neutral. Every aspect of the way we "do school" can be examined and reexamined in a struggle towards a more just, free and/ or democratic vision of education. He traced the systems of inequality from education to the workforce by deconstructing the conditions, roles, and responsibilities of workers. The unifying theme between the study of work and critical pedagogy was simple: Kincheloe argued that if schools were to be reformed, so must the workplace, and vice versa.

Within this line of research, Kincheloe argued for an integration of vocational education within academic tracks and the integration of the goal of preparing citizens, rather than workers, to vocational tracks. This integration of the skills, knowledge, and ways of knowing would create greater possibility for democratic workplaces in which workers self-manage, managers are directly involved with work sites, and everyone has access to a problem-centered, real-life, applied curriculum. These, according to Kincheloe, are the building blocks of a democratic society, in which schools prepare citizens, not cogs in a wheel. In this way Kincheloe's research and writing on preparation for work and the work place was the nexus of his writing on curriculum theory, indigenous/subjugated ways of knowing, and critical social theory in democratic societies.

Teachers as Researchers

The encroachment of positivism into education, as supported by federal educational policy, has reduced teaching to students learning standards and being evaluated using standardized tests. In this system, *so-called* "educational experts" create and agree to academic standards that states adopt and require to be taught, and they also develop the strategies for how best to teach their standards. Additionally, testing companies are hired by states to develop assessments aligned to the standards, which students must take and pass, and these tests are used to hold students and teachers accountable for learning and teaching. Kincheloe argued that this style of education only prepares students to be future workers who can follow instructions and not question authority. Standards-based education does not allow for students to explore multiple perspectives related to historical events or feel they have a voice in how knowledge is created. Rather, it uses "accountability" as a guise for controlling what students learn and how teachers teach; in doing so, it paves a path for "educational experts" and testing companies to make large profits. To break this insidious cycle, Kincheloe argued teachers must become educational researchers.

Kincheloe saw teachers as being in the best position to conduct educational research because of their everyday lived experiences in classrooms with students. For example, when "educational experts" who are removed from the classroom create methods for how to teach a standard, they are not considering who the students are; rather, they are prescribing a one-size-fits-all strategy for teaching a standard. This practice does not consider students' diversity, students' learning styles, or students' background knowledge; rather, it aligns with positivism by implying that there is only one best way to teach a particular standard. However, if teachers become researchers, they could work with students to discover the best methods for teaching the content, differentiate those methods for individual students and classes, and report their findings. In this way, teachers and students become active participants in creating knowledge. The works included in this theme center on how teachers can be empowered by being practitioners of research and how this empowerment can move education away from its current positivistic culture of testing and standards, and one-size-fits-all "best practice" approaches.

REFERENCES

Kincheloe, J. L. (1983). *Understanding the new Right and its impact on education.* Bloomington, IN: Phi Delta Kappa.

Kincheloe, J. L. (1989). *Getting beyond the facts: Teaching social studies in the late twentieth century.* New York, NY: Peter Lang.

Kincheloe, J. L. (2008). *Critical pedagogy: Primer.* (2nd ed.). New York, NY: Peter Lang Publishing.

Steinberg, S. (2009). Joe Kincheloe. Retrieved from http://www.freireproject.org/content/joe-kincheloe-0
Steinberg, S. (2010). Joe L. Kincheloe. Retrieved from: http://joekincheloe.com/

ANNOTATED BIBLIOGRAPHY

Herein is an annotated bibliography of some of Kincheloe's major works, including some of his most recent writings. Due to his prolific productivity this list should be viewed as highly selective. Included herein are many of his most commonly cited publications, as well as some that others have identified as seminal.

Kincheloe, J. (1995). *Toil and trouble: Good work, smart workers and the integration of academic and vocational education*. New York: Peter Lang.

First published in 1995, *Toil and Trouble* is currently in its third edition and was an early (the 7th) volume in the *Counterpoints: Studies in the Postmodern Theory of Education* series coedited by Kincheloe and Steinberg. In this book, Kincheloe described the political and social factors that connect schools to the economy and thus inextricably link school reform to workplace reform. He described the history and current systems of vocational education as separate from academic education and argued that a free and democratic society is consistently thwarted by systems of economics and education that divide the population into workers and managers; with separate and unequal education, workplace conditions and life prospects. In the spirit of critical bricolage, and as was his custom as a historian, Kincheloe insisted on the need to study the interactions of what it means to "work" and what it means to be educated in preparation for the workplace within an economic, political and sociocultural context. Rather than centering schooling, or work conditions, or economic factors in school, he insisted on the inseparability of school and work, and suggested revisions of both for the improvement of democracy. As he noted in the introduction to the book, the central question he explored is "If we possessed a vision of good work and economic democracy, what type of education would we need to prepare students for such a reality?" (p. ix).

Using a postmodern critique and critical theory, Kincheloe deconstructed the current reality of school and work and described an alternative vision. In this alternative, vocational and academic education would be integrated, for everyone's benefit. The knowledge and ways of knowing of subjugated workers and those assumed to be un-intellectual were viewed by Kincheloe not only as valid but vital to understanding and contributing to a workplace. Kincheloe described what role "smart workers" could play in productivity and democracy. Using the example of car factories where workers self-manage, Kincheloe described "smart workers" as skilled in communication, problem-solving, analysis—all those skills that had been reserved for managers, as workers were only taught to be managed: docile, compliant, and loyal. Essentially, then, managers would not be prepared to "manage" their workers, but rather to facilitate the efforts of workers who are uniquely prepared to "manage" themselves and their colleagues. If smart work were the goal, Kincheloe asserted, the lines between vocational and academic education would have to fade, as would the social differences and ways of preparing students in vocational or academic disciplines. Instead, an authentic, problem-based curriculum would have to emerge in which heterogeneous, rather than homogenously tracked groups would be most successful because the schoolwork they face would be complex and engaging.

Kincheloe, J. L., Steinberg, S. R., & Gresson, A. D. (Eds.) (1996). *Measured lies: The bell curve examined.* New York, NY: Palgrave MacMillan.

Within this edited volume, Kincheloe, Steinberg, and Gresson take on the highly controversial and popular work of Herrnstein and Murray (1994) entitled *The Bell Curve: Intelligence and Class Structure in American Life.* Herstein and Murray's work suggested that certain groups of people are unable to learn because of genetic factors linked to race. Thus, they argued, federal funds should not be spent on educating the presumably uneducable. Kincheloe and colleagues mounted an unabashed critique of this work, exposing the lies that were laced throughout Herrnstein and Murray's text. Within this edited volume, Kincheloe, Steinberg, and Gresson invited authors such as Henry Giroux, Michael Apple, William Pinar, Peter McLaren, Yvonna Lincoln, among many others, to respond to each chapter in *The Bell Curve.* In this way, this volume served to deconstruct the lies that were positioned as "truths," the latter of which constituted ethnocentric, racist claims couched as empirically grounded. The cultural capital inherent in claims of intellectual superiority, test scores, the very construct of intelligence, IQ tests, and various educational practices that define for others a single definition of success were made explicit, with each contributor teasing out the ways in which racism and intelligence were coupled and neutralized through supposed scientific evidence. Ultimately, within this volume, Kincheloe and his colleagues illustrated the ways in which "cognitive reductionism" (p. 37) serves to relegate certain groups of children as inept and not worthy of equitable educational access. Kincheloe acknowledged that the rejection of cognitive reductionism would surely agitate elites who consider their work to be brilliantly cutting-edge and locate themselves as the best and brightest.

Ultimately, Kincheloe and his colleagues essentially "reject[ed] the evaluation of students against a single standard of higher-order cognition" (p. 37).

Kincheloe, J. L. & Steinberg, S. R. (1998). Addressing the crisis of whiteness: Reconfiguring White identity in a pedagogy of whiteness. In J. L. Kincheloe, S. R. Steinberg, N. M. Rodriguez, & R. E. Chennault (Eds.), *White reign: Deploying Whiteness in America* (pp. 3–29). New York, NY: St. Martin's Press.

Rooted in the disparities between Whites and people of other cultural backgrounds, Kincheloe and Steinberg put forward a "pedagogy of whiteness" to help Whites understand how they are advantaged in Western societies. Although White supremacy began during the European Enlightenment, it has manifested to such a degree in modern society that White cultural capital—as reflected in the types of knowledge valued in schools and the methods used for scientific experimentation—has whitewashed society insomuch that Whites are unable to see its impact. In fact, when individuals claim neutrality by being "colorblind" they have become so saturated in whiteness that they are no longer able to see its influence. It is at this point that a "pedagogy of whiteness" is needed. Within this pedagogy, Kincheloe and Steinberg's aim was not for Whites to renounce their race; rather, they wanted them to reconceptualize their own ethnicity by understanding the privileges attributed to their race, engaging the perspectives and knowledge of diverse populations, and committing to living a life of antiracism and social justice. By taking these steps, Kincheloe asserted, Whites will hopefully begin to positively reconstruct a White ethnicity.

Semali, L. M., & Kincheloe, J. L. (1999). (Eds.) *What is indigenous knowledge?: Voices from the academy.* New York, NY: Falmer Press.

In this edited volume, Semali and Kincheloe and their contributors highlighted the central place of indigenous ways of knowing, being, and producing knowledge. The text served to highlight the ways in which modern, grand narratives, steeped in Westernized notions of knowledge, act to locate the knowledge and very personhood of the "other" as subordinate. Semali and Kincheloe warned the reader early on against the romantic ways in which the very term "indigenous" has been taken up in modern society, with such "knowledge" often constructed as "primitive, the wild, the natural" (p. 3). The authors highlighted that such orientations to indigenous ways of knowing have resulted in Westerners viewing the indigenous other as "less than" and thus deserving of a condescending attitude. Semali and Kincheloe called for an examination of the cultural, political, social, and historical ways in which the inclusion of indigenous ways of knowing benefit the academy. The introduction of this volume provides a prime example of the ways in which Kincheloe remained committed to being explicit about his own positionality, as he includes an explicit discussion of his personal history and the ways in which he seeks to monitor his own relationship with indigenous culture and knowledge. Ultimately, the text serves to invite the reader to consider how indigenous knowledge is a rich resource for "any justice-related attempt to bring about social change" (p. 15). The epistemologies deemed most appropriate by the academy, those often in opposition to indigeneity, are put into question, as the contributing authors challenge what has been cast as "normal science" (p. 15).

Kincheloe, J. (2001). Describing the bricolage: Conceptualizing a new rigor in qualitative research. *Qualitative Inquiry, 7*(6), 679–692.

Beginning by defining a *bricoleur* as "a handyman or handywoman who makes use of the tools available to complete a task" (p. 680), Kincheloe framed a debate about the rigor of researchers engaging in either disciplinary or interdisciplinary research. Coming from a perspective that states nothing is truly objective and all research can fit into a specific context, Kincheloe perceived researchers of specific disciplines as reducing a phenomenon from its context and limiting their research methods to ones that aligned with only their field. Kincheloe countered this research approach by supporting an interdisciplinary style that requires researchers to employ the epistemologies, ontologies, philosophies, and research methods of multiple disciplines to study phenomena. This interdisciplinary approach suggests that knowledge is not a fixed entity; rather, knowledge is continually changing based on its context. As such, an interdisciplinary approach is inherently more rigorous than one that de-contextualizes or takes only one view of the subject of inquiry. Kincheloe argued that an interdisciplinary approach is necessary to examine the complexity of a given phenomenon. Thus, methodological bricoleurs, who employ multiple perspectives and methodologies, have access to a new and more valid form of rigor in qualitative research.

Kincheloe, J. L. (2003). *Teachers as researchers: Qualitative inquiry as a path to empowerment* (2nd ed.). New York, NY: Routledge.

Beginning by outlining how positivism has influenced contemporary education, Kincheloe argued that teachers must become active educational researchers in order to democratize schools and teach students different knowledge paradigms. To ground his position, Kincheloe illustrated how positivism has promoted a standardized version of education as reflected in public education's current standards movement, which relies on high stakes tests to quantifiably measure student learning. Moreover, Kincheloe connected positivism's support for standardizing education to the work of "expert" educational researchers by explaining how quantitative research, which does not consider contextual factors and relies on reductionism to simplify phenomena to be studied, is the only type of research valued in contemporary education circles. In this positivistic system, teachers and students are reduced to engaging only the type of knowledge that will result in increased test scores. To democratize education, Kincheloe argued for teachers to become researchers who engage multiple disciplines to construct knowledge about their own practices. Although Kincheloe admits findings from action research lack generalizability, he argued generalizability is not the goal of action research that is conducted to inform the researcher's own practice. Further, he asserted that teachers who engage action research will uncover the power structures embedded in education and improve their instruction. Kincheloe concluded his book by offering a sample syllabus of a Foundations of Teacher Research course that would teach the action research skills teachers need to begin transforming education.

Kincheloe, J., & Berry, K. (2004). *Rigor and complexity in educational research: Conceptualizing the bricolage.* New York, NY: Open University Press.

In this coauthored volume, Kincheloe described the power of bricolage to expand research methods. Kincheloe, like Norman Denzin and Yvonna Lincoln, defined the term by citing its meaning in French. A *bricoleur* is a handyman who pragmatically uses whatever tools are available to complete a task. In qualitative research, bricolage is the process of using multiple methodological strategies as they are needed in the process of research. Rather than being controlled or predictable, the research situation is viewed as always unfolding and complex. He argued that moving towards bricolage involves a new level of researcher self-awareness and thus a new effort to maintain theoretical coherence. In this way, he highlighted the need to acknowledge research as a "power-driven act" in which researchers have to abandon the search for realism and claim a focus on their own position and how it shapes the production and interpretation of knowledge.

The next three chapters are used to explain the ways in which rigor and complexity are enhanced, rather than muddled, by a bricolage approach. He provided a critique of the traditional monological scientific strategies that attempt the "faux certainty of reductionist de-contextualization" (Kincheloe, 2004, p. x) in the name of objectivity and experimental design. Instead, Kincheloe suggested that bricolage is a way to construct a "practical science of complexity" (p. x), a way to employ forms of knowledge other than those traditionally associated with one discipline or another. In this way, Kincheloe demonstrated the possibilities of bricolage in his work on indigenous research methods and expressed his own commitments to identifying and describing disprivileged ways of knowing, especially by those employed by groups who have traditionally been marginalized and/or exploited. He argued that bricolage provides a way for new levels of analyses, for new kinds of data, and a new way of expressing what it means to be rigorous in qualitative research.

He then explored how research traditions and ways of identifying and positioning an object of study differ across disciplines, illustrating how they have functioned to exclude subjugated and indigenous insights in favor of a "Eurocentric, patriarchal, class elitist, and reductionistic lens" (p. xi) in which researchers perform and report research on others on their [the researchers'] own terms. Rather than clinging to disciplinary boundaries by tradition, pride or inertia, he argued that these boundaries should evolve along with the world around them.

The latter half of the book includes chapters by the co-editor, Kathleen Berry, who grounded Kincheloe's theoretical arguments by describing real examples and applications of bricolage. Her final chapters outline the structures of a bricolage approach and ways of systematically increasing complexity in qualitative research.

Kincheloe, J. L. (2008). *Critical pedagogy: Primer.* (2nd ed.). New York: Peter Lang Publishing.

In his introduction to critical pedagogy, Kincheloe first explained how we live in an age of positivism that uses reductionist research techniques to boil all phenomena down into bits of unquestionable knowledge. As related to education, power wielders identify the knowledge that students "need" to learn, package it as technical standards, and require it be the basis of achievement tests. In turn, these positivistic standards become the "essential knowledge" taught in schools. To counter such practices, Kincheloe drew on the work of criticalists—leaning heavily on the Frankfurt School Scholars, Paulo Freire, W. E. B. Du Bois, and Antonio Gramsci—to argue for the importance of expanding, rather than reducing what counts as knowledge and demonstrations of learning. He argued that it is important to comprehend how history, context, experience, personal identity, and power all interact with one another to form people's webs of consciousness, and that this shapes identities, societal politics, and control over how knowledge is produced and taught. With this understanding, Kincheloe urged individuals to use the bricoleur's interdisciplinary approach for understanding phenomena and to engage Freire's "radical love" to aid the oppressed. Radical love is not simply a term to be used or a theory to be memorized; rather, radical love speaks of a way of living in which individuals express their care, concern, and love for others who exist in oppressive environments. To engage radical love, individuals must rethink their personal identities, the types of knowledge they value, their actions in society, and what they can do for suffering people. In this way, critical pedagogy is dedicated to making the world a more egalitarian place.

Kincheloe, J. L. (2009). Contextualizing the madness: A critical analysis of the assault on teacher education and schools. In S. L. Groenke & J. A. Hatch (Eds.), *Critical pedagogy and teacher education the Neoliberal era* (pp. 19–36). New York, NY: Springer Publishing Company.

In this book chapter published posthumously, Kincheloe opened with a critique of how positivistic reductionism has resulted in an assault on education. In reaction to it, Kincheloe wanted teachers to engage students in a rigorous curriculum rooted in multiple, complex perspectives vis-à-vis knowledge. Kincheloe believed this type of teaching would result in the world becoming a more egalitarian place. To ground his position, Kincheloe first traced how early 20th century anticolonialist movements gave rise to the 1960s U.S. Civil Rights Movements. In reaction, the "Recoverists"—the controlling class generally consisting of White, heterosexual, affluent, Christian males—reframed the argument in the 1970s on the grounds that government programs related to affirmative action and multiculturalism were destroying America's most "treasured values" (p. 22). An obvious tension then developed between minorities and affluent, White Christians. Over the last several decades of the 20th century, the minority voices and perspectives lost the momentum gained during the 1960s, and Kincheloe explained how right-wing politicians and fundamentalist Christians seized the loss to advance their agenda of rational irrationality, anti-intellectualism, and positivism through policies such as the No Child Left Behind Act. To reverse this tide, Kincheloe urged teachers to engage a critical pedagogy, both to understand society's power structures and use such understanding to reshape the world.

Kincheloe, J .L. & Tobin, K. (2009). The much exaggerated death of positivism. *Cultural Studies of Science Education. 4,* 513–528.

In this 2009 article, Kincheloe and Tobin presented an overview of positivism to argue that positivism's claim to be scientific objectivity is false. Kincheloe and Tobin first provided an overview of positivism. Tracing positivism's roots to scientific reasoning and empirically-based research methods, the authors outlined how positivism is presented as an objective practice for scientific investigation that is generally accepted by Western scholars as the "correct" way to conduct research. The authors further substantiated their definition of positivism by discussing its central tenets. To defend their claim that positivism is a contradictory science, the authors explained how positivism removes the context from the study by not considering the temporality or politics of the investigated phenomenon, the researcher's reasons for conducting the research, or the perspectives of non-Western cultures. The authors view such omissions as the withholding of necessary information needed to deeply comprehend the research, which results in "crypto-positivism." This crypto-positivism is contradictory in that by removing the investigation's context to claim objectivity, researchers are able to manipulate their findings by omitting factors that influence their study.

Kincheloe, J. L., & McLaren, P. (2011). Rethinking Critical Theory and qualitative research, *Key Works in Critical Pedagogy*, *32*, 285–326.

In response to capitalism's globalization at the turn of the 21st century, Kincheloe and McLaren put forth a reconceptualization of critical theory. To do so, the authors outlined the evolution of critical theory and offered broad definitions of the theory's central tenets. The authors then discussed the role that critical hermeneutics and critical ethnography play in critical theory, arguing that all interpretations of culture are political and are part of specific historical and political contexts. However, Kincheloe and McLaren recognized that the epoch we live in, commonly referred to as a postmodern period, coupled with new technologies, including videos, the Internet, and digital images, has changed traditional methods of domination into a *hyper-reality*. This hyper-reality saturates individuals with messages engineered by capitalist organizations to control and exploit the global labor markets. Kincheloe and McLaren concluded that it is the work of criticalists to expose the manipulation and exploitation of the global workforce by transnational capitalists to end the dominant ideologies and hegemonies from continuing to worsen working conditions for laborers.

Kincheloe, J. L. & Steinberg, S. R. (2011). A tentative description of postformal thinking: The critical confrontation with cognitive thinking. In K. Hayes, S. Steinberg, & K. Tobin (Eds.), *Key Work in Critical Pedagogy: Joe L. Kincheloe* (pp. 53–76). Boston, MA: Sense Publishers.

Critiquing Piaget's theory of cognitive development on the grounds that it does not consider the context of a person's environment and reduces knowledge development to a series of stages, Kincheloe and Steinberg put forth their concept of postformal thinking. To explain postformal thinking, the authors outlined its four central tenets of etymology, pattern, process, and contextualization. Etymology requires that reflection is used to recognize how society, history, and politics influence thinking. Pattern then pushes back on using explication to order knowledge into accepted categories and instead argues for an implicate perspective (Kincheloe and Steinberg described "the implicate order" as one that uncovers the hidden patterns and meanings of phenomena that are situated in places that empirical research methods cannot access), which recognizes the interconnectedness of knowledge. Process refers to the deconstruction of a text to find its unintended message by keying in on what is not included in a text. Finally, contextualization is used to understand the environment and conditions (i.e., political climate, economic demands, and military conflicts) in which a text was created that works against Western science's push for generalizability. Kincheloe and Steinberg concluded that postformal thinking, such as Piaget's theory, is a social construction; however, it (postformal thinking) offers an alternative lens to what is traditionally accepted as higher order thinking.

CHAPTER 12

PETER MCLAREN

Intellectual Instigator

Lynda Kennedy

For nearly forty years Peter McLaren has been a provocateur, questioning and agitating against complacency in the profession of education as it plays out in the K–12 classroom and the university setting. Rooting his work in critical pedagogy, critical social theory and a Marxist humanist philosophy, McLaren has relentlessly pursued the ideal of a socially transformative education. The arc of his work began in his reflection on his own teaching and, as his critical consciousness developed, has expanded to advocacy for a global examination of oppressive structures and for an education that encourages individuals to come together as collaborative change agents in a globalized society—a society in which there is an ever increasing disparity of wealth and opportunity. Along the way he has worked with and inspired like-minded colleagues and new generations of critical, revolutionary pedagogues, written numerous books, chapters, articles and reviews, given hundreds of interviews and traveled to many countries around the world, presenting his work, inciting, and taking action. His writing is full of rich phrasing and a soaring Utopian vision of a world that could be. In the

Educating About Social Issues in the 20th and 21st Centuries, pages 237–256
Copyright © 2014 by Information Age Publishing
All rights of reproduction in any form reserved.

words of his colleague and long time friend, Joe Kincheloe, Peter McLaren should be considered "the poet laureate of the educational left" (McLaren, 2000, p. ix).

With his myriad writings and in his work as a teacher educator, Peter McLaren has long been one of the leading voices for the field of critical pedagogy. Though the term is used freely by many scholars, critical pedagogy is a label for an educational stance that is difficult to define. Its interpretation has morphed and changed over time and place in response to a growing and more sophisticated critical consciousness on the part of its adherents. McLaren himself has stated in many forums that there is no one definition of critical pedagogy, that each critical pedagogue would describe its meaning in his or her own way. Other, more specific, lenses have been employed by critical pedagogues, who ground their work in theoretical perspectives such as critical race theory and critical feminist theory.

Critical pedagogy, in turn, builds on the work of critical theorists such as Max Horkheimer, Theodor Adorno, Herbert Marcuse and others connected to the Institute of Social Research at the University of Frankfort (a group of theorists often referred to as the "Frankfort School") that began to gain recognition in the United States largely after World War II. Student movements and the "New Left" of the 1960's embraced critical theory and its questioning of the status quo. As Kincheloe (2005) writes, "The New Left preached a Marcusian sermon of political and personal emancipation from the conventions of dominant power" (p. 47), and gave voice to previously dominated groups such as women, African Americans and Latinos. Critical theory problematized accepted ideas of freedom and equality that were at work in the United States and other Western countries, focusing a new lens on the structural inequalities lurking beneath the surface of those societies. Among those structural disparities, and arguably the most impactful, were those that surrounded educational opportunity and access. Educators working to develop practices that raised consciousness about these structures and that, hopefully, would lead to empowerment by traditionally disenfranchised populations, embraced critical theory. A developing critical consciousness allowed students and teachers to question received knowledges and see them as arising from the limiting structures of a hierarchical society. Understanding the structures, individuals would then be better equipped to act for positive change. Into this heated atmosphere, during this time of burgeoning social awareness, Peter McLaren first stepped into the classroom.

A Canadian, McLaren was born in Toronto, Ontario, Canada. As a child and young man his family resided in both Toronto and Winnipeg, Manitoba. As an undergraduate he earned a bachelor of arts in English literature (with a focus on Elizabethan drama) at Waterloo University in 1973. He then matriculated at Toronto Teachers College and, ultimately, earned a Bachelor of Education at the University of Toronto. Completing his formal education he a Masters of Education at Brock University and a PhD at the famed Ontario Institute for Studies in Education at the University of Toronto (1983).

Prior to earning his doctorate, McLaren worked as an elementary and middle school teacher (1974–1979), including a school in Canada's largest public housing complex (Jane-Finch Corridor), where the struggles of the working class and poor community that lived there played out in the lives of the students he worked with daily. McLaren wrote about his experiences teaching in that community in his early work, *Cries from the Corridor: The New Suburban Ghettos,* originally published in 1980. Taking the form of journalistic entries of his daily experiences, the book shocked the Canadian public. It became a best seller, and sparked a heated public discussion on the state of schools in areas of poverty. Not all readers were enamored though. One reviewer in the *Canadian Journal of Education,* Gordon West (1981), stated, "McLaren announces at the beginning that this is not a work of fiction; it is equally not a balanced description of reality even in our worst schools in our worst areas" (p. 81). West later goes on to criticize McLaren's "gimmick" of opening each section by reporting incidents in a way meant to shock the reader. He also criticized the journalistic style, and its lack of accompanying analysis. Expressing concerns that the lack of analysis could indeed lead readers to blame the students, their families and their communities for the issues that plagued the schools, a more mature and scholarly McLaren later went back and critically examined this work himself. This re-examination led to the publication of *Life in Schools: An Introduction to Critical Pedagogy in the Foundations of Education* in 1989 which made use of excerpts from *Cries,* but now included a sophisticated theoretically grounded interpretation, reflecting his own growing critical consciousness and praxis. Several editions later, this work is still considered an essential text in social justice education.

After a year as a Special Lecturer in Teacher Education at Brock University, McLaren took a position at Miami University School of Education and Allied Professions in Ohio in 1985, and began to work closely with Henry Giroux, who is also well known for his work in critical pedagogy and cultural studies. Both McLaren and Giroux found grounding for their work in the theories of Marx and Paulo Freire, the latter of whom is considered by many as the father of critical pedagogy due to his work and its impact on the struggles of oppressed groups for liberation and self empowerment. Together McLaren and Giroux wrote, among other things, *Between Borders: Pedagogy and the Politics of Cultural Studies* in 1994, and McLaren has credited Giroux with bringing him to the United States as well as being a strong mentor and highly influential on his work. He equates their relationship as being like that of "a budding artist working with Picasso" (quoted in Engles,

2005 p. 3). McLaren's work began to take on a distinctly more political focus, with a more obvious Marxist bent, from this point forward.

Continuing to explore what it means to be a radical, critical pedagogue, and one who is inspired by the real world applications of Freire's pedagogy, McLaren came to believe that it was just as important for an educator to have a political stance as it was to have a theoretical grounding for his or her work. In order to truly foster and engage in societal change and social justice, educators must see their educational practice as embedded in a larger social/political/historical context. They must also develop a reflexive praxis that allows them to examine critically their decisions, their worldview, and all the structures that impact on their own and their student's lives. Through this practice, the educator becomes changed. In an interview with Dr. Joe Kincheloe, McLaren described how being a critical pedagogue changed him.

> For one thing, it has made me more aware of the contradictions in my life. . . . I am always ferreting out those contradictions that render me much more ineffective than I'd like to be when dealing with institutions, dealing with groups, policies, practices both pedagogical and critical. (McLaren, 2007)

In McLaren's view, students as well as teachers should experience a pedagogy that is "fundamentally concerned with understanding the relationship between power and knowledge" (McLaren, 1989, p. 180). He advocates that such a pedagogy should empower students to "exercise the kind of courage needed to change the social order when necessary" (McLaren, 1989, p. 182). Over the years, his work has become increasingly critical of postmodern social theory and its lack of grounding in the reality of the lived experience of workers and those in poverty and struggle.

As his career progressed, McLaren became progressively more engaged with the real-world application of critical pedagogy for supporting those in struggle and working toward a better, more humanist world. Connecting to these struggles though his writings, presentations and interviews, McLaren imagines a post-capitalist society in which all human beings are truly equal. On his personal website, McLaren states: "The critical pedagogy which I support and practice advocates nonviolent dissent, the development of a philosophy of praxis guided by a Marxist humanism, the study of revolutionary social movements and thought, and the struggle for socialist democracy." He goes on to say that his work draws inspiration from Paulo Freire, Raya Dunayevskaya, among others.

It can be argued that though McLaren cites many influences, there is a central core of Freirean radical love that flows through McLaren's work. The centrality of love to McLaren's pedagogy and praxis is noted by Freire's wife, Ana Maria Araujo Freire, in the foreword to McLaren's book, *Che*

Guevera, Paolo Freire, and the Pedagogy of Revolution (2000). Pondering the Canadian's feelings of solidarity for Guevera and Freire, she tells us that when she met McLaren he admitted, "He admired Paolo and Che above all because they had created the pedagogy of love" (p. xiv). Freire was indeed a major influence on McLaren. After meeting each other while McLaren was still a young academic, Freire arranged for McLaren to speak at a conference in Cuba in 1987. McLaren considered Freire a friend and mentor, and he has publically lamented the de-politicization of Freire's work when interpreted by others following Freire's death.

Some criticism exists of McLaren and indeed other critical theorists. Much of the criticism is focused on a perceived disconnect of the Utopian vision professed by many critical pedagogues from the day-to-day realities of the classroom. Some criticism also cites the underlying sexism that is still evident within the scholarship of critical pedadogy. In her review of McLaren's work, Mary Ann Doyle (1996), for example, suggests that even in McLaren's responses to criticism of his handling of gender issues, he failed to quite put into practice the ideals he advocated. In this regard, she writes, "Although it is clear that in McLaren's extended theorizing about issues of oppression he acknowledged issues of gender, it is in his articulations about what would constitute appropriate forms of resistance that he lost site of the contradictory effects of what he advocated" (Dolye, 1996 p. 30). Similar critiques have been made of Freire's work. These critiques highlight the difficulty inherent in shaking accepted norms and structures, even for a radical critical pedagogue. Like Freire, McLaren has evolved his theoretical frame and has proved his ability to re-engage with previous work through a refined lens. As part of his praxis, McLaren has revisited his work and re-examined it through an evolving critical consciousness. As previously mentioned, a good example of this is the publication *Life in Schools: An Introduction to Critical Pedagogy in the Foundations of Education.* The book, originally published in 1989, expanded on the work of *Cries from the Corridor,* which McLaren, along with critics of the book, had come to feel was too journalistic and lacked a theoretical analysis. In *Life in Schools,* he criticized his own pedagogy while in the classroom, and outlined a new framework for social justice education. He has subsequently continued to revise and revisit this work over several editions.

In more recent work, over the last decade or so, McLaren has advocated the need for scholars and educators to see education as dangerously embedded within capitalist society. He criticizes post modern education for failing to recognize the role of capital and capital production and relegating class struggle to an ambiguous place (McLaren & Farahmandpur, 2002). "Capitalism has been naturalized as commonsense reality," McLaren writes (2002), "even as a part of nature itself—while the term 'democratic education' has in my mind come to mean adjusting students to the logic of the capitalist marketplace" (p. 1).

McLaren has also written prolifically of the need for educators to have a global view, along with the damaging effects of a global capitalism, the subjection of education to the free market through the privatization efforts in the public school arena, and the dangers of the commodification of learning. He has also been eloquent on the weakening of what is thought of as critical pedagogy by the removal of the political and has equated some of the safer practices being cited as being part of a critical approach to the assumption that one is engaging in multicultural education if one includes holidays of different ethnic groups in the curricula. The antidote to this "safe" practice, which McLaren lambastes, is a *revolutionary*, critical pedagogy, in which real action is integrated into practice.

McLaren travels to engage workers and educators around the world and promotes a clearly activist, revolutionary agenda. As part of this agenda, for him, critical pedagogy has become a catalyst to a revolutionary struggle for freedom from oppression. As Kincheloe (2001) writes, when McLaren refers to the emancipation of teachers, he uses the phrase, "to evoke the image of teachers freeing themselves from the hegemonizing influences of larger sociological forces" (p. 368). Emancipation, freedom, revolution— these are all themes in McLarens' work which can excite. Indeed, there are many for whom his stance resonates as a needed, positive, hopeful stance of action in an increasingly passive world.

For others, though, there is more than discomfort caused by the critical lens McLaren turns on our society. Among these are those who likely to only want the revolution to go so far. A group of alumni from University of California, Los Angeles, where McLaren is on the faculty, created an organization un-affiliated with the University called the Bruin Alumni Association. On their website blazes the text, "Indoctrination, Not Education: Rampant Radicalism in the UCLA Graduate School of Education." Mini articles on the site list and lambast professors seen as radical, dangerous and prone to demagoguery. In the section devoted to McLaren, he is called a "dangerous and malevolent political force" (Jones, 2006). The author, Andrew Jones, goes on to criticize everything from McLaren's tattoos to what is described as "hate-America" topics of speeches delivered by McLaren in other countries, which is the reason, he postulates, for McLaren's popularity in other parts of the world.

In spite of a conservative backlash in the United States, McLaren has been honored around the world for his work. He has received numerous honorary doctorates including, Doctorate, honoris causa at the Universidad del Salvador, Buenos Aires, Argentina, Doctorate, honoris causa at the University of Lapland, Finland and is a Fellow of the Royal Society of Arts and Commerce (England). Along with works by Pierre Bourdieu, Paulo Freire,

Peter McLaren ▪ **243**

Ivan Ilich, Jerome Bruner, and Basil Bernstein, McLaren's *Life in Schools* was chosen in 2004 as one of the twelve most significant education books worldwide by an international panel of experts organized by The Moscow School of Social and Economic Sciences. In addition, three of his books (*Che Guevara, Paulo Freire, and the Pedagogy of Revolution; Life in Schools; and* the co-edited *Marxism Against Postmodernism in Educational Theory*) were winners of the American Education Studies Association Critics' Choice Awards for outstanding books in education.

McLaren's work has been recognized as so seminal to the field of education that several conferences and symposia have been centered on his work alone, such as the *Conference on the Work of Peter McLaren,* which was held as part of the official opening of The Peter McLaren Foundation of Critical Pedagogy (La Fundacion Peter McLaren de Pedagogia Critica) that was chartered at the University of Tijuana in July 2004. The Foundation is a nonprofit organization initiated and developed by a group of professors and educational activists in Mexico. McLaren's curriculum vitae described the foundation in the following manner:

> Adopting a multiracial, gender balanced, anticapitalist, antiracist and anti-imperialist pedagogical agenda, The Peter McLaren Foundation of Critical Pedagogy has been set up to advance a number of goals, including the fostering and development of revolutionary critical pedagogy, the undertaking of action research projects, the organization of conferences, the creation of centers of critical pedagogy and the establishment of public forums for debate, discussion, and political activism throughout Mexico and the Americas. The foundation is currently publishing a journal, *Aula Crítica,* in Spanish, with plans for Portuguese, French, and English editions. (McLaren, n.d.)

At a time when the economic disparity in Western countries continues to grow to extreme levels and the struggles in so many parts of the world seem to be never ending, it can be argued that the field of education needs the freedom a critical consciousness can bring. Educators need to be able to be in our world, living it, but also to be able to stand outside of it and see the structures enacting on our lived experience. We need forums for open dialogue about change and activism. We need hope, and most of all we need a revolutionary love for humanity. The work of Peter McLaren provides a touchstone for educators searching for this sort of transformational pedagogy.

REFERENCES

Bruin Alumni Association. (n.d.). Retrieved from http://www.bruinalumni.com/

Doyle, M. (1996). Review: Peter McLaren and the field of critical theory. *Educational Researcher,* 25 (4), 28–32. Retrieved from http://www.jstor.org/stable/1176778

Engles, S. (2005). Peter McLaren: Connecting pedagogy to social issues. *Forum*, 7(3), 3.

Giroux, H. A., & McLaren, P. (Eds.). (1994). *Between Borders: Pedagogy and the Politics of Cultural Studies*. New York: Routledge.

Jones, A. (2006). The GSEIS professoriate—Peter McLaren. Retrieved from http://www.bruinalumni.com/articles/gseis6.html

Kincheloe, J. (2005). *Critical pedagogy*. NY: Peter Lang Publishing, Inc.

Kincheloe, J. (2001). *Getting beyond the facts: Teaching social studies/social sciences in the twenty-first century*. NY: Peter Lang Publishing.

Kincheloe, J. (interviewer) & McLaren, P. (interviewee) (2007). Retrieved from *The Freire Project*, http://www.freireproject.org/content/peter-mclaren-video-interview

McLaren, P. (n.d.) Personal website. Retrieved from http://pages.gseis.ucla.edu/faculty/mclaren/

McLaren, P. (n.d.) Curriculum vitae. Retrieved from http://pages.gseis.ucla.edu/faculty/mclaren/mclarencv.pdf

McLaren, P. (1989) *Life in schools: An introduction to critical pedagogy in the foundations of education*. New York, NY: Longman.

McLaren, P. (1980). *Cries from the corridor: The new suburban ghettos*. Toronto, ON: Methuen Publications.

McLaren, P. (2000). *Che Guevara, Paulo Freire, and the pedagogy of revolution*. Boulder, CO: Rowman & Littlefield.

McLaren, P. (2002). *Educating for social justice and liberation*. Retrieved from http://www.zcommunications.org/educating-for-social-justice-and-liberation-by-peter-mclaren

McLaren, P., & Farahmandpur, R. (2002). Freire, Marx, and the new imperialism: Towards a revolutionary praxis. In J. J. Slater, S. M. Fain, & C. A. Rossatto (Eds.), *The Freirean legacy: Educating for social justice* (pp. 37–56). New York, NY: Peter Lang.

West, G. (1981). Review: Cries from the corridor, the new suburban ghetto. *Canadian Journal of Education*, 6(1), 81–83.

ANNOTATED BIBLIOGRAPHY

In terms of publications, McLaren has been particularly prolific. As of 2012, his curriculum vitae numbers well over 100 pages, much of it articles, books, chapters, talks, and interviews. Below is but a small sample of his works.

Books by McLaren

McLaren, P. (1980). *Cries from the corridor: The new suburban ghettos*. Toronto, ON: Methuen Publications.

In this early work, McLaren documents his early years teaching in Canada's largest public housing complex (known as the Jane-Finch Corridor), a suburban development outside of Toronto. The book is journalistic in its presentation. McLaren shares the daily episodes as they unfolded, described with little or no critical analysis or reference to wider issues and structures exerting their influences on the students, teachers and community—a criticism which he himself leveled at the work later. (See the annotation of *Life in Schools* below. Therein, McLaren basically revised *Cries in the Corridor*, and, in doing so, provided a critical analysis of what he reported on in *Cries in the Corridor*.) Nevertheless, the book was a best seller in Canada and sparked a major public conversation about schools in working class, poor and immigrant communities.

McLaren, P. (1989). *Life in schools: An introduction to critical pedagogy in the foundations of education.* New York, NY: Longman.

Originally published in 1989 and now in its 5th edition, this book is considered a seminal text in critical pedagogy. In it, McLaren revisits and repurposes the journalistic diary entries of *Cries from the Corridor* and adds context as well as analysis through sections on critical theory and pedagogy. Each edition contains another look at the autobiographical text, through an evolving critical lens. Intended to be read as an introduction to critical pedagogy, this work ably serves as an entry point into the basic underlying ideas and theoretical frameworks for becoming a critical pedagogue. However, there is some criticism regarding a lack of specificity around the use of language that could cause confusion to first time readers of critical pedagogy.

McLaren, P. (1993). *Schooling as a ritual performance: Towards a political economy of educational symbols and gestures.* 2nd ed. New York, NY: Routledge.

In this work, McLaren makes use of critical ethnography to explore cultural transmission through the symbolism embedded in the practice of schooling and the ritualized behaviors engaged in by all members of the school community, consciously or unconsciously, every day. The setting for the study, a Catholic school in Toronto, further underscores the connection between rituals, perceived and received knowledge, and power structures. The daily rituals and symbols, McLaren argues, re-enforces class, belief and social structures. McLaren's analysis is essential reading for any practicing educator who wishes to focus a lens on their own practice and cultural reproduction in their classroom or school.

McLaren, P. (1995) *Critical pedagogy and predatory culture: Oppositional politics in a postmodern era.* New York, NY: Routledge.

Bringing his theories about culture, power relations and capitalism to an examination of the intersections of media, postindustrial capitalistic society, identity, and schooling, McLaren discusses the provocation of desire, assimilation and the creation of a noncritical acceptance of the norm. As in most of his other works, he advocates for a politics of resistance, the development of a critical multiculturalism, a push-back against apathetic acceptance that capitalism and democracy are the same things, and a rejection of the idea that society/humanity should be moving towards a homogenous culture and an "othering" of those that don't fit "the paradigm." Includes a preface by Paolo Freire.

McLaren, P. (1997). *Revolutionary multiculturalism: Pedagogies of dissent for the new millennium.* Boulder, CO: Westview Press.

With a focus on understanding the role of whiteness and the privilege it brings, along with the need to decentralize it as a force in politics, this work highlights the interweaving of politics and practice not only for the world of education, but in other arenas of public discourse. McLaren calls for finding ways to build solidarity among oppressed groups, and fostering hope and agency in the face of discouraging structures. Also included is an interview with McLaren.

The book is comprised of the following chapters: "Introduction: Fashioning Los Olvidados In the Age of Cynical Reason"; 1. "Writing from the Margins: Geographies of Identity, Pedagogy, and Power" (with Henry Giroux); 2. "Liberatory Politics And Higher Education: A Freirean Perspective"; 3. "The Ethnographer as Postmodern Flâneur: Critical Reflexivity and Posthybridity as Narrative Engagement"; 4. "Jean Baudrillard's Chamber of Horrors: from Marxism to Terrorist Pedagogy" (with Zeus Leonardo); 5. "Gangsta Pedagogy and Ghettocentricity: The Hip-Hop Nation as Counterpublic Sphere"; 6. "Global Politics and Local Antagonisms: Research and Practice as Dissent and Possibility" (with Kris Gutierrez); 7. "Provisional Utopias in a Postcolonial World: An Interview with Peter McLaren" by Gert Biesta and Siebren Miedema); 8. Unthinking Whiteness, Rethinking Democracy: Critical Citizenship in Gringolandia); "Epilogue—Beyond the Threshold of Liberal Pluralism: Toward a Revolutionary Democracy"; and, "Afterword—Multiculturalism: The Fracturing of Cultural Souls."

McLaren, P. (2000). *Che Guevara, Paulo Freire, and the pedagogy of revolution.* Boulder, CO: Rowman & Littlefield.

In this work, with introductions by McLaren's longtime friend and colleague, Joe Kincheloe and Freire's wife, Ana Maria Araújo Freire, McLaren explores the scholarly work of his two heroes and how it can contribute to contemporary praxis. He writes with his usual passion of the dangers of capitalism and its growing global reach, finding in the work of the two revolutionaries of the title inspiration for a counter movement, a revolutionary pedagogy. Revolutionary pedagogy, McLaren argues throughout this work, acknowledges the centrality of class struggle, in contrast to the pedagogues who see themselves as "left" but who omit class and the oppressive structures of capitalism from their rhetoric.

McLaren, P. (2005). *Capitalists and conquerors: A critical pedagogy against empire.* Boulder, CO: Rowman & Littlefield Publishers.

This work is organized as a series of essays in which McLaren takes on many of his familiar themes. These include the problems inherent in the growth of global capitalism, neo-liberalism, an empire-building mindset, and the role of schools as a catalyst for social change. Especially timely, coming as it did when accusations of nation building began to be leveled at the United States vis-à-vis the prolonged conflict in the Middle East, McLaren urges us to not shy away from the political implications of educational work; indeed, he outlines the reasons as to why and how the removal of a radical stance from the contemporary practice of critical pedagogy contributes to the growth of inhumanity in the world.

McLaren, P. & Farahmandpur, R. (2005) *Teaching against Global Capitalism and the New Imperialism: A Critical Pedagogy*. Lanham, MD: Rowman and Littlefield.

This book is composed of the following ten chapters: 1. "Reconsidering Marx in Post-Marxist Times: A Requiem for Postmodernism?"; 2. "Freire, Marx, and the New Imperialism: Toward a Revolutionary Praxis"; 3. "Critical Pedagogy, Postmodernism, and the Retreat from Class: Towards a Contraband Pedagogy"; 4. "Critical Multiculturalism and the Globalization of Capital: Some Implications for a Politics of Resistance"; 5. "Globalization, Class, and Multiculturalism: Fragments from a Red Notebook"; 6. "Teaching against Globalization and the New Imperialism: Toward a Revolutionary Pedagogy"; 7. "Educational Policy and the Socialist Imagination: Revolutionary Citizenship as a Pedagogy of Resistance"; 8. "Teaching in and Against the Empire: Critical Pedagogy as Revolutionary Praxis"; 9. "Critical Revolutionary Pedagogy at Ground Zero: Renewing the Educational Left after September 11"; and 10. "Afterword."

Edited Volumes by McLaren and Others

Hill, D., McLaren, P. Cole, M., & Rikowski, G. (Eds.) (2002). *Marxism against Postmodernism in Educational Theory*. Lanham, MA: Lexingtoon Books.

The intent of this book is to, "...fuel the debate within the educational Left internationally regarding the need for useful theoretical work for the movement." It is comprised of twelve chapters: "Postmodernism in Educational Theory" by Glenn Rikowski and Peter McLaren; "Prelude: Marxist Educational Theory after Postmodernism" by Glenn Rikowski; "Breaking Signifying Chains: A Marxist Position on Postmodernism" by Peter McLaren and Ramin Farahmandpur; "Structuring the Postmodern in Education Policy" by Michael W. Apple and Geoff Whitty; "'Resistance Postmodernism'–Progressive Politics or Rhetorical Left Posturing?" by Mike Cole and Dave Hill; "Education, Capital and the Transhuman" by Glenn Rikowski; "Youth, Training and the Politics of 'Cool'" by Michael Neary; "Marxism, Class Analysis and Postmodernism" by Dave Hill, Mike Sanders and Ted Hankin; "Racism, Postmodernism and the Flight from Class" by Jenny Bourne; "Women, Work and the Family: Or Why Postmodernism Cannot Explain the Links" by Jane Kelly; "Recentering Class: Wither Postmodernism? Toward a Contraband Pedagogy" by Peter McLaren and Ramin Farahmandpur; and, "Postmodernism

Adieu: Toward a Politics of Human Resistance" by Peter McLaren, Dave Hill, Mike Cole and Glenn Rikowski.

Martin, G., Houston, D., McLaren, P., & Suoranta, J. (Eds.) (2010) *Havoc of Capitalism. educating for social and environmental justice.* Rotterdam, NL: Sense Publishers.

This book brings together an "interdisciplinary community of scholars to contribute to the dialogue about alternative global futures within the current context of environmental crisis." The book is comprised of the following three parts: Part I: Havoc: Katrian and the Crisis of Capital; Part II: Resilience: Indigenous Pedagogies and the Critique of Eco-Colonialism; and, Part III: Transformations: Pedagogy, Activism and the Environment of Justice.

Among some of the many chapters in this book are: "Critical Pedagogy 'After the Storm'" by Donna Houston and Gregory Martin; "The Media and Hurricane Katrina: Floating Bodies and Disposable Populations" by Henry A. Giroux; "Katrina and the Banshee's Wail: The Racialization of Class Exploitation" by Peter McLaren and Nathalia E. Jaramillo; "A Pedagogy of the Dispossessed: Toward a Red State of Decolonization, Sovereignty and Survivance" by Sandy Grande; "Denatured Spirit: Neo-Colonial Social Design" by Norm Sheehan, Janine Dunleavy, Tamar Cohen and Sean Mitchell; "(Re(a)d and White: Discussing Ethnicities and the Teaching of Whiteness" by Alison Sammel and Shauneen Pete; "Major Intentional Social Changes as a Political Perspective" by Olli Tammilehto; and "A Curriculum for a Secure Future: Agenda for Reform" by Alexander Lautensach and Sabina Lautensach.

McLaren, P., & Kincheloe, J. L. (Eds.) (2007). Critical Pedagogy: Where are we now? New York, NY: Peter Lang Inc.

In this book, the authors discuss "how the field of critical pedagogy should respond to . . . dire conditions [such as a growing concern that we are becoming a liberal nation-state with a increasingly antiliberal population and an electorate that is disinterested in politics] in a way that is theoretically savvy and visionary, while concurrently contributing to the struggle to improve the lives of those most hurt by them."

The following chapters comprise this book: "Critical Pedagogy in the Twenty-First Century: Evolution for Survival" by Joe l. Kincheloe; "Religion as Socio-Educational Critique: A Weberian Example" by Philip Wexler; "Critical Pedagogy and the Crisis of Imagination" by Eric J. Weiner; "Locations (or not) of Critical Pedagogy in Les Petites et les Grandes Histoires" by Kathleen S. Berry; "Neoliberal Non-Sense" by Pepi Leistyna; "The Politics and Ethic of Performance Pedagogy: Toward a Pedagogy of Hope" by Norman K. Denzin; "From Social to Socialist Media: The Critical Potential of the Wikiworld" by Juha Suoranta & Tere Vadén; "Globalizing Critical Pedagogy: A Case of Critical English Language Teaching in Korea" by Kiwan Sung; "Critical Pedagogy and Popular Culture in an Urban Secondary English Classroom" by Jeff Duncan-Andrade & Ernest Morrell; "Critical Pedagogy and Young Children's World" by Elizabeth Quintero; "Escola Cidadā and Critical Discourses of Educational Hope" by Gustavo E. Fischman & Luis A. Gandin; "Musicing Paulo Freire: A Critical Pedagogy for Music Education" by Frank Abrahams; "Reflections on the Violence of High-Stakes Testing and the Soothing Nature of Critical Pedagogy" by Valerie J. Janesick; "Pedagogy of Testimony: Reflections on the Pedagogy of Critical Pedagogy" by Luis Huerta-Charles; "Critical Pedagogy and Teacher Education: Radicalizing Prospective Teachers" by Lilia I. Bartolomé; "The Future of the Past: Reflections on the Present State of Empire and Pedagogy" by Peter McLaren; "Red Lake Woebegone: Pedagogy, Decolonization, and the Critical Project" by Sandy Grande; "The Poverty of Critical Pedagogy: Toward a Politics of Engagement" by Gregory Martin; "Frantz Fanon and a Materialist Critical Pedagogy" by Noah De Lissovoy; and, "Critical Pedagogy: Democratic Realism, Neoliberalism, Conservatism, and a Tragic Sense of Education" by William B. Stanley.

McLaren, P., & Leonard, P. (Eds). (1993). *Paulo Freire: A critical encounter.* New York, NY: Routledge

This volume includes chapters by such eminent thinkers as sociologist Stanley Aronowitz, Henry Giroux, Ira Shor, and the always provocative bell hooks, and McLaren, among others. This work allows McLaren and Leonard, as well as the other contributors, to explore the work of McLaren's friend and mentor, Paulo Freire. Liberation as a central theme is, of course, present, as is a deeper look at the role of political engagement and activism in pedagogy. This book is not meant to be simply a retelling or a celebration of Freire, but rather to allow the contributors to enter into a dialog with, and sometimes a critique of, Freire's work as it relates to their own work and theoretical lenses.

Giroux, H., Lankshear, C., McLaren, P., & Michael, P. (1996). *Counternarratives: Cultural studies and critical pedagogies in postmodern spaces.* New York, NY: Routledge.

Counternarratives develops a concept of "postmodern counternarratives" as a frame for exploring the politics of media, technology and education within everyday struggles for human identities and loyalties. The authors identify two forms of counternarratives. One functions as a critique of the modernist propensity for grand narratives. The second concept, which is the focus of the book, builds on the first; the idea of "little stories" addressing cultural and political opposition to the 'official' narratives used to manipulate public consciousness. Each marks an important point of contestation within contemporary education and culture: curriculum, pedagogy, literacy, media representations and applications of new technologies.

McLaren, P., & Jaramillo, N. (2007). *Pedagogy and Praxis in the Age of Empire: Towards a New Humanism.* Rotterdam, NL: Sense Publishers.

Written by two leading international exponents of critical pedagogy, this book is a pioneering attempt to create a Marxist humanist and feminist pedagogy for the new century. Critical pedagogy is discussed as an important revolutionary act in bringing about a socialist future.

Macrine, S., McLaren, P., & Hill, D, (Eds). (2010). *Revolutionizing pedagogy: Educating for social justice within and beyond global neo-liberalism.* London, UK: Palgrave Macmillan.

This book brings together a group of leading international scholars to examine the paradoxical roles of schooling in reproducing and legitimizing large-scale structural inequalities along the axes of race, ethnicity, class, sexuality, and disability. Through critical engagements with contemporary theories of class and cultural critique, the book questions the inherited dogma that underlies both liberal and conservative and also social democratic approaches to teaching and makes a spirited case for teaching as a critical and revolutionary act.

Articles

McLaren, P. (1985). Classroom symbols and the ritual dimensions of schooling. *Anthropologica, 27*(1/2), 161–189.

In this early work, McLaren delineates his understanding and usage of the term "ritual" and how it can be part of a conceptual framework for examining the creation of and transmission of culture in the classroom. Using fieldwork that also became the basis for the publication of *Schooling as Ritual Performance*, McLaren applies his framework to what he describes as "the toughest" Catholic junior high school in the city of Toronto. Written in a clear manner, with less jargon than is the norm in critical theory, McLaren argues for the relevance of using ritual to examine symbolic interactions in an institutional setting such as a school, and how it can be a useful tool in uncovering unconscious acceptance of and symbolic transmittal of ideologies, as well as bringing awareness to methods of resistance against prescribed norms in an educational setting.

McLaren P. (1992). Critical literacy and postcolonial praxis: A Freirian perspective. *College Literature.* October, (3/1), 7.

In this essay, McLaren examines the intersection of language, historical agency, power and experience. Language in particular is seen as tied to power and literacy practices to be practices of power. Language is tangled in context, gender, identity and power relations, so presenting students with a language of criticality is essential. Educators need to be critically aware of their own discourse and help students to also be critically aware. McLaren constructs his argument—which continues as a thread throughout his later writing—that Freire's work loses power when divorced from the socio- and geopolitical context from which it arose and in which it was practiced. Only in avoiding this reductionist view of Freire's work, can educators make full use of it to inform their practice to, as McLaren states, "shape history rather than rehearse it."

McLaren, P. (1993). Moral panic, schooling and gay identity: Critical pedagogy and the politics of resistance. *The High School Journal, 7*(1/2), 157–168.

In this piece, McLaren outlines the struggles of including LGBTQ (though that acronym was not used at the time of its writing) identity, issues, and history into the multicultural curriculum. More than any other group, gays have been victims of exclusion in teaching, even by those who would bring a critical lens to other issues, as, unlike race, there is an implied moral aspect for some. Teachers at the time feared backlash or even dismissal for even mentioning the subject, let alone discussing LGBTQ issues. This is an interesting piece to read in historical context and as an exercise in honesty about whether or not present day practice has become any less fearful or more inclusive in the language we use, the topics we broach and our willingness to resist political and social pressure to exclude issues and people from the curriculum and schools.

McLaren, P. (1998). Revolutionary pedagogy in post-revolutionary times: Rethinking the political economy of critical education. *Educational Theory, 48(4), 431–462.*

In this article, McLaren is extremely critical of the state of the "Left" in general and the Marxist educational Left in particular. The educational Left, he argues, has accepted global capitalism, and an active critique needs to be brought back into the conversation. With the collapsing of the economy and the disappearance of manufacturing, reduction of unions, pensions, and other benefits, the gulf between the labor and capital had reached a crisis point. McLaren outlines the dangers of the capital/labor divide and puts forth some ideas for a revitalization of the Left in education. Without a revolutionary agenda, McLaren argues, education becomes simply a subsector of the economy.

McLaren, P. (2005). Critical pedagogy and class struggle in the age of neoliberal globalization: Notes from history's underside. *The International Journal of Inclusive Democracy,* September, 2, (1). Retrieved from http://www.inclusivedemocracy. org/journal/vol2/vol2_no1_mcclaren.htm

The first section of this piece is entitled "Crisis in the American Left." The assertion that there is indeed a crisis is the starting point for this examination of the educational landscape in the second millennia. McLaren calls for a revival of the Marxist analysis of capital, and highlights the danger of the relationship between corporate sponsorship and scholarship—the commercialization of higher education. He also laments the "domestication" of critical pedagogy, criticizing the tendency to divorce the politics of difference—of sexism and racism—from class struggle. Here McLaren unequivocally calls for a revolutionary critical pedagogy.

McLaren, P. (2010). A Critical Pedagogy of Social Justice for Today's Workers. *Teacher Education and Practice, 23*(4), 482–487.

As the United States continued to sink even deeper into the financial, housing and labor crisis, McLaren called for critical pedagogues to reject capitalism completely, and lose their fear of being radical revolutionary fighters for social justice. McLaren outlines his belief that many who think of themselves as practitioners of critical pedagogy are reluctant to move beyond criticism into activism. It is only when this step is taken, he argues, that educators can fulfill their role in moving toward a more socially just society.

McLaren, P. (2011). Radical negativity: Music education for social justice. *Action, Criticism, and Theory for Music Education, 10*(1), 131–147.

In the wake of the "Great Recession" even McLaren admits to a difficulty of maintaining hope as well as an even more intense frustration with the incapacitated Left. Going further than in earlier work, McLaren calls for an alternative to capitalism—namely Socialism. He explains in more accessible language than is often used by critical theorists what he means by the term revolutionary critical pedagogy and outlines its relation to a Marxist humanist perspective. Using the work of Stephen Brookfield and John Holst, who examined the place of art in radical adult educational practice, McLaren cites several examples of music and lyrics that give voice to frustrations, describe injustices and are a call to resist oppression.

McLaren, P., & Farahmandpur, R. (2000). Reconsidering Marx in Post-Marxist Times: A Requiem for Postmodernism? *Educational Researcher, 29*(3), 25–33.

McLaren and his coauthor lament the tendency of the postmodern left to dismiss Marx and his theories as a failure and to remove discussion of labor and global capitalism from educational discourse. They outline the critiques leveled against Marxist theoretical frames and address each one in turn. They call for the use of Marxist analyses as a tool for examining globalization and neoliberal education policies, while still allowing for discourse centered on race, class, gender, sexual orientation, etc. They argue, these postmodern areas of discourse would be reinvigorated by an understanding of their interplay with the labor/capital struggle.

McLaren and Farahmandpur state their belief that the No Child Left Behind Act was informed by a neoliberal economic model that expects schools to perform like corporations. They lambast the almost complete focus on standardized testing as the measure of success, and the punitive use of test scores on schools with some of the highest needs. The policies, they argue, have shifted the field's focus from a quest for equality in education to a quest for adequacy. Throughout the piece, the authors pick apart the intensity of the return to a factory model of education and the irony of this return in the face of disappearing manufacturing jobs. They further express concern about the return to de facto segregation, the loss of the arts and the ease of access given to military recruitment.

McLaren, P., & Houston, D. (2004). Revolutionary ecologies: Ecosocialism and critical pedagogy. *Educational Studies, 36*(1), 27–45.

Taking on the idea of the "greening" of critical pedagogy, the authors examine the place of environmental issues and "eco justice" in educational practice. They explore schools as places of environmental injustice, interweaving this lens with the larger environmental discussion and as a piece of the structures on which a critical, revolutionary pedagogy can be brought to bear. The authors draw a line from capital and corporate lobbyists to policies disastrous for the environment. The environmental crisis looms so large, McLaren and Houston argue, that it must not be ignored by critical educators, who must foster in their schools a revolutionary and activist energy.

McLaren, P., Martin, G., Farahmandpur, R., & Jaramillo, N. (2004). Teaching in and against the empire: Critical pedagogy as revolutionary praxis. *Teacher Education Quarterly, 31*(1), 131–153.

Blatantly and extremely critical of the Bush-era post 911 war on terror and the "if you are not with us, you are against us" mentality that seemed to prevail, McLaren and his colleagues are urgent in their insistence that critical pedagogy step up as a counter balance to the trend of easy acceptance of this world view. No Child Left Behind is described as a framework for inserting a conservative ideology into schooling, of weakening the weakest schools and dumbing down the curriculum. Higher education is also critiqued, in particular the increasing reliance on adjuncts that may be with the institution for years but who are denied benefits, etc. and the ever-higher hoops required for full time faculty to attain tenure. The latter too is seen as part of the larger trend towards corporatization of education, with the corporate practices of downsizing, outsourcing and a disregard for those who labor. They call for critical pedagogues to add "revolutionary" into the mix, and the need to struggle for transformation of schools and for justice of the oppressed.

Giroux, H., & McLaren, P. (1984). Teacher education and the politics of engagement. *Harvard Educational Review,* 56 (3), 213–239.

Giroux and McLaren paint a picture of teachers as transformative intellectuals, or at least of their potential to be so. In this vision, schools can be places of political discourse, where student's critical awareness can be awakened and their role as active, participatory citizens can be developed. Giroux and McLaren express concern about the educational reforms being instituted at that time, and outline an approach to teacher education that would better prepare classroom teachers as critical pedagogues that value and encourage student voices.

Interviews With McLaren

McLaren, P. (2001). "Rage and hope: The revolutionary pedagogy of Peter McLaren: An interview with Peter McLaren." *Currículo sem Fronteiras, 1*(2): xlix–lix. Available at: www.curriculosemfronteiras.org

In this interview conducted by Mitja Sardoc, Educational Research Institute, Ljubljana, Slovenia, "McLaren clearly expresses his return to the Marxist roots, to a theory with a strategic centrality. After a period of incursions through the field of leftist postmodernism and poststructuralism, McLaren argues today that there are insuperable limitations in these approaches and criticizes the academic sycophants and their position towards these perspectives. To him, the return to the Marxist theory, as a way of both understanding and transforming social reality, is a natural process. However, McLaren stresses that Marxism should not be seen as a religion, emphasizing that he does not want to have anything to do with an inflexible perspective."

Pozo, M. (2003). Toward a Critical Revolutionary Pedagogy: An interview with Peter McLaren. *St. John's University Humanities Review*, Fall, 2(1), n.p.

This is an interesting and highly informative interview. The questions posited by Pozo and addressed in a good amount of detail by McLaren are as follow: Can you give us some background to your most well known book of critical pedagogy?; Can you describe your initial steps into critical pedagogy as a student and then as a professor?; So in your book *Life in Schools* we read of your personal growth as an inner city elementary school teacher to a future practioner (sic) of critical pedagogy. In 2000 your book, *Che Guevara, Paulo Freire and the Pedagogy of Revolution* seemed like yet another step in your life as an educator. Can you then describe the differences/similarities between the critical pedagogy you began with and the pedagogy of revolution you now practice? Most students are taught under a skills orientated type of education that basically prepares them to be workers and not, say, revolutionaries. What would you say differentiates a student taught by critical pedagogy as she enters the same world after graduation?; How does your classroom environment prepare students for a world that is often like a harsh wake-up call from life in a university where different groups mix together and academic success is said to be equally accessible to all?; I draw certain parallels from Paulo Freire's comments on the responsibility of the oppressed to that of some students who believe the sole purpose of an education is to provide the means to achieve material gains. In *Pedagogy of the Oppressed* Freire describes the dual task of the oppressed as self and social liberation. He writes, "In order for this struggle to have meaning the oppressed must not in seeking to regain their humanity (which is a way to create it) become in turn oppressors of the oppressors but rather restorers of the humanity of both" (p. 26). Have you encountered resistance from students to your ideas? And if so, how do teachers with similar concerns use critical pedagogy to convince students of such a heavy responsibility to not only their needs but those of the community?; How does critical pedagogy address the more standard pedagogy practiced so widely in most schools?; How do you see critical pedagogy surviving and growing in an atmosphere of rampant conservativism from school administrators?; Again, *in Che Guevara, Paulo Freire and the Pedagogy of Revolution* you quote an important passage from Freire. "Hoping that the teaching of content in and of itself will generate tomorrow a radical intelligence of reality is to take on a controlled position rather than a critical one. It means to fall for a magical comprehension of content which attributes to it a criticizing power of its own, 'The more we deposit content in the learner's heads and the more diversified the content is, the more possible it will be for them to, sooner or later experience a critical awakening, decide and break away'"(p. 157). Do you feel places like English or History Departments or even Composition Courses are viable sites for sustainable dissent and/or critical pedagogy? MP-How would you describe the roles teachers, students and workers play after 911? Let's address the Post-Modernist "legacy" in academics. Your critique of Post Modernism runs throughout your work and is an important yet often neglected argument against the hype of Post Modernist theories. Can you elaborate on your definition of Post Modernism and where you locate its shortcomings? As a student of critical theory it's easy to feel the sway of post structuralist "bohemia" and academic celebrities. But it seems so much of their "discoveries" of inadequacies or biased social structures have never been lost on those who lived through them. Do you think it has been a question of not having the "language" to adequately express such ideas from the perspectives of "minorities" or marginalized groups?; How has your implementation and study of people like Ernesto Guevara, Malcolm X and Rosa Luxembourg returned the lived experiences back to students taught under "detached" theories?; Henry Giroux has always called for teachers to be at the forefront of social/political issues. But do you think we see so very few "public" or "notable" radicals of color today because they are under pressure to curb their ideas on race, class or the War on "terror" in order to be perceived as non-threatening or loyal patriots?; Finally, do you feel class/race issues in the United States are often upstaged by the more "global" events and concerns?

McLaren, P. (Ed.) (2006). *Rage + Hope: Interviews with Peter McLaren: War, Imperialism, Critical Pedagogy.* New York, NY: Peter Lang.

This book is comprised of five interviews with McLaren: Interview 1: "Towards a Critical Revolutionary Pedagogy" by Michael Pozo; Interview 2: "Rage and Hope: The Revolutionary Pedagogy of Peter McLaren" by Mitja Sardoc; Interview 3. "The Globalization of Capital, Critical Pedagogy, and the Aftermath of September 11" by Lucia Coral Aguirre Munoz; Interview 4. "The Path of Dissent" by Marcia Moraes; and Interview 5. "Critical Multiculturalism and Democracy: A Conversation with Peter McLaren and Joe Kincheloe" by Shirley Steinberg.

Commentary About the Thoughts/Writings of Peter McLaren

Pruyn, M., & Huerta-Charles, L. M. (2005). *Teaching Peter McLaren.* New York, NY: Peter Lang Publishing.

Teaching Peter McLaren, the first volume in the Teaching Contemporary Scholars series, focuses on the work of educational scholars on the left who have made major contributions to the field. In this book, editors Marc Pruyn and Luis M. Huerta-Charles have assembled a notable group of contributors who reflect on, analyze, and critique over two decade's worth of scholarship produced by Peter McLaren.... Specifically, this book focuses on the nexus of education, critical theory, Marxism, globalization, and struggles for social justice via the work and theorizing of McLaren.

A review of this book stated the following: *Teaching Peter McLaren* is provocative, thorough, timely, engaging, challenging, reflective, critical, outstanding, unique, witty, and above all, a superb and needed contribution to the understanding of one of the most influential pedagogues of our times. In this book, Marc Pruyn and Luis Huerta-Charles put together the most comprehensive collection of articles addressing the contributions, changes, contradictions, influences, background, and potential of the ideas and praxis of a revolutionary scholar who has been a very creative, forceful, and brave voice for more than 30 years—Peter McLaren.

Eryaman, M. Y. (Ed.) (2009). *Peter Mclaren, Education, and the Struggle for Liberation.* New York, NY: Hampton Press.

This book is comprised of the following: Introduction—Understanding the Critical Pedagogy of Peter McLaren in the Age of Global Capitalism by Mustafa Yunus Eryaman; Interfering with Capitalism's Spell: Peter McLaren's Revolutionary Liminality by Samuel Day Fassbinder; Imagining the Impossible: Revolutionary Critical Pedagogy Against the 21st Century American Imperium by Valerie Scatamburlo-D'Annibale; Critical Pedagogy as a Collective Social Expertise in Higher Education by Juah Suoranta and Olli-Pekka Moisio; Remaking Critical Pedagogy: Peter McLaren's Contribution to a Collective Work by Gregory Martin; The Possibilities of Transformation: Critical Research and Peter McLaren by Brad J. Porfilio; Peter McLaren and the 3 Rs: Reflection, Resistance, and Revolution by David Gabbard; As Usual, the Critics are Always "Right": Political Pedagogues, That Haranguing Horowitz, and the Timely Interventions of Peter McLaren by Andrew Michael Lee; Embodying the Critical Pedagogy of Peter McLaren: The Cultural Expression of Papo de Asis and the Philippine Diaspora by Michael Viola; Radical Education in the Critical Moment: Envisioning a Revolutionary Praxis of Language, Teaching and Race in a Time of War by Arshad Ali; From Interpretive Progressivism to Radical Progressivism in Teacher Education: Teaching as Praxis by Mustafa Yunis Eryaman and Martina Riedler; An Interview with Peter McLaren: Comments on the State of the World-2005 by Michael F. Shaughnessy. Afterword by Peter McLaren.

Videos

McLaren, P. (Producer). (2007). *A Conversation With Peter McLaren.* Video retrieved from http://video.google.com/videoplay?docid=-72757753151 46302047

In this charming video, made in 2007, Joe Kincheloe and Peter McLaren, longtime friends and colleagues, discuss the basics of critical pedagogy and its personal as well as professional impact. Kincheloe interviews McLaren, asking how critical pedagogy has shaped his work as a scholar, his practice as an educator and how it has shaped his life. McLaren suggests that it is a struggle not to become incapacitated as one becomes increasingly aware of structural influences on those around you as well as oneself, yet he also speaks about the positive role a critical awareness can play in contributing to being a social justice educator and activist. The role of blues, humor and the importance of performance are also discussed.

CHAPTER 13

BELL HOOKS

Feminist Critique Through Love

Nancy Taber

INTRODUCTION

This chapter constitutes an exploration of the life and work of feminist bell hooks. She has written well over 30 books in the areas of cultural studies, education, writing, and children's literature. Her work has been enormously influential in the field of education as most of her work, regardless of its official discipline, relates to formal education, learning, and everyday pedagogy. She has been heavily influenced by authors as diverse as Paulo Freire, Toni Morrison, and Stuart Hall. Most of her books are written as a collection of essays, focusing on the ways in which gender, race, and class intersect in a white supremacist capitalist patriarchy. Her first academic book, *Ain't I a Woman: Black Women and Feminism,* was published in 1981, and, as of today, her latest is *Writing Beyond Race: Living Theory and Practice* (2013). Over the span of more than three decades, hooks has established and maintained her ongoing position as a key critical theorist and pedagogue whose work is integral to the way in which the field of education is conceptualized and investigated.

Educating About Social Issues in the 20th and 21st Centuries, pages 257–278
Copyright © 2014 by Information Age Publishing
All rights of reproduction in any form reserved.

As a white woman from a middle-class background, I am aware of the incongruity of my having this platform to construct a story of hooks' life and work. I do so with the utmost respect, and clarify that I am not an expert on hooks, nor should my telling of her work be any more important than another's. In fact, it is my hope that, in reading this chapter, readers will go to her work itself. I have purposely chosen to quote extensively from hooks, herself, in an attempt to give her voice some primacy over my own. I am conscious of hooks' words that "problems arise not when white women choose to write about the experiences of nonwhite people, but when such material is presented as 'authoritative'" (hooks, 1988, p. 48). This chapter, then, is not an authoritative piece on bell hooks, but an invitation to readers to interact with her work more directly.

As women, there is a "need to acknowledge that we all suffer in some way, but that we are not all oppressed nor equally oppressed" (hooks, 1984/2000, p. 59). Although "sexism, racism, and classism divide women from one another" (hooks, 1984/2000, p. 63), we "must learn to accept responsibility for fighting oppressions that may not directly affect us as individuals" (p. 64) in order to stand "united by shared interests and beliefs, united in our appreciation for diversity, united in our struggle to end sexist oppression, united in political solidarity" (p. 67). With that said, I write this chapter with the aim of honouring solidarity among women and listening across difference, in order to challenge white supremacist capitalist patriarchy.

As an Associate Professor in the Faculty of Education at Brock University, I use hooks' books in my courses at all levels of study as well as in my own research to assist in an exploration of the sociocultural implications of schooling/education/learning. Her work not only forefronts the experiences of women of colour, written by a black woman, but helps students understand that white privilege is central to racism, that "class privilege mediates and shapes perceptions about race" (hooks, 2003, p. 30), and sexism is not about men as the enemy but a "system of patriarchy" (hooks, 2000a, p. 12). Furthermore, students come to recognize that difference is not to be feared but should be problematized by having difficult and uncomfortable conversations. Learning is not about being safe but about challenging assumptions and ways of knowing. "Confronting one another across differences means that we must change ideas about how we learn; rather than fearing conflict, we must find ways to use it as a catalyst for new thinking, for growth" (hooks, 1994, p. 113). Finally, hooks' work highlights the fact that human learning occurs in various contexts: in curriculum, pedagogy, and educational institutions, as well as family, community, popular culture, and everyday life.

In this chapter, I begin with an exploration of elements of hooks' life that are relevant to her scholarship, particularly as she herself writes about the importance of her personal experiences to her development of theory. Due to the ways in which hooks continuously incorporates her life into her writing (with the exception of her first two academic books, *Ain't I a Woman* and *Feminist Theory*), this section also provides an overview of her work as a whole. I then discuss the main themes and concepts in her scholarship, particularly as it relates to the field of education. After a brief conclusion, I end with an annotated bibliography (all references used in this chapter can also be found there) that focuses on several of her most influential books, which address a diversity of topics.

BELL HOOKS: A LIFE OF CONTRADICTIONS

bell hooks was born as Gloria Watkins in Hopskinsville, Kentucky to a working-class black family. She was brought up with her five sisters, and one brother by her mother, and father, surrounded by extended family and community members. She began her schooling in segregated public schools, where her "teachers enact[ed] a revolutionary pedagogy of resistance that was profoundly anticolonial" (hooks, 1994, p. 2). Her teachers believed in the intelligence of black children, lived in their student's community, were familiar with their families, and nurtured their growth. Furthermore, the teachers engaged in a societal critique that challenged racist beliefs and actions, aiming to "uplift the race" (hooks, 1994, p. 2) through education.

This all changed with desegregation, as hooks completed high school at an integrated school that "sustain[ed] white supremacy and racial apartheid" (hooks, 1994, p. 24). In order to integrate the school, it was the black children who were forced to travel to white communities, spending an inordinate amount of time on school busses and made to arrive before the white children in order to avoid the possibility of any altercations. Black children like hooks felt isolated, as schooling was disconnected from community with no intent for liberation. "Knowledge was suddenly about information only. It had no relation to how one lived, behaved. It was no longer connected to antiracist struggle" (hooks, 1994, p. 3). Furthermore, integrated schooling taught "that obedience, and not a zealous will to learn, was expected of us" (hooks, 1994, p. 3). This obedience was intended to not only support rote learning and rule-following, but also the acceptance of white supremacy.

hooks often writes of the difficulties she faced growing up in a patriarchal household where, despite being loved and cared for, abuse and sexism taught her that "boy rights" (hooks, 1996, p. 29) were more important than girls'. In a third person narrative, hooks (1996) comments as follows:

> She was sent to bed without dinner. She was told to stop crying, to make no sound or she would be whipped more. No one could talk to her and she could talk to no

one. She could hear him [the father] telling the mama that the girl had too much spirit, that she had to learn to mind, that that spirit had to be broken. (p. 30)

hooks' love of writing was also disdained by her family, with hooks often writing in secret and destroying journals so no one would find them. "While I had been given permission to keep diaries, it was writing that my family began to see as dangerous when I began to express ideas considered strange and alien" (hooks, 1999, p. 6). hooks' desire to develop an autonomous voice by exploring her thoughts and feelings was viewed as senseless, even treacherous, as it challenged her family's working class beliefs vis-à-vis the importance of conformity, blue-collar labour, and patriarchy.

Nonetheless, her love of learning and books was somewhat supported:

My parent's ambivalence about my love for reading led to intense conflict. They (especially my mother) would work to ensure that I had access to books, but would threaten to burn the books or throw them away if I did not conform to other expectations. Or they would insist that too much reading would drive me insane. (hooks, 1988, p. 79)

Although her father "believed a woman with too much education would never find a husband (hooks, 2000b, p. 20), hooks states that her mother "constantly urged us to keep our minds on getting an education so we could get good jobs" (p. 20). She also advised that "cultivating the mind could place one outside the boundaries of desire" (p. 21), thus preventing one from being "dependent on a man for everything" (p. 21). Essentially, books and writing were essential to helping hooks survive her family life. They allowed her to "talk back" and "hold on to myself" (hooks, 1999, p. 5).

Beginning her postsecondary studies at a nearby college (whose name has, as far as this author has ascertained, never been disclosed), chosen for its proximity and relative inexpensiveness, hooks felt isolated due to her race and class. At the urging of a professor, she decided to transfer to Stanford University, where she hoped that "intellect was valued" (hooks, 2000b, p. 28). Instead, she again found that her class background was devalued and even demonized, particularly as she refused to renounce her own upbringing and culture (hooks, 1988). Academia valued those who conformed to expectations by speaking, dressing, acting, and thinking in specific ways that reflected a white middle-class background. hooks' black vernacular dialect and continual critique of authority were viewed as evidence that she did not fit in, as a scholar. Furthermore, her lack of disposable income marked her as different.

hooks continued to struggle with classism, racism, and sexism throughout her undergraduate studies at Stanford University, her graduate studies at Yale University and the University of California at Santa Cruz and even into her own professorship at such institutions such as Yale University, City

College of New York (CCNY) and Oberlin College. Despite harbouring the initial hope that universities could be sites of liberation, hooks soon came to the realization that a white supremacist capitalist patriarchy was endemic to the educational system itself; classrooms were "the place where the social order was kept in place" (hooks, 2000b, p. 36). Where she learned and taught mattered little, although she began to seek out institutions, such as CCNY, that were more diverse in terms of class and race.

Tellingly, at first, she resisted becoming a teacher partly because others' viewed teaching as the only path she could take due to the racism and sexism that restricted women's roles. She explains that "I had no desire to teach. I wanted to be a writer. I soon learned that working menial jobs for long hours did not a writer make and came to accept that teaching was the best profession a writer could have" (hooks, 2010, p. 3). These menial jobs were "in the world of the mundane. I worked at a bookstore, cooked at a club, worked for the telephone company" (hooks, 2000b, p. 36). Nonetheless, she "soon learned to love teaching" (p. 3), as is evidenced by her large body of work on the subject. It is ironic that these two passions, one that came early to her and one that she initially worked to avoid, have come together in her writing about teaching.

When she began writing for publication, hooks chose to use a pseudonym. Due to the difficulty in finding her own voice as Gloria Watkins, and the ambivalence with which her family approached writing and books, hooks (1988) felt that she needed to "construct a writer-identity that would challenge and subdue all impulses leading me away from speech into silence" (p. 9).

She "chose the name bell hooks because it was a family name [her great-grandmother's], because it had a strong sound. Throughout childhood, this name was used to speak to the memory of a strong woman, a woman who spoke her mind" (hooks, 1988, p. 161). hooks chose not to capitalize the first letters of the name as a way to differentiate herself from her great-grandmother, attaining her own distinct, yet connected, identity.

She also wanted to separate herself from her writing so that her content, not her ego, would be centred, leaving herself "open to challenge and change" (p. 163) without becoming too attached to her own ideas. She aimed to move her work away from a "cult of personality" (p. 164). Ironically, the name bell hooks is now famous, and is very much connected to Gloria Watkins. It could be argued that her pseudonym has created its own cult of personality. However, hooks explains that the use of a pseudonym keeps her grounded (hooks, 1988), allows her "playful" opportunities such as engaging in written dialogues with her two identities (hooks, 1994, p. 45). and "create[s] a meditative distance between me and my writing" (hooks, 1999, p. 115). She has also experienced instances when people speak to her, as Gloria Watkins, of hooks' work, without knowing they are the same person (hooks, 1988). Even though she tries to distance her identity (as expressed through her name) from her work, she does not separate her experiences. hooks is always willing to explore how her own life influences her writing.

hooks' eventually became a tenure-track professor at Yale University, with a cross-appointment in the English department and African-American Studies. Frustrated with a continual push-back against her teaching pedagogy and form of scholarship, particularly as it relates to her challenging of the status quo, hooks left the Ivy league to work in other institutions, such as City College in New York, where she felt she would have the opportunity "to teach students coming from poor and working class backgrounds similar to my own" (hooks, 2003, p. 17).

Regardless of where she was teaching, hooks aimed for an "engaged pedagogy" that is "more demanding than conventional critical or feminist pedagogy. For unlike the latter teaching practices [although encompassing many of their pedagogical elements], an engaged pedagogy emphasizes well-being" (hooks, 1994, p. 15) for students and teachers. After years of teaching in this way, continually challenging students', professors', and universities' ways of thinking, hooks began to feel "burnout":

> I knew it was time for me to take a break from the classroom when my mind was always someplace else. And in the last stages of burnout, I knew I needed to be someplace else because I simply did not want to get up, get dressed, and go to work. I dreaded the classroom. (hooks, 2003, pp. 14, 15)

While hooks ended up leaving the classroom, she has continued to teach outside of formal classrooms in ways that she finds fulfilling. She continues with her writing, gives speeches, facilitates workshops, and works with children. She has also begun to write children's books that portray young black boys and girls in positive ways, "challeng[ing] racism and sexism" (hooks, 2010, p. 141), while "aim[ing] to decolonize" (p. 144) children's "minds and imaginations" (p. 144).

The story of hooks' life is central to her theoretical scholarship. Knowing her story, which she is so open to sharing, can help readers gain a deeper understanding of her work.

TEACHING ABOUT SOCIAL ISSUES: THE INTERSECTIONS OF GENDER, RACE, AND CLASS

There are several main themes in hooks' work, each revolving around the central idea that issues of gender, race, and class intersect in complicated ways that cannot be separated. Although the theme of teaching/education is in its own distinct section below, it is entwined with each of the others.

WHITE SUPREMACIST CAPITALIST PATRIARCHY

hooks' use of the phrase "white supremacist capitalist patriarchy" is threaded throughout her work. She argues that one type of oppression cannot be separated from another. As such, they also cannot be put into hierarchical order; one is no more important than another, although they may function in varying ways in different people's lives. Furthermore, sexism, racism, and classism are not the result of individual actions (although they may be expressed as such) but are systemic forms of privilege and oppression. As hooks (1994/2008) says: there is a need "to accept the interlocking, interdependent nature of systems of domination and recognize specific ways each system is maintained" (p. 290). For instance, "racism has always been a divisive force separating black men and white men, and sexism has been a force that unites the two groups" (hooks, 1981, p. 99), which applies in reverse to women. White supremacy values whiteness over colour, privileging those who are white; capitalism values the "cultural code" of middle- and upper-class over the working class and poor, with a focus on money, consumerism, commodification, and class hierarchy; and, patriarchy esteems men and certain forms of masculinity.

Although hooks was, at one point, criticized for not critiquing heteronormativity and homophobia, she argues that an analysis of heteronormativity is embedded in her use of white supremacist capitalist patriarchy, although she does not make this explicit in her earliest work. Heterosexism, as hooks explains, is present in patriarchal thinking wherein men and women are expected to couple and have children, with the male as the head of the household. Therefore, "feminist movement[1] to eradicate heterosexism—compulsory heterosexuality—is central to efforts to end sexual oppression" (hooks, 1984/2000, p. 152).

While not everyone may enact overt forms of white supremacist capitalist patriarchy, it is embedded deeply in Western thinking and is often evidenced in more subtle actions, working to privilege white, middle- to upper-class men. It is not that men are perpetrators and women victims, but that "we all have capacity to act in ways that oppress, dominate, wound" (hooks, 1988, p. 21), as well as to resist and work for freedom. "By calling attention to interlocking systems of domination—sex, race, and class—black women and many other groups of women acknowledge the diversity and complexity of female experience, of our relationship to power and domination" (hooks, 1988, p. 21).

FEMINIST MOVEMENT

Women do not always perceive that they experience marginalization, oppression, and exploitation in their lives. In fact, "[u]nder capitalism, patriarchy is structured so that sexism restricts women's behaviour in some realms even as freedom from limitations is allowed in other spheres. The absence of extreme restrictions leads many women to ignore the areas in which they are exploited or discriminated against; it may even lead them to imagine that no women are oppressed" (hooks, 1984/2000, p. 5).

Such "imagining" is one of the reasons that hooks argues for feminist movement that is grassroots, going beyond academia into the community. In this regard, she has argued that "there will be no mass-based feminist movement as long as feminist ideas are understood only by a well-educated few" (hooks, 1984/2000 p. 113). It is for this reason that hooks writes in an accessible style that is understandable and connects to everyday life. Although she has been critiqued for this style (for instance, see Florence, 1998; Wallace, 1995), hooks argues that it is not only necessary but that being accessible does not mean her ideas are simplistic (hooks & West, 1991). As she has stated, "my goal as a feminist thinker and theorist is to take that abstraction [in theory] and articulate it in a language that renders it accessible—not less complex or rigorous—but simply more accessible" (hooks, 1988, p. 39). She decries the "tug-of-war that has existed within feminist movement between feminist intellectuals and academics, and participants in the movement . . . [who] are anti-intellectual" (hooks, 1984/2000, p. 113). What is required is to "unite theory and practice, to create a liberatory feminist praxis" (hooks, 1984/2000, p. 113) that values thought and action, scholarship and experience, in feminist movement.

hooks (1984/2000) defines "feminist movement" as what "happens when groups of people come together with an organized strategy to take action to eliminate patriarchy" (p. xi). In this definition, she does not specify who those "groups of people" are precisely because she believes that anyone can work against patriarchy, regardless of gender, race, or class.

Finally, feminist movement should be informed by feminist theory that provides groundwork for solidarity among women. "Feminist theory would have much to offer if it showed women ways in which racism and sexism are immutably connected, rather than pitting one struggle against the other or blatantly dismissing racism" (hooks, 1984/2000, p. 53). It can be difficult to work across differences, but hooks argues that it is essential.

WORKING TOGETHER WITH LOVE

Solidarity, acceptance, and love are required in order to build communities that can withstand the challenges of working together in a white supremacist capitalist patriarchy. hooks repeatedly calls for making connections through gender, race, and class. For example, as racism can work to separate women, white women and women of colour must work through issues of white privilege in order to meet the common goal of liberation. This does not mean that women should ignore differences, but should use them as a basis for challenging racism and connecting with each other. hooks argues that "feminist activists cannot bond on the terms set by the dominant ideology of the culture. We must define our own terms... [and] bond on the basis of our political commitment to a feminist movement that aims to end sexist oppression" (hooks, 1984/2000, p. 47).

Indeed, the same argument extends to men, particularly because "the reconstruction and transformation of male behaviour, of masculinity, is a necessary and essential part of feminist revolution" (hooks, 1988, p. 127). hooks connects the need to work across gender to that of race, as "after hundreds of years of antiracist struggle, more than ever before nonwhite people are currently calling attention to the primary role white people must play in antiracist struggle. The same is true of the struggle to eradicate sexism—men have a primary role to play" (hooks, 1984/2000, p. 83).

Additionally, it is necessary to work across class differences. Instead of demonizing those who are poor, which is a common occurrence in Western society, there are ways to support them:

> Those of us who are affluent, in solidarity with the underprivileged, bear witness by sharing resources, by helping to develop strategies for self-actualization that strengthen the self-esteem of the poor. We need concrete strategies and programs that address material needs in daily life as well as needs of the spirit." (hooks, 2000b, p. 130)

The Western system of capitalism has contributed to creating the conditions for poverty while simultaneously aiming for "disempowerment" of those who are poor (hooks, 2000b, p.124). As a result, their survival (as well as those who are part of the struggling working-class) has become increasingly difficult.

In order to engage in solidarity across gender, race, and class to challenge a white supremacist capitalist patriarchy, hooks (1988) emphasizes the need for love and caring: "embedded in the commitment to feminist revolution is the challenge to love" (p. 26). She calls for "love as the practice of freedom" (hooks, 1994/2008, p. 298), where love is not romantic, easy, and superficial, but deep, abiding, and steady in the face of conflict that recognizes and values difference. Love allows for acceptance as well as critical thought, with caring centred in community-building so that "critical exchange can take place without diminishing anyone's spirit ...conflict can be resolved constructively" (hooks, 2010, p. 162). Love itself is transgressive: "Love will always move us away from domination in all its forms. Love will always challenge and change us" (hooks, 2010, p. 163). This love also extends to self-love, as everyone holds some form of sexist, racist, and classist, beliefs, which are often internalized, resulting in feelings of shame (hooks, 1994/2008).

In order to learn to love, to "heal our wounds... recover and realize ourselves" (hooks, 1988, p. 3), hooks advocates for the exploration of personal experience. This is first noticeable in *Talking Back: Thinking Feminist, Thinking Black* when hooks (1988) explores the radical nature in "rooting... [her work] in personal reflection" (p. 3), arguing that the "public reality and institutional structures of domination make the private space for oppression and exploitation concrete—real. That's why I think it crucial to talk about the points where the public and the private meet, to connect the two" (p. 2). hooks (1988) also highlights the difficulties in doing so, due to a "fear of saying something about loved ones that they would feel should not be said" (p. 2), *and* how vulnerable it makes her. However, hooks (1988) argues that engaging with the personal has helped her to survive: "Openness is about how to be well and telling the truth is about how to put the broken bits and pieces of the heart back together again. It is about being whole—being wholehearted" (p. 2). Being whole and bringing in the personal is particularly pertinent to her work about teaching.

TEACHING AND LEARNING IN VARIOUS ASPECTS OF LIFE

There is a focus on teaching and learning throughout hooks' work, in the context of families, popular culture, feminist movement, women's literature, and formal education. Her first site for learning, her family, where she learned not only about love and community but about patriarchy, was, at times, confusing and contradictory.

> I was never taught absolute silence, I was taught that it was important to speak but to talk a talk that was in itself a silence. Taught to speak and yet beware of the betrayal of too much heard speech, I experienced intense confusion and deep anxiety in my efforts to speak and write. (hooks, 1988, p. 7)

By including these reflections in her work, hooks acknowledges the power of teaching-learning relationships in families, as well as the importance of studying them. In *Where We Stand: Class Matters*, hooks (2000b) "write[s] personally about my journey from a working-class world to class consciousness, about how classism has undermined feminism, about solidarity with the poor and how we see the rich" (p. viii). hooks (2000b) explores not only how she learned, but how others' valued learning, which was sometimes through formal education, and sometimes through conversation, the latter of which was, for her grandmother, "the place where everything must be learned—the site of all epistemology" (pp. 15, 16).

In her books that focus specifically on popular culture, hooks (1996/2009) explores the idea that, "whether we like it or not, cinema assumes a pedagogical role in the lives of many people" (p. 2). For hooks, such a pedagogical role also extends to other artifacts of popular culture, such as books, music videos, historical accounts, and even the concept of love. What is prevalent in these forms is "a culture of domination [which] is antilove. It requires violence to sustain itself. To choose love [in popular culture representations as well as professionally, and personally] is to go against the prevailing values of the culture" (hooks, 1994/2008, p. 293). People interact with culture, working to create, absorb, resist, "reimagine and re-envision" (hooks, 1996/2009, p. 12) it in a pedagogical relationship, not a one-way transmission.

As such, hooks (1996/2009) has found that "the use of movies as a pedagogical tool" (p. 3) helps students "engag[e] in an animated discussion deploying the very theoretical concepts that they had previously claimed they just did not understand" (p. 3). Popular culture assists students in not only engaging with theory, but applying it to their everyday lives.

With respect to teaching in particular, hooks wrote what became a trilogy largely centered on postsecondary education but applicable to a wide range of contexts. Its focus is on an engaged pedagogy that incorporates elements of feminist pedagogy as well as the work of critical theorist Paulo Freire and Buddhist monk Thich Nhat Hanh. hooks (1994) believes in "education as the practice of freedom" within a "pedagogy which emphasize[s] wholeness, a union of mind, body, and spirit" (p. 14). In order to practice such a pedagogy, it is essential to work towards "building community in the classroom" (hooks, 2010, p. 20). There are, however, significant challenges in attempting to do so in formal education, leading hooks (2003) to decry the ways in which "more often than not, the demands of academia . . . [are] at odds with intellectual life" (p. 186). In particular, the focus is too often on publishing as opposed to engaging in critical inquiry, teaching by rote instead of using transgressive pedagogy, and attending to administrative demands that detract from one's own scholarship and dedication to students.

hooks (1994/2008) argues that learning is somewhat distorted in postsecondary institutions, calling for "the *deinstitutionalization* of learning and of experience" (p. 274, italics in the original). Continuing, she asserts that "The more I've been in the academy, the more I think about Foucault's *Discipline and Punish: The Birth of the Prison* and the whole idea of how institutions work. . . . repression and containment" (hooks, 1994/2008, p. 275). hooks notes that such repression and containment works to confine learning, not broaden it. Creative, embodied, spiritual approaches focused on community and a critique of white supremacist capitalist patriarchy are typically not valued and often feared, particularly when emanating from the classroom of a black female professor. She notes that teaching, although an important vocation, can take a toll on critical pedagogues, who may need to take "time out" in order to recuperate and re-energize (hooks, 2003). Regardless, it is crucial that teaching is grounded in hope, "a place where paradise can be realized, a place of passion and possibility, a place where spirit matters, where all that we learn and know leads us into greater connection, into greater understanding of life lived in community" (hooks, 2003, p. 183).

CONCLUDING THOUGHTS

hooks' large body of work is testament to the importance and relevance of her ideas in today's world. As it crosses various disciplines of study, it is wide-ranging in its scope, explicating the multitude of ways in which a white supremacist capitalist patriarchy not only operates in Western society, but how it can and should be critiqued. By raising awareness about the interconnections between sexism, racism, and classism, and applying theory to practice through advocacy and activism, oppression and exploitation can be challenged and, eventually, if one works from a place of hope, diminished.

I end with the following words of hooks', demonstrating how critical theory, perhaps quite literally, saved her life, just as it can save the lives of others:

> When I am asked to talk about how I became "bell hooks," renowned writer and intellectual, I talk about the significance of critical thinking and how it helped me survive the racist, sexist, class elitism outside the home of my growing up and the dysfunction which sanctioned abuse, betrayal, and abandonment within the patriarchal home. (hooks, 2010, p. 183)

NOTES

1. Interestingly, hooks continually uses the phrase "feminist movement" without using an article ("the" or "a"). It is my belief that she does so intentionally to signify that "feminist" is not a noun, not a thing, but a verb, a living entity. As such, it is constantly changing, adapting, and evolving, incorporating new ideas, further developing theories, and attracting additional people.

REFERENCES

Florence, N. (1998). *bell hooks' engaged pedagogy: A transgressive education for critical consciousness*. Westport, CT: Bergin & Garvey.

hooks, b. (1981). *Ain't I a woman: Black women and feminism*. Boston, MA: South End Press.

hooks, b. (1984/2000). *Feminist theory from margin to center (2nd ed.).* Boston, MA: South End Press.

hooks, b. (1988). *Talking back: thinking feminist, thinking black.* Toronto: Between the Lines.

hooks, b. (1994). *Teaching to transgress: Education as the practice of freedom.* New York: Routledge.

hooks, b. (1994/2008). *Outlaw culture: Resisting representation.* New York: Routledge Classics.

hooks, b. (1996). *Bone black: memories of girlhood.* New York: Henry Holt and Co.

hooks, b. (1996/2009). *Reel to real: race, sex, and class at the movies.* New York: Routledge Classics.

hooks, b. (1999). *Remembered rapture: The writer at work.* New York: Henry Holt and Co.

hooks, b. (2000a). *Feminism is for everybody: Passionate politics.* Brooklyn: South End Press.

hooks, b. (2000b). *Where we stand: Class matters.* New York: Routledge.

hooks, b. (2003). *Teaching community: A pedagogy of hope.* New York: Routledge.

hooks, b. (2010). *Teaching critical thinking: Practical wisdom.* New York: Routledge.

hooks, b. (2013). *Writing beyond race: Living theory and practice.* New York: Routledge

hooks, b. & West, C. (1991). *Breaking bread: Insurgent black intellectual life.* Boston, MA.: South End Press.

Wallace, M. (1995). *For whom the bell tolls: Why America can't deal with black feminist intellectuals.* Voice Literary Supplement, 140, 19-24.

ANNOTATED BIBLIOGRAPHY

hooks, b. (1981). *Ain't I a woman: Black women and feminism.* Boston, MA: South End Press.

In this, her first academic book, hooks argues that race, gender, and class intersect and illustrates that by focusing on the ways in which, historically and contemporarily, black women's experiences differ from those of black men, white men, and white women. She explores how black women were sexually and racially oppressed in slavery, as opposed to black men's oppression which was due solely to race. In doing so, she critiques the ongoing myths of black women as matriarchs, amazons, mammies, and sapphires; and, examines black men's continued support of patriarchy. hooks goes on to discuss how the women's movement in the United States was/is racist and classist, with those in the movement often using the term and concept of "woman" as a stand-in for white privileged women to the exclusion of women of colour and those enmeshed in poverty. Nonetheless, she argues, despite backlashes and setbacks, black women have continued to work against racism and sexism.

hooks, b. (1984/2000). *Feminist theory from margin to center* (2nd ed.). Cambridge, MA: South End Press Classics.

The focus of this book is on feminist theory and feminist movement. hooks explains that she wrote this book due to the lack of material exploring "feminist theory that addresses margin and center" (p. xvii), as opposed to liberal feminist approaches that are derived too often from a white bourgeoisie lens. Additionally, she emphasizes the need to make feminism accessible to all women, not just those with a university education, through recognizing "the political importance of literacy" (p. 109), as well as working to "build mass awareness of the need for feminist movement through political education" (p. 163). She argues that the aim of feminist movement should be to build solidarity across races, classes, and genders as well as sexualities, by acknowledging and working through differences. Both men and women "have been socialized to passively accept sexist ideology... [and] must assume responsibility for eliminating it" (p. 73). Finally, hooks stresses that the goal of feminist movement is not reform but "total transformation of society" (p. 160) by "destroying dualism, eradicating systems of domination" (p. 165).

hooks, b. (1988). *Talking back: thinking feminist, thinking black.* Toronto, CA: Between the Lines.

In this book, hooks explores her growing awareness of the importance of including her own personal experiences and reflections in her writing. She argues that, in her lectures, she consistently discussed her life, that it "was that coming together of the idea, the theory, and shared personal experience that was the moment when the abstract became concrete, tangible, something people could hold and carry away with them" (p. 3). Therefore, she wanted to do the same in her writing. Weaving together theory and experience, hooks examines the "politics of domination" in feminist movement, education for liberation, white supremacy with its implications for black communities in general and black bodies (and minds) in particular, and homophobia. She also explains why she chose to take a pseudonym in that it allowed her to "claim an identity that affirmed for me my right to speech" (p. 162).

hooks, b. (1993). A life in the spirit: Reflections on faith and politics. *ReVision,* *15*(3), 99–104.

In this article, hooks discusses how mysticism, faith, and liberation theology are central to her own spirituality. She emphasizes the importance of service to others and working together in community. As she moved into adulthood, she began to distance herself from Christian doctrine which she perceived as dualistic and fear-oriented. In so doing, hooks explored other religions, finding a particular affinity with Buddhism. She believes that spiritual practice, love, and forgiveness are important in order to have hope, engage with the world, and honour each person's whole self.

hooks, b. (1994). *Teaching to transgress: Education as the practice of freedom.* New York, NY: Routledge.

In the first book of what became a trilogy on teaching, hooks focuses on teaching that emerges from an "interplay of anticolonial, critical, and feminist pedagogies" (p. 10). She explores the difficulty and importance of teaching for radical change as well as the concomitant need for teachers to embrace their own whole selves and those of their students. She brings in much of her own experiences as a student, professor, and scholar, which helps the reader to understand not only her argument with respect to "teaching to transgress" but how her own history influences her work. Most chapters are written in typical prose, but two are in the form of dialogues. In one, where hooks explores how Freire has influenced her teaching, she engages in "a playful dialogue with myself, Gloria Watkins, talking with bell hooks, my writing voice" (p. 45). This book is useful for those wanting to learn more about why radical pedagogy is so necessary and the implications of applying it in the classroom.

hooks, b. (1994/2008). *Outlaw culture: Resisting representation*. New York, NY: Routledge Classics.

Popular culture from the perspective of a gendered approach to cultural studies is the focus of this book. Herein, hooks explores the ways in which white supremacist capitalist patriarchy interacts with various American icons, including Madonna, Ice Cube, and Spike Lee, as well as with artifacts such as movies (*The Bodyguard, The Crying Game, Malcolm X*) and feminist books (by Naomi Wolf, Katie Roiphe). hooks critiques how American culture values money and commodities, demonizes the poor, causes shame to people of colour, and erases or alters Black history. In her final chapter, hooks calls for the need for love of self and others in order to transform society.

hooks, b. (1996). *Bone black: memories of girlhood*. New York, NY: Henry Holt and Co.

In this autobiographical book, hooks switches from first to third person in relating distinct yet connected stories of her childhood, writing from the perspective of her younger self. hooks' poetic writing reveals her struggles with the complexity of her feelings for her family, wrapped up as they are in the pain and love she experienced. In many of the chapters, hooks relates stories of the difficulties she faced as a girl in a large patriarchal family where she felt isolated, misunderstood, and abused. Often accused of being "crazy," because she refused to conform to gendered expectations, hooks found solace in books and in the dream of becoming a writer. Her stories about her home, community, school, and spiritual life highlight how she learned not only about white privilege, but "that men have the right to do whatever they want to do and that women must always follow rules" (p. 138). Nonetheless, she continued to resist, "making a world for myself" in "this place of words" (p. 183).

hooks, b. (1996/2009). *Reel to real: race, sex, and class at the movies*. New York, NY: Routledge Classics.

With a similar focus to that in *Outlaw Culture*, hooks deconstructs how movies too often essentialize black and black female experiences. As "cinema assumes a pedagogical role in the lives of many people" (p. 2) and is not a mirror to life but actively "make[s] culture" (p. 12), it is, she argues, crucial to interrogate and problematize the content of movies. And hooks does just that. In doing so, she critiques the ways in which movies, to a large extent, support a white supremacist capitalist patriarchy through their screenwriting, character development, plot choices, and casting. Among the movies she examines are: *Leaving Las Vegas, Pulp Fiction, Reservoir Dogs*, and *Waiting to Exhale*. She also engages in dialogues with several Hollywood industry filmmakers, exploring the reasoning behind some of the filmic choices they made.

hooks, b. (1997/1999). Representing whiteness in the black imagination. In R. Frankenberg (Ed.), *Displacing whiteness: Essays in social and cultural criticism* (pp. 165–179). Durham, NC: Duke University Press.

In this chapter in an edited book that interrogates whiteness, hooks explores how black people conceive the concept, both conceptually and in the reality of their everyday lives, sometimes associating it with terrorism and other times "pretend[ing] to be comfortable in the face of whiteness" (p. 169). She also discusses how, "socialized to believe the fantasy, that whiteness represents goodness and all that is benign and nonthreatening, many white people assume this is the way black people conceptualize whiteness" (p. 169). hooks calls for a move away from "evoking a simplistic, essentialist 'us and them' dichotomy" (p. 169), with a need for all people to acknowledge and work against racism. "Critically examining the association of whiteness as terror in the black imagination, deconstructing it, we both name racism's impact and help to break its hold. We decolonize our minds and our imaginations" (p. 178).

hooks, b. (1999). *Remembered rapture: The writer at work.* New York, NY: Henry Holt and Co.

The focus of this book is on hooks' writing with respect to her own authorial process, the content of her work, and the publishing industry. She begins with a discussion of the diary writing she did as a child, explaining how it allowed her to confront her shadow-self and eventually became transformational as she moved into adulthood. hooks emphasizes the passion and spirituality that is evoked when she writes, even given the difficulties faced in writing and publishing, particularly for a black woman. She speaks of the need to bring the self into writing, continually critiquing race, sex, and class. hooks explains how she became an academic in order to write, although she found that the demands of academia did not leave her as much time to write as she wanted. hooks also dedicates chapters to those women writers who have most influenced her, such as Zora Neale Hurston, Emily Dickinson, Ann Petry, Lorraine Hansberry, Toni Morrison, and Toni Cade Bambara.

hooks, b. (2000a). *Feminism is for everybody: Passionate politics.* Cambridge, MA: South End Press.

This book succinctly explains, demystifies, and challenges popular misconceptions about feminism, defining feminism as "a movement to end sexism, sexist exploitation, and oppression" (p. 1). As such, it argues that men *and* women need to be involved in working against "white supremacist capitalist patriarchy" (p. 4). In a straightforward and easy to understand manner, hooks explores feminism as it relates to such topics as women's bodies, beauty, race, class, imperialism, work, violence, family, sexuality, and love. It is a useful primer for introducing feminism in general to those unfamiliar with feminist movement, and hooks' approach to it in particular (with her stress on the interrelatedness of race, class, and gender).

hooks, b. (2000b). *Where we stand: Class matters*. New York, NY: Routledge.

In this book, hooks focuses on class as a central point of analysis, using it as a lens that is then connected to race and gender. She argues that American society works to occlude class, with citizens typically disregarding how it matters in everyday life. hooks uses her own experiences to describe how her family cuts across various classes, classifying her grandparents as poor, her immediate family as working class, and herself as now upper-middle class. She critiques the ways in which capitalism, embedded in a white supremacist capitalist patriarchy, encourages over-consumption, greed, and hoarding. Finally, hooks calls for "rethink[ing] class" (p. 163), as a beginning, by ceasing to disparage those who are poor and working class, "resisting unnecessary consumerism, living simply, and abundantly sharing resources" (p. 162).

hooks, b. (2003). *Teaching community: A pedagogy of hope*. New York, NY: Routledge.

This book builds on "*Teaching to transgress*" with a focus on teaching and learning within and outside the classroom. hooks discusses contexts such as formal classroom environments in universities, informal lectures and workshops, and the family. She emphasizes the need to build community in learning environments by working through fear in order to challenge racism and sexism as well as welcoming anti-racist whites as allies. She also explores the difficulties in teaching, explaining the need for "time outs" from teaching and the importance of valuing service to students. Learning should, she argues, incorporate wholeness through spirituality and a focus on learning for its own sake, as opposed to for a credential or work requirement.

hooks, b. (2010). *Teaching critical thinking: Practical wisdom*. New York, NY: Routledge.

In this final book of her teaching trilogy, hooks "highlight[s] issues and concerns that teachers and students placed before me and [that she] respond[s] to with short commentar[ies]" (p. 5). Each topic is addressed in very succinct chapters, building on her earlier work and in which she provides advice as to how to deal with specific teaching challenges. In doing so, she explores issues such as how to enact an "engaged pedagogy" that involves students in critical thinking for democratic education. She also highlights the negative effects of an education system that values meritocracy, individualism, and commodification in a "dominator culture." In response, she discusses the need to establish learning communities of love where teachers and students can work through conflict and are encouraged to critique white supremacist capitalist patriarchy. hooks believes that teaching is a "prophetic vocation" in which teachers and students should be recognized as whole beings, not just as minds but also as spiritual bodies.

hooks, b. (2013). *Writing beyond race: Living theory and practice*. New York, NY: Routledge.

In her latest book, hooks adds "imperialism" to her general description of life in the United States, "white supremacist capitalist patriarchy," thus creating the phrase and description: imperialist white supremacist capitalist patriarchy" (p. 4). Her use of imperialism is not new, as hooks has previously engaged with this concept, but its direct inclusion in her description of "systems of domination" (p. 4) now forefronts its importance. She explains its influence as "imperialist colonization became the belief system that supported the mass murder of indigenous natives, the blatant stealing of their lands, and the creation of segregated reservations" (p. 4), as well as the systematic "enslavement of black Africans" (p. 4). Furthermore, black history has been rewritten by ignoring "the presence of African individuals who came to the so-called new world before Columbus" (p. 4) as well as systematically enslaving African peoples. hooks candidly writes of her fatigue in (but continual commitment to) critiquing racism when white supremacy is so often denied. In particular, hooks works to "focus attention on issues of accountability, standpoint [i.e., positionality/perspective], and white supremacy" (p. 7) by "examin[ing] those cultural productions which give the surface appearance of addressing topics of race, gender, and class, while merely reinscribing ideologies of domination" (p. 7–8).

The primary cultural productions she examines in this book are media representations of Michelle Obama and a recent biography of Malcolm X, movies such as *Precious* and *Crash*, and books such as *The Immortal Life of Henrietta Lacks* and *The Help* (also a movie). In so doing, she builds on her previous work in cultural studies (for instance, her books *Outlaw Culture* and *Reel to Real*), demonstrating how gender, race, and class continue to operate in popular culture. hooks, again, also brings in her own experiences by writing of how, for her, "home is the only place where there is no race" (p. 184), which is why she "ground[s] myself in the homeplace" (p. 185). She explains how "turning away from images produced in the culture of imperialist white supremacist patriarchy by refusing television and being selective about other media protects my emotional well-being" (p. 185). Indeed, her entire book points to the insidiousness and danger of passively consuming popular culture artifacts as "the most powerful covert teacher of white supremacy is the mass media" (p. 12). Media images must be continually deconstructed, critiqued, and discussed in order to work against the ways in which "all children in this nation are inundated from birth on into adulthood with white supremacist thinking and practice" (p. 12).

hooks, b. & McKinnon, T. (1996). Sisterhood: Beyond public and private. *Signs*, *21*(4), 814–829.

This article is an interview of the first author by the second, prefaced with a discussion by hooks of her concerns about how she is represented in the media. hooks states that "it is rare that I am given an opportunity to talk with a progressive black female and to have some control over the way I am represented" (p. 815).

hooks and McKinnon met when McKinnon was a student, establishing a relationship that has sustained itself over the years. hooks terms this interview "unique" as "it begins from a location of intimacy" (p. 816) and trust. In the interview itself, the two dialogue about the interaction between feminist theory, practice, and politics; academic feminism; cultural criticism; engaging with students; and, public intellectualism. In discussing the need to connect private and public lives, hooks states that "private life as exhibitionism and performance is not the same thing as a politicized strategic use of private information that seeks to subvert the politics of domination" (p. 823). Feminist movement is a theme of the interview, with hooks concluding that "the challenge of where we go from here is to be able to create a new feminist movement that would be the site for the production of revolutionary feminist theory that is inclusive, that changes how people think and act" (p. 829).

hooks, b. & Sealey, K. (2008). Afterword: On the topic of film and education: A conversation with bell hooks. In Sealy, K. (Ed.), *Film, politics, & education: Cinematic pedagogy across the disciplines* (pp. 147–157). New York, NY: Peter Lang Publishing, Inc.

In Sealey's edited book on the use of cinematic pedagogy throughout all levels of schooling, this joint chapter presents a dialogue between hooks and the editor. hooks states that "because I feel like most of what people are learning about gender, race, class is coming from media and especially movies, to me movies become the perfect tool…for teaching critical thinking and critical theories" (p. 148). She speaks of being able to be entertained while at the same time engaging in societal critique. hooks brings in the concepts of literacy and engaged pedagogy in her discussion of film as "a pedagogical structure" (p. 155) to interrogate gender, race, class, and homophobia.

hooks, b., Wallace, M., Hacker, A., Taylor, J., Bell, D., Reed, I., et al. (1995). The crisis of African American gender relations: A symposium on the crisis of gender relations among African Americans. *Transitions, 66*, 91–175.

This symposium is a collection of responses to Orlando Patterson' s article ("Backlash"), previously published in *Transitions*, claiming that African-American men suffer more marginalization than African-American women, with the latter more well off from a societal standpoint than the former. The first essay, a "prospectus," summarizes Patterson's argument, with several essays following that engage with his work. hooks' response is first, wherein she vehemently opposes his view and his (mis)use of her own scholarship. Furthermore, she vilifies the journal editors' decision to publish such an antifeminist piece without "giv[ing] equal space to a profeminist perspective… [which] would have forfeited the attention-grabbing atmosphere of a sensationalist spectacle that is created by the request for critical responses to his essay" (p. 94). At the core of her critique of Patterson is that his "strategically undocumented insistence that there are ways that black females benefit from the existing social structure of white supremacist capitalist patriarchy merely distorts reality" (p. 95), particularly as he denies patriarchy and ignores class. hooks' response is followed by that of several others, who differentially agree/disagree with various elements of Patterson's article. This symposium is particularly useful in that it presents a variety of opinions on one topic, resulting in a dialogue of sorts (indeed, one essay is written as a dialogue) among scholars.

hooks, b. & West, C. (1991). *Breaking bread: Insurgent black intellectual life.* Cambridge, MA: South End Press.

In this book, bell hooks and Cornel West present an introduction to each other's work, interview each other, engage in dialogue, and contribute a sole chapter each on black intellectuals (West), and black women intellectuals (hooks). There is a focus on their relationship "as friends and comrades in struggle" (p. 2) in that, as hooks states, they have "the willingness to love compassionately, the willingness to engage intellectually with the kind of critical affirmation where we can talk, argue, disagree, even become disappointed in each other, yet still leave one another with a sense of spiritual joy and renewal" (p. 2). In his introduction to hooks' work, West addresses the "heavy price she pays" (p. 60) due to the difficulties inherent in her positionality as a black female scholar who writes in an accessible style typically not valued by academia: "She has insisted on doing her intellectual work—grappling with questions and issues usually eschewed by the academy—in her own style and in the interests of Black people" (p. 60). hooks' work, West concludes, "proposes a singular human struggle to be candid about one's self and contestory toward the dehumanizing forces in our world" (p. 62).

This book provides readers not only an understanding of the work of hooks and West, but a view as to how their perspectives interact, with each author demonstrating the possibility of simultaneously respecting and critiquing the other.

CHILDREN'S BOOKS

hooks, b. (1999). *Happy to be nappy.* Ilustrated by C. Raschka. New York, NY: Hyperion Books for Children.

In her first illustrated children's book, hooks presents a positive portrayal of black girls' hair and beauty, with a focus on self-acceptance.

hooks, b. (2002). *Be boy buzz.* Illustrated by C. Raschka. New York, NY: Hyperion Books for Children.

This illustrated children's book focuses on boys, with positive representations of black boys engaged in a number of activities, including playing and reading.

COMMENTARY

Carolissen, R., Bozalek, V., Nicholls, L., Leibowitz, B., Rohleder, P., & Swartz, L. (2011). bell hooks and the enactment of emotion in teaching and learning across boundaries. *South African Journal of Higher Education, 25*(1), 157–167.

In this journal article, the authors explore how they applied hooks' scholarship on a pedagogy of hope to their context of South African higher education. They provide an overview of hooks' work from her trilogy on teaching, discuss how she builds on Freire, and emphasize her use of autobiography. The authors undertook their project, "Community, Self, and Identity" (CSI) at the University of Stellenbosch, which "aimed to engage students across boundaries of universities, professions, race, gender and class to allow them to critically examine their assumptions about their disciplines through engagement with 'the other'" (p. 159). Herein, they focus specifically on their use of guest speakers to bring "a multitude of opportunities for identification, for being unsettled and for feeling affirmed" (p. 165). They conclude that "the value of emotion, biographies and human connectedness that bell hooks emphasizes as central to creating a pedagogy of hope was demonstrated by the teaching process and creative media used by guest speakers" (p. 165), resulting in "blurred boundaries between learners and educators" (p. 165). Participants in CSI were able to engage in transformative learning by meeting across difference, sharing aspects of themselves, and working through feelings of unsafeness. hooks' work on teaching was central to their success, demonstrating how her ideas can be applied to various contexts.

Davidson, M. & Yancy, G. (Eds.). (2009). *Critical perspectives on bell hooks.* New York, NY: Taylor & Francis. (e-book version)

This book, one in a series on *Critical Social Thought* (edited by Michael Apple), is a "critical yet supportive interrogation of what her [bell hooks'] work means in a large array of areas" (Apple, Series Editor's Introduction, p. ix). The editors begin this book with an introduction that provides an overview of hooks' work and life, emphasizing the bravery of her creative critique, which began in her childhood. They explore hooks' decision to use a pen name, the importance of which she attributes to theory as connected to experience, her focus on problem-posing and liberation, and her critique of the academy.

The book is divided into three main themes: critical pedagogy and praxis, dynamics of race and gender, and spirituality and love. The authors of each of the fourteen chapters discuss the ways in which their own scholarship and teaching has been influenced by hooks. For instance, in his chapter, Yancy explores "how hooks's critical pedagogy helps to frame my pedagogical engagement with predominantly white students within the context of teaching courses in philosophy where the central philosophical theme is race" (p. 34). In another chapter, Manuel focuses on how both children and adults reading hooks' children's books together can learn about literacy and societal critique. As a final example, Marcano argues that "hooks's corpus can be, and should be, considered a phenomenology of a black feminist consciousness"

(p. 112). These three chapters, although not encompassing the diversity of thought in this book, demonstrate the wide-ranging topics discussed. This book will assist readers in not only becoming familiar with hooks' scholarship, but understanding how others interpret and apply her work.

Florence, N. (1998). *bell hooks' engaged pedagogy: A transgressive education for critical consciousness.* Westport, CT: Bergin & Garvey.

An entry in the *Critical Studies in Education and Culture Series* (edited by Henry Giroux), this book focuses on the scholarship of bell hooks as it relates to social and educational theory, with a particular application of her work to third-world contexts. It provides a useful discussion of hooks' main concepts and provides an illuminating examination of how her ideas can be applied to other contexts.

Florence begins with an overview of hooks' work and life, discussing her main ideas as well as how her writing has been received by others (especially with respect to her nonacademic style and recurring self-disclosures).

The purpose of the first two parts on social theory (focusing on white supremacy, women's marginalization in the mass media, and classism in education) and educational theory (engaged pedagogy as discussed in *Teaching to transgress: Education as the Practice of Freedom,* 1994) is to provide background for Florence's exploration of how hooks' ideas (from a first-world context) might apply to Kenyan culture, economy, and educational system. She concludes that "a lot of issues raised by hooks are applicable to a Third World context. hooks' analysis of the United States resonates with cited literature on the Kenyan situation in terms of culture, gender, and class biases" (p. 225).

Wallace, M. (1995). For whom the bell tolls: Why America can't deal with black feminist intellectuals. *Voice Literary Supplement, 140,* 19–24.

In this article, Wallace, a feminist author who focuses on race, fervently critiques hooks for her use of personal experience and nonacademic writing style. She argues that hooks' work is self-indulgent, simplistic, and repetitive, with too little use of references and supporting evidence. Tellingly, Wallace's argument is similar to that what hooks herself has commented on in regard to how her work has frequently been devalued. Wallace provides a useful contrary opinion to those authors who have commended hooks' work for the specific reasons which Wallace critiques it (for instance, see hooks & West, 1991). In having access to multiple opinions, readers can make their own informed decisions as to the value, importance, and credibility of hooks' scholarship.

CHAPTER 14

KATHLEEN WEILER

A Feminist Scholar/Educator for Change: Gender, Class, and Power

Deborah Donahue-Keegan

Feminist, postcolonial, and postmodernist challenges have led critical educational theorists to reexamine their own assumptions and the ways their own thought could be examined as discursive practice. These challenges have led to tensions and conflicts within critical pedagogy, but at the same time they have led to a rich interchange and revitalization of the ways in which power is conceptualized as operating in schools and curricula, and in particular a much more complex understanding of the ways in which students and teachers are both subjected to and subjects of what we call education

—Kathleen Weiler (1992, p. 4)

The above statement by Kathleen Weiler (1992) from her introduction to the book *What Schools Can Do: Critical Pedagogy and Practice* encapsulates her own deeply rooted, substantive contributions to the "rich interchange and revitalization of the ways in which power is conceptualized as operating in schools and in curricula" (p. 4). It also reflects and encapsulates the profound impact of Weiler's dedication, as evidenced by her research and in her writing for over twenty-five years. She has generated "a much more

Educating About Social Issues in the 20th and 21st Centuries, pages 279–302
Copyright © 2014 by Information Age Publishing
All rights of reproduction in any form reserved.

complex understanding of the ways in which students and teachers are both subjected to and subjects of what we call education" (Weiler, 1992, p. 4).

An Emeritus Professor of Education at Tufts University, Kathleen Weiler is a distinguished scholar who has "focused on the social, historical, and political context of education in relation to questions of gender, and includes ethnographic studies of classroom teaching, feminist theory and pedagogy, and historical studies of women educators in the American West" (http://ase.tufts.edu/education/faculty/weiler.asp). Weiler's scholarship has been grounded by her ongoing development of a critical theory of schooling that bridges "the most critical aspects of reproduction theory...with those aspects of feminist theory that stress the importance of consciousness, experience, and the subjective side of human relations" (Giroux and Freire, 1988, p. ix).

In writing across disciplines—critical studies in education, history, and anthropology—Weiler's evolved capacity for courageous intellectual critique and simultaneous perspective-taking—whether of world-renowned figures such as John Dewey or Paulo Freire, or of little known school systems or educators—has had a profound impact on the deeper layers of the education landscape in the United States. This is particularly true in terms of her complex, multifocal (race, class and gender) scholarship vis-à-vis her feminist analysis of women's work in schools/classrooms. The profound impact of the latter is clearly addressed—in a foreseeing way—in Henry Giroux and Paulo Freire's introduction to Weiler's *Women Teaching for Change*:

Women Teaching for Change challenges the reader to understand schooling and critical pedagogy as a form of cultural politics. By utilizing the concept of "voice" as a pedagogical category to examine the interaction of teachers and learners and the knowledge they both bring to the classroom, as well as the knowledge they produce together, Weiler extends the notion of radical praxis far beyond the ways in which it has been employed in radical educational theory. She rightly criticizes those dogmatic strands within critical pedagogy, which assume that a theoretically correct position is all that is needed for students to acquire an alternative reading of the world. She also rejects the prevailing notion that pedagogy necessarily follows from the production or transmission of knowledge. Rather, she takes the position that pedagogy is an integral aspect of knowledge production itself. Finally, Weiler lucidly demonstrates in her study how pedagogy is always part of the dynamic of production, with the teacher rendered as theorist/learner and the student as learner/reader/critic. With a similar clarity of insight, she analyzes how pedagogy, as part of the process of exchange that takes place within asymmetrical relations of power, always engages specific cultural forms and experiences, which generate different sets of understandings for teachers and students with respect to the categories of gender, race, and class (p. 2).

KATHLEEN WEILER'S REFLECTIONS
ON FORMATIVE EXPERIENCES

It is my profound honor to know Kathleen Weiler. In the spring of 2008, Kathleen hired me to teach the *Education for Peace and Justice* course she had iteratively developed, with other Tufts University Department of Education faculty, over a number of years. Her work continues to inform this course, which I continue to teach. During the process of preparing for and writing this chapter, I have thoroughly enjoyed learning more about the breadth and depth of Kathleen Weiler's research and writing over the past twenty-five years.

When I presented Kathleen with a number of questions about the formative, subjective experiences that have shaped her views, perspectives and sociomoral proclivities, she replied with thoughtfully composed written responses. With her permission, I include her exact words below, in response to the following questions: What were some key formative experiences for you, as a child/adolescent/young adult—in and outside your family, in your schooling as a child, high school student, and university student? How did you become so interested and immersed in critical theory? What were your goals in choosing to go to graduate school? What books and scholars have most influenced your thinking? How and why did you choose Henry Giroux as your doctoral advisor/mentor? What was it like, for you, to be advised/mentored by Giroux? To follow are Kathleen Weiler's words, in response to this inquiry:

> I grew up in a small rural town in central California, an only child. My father was a lineman for the gas and electric company and my mother was an elementary school teacher who was greatly loved by her students and respected by parents and people in the town. My own experience taught me the value of the work of teaching and also the contradiction between people's lived experience and the way teaching and teachers are presented politically. I knew from my own life how teaching is both unrecognized and all too often denigrated in political discourse, and at the same time respected and valued at the level of the immediate relationships of children, families, and teachers.
>
> I was one of the very few students, from my high school, who went on to a four-year college. I received a scholarship to Stanford. The early 1960s were not a positive time for women students. At Stanford, class was unrecognized; I only knew one other student whose father belonged to a union, for example. There were only a handful of African American, Mexican American, and Asian American students. Almost everyone else I met was white, and from professional or wealthy families. But this was not remarked upon. The privilege of the students and those in power—along the lines of race, class, gender, or any other form of identity—was simply not acknowledged.

I studied history and was particularly interested in what we then called intellectual history, the development of ideas over time, but there was very little concern with social history or the way broader events and ideas shape individual lives. It was a traditional undergraduate education focusing on the ideas of "great men," with little interest with social movements or connecting ideas to the social conditions that generated them . . . and certainly not even a mention of the idea that thinkers were socially positioned or privileged. There was a belief that philosophers were truth seekers. The fact that these truth seekers we studied were all white men was not even considered; nor was the fact that there were no women professors in the history department. Only women bore gender, only people of color bore race; gays and lesbians were pariahs.

In many ways the most powerful education for me was after I graduated and lived through the social movements of the later 1960s, when the ideas of class and race and gender were raised and became central to politics and our lives. The civil rights movement, the organizing against the Vietnam War, and the women's movement, all challenged the ideas that had dominated my undergraduate education.

As was true of many other women of my generation, I married immediately after graduating. I had two children, and worked as a high school teacher. Although I enjoyed teaching, I still had a desire to study and write. Since my experience was in schools, it was natural for me to turn to the study of education. It was my great good fortune that Henry Giroux was an assistant professor at Boston University at that time, just beginning his career.

It was through Henry that I was introduced to critical theory and to the work of other scholars who were applying Marxist and critical theory to education, both in the United States and in other countries. Henry was in contact with these thinkers and brought their work into his courses and seminars. The most influential thinkers for me were probably Gramsci and Freire, but I was also concerned to explore feminist theory as well. I was influenced by the work of other feminist educational theorists who were undertaking research at this time—Madeleine Arnot, Gaby Weiner, Miriam David in England, Jane Gaskell in Canada, Lyn Yates and Marjorie Theobald in Australia, Sue Middleton in New Zealand. My doctoral thesis was an attempt to use both critical theory and feminist theory to understand the work of feminist high school teachers. It was published as *Women Teaching for Change* in a series edited by Henry Giroux and Paulo Freire.

After I completed my doctorate I moved to university teaching at Tufts University. At Tufts, I was influenced by scholars in other fields—particularly in Peace and Justice Studies, and American Studies. And I met other feminist educators working in the United States—Sari Biklen among many others—who greatly enriched my own thinking. My subsequent research moved both to theory but most significantly to the history of women in education. My second book, *Country Schoolwomen*, is a local history of women teachers in the area of California where I grew up, and my most recent book, *Democracy and*

Schooling in California: The Legacy of Helen Heffernan and Corinne Seeds, is a joint biography of two progressive California educators. Although I have moved to historical research, I have maintained a critical perspective and a strong belief that scholarship is deeply political.

Weiler's activist approach within the realm of academics embraces "all intellectual work as political" (Weiler, 1992, p. 5). As she contends in *What Schools Can Do*, "critical pedagogy links education with an analysis of politics and economics, and takes as central the belief that schools are places where social analysis and the empowerment of students can take place" (Weiler, 1992, p. 2). Weiler's intellectual, and moral commitment to critical pedagogy as a centering conceptual approach developed and solidified during her time as doctoral student at Boston University in the early 1980s, when she was an advisee and mentee of Henry Giroux. Her expansive scholarship since that time is evidenced by her impressive list of publications (sole authorship of three books; editor, coeditor and coauthor of six books in total; author of 19 book chapters; 30 articles and reviews, and over 80 conference presentations and invited lectures since 1985) and numerous prestigious fellowships and awards.

A WOMAN WRITING FOR CHANGE

In cases where the gender, race, or class of teacher and student are different, feminist teaching creates conflicts on various levels. But that conflict can become the text for counter-hegemonic teaching. What is important is not to deny conflict, but to recognize that in a society like the United States, which is so deeply split by gender, race, and class, conflict is inevitable and only reflects social and political realities. But recognition of conflict, oppression, and power does not mean their acceptance. It means making them conscious so they can be addressed and transformed (Weiler, 1988, p. 145).

In the above statement, which is from her first published book, *Women Teaching for Change: Gender, Class, & Power*, in 1988) Kathleen Weiler identifies the perennial tension, and conflict, involved in the work for counter-hegemonic, emancipatory social change. In *Women Teaching for Change*, which was grounded in her in-depth study of teachers and administrators in/across two large urban schools, Weiler explores the possibilities that can result from such a process, as facilitated by feminist educators, within the domain of schooling. Through the lens of feminist theory, she illuminates how structural forces and agency "act upon" the "life histories, consciousness, and practice" of feminist educators, in public high schools (Weiler, 1988, p. 145). Weiler points to how feminist teachers "conscious of their own gendered, classed, and raced subjectivities as they confirm or challenge the lived experiences of their students" (1988, p. 145) are positioned, and hence, more apt, to constructively address the tensions that come with conflict, power, and oppression vis-à-vis the intersection of structural forces and agency. Concomitantly, Weiler asserts that feminist educators are best positioned to initiate and further transformative change through, and within, the realm of schooling.

To move towards realizing such emancipatory social change, Weiler (1988) argues that it is essential to view teachers and students as "multilayered subjects" in that such an approach will most likely reveal "the complex interrelationship of teachers and students as they negotiate and mediate meaning in the classroom" (p. 126). On this, as well as other, central points presented in *Women Teaching for Change*, Weiler holds up and draws on the work of Paulo Freire, whom she perceives as "perhaps the most influential" of critical educational theorists. On the subject of subjects and subjectivities and the influence of Freire, she writes:

> In Freire's pedagogy, students must embark upon the process of investigating those historical processes that have led to their class, gender, and race interests and power. They explore both their oppression and their power in the light of moral and political questions of justice and equality. But teachers are also subjects, with historically situated interests. (Weiler, 1988, p. 126)

In terms of the interlinked subjectivities of teachers and students in schools/classrooms, Weiler underscores how conflict is inescapably part of the dynamics of the learning and teaching process, a process that is always gendered, raced, and classed:

> The classroom is always a site of conflict, and will be a site of conflict for the feminist or critical teacher trying to create a counter-hegemonic vision just as much as it will be for a traditional or authoritarian teacher. This is precisely because students are agents and creators of meaning in both settings...Students also are gendered, raced, and classed; they therefore "read" texts and classroom social relationships according to those subjectivities. (1988, p. 137)

In *Women Teaching for Change*, Weiler illuminates the vital contributions of the feminist educators she came to know through her in-depth exploration of their work in public, urban high schools—teachers and administrators who "do not envision the basis of their teaching as solely the transmission of 'facts,' but more the recognition of the value of students' own voices, subjective experiences of power and oppression, and the worth of their class and ethnic cultures" (Weiler, 1988, p. 149).

RESPECTFULLY CALLING OUT PAULO FREIRE

In 1991, three years after the release of her seminal book, *Women Teaching for Change*, Weiler published her similarly consequential *Harvard Educational Review* article, "Freire and a Feminist Pedagogy of Difference." In this article, she presents a substantive and pointed critique of Paulo Freire's liberatory pedagogy. As Weiler (1991) explains, this "philosophical and theoretical" article was "an elaboration of further thinking and discussions with feminist scholars" immediately following the publication of her 1988 book (p. 449). During that three-year period, she tossed a curved ball vis-à-vis Freire's conceptualization of liberatory pedagogy.

At the outset, Weiler (1991) transparently states her overarching purpose in writing the article: to point "to ways in which the project of Freirean pedagogy, like that of feminist pedagogy, may be enriched and re-envisioned" (p. 453). To this end, she situates a substantive critique of Freire within an initial discussion of the profound value of his theory of liberatory education, a discussion that points to the parallels between feminist and Freirean pedagogies, both of which "rest upon visions of social transformation" (Weiler, 1991, p. 450). The following excerpts encapsulate Weiler's main challenges to Freirean pedagogy as raised in her 1991 article:

> From a feminist perspective, Pedagogy of the Oppressed is striking in its use of the male referent. . . . Much more troublesome, however, is the abstract quality of terms such as humanization, which do not address the particular meanings imbued by men and women, Black and White, or other groups. (p. 453)

> By framing his discussion in such abstract terms, Freire slides over the contradictions and tensions within social settings in which overlapping forms of oppression exist. . . . The possibility of a contradictory experience of oppression is absent. (p. 453)

> Without recognizing more clearly the implicit power and limitations of the position of teachers, calls for a collective liberation or for opposition to oppression slide over the surface of the tensions that may emerge among teachers and students as subjects with conflicting interests and histories and with different kinds of knowledge and power. (p. 455)

Concomitantly, Weiler identifies three key questions not addressed by Freire in *Pedagogy of the Oppressed*, and notes how they point to a myopic vision in view of feminist theory/pedagogy in the early 1990s:

> How are we to situate ourselves in relation to the struggles of others? How are we to address our own contradictory positions as oppressors and oppressed? Where are we to look for liberation when our collective "reading of the world" reveals contradictory and conflicting experiences and struggles? The Freirean vision of the oppressed as undifferentiated and as the source of

unitary political action, the transparency of the subjectivity of the Freirean teacher, and the claims of universal goals of liberation and social transformation fail to provide the answers to these questions. (p. 455)

Weiler (1991) proceeds by calling for, and presenting, "a more situated theory of oppression" via feminist pedagogy—an approach that, she argues, "suggests new directions that can enrich Freirean pedagogies of liberation" (p. 460):

> In the complexity of issues raised by feminist pedagogy, we can begin to acknowledge the reality of tensions that result from different histories, from privilege, oppression, and power as they are lived by teachers and students in classrooms. To recognize these tensions and differences does not mean abandonment of the goals of social justice and empowerment, but it does make clear the need to recognize contingent·and situated claims and to acknowledge our own histories and selves in process...grounded in the collective analysis of experience and emotion. (p. 470)

Fast forward a decade, to the 2001 publication of the book *Feminist Engagements: Reading, Resisting, and Revisioning Male Theorists in Education and Cultural Studies,* which Weiler edited. This book was the product of further thinking, dialogue and debate among feminist educators since the 1991 publication of her *Harvard Educational Review* article. Her substantive work on and in this book, particularly her writing of the introduction and the chapter entitled "Rereading Paulo Freire" compellingly conveys and represents her evolved thinking and meaning-making since the publication of this 1991 article, and since Freire's death in the late 1990s. The following two excerpts from her chapter, "Rereading Freire," capture, respectively, her capacity to hold and navigate both her sense of deep respect for and appreciation of Freire's life work, and her tenacious critique regarding facets of his theory:

> In this reading of Freire I take up a number of what I see as problematic aspects of his theory. But at the same time, and in a fundamental way, I want to assert my respect for Freire and for his passionate commitment to social justice, his steadfast stance on the side of those who suffer.... Freire articulated a set of values based on compassion and respect for all human beings. His humanity and respect for students as "knowers of the world" have deep resonance for feminists who are seeking to develop an education and pedagogy for women. (p. 74)

> Perhaps the most troubling evidence of the ongoing assumptions of patriarchal privilege in Freire's thought emerges in interviews with Freire and his response to feminist criticisms.... Freire adopts the language of multiple oppression and acknowledges feminist criticisms, [yet] his claim that his own work is feminist is somewhat suspect.... He fails to provide us with any examples of what he means by "feminism" (p. 80).

ADDRESSING THE COMPLEX RELATIONSHIP
BETWEEN/AMONG EDUCATION FEMINISTS

The relationship between education feminists who share a commitment to education as a site for possible progressive political action and critical and democratic male theorists continues to be complex. Education feminists, like others, must consider not only their relationship to a male intellectual and political tradition that has more often than not ignored and excluded them, but also to the relationships among women themselves across divides of race, class, and sexuality (Weiler, 2001, p. 2).

In *Feminist Engagements*, Weiler interweaves her sharp analysis and perceptive observations vis-à-vis feminist pedagogy and education feminists within the context of, and through, a critical lens regarding patriarchy. Like the other essays in the book, Weiler's "offers a new and challenging perspective on the work of classic educational and cultural theory by examining this work through the lens of gender" in terms of critical engagement (p. 6); yet, she explains, these essays "are not monolithic in approach" in that "they take a number of different stances in relation to the male theorists who have influenced them" (p. 5), depending, in part, Weiler observes, "on the social location of the feminist critic and in part on the historical and political context, the strategic need to make theoretical alliances for common political goals" (p. 5).

Concerning social location, historical and political contexts, Weiler reflects on her own assumptions and perspectives in connection to a question once publicly asked of her during a national education conference: "Given the complexities of feminist educational thinking, how then do I, a white woman from the United States, approach the work of a Brazilian man who spoke for the subjugated and oppressed?" (2001, p. 73). Having reflexively and deeply explored this question since her beginning days as a scholar, Weiler explained/explains that this reflection led her to consistently "consider the ways [her] own social and historical location of privilege has shaped [her] critique of Freire" (p. 73).

Weiler's (2001) intentional reflections on her "own social and historical location of privilege" concurrent with her ongoing, systemic exploration and analysis of "the social and historical construction of . . . existing social and cultural definitions of men's and women's natures" (p. 11) set her apart from the feminist theorists many educators, particularly in the United States, tend(ed) to associate with feminist pedagogy: those who engage in a "maternal discourse" that holds "teaching as similar to mothering" (p. 69). The following excerpt from her chapter in *Feminist Engagements*, Weiler points to the "theoretical weaknesses and dangers of this maternal discourse" (p. 70) vis-à-vis feminist pedagogy:

For many educators, feminist pedagogy in the United States is understood in a discourse that has emerged from developmental psychology. Feminist theorists who celebrate teaching as similar to mothering argue, echoing Carol Gilligan [In a Different Voice, 1982], that women students approach knowledge through a connection with their own emotional and personal lives, and that women are alienated by competitive and antagonistic classroom relationships. While the work of these scholars has been valuable in calling into question competitive and hierarchical forms of classroom pedagogy and academic knowledge, it is also open to criticism on a number of levels. The developmental work of Gilligan and her group, for example, has frequently been criticized for its implication that the experiences and attitudes of white middle class girls and women are representative of all women, and for failing to explore the possibility that women may act in particular ways not because of essential womanly qualities, but in response to specific experiences of oppression (Thompson, 1998). The theoretical weaknesses and dangers of this maternal discourse operate not only in terms of epistemological shortcomings, but also in the potentially dangerous implications of accepting existing social and cultural definitions of men's and women's natures as in some ahistorical sense true. By failing to explore and analyze the social and historical construction of these ideas of women's natures, such approaches tend dangerously toward recasting the same old story of Western patriarchy (pp. 69–70).

CONFRONTING "HISTORICAL AMNESIA"

In the intervening years between the publication of her *Harvard Educational Review* article and *Feminist Engagements*, Weiler was prolific. She generated numerous articles and chapters, as well as a second book: *Country Schoolwomen*. Published in 1998, ten years after *Women Teaching for Change*, in Feminist *Engagements* Weiler confronts what she asserts is the longstanding "historical amnesia" vis-à-vis the complex history of women teachers in the United States. In the introduction, she expresses her deeply personal and poignant motivation for what proved to be an extensive personal research project: "to understand and remain connected to my mother's world" (p. 2). Her mother, a beloved schoolteacher deeply committed to her work, died just after Weiler had "completed [her] doctoral thesis, a study of urban women teachers" (p. 2). During the process of conducting research for and writing *Country Schoolwomen*, Weiler reflects that she "confronted not only [her] own personal loss, but also the loss of a wider world that [had] been forgotten" (p. 2).

Throughout *Country Schoolwomen*, Weiler (1998) meticulously traces "ideological shifts in the meaning of the schoolteacher" (p. 34) in the context of, and in relation to, broader historical movements—particularly as mirrored by "changes in state structures and in the context of local school settings, communities, and families" (p. 17). In looking at the period between the mid-nineteenth century, when women began to outnumber men as public school teachers, to the mid-twentieth century, when feminist historians "began a project to recover women's lives from the oblivion to which they had been relegated" (p. 5), Weiler (1998) provides a complex analysis of how the interweaving of historical movements and altering ideologies shaped the construct of the woman teachers—specifically during the 100 year period, from 1850–1950, in California's rural Kings and Tulare Counties. Of this period she writes, "[c]onceptions of gender, representations of men and women teachers, and direct struggles between men and women in education over issues of power and authority are central to [this] history" (p. 79).

Weiler (1998) assiduously delineates the historical context that sets the stage for her analysis of collected documents (school records, state papers, etc.) and narrative accounts, drawing on thirty interviews she conducted, of retired women schoolteachers. Their stories reflect diverse perspectives on the socio-political landscape, and the ways that "the work of teachers in California was gradually transformed" during the first half of the twentieth century (p. 124). She weaves together and presents her analysis of the women teachers' narratives in compelling ways. Of her anchoring concern in exploring this rich interview data, Weiler (1998) writes:

> My examination of these teachers' narratives is concerned with the ways in which unconscious assumptions and imaginative paradigms organize and shape teachers' understanding of the world and of their actions in it. In their stories, [these] teachers present themselves and their life choices in ways that challenge hegemonic definitions of women teachers as mothering, self-sacrificing, and passive; at the same time, the narratives contain unacknowledged contradictions and a kind of dissonance with regard to accepted conceptions of society and gender. I have read these stories for both structure and culture, on the one hand documenting the materiality of these teachers' lives—the organization of families, of schooling, and of the social world—on the other hand examining the selective quality of memory, the ways in which the past is framed as narrative, the representations through which value is given to lives (p. 161).

LIBERATORY TEACHING

Kathleen Weiler was an active member of Tufts University's Department of Education for twenty-four years, from 1987–2011. During that time, simultaneous to her leadership within that department as well as within the Peace and Justice Studies and Women's Studies programs, Weiler practiced liberatory teaching as she worked with countless preservice educators. In the introduction to a special issue ("Teacher Education and Social Justice") of *The Radical Teacher* (Winter 2002–2003), Weiler and Frinde Maher, her coauthor, argue that providing courses that focus on class, race, and gender vis-à-vis the history of schooling/education as a part of teacher education programs is essential: "Too often, teacher education is seen as the mastery of the content of specific disciplines and teaching techniques to be used in isolated classrooms. The rich tradition of historical struggles over education and the collective work of teachers is lost" (Weiler and Maher, 2002–2003, p. 4). Weiler (2002–2003) goes on to describe a substantive teacher education course—centered on the dimensions of class, race, and gender vis-à-vis the history of schooling/education—that she, and others, iteratively developed and taught at Tufts, for a number of years:

> This course, Class, Race, and Gender in the History of U.S. Education, views the history of education in the United States as a story of struggle over knowledge and power. The course addresses the meaning of education, both informal education and state-controlled schooling, for different groups, including Native Americans, African Americans, women of different classes and ethnicities, and immigrants from a variety of cultures. It explores the growth of the state as well as the actions of subjugated groups, who have seen education as central in their fight for civil and political rights. It is founded on the belief that teachers need to understand their own work in the context of a broader historical and political enterprise. (p. 4)

In the opening paragraph of their coauthored introduction, Weiler and Maher (2002–2003) invite all concerned about "teacher education and social justice" into a crucial dialogue about the movement to further standardize and privatize the U.S. education system—a movement that tenaciously continues, a decade into the 21st century. In their introduction, and embedded in the compelling collection of articles, is the understanding that "teachers and teacher educators cannot just close their classroom doors and teach 'progressively;' they need to be aware of the historical and political bases of the current struggles over the schools" (p. 4). They also emphasize the critical "need [for teachers] to talk to their students and their colleagues in new ways, and see their schools and communities as well as their classrooms as places for these dialogues" (Weiler and Maher, 2002–2003, p. 4). In doing so, they argue as follows:

> When progressive people today think about teacher education, they often focus on the discrepancy between the ideals of radical teaching and the realities of contemporary public schools. The articles on teacher education in this issue and the next confront these contradictions in various ways, both by examining aspects of the current situation and offering approaches to dealing with these issues in our classrooms. On one hand, examples of transformative pedagogy, the need to respect and encourage the voices of students, and curriculum which critiques popular culture and analyzes social inequities are invaluable to prospective teachers. Moreover, progressive programs educating prospective teachers need to include both models of progressive peda-

gogy and curriculum and courses exploring the historical and contemporary politics of education, to give prospective teachers tools of analysis and action. On the other hand, calls for liberatory teaching can appear to ring hollow notes in underfunded and inequitable public schools, where knowledge and teaching practices are increasingly standardized and monitored through high stakes testing. Analysis of the political context of teacher education is essential to an informed practice of teacher preparation (Weiler and Maher, 2002–2003, p. 2)

STRUGGLING FOR ISSUES THAT ARE
STILL CRUCIAL AND STILL UNRESOLVED

Just over a year after the "Teacher Education and Social Justice" issue (Winter 2002–2003) of *The Radical Teacher* appeared, Weiler (2004) published an article entitled "What Can We Learn From Progressive Education?" in *The Radical Teacher*. In this essay, Kathleen Weiler (2004) explores "the break between the educational ideas of pre-World War I progressives and the child-centered educators of the 1920s, as a way of raising questions about what progressive education has meant historically—and can mean in the future" (p. 5) Therein, she juxtaposes how John Dewey, and his daughter, Evelyn Dewey, portray—in their 1915 book, *Schools of To-Morrow*—public schools for working-class children/families and their portrayal of child-centered private schools for children of privilege, asserting that, "their discussion of these two schools makes clear their implicit acceptance of class and race, and the role of schools in preparing future workers to take up positions within this structure" (Weiler, 2004, p. 6). More broadly, Weiler (2004) argues that the Deweys, and other early progressive educators, largely failed "to address the deep inequalities of their society" (p. 9) by not examining their own social location privileges, and taking into account the impact of "the societal forces of racism, sexism, and class privilege" on the lives of and opportunities for children (p. 9).

"And yet," Weiler attests, "despite the limitations of their vision, many of the early progressive educators, like the Deweys, were utopian in the best sense of deeply desiring a more just and worthy society" (p. 9). She continues, "Surely their ideals—respect for each student, confidence in every child's ability to know, a belief that learning should be joyous and creative—are admirable. They tried hard to navigate the contradictions of liberalism and radicalism, in ways forgotten by child-centered popularizers of the conservative 1920s (p. 9).

Weiler concludes the essay with the following admonition: "We who live in a similar conservative moment can learn by reviewing how the Deweys and their allies struggled with issues that are still crucial, and still unresolved" (p. 9)

Nearly a decade later, in 2013, market-based reform constituencies have colluded, at an accelerated pace, in forming a movement to dismantle public education, and, concurrently, to devalue traditional educator preparation programs based at institutions of higher education (IHEs). Fast-track routes to preliminary licensure are viewed by proponents as an effective solution to the "problem" of university-based educator preparation programs, which, as Kumashiro (2010) asserts "have long faced public criticism for being ineffective in preparing teachers [by] overlapping movements...that make attacks on public education and teacher education seem like 'common sense'" (p. 56). This trend mirrors the conceptualization and approach touted in Race To The Top (RTTT), the Obama administration's signature education program currently driving federal/state policies and practice. Teaching and learning, in public schools across the country, have been scripted and quantified in unprecedented ways, as a result of iteratively persistent, variation-on-a-theme education policies.

Though it has been twenty-five years since the publication of *Women Teaching for Change*, Weiler's call, via her impeccably conceptualized analysis, is still timely and relevant a decade into the 21st century, and will continue to be so for the foreseeable future. The following excerpt from Giroux and Freire's (1988) introduction to *Women Teaching for Change* underscores the continued—and, arguably, now more than ever—relevance of Weiler's 1988 clarion challenge: "Hers is a narrative produced through ideological considerations and interests that confront the realities of school life through a project of possibility, that is, through a project that attempts to study reality in order to change it, to interrogate schooling as an arena of conflict and contestation. She writes in order to promote counterhegemonic strategies, which might prove useful to those...who are struggling to improve the quality and purpose of schooling in the interests of creating a more just, radically democratic society" (p. xii).

Although Kathleen Weiler has moved onto historical research as exemplified in *Country Schoolwomen* and *Democracy and Schooling in California: The Legacy of Helen Heffernan and Corinne Seeds*, she has maintained a critical perspective and a strong belief that scholarship is deeply political. Evident throughout her writing is her grounded sense of hope with regard to education and schooling—past and present—particularly in terms of gender, race, class and power. In this way, she echoes Freire's fervent belief, as expressed in *Pedagogy of the Oppressed*: "Hopelessness is a form of silence, of denying the world and fleeing from it" (Freire, 1968, p. 91). In Weiler's 2003 article, "Paulo Freire: On Hope," she writes, "For [Freire], those who reject hope, who discount human agency and the possibility of a better world as utopian idealism are themselves actively contributing to an oppressive world by encouraging fatalism" (p. 34).

A sense of grounded hope for "the possibility of a better world" is echoed throughout her own writing. This is reflected in the following excerpt from

"Feminism and the Struggle for a Democratic Education in the United States," written during Weiler's early years as a scholar:

> The problems facing education reflect decisions and choices that have been made about the use of resources, the distribution of wealth and concentration of power, and the value of human lives.... Just as exploitation and oppression are human acts that both are grounded in and create identities of center and margin, so political resistance and a demand for transformation are human acts grounded not in essential identities but in the political imagination and in collective work in the world (p. 224).

Anchored in hope, ethics, and a thirst for social justice, Kathleen Weiler has had a profound impact as a scholar focused on gender, class and power as it relates to the field of education in the United States and beyond.

NOTES

1. According to Weiler (1988), "counter-hegemony implies a more critical theoretical understanding [than resistance], and is expressed in organized and active political opposition" (p. 54).

REFERENCES

Dewey, J. & Dewey, E. (1915). *Schools of to-morrow.* New York, NY: E.P. Dutton & Co.

Freire, P. (1970). Pedagogy of the Oppressed. New York: Herder and Herder.

Giroux, H. & Freire, P. (1988). Introduction, pp. ix–xiv. In K. Weiler's *Women teaching for change: Gender, class & power.* New York: Bergin & Garvey Publishers.

Kumashiro, K. (2010). Seeing the Bigger Picture: Troubling Movements to End Teacher Education. *Journal of Teacher Education 2010, 61,* 56.

Weiler, K. (1988). *Women teaching for change: Gender, class, & power.* New York: Bergin & Garvey Publishers, Inc.

Weiler, K. (1991). Freire and a feminist pedagogy of difference. *Harvard Educational Review, 61*(4), 449–474.

Weiler, K. (1992). Introduction, 1–12. In K. Weiler and C. Mitchell (Eds.), *What schools can do: Critical pedagogy and practice.* New York: State University of New York Press.

Weiler, K. (1998). *Country schoolwomen: Teaching in rural California, 1850–1950.* Stanford, CA: Stanford University Press.

Weiler, K. (2001). Rereading Paulo Freire. In K. Weiler (Ed.), *Feminist engagements: Reading, resisting, and revisioning male theorists in education and cultural studies* (pp. 67–87). New York, NY: Routledge Press.

Weiler, K. (Ed.) (2001). *Feminist engagements: Reading, resisting and revisioning male theorists in educational and cultural studies.* New York, NY: Routledge Press.

Weiler, K., & Maher, F. (Eds.). (2002). Teacher education and social justice I [Special issue]. *The Radical Teacher, Fall*(64).

Weiler, K., & Maher, F. (Eds.). (2002). Introduction to teacher education and social justice. *The Radical Teacher, Fall, 64*, 2–4.

Weiler, K., & Maher, F. (2002). Teacher education and social justice II. *The Radical Teacher, Winter*(65), 2–4.

Weiler, K. (Winter 2002–2003). Hope and history: What do future teachers need to know? [Special issue]. *The Radical Teacher, Winter*(65), 11–17.

Weiler, K. (2004). What can we learn from progressive education? *The Radical Teacher, May*(69), 4–9.

ANNOTATED BIBLIOGRAPHY

Weiler, K. (2011). *Democracy and schooling in California: The legacy of Helen Heffernan and Corinne Seeds.* New York, NY: Palgrave Macmillan.

In her most recent book, *Democracy and Schooling in California,* Kathleen Weiler provides an historical analysis of the intertwined stories of two women (Helen Heffernan and Corinne Seeds) recognized as progressive education movement leaders between the early 1920s to the mid-1960s. Heffernan was the California Commissioner of Rural and Elementary Education from 1926 to 1965. Between 1925 and 1957, Seeds was the Director of the University Elementary School at the University of California in Los Angeles.

The book is comprised of the following chapters: 1. Working Girls of the Golden West; 2. The Child and the Curriculum; 3. Dare the School Build a New Social Order?; 4. Was Progressive Education Progressive?; 5. Love and War; 6. Prejudice; 7. The Battle of Westwood Hills; 8. Exporting Democracy/Defending Democracy; 9. "Progressive" Education is Subverting America; 10. How to Teach the California Child; and Epilogue: The Long Retreat from Democratic Education.

In their respective ways, each of these women exercised leadership to mobilize school districts to embed progressive education practices in public schooling, statewide. Weiler explores both the struggles within the state of California vis-à-vis public education, and the concomitant ways that Heffernan and Seeds moved the state to the forefront of progressive education and served as an exemplar of democratic education.

Weiler, K. (1998). *Country schoolwomen: Teaching in rural California, 1850–1950.* Stanford, CA: Stanford University Press.

In *Country Schoolwomen,* Weiler confronts longstanding "historical amnesia" (p. 17) regarding the complex history of women teachers in the United States. The book is comprised of the following chapters: 1. Women's History and the History of Women Teachers; 2. Gender and the Growth of the Educational State: California, 1850–1940; 3. Culture, Schools, and Community: Tulare and Kings Counties; 4. Subjugated Knowledge: Lives of Women Teachers, 1860–1920; 5. Memory and Identity: Lives of Women Teachers 1920–1940; 6.

The Work of Teaching in Rural Schools, 1920–1940; 7. Men Take Control, 1940–1950; and Conclusion.

Weiler examines the period between the mid-nineteenth century, when women began to outnumber men as public school teachers, to the mid-twentieth century, when feminist historians "began a project to recover women's lives from the oblivion to which they had been relegated" (p. 5). In doing so, Weiler meticulously traces "ideological shifts in the meaning of the school-teacher" (p. 34) within the context of, and in relation to, broader historical movements—particularly as mirrored by "changes in state structures and in the context of local school settings, communities, and families" (p. 17). Throughout she provides a substantive, complex analysis of how the interweaving of historical movements and altering ideologies shaped the construct of woman teachers from 1850 to 1950 in California's rural Kings and Tulare Counties. Of this period she writes, "Conceptions of gender, representations of men and women teachers, and direct struggles between men and women in education over issues of power and authority are central to [this] history" (p. 79). Weiler presents their stories in intricately complex and compelling ways.

Weiler, K. (1988). *Women teaching for change: Gender, class, & power.* Westport, CT: Bergin & Garvey Publishers.

Comprised of seven chapters 1. Critical Educational Theory; 2. Feminist Analyses of Gender and Schooling; 3. Feminist Methodology; 4. The Dialectics of Gender in the Lives of Feminist Teachers; 5. The Struggle for a Critical Literacy; 6. Gender Race and Class in the Feminist Classroom; and 7. Conclusion, in Women Teaching for Change, Weiler explains how structural forces and agency "act upon . . . [the] life histories, consciousness, and practice" (p. 55) of feminist educators through her in-depth study of teachers and administrators in two large, urban public high schools. Throughout, she points to how feminist teachers who are "conscious of their own gendered, classed, and raced subjectivities" (p. 137) are positioned, and hence, more apt, to constructively address the tensions that come with conflict, power, and oppression vis-à-vis the intersection of structural forces and agency. In so doing, Weiler claims that these educators are ultimately positioned to initiate and promote transformative change through, and within, the realm of schooling.

To move towards realizing such emancipatory social change, Weiler argues that it is essential to view teachers and students as "multi-layered subjects" in order to reveal "the complex interrelationship of teachers and students as they negotiate and mediate meaning in the classroom" (p. 126).

Weiler, K. (Ed.). (2001). *Feminist engagements: Reading, resisting, and revisioning male theorists in educational and cultural studies.* New York, NY: Routledge Press.

Feminist Engagements was the product of further thinking, and countless discussions among feminist theorists, after the publication of Weiler's ground-breaking *Harvard Educational Review* (HER) article in 1991, "Freire and a Feminist Pedagogy of Difference." It is comprised of the following chapters: Introduction by Kathleen Weiler; John Dewey, Progressive Education, and

Feminist Pedagogies: Issues in Gender and Authority by *Frances Maher*; Du-Bois and the Invisible Talented Tenth by *Cally L. Waite*; Remembering and Regenerating Gramsci by *Jane Kenway*; Rereading Paulo Freire by *Kathleen Weiler*; The Dreamwork of Autobiography: Felman, Freud, and Lacan by *Alice Pitt*; Bernstein's Sociology of Pedagogy: Female Dialogues and Feminist Elaborations by *Madeleine Arnot*; Coming to Theory: Finding Foucalt and Deleuze by *Elizabeth Adams St. Pierre*; Stuart Hall, Cultural Studies: Theory Letting You Off the Hook? by *Annette Henry*; and Ten Years Later, Yet Again: Critical Pedagogy and Its Complicities by *Patti Lather*.

As Weiler explains in the introduction to *the book*, while the authors of the respective chapters "take a number of different stances in relation to the male theorists who have influenced them" (p. 5), three conceptual approaches are represented: a critical feminist analysis; an appropriation of male theorist conceptualizing, to concerns of feminists, with minimal critique; and a critical appropriation of male theorist conceptualizing vis-à-vis feminist analytical thinking. Weiler asserts that the diverse perspectives represented in this collection of essays together offer "a new and challenging perspective on the work of classic educational and cultural theory by examining this work through the lens of gender" (p. 6).

Weiler, K., & Arnot, M. (Eds.). (1993). *Feminism and social justice in education: International perspectives*. Washington, D.C.: Falmer Press.

Feminism and Social Justice in Education includes chapters authored by feminist educators from five different English-speaking, industrialized countries (Australia, Canada, New Zealand, the United Kingdom, and the United States). The contents of the book are: Introduction by *Madeleine Arnot*; Theories of Family Change, Motherhood and Education by *Miriam E. David*; The Social Construction of Black Womanhood in British Educational Research: Towards a New Understanding by *Heidi Safia Mirza*; Getting Out From Down Under: Maori Women, Education and the Struggles for *Mana Wahine* by *Linda Tuhiwai Smith*; Shell-Shock or Sisterhood: English School History and Feminist Practice by *Gaby Weiner*; Other Mothers: Exploring the Educational Philosophy of Black American Women Teachers by *Michele Foster*; A Post-Modern Pedagogy for the Sociology of Women's Education by *Sue Middleton*; Contradictions in Terms: Women Academics in British Universities by *Sandra Acker*; Feminism and Australian State Policy: Some Questions for the 1990s by *Lyn Yates*; A Crisis in Patriarchy? British Feminist Educational Politics and State Regulation of Gender by *Madeleine Arnot*; and, Feminism and the Struggle for a Democratic Education: A View from the United States by *Kathleen Weiler*.

According to Arnot's introduction, the book was conceptualized at the 1991 American Educational Research Association's annual conference in Chicago, and compiled in response to two merging trends at the time: new currents of thought vis-à-vis postmodernist and postcolonial theories; and, the "economic recession and the emergence of free market philosophies [that] had generated a crisis in education and a new pattern of educational reform" (p. 2).

As Weiler explains, she and Arnot, along with the contributing authors, all leading feminist scholars at the time, shared the same overarching concern "about the future of education for women in societies marked by the resurgence of right-wing ideology and the conservative control of the state" (p. 210). While the book's chapters "reflect differences in national circumstances... ,all [chapters] share a commitment to social justice and see education as a key arena of struggle for women and other excluded and oppressed groups" (p. 210).

Weiler, K., & Mitchell, C. (Eds.). (1992). *What schools can do: Critical pedagogy and practice.* Albany, NY: State University of New York Press.

This book is comprised of two sections, Theorizing Power/Knowledge, and Pedagogies of Possibility. Chapters in Section I include: Introduction *by Kathleen Weiler;* The Hope of Radical Education by *Henry A. Giroux;* Schools and Families: A Feminist Perspective by *Madeleine Arnot;* Sex, Pregnancy, and Schooling: Obstacles to a Critical Teaching of the Body by *Laurie McDade;* Presence of Mind in the Absence of Body by *Linda Brodkey and Michelle Fine;* Knowledge, Power, and Discourse in Social Studies Education by *Cleo Cherryholmes;* Multicultural Education: Minority Identities, Textbooks, and the Challenge of Curricular Reform by *Cameron McCarthy;* Culture, Pedagogy, and, Power: Issues in the Production of Values and Colonialization by *Thomas S. Popkewitz.*

Section II is comprised of the following chapters: Decentering Discourses in Teacher Education: Or, the Unleashing of Unpopular Things by *Deborah P. Britzman;* The Politics of Race: Through the Eyes of African-American Teachers by *Michele Foster;* The Art of Being Present: Educating for Aesthetic Encounters by *Maxine Greene;* Schooling, Popular Culture, and a Pedagogy of Possibility by *Henry A. Giroux and Roger I. Simon;* Critical Mathematics Education: An Application of Paulo Freire's Epistemology by *Marilyn Frankenstein; and* Writing Pedagogy: A Dialogue of Hope by *Anne-Louis Brookes and Ursula A. Kelly.*

Collectively, the essays explore the inextricable links between schooling, economics, and politics. Though each essay is framed by a critique of educational systems, on both macro and micro levels, all are anchored in possibility. The authors present varying perspectives (most notably along the lines of feminist critiques, cultural politics, and anti-racist approaches) on how teaching and learning in public schools can be proactively transformed with a focus on benefiting children/adolescents in K–12 schools. All of the essays were originally published in the *Journal of Education,* published by Boston University's School of Education.

Mitchell, C., & Weiler, K. (Eds.). (1991). *Rewriting literacy: Culture and the discourse of the other.* New York, NY: Bergin & Garvey.

This book is the first in the series entitled *Literacy, Difference, and the Politics of Border Crossing.* The contents of the book include: Series Introduction: Literacy, Difference, and the Politics of Border Crossing by *Henry Giroux;* Preface by *Candace Mitchell;* Literacy, Discourse, and Power: What Is Literacy? by *James Paul Gee;* Discourses of Power, the Dialectics of Understanding, the Power of

Literacy by *Adrian T. Bennett*; The Struggle for Voice: Narrative, Literacy, and Consciousness in an East Harlem School by *Michele Sola and Adrian T. Bennett*; "Gimme Room": School Resistance, Attitude, and Access to Literacy by *Perry Gilmore*; Multiple Ways of Constructing Reality: The Narrativization of Experience in the Oral Style by *James Paul Gee*; Hearing the Connections in Children's Oral and Written Discourse by *Sarah Michaels*; Discourse Systems and Aspirin Bottles: On Literacy by *James Paul Gee*; The Politics of Reading and Writing: The Importance of the Act of Reading by *Paulo Freire*; The Politics of an Emancipatory Literacy in Cape Verde by *Donaldo Macedo*; Tropics of Literacy by *Linda Brodkey*; The Construction of School Knowledge: A Case Study by *Jan Nespor*; Benjamin's Story by *Jonathan Kozol*; Petra: Learning to Read at 45 by *Pat Rigg*; Literacy, History, and Ideology: How Illiteracy Became a Problem and Literacy Stopped Being One by *James Donald*; Hegemonic Practice: Literacy and Standard Language in Public Education by *James Collins*; and, Popular Literacy and the Roots of the New Writing by *John Willinsky*.

Giroux lauds the authors of the book's chapters for their respective contributions in discussing "what it means to restructure school curricula in order to address the needs of those groups who traditionally have been generally excluded within the dominant discourse of schooling" (p. ix).

BOOK CHAPTERS

Weiler, K. (2011). Freire and a feminist pedagogy of difference. In K. P. Afolabi, C. Bocala, R. C. DiAquoi, J. M. Hayden, I. A. Liefshitz, & S. S. Oh. (Eds.) *Education for a multicultural society* (pp. 319–348). Cambridge, MA: Harvard Education Press. [Reprinted from *Harvard Educational Review, 61(4)*, 449–474)]

This article was originally published in 1991 in the *Harvard Educational Review*, three years after the release of her first book, *Women Teaching for Change*. Herein, Weiler presents a substantive and pointed critique of Paulo Freire's liberatory pedagogy. She boldly develops further what both Freire and Henry Giroux referred to, in their introduction, as her "important conceptual advance" (p. ix), *Women Teaching for Change*. As Weiler explains, this article was generated from in-depth dialogue among feminist scholars, following the publication of her 1988 book.

As a spokesperson for critical feminists' Weiler states her purpose, is to point "to ways in which the project of Freirean pedagogy, like that of feminist pedagogy, may be enriched and re-envisioned" (p. 453). To this end, she situates a substantive critique of Freire within an initial discussion of the profound value of his theory of liberatory education, and provides a discussion that points to the parallels between feminist and Freirean pedagogies, both of which "rest upon visions of social transformation" (p. 450).

Weiler, K. (2008). Paulo Freire: On hope. In J. Entin, R. Rosen & L. Vogt (Eds.), *Controversies in the classroom: A radical teacher reader* (pp. 167–174). New York, NY: Teachers College Press.

"Paulo Freire: On Hope" is the epilogue chapter of *Controversies in the Classroom: A radical teacher reader*, a collection of essays reprinted from fifteen years of the *Radical Teacher magazine*. In her essay, Weiler hearkens the hope-laden vision and messages of Paulo Freire wrote specifically for teachers in public schools. She addresses the vast number of teachers who experience, or border experiencing, stress, burn-out and a sense of despair given the restraints and demands of the mainstream corporate-based education reform movement. She points to Freire's influence in the 1960s, a time when many U.S. educators were inspired and guided by Freire vis-à-vis expanding views and sense of possibility with regard to progressive education in practice.

Weiler, K. (2007). Gender. In D. Gabbard (Ed.), *Knowledge and power in the global economy*, 2nd ed. (pp. 113–120). Mahwah, NJ: Lawrence Earlbaum.

Weiler's chapter, "Gender," delineates how neoliberal and neoconservative pulls on the cultural, economic, and political landscape in the United States, and have impacted women, feminism, and feminist pedagogy. Her main message to feminist educators is "... to continue locating their analysis and practice in order to capture the complexity of gender and build a more progressive analysis and program for education" (p. 120).

Weiler, K. (2001). Rereading Paulo Freire. In K. Weiler (Ed.), *Feminist engagements: Reading, resisting, and revisioning male theorists in education and cultural studies* (pp. 67–88). New York, NY: Routledge Press.

In this chapter, Weiler critiques Freire's assumptions regarding male privilege, through the lens of feminist pedagogy. She names and delineates the often overlooked flaws in Freire's frequently cited and venerated ideas because of how his passionate work for social justice speaks to, on surface levels, many issues of concern to feminist theorists.

Weiler, K. (1993). Feminism the struggle for a democratic education: A view from the United States. In K. Weiler and M. Arnot (Eds.), *Feminism and social justice in education: International perspectives* (pp. 210–225). Washington, D.C.: Falmer Press.

Collectively, the chapters in the book, *Feminism and Social Justice in Education* call for a profound shift in policy trends in order to realize the promise of authentic democratic education. In Weiler's words, these shifts depend "on the ideal of a society that is inclusive and celebrates the rich diversity of human beings, not as 'capital,' but as creative, intelligent, and feeling beings open to the rich possibilities of human life" (p. 223). Her chapter, "Feminism and the Struggle for a Democratic Education in the United States," focuses on the grounded hope echoed by all of the contributing authors. In synthesizing the main themes across the collection of essays, she points to the authors' overarching collective belief in the possibility of ethical choices and actions that can lead to transformative changes—to realize greater justice and equity—within the education system. In Weiler's words, all of the authors hold a conviction "that just as exploitation and oppression are human acts... so political resistance and a demand for transformation are human acts grounded not in essential identities but in the political imagination and in collective work in the world (p. 224).

Weiler, K. (1993). Feminism and the struggle for a democratic education: A view from the United States. In K. Weiler and M. Arnot (Eds.), *Feminism and social justice in education* (pp. 210–225). Washington, D.C.: Falmer Press.

In the final chapter of this book, Weiler explains the common aim of all of the authors in the book is "... to theorize a more just education for women while moving beyond a one dimensional theoretical perspective that focuses only on gender" (p. 213). The key challenge for feminist theorists, in the early 1990s, she writes, "is to try to take account of and comprehend the complexity of all forces of identity formation acting upon women in relation to educational institutions and policies in a rapidly changing world" (p. 213). These feminist scholars were galvanized, to address this challenge, through the influence of Gramsci (1971), specifically "his formulation of hegemony and the ways in which powerful groups constantly struggle to control and dominate discourse and set the parameters of political understanding and action" (p. 215).

Weiler, K. (1992). Teaching, feminism, and social change. In C. M. Hurlbert & S. Totten (Eds.), *Social issues in the English classroom* (pp. 322–337). Urbana, IL: National Council of Teachers of English.

This essay, as the epilogue chapter of the book, *Social Issues in the English Classroom,* centers on this pivotal message: "We need to struggle collectively to create social change in vitally needed, more humane directions" (p. 323). Her timely call focuses on how those "who hope for a more just and humane world [must] think seriously about the ways we can work in our own lives to attain our goals [in contributing to] the building of a more just society" (p. 323). In exploring this appeal in terms of education and schooling, she refers to and juxtaposes the writings of "two women of radically different lives and circumstances: Virginia Woolf and Audre Lorde" (p. 330). In juxtaposing and analyzing the writing of both Woolf and Lorde, Weiler identifies an overarching theme across their work—both authors call for a widening of the feminist lens, to more deeply examine, as an ongoing process of conscientization, the impact of oppression and injustice on both women and men in society.

ARTICLES AND REVIEWS

Weiler, K. (2004). What can we learn from progressive education? *Radical Teacher,* 69, 4–9.

Kathleen Weiler explores "the break between the educational ideas of pre-World War I progressives and the child-centered educators of the 1920s, as a way of raising questions about what progressive education has meant historically—and can mean in the future" (p. 5) She focuses on a generally lesser known text written by John Dewey, and his daughter, Evelyn Dewey, published in 1915:

Schools of To-morrow. In comparing the Deweys' portrayal of public schools for working-class children/families with their portrayal of child-centered private schools for children of privilege, she asserts, "*Schools of To-morrow* is a complicated text. It juxtaposes the freedom of privileged children to learn through play with the mastery of manual skills for the working class children of Gary and Indianapolis" (p. 8). Regarding the two "working class" public schools portrayed in the book, Weiler observes, "Their discussion of these two schools makes clear their implicit acceptance of class and race, and the role of schools in preparing future workers to take up positions within this structure" (p. 6)

In sum, Weiler argues that the Deweys and other early progressive educators largely failed "to address the deep inequalities of their society" (p. 9) by not examining their own social location privileges, and taking into account the impact of "the societal forces of racism, sexism, and class privilege" (p. 9) on the lives of and opportunities for children.

Weiler, K. (2002–2003). Hope and history: What do future teachers need to know? *Radical Teacher*, 65, 2–4.

In this essay, Kathleen Weiler argues for the importance of providing courses on the history of education as a part of teacher education programs: "Too often, teacher education is seen as the mastery of the content of specific disciplines and teaching techniques to be used in isolated classrooms. The rich tradition of historical struggles over education and the collective work of teachers is lost" (p. 4). She goes on to describe a substantive course she and others developed and taught over a number of years at Tufts University: Class, Race, and Gender in the History of U.S. Education. It is a course that "views the history of education in the United States as a story of struggle over knowledge and power" (p. 4).

Weiler, K. (1997). Reflections on writing a history of women teachers. *Harvard Educational Review*, 1(67), 635–657.

Weiler takes a meta-reflective look at the historiography of her research on women teaching in rural California schools, from 1850–1950. Weiler "raises questions about the nature of knowledge, the influence of language in the social construction of gender, and the importance of an awareness of subjectivity in the production of historical evidence" (http://hepg.org/her/abstract/204). In her conclusion, Weiler reflects on the complicated experience that comes with analyzing historical narratives through a feminist and reflexive lens.

Weiler, K., & Maher, F. (2002). Introduction: Teacher education and social justice, Radical *Teacher*, *64*, 2–4.

In their opening paragraph Weiler and Maher implicitly invite all involved in and concerned about "teacher education and social justice" into a crucial dialogue about the movements to further standardize and privatize the U.S. education system. Throughout their introduction, and embedded in the excellent, compelling collection of articles, is an assertion—both explicit and implicit—that "teachers and teacher educators cannot just close their classroom doors and teach 'progressively'; they need to be aware of the historical and political bases of the current struggles over the schools" (p. 4). Concomitantly, they emphasize the "need to talk to their students and their colleagues in new ways, and see their schools and communities as well as their classrooms as places for these dialogues" (p. 4).

CHAPTER 15

CHRISTINE SLEETER

Sara Carrigan Wooten, Reagan Mitchell, Kenneth Fasching-Varner, and Roland Mitchell

Education either functions as an instrument which is used to facilitate integration
of the younger generation into the logic of the present system and bring
about conformity or it becomes the practice of freedom, the means by which men
and women deal critically and creatively with reality and discover
how to participate in the transformation of their world.
—Paulo Freire (1970)

CHRISTINE SLEETER, THE PERSON
BEHIND THE SCHOLAR AND ACTIVIST

Christine Sleeter grew up in a small segregated community in Southern Oregon (Sleeter, 2008a). In her town, she says, there was very little representation of difference, particularly racially.

Sleeter (2008a) talks about growing up with a sanitized perspective of American history that is at odds in many ways with the scope and approach to scholarship she has gone on to produce in terms of expansive understandings of multicultural education. Citing some of the metanarratives about U.S. history found in Lowen's (2008) *Lies My Teacher Told Me*, Sleeter (2008a) states, "I learned that racism ended with the Emancipation Proclamation,

Educating About Social Issues in the 20th and 21st Centuries, pages 303–322
Copyright © 2014 by Information Age Publishing
All rights of reproduction in any form reserved.

that American Indians were "noble" figures in history, and that U.S. history is largely a story of steady progress toward freedom and justice" (p. 116). In the process of learning about her own family background Sleeter (2008a) determined, through DNA testing, she was 6% sub-Saharan African, not Cherokee as she had been led to believe by her own family members. Sleeter (2008a) writes, "I carry a history and legacy of not only European American immigration, but also of Appalachia, of slave ownership, of African Americans passing as White and leaving family behind, and of Jim Crow" (p. 121).

Initially, Sleeter examined her own racial and ethnic history solely out of a personal interest in her identity. Given her work in multicultural education it seems natural that she went on to publish about this identity work, relative to engaging preservice teachers about their identities. Sleeter suggests that family history work can be used to trouble one's own history and the relationship between identity and privilege. Sleeter's use of modeling the complexities of coming to understand one's own identity is consistent with her career first as a teacher, then as a scholar and activist.

Sleeter began her teaching career as a learning disabilities instructor in 1972 at Roosevelt High School in Seattle, Washington. She remained there for five years before entering the doctoral program in Curriculum & Instruction at the University of Wisconsin–Madison, where she served as a teaching assistant until 1982. Sleeter was awarded her first professorship in 1982 in the Department of Education at Ripon College in Wisconsin. She taught there for three years before joining the School of Education at the University of Wisconsin–Parkside, where she remained for nine years and was granted full professorship status. In 1995, she made the long journey to California to assume a full professorship in the College of Education and Professional Studies at California State University, Monterey, a recent addition to the California State University system. In 2004, she retired and was awarded emerita status. Sleeter continues to teach, though, and has enjoyed numerous visiting professorships, including at San Francisco State University from 2009 until 2011. Earlier in her career she also held summer positions at the University of Washington (1987, 1999, and 2007).

Sleeter holds four degrees. She obtained her Bachelor of Arts in Political Science from Willamette University in 1970. Sleeter earned an additional Bachelor of Arts degree in Secondary Education from Central Washington State University in 1972. In 1977, she received a Master of Arts in Curriculum & Instruction with a concentration in learning disabilities from Seattle University. In 1981, she was awarded her PhD in Curriculum and Instruction from the University of Wisconsin–Madison in 1981. Her doctoral dissertation was entitled, "Student Friendships and Cultural Knowledge Related to Human Diversity in a Multiracial and Mainstreamed Junior High School."

Similar to so many stories of great educators who found themselves immersed in the passion of teaching through somewhat roundabout or serendipitous means, Christine Sleeter initially entered an urban education program in Seattle, Washington, because she thought living in Seattle sounded thrilling (Dade, 2013). As a part of that program, she was required to live in the Black and White working class neighborhood of the school that she was assigned to. This arrangement allowed her to get acquainted with the African American high schoolers she was working with as well as their parents and others living in the neighborhood.

As the Civil Rights movement was winding down in the early 1970s, the young Sleeter believed that racism within the United States had been largely resolved (Akande, 2012). However, as a result of living in a community far different from the one that she grew up in, she underwent a radical reeducation regarding the continuing role of racism within the United States. Through these experiences, Sleeter developed a profound respect for coalition building and learning from people who had life experiences completely different from her own. Concomitantly, during this period of teaching in urban Seattle, she came in contact with a group of multi-racial educators who were trying to develop multicultural education curricula for elementary schools, as those spaces became increasingly diversified. As a White woman new to that particular urban Seattle community, Sleeter struggled with how to situate herself within those conversations:

> I recognized that in diverse contexts, Whites too often just take over or assume that we can figure out answers by ourselves. I struggled with whether it would be better just to step back and not become involved or to become involved and, in the process, learn to collaborate and share power. I realized that not becoming involved is not a solution because then things never change. (Interview with Sleeter, Howe & Lisi, 2013, p. 210)

These early experiences continue to impact Sleeter's work as an educator, activist, and scholar, as she understands that the process of engaging issues of race and power, "isn't something I've finished or anticipate finishing," (Interview with Christine Sleeter, Howe & Lisi, 2013, p. 210).

Sleeter is an incredibly prolific author, having published more than 70 articles in peer-reviewed journals. Her voluminous work has been translated from English into Spanish, Korean, French, and Portuguese (Howe & Lisi, 2013, p. 209). Additionally, Sleeter has served on the editorial boards of such prestigious journals as the *Journal of Negro Education*, the *American Educational Research Journal, Race, Ethnicity, and Education*, and *Educational Researcher*.

Christine Sleeter is a renowned international scholar whose work has been recognized and acclaimed by critical educators spanning the globe. In part, this is reflected in the prodigious amount of invited speaking engagements she has commanded, both within the United States and internationally (i.e., Taiwan, South Korea, the Netherlands, Chile, India and Spain).

In all, she has delivered talks at over seventy universities within the United States and abroad. The topics of her talks range from neoliberalism and capitalism within education to issues of freedom and democracy within teaching, and the promotion of equity in diverse educational spaces.

Over the course of her career, Sleeter has received numerous awards for her exceptional scholarship and contributions to the field of education. Those awards include the National Association for Multicultural Education Research Award, the American Educational Research Association Social Justice in Education Award (given to those "individuals who have advanced social justice through education research... [and] exemplify the goal of linking education research to social justice"—AERA, 2013), the American Educational Research Association Special Interest Group Multicultural and Multiethnic Education Lifetime Achievement Award, and the Chapman University Paulo Freire Education Project Social Justice Award (which is awarded to those who honor the mission of the Paulo Freire Education Project by, "[bringing] to bear a synthesis of progressive/critical and ethical/democratic practices upon both formal and informal educational contexts"—PFDP, 2013).

The diversity and breadth of Christine Sleeter's work in multicultural education has made a profound, lasting impact on the field of education. In this chapter, we will provide a brief glimpse into the work of a scholar whose intellectual contributions cannot be overstated. Christine Sleeter's academic life has been devoted to asking questions about the role of critical theory in multicultural education, the place of multicultural education within teacher preparation and education programs, and the field of teacher education vis-à-vis the alarming rise of neoliberal influence on educational policy in the United States. Though her career spans the course of forty years, beginning with her work as a learning disabilities teacher in 1972, the questions that Sleeter has wrestled with remain pertinent through today. Those questions include, for example: What is multicultural education? (Banks, 1993; Bennett, 2001; May & Sleeter, 2010; Sleeter & McLaren, 2009); What are the aims of multicultural education and what is its utility for critical practices in teacher education? (Beyer, 2001; Fox & Gay, 1995; Sleeter, 1992; Sleeter, 2009a, 2009b, 2009c); and How do dominant constructions of (dis)ability within education policy impact children with different learning styles and disrupt the learning process? (Sleeter, 1987b, 1995). Herein, we provide a succinct overview of some of the most salient themes of Christine Sleeter's scholarly work and discuss the ongoing significance of her intellectual legacy, particularly for those who are similarly committed to delving into such issues and concerns.

From this point forward, we basically center a number of Sleeter's major theoretical arguments. A portion of this chapter is devoted to how Sleeter herself has articulated the aims of her career and the commitments she has made to multicultural education specifically. We conclude with an annotated bibliography of many of Sleeter's major works and those of other scholars who have been influenced by her expertise.

MAJOR THEORETICAL ARGUMENTS

Christine Sleeter has made remarkable contributions to the field of education, generally, and the areas of multicultural education, antiracist education, and teacher education, specifically. Some of the guiding theoretical frameworks in Sleeter's work include critical race theory (Sleeter & Delgado-Bernal, 2004; Yosso, 2002), critical disability studies (Sleeter, 1987a, 1987b, 1988, 1995, 1998), and critical pedagogy (Sleeter, 2011c; Sleeter & Delgado-Bernal, 2004; Sleeter & McLaren, 1995). Sleeter is one of the premier multicultural education scholars of our time, having generated a tremendous amount of knowledge on the application of multicultural education in the education of preservice teachers (Sleeter & McLaren, 1995; Boyle-Baise & Sleeter, 2000; Sleeter, 1993a, 1993b, 2011d), and remains deeply invested in and concerned about the policy implications of the venture capitalist takeover of public education (Sleeter, 2004, 2005, 2008b, 2009c). Present throughout Sleeter's work is a commitment to culturally responsive pedagogy that seeks to decolonize a standards-based curriculum (Gay, 1995, 2010; Sleeter, 2010b; Sleeter & Cornbleth, 2011). Part of this work is embedded in a tradition of recognizing and resisting the ongoing White supremacist aims of education (Gillborn, 2005; Giroux, 1992; Grande, 2000; Sleeter, 2010c; Castagno & Brayboy, 2008).

The intellectual commitment Sleeter has made in regard to carrying out an examination of structural and institutional power within education is substantial (Grant & Sleeter, 1986a, 1986b; Hoffman, 1996). Critical theory, feminist theories, postcolonial theory, critical race theory, queer theory, and critical disabilities theory are all major components of her work. These frameworks have allowed her to more thoroughly examine the "interlocking structures of race, class, gender, and disability, how these structures are reflected in inequities in schools and universities, and how teachers, teacher educators, and communities might resist" (Sleeter, 2010a).

As a former learning disabilities instructor, Sleeter maintained a steady focus on disability studies within the context of racial and class discrimination in education. One example of how Sleeter situates her critique regarding elementary and secondary schools comes in addressing special education categories. Sleeter (2010a) asserts that the category of learning disabilities arose as an attempt by White middle class parents to differentiate and demarcate their children from the minority students of low-income backgrounds with a history of low-achievement. She notes that the category came into prominence in the 1960's and that it was educators who developed the four syndromes of (mental retardation, slow learner, economically disturbed, and culturally deprived) to explain the failure of lower class and minority students. As Ferri & Connor (2006) assert, disability categories, especially the "soft" categories that require subjective judgment in making referrals and diagnosis decisions, cannot be separated from other mechanisms through which professional class Whites continue to segregate children of color.

Sleeter recalls feeling troubled during her time as an LD instructor that the job required her to classify students who were failing in classrooms as disabled, and to invoke a brain-based rationale in order to teach them. Sleeter (2010a) states that organic damage was presented as the basis of the learning disabilities category because: (a) it suggested that the disability could be overcome or recovered from; (b) the reading deficiencies in White middle class children were addressed and did not result in an interrogation regarding the quality of their households; and, (c) it distinguished the category of learning disability from mental retardation, while simultaneously situating the child in both spaces. Furthermore, Sleeter (2010a) identifies 1968 as the year learning disabilities was sanctioned, thus creating a space by which financial resources where designated to establish classes and train teachers. Sleeter's critique of the category of learning disabilities calls on all educators to question the degree of inaccuracy a structure developed on flawed foundations reinscribes on children. Pushing against this educational psychological approach to children who learned differently, Sleeter argues that helping general education teachers to learn how to teach a wider diversity of students more effectively is a better and much more sagacious solution (Sleeter, 2010a).

In recent years, Sleeter's zeroed in on the neoliberal drive for school accountability. The powered capitalist motivations that are imbedded within the standards and accountability movement in education is an area of focus that Sleeter has highlighted as being of particular importance. She has identified two major ideological views of society that have emerged in tension with one another over the course of the past forty to fifty years (Education Radio, 2012). The first is the view that the success of a society can be measured in terms of how well it serves those who live within it. The second measures the success of a society by how well it develops and proliferates mechanisms of profit accumulation. Inherent in the latter view is the argument that the democratization of social services undercuts the ability of a society to generate wealth. However, as Sleeter has noted, this view of societal purpose has almost exclusively resulted in those at the top of capitalist markets being the sole beneficiaries of the profits they generate.

Since the 1980s, business has become the driving force of standardization and accountability within education (Education Radio, 2012). This shift has served to undermine and undo the movement to democratize curriculum (Kumashiro, 2010). With an exclusive focus on the achievement gap, other issues that are actively serving to undermine equitable education are being silenced and ignored. Sleeter notes the impact that this has had on teacher education, where the focus is now on training future educators to implement a rigid curriculum, while teacher education programs in universities and colleges are rapidly being undermined and replaced by organizations tied to venture capitalists. Education as a frontier of corporate profit-making and the subversion of democratic ideals is central to Sleeter's recent work and critical commentary (Sleeter 2007, 2008b, 2008c, 2009c, 2010d).

Sleeter operationalizes her neoliberal critique via an examination of United States-based teacher education programs (2008b, 2008c, 2009c). She roots her criticism in reference to the reverberations of deficit oriented educational programs such as "A Nation at Risk" and "No Child Left Behind." Standards and accountability, modeled on corporate measures of assessment as well as profit-centered policy, have increasingly become the sole means of assessing student success and engagement (Au, 2009; Bohn & Sleeter, 2000; Kumashiro, 2008). In response to the recent tide of education policy "reform," Sleeter extends her analysis to include neo-conservatism. According to Sleeter (2008c), this forms the impetus by which education adopts a corporate paradigm. The school is consequently transformed into a feeder system for all levels of the corporate workforce.

Sleeter's (2008b) critique also considers the impact of all of this on preservice teacher preparation. In that regard, she takes issue with the predominantly White population of college students recruited to teach. Sleeter posits that homogeneity occurs due to teacher education programs' primary emphasis on "academic ability" (Sleeter, 2008b, p. 1949), which results in the further perpetuation of dominant cultural epistemologies. Sleeter's solution to this issue is the critical need to radically diversify recruiting measures by teacher education programs in order to incorporate and attract preservice teachers from marginalized communities (Sleeter & Thao, 2007). Additionally, Sleeter (2008b) critiques the negation of multiple cross-cultural field experiences in marginalized communities, suggesting instead that teacher education programs should require their students to have unfamiliar field encounters. Requiring this, according to Sleeter (2008b), would help preservice teachers to make connections with their students' cultural backgrounds as well as challenge them to confront the entrenched stereotypes they embody.

Sleeter has attended to the historical roots of multicultural education, citing the Civil Rights movement as a major impetus for societal as well as classroom transformation (International Journal of Multicultural Education, 2013). Along this line, she views multicultural education as a critical component of broader social justice work within the United States, specifically.

Sleeter builds on her resistance continuum by asserting the need for deeper discussions of multiculturalism in education. Her concerns arise from the destructive legacies of "A Nation at Risk," "No Child Left Behind," and more currently "color-blindness" and "post racialism." Historically, Sleeter (1996a, 1996b) reminds us, multiculturalism's foundation was built on the resonances of the Civil Rights Movement. However, she highlights the problem with current conceptualizations of multiculturalism as resulting from White educators' nonacknowledgement of its rootedness in progressive and radical social movements. Sleeter (1996a) takes her critique further in warning against reducing multiculturalism to a series of teaching techniques (p. 233). She asserts that *multiculturalism only becomes transformative* when understood as a dialogue between teachers and community members. Furthermore, she situates multiculturalism as social movement which positions the teacher and the community in coalition with each other for the express purpose of "pressur[ing] schools to serve their interests and those of their children" (Sleeter, 1996b, p. 242).

THE CONTINUING CALL TO WORK

Beginning in 2008, Sleeter (2008a) turned her scholarly attention to what she refers to as her Critical Family History project. On her website devoted to this project, Sleeter (2013) briefly discusses the origins and rationale of Critical Family History:

> Critical family history research is a term I coined in the process of placing family history within an analysis informed by critical theoretical traditions. Insights from critical theoretical traditions guide analysis of how one's family has been constructed historically within and through relations of power. To be useful, a critical theory identifies specific unjust social relationships, the roots of those relationships, and how they can be changed. Since multiple critical theories have emerged in connection with multiple social movements, I drew on insights from critical theory, critical race theory, critical whiteness studies, and radical humanist feminism. (Critical Family History, 2013)

Sleeter's work in this area is in keeping with other theoretical work that identifies the family unit as an institution itself, replete with sociocultural silences, erasures, and revisionist narratives that serve to maintain hegemonic racial ideologies (Laslett, 1973; Collins, 1998). The work of historical memory making has proven to be a useful teaching strategy *with* White preservice teachers, whose superficial understandings of race and racism often inspire oversimplified and uncritical reflections on their family histories

(Sleeter, 2008a). Sleeter insists that multicultural education is an absolute necessity for preservice teachers because:

> ...they will become multicultural educators, whether they intend to or not. All classrooms have diversity within them, even if students are all of one racial background. And increasingly, places that used to be racially homogeneous are not anymore. Teachers today can anticipate teaching racially diverse students at some point in their lives. The question isn't whether to become a good multicultural educator but rather whether to become a good educator in a multicultural context. (Interview with Christine Sleeter, Howe & Lisi, 2013, p. 210)

Sleeter is committed to ensuring that the groups of educators she works with are diverse in terms of race, ethnicity, and gender. She views spending time developing relationships and working from consensus as essential components of multicultural education. Such coalition building, which makes space for people to voice their differences, is absolutely crucial to the project of multicultural education and breaking down inherent distrust that has built up (Akande, 2012).

Because Sleeter remains a strong advocate for the continued presence of multicultural education, she is continually frustrated by leftist educators who have deemed multicultural education "soft" and who see it as skirting issues of power. She maintains that as a country, we, in the United States, collectively do not really engage in conversations about race or racism outside of major incidents that grab the attention of the national news media. Racism in the United States has increasingly come to be carried out through covert (and overt) mechanisms in public policy, making the identification of racist acts significantly more difficult, as the public perception of racism remains driven by a pathological individual act of physical violence archetype (Bonilla-Silva, 2001; Nagda, Gurin, & Lopez, 2003; Vaught & Castagno, 2008). Public policy, as a site of institutional racism, has contributed to overwhelming poverty within segregated, impoverished urban areas, rendering progressive, responsive educational policy all but futile (Anyon, 2005; Sleeter, 2011b). Given the subversive nature of this Post-Civil Rights racism syndrome, Sleeter has noted that White people often do not learn to talk about racism, but rather are taught to understand conversations about race and racism as impolite (Sleeter, 2011b). In her role preparing students for urban teaching, Sleeter has routinely encountered students who are markedly uncomfortable in even discussing racism. As a consequence, one of the frameworks that she spends a substantial amount of time on teaching is institutional racism within both society and schools and the effects thereof, along with a focus on what kinds of structural changes need to be made and how to effectively engage in the type of work that brings about such changes (Blog Talk Radio, 2010).

With the current educational policy climate in the United States exclusively focused on a superficial understanding of the achievement gap, Sleeter advocates for a deeper framing that identifies how the teaching and learning of students who are culturally and linguistically diverse might be strengthened. Within this project, multicultural education remains imperative. Multicultural education has been an important venue since the 1970s for naming and examining ways in which racism works and how racism intersects with class (Kincheloe, 1997; Mansfield & Kehoe, 1994). Multicultural education also works on a practical level to build a sense of "we" that is diverse. While the term "multicultural education" prompts many people who are unfamiliar with its work to think of cultural awareness activities, Sleeter rejects this connotation. Instead, civil rights and social justice activism that gave birth to multicultural education is (or should be) at the core of its work (Nagda, Gurin, & Lopez, 2003; Oakes & Lipton, 2006; Shor, 1992; Sleeter 1996a, 1996b, 2009c, 2010d, 2012).

Sleeter's work serves as a reminder of the importance in maintaining humility, the most resonate feature of the intellectual tributaries of her work. Sleeter's brief background that opens this chapter speaks about the "radical reeducation" she underwent as a result of being compelled to live and work in a community that was the cultural opposite of her own. Sleeter's openness in the face of her "radical reeducation" is a reminder to educators of the necessity to maintain humility and to understand it as source for engaging in transformative community and schooling practice.

This brief chapter on Christine Sleeter's life, works, and intellectual commitments is by no means complete. Rather, we invite our readers to approach this discussion as a combination of introduction and homage to an individual who has committed her life to inciting others to identify, question, and resist the oppressive structures permeating our educational systems. Sleeter's discourse calls for a disavowal of complacency as well as a critical need to move beyond an over reliance on academic jargon in place of holistic praxis. However, praxis for Sleeter does not constitute a series of educators stepping in from ivory towers to monitor marginalized communities. Praxis in her world emerges as coalitions between teachers and community members work closely together to place an emphasis on putting power back in the hands of the community. In Sleeter's hands, critical pedagogy, multiculturalism, and anti-racist education move from fashionable terminology, inserted into everyday speech as markers of superior intellectualism within the academy, to calls for action, for the express and critical purpose of opening doors to engage overlooked and negated voices.

REFERENCES

Akande, Y. (2012). Making the case featuring Christine Sleeter. WJCU Radio. Retrieved from http://www.wjcu.org/2012/07/20/making-the-case-featuring -christine-sleeter

American Educational Research Association. (2013). Social justice in education award. Retrieved from http://www.aera.net/AboutAERA/Awardsand-Honors/SocialJusticeinEducationAward/tabid/12787/Default.aspx

Anyon, J. (2005). *Radical possibilities: Public policy, urban education, and a new social movement.* New York, NY: Routledge.

Au, W. (2009). *Unequal by design: High-stakes testing and the standardization of inequality.* New York, NY: Routledge.

Banks, J. A. (1993). Multicultural education: Historical development, dimensions, and practice. *Review of Research in Education, 19*(1993), 3–49.

Bennett, C. (2001). Genres of research in multicultural education. *Review of Educational Research, 71*(2), 171–217.

Beyer, L. E. (2001). The value of critical perspectives in teacher education. *Journal of Teacher Education, 52*(2), 151–163.

Blog Talk Radio. (2010). Multicultural education scholars speak out. Retrieved from http://www.blogtalkradio.com/real-life/2010/11/09/multicultural-education -scholars-speak-out-guest-dr-christine-e-sleeter

Bohn, A. P. & Sleeter, C. E. (2000). Multicultural education and the standards movement: A report from the field. *Phi Delta Kappan, 82*(2), 156–159.

Bonilla-Silva, E. (2001). White supremacy and racism in the post-civil rights era. Boulder, CO: Lynne Rienner Publishers, Inc.

Boyle-Baise, L. & Sleeter, C. E. (2000). Community-based service learning for multicultural teacher education. *Educational Foundations, 14*(2), 33–50.

Castagno, A. E. & Brayboy, B. M. (2008). Culturally responsive schooling for indigenous youth: A review of the literature. *Review of Educational Research, 78*(4), 941–993.

Collins, P. H. (1998). It's all in the family: Intersections of gender, race, and nation. *Hypatia, 13*(3), 62–82.

Critical Family History. (2013). Retrieved from https://sites.google.com/a/christinesleeter.org/critical-family-history/

Dade, K. (2013). Interviews from the field: Dr. Christine Sleeter with Dr. Karen Dade. *International Journal of Multicultural Education.* Retrieved from http://ijme-journal.blogspot.com/2013/02/interviews-from-field-dr-christine.html

Education Radio. (2012). Audit culture: Snuffing the life out of teacher education. Retrieved from http://education-radio.blogspot.com/2012/02/audit-culture-snuffing-life-out-of_05.html?spref=fb

Ferri, B. A. & Connor, D. J. (2006). *Reading resistance: Discourses of exclusion in desegregation and inclusion debates.* New York, NY: Peter Lang.

Fox, W. & Gay, G. (1995). Integrating multicultural and curriculum principles in teacher education. *Peabody Journal of Education, 70*(3), 64–82.

Freire, P. (1970). *Pedagogy of the oppressed.* New York, NY: Herder and Herder.

Gay, G. (1995) Mirror images on common issues: Parallels between multicultural education and critical pedagogy. In C. E. Sleeter & P. McLaren (Eds.), *Multicultural education, critical pedagogy, and the politics of difference.* New York, NY: SUNY Press.

Gay, G. (2010). *Culturally responsive teaching: Theory, research, and practice.* New York, NY: Teachers College Press.

Gillborn, D. (2005). Education policy as an act of white supremacy: Whiteness, critical race theory, and education reform. *Journal of Education Policy, 20*(4), 485–505.

Giroux, H. A. (1992). Post-colonial ruptures and democratic possibilities: Multiculturalism as anti-racist pedagogy. *Cultural Critique, 21*(1992), 5–39.

Grande, S. (2000). American Indian identity and intellectualism: The quest for a new red pedagogy. *International Journal of Qualitative Studies in Education, 13*(4), 343–359.

Grant, C. A. & Sleeter, C. E. (1986a). Educational equity, education that is multicultural and social reconstructionism. *Journal of Educational Equity and Leadership, 6*, 105–118.

Hoffman, D. M. (1996): Culture and self in multicultural education; Reflections on discourse, text, and practice. *American Educational Research Journal, 33*(3), 545–569.

Howe, W. A. & Lisi, P. L. (2013). *Becoming a multicultural educator: Developing awareness, gaining skills, and taking action.* New York, NY: Sage Publications.

International Journal of Multicultural Education. (2013). Personal Interview. Available at ijme-journal.blogspot.com/2013/02/interviews-from-field-dr-christine.html

Kincheloe, J. L. (1997). *Changing multiculturalism.* Buckingham, UK: Open University Press.

Kumashiro, K. K. (2008). *The seduction of common sense: How the Right has framed the debate on America's schools.* New York, NY: Teachers College Press.

Kumashiro, K. K. (2010). Seeing the bigger picture: Troubling movements to end teacher education. *Journal of Teacher Education, 61*(1-2), 56–65.

Laslett, B. (1973). The family as a public and private institution: An historical perspective. *Journal of Marriage and Family, 35*(3), 480–492.

Lowen, J. W. (2008). *Lies my teacher told me. Everything your American history book got wrong.* The New Press, New York: NY.

Mansfield, E. & Kehoe, J. (1994). A critical examination of anti-racist education. *Canadian Journal of Education / Revue canadienne de l'éducation, 19*(4), 418–430.

May, S. & Sleeter, C. E. (Eds.) (2010). *Critical Multiculturalism: Theory and Praxis.* New York, NY: Routledge.

McLaren, P. (1999). A pedagogy of possibility: Reflecting upon Paulo Freire's politics of education. *Educational Researcher, 28*(2), 49–56.

Nagda, B. A., Gurin, P. & Lopez, G. E. (2003). Transformative pedagogy for democracy and social justice. *Race Ethnicity and Education, 6*(3), 165–191.

National Association for Multicultural Education. (2011). Is multicultural education relevant today? Retrieved from http://nameorg.org/nameblog/2011/06/is-multicultural-education-relevant-today/

Oakes, A. & Lipton, M. (2006). *Teaching to change the world.* New York, NY: McGraw-Hill Higher Education.

Paulo Freire Democratic Project. (2013). The PFDP award for social justice. Retrieved from http://www.chapman.edu/ces/research/democratic-project.aspx

Shor, I. (1992). *Empowering education: Critical teaching for social change.* Chicago, IL: University of Chicago Press.

Sleeter, C. E. (1987a). Definitions of learning disabilities, literacy, and social control. In B. Franklin (Ed.) *Learning Disability: Dissenting Essays.* Barcombe, UK: Falmer Press, pp. 67–87.

Sleeter, C. E. (1987b). Why is there learning disabilities? A critical history of the birth of the field. In T. S. Popkewitz (Ed.), *The Formation of the School Subject Matter: The Struggle for an American Institution,* Barcombe, UK: Falmer Press, pp. 210–237.

Sleeter, C. E. (1988). The social construction of learning disabilities: A reply to Kavale and Forness. *Remedial and Special Education,* 9, 53–57.

Sleeter, C. E. (1992). Restructuring schools for multicultural education. *Journal of Teacher Education, 43*(2), 148–156.

Sleeter, C. E. (1993a). Multicultural education: Five views. *Education Digest, 58*(7): 53–57.

Sleeter, C. E. (1993b). Power and privilege in White middle class feminist discussion of gender and education. In S. K. Biklin & D. Pollard (Eds.), *Gender and Education,* (pp. 221–240) Chicago: National Society for the Study of Education.

Sleeter, C. E. (1995). Radical structuralist perspectives on the creation and use of learning disabilities. In T. Skrtic (Ed.), *Disability and Democracy* (pp. 153–165). New York, NY: Teachers College Press.

Sleeter, C. E. (1996a). *Multicultural Education as Social Activism.* New York, NY: SUNY Press.

Sleeter, C. E. (1996b). Multicultural education as a social movement. *Theory into Practice, 35*(4), 239–247.

Sleeter, C. E. (1998). Yes, learning disabilities is political; what isn't? *Learning Disability Quarterly, 21*(4), 289–296.

Sleeter, C. E. (2004). Standardizing imperialism. *Rethinking Schools, 19*(1), 26–29.

Sleeter, C. E. (2005). Empire building for a new millennium: State standards and a curriculum for imperialism. In L. L. Karumanchery, (Ed.), *Engaging Equity: New Perspectives on Anti-Racist Education* (pp. 81–98). Detselig Enterprises.

Sleeter, C. E. (Ed.) (2007). *Facing Accountability in Education: Democracy and Equity at Risk.* New York, NY: Teachers College Press.

Sleeter, C. E. (2008a). Critical family history, identity, and historical memory. *Educational Studies, 43*(2), 114–124.

Sleeter, C. E. (2008b). Equity, democracy, and neoliberal assaults on teacher education. *Teaching and Teacher Education, 54*(8), 1947–1957.

Sleeter, C. E. (2008c). Teaching for democracy in an age of corporatocracy. *Teachers College Record, 110*(1), 139–159.

Sleeter, C. E. (2009a). Developing teacher epistemological sophistication about multicultural curriculum: A case study. *Action in Teacher Education, 31*(1), 3–13.

Sleeter, C. E. (2009b). Pedagogies of inclusion in teacher education. In S. Mitakidou, E. Tressou, B. B. Swadener, & C. A.Grant (Eds), *Beyond pedadodies of exclusion in diverse childhood contexts* (pp. 149–166). New York, NY: Palgrave Macmillan.

Sleeter, C. E. (2009c). Teacher education, neoliberalism, and social justice. In W. Ayers, T. Quinn, & D. Stovall (Eds.), *The Handbook of Social Justice in Education* (pp. 611–624). New York, NY: Routledge.

Sleeter, C. E. (2010a). Building counter-theory about disability. *Disability Studies Quarterly, 30*(2), NP.

Sleeter, C. E. (2010b). Culturally responsive pedagogy: A reflection. *Journal of Praxis in Multicultural Education, 5*(1), 116–119.

Sleeter, C. E. (2010c). Decolonizing curriculum: An essay review of The Sacred Hoop. *Curriculum Inquiry, 40*(2), 193–203.

Sleeter, C. E. (2010d). Federal education policy and social justice education. In T. K. Chapman & N. Hobbel (Eds), *Social Justice Pedagogy Across the Curriculum* (pp. 36–58). New York, NY: Routledge.

Sleeter, C. E. (2011a). Becoming white: Reinterpreting a family story by putting race back into the picture. *Race Ethnicity and Education, 14*(4), 421–433.

Sleeter, C. E. (2011b). Reexamining social inequality in schools and beyond: A conversation with Christine Sleeter (pp. 67–74); and Afterword (pp. 183–186). In P. W. Orelus (Ed.), *Rethinking race, class, language and gender.* Lanham, NJ: Rowman & Littlefield.

Sleeter, C. E. (2011c). Reflections on my use of multicultural and critical pedagogy when students are white. In K. L. Koppelman (Ed.), *Perspectives on human differences* (pp. 315–319). Boston, MA: Pearson.

Sleeter, C. E. (2011d). Rethinking Schools and the power of silver. *Rethinking Schools, 26*(1), 18–19.

Sleeter, C. E. (2012). Working to awaken: Seeing the need for multicultural education. In L. G. Denti & P. A. Whang (Eds.), *Rattling chains: Exploring social justice in education* (pp. 13–18). Boston, MA: Sense Publishers.

Sleeter, C. E. & Cornbleth, C. (Ed.) (2011). *Teaching with Vision: Culturally Responsive Teaching in Standards-Based Classrooms.* New York, NY: Teachers College Press.

Sleeter, C. E. & Delgado Bernal, D. (2004). Critical pedagogy, critical race theory, and antiracist education: Their implications for multicultural education, (pp. 240–260). In J. A. Banks & C. M. Banks (Eds.), *Handbook of Research on Multicultural Education* 2nd ed. San Francisco, CA: Jossey Bass.

Sleeter, C. E. & McLaren, P. (Eds.). (1995). *Multicultural Education and Critical Pedagogy: The Politics of Difference.* Albany, NY: SUNY Press.

Sleeter, C. E. & McLaren, P. (2009). The origins of multiculturalism. In Wayne Au (Ed.), *Rethinking Multicultural Education* (pp. 17–20). Milwaukee, WI: Rethinking Schools, Ltd.

Sleeter, C. E. & Thao, Y. J. (2007). Guest editors' introduction: Diversifying the teaching force. *Teacher Education Quarterly, 34*(4), 3–8.

Vaught, S.E. & Castagno, A.E. (2008). I don't think I'm a racist': Critical race theory, teacher attitudes, and structural racism. *Race Ethnicity and Education,* 11(2), 95–113.

Yosso, T. J. (2002). Toward a critical race curriculum. *Equity & Excellence in Education, 35*(2), 93–107.

ANNOTATED BIBLIOGRAPHY

WORKS BY SLEETER

Sleeter, C. E. (1986). Learning disabilities: The social construction of a special education category. *Exceptional Children 53,* 46–54. (Reprinted in S.B. Sigmon (Ed.) *Critical voices in special education.* Albany: SUNY Press, 1990, 21–34.)

In this chapter Sleeter provides a critical examination of the emergence of learning disability categories in the early 1960's as a result of the perception that America had to ratchet up its educational system to rival that of the Soviet

Union. Along with the Soviet's launching of Sputnik in 1957 and political reform movements of the time that in the United States that linked education to national security, the inability of specific segments of the population to meet the prescribed standards caused the government to create five categories that Sleeter argues were grounded in issues of race and class. According to Sleeter, these categories afforded some protection for struggling white middle class children while simultaneously developing a stigma for poor children of color.

Sleeter, C. E., & Grant, C. A. (1987). An analysis of multicultural education in the U.S.A. *Harvard Educational Review, 57*, 441–444.

Cited over 475 times in scholarly literature, this piece by Sleeter and Grant provides a seminal set of insights into the scholarly literature up to and through the mid-1980's with a critical perspective that highlighted the limits of the literature, particularly the overemphasis on discrete or isolated components of multiculturalism. Since the mid-1980's this article and its taxonomy, which helped readers to understand and situate the literature, have served to not only provide an overview of the foundational literature in the field of multicultural education and as a catalyst for continued work in the field. Sleeter and Grant are often drawn upon by leading scholars in multicultural education, including James Banks, John Ogbu, Marilyn Cochran-Smith, Gloria Ladson-Billings, Mica Pollock, Sonia Nieto, and Kevin Kumashiro, among many others.

Sleeter, C. E. (1989). Multicultural education as a form of resistance to oppression. *Journal of Education 171*(3): 51–71. (Reprinted in E. F. Provenzo, Jr. (Ed.) *Foundations of Educational Thought,* 2008, London, Sage Publications.)

In this article Sleeter takes head on numerous critiques of multiculturalism, from conservative appeals for color blind objectivists approaches to education to more transformationalist critiques of the limitations of multiculturalism's inherent liberal grounding. By chronicling 25 years of the influence of multiculturalism on education Sleeter makes recommendations about the potential for political resistance within the field of education and the resulting challenge to confront oppressive societal structures.

Sleeter, C. E. (Ed.). (1991). *Empowerment through multicultural education.* Albany, NY: SUNY Press.

Organized into three sections, with a total of fourteen chapters, Sleeter's edited volume predates Ira Shor's work on empowerment in education, and brought together multi-disciplinary perspectives to confront how underrepresented groups are disempowered through schooling, to think through what strategies could be enacted upon within educational contexts, and the role that teacher education might play in an empowering type of education. Throughout the text, persistent themes of dialogue, engagement, and connection are explored within the context of thinking through the value and role of empowerment in education. This text, along with its contemporaries such as Shor's *Empowering*

Education (see the annotation below) provided an emerging set of perspectives on the transformative role of education in the early 1990's.

Sleeter, C. E. (1996). *Multicultural education as social activism.* Albany, NY: State University of New York Press.

Sleeter's examination of multicultural education is made powerful through her use of an auto-ethnographic narrative. She is not afraid to implicate her role as a white woman in her discussions of race and schooling. Furthermore, Sleeter discusses important ideas regarding her own classroom experience at the collegiate level vis-à-vis race and schooling. Perhaps most significantly, Sleeter situates her musings in the context of today's globalized society.

Sleeter, C. E. (1996). Multicultural education as a social movement. *Theory into Practice, 35*(4), 239–247.

In this powerful piece, Sleeter notes that most of the foundations for multicultural education were spawned as a result of key issues addressed in various social movements of the 1960s and 1970s. Sleeter traces why current (at the time, though we would argue this has continued even more since Sleeter wrote this piece) educators who commit to multiculturalism have not themselves ever participated in social movements. The disconnect, Sleeter suggests, is that multiculturalism may very well be taken up by well-meaning and well intentioned educators, but those same educators are not experienced at or inclined to participate in social change as activists like those who helped to lay the groundwork for multicultural education were inclined to do. Sleeter offers that multicultural education is, metaphorically, often reduced to (a) therapy, (b) teaching techniques, and/or (c) academic discourses. Sleeter discusses why "social movement" may be a better albeit less discussed metaphor for the hopes of multicultural education.

Sleeter, C. E. (2003). Teaching globalization. *Multicultural perspectives, 5*(2), 3–9.

Sleeter examines a number of metaphors in order to discuss globalization and education, particularly as it shaped up in the wake of 9/11 in the United States, and then moves beyond the metaphors, suggesting that "... increasingly, schooling is helping to serve global imperialism" (p. 9). Sleeter offers a number of teaching resources that she asserts are capable of helping to redefine and rethink the meaning of globalization, ultimately arguing that the time has passed to think about whether or not globalization will affect education and that what needs to be done is to understand how education will play a part in determining the role of discourse about "the kind of society we wish to be building" (p. 9).

Sleeter, C. E. (2005). *Un-standardizing curriculum: Multicultural teaching in standards-based classrooms.* New York, NY: Teachers College Press.

Sleeter's primary audience is teachers whose professional autonomy has been continually shrinking as a result of increased state-sanctioned prescriptive approaches to teaching. The primary focus of the book is on curriculum because Sleeter believes that curriculum lacking recognition of the culturally relevant and intellectually rich influence of multiculturalism risks denying students foundational knowledge for being informed citizens in a culturally diverse democratic society.

Sleeter, C. E. (Ed.) (2007). *Facing accountability in education: Democracy and equity at risk.* New York, NY: Teachers College Press.

This edited volume provides insights from leading scholars—including Barbara McCombs, James Scheurich, Jim and Cherry Banks, Laurence Parker, David Gillborn—into what accountability in education could possibly mean in the 21st century. In doing so, they draw on key ideas and concepts of equity, school reform, race and racism, and political ideologies. According to Sleeter, the volume and chapter authors have "...deep concern for democracy, equity, and particularly the experiences and futures of young people from communities that historically have not been well served by schools and other social institutions" (p. 10).

Sleeter, C. E. (2008). Equity, democracy, and neoliberal assaults on teacher education. *Teaching and Teacher Education, 54*(8), 1947–1957.

In this article Sleeter moves beyond a simple critique or theorization of the impact of neoliberalism on the United States educational system to offering actual concrete recommendations on ways that educators, families, and engaged citizens in general can collaborate with underserved communities to establish pockets of resistance. In this article Sleeter primarily focuses on taking up this effort via preservice teachers and teacher education programs. In doing so, she recommends addressing the following: recruitment and admission, early fieldwork, professional coursework, student teaching, and ongoing professional development.

Sleeter, C. E. (2008). Teaching for democracy in an age of corporatocracy. *Teachers College, Record 110*(1), 139–159.

Teaching for Democracy in an Age of Corporatocracy draws attention to the inherently undemocratic aspects of the No Child Left Behind (NCLB) educational movement, particularly as it applies to teachers whose practice is grounded in democratic education. Sleeter's ability to link NCLB to what she describes as "corporatocracy" highlights the tensions between education's role in supposedly equipping students to participate in a democratic society versus what Sleeter highlights as a much more nefarious effort to prepare students to function in a purely consumerist society.

Sleeter, C. E. (Ed.) (2011). *Professional development for culturally responsive and relationship-based pedagogy.* New York, NY: Peter Lang.

The authors in this edited text address an educational conundrum in which colonialism, global migratory patterns, competition for educational resources, current technological advancements, and untimely a myriad of numerous other conditions has resulted in a disconnect between an ever-increasing racial, cultural, and linguistically diverse student population (generally including Indigenous students, students of color, students whose families live in poverty and new immigrants are experiencing a disparity of educational opportunity) and a disproportionally homogeneous teacher population.

Sleeter, C. E., & McLaren, P. (Eds.). (1995). *Multicultural education and critical pedagogy: The politics of difference.* Albany, NY: SUNY Press.

The forward of *Multicultural Education and Critical Pedagogy* asserts that the text sets out to "understand the myriad complex of social, historical, economic, and cultural relations that influence learning and quality of life" for the yet to be born. The writing of the text against the backdrop of the 1993 Los Angeles race riots powerfully illustrates the point that each of the contributors in this edited text struggle to make, which is society has become ever-increasingly diverse and old conventions that are ill-equipped to understand the nature of a multicultural society must give way to more critical and profound understandings for the establishment of a working democracy.

Sleeter, C. E., & Soriano, E. (Eds.) (2012). *Creating solidarity across diverse communities: International perspectives in education.* New York, NY: Teachers College Press.

This important edited volume exhibits Sleeter's reach beyond just the context of the United States. The volume brings to bear multiple perspectives from around the world to explore what solidarity looks like within and across diverse community contexts. In the editing of this book, Sleeter and her co-editor Soriano show how "glocality" operates—the idea that the global and local both simultaneously matter. Within the "glocal" approach the contexts discussed provide significant fodder for readers within their own local contexts. At a more fundamental level, this text helps bring to light to the fact that commitment to social justice and transformational educational opportunities are global commitments and concerns.

RELATED WORKS

Asher, N. (2007). Made in the (multicultural) U.S.A.: Unpacking tensions of race, culture, gender, and sexuality in education. *Educational Researcher, 36*(2), 65–73.

Drawing from work in multicultural education, including Sleeter's, Asher pushes beyond the traditional boundaries of the field. In doing so, Asher examines how sexuality and Asian American identities receive little attention and representation within multicultural discourses. Asher attempts to move the conversation beyond representation within the confines of stereotypes, and toward a situation in which self-reflexivity becomes a site within multicultural classes to model critical participatory democratic engagement.

Au, W. (2009). *Unequal by design: High-stakes testing and the standardization of inequality.* New York, NY: Routledge.

Unequal by Design provides readers a thorough look at the roots of standardized testing, from its precursors in the Eugenics and Social Efficiency Movements through its current manifestation in such contemporary educational reforms as No Child Left Behind. In the tradition of noted educational historians like James Anderson, William Watkins, and educational sociologists like Annie Winfield, Au's text illustrates the ways in which struggles for social justice are deeply ingrained in the political economy of schooling, in general, and standardized tests, in particular.

Banks, J. A. (1993). Multicultural education: Historical development, dimensions, and practice. *Review of Research in Education, 19*(1993), 3–49.

In this historic article, Banks outlines the historical contour of the early ethnic studies movement, with a specific focus on African American studies programs. The article calls for a more comprehensive history of the intergroup education movement. Banks concludes with questions concerning the extent to which ethnic studies programs were institutionalized within schools and the subsequent impact on both the schools and the programs of such institutionalization.

Gay, G. (2010). *Culturally responsive teaching: Theory, research, and practice (2nd Edition)*. New York, NY: Teachers College Press.

Culturally Responsive Teaching, first published in 2000, has been an important and enduring text in the foundation of culturally engaged practice. Sleeter's work is highlighted in this text in a section on "ethnic and culturally diversity in curriculum content." It addresses the thoughtful contributions of Sleeter's work in both the fields of multiculturalism and culturally relevant teaching.

Gillborn, D. (2005). Education policy as an act of white supremacy: Whiteness, critical race theory, and education reform. *Journal of Education Policy, 20*(4), 485–505.

Gilborn draws from Critical Race Theory (CRT) as a means of analyzing education policy in England. The piece connects with much of Sleeter's considerations vis-à-vis inequity, often times centered within racial discourses, that is pervasive not only in the United States but abroad. Gillborn argues that white supremacy is not exempt in educational policy making decisions, specifically arguing that educational policy makers, often white males, promote what he calls tacit intentionality, making education policy itself white supremacist. While Gillborn credits CRT for furthering a line of thinking in race research that examines the role of whiteness and exploitation, he specifically credits Sleeter as having promoted similar thinking prior to the advent of CRT in education.

Grant, C. A., & Sleeter, C. E. (2007). *Doing multicultural education for achievement and equity.* New York, NY: Routledge Falmer.

Covering a wide range of ideas in multicultural education, ranging from the formation of teachers, to what supportive classrooms look like with respect to academic achievement, to the role of testing and assessment, and even how to move ideas and action beyond the classroom environment, this text has served as an approachable work for understanding the multiple dimensions of multicultural education. Grant and Sleeter organized their work into seventeen building blocks for what they call "fantastic teachers" (p. 4) as a means of situating the journey to becoming a (multicultural) educator. The thrust of the book promotes the notion that educators must have an active role in the development of educational equity for all students.

Grant, C. A., & Sleeter, C. E. (1988b). A rationale for integrating race, gender, and social class. In L. Weis (Ed.), *Class, race, and gender in U.S. education*. Buffalo, NY: SUNY Press, pp. 144–160.

Grant and Sleeter present a discussion of ethnographic inquiry into the practice of educators in urban school settings. They concluded that the research at the time placed too much emphasis on determining approaches and outcomes for teachers. Grant and Sleeter go on to suggest that teachers themselves should be part of determining the approaches, aims, and outcomes of education.

Kincheloe, J. L. (1997). *Changing multiculturalism*. Buckingham, UK: Open University Press.

The change that Kincheloe refers to in the title of this timely text is a both a critical and practically grounded approach to multiculturalism. The political landscape of the late 1990's when this text was written featured a resurgence of what Kincheloe characterized as angry whites invested in guarding the vestiges of institutionalized racial hegemony. Against this backdrop *Changing Multiculturalism* considers the production of racialized, gendered and class based subjectivities as a means for rethinking schools and schooling.

Kumashiro, K. K. (2008). *The seduction of common sense: How the Right has framed the debate on America's schools*. New York, NY: Teachers College Press.

Kumashiro, a leading expert in multicultural education, reframes the debate in education by taking a critical perspective of both left and right ideology that has dominated educational discourse, particularly in the wake of *No Child Left Behind*. Like Sleeter, Kumashiro is interested in how social justice and issues of equity and multicultural education have been stifled among the myriad educational reforms that have most often lacked substance or commitment to move become anti-oppressive in nature.

Shor, I. (1992). *Empowering education: Critical teaching for social change*. Chicago, IL: University of Chicago Press.

Like much of Sleeter's work, Ira Short examines and critically analyzes the mechanism that prevents education from reaching its potential to empower and impassion the very people receiving education. Drawing on a variety of situations and teaching exemplars from across the K–20 spectrum, Short blends themes of critical theory, democratic commitment, and transformative pedagogy throughout the book. While Shor neither directly draw on Sleeter's work nor spends significant space focusing on multicultural education, this text connects directly both with Sleeter's, particularly around how traditionally underrepresented groups might be empowered through education as a means of engaging social change.

CHAPTER 16

WILLIAM F. TATE, IV

Mathematics, Critical Race Theory, and Social Justice: A Formula for Equitable Access and Opportunity to Learn

Charlene Johnson Carter and Michael Carter

INTRODUCTION

William F. Tate is a child of fortune, if not a child of privilege. He was fortunate to have ample family and community support throughout his life. Both parents had degrees and, growing up, Tate had the benefit of their friends from the educational arena and others in the neighborhood supporting him in his endeavors (Ladson-Billings, 2005). The example set by his parents, combined with the persistent encouragement of his grandmother, all but guaranteed that Tate would attain at least an undergraduate degree.

Beginning with a degree in economics, Tate's initial career choice was to become a high school mathematics teacher. Encouraged by family and community, Tate obtained a doctorate in mathematics education. Tate's background as a Black Catholic and the support of his family have been

Educating About Social Issues in the 20th and 21st Centuries, pages 323–343
Copyright © 2014 by Information Age Publishing
All rights of reproduction in any form reserved.

instrumental to his success and his drive to enhance life's opportunities for students of color. As he explained to Ladson-Billings (2005), "showing up," i.e., being there when no one expects you and/or to begin the process is critical to achieving anything in life.

Other significant influences on Tate's choice in regard to his life's work are Holy Angels Catholic (elementary) School in Chicago, Illinois, and Father Gene Clemons, the parish priest at the school. Holy Angels serves African Americans on Chicago's "south side." The school is recognized for having a culturally relevant curricular and instructional program; that is, it takes an Afrocentric approach to educating students and exemplifies its commitment to social justice (Ladson-Billings, 2005; Tate, 1994a). Father Clemons, an outspoken advocate for Black children, not only proposed that Black Catholic churches adopt a Black child from foster care but, amid much controversy, adopted one himself (Ladson-Billings, 2005, p. 100). Tate attributes his success as a mathematics educator to his early education in this empowering, safe, and socially validating environment where he experienced the realities of social justice at a young age (Tate, 1994a).

Tate received neither justice nor affirmation while at the Catholic high school Chicago's Archbishop Quigley Preparatory Seminary. Fortunately, that experience was neutralized by the foundation established in his elementary school years and the family and community support he was graced with that affirmed him and his ability to achieve. Both of the educational environments he experienced during his formative years influence his research into the discrepancy in achievement of African-American students in mathematics sciences:

> Now that I live in an urban city again, I view the kids almost like they're my own and the questions I raise in my research are the questions I would raise if I were trying to understand the environment that my own children were in.... So I see it as—I'm almost like an elected representative, since I came from an urban environment and largely one that was supportive for me. I see myself as an agent on behalf of those kids. (Ladson-Billings, 2005, p. 105)

This agency permeates his work. For Tate, research complies with an imperative to serve and inform society (Tate, 2006). When discussing his scholarship with Ladson-Billings (2005) Tate distinguished a "we" career from the "me" career that seems to predominate in the academy:

> ...and I am really trying to work on having a "we" career where it is about a broader set of people than just the work. It's about helping people; it's about exposing all forms of inequality and so, for me, my work is intricately tied to the people, whereas I see a lot of my colleagues who seem to write for their own self-gratification or...crass careerism. (p. 108)

This quest is evidenced in his bold scholarship that has a penchant to be thought-provoking. From his initial prodding of the academy at University of Wisconsin, Madison where, he, along with Ladson-Billings, served as assistant professors, addressed the "taboo" topic of race (Ladson-Billings, 2005; Ladson-Billings and Tate, 1995) to his most recent position as Edward Mallinckrodt Distinguished Professor in Arts & Sciences at Washington University in St. Louis, Tate continues to provoke dialogue on the academic advancement of students of color.

SOCIAL JUSTICE

The complexity, range and potential of social justice are reflected in William Tate's scholarship vis-à-vis race, mathematical sciences and geography of opportunity. Essentially, he demonstrates how opportunity to learn for students of color is governed by systemic factors that permeate that area of instruction. His micro-level research examines the effects of culturally imbued variables such as culturally relevant pedagogy for teaching mathematical sciences on the learning and achievement of African-American students in urban environments. Systemically, he investigates how access and opportunity to learn in the mathematical sciences for students of color is influenced by macro-level variables (tracking, teacher quality and fiscal management). As coauthor of the premier treatise that applied the legally based Critical Race Theory (CRT) to education, Tate elucidated race as an exigent variable for establishing equity in educational processes. For Tate, race, in conjunction with poverty and urban environments, is germane to the nature and quality of instruction and, therefore, to learning in mathematical sciences. He makes the case that this convergence of factors creates a civil rights issue because of its impact on the participation of certain citizens in our democratic society. Although his work spans several areas, this chapter's focus is on his contributions to CRT, education of African-American students in mathematics/science, and, geography of opportunity.

Endemic to the struggle for social justice is the interrogation of existing societal structures and their philosophical foundations (power, equity, and entitlement). Education is one of those structures. While education is frequently perceived as some that is totally, it is also capable of instituting and implementing and reinforcing that which is negative. Thus, for example, while it can provide the impetus for greater inclusion, egalitarianism, and progress toward social justice, it is also true that it can be used to maintain a particular system of power and its associated substructure. As Freire (1987) notes,

> There is no such thing as a neutral educational process. Education either functions as an instrument which is used to facilitate the integration of the

younger generation into the logic of the present system and bring about conformity to it, or it becomes "the practice of freedom," the means by which men and women deal critically and creatively with reality and discover how to participate in the transformation of their world. (p. 152)

Neutrality and objectivity are embraced as cornerstones of mathematical sciences,[1] apparently because of their form and function. Tate's scholarship eviscerates this perception and the entrenched belief that high achievement in mathematical sciences is attainable by only a select, elite few, and he does so by exposing biased axioms and practices (Hogrebe & Tate, 2012, Tate, 1995c, 2008a). The elitist, Eurocentric canon that pervades these disciplines is exposed to reveal misguided precepts regarding neutrality and objectivity, and concomitant practices that are ineffective for students of color. (Tate, 1994b, 2001, 2004).

For Tate (1994b, 2001), proficiency in mathematics is a civil right in that it affects civic engagement and involvement in democracy:

If students learn in school to analyze and critique mathematical situations....they will be prepared for public discussions about the development and implementation of the mathematical models that are used in social decision-making. Such preparation is radically different from merely preparing students to add, subtract, multiply and divide accurately. Our highly technological society requires that all students, not just African-American students, be prepared to use mathematics to defend their rights. The curriculum and pedagogy of mathematics should support this objective. (p. 483)

This right is central to his work. His personal journey to a career in mathematics was facilitated by a culturally relevant environment that provided insight into the potential benefits from acknowledging and acting on this belief (Tate, 1994a). His success and that of others in the environment led him to wonder why these types of affirming experiences are not ingrained in administrators and teachers in low-performing schools serving students of color.[2] His study of Critical Race Theory (CRT), a legal, interdisciplinary theory regarding race and its systemic effects on societal and legal issues, provided answers to the question (Ladson-Billings, 2005). Convinced that the theory would help to illumine a number of educational issues for students of color, Tate and Ladson-Billings worked to disentangle and apply it to education (Ladson-Billings, 2005). Its application is evident in several of Tate's works regarding how mathematical sciences are advanced and taught within large, urban educational settings involving students of color.

This chapter focuses on Tate's contributions to CRT, mathematical sciences, and geography/geospatial research. Works selected are emblematic of his analysis of the salience of race for assessing educational access and opportunity to learn. This position challenges overriding presumptions that "color-blindness," meritocracy, and neutrality ensure equity within the educational system. This position and analysis is explicated with "boundary crossings," paradigmatic challenges, and interdisciplinary sources.

Critical Race Theory

The publication Ladson-Billings and Tate's (1995) "Toward a Critical Race Theory of Education," precipitated a discourse on race, a subject previously un-theorized within education. Up until that point in time, models linking educational equity to socioeconomic status and gender dominated the discourse on factors impacting educational equity. All too often, however, the effect of race on educational achievement was obfuscated—possibly because of the history of oppression and exploitation within the United States (Ladson-Billings & Tate, 1995; Tate, 1997; Tate, 1994a). Tate worked with Ladson-Billings to fashion CRT into a formal analytical framework for studying and addressing educational inequity. Ladson-Billings (2005) credits Tate with initiating and managing the process of adapting the theory.

The history of desegregation litigation in the United States is largely based on the experiences of people of African descent and includes cases such as the following: *Roberts v. City of Boston*, 1850; *Dred Scott v. Sanford*, 1857; *Plessy v. Ferguson*, 1896; and the *Brown v. Board of Education* decisions of 1954 and 1955. This history, in conjunction with the gains and limitations of the Civil Rights Movement, served as the catalyst for the expansion of CRT (Tate, 1997; Bell, 1987). These socio-historical events are evidence of the momentous role race has played and continues to play in our society. More importantly, they demonstrate that insidious, systemic racism is not only centuries old in the United States, but continues unabated. With its primary theoretical pillars in interest-convergence, property rights, and voice scholarship, CRT illumines the continued existence of racism and yields a research agenda to investigate, deconstruct and interpret its effects on various groups (Dixson & Rousseau, 2005; Ladson-Billings & Tate, 1995; Tate, 1997). From an initial focus on African Americans, CRT has expanded exponentially to include a number of disenfranchised groups (i.e., Latinos/Latinas (LatCrit), Asian Americans (critical Asian American legal studies), and women (Critical race feminism)) (Lynn and Parker, 2006). In a touch of irony, even "whiteness" as a racial construct and surreptitious variable affecting societal functioning has been studied (Tate, 2003).

Among the constructs in CRT used to explicate the ways in which race influences perceptions and definitions of phenomena, Crenshaw's delineation of the expansive and restrictive properties of anti-discrimination law are of particular interest in relation to Tate (1997):

Crenshaw identified two distinct rhetorical visions of equality in the body of antidiscrimination law: one termed the *expansive* view and the other the *restrictive* view. The expansive view stresses equality as an outcome and seeks to enlist the power of the courts to eliminate the effects of racial oppression. In contrast, the restrictive view of equality, which coexists with the expansive view, treats equality as a process.... The primary goal of antidiscrimination law, according to the restrictive view, is to stop future acts of wrongdoing rather than correct present forms of past injustice. (Tate, 1997, p. 228)

This contrast is referenced in several of Tate's works on mathematics (Tate, Ladson-Billings & Grant, 1993; Rousseau & Tate, 2003, Tate, 1993; Tate, 1994b), including some predating Tate's seminal article with Ladson-Billings (1995). The distinction is used to demonstrate differences in the motives underlying the goals of race-based litigation and their concomitant effects on interests related to a case. This differential is used to demonstrate that goals and instructional methods arising from a certain perspective may have adverse effects when used to teach mathematics to students of color. It is also used to illustrate the complexity and implications of "mathematizing" social issues and/or relying on quantitative measures as indicators of equity (Tate et al., 1993).

MATHEMATICAL SCIENCES, SOCIAL JUSTICE, AND AFRICAN-AMERICAN STUDENTS

Tate's credential as a Ph.D. in mathematics is evident in his writing. He frequently frames logic and theorizes concepts in mathematical and/or scientific terms, e.g., "binary perspectives" (Tate, 2003). However, his work is also an exemplar of the "boundary crossing" and "paradigmatic shifts" he suggests is absolutely essential in addressing issues of inequity. Keenly aware of the importance of literacy in mathematics and science for fully functioning in a democratic society, he devised a logical proof to show that mathematical/scientific skills are not only integral to the economic progress of students but also to their optimal involvement in the democratic process. Terms such as civic engagement, democracy, and citizenship are woven throughout his writings. It is evident that Tate considers skill in mathematics and the associated areas of science and technology akin to reading and writing in terms of their impact on one's ability to function unimpaired in contemporary society. At one and the same time, as noted above, he is adamant that race and poverty have implications for the acquisition of these requisite skills. In that regard, Tate demonstrates how the confluence of race and poverty creates systemic barriers to achievement for students of color. Moreover, he presents theoretical and empirical evidence on how those barriers can be overturned. Providing access and opportunity across multiple dimensions is shown to be crucial to both involvement and success for students of color in mathematical sciences. Helpfully, Tate models issues and solutions in the context of Venn diagrams to show how the application of culturally relevant pedagogy (Ladson-Billings, 1994) and "centricity" can breach concentric barriers arising from the social and political context of mathematics, color-blindness, tracking (curricular and ability), and opportunity-to-learn (Tate, 1994a, 1994b, 1995a, 1995b).

Why and how instruction lacking cultural relevance constitutes a "foreign pedagogy" for students of African descent was articulated by African-American historian Carter G. Woodson as far back as 1933:

> And even in the certitude of science of mathematics it has been unfortunate that the approach to the Negro has been borrowed from a "foreign" method. For example, the teaching of arithmetic in a backwards county in Mississippi should mean one thing in the Negro school and a decidedly different thing in the white school. The Negro children, as a rule, come from the homes of tenants and peons who have to migrate annually from plantation to plantation, looking for light which they have never seen. The children from the homes of white planters and merchants live permanently in the midst of calculations, family budgets, and the like, which enable them sometimes to learn more by contact than the Negro can acquire in school. Instead of teaching such Negro children with less arithmetic, they should be taught much more than the white children, for the latter attend a graded school consolidated by free transportation when the Negroes go to one-room hovels to be taught without equipment and by incompetent teachers educated scarcely beyond the eighth grade. (Woodson, 1933/1990, p. 4)

Conditions outlined by Woodson almost 80 years ago—content unconnected to the students' experience, less instruction when more was needed given their lived realities, and less-than-adequate resources and trained educators—remain true for students of color today. Woodson's insights are referenced in several of Tate's writings as evidence that inequitable treatment is neither happenstance nor circumstantial but is a vestige of a legacy of systemic racism. "Centricity" is presented as a way to address this heritage of injustice caused by inadequate cultural congruence. It has the capacity to boost academic achievement by making students' own cultural experiences the common pedagogical denominator in learning. In this regard, Tate (1994) has said:

> I have argued that one barrier to an equitable mathematics education for African-American students is the failure to "center" them in the process of knowledge acquisition and to build on their cultural and community experiences. Molefi Asante defines the concept of centricity as "a perspective that involves locating students within the context of their own cultural references so that they can relate socially and psychologically to other cultural perspec-

tives." The concept of centricity can be applied to any culture. "For the white students in America," Asante continues, "this is easy because almost all the experiences discussed in American classrooms are approached from the standpoint of white perspectives and history." (p. 479)

The significance of culturally relevant pedagogy and the consequences of its ubiquitous influence in social and political contexts are also recognized by the National Council of Teachers of Mathematics (NCTM). For example, the professional standards of NCTM regarding the teaching of mathematics include the following:

Teachers should know:

- how students' linguistic, ethnic, racial and socioeconomic background influence their learning of mathematics; and
- the role of mathematics in society and culture, the contributions of various cultures to the advancement of mathematics, and the relationship of school mathematics to other subjects and realistic applications. (as cited in Rousseau & Tate, 2003)

In his work, Tate provides pedagogical exemplars from real classrooms as additional support for the benefits of culturally relevant approaches that are centered on the lived realities of students. In doing so, for example, he discusses a group of middle level students in south Dallas (Texas) who addressed the issue of liquor stores being allowed in the vicinity of schools in their district but not in certain districts outside their community. Details regarding the teacher's approach to teaching mathematical sciences and the students' use of mathematics to investigate the issue and present it to city officials are included in several of his writings (Tate, 1994b, 1995a, 1995b, 2008a). In his 2008 presidential speech at the American Educational Research Association's annual meeting, Tate emphasized that the students were able to understand and effectively use mathematics to analyze an issue of interest, convey a message, support a position, and visually present data (Tate, 2008a). This example has also been used to underscore the efficacy of mathematics' communication that is situated in students' lived realities (Tate, 1994b, 1995a), and how geography affects opportunity and access to education, health, among other resources (Tate, 2008).

Tate also presents examples as to how word problems can be used to challenge the "neutrality of numbers." One illustration involves the choice between a weekly rail/subway pass costing $16.00 and a daily, one-way pass that costs $1.50 for transportation to work. The question posed is: which is the better choice? The "correct" answer, the daily pass because one saves $1 ($3.00/round trip for five days = $15.00), is based on the 40-hour, eight-to-five, five-days per week work model common in white, middle-class homes. However, African-American students tended to select the weekly pass as the better choice. When asked to explain their answer, many offered multiple reasons for the preference. The weekly pass could be used more than five times a week, a valuable benefit to wage-earners holding multiple jobs. The weekly pass could also be used by more than one person if members of a household work different shifts. In this setting, the weekly pass is indeed the most reasonable, and cost-saving, choice. This crystallizes the juxtaposition of the students' realities against what is to them a mis-specified model of their existence—one individual working eight hours per day, five days per week.

Another case involves a preservice teacher who, during the Thanksgiving season, used examples of pumpkin pies as counting items to hold the attention of five second-grade students struggling with word-problems. When the African-American student in the group appeared disinterested and not fully engaged in the discourse/lesson, the preservice teacher attributed it to the student's lack of interest in mathematics. When Tate discussed the situation with the teacher, he offered an alternative perspective on the student's apparent detachment. He explained that an African-American family is more likely to have sweet potato pie than pumpkin pie at Thanksgiving. While the cultural relevance and centricity of the pumpkin pies may have heightened the attention of the students of European descent, this may not have been true for the student of African descent. This unintentional bias had implications for the student's engagement and for the teacher's assessment of the underlying cause of the behavior (Tate, 1994b). These examples are employed by Tate in his works to illustrate the implications of cultural relevance for working mathematical word problems within the seemingly neutral, objective discipline of mathematics (Tate, 1994b, 1995b).

In addition to the micro-level analysis of classrooms, Tate conducts macro-analysis of the implications of the range of systemic issues vis-à-vis tracking and resource allocation in regard to achievement in mathematics by students of color. Tate's work presents the deleterious effects of tracking on students of color and students of lower socioeconomic status, including there being a major impediment to learning—not to mention, access to higher level education (Tate, 1994a, 1995a, 1995b, 1995c, and 2008b). The issue of tracking is addressed comprehensively by Oakes (2005).

Research indicates that coursework in geometry is a significant predictor of the likelihood of attending college. However, prerequisite courses are required before one is able to take geometry. Tate refers to this situation as curricular tracking which is related to resource allocation because of the dearth of prerequisite courses in those urban schools where impoverished students of color predominate (Tate, 1993, 2004, 2008a, 2008b).

Other resources in short supply in urban schools are adequate technology and skilled fiscal management that adequately addresses the higher NCTM standards for in-depth analytical skills (Tate, 1993, 2008b). These and other issues such as a constructive vs. a behavioral approach to mathematics instruction (Tate, 1995c) and reliance on color-blindness as surety for equity in mathematics instruction (Rousseau & Tate, 2003), are integral to ready access to such courses and the opportunity to learn for students of color in mathematics.

Tellingly, Gutstein and Peterson (2005) collected several works including Tate's article, "Race, Retrenchment and the Reform of School Mathematics" (1994b) in their book, *Rethinking Mathematics: Teaching Social Justice by the Numbers*. This compilation was assembled to provide an impetus for teachers to weave social justice into mathematics lessons so students:

- recognize the power of mathematics as an essential analytical tool to understand and potentially change the world, rather than merely regarding math as a collection of disconnected rules to be rotely memorized and regurgitated;
- deepen understanding of important social issues such as racism, sexism, classism and ecology;
- connect math with [the students'] own cultural and community histories and [so that they] can appreciate the contributions that various cultures and people have made to mathematics;
- help the students come to own power as active citizens in building a democratic society and thus equipped to play a more active role in that society; and
- help the students to become more motivated to learn important mathematics. (Tate cited in Gutstein & Peterson, 2005, p. 1)

These goals are aligned with NCTM professional standards for teachers of mathematics regarding teaching, understanding, and using mathematics to attain benefits to society beyond "counting numbers." An in-school application of mathematics that is rarely seen out of school involves counting numbers void of any context. To motivate students to see the utility of mathematics in addressing personal and social situations, and understanding mathematics in out-of-school contexts is needed. The theme of the book, advocacy for teaching social justice in mathematics, is in line with Tate's scholarship and stance that appropriate education in the mathematical sciences is a civil rights issue.

Recently, Tate's toolkit for dissecting the inequity within society and schooling expanded to include the geography of opportunity and geospatial research (Hogrebe & Tate, 2012; Tate, 2008a). He uses these two to further expose the systemic and concentric aspects of impediments to opportunity to learn in the mathematical sciences. However, his conclusions have implications across disciplines. He provides an intriguing view of the link between business development and community development—the two are systemically structured to the benefit of some and disenfranchisement of others. Tate demonstrates how this relationship is used to advance political and societal agendas. The methodology of geospatial research, because of its visual appeal and ability to engage interested parties, including community members, policymakers, and business personnel, is a valuable instrument for engaging stakeholders in the discourse on these issues (Tate. 2008a).

CONCLUSION

Tate's research/scholarship is truly revelatory in that it highlights and deconstructs multifaceted issues (particularly race and poverty) confronting students based on background; in particular. Furthermore, his work remains a singular beacon illuminating the potential of students of color to achieve in all disciplines. Emphasis is placed on mathematical sciences, an area largely regarded as academically off-limits to most students of color because of the perception that it is beyond their abilities. Social justice without equitable access and outcomes within the educational system is an impossibility. Tate's scholarship makes this clear and calls for a reconsideration of the paradigms of deficiency that prevail regarding the abilities of students of color.

In her presentation about teacher educators of African descent, Ladson-Billings (2005) configures them via heroic figures she feels "...might be emblematic of [his/her] principles and perspectives" (p. xvi). Thus, for example, she links Tate to Nat Turner, but with this caveat:

> Anyone who knows Bill Tate might be shocked to see him compared to Nat Turner. Bill is kind, rational and level-headed. However, those who know him well know that a special fire burns beneath that cool exterior. As his friend and colleague, I have been privy to that side of his personality and have seen it at work in his scholarship, teaching and service. (p. 99)

This is, indeed, an apt depiction of Tate and his work...Ladson-Billings further explains that Nat Turner was very intelligent and committed to his cause.

Another Tate attribute that brings to mind Nat Turner is the courage of his convictions being evident in his work. With distinction and consistency, he focuses on adequate knowledge of mathematical sciences as a basic civil right in relationship to full participation in a republic such as the United States. He calls on empiricists to constantly ask themselves, "To what end is this research being conducted?" He summons us to arm ourselves with ethics and courage and to seek answers to questions and solutions to problems that may not be popular, but are necessary for the progress of marginalized people (Tate, 2006). In reading his works, one acquires a sense of the magnitude of the agenda in social justice but, more importantly, an informed perspective regarding its significance for the healthy development of the country and its citizen.

Whether illuminating how the traditional epistemologies and structures of mathematical processes mitigate against learning and achievement by students of color, specifically African Americans, or developing a legal theory to explain inequity in educational processes, Tate's scholarship is expansive in incorporating knowledge from several distinct areas to support his arguments. The artfully crafted logic of his position on structures and effects of inequitable educational practices underscores an in-depth understanding of these diverse issues and topics. Perhaps most significantly, Tate emphasizes that current policies and practices dramatically affect both opportunity and access to knowledge/information, and that policymakers and educators need to be cognizant of the critical need to create policies and implement practices that enhance, versus thwart, students' futures as economic agents and citizens. This chapter provides only a sampling of his voluminous work that contributes to his efforts in the latter regard.

NOTES

1. The term "mathematical sciences" is used as a general, inclusive term for mathematics and its associated disciplines of science, technology and engineering. Tate refers to them as SMET, whereas the contemporary term is STEM; for this chapter, mathematical sciences will be used to identify these areas. When referring only to mathematics, the term "mathematics" is used because this is how Tate references the discipline throughout his writings.
2. The term, "students of color" is used when the discussion centers on students who are not of European descent. African American or students of African descent are used when Black students are the specific focus of the discourse.

REFERENCES

Bell, D. (1987). *And we are not saved: The elusive quest for racial justice.* New York, NY: Basic Books.

Dixson, A., & Rousseau, C. K. (2005). And we are still not saved: Critical race theory in education ten years later. *Race, Ethnicity and Education, 8*(1), 7–27.

Freire, P. (1987). *Pedagogy of the oppressed.* New York: Continuum Publishing Corporation.

Gutstein, E., & Peterson, B. (Eds.). (2005). *Rethinking mathematics: Teaching social justice by the numbers.* Milwaukee, WI: Rethinking Schools, Ltd.

Hogrebe, M. C., & Tate, W. F., IV (2012). Geospatial perspectives: Toward a visual political literacy project in education, health, and human services. *Review of Research in Education (36),* 67–94.

Ladson-Billings, G. (1994). *The dreamkeepers: Successful teachers of African American children.* San Francisco: Jossey-Bass.

Ladson-Billings, G. (2005). *Beyond the big house: African American educators on teacher education.* New York, NY: Teachers College Press.

Ladson-Billings, G., & Tate, W. F., IV (1995). Toward a critical race theory of education. *Teachers College Record, 97*(1), 47–68.

Lynn, M., & Parker, L. (2006). Critical race studies in education: Examining a decade of research on U.S. schools. *The Urban Review, 38*(4), 257–289.

Oakes, J. (2005). *Keeping track: How schools structure inequality* (2nd ed.). New Haven, CT: Yale University Press.

Rousseau, C., & Tate, W. F. (2003). No time like the present: Reflecting on equity in school mathematics. *Theory Into Practice, 42*(3), 210–216.

Tate, W. F., Ladson-Billings, G., & Grant, C. A. (1993). The Brown decision revisited: Mathematizing social problems. *Educational Policy, 7*(3), 255–275.

Tate, W. F., IV. (1993). Advocacy versus economics: A critical race analysis of the proposed national assessment in mathematics. *Thresholds in Education, 19,* (1–2), p. 16–22.

Tate, W. F. (1994a). From inner city to ivory tower: Does my voice matter in the academy? *Urban Education, 28*(3), 245–269.

Tate. W. F. (1994b). Race, retrenchment, and the reform of school mathematics. *Phi Delta Kappan, 75(6),* 477–484.

Tate, W. F. (1995a). Mathematics communication: Creating opportunities to learn. *Teaching Children Mathematics, 1*(6), 344–341.

Tate, W. F. (1995b). Returning to the root: A culturally relevant approach to mathematics pedagogy. *Theory into Practice, 34*(3), 166–173.

Tate. W. F. (1995c). School mathematics and African American students: Thinking seriously about opportunity-to-learn standards. *Educational Administration Quarterly, 31(3),* 424–448.

Tate, W. F., IV. (1997). Critical race theory and education: History, theory, and implications. In Apple, M. W. (Ed.) *Review of Research in Education* (22), 195–247.

Tate, W. F. (2001). Science education as a civil right: Urban schools and opportunity-to-learn considerations. *Journal of Research in Science Teaching, 38*(9), 1015–1028.

Tate, W. (2003). The "race" to theorize education: Who is my neighbor? *Qualitative Studies in Education, 16*(1), 121–126.

Tate, W. F. IV (2004). Chapter 5: Political economy, and the scientific education of African Americans. *Review of Research in Education, (28),* 147–184.

Tate, W. (2006). Afterword: In the public interest. In G. Ladson-Billings, & W. F. Tate, (Eds.), *Education research in the public interest: Social justice, action and policy* (pp. 247–260). New York: Teachers College Press.

Tate, W. F., IV. (2008a). "Geography of Opportunity": Poverty, place, and educational outcomes. *Educational Researcher, 37*(7), 397–411.

Tate, W. F., IV. (2008b). The political economy of teacher quality in school mathematics: African American males, opportunity structures, politics and method. *American Behavioral Scientist, 51*(7), 953–971.

Woodson, C. G. (1933/1990). *The mis-education of the Negro.* Trenton, NJ: Africa World Press.

ANNOTATED BIBLIOGRAPHY

Hogrebe, M. C., & Tate, W. F., IV (2012). Geospatial perspectives: Toward a visual political literacy project in education, health and human services. *Review of Research in Education*, (36), 67–94.

Place and space (i.e., geography) are shown to be highly influential for determining access to educational, health, and other resources necessary for active involvement in a democracy. Addressing the "social formation of inequality," the authors outline how physical/building systems and intangible social systems are affected by space and location. Geospatial methods, specifically geographic information system (GIS), provide a contextual dimension that includes location, distance and relative position on earth, which contributes to greater understanding of how opportunity is structured within communities. These methods, because of their visual and spatial components, have been found useful for facilitating discourse among various stakeholders, including community members, policy makers, education administrators, legislators, etc. These discussions increase the likelihood of developing effective, relevant policies for mediating the educational, health, and social issues indicated by the results of these investigations. The use and efficacy of diverse statistical methods that employ GIS or PGIS (participatory geographic information systems), including quantitative, qualitative and mixed methods, are demonstrated. The civic engagement and duty that are involved is stressed. The authors make a compelling case for why spatial intelligence that is integral to mathematical, science, engineering and technical education needs to be given attention in the educational arena of general education.

Ladson-Billings, G. & Tate, W. F. IV. (1995). Toward a Critical Race Theory of education. *Teachers College Record, 97*(1), 47–68.

A treatise considered the seminal work in the application of the legal/interdisciplinary concept of Critical Race Theory (CRT) to education. Indeed, this is a foundational, theoretical framework for conceptualizing race as an intervening variable for educational effectiveness and processes. Critical Race Theory, as developed in regard to its legal application, was predicated on three key principles: race as endemic to U.S. society, sociohistoric reality of property rights vs human/civil rights in U.S. society, and the intersection of the latter two in deciding/determining justice, and then subsequently applied to educational issues by Tate and Gladson-Billings, among others. The case for race as an intervening characteristic vis-à-vis educational processes is predicated on that it is distinct from gender and socioeconomic status. CRT espouses race as having an inherent, unique, socio-historical perspective from which to challenge the status quo and attain social justice. This position is contrasted with the classical multicultural paradigm emphasizing "diversity," thereby cloaking race in a mire of assimilation and status quo maintenance. Like the architects of CRT who paid tribute to their intellectual forefathers who demarcated battle lines in civil rights and antidiscrimination law, Ladson-Billings and Tate pay homage to those in multicultural education who initiated the foray into the recognition of difference, but the former offer an extension to such an approach.

Rousseau, C. & Tate, W. F. (2003). No time like the present: Reflecting on equity in school mathematics. *Theory Into Practice, 42*(3), 210–216.

The need for teacher reflection regarding equity even in a seemingly neutral area like mathematics is established in this article. Content changes in mathematics (i.e., the shift in focus from fact-based, rote memorization to emphasis on analytical perspectives) is discussed in conjunction with changes in professional standards for teaching mathematics. Higher priority is placed on a teacher's knowledge of content and of his/her students. Both changes have been strongly advocated by the National Council of Teacher of Mathematics (NCTM) and have potentially significant consequences for achievement by students of color due to teacher expectations and class placement trends. Using the results of a study with mathematics teachers working with lower-tracked classes where students of color were overrepresented, it is shown that the teachers' tended to pay more attention to equality of process rather than equality of outcomes (a restrictive vs. an expansive view from CRT). Equality of process was intrinsic to the colorblindness teachers reported as reflective of an unbiased environment for student achievement and, more importantly, for measuring teachers' effectiveness in the classroom. The authors determine that the inadequacies in these perspectives make them of little use in employing a social reconstructionist approach to mathematics instruction. They conclude with questions to guide reflections on equity that are reflective of NCTM standards regarding teacher's need to be cognizant of and use of student background for mathematics instructions.

Tate, W. F., IV. (1997). Critical race theory and education: History, theory, and implications. In Apple, M. W. (Ed.), *Review of Research in Education,* (22), 195–247.

In this chapter Tate outlines the major tenets of CRT, its history in legal scholarship, and its applicability for scholarship involving systemic inequity in the educational system. An extensive history of litigation arising from the quest for equality and desegregation is accompanied by a description of how CRT originated out of the inability of other theoretical perspectives, including Critical Legal Studies (CLS) and realism, to expose the endemic nature of race and racism in U.S. society and politics. CRT confronts, extricates and deciphers the codes of color-blindness and meritocracy to better understand the effects and implications of race for legal decisions and, consequently, on spillovers to other social domains, including educational processes. Focusing on the contributions of three major writers in CRT (Derrick Bell, Richard Delgado, and Kimberle Crenshaw), the history and major tenets of the theory are further explored. To provide a broader and more comprehensive perspective on the legal theory, criticisms of the varied areas are also presented. Educational implications, boundary crossings, and the interdisciplinary nature of the theory are stressed throughout the chapter.

Tate, W. F., Ladson-Billings, G., & Grant, C. A. (1993). The *Brown* decision revisited: Mathematizing social problems. *Educational Policy, 7*(3), 255–275.

This chronicle of the legal struggle of African Americans to attain educational parity includes cases, arguments and rationales based on a social construct, i.e., equal schools will lead to increased economic opportunities and a decreased sense of inferiority. Beginning with articles of the Constitution and the objectification of people of African descent via a mathematical construct (The Three-Fifths Compromise), the importance of the sociocultural and sociopolitical setting surrounding court decisions and their corresponding effects is shown. The restrictive and expansive perspectives on antidiscrimination litigation *are* used to interrogate the outcomes and goals of both *Brown* decisions (1954 and 1955). Using mathematical precepts, the cases, decisions, and outcomes are analyzed for their logic and compatibility with either the expansive or restrictive viewpoints. How the two views interacted with a plaintiff's or defendant's position in the cases are also discussed. Notably, people of African descent who identified with plaintiffs held the expansive view and expected equality in schooling to occur as an outcome of a favorable ruling. Conversely, those whose interests and actions held to the restrictive view favored a process for addressing discrimination, while continuing to adhere to the status quo in all other ways. The authors, ascribing to an expansive view and attention to outcomes, discuss changes in curriculum, instructional practices, student interactions, school climate, and parental involvement as constituting prerequisites for realizing the vision of truly equal schools.

Tate, W. F., IV. (1993). Advocacy versus economics: A critical race analysis of the proposed national assessment in mathematics. *Thresholds in Education, 19,* (1–2), 16–22.

Referencing the *Plessy v. Ferguson* decision, Thomas Jefferson's views on the intellectual capacity of African Americans, and the belief that Euro centrism and elitism are prevalent in mathematics education, Tate outlines how the voluntary nature of the mathematics' assessment proposed by the America 2000 plan, which was developed in 1991, preserves and increases inequitable mathematic achievement for African-American students. Included in this analysis is the philosophic foundation of the legislation/programs and economics that are implicated in the national mathematics assessment. Using interest-convergence and symbolic index principles of CRT, it is shown how the structure of this mathematics assessment burdens some groups (the poor, African Americans) while benefitting others (the affluent, of European descent). To explicate his points, Tate uses ideas and theories from economics and mathematics to show how mathematics is marketed as elitist and European in nature, and, therefore, likely to be viewed as unattainable by those of African descent. These variables contribute to the lack of mathematical progress by students in schools with large percentages of poor and African-American children.

Tate. W. F. (1994). Race, retrenchment, and the reform of school mathematics. *Phi Delta Kappan, 75(6),* 477–484.

The discipline of mathematics, how race/culture influences the pedagogy used to teach it, and using mathematics to analyze social phenomenon are scrutinized here. Tate outlines how race and/or culture affect pedagogy, and how competency in mathematics is aligned with democracy and civic engagement. To make this point, he lays out how the emphasis in mathematics has shifted from concentrating on the fundamentals to more in-depth, analytical skills. Professional standards for teaching mathematics have been broadened to include understanding how a student's cultural background influences learning in mathematics and the need to relate mathematics to multiple societal contexts. The implications of these changes for understanding mathematical concepts and the progress of African-American students in light of historical realities concerning resource availability and "foreign" pedagogy are discussed. Tate makes the case that an absence of "centricity" and the failure to effectively interrogate conflicts in mathematical theory and its use in society obstructs African-American students inform becoming engaged in mathematics. Using examples from his own experiences with pre/in-service educators who were teaching mathematics to African-American students, Tate sheds valuable light on the possible consequences of a culturally determined pedagogy.

Tate, W. F. (1994). From inner city to ivory tower: Does my voice matter in the academy? *Urban Education, 28(3),* 245–269.

Using his own experience in the empowering environment of a culturally relevant elementary school, Tate provides insights into what can be achieved in specific instances and overall by mathematics curriculum and instruction that "centers" African-American students in their realities. Reflecting on the two themes of centricity and conflict (endemic to most theoretical stances and life endeavors) that were integral to his elementary school's philosophy and instruction, Tate demonstrates how what he learned at an early age at the school served him throughout his life. The effects of this culturally-grounded approach are discussed (i.e., number of college graduates, number of students who took higher-level mathematics courses, community and parental involvement, etc.). Tate attributes his success as an African-American male mathematics educator and the success of family and friends in other "rare bird" career areas to what they experienced within the challenging but affirming centric environment. Although published before the landmark article on CRT that Tate coauthored with Ladson-Billings, he uses CRT (voice, property vs. human rights, and personal narratives) in combination with Afrocentricity to create a framework for analyzing his educational experiences in mathematics and science and their influence on his cultural and economic independence.

Tate. W. F. (1995). School mathematics and African-American students: Thinking seriously about opportunity-to-learn standards. *Educational Administration Quarterly, 31(3)*, 424–448.

The meaning of "opportunity to learn" in regard to African-American students and mathematics education given the new mathematics standards and their aftermath for instruction is examined within this article. According to Tate, "The call for new mathematics standards represents an epistemological shift in school mathematics from a shopkeeper (basic skills) philosophy of mathematics pedagogy to a constructivist, technology-driven vision of mathematics instruction." (p. 437) Cognitively Guided Instruction (CGI) is used as an example of an approach that embodies the latter type of epistemology because it is more constructivist in nature than the behaviorist approach traditionally taught in the "shopkeeper (basic skills)" focus. Such a change, while desirable given the need for deeper understanding of mathematics concepts, has significant cultural and fiscal implications for African-American students, especially those in poverty and/or urban schools. Tate demonstrates the cultural dimensions of the content and instruction used to effectuate these revised standards by way of examples involving seemingly neutral assessment problems that are European and middle class in context. Differences in meaning and interpretation for students who are not likewise situated (that is, not of European descent and of the middle class) are discussed in respect to the subtexts in mathematics pedagogy that is closely aligned with the experiences of the white middle class. Tate highlights the fiscal responsibilities that accompany this paradigmatic and epistemological shift in mathematics instruction. Many urban, inadequately funded schools with high concentrations of students of color, do not have the resources to make the requisite changes for realizing the goals of the revised standards. Tracking and little access to rigorous mathematics instruction and/or higher level mathematics courses are also examined vis-a-vis their consequences for the opportunity of African-American students to learn and achieve in the area of mathematics.

Tate, W. F. (1995). Mathematics communication: Creating opportunities to learn. *Teaching Children Mathematics, 1(6)*, 344, 7 pages.

Building on the assertion by African-American historian and educator Carter G. Woodson that there are two environments for learning mathematics – one within the school and another outside the school, Tate shows how communication (i.e., voice/experience) is integral to learning mathematics principles that are not neutral or "color-blind." In addition, he shows why mathematics is socially and culturally situated and the implications this condition has for participating in a democracy. Professional standards (NCTM) for teachers of mathematics regarding the need to be familiar with students' backgrounds and the role of mathematics in society are discussed in conjunction with centricity. How using communication that enlists students' lived realities as mathematics learning material differs from more traditional approaches is illustrated by juxtaposing experiences and outcomes of preservice and in-services educators who employed centrist approaches versus those of educators who utilized the traditional approaches. Tate explains why higher-level concepts in mathematics are learned more completely when students' realities are honored and used. Additionally, with in-depth understanding, mathematics becomes an instrument of change and facilitates students' involvement in the democratic process by taking knowledge "outside the school" as Dr. Woodson recommended 70+ years ago.

Tate, W. F. (1995). Returning to the root: A culturally relevant approach to mathematics pedagogy. *Theory into Practice, 34*(3), 166–173.

Tate makes the case for cultural relevance in teaching mathematics by focusing on how the students in one middle school class were able to use mathematics to address community/school issues/concerns. After justifying the need for cultural relevance in reference to Woodson's indictment of mathematics education in particular and schooling in general for lacking relevance to the realities of students of African descent ("foreign pedagogy"), Tate explains Afro-centric and culturally relevant ideology. The need to center African Americans within their own cultural context to expedite learning across all areas, and specifically in mathematics, is determined to benefit scholarly achievement and facilitate full engagement in a democracy. The teacher's multifaceted approach to mathematics and science is an exemplar of the culturally relevant approach to mathematics and of the empowerment, mathematics achievement, and social activism that emanate from it.

Tate, W. (2001). Science education as a civil right: Urban schools and opportunity-to-learn considerations. *Journal of Research in Science Teaching, 38*(9), 1015–1028.

The article begins with a quote from former civil rights activist Bob Moses, president of the Algebra Project, a program focused on enhancing mathematics education for students of color (http://www.algebra.org), who equates educational access and literacy in mathematics and science to voting rights. According to Moses, both of the latter are civil rights that should be afforded to all citizens in order to provide for full participation in our democratic system. This opens into a discussion/explication of the litigation over desegregation of school systems that began in 1850 and progressed through the Brown decision of 1954 and onto the 1990s. Tate notes that systemic resistance to desegregation continues through today as evidenced in tracking practices by ability and curriculum, which is very prominent in the sciences. Scientific knowledge is vital for fully functioning in society because of its link to mathematics, technology, and engineering, fields that affect not only economical potential but also citizenship and civic involvement. Theoretical positions addressing opportunity to learn—including quality (i.e., of instruction), time (i.e., needed to learn) and assessment (i.e., is the curriculum sufficient to for students to perform successfully on standardized tests)—are presented in conjunction with the political realities that affect the manifestations of these concepts within urban schools that serve the poor and students of color. Tate asserts that "...future research on urban school-based science should seek to understand how time, quality, and technology influence students' understanding in the domain of science." (p. 1019). Examples of effective programs for addressing these issues are discussed.

Tate, W. F. IV (2004). Chapter 5: Political economy, and the scientific education of African Americans. *Review of Research in Education, (28),* 147–184.

Beginning with Thomas Jefferson's comments that Benjamin Banneker's (an African-American scientist/engineer integrally involved in the design of Washington, D.C.) abilities are an anomaly given the lack of intellectual ability of African Americans, Tate outlines the continuing societal ambivalence toward the efficacy of adequate education for African Americans, in general, and in the sciences (mathematical, natural and physical), specifically. Historical and contemporary implications of this conundrum are discussed herein. Trend data from the National Assessment of Educational Progress (NAEP), along with the number of college and university degrees issued in the sciences, show that although gains were made by African Americans in scientific attainment in the later decades of the twentieth century, they were not on par with the scientific and technological gains made in education and contemporary society. Tate shows how mathematics, and to some degree science, have been integral to the education of individuals in the United States because of their relationship to advancement. African Americans historically were not privy to this or other types of knowledge until the *Brown* decision. This judgment is analyzed in light of the social sciences employed to argue the merits of the case and the historical background leading up to the case. Tate draws on the fields of history, sociology, economics and psychology to explain the importance of scientific attainment for African-American students and the *Brown* decision as emblematic of the various issues that must be confronted in order to advance toward this goal.

Tate, W. F., IV. (2008). "Geography of Opportunity": Poverty, place, and educational outcomes. *Educational Researcher, 37*(7), 397–411.

This article is an expanded version of Tate's Presidential Address at the 2008 American Educational Research Association (AERA) annual meeting *(site/ address for viewing the lecture,* http://www.cmcgc.com/Media/Synch/280324/ Video/370-V/default.htm)

Case studies from Dallas, Texas and St. Louis, Missouri, are used to illustrate how geography (place/location) determines the availability and viability of economic opportunities within a geographical space by affecting industries' willingness to locate and grow within an area. In regard to Dallas, Tate outlines how the Texas telecommunications research and development industry came to be in North Dallas. Subsequent to adopting this location, there was significant growth in higher educational institutions and in technical and retail industries. With this growth in industry, retail, and institutions of higher education, the schools within the area became of the highest caliber. Tate compares development and realities in North Dallas to the very different prospects and realities for South Dallas, a section of the city largely comprised of poor African Americans, where there is an inordinate number of liquor stores but limited buildings for commercial businesses. In St. Louis, a number of low socioeconomic status residents were displaced in the name of urban renewal and metropolitan research development to make room for the affluent. The resultant redistribution of residents in the city's neighborhoods shows how the reconstituted communities differed in terms of economic indicators (e.g., income, home pricing, the number who qualified for free and reduced-price lunch, etc.), and the impact these changes had on school variables, including proficiency in 10th grade mathematics and science, as reflected in state-wide tests.

CHAPTER 17

GLORIA LADSON-BILLINGS

Race, Voice, and Social Justice

Charlene Johnson Carter

As an undergraduate student at the University of Cincinnati I was involved in a Black Drama course where a major part of the class involved acting out scenes from varied dramatic pieces, i.e., plays, movies, and television shows. Our task was to authentically portray the character. The performance/portrayal of characters took place in front of the class, after which it was critiqued afterwards by the professor and one's peers. The discourse regarding the portrayal was offered to enhance not only the performance of the actor but also to offer insights for others in class when it was their turn in the spotlight. Our professor, Dr. AJ, an African American female from North Carolina, was known for her straightforward manner of commenting on our performances and for her southern "twang."

During one of our class readings, a student known in our circles for her formal style of speaking, what we called "speaking the King's English," was reading lines from a play in (what she considered) a southern accent. When she finished her lines, Dr. AJ smiled and asked in her Southern tongue, "What was that?" The student, aware that Dr. AJ's smile was

Educating About Social Issues in the 20th and 21st Centuries, pages 345–361
Copyright © 2014 by Information Age Publishing
All rights of reproduction in any form reserved.

unconvincingly camouflaging her disapproval, explained that she was getting into the "southerness" of the character by using her mode of language, i.e., a southern accent. Our professor responded, "Really" (less of a question and more of a statement). After a pause, she said, "This is a Black character and [looking at my classmate and then the class] . . . .Black southerners don't talk like white southerners."

The class was puzzled and somewhat curious because in our Midwestern minds and world views, southern was southern. However, when Dr. AJ stated this, most of us, having some southern roots (parents, grandparents, uncles, aunts, etc.), had to stop and rethink our initial perspective that our peer had appropriately captured the essence of the character. As we ruminated over it, we had to agree with Dr. AJ that her pronunciation and manner of speaking as well as that of our southern-speaking relatives did not sound like the ones prevalent in movies, television shows, and other forms of media. Although our lived realities ran counter to those promulgated by the media, we had willingly accepted this alternative perspective because of its prominence and acceptability within larger society. Dr. AJ was not so inclined. The authenticity of her lived experience was lost in the interpretive stance taken by my classmate and for personal as well as professional reasons she felt compelled to address it.

I chose to begin this chapter on Gloria Ladson-Billings and her contributions to social justice with this personal experience for several reasons. First, it is emblematic of the narrative and counter-storytelling that is a major precept of Critical Race Theory (CRT), a legally-based concept/theory that explicates inequities within the legal system based on race and racism (Tate, 1997), and because, in 1995, Ladson-Billings and Tate wrote their signature piece where they applied this legally-based theory to education and its inequitable treatment of students of color. Second, it reflects how voice can be distorted and misapplied when others' perceptions and interpretations prevail over the lived experiences of the speakers. Third, race as a salient variable for not only language but the interpretation of experience and voice is reflected in the story. Last, the effects of highlighting or manifesting the inconsistencies between what is authentic and what is misinformation influences the discourse that facilitates the praxis Freire (1987) discusses as integral to action and meaningful work. Ladson-Billings' scholarship embodies all four of these attributes. Focusing on two areas of her work, (a) successful teaching/pedagogy for poor, Black[1]/students of color, and (b) CRT for understanding the inequities that persist in education, Ladson-Billings' contribution to social justice will be examined herein.

Endemic to social justice is the recognition, acknowledgement and valuing of voice from varied individuals. Although this is touted as a key and significant goal by many, it remains an elusive goal because of the historical legacy of inequity and hegemony, mainly based on sociopolitical characteristics, that exists in the United States. As with my classmates, voice can become a manifestation of observations and perceptions that are not always accurate. Having power has profound implications for hearing and manifestation of voice. More specifically, what often masquerades as voice is re-stating ideas, concepts and experiences that coincide with conventional perceptions that are usually purported by those in power.

Indeed, sociopolitically and socioculturally, certain voices are valued over others. Privileged positionality (Arber, 2000; Milner, 2007) has implications for whose voice is heard and acknowledged. Cognizant of this reality, those not in power will often remain silent or, as with my drama class, repeat the prevailing cant in order to be heard. Nowhere is this more apparent than when racism or racial disparities are discussed. The ones at the center of this discourse, people of color. i.e., the oppressed, are frequently the subject being discussed by the ones legally responsible for and/or benefiting from the disparities—in other words, those in power. "The success of the desegregation model of equality was, and continues to be, contingent upon its ability to adapt to a cultural ethos of White self-interest" (Tate, Ladson-Billings, and Grant, 1993).

Ladson-Billings' commitment is to have the voices of Black educators and their students heard within a relevant, meaningful context that honors cultural traditions, beliefs and actions. In this regard, her scholarship counteracts the deficit theories regarding Black cultural traditions. This theme is evident throughout her work. Honored as the Brown speaker for American Educational Research Association (AERA) in 2011, Ladson-Billings (2011) spoke of the need for a paradigmatic shift that is needed in order to maximize the skills of students of color. This same idea is repeated in one of her earlier articles (Ladson-Billings, 1990), indicating her ongoing commitment to this quest.

Ladson-Billings has been at the forefront of the struggle to recognize the salience of race for educational processes. Beginning with her concept of culturally relevant pedagogy/teaching through Critical Race Theory (CRT), her scholarship is an urgent call for recognition of how being Black affects educational achievement and progress. The discourse concerning this issue is oftentimes cloaked in others' realities versus the realities of those being discussed, and that is profoundly problematic. The voices of those being examined need to be present at this discussion rather than a distortion based on someone else's reality. As Lisa Delpit put it early in her career, "We must keep the perspective that people are experts in their own lives" (cited in Ladson-Billings, 2005, p. 132). These words epitomize the guiding force for Ladson-Billings' work. Significantly, she dismisses and counters the deficit model regarding Black children and their educational progress or lack thereof. Conversely, her scholarship is directed towards explaining and/or providing a rationale for educating Black students by focusing on their strengths. But she does not leave it there; rather, she also provides ample evidence that there is much to be heard and used to meet the varied needs of Black students—the latter of which constitutes a major tenet of her theory of culturally relevant teaching/pedagogy.

An activist by all accounts, Ladson-Billings focuses on both the micro (classroom teachers) and macro (societal and systemic educational) variables that contribute to the misunderstanding and misinterpretation of the cultural capital Black students bring with them to school (Boykin, 1994). Her writings exemplify how teaching to the strengths of Black students is not only possible but essential. She also questions the prevailing perspectives regarding the perceived "problem" involved in educating Black students because of home lives or cultural deprivation. Recognition of racism as endemic to society and therefore a contributing factor to the inequitable treatment and recognition of students of color is a major tenet of CRT. In the article, "Your Blues Ain't Like Mine: Keeping the Issues of Race and Racism on the Multicultural Agenda," she articulates the salience of race for multicultural education because of its effects on voice and the experiences of people (Ladson-Billings, 1996). This article follows her now classic article with William Tate on the application of Critical Race Theory to education (Ladson-Billings & Tate, 1995). Noting the lack of attention to theorizing about race within educational scholarship, she and Tate applied CRT, an interdisciplinary, legally-based theory, to education.

Ladson-Billings' scholarship is reflective and action-oriented. The quintessential educator, her work reflects her varied areas of experience as a former social studies and language arts middle-school teacher, teacher educator, and, anthropologist. In her work she references an eclectic array of scholars, running the gamut from Paulo Freire, Peter McLaren, Joyce King, Lisa Delpit, and Henry Giroux to Marcus Garvey, W. E. B. Dubois, Carter G. Woodson, Frantz Fanon, Derrick Bell, and Toni Morrison. She often references legal scholars applying their ideas to educational inequity. She epitomizes the interdisciplinary approach, one which many proclaim as the most effective educational approach.

Her contributions are theoretical, practical and empirical. Theoretically and practically, her culturally relevant pedagogy/teaching theory that is based on the practices and dispositions of educators successful in their teaching of students who are poor and Black, is a major contribution to the field. She differentiates this approach from others with a focus on culture by also emphasizing academic achievement, cultural competence and sociopolitical consciousness. The efforts of such educators are not offered as a prescription, magic pill or all encompassing remedy for addressing the varied needs of Black students; rather, she demonstrates the sagacity and efficacy of using multiple variables that need to be addressed in reaching and teaching Black students. Success is shown to be predicated on teacher beliefs about the students, themselves as educators and the profession itself. More specifically, these teachers felt their purpose was to empower students intellectually.

The "fit" involves "plugging" students into the existing order regardless of its suitability or congruence with personal identity. Society, (i.e., status quo) is considered the ideal and these approaches seek to somehow accommodate students to its ways, beliefs, and tenets via educational content and practices. Conversely, culturally relevant teaching/pedagogy recognizes and celebrates the individual, what he/she brings to the educational process, and the potential of these contributions for societal enhancement. Culturally relevant pedagogy theoretically and practically seeks to build a bridge to "self" (the student him/herself), whereas the assimilationist approach seeks to build a bridge to "them" (the larger society). By honoring self, education is used to enhance personhood thereby facilitating engagement with and in the larger society from an empowered, self-directed stance; the other involves finding a place within the existing status quo regardless of logic, thereby maintaining it.

Ultimately, the path to social justice involves increased access for a range of individuals so that equity for all becomes a reality. In order for this to occur, prevailing ideologies and ethos are challenged by those most affected but least visible within the societal hierarchy of power. This requires an empowered, informed stance that challenges the prevailing order with an eye towards a situation that benefits all and not just the select few who benefit from whatever iteration the society undergoes.

Theoretically, Ladson-Billings' application of CRT to her scholarly endeavors in the field of education has brought race to the center of the discourse vis-à-vis the many and varied systemic issues that affect the schooling and education of students who are Black/of color. Over the years her work has highlighted, explored and analyzed systemic racism and its pernicious effects on education policy and practices. Her efforts constitute an exemplary commitment to addressing educational inequity based on systemic racism.

> Empirically, Ladson-Billings counters the neutral, objective stance of the positivist tradition by engaging in what she calls, a "methodologically messy" style whereby she integrates her scholarly tools with her cultural knowledge and personal experiences. (1994, p. xi).

In one of her books, *The Dreamkeepers: Successful Teachers of African American Children*, Ladson-Billings (1994), noted the following: "I have written this book with three voices: that of an African American scholar and researcher, that of an African American teacher, and that of an American woman, parent, community member. Thus, the book offers a mixture of scholarships and story—of qualitative research and lived reality" (p. x). In fact, she follows this path throughout her work.

Her use of storytelling as used by Bell (1992) and other CRT scholars is also prevalent in most of her work also. Stories, critical incidents and/or scenarios are used in the majority of her work to further explicate points being made. She also makes use of "portraiture" (Lawrence-Lightfoot & Davis, 1997) in her work (see, for example, *Beyond the Big House*). In each of her works, readers become more aware of her lived life and beliefs. Reflecting her anthropological education/preparation, her role and stance as researcher is transparent in each of her writings. Furthermore, in each of her publications she discusses and explains the theoretical and conceptual framework for her work.

The impact of Ladson-Billing's work has been felt by large swaths of the educational community. For those marginalized, however, her work virtually provides a sense of sanity and serves as a beacon for how scholarly work can be used to advance, address and impact vitally significant issues. As a scholar of color, her research provides theoretical and empirical support for key positions/stances vis-à-vis the lives and education of those marginalized, and empowers others to forge their own research agendas based on the lived experiences of students of color. By making use of various historical figures and storytelling as a mode of empiricism, Ladson-Billings provides ample evidence that defining and constructing knowledge is not only the purview of the Western canon.

Significantly, I have written this chapter whereby my positionality is transparent. In that regard, my selection of works highlighted in the annotated bibliography is based on my view of the salience of the information from a historical, cultural and scholarly perspective. Put another way, the works selected are those that I believe serve as exemplars of Ladson-Billings' most provocative and thought-provoking scholarship regarding the issues confronting Black students in today's classrooms. Keeping with the ideology regarding the honoring of voice, each annotation is preceded by a quote from the source. Such quotes embody the ideas of Dr. Ladson-Billings vis-à-vis her most critical concerns. Included are publications regarding culturally relevant teaching/pedagogy, CRT and the implications of the *Brown* decisions (1954 and 1955) for educational equity for students who are Black/of color and are poor.

It seems fitting to conclude with a lyric from "95 South (All of the Places We've Been)," a song written by Gil Scott Herron and Brain Jackson in tribute to Ms. Fannie Lou Hammer, a noted American voting rights activist and civil rights leader, who was instrumental in establishing the Mississippi Freedom Summer for the Student Nonviolent Coordinating Committee (SNCC):

I can't stop and give up on them. Their light that shines on, inspires me to climb on from all the places we've been. (Scott-Herron, 1977)

Thus, it is with Dr. Ladson-Billings' scholarship. Her work honors those who came before us and reminds those to come the critical need to continue in the quest for social justice.

NOTES

1. The term, Black will be used interchangeably with African American to refer to students of African descent.

   Black is capitalized throughout. This follows Toure who, at the outset of his book, *Who's Afraid of Post-Blackness: What It Means to Be Black Now* (2011), stated the following: "I believe "Black" constitutes a group, an ethnicity equivalent to African American, Negro, or, in terms of a sense ethnic cohesion, Irish, Polish, or Chinese." (p. vii)

REFERENCES

Arber, R. (2000). Defining positionality within politics of difference: Negotiating spaces 'in between.' *Race, Ethnicity and Education*, 3(1), 45–62.

Bell, D. (1992). *Faces at the bottom of the well: The permanence of racism.* New York, NY: Basic Books.

Boykin, W. (1994). Afrocultural expression and its implications for schooling. In Hollins, E. R., King, J. E., & Hayman, W. C. (Eds.), *Teaching diverse populations: Formulating a knowledge base.* Albany, NY: State University of New York Press.

Brown v. Board of Education, 347 U.S. 483 (1954).

Brown v. Board of Education, 349 U.S. 294 (1955).

Freire, P. (1987). *Pedagogy of the oppressed.* New York: Continuum Publishing Corporation.

Ladson-Billings, G. (1990). Like lightning in a bottle: Attempting to capture the pedagogical excellence of successful teachers of black students. *International Journal of Qualitative Studies in Education, 3*(4), 335–344.

Ladson-Billings, G. (1994). *The dreamkeepers: Successful teachers of African American teachers.* San Francisco: CA: Jossey-Bass.

Ladson-Billings, G. (1996). "Your blues ain't like mine": Keeping issues of race and racism on the multicultural agenda. *Theory Into Practice, 35*(4), 248–255.

Ladson-Billings, G. (2011). *Through a glass darkly: The persistence of race in education research.* Eighth Annual Brown Lecture in Research: American Educational Research Association.

Ladson-Billings, G. (2005). *Beyond the big house: African-American educators on teacher education.* New York, NY: Teachers College Press.

Ladson-Billings, G., & Tate, W. F. (1995). Toward a critical race theory of education. *Teachers College Record, 97*(1), 47–68.

Lawrence-Lightfoot, S., & Davis, J. (1997). *The art and science of portraiture.* San Francisco: Jossey-Bass.

Milner, R. H. IV. (2007). Race culture and researcher positionality: Working through dangers seen, unseen and unforeseen. *Educational Researcher,* 36(7), 388–400.

Scott-Herron, G. (1977). 95 South (All of the places we've been). *On Bridges* [Vinyl Record Album]. New York: Arista Records.

Tate, W. F. IV. (1997). Critical race theory and education: History, theory and implications. In M. Apple (Ed.), *Review of Research in Education* (vol. 22, pp. 195–247). Washington, DC: American Educational Research Association.

Tate, W. F., Ladson-Billings, G., & Grant, C. A. (1993). The Brown decision revisited: Mathematizing social problems. *Educational Researcher,* 7(3), 255–275.

ANNOTATED BIBLIOGRAPHY

Ladson-Billings, G. (1990). Like lightning in a bottle: Attempting to capture the pedagogical excellence of successful teachers of black students. *International Journal of Qualitative Studies in Education,* 3(4), 335–344.

"For purposes of this study, successful teaching allows black students to 'choose' academic excellence without losing a sense of personal and cultural identity. The ability to foster the choice of academic excellence and maintenance of cultural integrity represents what is meant by pedagogical excellence. This study has located eight such teachers."

This article outlines the qualitative research methodology employed, and the rationale for this approach, to examine and explain the effective teaching practices used by eight successful teachers of Black students. Ladson-Billings begins the article by outlining the social and community context for the schools involved in her study. Different definitions of success held by different constituents including parents and administrators are explored. A "community nomination process," which involves relying on those most vested in the schools and the students was used, and thus parents as well as educators were asked to nominate teachers believed to be successful the former's children. Teachers selected for the study were those cited by both parties. Preliminary analysis of the interview data of the eight teachers are discussed. This article appeared prior to the publication of the book, *Dreamkeepers,* where the results of the study are discussed in full.

Ladson-Billings, G. (1994). *The dreamkeepers: Successful teachers of African American-children.* San Francisco, CA: Jossey-Bass.

"I made a distinction between *excellent teaching* and *excellent teachers* purposely. Although each of the teachers who participated in my study are superb individually, this book looks at a teaching ideology and common behaviors, not at individual teaching styles" (p. 13).

In this book Ladson-Billings explains the development of her culturally relevant teaching/pedagogy theory. She juxtaposes culturally relevant teaching/pedagogy with "assimilationist" teaching to explicate how building on culture to develop the individual is different from using it to assist him/her to "fit" in the existing social order. The point is made that culturally relevant teaching does not involve prescribed steps to follow but rather is predicated on a teacher's dispositions pertaining to conceptions of self and others; the structuring of classroom interaction; and, the teacher's conception of knowledge. Profiling eight successful teachers (five of African descent and three of European descent) from low-income, majority African American schools, Ladson-Billings provides ample evidence for how these major tenets are differentially operationalized within classrooms. The book covers the foundational ideas for the study, the methodology employed, and interview and observational data from each teacher and her classroom.

Ladson-Billings, G. (1995). Toward a theory of culturally relevant pedagogy. *American Educational Research Journal, 32*(3), 465–491.

"My own interest in these issues of teaching excellence for African American students came as a result of my desire to challenge deficit paradigms... that prevailed in the literature on African American learners. Partly as a result of my experiences as a learner, a teacher, and a parent, I was convinced that, despite the literature, there were teachers who were capable of excellent teaching for African American students. Thus, my work required a paradigmatic shift toward looking in the classrooms of excellent teachers, *through* the reality of those teachers" (p. 472).

This article provides a backdrop for the development of culturally relevant pedagogy theory as the predecessor to the development of a culturally relevant theory of education. Discussing the varied theoretical perspectives vis-à-vis educational research (e.g., the logical positivist tradition, action research, grounded theory, etc.), Ladson-Billings explicates how such paradigms have profound implications for teachers, teaching, students and learning. She goes on to explain how her personal involvement in the research regarding successful teachers for Black children reflects many aspects of the Black feminist tradition as proposed by Patricia Hill Collins (2000). A primary focus is on personal experience, dialogue and the intersection of the two. Using the research conducted on eight teachers as examples of how the tenets of culturally relevant pedagogy are manifested, Ladson-Billings demonstrates the viability of educational research with pedagogy at its core. In addition to a micro-analytic perspective, she goes on to provide a macro-analytical view by examining various theoretical perspectives regarding educational reform, teacher education and culture as a mediating factor for these processes. Ultimately, Ladson-Billings considered the vitality and significance of the intersection of these two perspectives in proposing a culturally relevant theory of education.

Willis, A. I. & Lewis, K. C. (1998). Focus on research: A conversation with Gloria Ladson-Billings. *Language Arts, 75*(1), 61–70.

"Language is so incredible, so powerful, that I don't think you can think about calling yourself culturally relevant if you have not considered the power of language."

In this interview, Ladson-Billings is asked about the application of culturally relevant pedagogy to language arts. To address this question, she refers to the broader area of literacy, discussing its multifaceted effects and contributions to the empowerment of people/students. Referring to the Civil Rights Movement and varied African Americans who worked to procure equal voting/citizenship rights, she makes the case that literacy is broader than learning the alphabet in that it links people to each other and the world. She further expounds on the need for educators to become aware of culture and its importance for learning. To be effective in developing the literacy skills of all students, Ladson-Billings refers to the ideology and practices of the eight effective teachers of African American students in her book, *The Dreamkeepers*. She further explains that educators must first become aware of their personal cultural heritage and all of its manifestations and uses within classrooms. Referring back to her work with seventh- and eighth-grade students, Ladson-Billings discusses the positive effects to be gained by committing to meet the literacy needs of all students. She recommends that educators remain vigilant in the quest to find beneficial methods for teaching varied ability/skill levels versus remaining fixated on life circumstances as a reason for allowing some to fail.

Ladson-Billings, G. (2001). The power of pedagogy: Does teaching matter? In Watkins, W. H., Lewis, J. H. & Chou, V. (Eds.) Race *and Education: The roles of history and society in educating African American students.* (pp. 73–88). Boston, MA: Allyn and Bacon.

"Thus, the goal of education becomes how to 'fit' students constructed as 'other' by virtue of their race/ethnicity, language or social class into a hierarchical structure that is defined as a 'meritocracy.' However, it is unclear how these conceptions do more than reproduce the current inequities. (p. 76) ... Pedagogy must provide a way for students to maintain their cultural integrity while succeeding academically" (p. 79).

This chapter begins with an overview of the research and major ideas regarding teaching children of color, with special emphasis on African American students, based on cultural realities. Learning styles research in conjunction with the varied cultural concepts steeped in anthropology (including cultural congruence, cultural appropriateness, cultural responsiveness, cultural compatibility, and mitigating cultural discontinuity) are reviewed for their meanings and explanations for students of color and their educational progress. Noting the prevalent adherence to accommodating the culture of people of color to the culture of the larger society, Ladson-Billings offers her theory of culturally relevant pedagogy as one of several approaches that focus on the success of students of color via pedagogical approaches that build on their culture. The three major tenets of culturally relevant pedagogy—cultural competence, sociopolitical consciousness and academic achievement—are explained. Each, Ladson-Billings explains, is fundamental to the success of students of color, and through their inclusion in the pedagogy, academic success is not achieved at the expense of cultural identity. Drawing on the research of several theorists renowned for their pedagogy for students of color (e.g., Jackie Jordan Irvine, Carol Lee, Joyce King, Michele Foster, Eugene Garcia, Lisa Delpit, and Mark Haberman), she outlines several approaches that have proven successful. Noting the inequitable knowledge base, subject as well as cultural, of many educators in schools with large numbers of students of color, she concludes that there is much to be learned about pedagogy, including teachers and teaching, that contributes to the success of all students, especially those considered marginalized.

Ladson-Billings, G., & Tate, W. F. IV. (1995). Toward a critical race theory of education. *Teachers College Record, 97*(1), 47–68.

"The 'voice' component of critical race theory provides a way to communicate the experience and realities of the oppressed, a first step on the road to justice. As we attempt to make linkages between critical race theory and education, we contend that the voice of people of color is required for a complete analysis of the educational system" (p. 58).

Building on critical race theory (CRT) that originated in legal studies as a means to address the continued inequities that beset people of color within the legal system, Ladson-Billing and Tate filled a theoretical void regarding the salience of race in educational scholarship. As the authors state, "...we attempt to theorize race and use it as an analytical tool for understanding school inequity."

Noting that the theoretical framework for CRT includes race as an influential factor for societal inequity; property rights as integral to the founding and functioning of society in the United States; and, lastly, the intersection of race and property rights for defining one's positionality and value within our society, Ladson-Billings and Tate provide an in-depth analysis of how these foundational principles were conceptualized within legal studies and their pertinence for explicating the study of educational inequity.

Also addressed is how storytelling as a form of scholarship serves to counter notions of neutrality (e.g., knowledge is factual and unbiased), objectivity (e.g., statistics and quantitative measures are impartial) and meritocracy (e.g., everyone has a chance/opportunity to succeed within our present system). In addition to references to the architect of CRT, former Harvard law professor, DerrickBell, other African American giants/heroes—including Toni Morrison, Nobel Laureate for Literature; Marcus Garvey, nationalist and activist; W. E. B. Dubois, acclaimed African American educator and cofounder of National Association for the Advancement of Colored People; and, Carter G. Woodson, the noted historian and educator who is considered Father of Black History month and author of the classic, *The Miseducation of the Negro*—are discussed in relation to the pervasiveness of race and its effects on the life experiences of people of African descent.

Ladson-Billings, G. (1996). "Your blues ain't like mine": Keeping issues of race and racism on the multicultural agenda. *Theory Into Practice, 35*(4), 248–255.

"My attempt to reposition race on the multicultural agenda is not an argument to substitute one single explanation strategy for another. Rather, I want to examine the ways that race, a social construct with powerful social and political implications, has been muted in the current multicultural paradigm or pitted against other subjectivities—particularly class and gender—to render it "un-discussable" as a difference or a site of struggle" (p. 249).

Beginning with an excerpt from a book of the same name as the title of the article, *Your Blues Aint' Like Mine* by Bebe Moore Campbell, Ladson-Billings explains why race remains a salient variable for developing equitable schools. Her explanation is juxtaposed against claims made by sociologist, William Wilson (author of *The Declining Significance of Race, 1978*) that class, not race, was the deciding factor for the quality of people's lives in Chicago's inner cities.

As explained by Ladson-Billings, Campbell's book provides a fictionalized account of the killing of Emmett Till, a well-known case of the 1955 mutilation and killing of a fourteen year old African American male in Mississippi based on an accusation that he had whistled at a white woman, and the effects of such a horrific, race-based event on the community—White and Black. Following Campbell's lead, Ladson-Billings discusses how race is experienced by white preservice and in-service teachers when the issue of race is raised. Using examples from her classes and professional development workshops, Ladson-Billings shows how issues of race and culture are variously defined, experienced and examined based on one's positionality (race and socioeconomic status). These differences warrant further discussion and examination to ensure equitable practices are developed and implemented.

Ladson-Billings, G. (2006). From the achievement gap to the education debt: Understanding achievement in U.S. school. *Educational Researcher*, 35(7), 3–12.

"Over the last 7 years, the number of children living in poverty in the U.S. has grown by 11.3% to approach 1.3 million. More than a million children have fallen into extreme poverty (22% increase) over the past 5 years, now gripping over 5.6 million children . . . Extreme poverty means living with an annual income below $7,870 for a family of three. To isolate the 'achievement gap' in the midst of all of these other disparities seems wrong-headed and disingenuous" (p. 318).

In her 2006 presidential address to the annual conference of the American Educational Research Association, , Ladson-Billings turned upside down (or, if you will, capsized) the traditional discourse regarding educational differences between students of color, namely African American, Latino, Native American and Asian, and those of European descent. She addresses head on the "achievement gap" and provides an alternative rationale for the disparities that takes into account the larger context within which education takes place. Beginning with the Census categories for race, Ladson-Billings provides an economic, a historical, a sociopolitical, and an educational framework for reframing this discourse as an education debt that must be paid if our future is to survive and flourish while maximizing our human capital resources.

Tate, W. F., Ladson-Billings, G. & Grant, C. A. (1993). The Brown decision revisited: Mathematizing social problems. *Educational Policy*, 7(3), 255–275.

"The shortcomings in Brown is that the court proposed an essentially mathematical solution to a sociocultural problem. More specifically, the Supreme

Court looked at the sociocultural reality of African American students—that they were consigned to substandard, ill-equipped schools—and proposed that by physically manipulating the students' school placement the problem of inequality would be addressed" (p. 259).

The authors chronicle the struggle to attain educational equality via the courts up to *Brown v. Board of Education* (1954 and 1955). Within this legislative history, sociocultural and sociopolitical realities are outlined as a reflection of the decisions handed down by the courts previous to *Brown* (1954). The authors challenge this legal struggle in terms of its premise, theoretical orientation and outcomes. Beginning with the objectification of people of African descent as "three-fifths" (Three Fifths Compromise, 1787) of a person, the authors outline how mathematizing personhood allowed us to be considered in purely mathematical terms and never as humans. In this regard, seeking "equality" as a mathematical concept is challenged for its viability given that what was at stake was/is a societal issue. Two vantage points, expansive and restrictive, regarding the *Brown* decision are discussed. African American parents held the expansive view that their children reaping the same (equal) educational benefits as White children constituted the major outcome. The restrictive vantage point whereby the emphasis is on the legal process over the actual outcomes is more in line with White interests. The implications of the continuance of the restrictive view are discussed.

Ladson-Billings, G. (2005). *Beyond the big house: African American educators on teacher education.* New York, NY: Teachers College Press.

"Although this discourse [regarding teacher education] impacts everyone involved in teacher education, it creates a particular tension for African American teacher educators who have dedicated their scholarly careers to equity, social justice and fighting racism and other forms of oppression. The particular tension is tied to the African American teacher educators' embodiment of race and what they come to represent in the academy. Thus, if they fail to take up this discourse, they may be seen as out of step with the standards and conventions of the profession. If they fail to challenge this discourse, they may be seen as so fully assimilated into the system—so much a part of the Big House—that they are incapable of affecting change" (p. 14).

This book provides insight into the perspectives of seven African American teacher educators—Joyce King, Carl Grant, Jacqueline Jordan Irvine, Geneva Gay, William Tate, Cherry A. McGee Banks and Lisa Delpit—regarding their work and their role within the academy. Metaphorically speaking, the "Big House" is used to denote the academy as a place where these teacher educators work but have questionable status given their race and stance on issues of interest for African American children, their parents and communities. As in slavery days, when people of African descent were differentiated by where they worked, i.e., the big house (master's house) or the field, Ladson-Billings captures the dichotomy and ambiguity of working in but not feeling a part of the academy. While one's scholarship centers on subject matter (i.e., students/people of African descent) that is integral to one's life and/or reality, in the academy this reality is tangential and inconsequential to the culture and ethos that prevails within it. Thus, one ends up working *in* but *is* not considered part of the (academic) community.

The teacher educators were interviewed about how their educational histories/biographies led them to the academy, and how their experiences with colleagues and others within the academy affected their progress (or lack thereof) therein. Ladson-Billings' portraiture methodology and research stance are thoroughly explained prior to the discussion of the interviews as well as within the analysis of each. Interestingly, another metaphoric device Ladson-Billings makes use of is that of "historical and/or legendary personalities" (p. xvi) which she applies to each teacher educator as a means of capturing the essence of the person being portrayed and to inform and educate the reader about historical figures.

Ladson-Billings, G. (2007). Pushing past the achievement gap: An essay on the language of deficit. *Journal of Negro Education, 76*(3), 316–323.

"I argue that we need to change the discourse from achievement gap to what I have termed as an 'education debt.' ..., the gap in which language places the onus of underachievement on the students, their families, and in some cases individual teachers. It admonishes them that they need to catch up. When we speak of an education debt we move to a discourse that holds us all accountable. It reminds us that we have accumulated this problem as a result of centuries of neglect and denial of education to entire groups of students" (p. 321).

This article is an extension of Ladson-Billings' presidential speech at the 2006 AERA annual meeting. After discussing the semantic and substantive concerns with the term/concept of an "achievement gap," given the unheeded societal conditions that contribute to the lack of educational progress of poor students of color, she focuses on five common explanations frequently given for this phenomenon:

- The parents just don't care;
- These children don't have enough exposure/experiences;
- These children aren't ready for school;
- Their families don't value education; and
- They are coming from a "culture of poverty" (p. 318)

Examining each of these explanations, she "unpacks" the contradictions, ill-advised rationales, and pedagogical implications embedded within them. In her conclusion, the disaster caused by Hurricane Katrina is compared to that of the one caused by the flooding of the Red River in Grand Forks, North Dakota as further indication of how even in tragedies, race and poverty affect experiences and outcomes.

Ladson-Billings, G. (2006). The meaning of Brown ... for now. *Yearbook of the National Society for the Study of Education, 105*(2), 298–315.

"My stance as a racial realist makes me sound both cynical and hopeless. The promise of *Brown* seems to have evaporated in that small moment of civil activity in the 1960s. However, I am not without hope. It is just my hope has moved away from waiting on justice to prevail in the courts and for a conscience to be awakened in white middle-income communities. I have learned the limits of liberalism when whites believe that it is possible to have justice without having to give up anything. My hope now resides in parents and community organizers who believe that they have a right and responsibility to demand excellent education." (p. 310).

This article begins by referring to the devastation of Hurricane Katrina and its differential effects on its citizens based on income and race—poor African Americans compared to the wealthier white citizens of New Orleans. Against this backdrop, Ladson-Billings uses a CRT lens to analyze the meanings of both *Brown* decisions (1954 and 1955) vis-à-vis the issue of educational equity in contemporary society over fifty years since its passing. Using three perspectives/scenarios—racial optimists, racial liberals and racial realists—she outlines a continuum of beliefs regarding the efficacy of the Brown decision for today's educational system. Racial optimists believe in the inherent goodness of the system and based on this belief would expect the same decision fifty plus years later. Similar to the racial optimists, racial liberals believe the decision would be the same today but see the process as unfinished. However, they expect the process to continue and with incremental changes being made, the maximum benefits of the decision will be realized. The racial realists view the decision as not being about the liberation of Black people as long as the benefits hinder or affect those of white people. After providing an overview of CRT and its legal history, three scenarios that represent the three positions/stances are provided. In the end, its historical significance is acknowledged but its promise and fulfillment is questioned.

Ladson-Billings, G. & Donnor, J. (2005). The moral activist role of critical theory scholarship. In Denzin, N. K. & Lincoln, Y. S. (Eds.) *The Sage handbook of qualitative research*, (3rd ed.) (pp. 279–301). Thousands Oaks, CA: Sage Publications, Inc.

"Actually, we point to the limits of the academy and suggest that committed intellectuals must move into spaces beyond the academy to participate in real change. Thus, we speak to an audience who is willing to search for a revolutionary hiatus" (p. 297).

"In his book, *Ethical Ambitions*, legal scholar Derrick Bell (2002) addresses a question that plagues many scholars of color: 'How can I succeed without selling my soul?' He argues that the qualities of passion, risk, courage, inspiration, faith, humility, and love are the keys to success that maintain one's integrity and dignity. He contends that scholars must consider these as standards of behavior in both scholarship and relationships. Clearly, this is a different set of standards than those the academy typically applies to research and scholarship. But, how well have the usual standards served communities of color?" (p. 288).

Two quotes are included here due to complexity of the ideas inherent in this chapter. Ladson-Billings and Donnor provide personal, societal and educational examples of how race and other characteristics render individuals as

"Other" within academe and the larger society. These characteristics remain salient for determining the treatment and status of people within power relations where whites are involved. They use several examples to make this point, including the case of O. J. Simpson and other controversial figures that exemplify how one's stature can be compromised based on societal context. In the case of O. J. Simpson, the authors state their interest is not in/with his guilt or innocence. Rather, they illumine the process of his perceived state of transcending race being annihilated, thereby removing him from favored, "honorary white" status (because of his athletic prowess and social accord with rich people of European descent) to being depicted as a disgraced figure who fell from favor. The authors also share examples of instances when they, personally, experienced such a transcending of race as a result of their status as acclaimed professionals. As with O. J., societal perspectives and effects on dominant order determine what is studied, how and to what ends.

Focusing on the moral and ethical issues underlying varied epistemological areas, the authors explore liberal ideology, ethical activism, and revolutionary "habitus." In-depth analysis of the varied theoretical positions regarding research epistemologies and their implications for varied people of color is provided. The authors state their goal to mobilize "scholarship that will take a stance on behalf of human liberation" (p. 281) is an ambitious but needed one.

Ladson-Billings, G. (2004). New directions in multicultural education: Complexities, boundaries and Critical Race Theory. In Banks, J & Banks, C. A. M., (Eds.), *The handbook of research on multicultural education*, (2nd ed.) (pp. 50–65). San Francisco, CA: Jossey Bass.

"Both scholars and classroom teachers must look for opportunities, new ways to think and learn about human diversity and social justice. They must be willing to push innovation in multicultural education. Multicultural education must be open to conflict and change, as is true of any culture and cultural form if it is to survive. Multicultural education, like jazz, must remain 'gloriously inclusive'" (p. 63).

Using a jazz metaphor, Ladson-Billings discusses the different "syncopations" of multicultural education and how these varied interpretations influence the construction of knowledge in this area. Outlining how jazz has grown and changed, the same case is made for multicultural education noting it needs to move beyond the study of "other" to the study of the varied cultural expressions and practices that culminate in the lived experiences of human beings. Using King's (2001) and McLaren's (1994) analysis of multicultural education and how conservative and liberal discourse affects its promulgation of knowledge that actively resists the status quo, Ladson-Billings discusses the evolution of multicultural education to its present state.

Ultimately, Critical Race Theory is discussed as a heuristic for interrogating the curriculum and instructional practices for their effectiveness in liberating students.

Ladson-Billings, G. (2006). It's not the culture of poverty, it's the poverty of culture: The problem with teacher education. *Anthropology and Education Quarterly*, 37(2), 104–109.

"If we are serious about students learning about culture, we need to help them first become careful observers of culture, both in the communities in which they will teach and in themselves. Far too many prospective teachers believe that they are without culture. They assume their participation in the dominant culture makes them immune to culture." (p. 109)

This article is based on Ladson-Billings' George and Louise Spindler Award (2004 recipient) Lecture given in 2005 at the Council on Anthropology and Education business meeting. Ladson-Billings decries the fact that prospective and veteran teachers have limited coursework that addresses anthropology/ culture, and discusses its implications for learning. She further argues that although a greater emphasis and more attention is given to psychology and its meaning for educational progress, limited application of both constructs in school settings by educators have an ill effect in meeting the needs of the students with whom they work.

Using vignettes (what she calls, "critical incidents") from her work with pre-service educators, Ladson-Billings shows how self-esteem and culture have become the watchwords or excuses for students' lack of progress and/or behavioral problems in the classroom. She illustrates how an in-depth understanding of culture and how it is endemic to a person's way of life is not missing only in teacher education but also in the larger society. Rather than being used to decipher the meaning of human behavior in classrooms to better instruct students, it has become an excuse to not meet their needs.

CHAPTER 18

THE SCHOLARSHIP OF CARLOS ALBERTO TORRES

A Dialectic of Critique and Utopia

Christine Brigid Malsbary and Winmar Way

INTRODUCTION

Carlos Alberto Torres is one of the foremost critical theorists of education. Throughout his career and in his prolific scholarship Torres has rigorously critiqued educational injustice and advocated for educational equity, a natural fit for this volume's focus on social issues. Torres' epistemological approach to social issues is similar to that of Michael Apple, Jean Anyon, Henry Giroux, among other critical educators highlighted in this volume. Much of his analytical practices stem from his early involvement with Paulo Freire and the peasant movement in Latin America, a connection that will be discussed in greater depth later in this chapter. As such, Torres is set apart from most mainstream educational scholarship by his ability to accurately diagnose the workings of hegemony in education, and then *push past* critique and deconstruction to offer solution and possibility. In this chapter, we provide a narrative that discusses the progression of Torres'

Educating About Social Issues in the 20th and 21st Centuries, pages 363–382
Copyright © 2014 by Information Age Publishing
All rights of reproduction in any form reserved.

363

social concerns in education during his scholarly tenure. We then provide an annotated bibliography of relevant works ranging from articles to books.

It is worth noting that the coauthors of this chapter are former students of Carlos Alberto Torres at UCLA. In 2011, both authors were involved in a class named *Politics and Education* (Way as a student and Malsbary as the Teaching Assistant). Torres' hallmark seminar, it was consistently filled to capacity with graduate and undergraduate students, Visiting Professors from countries like China, Korea, and Italy, among other intellectuals. We came to know Carlos Alberto Torres as an erudite, passionate scholar learned in the classical texts of the social science and the humanities, and a generous and caring advisor, mentor and friend.

Politics of Education was a *tour de force,* capturing over two decades of Torres' epistemological approach to social issues. Torres firmly believes that education has a unique ability to empower people to direct intellectual, cultural, economic, and social development for themselves and for their communities. The seminar demonstrated how social contexts can impact and limit the possibilities of education and human development. During the decades marking his teaching and scholarly career, Torres has been intimately concerned with the relationships of power, the state and education. As such, over the years, he has delineated the workings of capitalism and the state in education, focusing particularly on globalization and neoliberalism; indeed, neoliberalism was a concern of Torres' for decades, far before it became a popular topic in the academy in North America. He has also looked carefully at issues of identity, examining how identity markers like class, race, and gender can marginalize individuals and communities and hinder their access to quality education. All of these issues were examined in *Politics and Education.*

Politics and Education also examined the liberatory offerings of social movements and the work of Paulo Freire, who is widely considered the father of critical pedagogy. The structure of the seminar—from critique to hope—was classic Torres, a basic discursive structure recognizable in much of his published works. He understands and appreciates the despair that social justice educators can experience when analyzing the challenges facing educational programs globally, and was careful to guide us back to positions of possibility and hope. Throughout the academic term in which we participated, students were encouraged to bring their own knowledge and experience to the table, discussing, among other topics, their involvement in nonformal and formal education structures and protest movements such as the-then emerging Occupy Wall Street movement.

Throughout the course, Torres maintained a systematic conversation around critical education problems and praxis. In that sense, being a student of Torres was like an invitation to a dinner party (and Torres held many, in the spirit of, as he likes to say, *mangia con tutti*) where international scholars in areas like education, sociology, and cultural studies met and mingled, laughed, and argued solutions to intractable social issues like poverty and hegemonic oppression. Many scholars of comparative education and globalization were at these *salons*, given Torres' stature in the Comparative and International Education Society (CIES), of which he was president from 1997–1998.

In his teaching, mentoring, lectures, and writing, Carlos Alberto Torres balances eviscerating and systematic critiques of the fruits of global capitalism and the State with a steadfast belief in the power of the marginalized to act democratically for their own freedom.

Torres also believes deeply in the reading classic theory; a means, if you will, of interacting with scholars from eras gone as if they were contemporaries. As he once told his students:

> We all stand on the shoulders of giants, or at least we should be. For me to read is to encounter the classics, and the 'derivations' that emerge from the classics as much as to get informed from current events, theories, paradigms, or programs. Machiavelli once said that when he gets to his house, he would change his clothes and put on special robes to "meet" in his studio the classics. This admonition (*ceteris paribus* mass media) should have more currency today than ever. (Personal Communication, Spring, 2008)

WHO IS TORRES?

Torres came of intellectual age in Argentina. His childhood was marked by poverty, but also a caring and tight-knit family. His father became a soldier through a newly formed government program. Social mobility eventually took its course and the family made middle class wages, but Torres' formative years were meager. As a young child he lived in a shantytown, later moving to a neighborhood that bordered the refuse area in Buenos Aires. During his free time when he was in elementary school, Torres worked in his parents' leather workshop making and delivering women's purses, a job that he hated but that was necessary for the family's economic survival.

Torres attended what he considered an excellent Catholic school in his teenage years that was the center of his life and his neighborhood. He attended school for long hours in the mornings and evenings during the weekdays. On Saturdays, the young Torres took more classes and then played ping-pong or soccer at the school in the afternoon.

Torres called his high school teachers "dedicated career teachers," and that they greatly impacted his formative education. In secondary school, his teachers were not professionally-trained teachers but rather local parents who came to the school to teach courses on their professional specialties, like law.

Torres has said that he was a "poor" student who was disengaged until the final year of high school when he took his first course in political economy. Torres was surprised by how easily he understood the content of the course, and was the only one in the class who could explain what a rate of return was to the teacher.

Still later, he happened upon sociology during a university course on management and labor that he was taking as part of his studies in business management. For the course paper, Torres interviewed a famous religious figure who had created a new model of community organization in, as Torres put it, one of the poorest and most dispossessed neighborhoods of Buenos Aires. The organizers challenged Torres to contemplate the question: "Is managing labor an act of oppression or is it charity?" Torres concluded that it was oppression, and subsequently joined a group that went to neighboring Colombia for three months to work with youth, teaching sociology, theology and farming.

After returning to Argentina, Torres switched the focus of his university studies to political philosophy, and suddenly found himself surrounded by people who challenged him to develop an intellectual life and mobilized him to act as a student leader in the university protests sweeping the country. During his final university exams, Torres received the highest marks possible. Highly impressed with Torres' thinking vis-à-vis politics and sociology, Hegel, Marx and others, the professor overseeing Torres' exams asked Torres to step into a position as General Secretary for a new Institute of Science and Technology.

Ultimately, Torres moved into conducting sociological research. Since that period, Torres has written over 300 peer-reviewed articles and numerous books. Torres sees contributing to intellectual life as one of forming ideas across disciplines due to an abiding passion and interest versus simply generating work because it is tied to one's title and related academic position.

Torres' earliest intellectual passion was the theology of liberation. He defines theology of liberation as having a "preferential option for the poor." The latter position, Torres says, has guided his life.

Tellingly, Torres' education unfolded against the backdrop of dramatic political and economic unrest in Argentina. President Juan Perón was deposed in 1955, which was followed by a military dictatorship during the years that Torres was finishing secondary school and entering university. For three brief years he experienced democracy, but concluded his university years under a second, brutal dictatorship.

After marrying, Torres lived on a commune, eventually leaving when several members who were planning on joining the group were kidnapped by the government. Torres, his wife and their two children fled to a remote region, remaining there while Argentina was engulfed in horrendous problems of financial instability, inflation, endemic corruption, international isolation and violence.[1] During that period, Torres wrote his first book, a critical reading of the work of Paulo Freire. He gave the book to Freire's editor a week after the military dictatorship ended in 1976. Freire's editor convinced Torres that that it was no longer safe for him to remain in Argentina, and thus Torres left his homeland, moving his family to Mexico where he began his graduate studies and then subsequently to the United States where he studied at Stanford University.

It is clear from Torres' life where his intellectual interests and dedication to education and social justice have stemmed. As faculty at UCLA, he reminded his students that their collaboration with each other reflected the politics of relations at work in the larger society. In other words, he encouraged his students to focus on their basic values and emphasized that an inability to solve differences in the context of a community of learning meant that it would also be impossible to do so in the larger and more complex society.

Now, we turn to a discussion of Carlos Alberto Torres' historical significance, and his dedication to a critical perspective towards social issues in education, especially adult education.

INTELLECTUAL BIOGRAPHY OF CARLOS ALBERTO TORRES

Torres has been globally recognized for his contributions as a theorist, particularly in the field of Comparative Education. Torres' seminal contribution is as a political sociologist of education who seeks to understand the relationship between education, social groups, and the state. His primary interests lie in questioning power, influence and authority, and explaining the process of decision-making and educational planning. Torres has focused on understanding why a given policy is created and implemented, how historical-structural, systematic, symbolic, and organizational processes contextualize the development of policy, what the effects of policy are on communities, and what kinds of social questions can be asked as a result. He has published mostly in the area of adult education[2] and specifically on policy creating and implementation in Latin America, although he has worked on educational issues in Egypt, Korea and Canada, among other nations.

Torres' faculty appointment at UCLA in Los Angeles in 1990 marked the beginning of the highly productive middle years of his career. While at UCLA, he turned his attention to the issue of multiculturalism in culture. This development was in conjunction with his sensitivity to social context: Los Angeles is a city marked by racial strife, notably captured during the events of the L.A. Uprising (popularly called the "Rodney King riots") in 1992. At the same time, Torres's writing shifted to "meta-theory," whereby he would assemble critical interpretations of cultural and social reproduction theory, theories of the state, analyses of multiculturalism, feminism and other approaches to social diversity, inequality, and the struggle for social justice education. During a keynote address at the conference of the Comparative and International Education Society, Torres outlined the beginnings of what would later become one of his most influential books, *Education, Democracy, and Multiculturalism: Dilemmas of Citizenship in a Global World*. Published in 1998, *Education, Democracy, and Multiculturalism* is a meta-theoretical discussion of social issues. In it, Torres theorizes about theory, evaluating a variety of perspectives' usefulness for research and teaching, while noting and commenting on gaps, slippages, and overlaps amongst and between ideas. The book also provides a framework for liberatory possibility. In regard to the question of a multicultural democratic citizenship and the virtues of civility he writes as follows:

> Civic virtues point to a sense of solidarity that unites individuals around common goals . . . These goals are, at the very least, how to survive and live together in our contemporary, diverse society... learning how to thrive as a community of communities, as a culture of cultures drawing from our cultural diversity as a cultural strength, and promoting affirmative action, broadly understood, as a useful policy. (Torres, 1998, p. 247)

Here, Torres demonstrates the humanity at the center of his theoretical life. That is, he is able to identify and denounce discriminatory policies and actions towards persons based on their identity, while concurrently avoiding the social distancing that can come from excessive attention to personal markers of identity (e.g., gender, race, class) by seeking out ways to create solidarity across difference.

Torres' interest in multiculturalism in culture has produced several other influential texts. After his tenure as president of Comparative International Educational Society, Torres coedited the first edition of *Comparative Education: Dialectics of the Global and the Local* (2003) with long-term collaborator Robert Arnove. *Comparative Education* showcased the diversity of the field, with studies on education for development, institutional analyses, and research in area studies. Now in its fourth edition (2013), this collection of essays edited by Arnove, Torres and now Frantz, bears the stamp of Torres' exhortation to take context into account and thus to take notice of the undeniable presence of politics in education and educational research. His interest in multiculturalism has continued most recently in the provocatively titled *Multiculturalism is Dead*, a coauthored book with the Italian scholar Massimiliano Tarozzi. In this work, Torres once again points towards the usefulness of comparative analysis in his comparison of the intercultural movement in Europe with the multicultural movement in North America, drawing from the comparison the most valuable lessons of each for social justice scholars and educators. Torres and Tarozzi direct their critical/analytical gaze to policy, media, political discourse, along with cases of individual schools, as they analyze the effect of immigration on minority education and the multicultural social engagement, the state, and teachers.

Next, we turn to the origins of Torres' approaches to the dialectic of critique and possibility in education. To do so, we review his original social concern: adult education in his home context of Latin America.

THEORY IN ACTION: ADULT EDUCATION, AND THE ROLE OF THE STATE IN LATIN AMERICA AND BEYOND

Torres's dissertation, completed in 1983, was entitled *Educational Policy Formation and the Mexican Corporatist State: A Study of Adult Education Policy and Planning in Mexico (1970–1982)*. It addressed several of the fields that Torres would contribute to throughout his career—especially Latin American Studies and the Political Sociology of Education—and introduced the social issues that have continued to be of concern to him for the last 25 years. Among those social issues are: people who are marginalized in society because of class, race, gender or other identity markers, and how adult education (the practice of teaching and training adults, especially in the work place) can benefit the marginalized. Adult education is a sub-set of nonformal education initiatives in general but specifically focuses on learning and training adults, often in the workplace. As he wrote in *Adult Education as Public Policy: A Perspective from Latin America* (1998a), the adult education clientele in Latin America was composed mostly of peasants, the indigenous, urban marginals and low-wage recent migrants. Elsewhere he explains:

> Although adult education claims to address the educational needs of the most disadvantaged groups of society, it seems that it only makes a contribution to a select group of people.... Far from being a vehicle for the advancement of the working classes and marginal groups as a whole, it seems that adult education has been more successful in identifying potential role models or leaders...educating them in such a way as to remove them from their original culture (Shugurensky & Torres, 1994, p. 132).

In his dissertation, Torres documented the failure of adult education in Mexico. He argued that adult education initiatives had failed because they had neither supported adult learners to retain their culture as they were educated, nor served as a vehicle towards economic improvement for entire communities of marginalized workers. After completing his dissertation, he went on, in later work, to discuss those contexts in which adult education had been more successful. Torres' turn from discussing failure to success was in keeping with his hopeful epistemology and efforts to describe how we can move towards the "utopia" envisioned by his mentor, Paulo Freire. Torres' writing as a way to understand *what works* in education is evident in his discussions of examples from adult and nonformal education in Cuba, Nicaragua and Grenada (Torres, 1991). The success of Cuba's literacy campaign was tremendous. According to Fagen (1969), the collaboration of nearly 10,000 students and scholars with over 170,000 adult volunteers resulted in increased national unity between Cuban youth and the isolated poor of the mountains. Thus, Torres argues, class alliance was an important outcome of the Cuban revolution. Additionally, adult education became important in postrevolution societies because it combined productive labor with literacy and encouraged a "popular education," whereby adults didn't have to leave the field in order to spend time in school way from their primary work on the land. ("Popular education" is a kind of education that is concerned with class inequalities, political struggle, and social transformation. Popular education is a more clearly delineated concept in Latin America, where it is referred to in Spanish as *educación popular* or in the Portuguese as *educação popular*. Popular here refers to the "popular classes," which include peasants, the unemployed, the working class and sometimes the lower middle class. The designation of "popular" is meant most of all in contrast to that of the education of the upper class and upper middle classes.)

As the examples of Cuba, Nicaragua and Grenada showed, revolutionary governments were able to use alternative educational programs like popular education in order to bring the populace of their transitional societies into the fold of the state through the use of nonalienating methods. More specifically, bringing people into the fold of the state was to increase their belief that the state's socialist agenda was eliminate. Popular education in Cuba, Nicaragua and Grenada was democratic and could involve educators meeting the populace in their homes and the places where they worked. The context of popular education is important here, and Torres draws on the arguments of Thomas La Belle, a critical adult education specialist who was Torres' mentor at UCLA. As La Belle wrote in 1986: "nonformal education made such strong contributions to the pre- and postrevolutionary movements [because of] its interaction with the social structures of these societies . . . .The radical transformation of such structures provided the impetus for a more equitable distribution of power and resources" (quoted in Torres, 1991, p. 243). In revolutionary societies such as Cuba, Nicaragua and Grenada, local-level politics flourished. The state was able to initiate broad-based social development beginning at the local level.

Torres (1991) made the argument that the state itself can be colonized by certain groups in civil society who then use educational mechanisms as compensatory legitimation,[3] and that adult education can be a powerful mechanism of such a type of legitimation, as used by the postrevolutionary Cuban state: "The combined strategy of polytechnic education and a very elaborate system of nonformal education resulted in adult education programs that, unlike compensatory programs carried out in the rest of Latin

America [e.g., Mexico], are developed mostly at the workplace, enhancing technological, scientific and social knowledge related to work" (p.116). Additionally, the Cuban Revolution's origins in the mountains presented the insurgents with the challenge of spreading their mobilization and learning campaigns to the urban centers of government. Here again, Torres' focus on the social context of education clarifies nuanced differences in state policies; that is, Torres focuses on the social context to challenge normative ideas that policy is monolithic. Torres sees policy as a lived experience that is negotiated contested, adapted and changed according to the needs to the individual.

From his work on his dissertation through his comparative work, Torres moved from critique of the state in his work in Mexico to documenting educational possibilities based on the nature of the state in Cuba and other post-revolutionary societies. As discussed, this dialectic of critique and possibility would continue to thread its way throughout the next few decades of his career. For example, in 2009, Torres' focus on adult education policy led to his involvement in the drafting of a United Nations report exploring the relationship of Adult Education to global Millennium Development Goals. In that document,[4] Torres argues that adult education has a special ability to become a method for social change and empowerment, but that state economic policies and policy makers who do not consider the actual cultural needs of the populations they claim to serve place economics before humans, significantly reducing the chances of creating a more equitable society.

Ultimately, Torres' rich theoretical work on education policy, politics and the state has been produced *not* for theory's sake alone, *but because* of Torres' concern for the everyday lives of marginalized people. Essentially, Torres is a grounded theorist; in that respect, he has empirically traced the effect of macro-level practices and processes on the everyday lives of those people who are the most vulnerable in society. As discussed previously, Torres' upbringing in Argentina during the time of the *Revolución Argentina,* a bloody military takeover that began in 1966 as Torres entered the university as a student, undoubtedly made an impact on his intense social justice sensibilities. To further understand Torres' theoretical stance on social issues it is important to understand his relationship with the late Paulo Freire, a fellow Latin American, critical educator, and Torres' mentor.

"IF YOU SCRATCH A THEORY, YOU FIND A BIOGRAPHY": TORRES' WORK ON FREIRE, TEACHING AS A POLITICAL/ BIOGRAPHICAL/PERSONAL ACT, AND HIS MOVE TOWARDS A POLITICAL SOCIOLOGY OF EDUCATION

Before his death on May 2, 1997, Paulo Freire had become a friend and collaborator of Torres and his students. As one of the giants of the adult education movement, Freire's echo is traceable in Torres' focus on the critical importance of culture and education in healing the class struggle in Latin America, and around the world. Like Freire, Torres' writing on adult education is full of hope. As Torres often said to his students: *You are either with Freire or against Freire, but never without Freire.* By this he meant that those who are concerned with the making their way in the world are either acting *with* a vision of possibility, or *against* the possibility of social transformation. Life (and education) is always political, in Torres' view. It is impossible not to take a stand, because neutrality doesn't exist. As Torres explained to his students:

> For Critical Theorists' research cannot be separated from political struggle, hence scholarship and activism are inevitably part and parcel of our life journey. Paulo Freire has argued that politics and education cannot be easily dissociated, not even for purely didactic purposes. We conduct research and teaching to change the world, not simply to observe as the detached scientist what happens around us, or to manipulate knowledge as social *'alquimia'* or as social engineering. (Personal Communication, 2012)

In addition to Torres' work as a re-inventor of Freirian thought, his scholarship on Freire demonstrates once again his interest in how educational policy can contribute to the development of both formal and nonformal education systems that support men, women and children to become whole, as well as agents of their own development. One notable project along this line was his mentorship of Pilar O'Cadiz who wrote her dissertation on Freire's tenure as head of the education system of Sao Paulo, a dissertation that eventually became a coauthored book with Torres and Wong.[5] While Freire is known for his inspiring writing and praxis in the area of adult and popular education, his work as an administrator in Sao Paulo, Brazil was an important moment for Torres and his coauthors to document because it demonstrated how Freirean pedagogy could become praxis within a bureaucratic system. In *Education and Democracy*, O' Cadiz, Torres, and Wong describe how theories of the state, social movements, and democracy were translated in Freire's work to empower teachers to become agents who could negotiate systems.

Torres' focus on teachers runs throughout his scholarship, beginning from his work with and on Freire, who was infinitely concerned with the position of teachers as free agents. As Torres has received accolades for his theoretical work and research, it might surprise some to discover that Torres' interest in comparative, international and area studies has not been limited to issues of policy and educational planning. In fact, Torres has viewed himself primarily as a teacher. Throughout his tenure as a professor, he has been deeply committed to building and maintaining institutes dedicated to the legacy of Paulo Freire. This work manifests itself in the work of the Paulo Freire Institute (PFI) at UCLA, the only such institute in North America, of which Torres is the founder and director. The genesis for this institute was a conversation between Torres and Freire a few years before Freire's death; during this conversation, Freire told Torres that he ardently hoped that his [Freiere's] work not be *repeated* but instead *reinvented* based on the issues, needs and desires of those disempowered by the problems of their historical period.

Through PFI, Torres has created spaces for his students to develop Freirean practices (thinking and efforts, with an eye towards praxis), in addition to running workshops and programs for social justice educators from around the world. Additionally, PFI is home to the California Association for Freirean Educators (CAFÉ), a student-run organization that hosts an annual conference where teachers, community activists, and established, emerging and young scholars present, examine and discuss Freirean methods of teaching in different contexts such as adult education, special education, immigrant populations in the United States and critical media literacy. This conference has been described to Way, one of the authors of this chapter, as "a hidden gem" by a participant in reference to the level of intimacy that coalesces from the personal and political commitment of the people who congregate and engage with rich and fevered discussion.

Torres has also offered workshops on educational research and teacher education workshops through the network of Paulo Freire Institutes in Taiwan, Korea, Japan and, most recently, Italy. As a teacher, Torres has always been deeply concerned with the ability of other teachers to succeed, in ways that are meaningful and authentic. In that regard, he has been preoccupied with the question of how the identity of teachers impact their work. In this respect, Torres wants to know who teachers are, where they come from and what relation they have to their communities and the state.

Spaces that Torres creates, like PFI, have provided the opportunity for social justice educators to build counter-culture communities that have challenged the currently dominant neoliberal, instrumentalist approach to education. This again is pure Torres, indicative of his belief in a dialectical presence in the world, between the global and local, and between critique and utopia.

Torres is well acquainted with the seeming perdurable and certainly dire situation facing teachers in Los Angeles, and is so both as a result of his family's involvement in the schools and his own research. In 2011, he mobilized his students at PFI to apply and receive funding from the University of California Institute for Research on Labor and Employment to conduct a day-long workshop for teacher educators called "Teachers as Displaced Laborers." It was created as a response to neoliberal reforms now taking place in L.A. and around the nation and world. In Los Angeles, these reforms have manifested themselves in the devaluing of the teaching force and the so-called "pink-slipping" (laying off) of over 8,500 teachers in the Los Angeles School District following the economic downturn in 2007. The small workshop included individuals from the adult education office who had been pink-slipped. Teachers in today's society face a heavy burden and it is not our intention to suggest that a single day workshop could reduce the complexities of issues that they face. Nevertheless, their feedback forms indicated that they felt energized and reconnected to their passion for teaching as a political act of courage. This is in the spirit of the Freirian philosophy of *conscientizacao,* whereby creating a space for liberatory discussion can alleviate the sense of isolation that can be as crippling as unjust social policy. To struggle is human, but to struggle alone is debilitating. Through the ways in which he created community, Torres enacted pedagogically what has recently been termed "compassionate listening," an act that "recognizes the suffering of others in ways that open up possibilities for healing and transformative communication" (Garrison, 2010).

Teaching, then, is personal and political for Torres. In every instance of his work, scholarship, service, and his own classes, he puts theory into action and helps make the biographical political. His deep sense of empathy allows him to focus his teaching and theory development both on the micro-level of person-to-person interaction—as described above vis-à-vis the situations/events of the Paulo Freire Institute, CAFÉ, educator programs and the teacher labor workshop—*and* the macro-level of the political sociology of and critical theory in education. His ability to connect broad global and national educational goals with work in classroom and schools is reflected in the scholarship of his students, his colleagues and members of the community with whom he works.

As expressed in the subheading of this section, Carlos Alberto Torres has connected the events of his own biography to his scholarly interests, and encourages others to do so as well. In a collection of interviews with critical theorists called *Education, Power and Personal Biography: Dialogue with Critical Educators,* Torres (1998b) connects the biographies of influential teachers like Gloria Ladson-Billings, Maxine Greene, and Geoff Whitty with their social preoccupations. The book also contains an interview with Paulo Freire. In the chapter, it is possible to see the mentor-mentee relationship that Freire and Torres had and extrapolate how it has influenced Torres' epistemology. For example, at one point, Freire tells Torres:

> My great preoccupation is method as a means to knowledge. Still, we must ask ourselves: to know *in favor of what* and therefore, *against what* to know; *in whose favor* to know, and *against whom* to know. . . . We must also know that it is always education which brings us to the confirmation of another obvious fact, which is the political nature of education. (cited in Torres, 1998, p. 99)

The issue of "in whose favor do we research and know what we know" is the great preoccupation of many of those whom Torres interviewed for *Education, Power and Personal Biography,* and those which whom he has maintained close collaborative working relationships over the years. As his friend Michael Apple would write in his introduction to *Globalizations and Education,* a slim collection of essays published in 2009 that showcased much of Torres' best work:

> Carlos is not simply a follower of Freire, to say the least. He is a critical sociologist of education, which his own major contributions and affiliations. And a critical sociology is always grounded in two questions: (1) "Sociology for whom?" and (2) "Sociology for what?" (Apple, Foreword, p. xvi)

Apple is right. Torres is not a follower—he is too loyal to Freire's adage that we must *reinvent* Freire, not copy. Torres reinvents Freire out of his deep love for Freire, both the person and the intellectual heritage that Freire left as his legacy. Torres often says that Freire's greatest concern, before his death, was what neoliberalism would do to the world. Torres' latest writing is concerns a scathing critique of neoliberalism, particularly in two publications: (a) a book published in 2009 entitled *Education and Neoliberal Globalization,* and (b) a 2011 article entitled *Dancing on the Deck of the Titanic?* In these works, Torres' attention was captured by the economic turmoil and questions of national identity surfacing in Europe. *Dancing on the Deck of the Titanic?* examines how current social movements change the state's role in education. He discusses the Conference on Adult Education based in Geneva and cautions social movements of the necessity of state involvement in long-lasting, far-reaching social change/revolution. Through this scholarly effort, Torres comes full circle. From his roots in adult education, through his writing and work on multiculturalism, democracy and the state, to his focus on neoliberalism, Torres offers a different kind of scholarship. His teaching, writing—and his friendship—inspires the people around him to reach into their own humanity and their deepest longings, and fight their way to what is good, what is possible, and what is compassionate.

NOTES

1. The 1976 Argentine coup by right-wing military officers overthrew Isabel Perón on March 14, 1976. The military junta that took over remained in power until 1983. While political repression existed prior to the coup, it was ratcheted up following the coup, and the "Dirty War," as it has come to be known as, resulted in the "disappearances" of between some 7,000 to 30,000 people.
2. Torres works primarily in the area of adult education, and has also worked in popular education, and nonformal education. These three areas, while over-

lapping and often used synonymously, can also be implemented as distinct methods of educating.

3. Education as compensatory legitimation is a concept developed by Hans Weiler (1986). Building on the work of Jurgen Habermas and Claus Offe, Weiler contends that the inability of the capitalist state to distribute wealth equitably results in a crisis of legitimacy in the power of the state, and the seeks to rectify this diminished legitimacy through educational policies.

4. See Chapters One and Two of *Global Report on Adult Education and Learning*, published by UNESCO Institute for Lifelong Learning in 2009.

5. O'Cadiz, M. d. P., Wong, P. L., & Torres, C. A. (1998). *Education and Democracy: Paulo Freire, Social Movements and Educational Reform in Sao Paulo*. Boulder, CO: Westview Press.

REFERENCES

Apple, M. (2009). Foreword. In C. A. Torres (Ed.) *Globalizations and education: Collected essays on class, race, gender, and the state*. New York, NY: Teachers College Press.,

Arnove, R., & Torres, C. (Eds.). (2003). *Comparative education: The dialectic of the global and the local*. New York, NY: Rowman & Littlefield Publishers, Inc.

Fagen, R. R. (1969). *The transformation of political culture in Cuba*. Stanford, CA: Stanford University Press.

Garrison, J. (2010). Compassionate, Spiritual, and Creative Listening in Teaching and Learning. *Teacher's College Record, 112*(11), 2763–2776.

La Belle, T. (1986). *Nonformal education in Latin America and the Caribbean: Stability, reform or revolution?* New York, NY: Praeger.

O'Cadiz, M. d. P., Wong, P. L., & Torres, C. A. (1998). *Education and Democracy: Paulo Freire, Social Movements and Educational Reform in Sao Paulo*. Boulder, Colorado: Westview Press.

Shugurensky, D., & Torres, C. A. (1994). The Politics of adult education in comparative perspective: Models, rationalities and adult education policy implementation in Canada, Mexico and Tanzania. *Comparative Education, 30*(2), 131–152.

Tarozzi, M., & Torres, C. (2011). Multiculturalism is Dead. Unpublished manuscript.

Torres, C. (1998). Adult education as public policy: A perspective from Latin America. *Prospects: Quarterly Review of Education 18*(3), 79–88.

Torres, C. (1998). Democracy, education, and multiculturalism: Dilemmas of citizenship in a global world. *Comparative Education Review, 42*(4), 421–447.

Torres, C. A. (1998c). *Education, power and personal biography: Dialogues with critical educators*. New York, NY: Routledge. (Portuguese translation, 2000; Spanish translation, Siglo Veintiuno Editores, 2004.)

Torres, C. A. (1983). *Educational policy formation and the Mexican corporatist state: A study of adult education policy and planning in Mexico (1970–1982)*. Stanford University, Stanford, CA.

Torres, C. A. (1991). The state, nonformal education and socialism in Cuba, Nicaragua and Grenada. *Comparative Education Review, 35* (1), 110–130.

Torres, C. A. (1998a). Adult education as public policy: A perspective from Latin America. *Prospects, Quarterly Review of Education 18*(3), 79–88.

Torres, C. A. (1998b). *Education, power and personal biography: Dialogues with critical educators.* New York, NY: Routledge. (Portuguese translation, 2000; Spanish translation, Siglo Veintiuno Editores, 2004.)

Torres, C. A. (2009). *Globalizations and education: Collected essays on class, race, gender, and the state.* New York, NY: Teachers College Press.

Torres, C. A. (2009b). *Education and neoliberal globalization.* New York and London: Routledge.

Torres, C. A. (2011). Dancing on the deck of the Titanic? Adult education, the nation-state and new social movements. *International Review of Education, 57*(1–2), 39–55.

Torres, C. A., & Van Heertum, R. (2008). Education and domination: Policy and practice reform through a critical theory lens. In Sykes, G., Schneiber B., Plank, D. N. & Ford, T. G. (Eds.), *Handbook of Education Policy Research* (pp. 221–239). New York, NY: Routledge.

ANNOTATED BIBLIOGRAPHY OF SELECTED WORKS

Herein, we have chosen to showcase a group of texts that represent the major issues pertinent to Torres thoughts and efforts germane to the focus of social issues in education. This annotated bibliography is not exhaustive, rather, it represents an introduction to Torres' thinking and writing. We have included only those coauthored works that Torres wrote in conjunction with his long-term collaborators and students.

Arnove, R. F. & Torres, C. A. (2007). *Comparative education: The dialectic of the global and the local.* Lanham, MD: Rowman & Littlefield.

Long-time collaborators, Arnove and Torres epistemologically map the field of comparative education at the turn of the 21st century, as education around the world is affected by forces of globalization. Similar to the way that the first generation of comparative educators in the 19th century looked closely at the role of education in nation-building, subsequent generations of comparative educators have examined how education systems deal with global and local influences along various scientific, pragmatic and global dimensions. Torres challenges new generations of comparative educators to fully take into account politics and power in theorizing about education, particularly in area studies and ethnic studies, multiculturalism in the United States and interculturalism in Europe, and minority education.

Herrera, L., & Torres, C. A. (2006). *Cultures of Arab schooling: Critical ethnographies from Egypt.* Albany, NY: State University of New York Press.

The book presents scholarship on politics, religion, urban poverty and teacher education in Egyptian schools. The editors argue that Critical Social

Theory is needed to guide the ethnographic study of schooling processes in order to shed light on the mechanisms of cultural and social reproduction in education, especially in the context of late 20th century Arab world, where such a critical analysis is risky yet potentially powerful. Torres, in his concluding essay, speculates on the possibility of Freirean liberatory education for democratic development in the Arab world, highlighting how the concurrent use of a normative and analytic lens in education through critical theory is important in the educational struggle in the Arab world.

Morrow, R. A., & Torres, C. A. (2002). *Reading Freire and Habermas: Critical pedagogy and transformative social change.* New York, NY: Teachers College Press.

A theoretical work that introduces the complementariness of Habermas' and Freire's thinking, especially in the overlap between Habermas' theory of communicative action and Freire's dialogical subject. The authors highlight the importance of locating the development of subjectivity and identity in contexts and dialogue.

Morrow, R. A., & Torres, C. A. (1995). *Social theory and education: A critique of theories of social and cultural reproduction.* Albany, NY: State University of New York Press.

A collection of essays that brings together social theories such as structural functionalism, social/cultural reproduction, Marxism, and critical theory, this volume examines theories of reproduction in education. The authors link cultural reproduction and poststructuralism together to examine agency and structure along the axes of race, class and gender in education. For example, they describe how Popular Public Schooling stands in contrast to techno-rational approaches to education; in short, the education of the popular classes inherently draws on political standpoints to education which can never separate educational reform from the dignity of the individual and support of his or her freedom to act. (Popular Public Schooling is a political orientation towards education that challenges the status and power accorded to scientific (e.g., educated) thought of upper classes and not to wisdom that arises from collective experiences of the proletariat. This type of public education builds upon Bourdieu's notion of students' habitus to urge the creation of schools that reconcile opposing experiences in home and in school; thus, popular public schooling seeks to make the relationship between school and home mutually reinforcing.)

O'Cadiz, M. P., Wong, P., & Torres, C. A. (1998). *Education and democracy: Paulo Freire, social movements, and educational reform in São Paulo.* Boulder, CO: Westview Press.

As discussed in the narrative section of this chapter, this volume critically examines the ideas and performance of Paulo Freire as secretary of education in Brazil in the early 1990s during the socialist democratic administration of the Workers' Party in São Paulo. With an emphasis on theory, the authors discuss the relationships between the state and social movements as well as the relationships between teachers and curriculum reform. In so doing, they critically examine the intersection of politics and education in educational reform in one of the major urban centers of Latin America. A central focus of the book is the project of inter-disciplinarity in teachers' training, an essential principle of the Freirean approach. By concentrating on classrooms, schools, and teachers, this book constitutes an assessment of an original, far-reaching, and radical process of educational reform.

Rexhepi, J., & Torres, C. A. (2011): Reimagining Critical Theory. *British Journal of Sociology of Education, 32*(5), 679–698.

Coauthored with one of Torres' students, this meta-theoretical work discusses the relevance of critical theory to social analysis, and its value as a normative and analytical approach. The authors argue for examining the historical present to inform future social change. The authors suggest using critical theory to inform empirical work to avoid a situation in which there is a so-called end of history.

Schugurensky, D., & Torres, C. A. (1994). The politics of adult education in comparative perspective: Models, rationalities and adult education policy implementation in Canada, Mexico and Tanzania. *Comparative Education, 30*(2), 131–152.

In this article, written with Freirian scholar Schugurensky, Torres explores relationships among the state, ideology, and adult education actors. Based on systematic empirical work, the authors theorize main commonalities and differences in three adult education systems: Canada, Mexico, and Tanzania, three countries with highly sophisticated adult education systems. The authors place emphasis on the manner in which national case-studies relate to overall global processes. Specifically, they focus on how a particular organization of the state and hegemonic ideology affects the views of policymakers, teachers and other actors. This piece showcases the emergence of a key concern of Torres' body of scholarship, namely, how education is a site of political struggle where social reproduction and the business model wage war on democracy and opportunity.

Torres, C. (1998). Adult education as public policy: A perspective from Latin America. *Prospects, Quarterly Review of Education, 18*(3), 79–88.

In this critique of adult education, Torres links the interaction between the capitalist economy in Latin America to the state and policy actions. Here, Torres argues from a critical standpoint to note that policy rationales are "wishful thinking" that lack a critical theory of the social functions of adult education in development. Torres notes that policy makers would be better served by understanding the segmented labor economies of Latin America to design realistic education programs for adults. This article is useful to both critical educators and scholars of Latin America.

Torres, C. A. (1992). *The church, society and hegemony: A critical sociology of religion in Latin America.* Westport, CT: Praeger.

This book uses the analysis of Marx, Durkheim, Weber and Gramsci on religion as a social, cultural and political process related to capitalism. Torres offers a framework for understanding the dominant Catholic Church in Latin America, offering Argentina as an example. Torres develops a typology of neo-Christianity, socialism and social Christianity. This article highlights a less obvious strand in Torres scholarship, his attention to religion and faith in both hegemonic processes and social movements.

Torres, C. A. (2011). Dancing on the deck of the Titanic? Adult education, the nation-state and new social movements. *International Review of Education, 57,* 39–55.

In this retrospective article, Torres speculates on the current contradictions and future prospects of adult education, given how globalization makes changes to the nation-state. Torres points to the paradox of a recent situation—namely, Lula, president of Brazil and a union leader who spoke at the World Social Forum (WSF) received an award from WSF's antithesis, the World Economic Forum later the same year. This example illustrates the idea of relationship building for the greater good. Taking the meeting of CONFINTEA VI, the sixth Conference on Adult Education that took place in the city of Belém in the state of Pará (Brazil), as a starting point, where there was a consensus as to the importance of "civil society" in developing adult education programs, Torres poses the question of an alliance between social movements/civil society and the nation-state, asking whether such alliances or partnerships can be established.

Torres, C. A. (1998). *Education, power, and personal biography: Dialogues with critical educators.* New York, NY: Routledge.

A personal favorite of ours, this volume beautifully documents the growth of a tradition of study in the United States. Through in-depth interviews, Carlos Alberto Torres asks seminal educational thinkers to talk about the relationship between their personal experiences and their academic work. The reader will learn, by reading these intellectual, political and personal biographies (as well as "listening" to the voices of the speakers), how and why these individual scholars have struggled for more than three decades to expand the borders of critical education studies. Interviews with Henry Giroux, Herbert Gintis, Martin Carnoy, Maxine Greene, Michael Apple, Samuel Bowles, Paulo Freire, Gloria Ladson-Billings and Geoff Whitty are included.

Torres, C. A. (2009). *Globalizations and education: Collected essays on class, race, gender, and the state.* New York, NY: Teachers College Press.

This book is an excellent introduction to the thinking of Carlos Alberto Torres. It is organized as a selection of his thinking comprised of short essays that range from issues of gender, citizenship, democracy, neoliberalism and the role of the state in education. Per one of his trademark interests, Torres develops theoretical frameworks in political sociology, particularly marrying the critical modernist perspectives of Hegel and Paulo Freire as they are applied to education. As such, Torres speculates on the possibility of extending Freire's pedagogical work in Brazil and in Guinea Bisseau in the spirit of *a luta continua.*

Torres, C. A. (2011). Public universities and the neoliberal common sense: Seven iconoclastic theses. *International Studies in Sociology of Education, 21*(3), 177–197.

In this essay, which Torres described as polemical, Torres outlines the current conditions of neoliberalism that has permeated the logic of the university in the form of a new common sense, which he defines in his first thesis or argument as the existence of unbalanced power in everyday life that is underwritten by dominant structures. Neoliberal common sense, with its emphasis on private over public and on the market over the state, has impacted the university in the following ways: it has challenged their autonomy, encouraged the privatization of them, fostered their transformation into transnational institutions of knowledge production, and contributed to the creation of academic capitalism.

Torres, C. A., & Noguera, P. (2008). *Social justice education for teachers: Paulo Freire and the possible dream.* Rotterdam, NL: Sense Publishers.

These pieces resulted from a series of workshops given at the Paulo Freire Institute at UCLA by prominent Freirean educators from Brazil, the United States, Portugal, Canada and New Zealand. They deal with pedagogical issues such as the use of technology, the lessons Pedro Noguera learned as a new teacher when he brought "Freire to the 'hood'," and indigenous knowledge, all showcasing Freirean praxis and its far-ranging applications.

Torres, C. A., & Puiggrós, A. (1997). *Latin American Education: Comparative perspectives.* Boulder, CO: Westview Press.

This work, with fellow Argentine education administrator and Professor Adriana Puiggrós, includes chapters on basic education, higher education, privatization and the role of women's education in countries such as Mexico, Argentina and Cuba. The authors systematically question the impact of the structural adjustment programs across Latin America and related economistic ways of viewing education. For example, they ask: what is the influence of introducing user fees into the Argentine university? What are the effects of expanding nonformal education to women in Cuba? The core issue, here, is the relevance of the state and social context in human development in Latin American countries, particularly during a time of neoliberal policies.

Torres, C. A., & Teodoro, A. (2007). *Critique and utopia: New developments in the sociology of education in the twenty-first century.* Lanham, MD: Rowman & Littlefield.

This work is a collection of essays in two parts. The first part deals with new developments in the sociology of education in light of globalization. It includes essays on human rights and citizenship education, public choice in education and multiculturalism in Europe. The second part contains essays on classical sociologists of education such as Basil Bernstein, Pierre Bourdieu and Paulo Freire. The editors use Wallerstein's term "utopistics" to encourage renewed critique to imagine a postneoliberal era.

Torres, C. A., & Van Heertum, R. (2008). Education and domination: Policy and practice reform through a critical theory lens, pp. 221–239. In Sykes, G., Schneiber B., Plank, D. N. & Ford, T. G. (Eds.). *Handbook of Education Policy Research*. New York, NY: Routledge.

This chapter defines critical theory and traces its rise from Marxism to the Frankfurt School, and includes recent contributions by feminists and Scholars of Color. The authors describe the role of critical theory in knowledge production generally and specifically in education research that has to deal with political ideologies. The chapter ends with a critical theory analysis of the policies in the United States' educational mandate, No Child Left Behind.

CHAPTER 19

ELIZABETH ELLSWORTH

Kenneth J. Fasching-Varner, Margaret-Mary Sulentic-Dowell, Roland W. Mitchell, and Desiree R. Lindbom-Cho

Because if I am not what I've been told I am, then it means that you're not what you thought you were either! And that is the crisis
—James Baldwin (1969).

In the quote above, James Baldwin (1969) articulates a concern at the heart of the work of Elizabeth Ellsworth. More specifically, Baldwin (1969) is addressing what it means to be himself in the context of a society that created an image and idea of who he was supposed be as a Black male. Baldwin (1969) not only rejects the control exerted by dominant groups in trying to decide and frame who he was, but simultaneously questions the larger social construct of knowledge by questioning who the knowers are, or ultimately who *they* think they are. Such concerns vis-à-vis what constitutes knowledge, an active questioning of the notion that knowledge is already made, and what the role of representation (i.e., how identity is represented, how society is represented, etc.) is relative to the school curriculum, media, and pedagogy are at the heart of Elizabeth Ellsworth's work as a social scientist, scholar, and activist.

As a scholar, Elizabeth Ellsworth has made a lasting impression on the literature and scholarship related to pedagogical epistemology, representation of identity and society, the role of media, as well as pedagogical power (that is, the strength that teaching as a medium to communicate ideas).

Educating About Social Issues in the 20th and 21st Centuries, pages 383–402
Copyright © 2014 by Information Age Publishing
All rights of reproduction in any form reserved.

This chapter presents an overview of key aspects of Ellsworth's work as a critical theorist in the field of education.

The discussion of Ellsworth's work, which often has had implications for those interested in the constructs of diversity and equity, is particularly timely. In the wake of the election of Barack Obama as president of the United States many scholars and activists as well as many within what might be deemed the general citizenry were hopeful about the direction the United States was seemingly taking relative to issues of diversity and the related epistemological underpinnings of living and being in a diverse society (Clark, Fasching-Varner, & Brimhall-Vargas, 2012). This was, after all the election of (a) the first African-American, (b) an election in which a female candidate, Hillary Clinton, was positioned as a viable candidate for President, and despite one's political like or dislike for her, another woman, Sarah Palin, was positioned as the second viable female candidate for the office of Vice-President (the first being Geraldine Ferraro in 1984). The country it seemed was changing. What many have found in the Obama-era, however, are personal, academic, epistemological, and ultimately paradigmatic attacks on diversity, coming from conservative, neo-conservative, and neo-liberal groups alike, who, similar to those who thought they knew Baldwin, have enjoyed controlling not only what we think knowledge is, but who gets to possess the privilege of knowledge, and how knowledge is interacted with, created, and manifested. The related assaults on diversity, epistemology, and pedagogy—all of which trace back to Ellsworth's work—certainly existed prior to the Obama-era. The visibility and intensity of the assault, however, has increased significantly concurrent with the first presidency of an African-American (Arnsdorf, 2011; Exec. Order, 2011; King & Smith, 2011; Patterson, 2009; Tapia, 2009). Scholars and readers of Elizabeth Ellsworth's work have the opportunity to see how her work serves as a scaffold or tool in understanding how to break with epistemological traditions that frame all knowledge as premade, rested within frameworks of dominance, and controlled.

This chapter provides a historical overview of Elizabeth Ellsworth's work, an exploration of significant theories related to teaching and teaching social ideas expressed in Ellsworth's work, along with an exploration of her major accomplishments. It concludes with an annotated bibliography of Ellsworth's most significant contributions as well as pieces that appear to have influenced Ellsworth's thinking and pieces by various thinkers across the curriculum who have been influenced by Ellsworth.

HISTORICAL OVERVIEW OF ELIZABETH ELLSWORTH

Elizabeth Ellsworth is an immense talent—a distinguished and inspirational scholar. To attempt to define or even select the appropriate words to classify her body of work almost defies logic, for Ellsworth is a complex and provocative intellectual who questions labels, pedagogical movements, approaches, and constantly unsettles the boundaries those in the academy are so fond of drawing (Ellsworth, 1997a, 2005). To demarcate her scholarly interests feels a little bit like trying to establish the limits of her talents, her influence, and her thinking as she represents many schools of thought. Ellsworth may be a curriculum theorist (Ellsworth 1989a, 1989b, 1997a; Orner, Miller & Ellsworth, 1996; Ellsworth & Miller 1996), an ardent though difficult-to-peg feminist scholar (Roman, Christian-Smith, & Ellsworth, 1988), a principal contemporary theorist regarding representation (Ellsworth, 1997a, 1997b, 2005), and an individual who has had an impact on action research, teacher research, culture, curriculum integration, and online environments and communications media (Ellsworth 2005; Ellsworth & Kruse 2007a; 2007b; Ellsworth and Whatley 1990; Ellsworth & Kruse, 2007a, 2007b), though she may not know herself as any one of things, nor may she wish to be represented as such, a theme of Ellsworth (2005) more recent work. While we do not wish to limit who Ellsworth is, even through praise, the aforementioned areas of expertise represent the areas of focus in Ellsworth's scholarly work. In particular, her work with mediated learning environments and media (Ellsworth, 2005; Ellsworth & Kruse 2007a, 2007b; Ellsworth & Whatley, 1990, pedagogical critique and approaches (Ellsworth 1989a, 1989b, 1997a; Orner, Miller & Ellsworth, 1996; Ellsworth & Miller, 1996) are most noteworthy.

Her record is fairly simple to trace and present. (See the accompanying annotated bibliography for more details on specific works). Ellsworth's influence, however, is far reaching. She has impacted numerous fields of inquiry in profound ways from education to architecture, from feminist studies to mass communication, and from mass and other media to activism.

BACKGROUND

Elizabeth Ellsworth earned three degrees, all from the University of Wisconsin System. From the University of Wisconsin-Milwaukee, Ellsworth earned a Bachelor of Arts in Mass Communication in 1971 and a Master of Arts in Communication in 1975. For her MA Ellsworth pursued a concentration in history along with the criticism of documentary film. From the University of Wisconsin-Madison, Ellsworth earned a Doctor of Philosophy in Communication in 1984, focusing on the theory and criticism of film and mass media. Ellsworth's dissertation, "The Power of Interpretive Communities: Feminist Appropriations of Person Best," examined the relationship between audience interpretive strategies and social change.

Ellsworth's accomplishments are remarkable. Over the years (beginning in 1979) she has been a prolific author of books, journal articles, and book chapters. She has lectured widely, both in the United States (including as a distinguished lecturer/scholar at Teachers College, Columbia University) as well as internationally (including The Centre for Cross-Faculty Inquiry at the University of British Columbia). In addition, she has been awarded grants from such entities as New York State Council for the Arts, Parson's School of Design, and the Memorial Foundation for Jewish Culture.

In terms of teaching appointments and experience, Ellsworth's accomplishments are many and the sphere of her influence wide. She spent eighteen years at the University of Wisconsin-Milwaukee where she earned Full Professor status (1984–2002). While there, she also served as Vice President for Research and Development for Rethinking (2000–2001), where she worked on the development of education media. From 2001 through 2002, she served as the Director of Educational Programs at Teachers College, Columbia University (2001–2002). Since 2004, Ellsworth has been at The New School in New York City, where she is a professor of media studies and is also Associate Provost for Curriculum and Learning.

ON-GOING INFLUENCE

Elizabeth Ellsworth's influence ranges across a broad array of topics/issues, including but not limited to the following: emergent ways of knowing, invisible pedagogies, power relationships, and classroom spaces as power differentials. She is also renowned for her work to improve and inform museum exhibits, online learning environments, and new communication media. Ellsworth transcends multiple disciplines through the intersectional nature of her work, making her "among the earliest writers to engage . . . whiteness studies, critical race studies, queer studies, and postcolonial studies in educational research" with other frameworks such as museum studies, environment studies, and architectural studies for example, which are typically not often connected to the aforementioned fields (Kumashiro, 2012). To understand the wide reach and influence that Ellsworth has had on the academy one need only look at the scholarly works that cites Ellsworth. For example, Ellsworth's (1989a; 1993e) article, "Why Doesn't This Feel Empowering? Working Through the Repressive Myths of Critical Pedagogy" in the *Harvard Educational Review* has been cited by 2, 140 other scholarly texts, including works by leading theorists such as Michael Apple (1996), Ladson-Billings (1995), and Marilyn Cochran-Smith (1993), and Pennycock (1995). Ellsworth's (1997a) book "Teaching Positions: Difference, Pedagogy, and the Power of Address" has been cited 633 times by such notable scholars as Pinar (2004), Slattery (2006), and Kumashiro (2000).

Finally, Ellsworth's (2005) *Places of Learning: Media, Architecture, Pedagogy*, a fairly recent addition to scholarly literature, has already been cited 235 times in scholarly literature. Besides her influence on scholarly texts, Ellsworth's outreach to scholarly communities is also significant. As an example, the 2012 Curriculum and Pedagogy conference organized its call for proposals based on the following fourteen words of Ellsworth (2005): "Use what has already been thought as a provocation and a call to invention" (p. 165). This overview, however brief, provides a good sense of the scope and magnitude of Ellsworth's reach as a scholar.

MAJOR THEORIES: TEACHING AND TEACHING ABOUT SOCIAL ISSUES

Elizabeth Ellsworth has raised provocative and important issues about teaching, specifically the paradoxes of teaching. Perceiving teaching as a site of cultural production, Ellsworth argues that knowledge cannot exist outside of the context of its use, or perhaps more pointedly, knowledge cannot exist outside of the very interest and intentions for which it was construed and constructed (Ellsworth, 2005). Ellsworth has posited several challenging, vexing, and interrelated issues vis-à-vis teaching, namely, social positioning, the politics of appearance, and the paradoxes of teaching. Social positioning (the way in which film and media appeal to ideas about identity, such as what films are positioned to be received by adolescent males, or lesbian academics, or married couples, and so on) has become a hallmark of Ellsworth's work and interests, which appear in her scholarship beginning in the 1980's (Ellsworth, 1986). At, and of, the time, Ellsworth and colleagues explored the theorization of "reception" that challenged perceptions in media studies that intersected with critical culture studies and feminist film criticism. Delving onto the "problematics of pleasure," Ellsworth and colleagues explored the boundaries between private and public issues vis-à-vis reception, examining their own views and perceptions in terms of social positioning.

Ellsworth has always been on the cutting edge of scholarship, as demonstrated through her exploration and critique of the politics of appearance (the ways in which appearance is demonstrated and communicated in media to make people feel and understand certain things). Ellsworth's work has challenged traditional conventions of appearance in many venues including academic ones. In particular, Ellsworth (1996) has challenged the academy's traditional ways of listing authors, deciding at times to list authors not by order of contributional merit or an alphabetical listing but instead according to how pleasing they might sound, one after the other (p. 73). Juxtaposed to this bold challenge to academia, Ellsworth (1996) has pushed scholarly thinking, urging educators to "remap some of our assumptions about and discussions of pedagogy." (p. 75) Ellsworth's contributions surrounding the politics of appearance has influenced how academics and educators think about the traditional boundaries in classrooms, such as how student self-select and group themselves, how students self-identify, how classroom space is physically organized, impact learning. Ellsworth's contemplations serve a cautionary role for all educational researchers to more deeply question what we do and why we do research.

Ellsworth's use of questions is masterful and stimulating in terms of its impact on the teaching of social issues, as she explores what she terms the paradoxes of teaching (1998a). She confronts the boundaries of teaching and learning with penetrating questions about what it means to teach and what it means to learn. A common theme, or thread, running throughout her body of contributions to the academy are her questions (Allen, Haralovich, & Ellsworth, 1978; Ellsworth, 2008, 2007, 2005, 2004, 2002, 1999, 1998a, 1998b, 1997a, 1997b, 1996, 1994, 1993a, 1993b, 1993c, 1993d, 1992a, 1992b, 1991, 1990a, 1990b, 1989a, 1989b, 1988a, 1988b, 1987a, 1987b, 1987c, 1986, 1984, 1979; Ellsworth & Whatley, 1990; Roman, Christian-Smith, and Ellsworth, 1998; Ellsworth & Larson, 1986; Ellsworth, Larson & Selvin, 1986; Ellsworth & Selvin, 1986). She has posed inspiring, exciting, and perplexing questions about the role of teacher, the position of learners, the art and science of teaching, and the act of building knowledge. For Ellsworth, teaching and constructing knowledge are events full of ambiguity. Knowledge is situated, postulates Ellsworth, and she claims a teacher can never truly or fully understand the extent of what she teaches. Similarly, a teacher cannot adequately plan for or control what a learner might learn. Learning shifts as contexts and learners change. According to Ellsworth (1998a), teaching is a "never finished moment of affirming and engaging an ongoing cultural production (p. 442). As such, Ellsworth provides a cautionary tale about what we as teachers assign as learning experiences. She views many writing assignments as incidences wherein teachers "force" a learning or understanding of a text. Rather, Ellsworth recommends students be given wide choice and options, emphasizing learning processes. Terming this stance "response-ability," Ellsworth (1996) suggests asking students what value a reading may have to their current situation, no matter whether they are generating a perspective, searching for a topic, approaching exams, or preparing a defense. Above all, Ellsworth emerges as a true student advocate, stressing the importance of what a student needs over what a teacher feels is necessary knowledge or considerations. In the process of her work, Ellsworth often connects to ideas of the hidden curriculum and how hidden curricula affects learners (Apple & King, 1983; Cornbleth, 1984; Giroux & Penna, 1983; Martin; 1983). Again, Ellsworth emphasizes that learning should *always* be about what a learner needs. In the ten years since the passage of the No Child left Behind (NCLB) Act (2001), this view seems new and innovative, almost a response to the prescriptive, formulaic teaching that has become the norm in the last decade. However, Ellsworth was promoting this notion of learning pre NCLB. For Ellsworth, placing the learner and his/her needs at the heart of teaching is simply responsible teaching. She recommends that teachers continually "place themselves as learners" (be aware of themselves as learners and what that means and feels like), and thus, continually work to be cognizant of what students need in the way of pedagogy.

MAJOR ACCOMPLISHMENTS/CONTRIBUTIONS WITH RESPECT TO TEACHING ABOUT SOCIAL ISSUES

Perhaps the most noteworthy of Ellsworth's contributions are her views on identity and her examinations of the visual representation and language used in educational film. In addition, her questioning as to whether critical pedagogy is repressive is a major contribution regarding social issues in education.

Ellsworth argues that the use of static categories (constructs that do not change) has serious repercussions for teaching about social and cultural issues. Ellsworth has been influential in helping scholars and educators understand the presence of "others" that are taken for granted or otherwise ignored by groups who hold dominant positions within the academy; this strand of social thinking connects with other scholarship that has refocused the center (hooks, 1983) and made visible the foundational presence of nondominant groups in literature (Morrison, 1993). Ellsworth perceives difference to be fluid and contingent, not fixed, and, consequently, argues that when we attune to and honor differences we are able to grow as a scholarly community, pushing the epistemological boundary waters of what counts as knowledge, how is knowledge made, produced, experienced, and what are our roles are as thinking-feeling creatures in the act of learning.

As previously mentioned, Ellsworth (1989a) has questioned whether critical pedagogy as a field is in actuality repressive, as it perhaps has not properly attuned to what might be a sentipensante (feeling-thinking) pedagogy (Rendón, 2008), where thinking and feeling are valued, and hegemony is not replicated through what is framed as the act of being critical. In other words, a sentipensante approach rejects privileging only intellectual development, particularly to the exclusion of the whole person who thinks and feels. Such an approach is inherently relational, democratic, active, and ultimately "...focused on the shared construction of meaning" (Rendón, 2008, p. 17). If we believe that a relational, democratic, active, and shared approach to the construction of knowledge is valid, we consequently have to recognize that all isimistic behaviors are played out in what amount to multiracial, multigendered, multiclassed, multibeing environments so as to get at the root of how hegemony operated within society.

Trying to define or elucidate Elizabeth Ellsworth's impact on education is a daunting task. Ellsworth has influenced many academics to question all aspects of their research, classroom practices, and ways of labeling and identifying what they purportedly see and what they do.

Essentially, Ellsworth has prodded researchers and educators to question their motives, question purposes, and themselves, openly and continuously. In that regard, she has urged scholars to question why they do research and for whose purpose.

CONCLUSION

It is a real struggle to bring this chapter to a close or the linear organization of a chapter like this stands in opposition to much of what Ellsworth has herself engaged with, particularly in terms of how knowledge is represented. As this part of the chapter transitions to the annotated bibliography we recognize the challenge of representing the work of such a creative scholar who has resisted forms of representation generally perceived as epistemologically firm.

Ellsworth's efforts in such diverse fields as media, popular culture, visual arts and environmental activism certainly make her unique. Ellsworth, as both parts of this chapter (the overview and the bibliography) demonstrate, has produced a body of scholarship that matters and, significantly, adheres to no arbitrary intellectual, social or cultural boundaries.

REFERENCES

Apple, M., & King, N. (1983). What do schools teach? *The hidden curriculum and moral education: Deception of discovery* (pp. 82–99). Berkeley, CA: McCutchan Publishing Corporation.

Apple, M. (1996). *Official knowledge: Democratic education in a conservative era.* New York, NY: Routledge.

Arnsdorf, I. (2011, August 18). Obama orders improved workforce diversity effort. *The Washington Post.* Retrieved from http://www.washingtonpost.com/local/dc-politics/executive-order-to-push-agencies-on-federal-workforce-diversity/2011/08/18/gIQAng5POJ_story.html

Baldwin, J. (1969). A talk to teachers. In *The price of the ticket: Collected non-fiction 1948–1985* (pp. 325–332). New York, NY: St. Martin's Press. (Reprinted from The Negro child—his self image in *The Saturday Review.* 1963, December.)

Clark, C., Fasching-Varner, K. J., Brimhall-Vargas, M. (2012). *Occupying the academy: Just how important is diversity work in higher education.* Lanham, MD: Rowman and Littlefield.

Cochran-Smith, M. (1993). *Inside/outside: Teacher research and knowledge.* New York, NY: Teachers College Press.

Cornbleth, C. (1984). Beyond hidden curriculum? *Journal of Curriculum Studies, 16*(1), 29–36.

Ellsworth, E. (1984). Incorporation of feminist meanings in media texts. *Humanities in Society, 7*(1/2), 65–75.

Ellsworth, E. (1986). Illicit pleasures: Feminist spectators and *Personal Best. Wide Angle, 8*(2), 45–58.

Ellsworth, E. (1987a). Educational films against critical pedagogy. *Journal of Education, 169*(3), 32–47.

Ellsworth, E. (1987b). Media interpretation is a social and political act. *Journal of Visual Literacy, 8*(2), 27–38.

Ellsworth, E. (1987c). The place of video in social change: At the edge of making sense. *Frame/Work, 34,* 26–34.

Ellsworth, E. (1988a). Educational media, ideology, and the presentation of knowledge through popular cultural forms. *Curriculum and Teaching, 3*(1 & 2), 19–31.

Ellsworth, E. (1988b). Illicit pleasures: Feminist spectators and Personal Best. In L. Roman, L. K. Christian-Smith, & E. Ellsworth, (Eds.), *Becoming feminine: The politics of popular culture.* Philadelphia, PA. The Falmer Press.

Ellsworth, E. (1989a). Why doesn't this feel empowering? Working through the repressive myths of critical pedagogy, *Harvard Educational Review, 59*(3), 297–325.

Ellsworth, E. (1989b). Educational media, ideology, and the presentation of knowledge through popular cultural forms. In H. Giroux & R. Simone (Eds.), *Popular culture: Schooling and everyday life* (pp. 47–66). New York, NY: Bergin and Garvey.

Ellsworth, E. (1990a). The question remains: How will you hold awareness of the limits of your knowledge? *Harvard Educational Review, 60,* 396–405.

Ellsworth, E. (1990b). Illicit pleasures: Feminist spectators and Personal Best. In P. Erens (Ed.), *reprinted* in *Issues in Feminist Film Criticism* (pp. 183–196). Bloomington, IN: Indiana University Press.

Ellsworth, E. (1991). I pledge allegiance: The politics of reading and using educational documentaries. *Curriculum Inquiry, 21*(1), 41–64.

Ellsworth, E. (1992a). Teaching to support unassimilated difference. *Radical Teacher, 42,* 4–9.

Ellsworth, E. (1992b). Why doesn't this feel empowering? Working through the repressive myths of critical pedagogy. In C. Luke & J. Gore (Eds.), *Feminisms and critical pedagogy* (pp. 90–119). New York, NY: Routledge, 1992.

Ellsworth, E. (1993a). *AIDS: Cultural Analysis/Cultural Activism* (Review of the book). *Educational Studies, 24.*

Ellsworth, E. (1993b). Claiming the tenured body. In D. Wear (Ed.). *The center of the web: Women and solitude* (pp. 63–74). Albany, NY: SUNY Press.

Ellsworth, E. (1993c). I pledge allegiance: The politics of reading and using educational documentaries. In C. McCarthy & W. Crichlow (Eds.), *Race, identity, and representation in education* (1st ed.). (pp. 201–219). New York, NY: Routledge, 1993.

Ellsworth, E. (1993d). Why doesn't this feel empowering? Working through the repressive myths of critical pedagogy. In K. Geismar & G. Nicoleau (Eds.), *Teaching for change: Addressing issues of difference in the college classroom.* Boston, MA: Harvard Educational Review.

Ellsworth, E. (1993e). Why doesn't this feel empowering? Working through the repressive myths of critical pedagogy. In L. Stone (with G. M. Boldt) (Eds.), *The education feminism reader* (pp. 300–327). New York, NY: Routledge.

Ellsworth, E. (1994). Representation, self-Representation, and the meanings of difference: Questions for educators, in R. Martusewicz & B. Reynolds (Eds.), *Inside/out: Contemporary critical perspectives in education* (pp. 99–108). New York, NY: St. Martin's Press.

Ellsworth, E. (1996). Situated Response-ability to student papers. *Theory into Practice, 35,* 138–43.

Ellsworth, E. (1997a). *Teaching positions: Difference pedagogy and the power of address.* New York, NY: Teachers College Press.

Ellsworth, E. (1997b). Double binds of whiteness. In M. Fine, L. Weis, L. C. Powell, & L. Mun Wong (Eds.), *Off white: Readings on race, power, and society* (pp. 259–269). New York, NY: Routledge.

Ellsworth, E. (1998a). A response to Margery Osborne: Teacher as knower and learner: Reflections on situated knowledge in science teaching. *Journal of Research in Science Teaching, 35,* 441–442.

Ellsworth, E. (1998b). Multicultural research in the making. In C. A. Grant (Ed.), *Multicultural research: A reflective engagement with race, class, gender and sexual orientation* (pp. 24–36). Philadelphia, PA: Falmer Press.

Ellsworth, E. (1999). Why doesn't this feel empowering? Working through the repressive myths of critical pedagogy. In B. Pescosolido & R. Aminzade (Eds.), *The social worlds of higher education: Handbook for teaching in a new century* (pp. 487–495). Indiana University Press, 1999.

Ellsworth, E. (2002). The United States Holocaust Memorial Museum as a scene of pedagogical address. *Symploke: A Comparative Theory and Literature Journal, 10*(1), 13–31.

Ellsworth, E. (2004). The U.S. Holocaust Memorial Museum as a scene of pedagogical address. In J. R. Di Leo & W. R. Jacobs (Eds.), *If classrooms matter: Progressive visions of educational environments* (pp. 95–113). New York, NY: Routledge.

Ellsworth, E. (2005). *Places of learning: Media, architecture, pedagogy.* New York, NY: Routledge.

Ellsworth, E. (2007). What might become thinkable and do-able if we stop treating curriculum/teaching theory and practice as separate domains of academic research? *Journal of Curriculum and Pedagogy, 4*(1), 80–83.

Ellsworth, E. (2008). *Spatial Theories of Education: Policy and Geography* (book review). *Teachers College Record, 287.*

Ellsworth, E., Allen, J., & Haralovich, M. B. (1978). Taking charge of media experience. *Journal of the Wisconsin Communication Association, 9*(1), 48–54.

Ellsworth, E., & Kruse, J. (2007a). Becoming human | Artist: Moving in accord with the change that makes the world. *Performance Paradigm, 4.* Retrieved from http://www.performanceparadigm.net/

Ellsworth, E., & Kruse, J. (2007b). Limit cases. *Polar Inertia Journal, 29.* Retrieved from http://www.polarinertia.com/aug07/limit01.htm

Ellsworth, E., & Larson, M. K. (1986). Critical media analysis, radical pedagogy, and MTV. *Feminist Teacher, 2*(1), 8–13.

Ellsworth, E., Larson, M. K., & Selvin, A. (1986). MTV presents: Problematic pleasures. *Communication Inquiry, 10,* 55–63.

Ellsworth, E., & Miller, J. L. (1996). Working difference in education. *Curriculum Inquiry, 26,* 245–264.

Ellsworth, E., & Selvin, A. (1986). Using transformative media events for social education. *New Education, 8*(2), 70–77.

Ellsworth, E., & Whatley, M. H. (Eds.). (1990). *The ideology of images in educational media: Hidden curriculums in the classroom.* New York, NY: Teachers College Press.

Exec. Order No. 13,583. (2011). Retrieved from http://www.whitehouse.gov/the-press-office/2011/08/18/executive-order-establishing-coordinated-government-wide-initiative-prom.

Giroux, H., & Penna, A. (1983). Social education in the classroom: The dynamics of hidden curriculum. In H. Giroux & D. Purpel (Eds.), *The hidden curriculum and moral education: Deception of discovery* (pp. 100–121). Berkeley, CA: McCutchan Publishing Corporation.

hooks, b. (1983). Feminist theory: From margin to center. Boston, MA: South End Press.

King, D., & Smith, R. (2011). *Still a house divided: Race and politics in Obama's America.* Princeton, NJ: Princeton University Press.

Kumashiro, K. K. (2000). Toward a theory of anti-oppressive education. *Review of Educational Research, 70*(1), 25–53.

Kumashiro, Kevin (Personal communication, 2012)

Ladson-Billings, G. (1995). Toward a theory of culturally relevant pedagogy. *American Educational Research Journal, 32,* 465–491.

Martin, J. (1983). What should we do with a hidden curriculum when we find one? In H. Giroux & D. Purpel (Eds.), *The hidden curriculum and moral education: Deception of discovery* (pp. 122–13). Berkeley, CA: McCutchan Publishing Corporation.

Morrison, T. (1993). *Playing in the dark: Whiteness and the literary imagination.* New York, NY: Vintage.

No Child Left Behind. (2001). *Public Law No. 107–1110, 115 Stat. 1425, 2002.* One hundred seventh Congress of the United States of America.

Orner, M., Miller, J. L., Ellsworth, E. (1996). Excessive moments and the educational discourses that try to contain them, *Educational Theory, 46*(1), 71–91.

Patterson, O. (2009, August 14). Race and diversity in the age of Obama. *New York Times.* Retrieved from http://www.nytimes.com/2009/08/16/books/review/Patterson-t.html

Pennycook, A. (1995). *The cultural politics of English as an international language.* Boston, MA: Addison-Wesley.

Pinar, W. (2004). What is curriculum theory? Mahwah, NJ: Lawrence Erlbaum Associates.

Rendón, L. (2008). Sentipensante *Pedagogy: Educating for wholeness, social justice and liberation.* Sterling, VA: Stylus Publishing.

Roman, L. G., Christian-Smith, L. K., & Ellsworth, E. A. (Eds.). (1988). *Becoming feminine: The politics of popular culture.* New York, NY: Falmer Press.

Slattery, P. (2006). *Curriculum development in the Postmodern Era: Teaching and learning in an age of accountability* (2nd ed.). New York, NY: Routledge.

Tapia, A. (2009). *The inclusion paradox: The Obama era and the transformation of global diversity.* Lincolnshire, IL: Hewitt Associates.

ANNOTATED BIBLIOGRAPHY

Apple, M. W. (2000). *Official knowledge: Democratic education in a conservative age* (2nd ed.). New York, NY: Routledge.

Apple touts Ellsworth and colleagues' edited book, *Becoming Feminine*, as "some of the most elegant discussions of how we need to think about … 'cultural silences'" (p. 187). He also footnotes the importance of Ellsworth's articles "Illicit Pleasures" and "Why Doesn't This Feel Empowering?" as works to enhance his own critical discussion. Through a series of essays, Apple positions himself in direct opposition with the largely accepted "norm" of public education whereby racial minorities, people of lower socioeconomic classes, and other groups outside of conservative right mainstream society are systematically disenfranchised.

Ellsworth, E. (1987b). Media interpretation is a social and political act. *Journal of Visual Literacy, 8*(2), 27–38.

In this article, Ellsworth posits challenging questions for the fields of educational technology, cognitive psychology and sociology of education in regard to the kinds of interpretations particular media texts and social events (going to parties, online chats, classroom interactions, political rallies, etc.) surrounding them offer students. Through the chapter, Ellsworth raises concerns about the social implications of educational communication and calls for research agendas informed by questions quite different than those asked about how individuals process information. Instead, Ellsworth is much more interested in how and why audiences attach particular meanings to particular media texts. And, further through this line of argumentation, "what kinds of opportunities educational media offers students for engaging in interpretation" (pp. 27–28).

Ellsworth, E. (1989a). Why doesn't this feel empowering? Working through the repressive myths of critical pedagogy, *Harvard Educational Review, 59,* 297–324.

In this oft-cited article, Ellsworth conducts an inquiry into her own practice and positionality as a white, middle-class woman teaching in a racially diverse class. The course was focused on anti-racist approaches to education. Her critique of then current (1980s) discourses of critical pedagogy resulted in this article becoming one of her most provocative works. She suggests that foundational critical pedagogy concepts such as "empowerment," "student voice," "dialogue," and even "critical" are repressive myths that sustain relations of domination and "banking education" (298). At the conclusion of the article, Ellsworth problematizes critical theory's tendency to situate one group as having the more informed perspective and subsequently its attempt to enlighten the (racially, economically, gender, sexuality etc.) less informed group. Despite, the altruistic aims associated with critical pedagogy, Ellsworth's keen perspective brings to the surface the ways that the rules of reason and rationalism inherent to critical pedagogy can also be used to perpetuate the oppressive forces that critical pedagogues set out to disrupt.

Ellsworth, E. (1991). I pledge allegiance: The politics of reading and using educational documentaries. *Curriculum Inquiry, 21*(1), 41–64.

Herein, Ellsworth conducts an inquiry into the use of educational media to manipulate strong emotions (primarily fear and desire) to coax learners into what she refers to as a "child-like allegiance" to the ideological projects of specific curriculums. Ellsworth provides illustrations of the hidden curriculum within these media representations by juxtaposing classic educational documentaries from 1930 through 1965 against propaganda and social issue documentaries from the same era. The theoretical lens that she uses to bring to the surface the functioning of the ideological machinations on the part of the producers of these films includes contemporary approaches to cultural studies, specifically the concept of audience positioning and the politics of reading (p. 44).

Ellsworth, E. (1996). Situated Response-ability to student papers. *Theory into Practice, 35*, 138–43.

Situated response-ability reflects Ellsworth's work at applying the philosophical and theoretical to the practice of classroom teachers. The theory to practice application discussed in the article occurred in her graduate seminars on educational media and theories of representation. For the theoretical aspects of the class, Ellsworth taught the work of Ellen Rooney and Shoshana Felman. Through their scholarship, both Rooney and Felman challenge the notion that there is any "innocent" reading of the world. According to Ellsworth, "Rooney and Felman seem to agree, reading the world and "insight" or "comprehension" about the world are always performative—which always involves a strategy for constructing knowledge and never [constitutes] a moment of pure mirroring of the text in the reader" (p.139).

Consequently, the for-referenced approach to reading caused Ellsworth to alter the assignments to reflect the same level of epistemology under construction as reflected in Rooney's and Felman's ideas. This refocusing of her approach to assigning writing assignments and readings prompted Ellsworth to query, "right now I am thinking of this practice as part of my work as a teacher to use the reading of student papers in the continual struggle to become aware, that is, to situate my readings of student papers in their projects and questions—and from that place, to be able to respond as a teacher to those inaudible messages from students and from myself about our processes and projects in seminar" (p.141).

Ellsworth, E. (1997a). *Teaching positions: Difference pedagogy and the power of address.* New York, NY: Teachers College Press.

In this book, Ellsworth explores the complexity of classroom teaching in a context where both teachers and students have been socialized to repress difference as a starting point in the educative venture. In classic Ellsworth fashion, the text draws on an interdisciplinary approach to inquiry informed by cultural studies, performance studies, critical theory, media studies and women's studies. Ellsworth states that the aim of the text is to "take up the question of pedagogy and pursue it into some unlikely places...like film studies, psychoanalytic literary criticism and educational documentary films" (p.1). At the core of the text, notions of how to be in relation with students are explored in regard to developments concerning the concept of "address" in film and literary studies. Teachers are challenged to think deeply about who they are and ultimately how they are in relation to their students.

Ellsworth, E. (1998a). A response to Margery Osborne: Teacher as knower and learner: Reflections on situated knowledge in science teaching. *Journal of Research in Science Teaching, 35*, 441–442.

In this short but extremely insightful response Ellsworth succinctly outlines her thinking on the role of teaching as a site of cultural production. Specifically, Ellsworth is drawn to Osborne's convention that one who teaches the same courses year after year comes up against the limits of her own knowledge— and of knowledge itself. Of particular significance is Ellsworth's description of herself as "one among many and not The One Who Knows, and as one whose teaching is also a participation in the making of culture and not just the transmission of information" (p. 144). Ellsworth's pervasive destabilization of binary conceptions of teachers and learner and the danger associated with introducing knowledge as prefabricated is powerfully illustrated in this response.

Ellsworth, E. (2002). The United States Holocaust Memorial Museum as a scene of pedagogical address. *Symploke: A Comparative Theory and Literature Journal, 10*(1), 13–31.

In this article Ellsworth considers the role of the actual architecture of the U.S. Holocaust Museum in Washington D. C. as a space for teaching and learning about events that exceed the teachable or are un-representable. Ellsworth highlights the strength vis-à-vis the accomplishments of the architect and exhibit designers of the U.S. Holocaust Memorial Museum given the philosophical and pedagogical problems that challenge any attempt to teach or memorialize the Holocaust. As in other essays, books and articles penned by Ellsworth, in this article she highlights the benefits associated with the fluid and malleable types of knowledge that arise from trying to understand that which is "inconceivable." Against this backdrop, Ellsworth comments that "teaching and representing such traumatic histories brings educators up against the limits of our theories and practices concerning pedagogy, curriculum, and the roles of dialogue, empathy, and understanding in teaching about and across social and cultural difference" (p 13).

Ellsworth, E. (2005). *Places of learning: Media, architecture, pedagogy.* New York: Routledge.

Ellsworth challenges readers to consider knowledge as constantly in the making as opposed to being static—already constructed—prior to the transactions between individuals in learning environments. Learners and teachers are challenged to consider their embodied roles in constructing knowledge as well as the pedagogical possibilities that can occur through new epistemic constructions. Additionally in *Places of Learning*, Ellsworth continues the vein of her research that considers where learning occurs in order to recognize what she terms "anomalous places of learning" or, that is, places outside of schools that provoke us to rethink what happens in formal educational context. A particularly powerful illustration of this strand of her thought focuses on the role of the U.S. Holocaust Memorial Museum's uses of media and architecture that provides a "powerful pedagogical pivot space that puts inside and outside the classroom in perspective" (p.51).

Ellsworth, E. (2007). What might become thinkable and do-able if we stop treating curriculum/teaching theory and practice as separate domains of academic research? *Journal of Curriculum and Pedagogy, 4*(1), 80–83.

In this article Ellsworth challenges all involved in the educative venture to imagine 'thresholding' into previously unlived ways of being alive and thoughtful in relation to the world, self, and others. Consequently, from this vantage Ellsworth returns to a familiar topic asserting that teachers should let go of their dependence on already-known curriculum in pursuit of what she refers to as a vast and endless sea of knowledge in the making. While this article is as provocative as much of her other work, it is much more poetic and fanciful.

Ellsworth, E., & Kruse, J. (n. d.). *smudge* (website). Retrieved from http://smudg-estudio.org/

Perhaps Ellsworth's most telling project is her collaboration with Jamie Kruse, a website dubbed *smudge*. The homepage states, in part, the following: "Our current project meets sites and moments where the geologic and the human converge. We creatively respond to the complex forces we encounter there: the natural, built, historic, social, strategic and the imagined." Readers can click on a link to the authors' projects, a series of photographs that make the relationship between humans and the earth starkly and concretely visual. For each project, informative writings and/or other graphics such as maps and charts highlight the interdisciplinary nature of this complex relationship.

Ellsworth, E., & Miller, J. L. (1996). Working difference in education. *Curriculum Inquiry, 26*, 245–264.

"Working Difference in Education" reflects Ellsworth's collaboration with another prominent scholar/teacher educator Janet Miller. In the article they explore ways to develop forms of pedagogical address missing in current iterations of multiculturalism. Their aim is that these new forms of address may productively shift some of the tensions associated with teaching about racial, economic and cultural difference. The discussion of seeking out these inherent differences as a space for future epistemic ventures is a constant within Ellsworth's scholarship. And as readers familiar with Ellsworth's work should expect, Ellsworth constantly seeks material illustrations of the theoretical concepts described in her work. Consequently, the illustration of a working/productive type of difference and fluid positionality that she and Miller build upon in the article is Patricia Williams' book, *The Alchemy of Race and Rights: Diary of a Law Professor.* Williams is a black woman, professor, Harvard-educated scholar/lawyer. Given the interlocking and pervasive influence of systemic racism and patriarchy on the lives of women of color Ellsworth and Miller argue that Williams' memoir provides a much needed, detailed account of how she works the meanings and uses of her "oxymoronic" positioning's or differences.

Ellsworth, E., & Whatley, M. H. (Eds.). (1990). *The ideology of images in educational media: Hidden curriculums in the classroom.* New York: Teachers College Press.

This co-edited book represents yet another illustration of Ellsworth's pursuit to move her scholarship from the perceived Ivory Tower to the broader community. The text is composed of the collection of papers presented at a session entitled "Ideology of Images in the Classroom: Educational Film, Television and Textbook Telegraphs" held at the 1988 annual meeting of the American Educational Research Association (AERA) in New Orleans, Louisiana. The participants consider the collection of their papers to fill a significant void between the fields of Curriculum Theory and Sociology of Education. Ellsworth and Whatley assert that the primary contribution of this text to this gap in literature is that it reflects scholars' efforts to conduct research into the ideological influence of images in educational settings and particularly their presence as "the most hidden of hidden curriculums" (p. 1).

Ellsworth's actual contribution, "Educational Films Against Critical Pedagogy," argues that "teachers committed to constructing classroom practices against racism, sexism, classism and other oppressive formations must often do so in spite of the curriculum materials, including educational films, available to them" (p. 5).

This text, and specifically Ellsworth's chapter, further conceptualized Ellsworth's critique of key aspects of critical pedagogy, and the AERA session that spurred the creation of the text also helped to create one of the most innovative and provocative Special Interests Groups within AERA: "Media, Culture and Curriculum."

Ellsworth, L. (1979). *Frederick Wiseman: A guide to references and resources.* Boston: G.K. Hall & Co.

Frederick Wiseman: A Guide to References and Resources, published under "Liz" as opposed to "Elizabeth" Ellsworth, provides readers a glimpse into Ellsworth's talents squarely placed in the field of media studies. The early portions of the text reflect Ellsworth's research initially prepared in 1976–1978 for her master's thesis project at the University of Wisconsin-Milwaukee. In the text, she chronicles the films of iconic filmmaker Frederick Wiseman. For various reasons—from critical acclimation to an illustration of the ways that institutions like hospitals and schools act as agents of social change—Ellsworth chose five of Wiseman's most provocative films *Titicut Follies, High School, Hospital, Primate* and *Meat* for analysis.

Kamler, B., & Thomson, P. (2006). *Helping doctoral students write: Pedagogies for supervision.* New York: Routledge.

In addition to a myriad of practical information for advisors and committee members of doctoral students, Kamler and Thomson also examine herein what the goal of every advisor and student should be: the ability to "smudge" (p. 18) one's self. The authors appreciate Ellsworth's view of "smudge," where learning is happening, a place between knowing one thing and another or even between one's previous self-awareness and one's new knowledge of identity. Ellsworth's work emphasizes an openness of pedagogy, and the authors agree that being an open and flexible pedagogue creates a space for students to "allow students freedom to choose what to become" (p. 19).

Kumashiro, K. K. (2000). Toward a theory of anti-oppressive education. *Review of Educational Research, 70*(1), 25–53.

Kumashiro posits that there are four major ways in which educational research literature addresses anti-oppressive education, or education that works against oppression: (a) Education for the Other, (b) Education About the Other, (c) Education that is Critical of Privileging and Othering, and (d) Education that Changes Students and Society. Kumashiro notes that each way of researching oppressive education has benefits and deficits. In particular, he discusses Ellsworth's appeal to educators to disrupt normalized viewpoints with students by asking them to examine what has *not* been stated by a person, text, or society. Thus, he hopes educators will utilize an "amalgam" (p. 45) of the approaches outlined, and that academics will continue to search for other perspectives on and implications for anti-oppressive education.

Kumashiro, K. K. (2009). *Against Common Sense: Teaching and Learning Toward Social Justice.* New York: Taylor and Francis.

Kumashiro models the limits of common sense as an approach to teaching, arguing that common-sense approaches and mindsets ultimately maintain hegemony, privilege for some, and marginalization for others. The text is concerned with how common sense is replicated and modeled in the curriculum. Kumashiro draws from the practice of teaching to model the theory of teaching. To that extent this text demonstrates a social justice praxis.

Ladson-Billings, G. (1995). Toward a theory of culturally relevant pedagogy. *American Educational Research Journal, 32*, 465–491.

Gloria Ladson-Billings is a highly regarded and recognized scholar who, like Elizabeth Ellsworth, is concerned with issues of racism in the educational setting of school. This landmark article examines the pedagogies of five educators who teach African-American students. The participant pool, interestingly, was selectively chosen through the input of community members who felt respected by the teachers and felt their children were actively engaged in the classroom.

Through interviews and observation, Ladson-Billings discovered that these teachers (five black and three white women) had a number of commonalities including some of the following: high expectations for their students and the belief that their students could learn, the development of strong social relationships with their students, and that knowledge of some concept is not a given construct but one that is ever-changing and constructed.

Morrison, T. (1993). *Playing in the dark: Whiteness and the literary imagination.* New York: Vintage.

This seminal work in literary analysis challenges dominant positions about representation within American Literature. Morrison argues that the Africanist presence is foundational to all American literature. This work represents a suggested paradigmatic shift in regard to how readers should view the foundations of American literature, which would result in readers beginning to understand the necessity of an Africanist presence to move forward the interests of white characters and plots. Morrison supports her arguments by showing the Africanist presence in classic American literature works by Edgar Allen Poe, Willa Cather, and Ernest Hemingway among others. Morrison moves beyond challenging what representation should be by systemically pointing out what is in literature already and why the real foundation of literature, with its Africanist presence, moves beyond what dominant groups have imagined the foundation to be.

Orner, M., Miller, J. L., Ellsworth, E. (1996). Excessive moments and the educational discourses that try to contain them. *Educational Theory, 46*(1), 71–91.

This provocative article situates the cumulative thought of thee intellectually diverse scholars on the excesses that have arisen in educational discourse as a result histories of repression. The authors have numerous years of teaching, writing and researching together and the resulting interplay between the authors concerning excessive moments in education when considering pedagogy, location, student writing and school change research, affords readers' purview to the multiple relationships that Orner, Miller and Ellsworth had begun to draw for themselves vis-à-vis their collective research as well as their individual bodies of scholarship.

This focus on recognizing difference and seeking the knowledge that resides in the repressed aspects of particular educational discourse is a constant in Ellsworth's work. The authors describe being called to repressed excesses as, "We have been drawn to the notion of 'excess' and 'excessive' as a means for examining the repressed in our own sites of theory and practice" (p. 71). In a classic example of "Ellsworth reflexive praxis," the authors of this article remain firmly within the scope of the analysis/critique.

Pennycook, A. (1995). *The cultural politics of English as an international language.* Boston, MA: Addison-Wesley.

Pennycook's text, in a vein similar to Ellsworth, urges teachers of the English language as well as academics who study English to examine the historical and philosophical underpinnings of their disciplines. He posits that the global spread of English is rooted in politics and the hegemonic influences of one culture over another; as the adage proclaims, "The sun never set on the British Empire." He also, however, notes that the English language is not just a symptom of imperialism, but also a language of self-agency whereby people have the ability to oppose those in power.

Pinar, W. (2004). *What is curriculum theory?* Mahwah, NJ: Lawrence Erlbaum Associates.

Pinar's modest book title may be misleading, for the first part of his text is audaciously entitled "The Nightmare That Is the Present." His desire is that U.S. citizens awaken to the reality of discussions about education and what they really mean, illustrating his point through the (mis)representation of the knowledge of historical events both north and south of the Mason-Dixon Line. He also spends much time looking at Ellsworth's work on social relationships and communication, "modes of address" in the school setting as a bridge to his call for "Self Mobilization and Social Reconstruction."

Rendón, L. (2008). Sentipensante *Pedagogy: Educating for wholeness, social justice and liberation.* Sterling, VA: Stylus Publishing.

Sentipensante Pedagogy challenges scholars to take pause and evaluate if they have lost in balancing what academic education might mean as opposed to education for life. Rendón transcends disciplines to weave together the aesthetic, cognitive, emotional, and intuitive frames of reference that might drive pedagogical orientations. In doing so, she draws from her own auto-ethnographic experiences growing up in a rural area as a Latina in poverty to model for other educators how they might draw from their own auto-ethnographically informed thinking-feeling orientation to unlock the potential of pedagogy.

Roman, L. G., Christian-Smith, L. K., & Ellsworth, E. A. (Eds.). (1988). *Becoming feminine: The politics of popular culture.* New York: Falmer Press.

The collection of works in this edited text illustrates the referenced breadth and depth of Ellsworth's interdisciplinary interests. Primarily situated in the fields of cultural studies with a specific focus on the role of popular culture in the construction and transformation of feminists' identities, the authors in the text take up provocative issues such as adolescent romance novels and embodiment ("Lessons from a Catholic High School"), and films about lesbian student culture in and out of school.

Ellsworth's actual contribution to the book explores the ways that feminists reviewers used their interpretations of the mainstream film *Personal Best* to construct and engage in a public debate to determine which "feminist" social subjectivities would count as the basis for concrete political action (p. 103). The pursuit of what Ellsworth terms as "concrete political action" permeates significant parts of her work, fuel her critique of purely academic discussions of school and society and are evident in the progression of her destabilizing both disciplinary and universities and community boundaries.

Slattery, P. (2006). *Curriculum development in the Postmodern Era: Teaching and learning in an age of accountability* (2nd ed.). New York: Routledge.

Slattery begins his text with a historical look at curriculum studies as a field and then examines current and pointed issues such as hermeneutics; gender, sexuality, race, and ethnicity; and postmodern philosophies within curriculum studies. He leans heavily on Ellsworth's musings as a white woman academic teaching a diverse population of students to note that, all too often, white males are the only ones engaged in and creating discourse about multiculturalism. Like Ellsworth, he wonders how students and teachers can construct their own knowledge and make meaning in a classroom where school structure can and does impose certain values upon them, grounding his ideas on curriculum in the current Postmodern Era.

Sleeter, C. E. (1996). *Multicultural education as social activism.* Albany: State University of New York Press.

Sleeter's examination of multicultural education is made powerful through her use of auto-ethnographic narrative. She is not afraid to implicate her role as a white woman in her discussions of race and schooling. Sleeter draws on Ellsworth to note specifics regarding her own classroom experience at the collegiate level, noting that "in raising questions about multiple identities within subjects, and the interplay between rational thought and desire, such works probe subtle and often unanticipated dynamics that occur in classrooms in which critical or feminist pedagogies are employed" (p. 119). Perhaps most significantly, Sleeter situates her musings in the context of today's globalized society.

CHAPTER 20

GLORIA ANZALDÚA'S RADICAL VISION FOR SOCIAL AND POLITICAL TRANSFORMATION

Breaking Boundaries, Building Bridges, Changing Consciousness

Suniti Sharma

INTRODUCTION

In keeping with critical theory's historical commitment to human emancipation and freedom from oppression, Gloria Anzaldúa's (1942–2004) writing is revolutionary and subversive on many levels, articulating a radical vision and creating spaces for teachers and students to work toward social and political transformation. Anzaldúa's commitment to social justice is based on critique of ideological and institutional conditions that perpetuate racism, sexism, classism, and homophobia; deconstruction of the dynamics of power, knowledge, and domination; construction of an emancipatory language for engaging with identity and difference; and

Educating About Social Issues in the 20th and 21st Centuries, pages 403–431

403

envisioning radical pathways to social and political transformation. As a seventh generation Mexicana on the American side of the U.S.–Mexico border, Anzaldúa's Chicana identity, the lived experience of marginality, and diverse teaching experiences, are critical to her writing, theorizing, and activism.

ANZALDÚA'S LIFE AND INFLUENCES

Anzaldúa's academic and activist focus was profoundly influenced by several key issues and moments in her life, including physical issues, her early years growing up along the U.S.–Mexico border; her Chicana-Mexican-Aztlán cultural roots; her educational experiences as a student, teacher, and activist; and her lifelong struggles with health issues. According to the *Gloria Evangelina Anzaldúa Papers, 1942–2004* archived at The University of Texas, Austin, (UTA) Anzaldúa was born on September 26th, 1942, in Raymondville, South Texas, where her parents worked as share croppers and migrant farm workers.

Having witnessed firsthand the subjugation of Chicana women in her family convinced Anzaldúa of the critical importance of feminist work and the need for women to voice their resistance to patriarchal, heterosexual narratives and identity. In *Borderlands/La Frontera*, (1987) Anzaldúa speaks of the humiliation her grandmother experienced at the hands of her grandfather who had three mistresses and treated women as sexual objects which strengthened Anzaldúa's resolve to fight for the emancipation of women from the imposition of history, society, religion and culture.

Anzaldúa's early years along the border were marked by first-hand experience with the U.S. Border Patrol, exploitation of cheap Mexican labor, the displacement of family members on both sides of the border, and the terrorization of documented and undocumented Mexican and U.S.–Mexican communities along the Rio Grande Valley. All of these experiences, as well as others, influenced her academic and activist work in major ways.[1]

From an early age, Anzaldúa (2009b) was painfully conscious of her body as a marker of difference and felt alienated from the "nightmare" of her own body and sexuality. Due to an unusual hormonal imbalance that led to menstruation in infancy and puberty at six years of age, Anzaldúa experienced constant humiliation and shame, and made every attempt to hide her "body that was a freak" (p. 84) from others. Explaining her sexuality, Anzaldúa (1987) states that she felt queer in terms of being alienated from her own body, however, her queer sexual orientation was a conscious choice, not a biological given. In an interview with Héctor Torres (1992), Anzaldúa discusses breaking ties with her mother and her sister for three years after the publication of *This Bridge Called My Back*, as her family refused to accept her sexual orientation. Anzaldúa saw this rejection by her family further compounded by a homophobic Chicano culture, and alienation from the Church as a betrayal that is rearticulated as a recurring theme that permeates her writing—the female body as a powerful, social and cultural text and her Chicana, feminist, queer subversion of this text.

Keen to educate his children, Anzaldúa's father settled in Hargill, a small border town in Texas; however, his early death in a car accident forced Anzaldúa to continue working in the fields through high school and college. These early years spent in South Texas had a lasting impact on Anzaldúa's writing and shaped her struggles against the legacy of racial discrimination and *Tejano* (Texans of Mexican descent) land dispossession at the U.S.–Mexico border of South Texas.

A major influence on Anzaldúa's writing were her educational experiences, elementary school through university. Reflecting on her high school experiences, Anzaldúa (1987) recalls being punished for speaking Spanish in school and for speaking with a Mexican accent. Angered with Anzaldúa for her accent and language, a teacher scolded her saying, "If you want to be American, speak 'American.' If you don't like it, go back to Mexico where you belong" (Anzaldúa, 1987, p. 75). At Pan American University, Anzaldúa recollects that the Chicano students were required to take two speech classes to get rid of their Mexican accents. Throughout her writing, Anzaldúa explores themes related to establishing a sense of identity and voice—gender, race, nationality, and language.

In an interview with Andrea Lunsford (1997), Anzaldúa recalls that growing up as a child she attended school, did household chores, and worked in the fields, leaving no time for studying. Sharing the room with her siblings, Anzaldúa remembers reading with a flashlight under the covers and in order to prevent her younger sister from telling her mother about this, Anzaldúa distracted her sister by telling her stories based on the day's experiences. According to Anzaldúa, the short stories turned into a series of stories, embellished each day as she combined family history, cultural myths, and fact and fiction to keep her sister entertained.

Anzaldúa also recalls that as a young child and through adolescence she escaped into the world of writing journals in order to distance herself from her family that was "very verbal" and "fought a lot" (Lunsford 1997, p. 5), the pain of her physical hormonal condition, and the struggles she faced as a Mexican American in an Anglo world. Thus writing became a "liberatory goal" that was both an escape and a form of creativity offering "possibilities for people to look at things in a different way" (p. 6).

Speaking with Lunsford (1997), Anzaldúa remembers that when in high school she excelled in academic work and was one of two Mexican-American students in an accelerated section, however, the Anglo students looked down on her and the teachers ignored her while assisting the Anglo students, making her feel that advanced placement was "like a put-down rather than praise" (p. 22). Similarly, as a college student, Anzaldúa notes that her writing was being "put-down" by her teachers who considered her work subjective and criticized her for not "following the rhetoric of Aristotle and Cicero" (p. 23) making her feel that she was being punished for being a Mexican. Anzaldúa articulates the tension among her educational experiences of rejection at the hands of her teachers, her love of reading and writing of English which she perceived as the language of domination and her close connection with her Mexican cultural roots through use of multiple languages and cultural code-switching in her writing. Despite everything, by the time she graduated from Edinburg High School in 1962, she had become a prolific writer and poet.

In her interview with Lunsford, Anzaldúa speaks highly of her professor and role model, James Sledd at the graduate school in The University of Texas, Austin, who was the first person to encourage her cultural writing that reflected her Chicana-Mexican-Spanish historical influences and experiences. Other early influences on her writing were Julio Cortazar, an Argentinean writer who wrote hybridity and in-between spaces and identity and Jane Austen's *Jane Eyre* which she read thirteen times. Jane Eyre's strong will and assertiveness in resisting traditional gender roles assigned to women, inspired Anzaldúa to think about "my feminist ideas, my gender liberation ideas" (Lunsford 1997, p. 20) that served as a key theme in her writing.

In 1969, Anzaldúa received her BA in English, Art, and Secondary Education from Pan American University, and went on to earn an MA in English and Education from the University of Texas at Austin in 1972. Speaking about her choice of subjects at the college level, Anzaldúa notes that she chose art as she was passionate about art, and English because she had never taken any Spanish courses nor had she taken any courses in which theory was taught in Spanish. Although Anzaldúa majored in literature and art education and was keen to teach art she was unable to get a teaching position in a public school as an art teacher, therefore, began teaching English composition.

In March of 1969, the first National Chicano Youth Liberation Conference was held that drafted the basic premises for the Chicana/Chicano Movement. The following year Chicanas/Chicanos at the University of California, Santa Barbara came together, resulting in the formation of the Chicano/a Studies Program. Rejecting terms such as "Mexican-American" that symbolized assimilation and "Hispanic" as an Anglicized term, Chicano/a activists distinguished their cultural and political position by using the term Chicano/a. For Anzaldúa, this act of naming, combined with her own Chicana, identity was the culmination of a period of intense political activism signaling a new level of political consciousness, critical to her development as a theorist-writer-activist.

While enrolled at Pan American University from 1965–1968, Anzaldúa was a full time student in the evening, a teacher's aide in the day time, and a farm worker on the weekends. She notes that after graduating in English, art, and secondary education, she spent the next three years from 1969–1973, teaching in various school districts of San Juan, Texas. Although interested in working at the high school level, according to the general perception in schools, "Mexicans are only 'good enough' to teach elementary" so Anzaldúa taught five-year olds in a bilingual school for a year, emotionally disturbed children for another two years before being moved to the high school level. During this period, Anzaldúa attended summer courses at The University of Texas, Austin, graduating with a master's in English and education. Thereafter, she moved to Indiana working as a liaison between migrant farm workers' children and the Indiana public school system from 1973–1974. In September 1974, Anzaldúa returned to The University of Texas, Austin as a doctoral student, leaving for California in 1977.

By her own account, Anzaldúa's (1981) time at UTA was significant in giving her a sense of direction toward writing and activism. Enrolled as a doctoral student at UTA, Anzaldúa recalls the negative reception of her doctoral proposal and criticism she received for writing about her Chicana life-experiences, as well as for her unique style of writing in multiple languages. Frustrated, Anzaldúa moved to San Francisco, dedicating her life to writing, teaching, and activism. In 1988, Anzaldúa was accepted into the PhD program in literature at the University of California, Santa Cruz (UCSC) and began her dissertation entitled, *Llaronas-Women Who Wail: (Self) Representation and the Production of Writing, Knowledge, and Identity*. Anzaldúa was posthumously awarded a PhD in Literature as she died in May 2004 of diabetes related complications.

The years 1974 and 1977, while enrolled at the University of Texas, Austin, were critical to Anzaldúa's growth as an activist, especially her work with the political group, Movimiento Estudiantil Chicano de Aztlán (MEChA) (Movement of Chicano students of Aztlán), during which she participated in farm worker protests and worked within feminist organizations and consciousness-raising groups.

Anzaldúa taught a course at the University of Texas, Austin, called *La Mujer Chicana* (*The Chicana Woman*) and became aware of the marginalization of women-of-color from academia, the exclusion of U.S. women-of-color from academic publishing, and the subordination of feminist women-of-color by white feminism. This awareness resulted in Anzaldúa's first edited anthology composed entirely by women-of-color, *This bridge called my back: Writings by radical women-of-color* (1981).

After moving to California, Anzaldúa continued to teach a women's studies course at UCSC and published the course readings she had assembled as an edited anthology, *Making Face, Making Soul/Haciendo Cara* (1990). Anzaldúa also taught through Vermont College's Adult Degree Program, held various visiting faculty appointments, and taught through workshops at the Women's Voices writing workshop at UCSC. Throughout the 1980s and 1990s, Anzaldúa corresponded with several contemporary women scholars and activists such as Norma Alarcon, Ruth Behar, Beth Brant, Chrystos, Shelley Fisher Fishkin, Melanie Kaye/Kantrowitz, Ana Louise Keating, Cherrie Moraga, Emma Perez, Norma Cantú, and Chela Sandoval, some of whom became her closest friends and writing associates.

In her writing, Anzaldúa used her experiences as a colonized Mexican/Aztlán Indian who had to continually negotiate multiple identities of oppression and resistance. According to Anzaldúa (2002), her sense of empowerment came from the power of ideas, as aggression and domination were to be resisted with new and innovative concepts, not weapons. Anzaldúa transformed her personal struggles; her brown skin and mixed accent; her childhood in the Rio Grande Valley of South Texas; experiences as a Mexican-American in an Anglo dominated society; her Chicana feminism and queer identity; her art and spirituality into a lifetime devoted to writing poems, short stories, essays and letters of resistance, hope, and consciousness building.

Writing from the position(s) of "Chicana, *tejana* (Texan of Mexican descent) working-class, dyke-feminist poet, writer-theorist" (Anzaldúa 2009, p. 164), Anzaldúa's multiple naming of identities is a strategic epistemological position for resisting systems of oppression in her political struggle for social justice. As she states, naming is "how I make my presence known, how I assert who and what I am and want to be known as," how she documents her unique personal and collective history assuring she is not "erased, omitted, or killed" (Anzaldúa 2009b, p. 164). At the forefront of Chicana, feminist and queer thought, the power of Anzaldúa's work, especially for educators teaching about social issues through a social justice lens, comes from her call for political action and conversations across theoretical approaches and academic disciplines within a complex series of coalitions across differences based on a heterogeneity of experiences.

In the foreword to her first published coedited anthology, *This Bridge Called My Back* (1981), Anzaldúa calls on U.S. Third-World feminists and educators, diverse women-of-color, and, in fact, all oppressed groups of women, to participate in the emancipatory project of breaking boundaries in order to resist oppressive practices, building bridges across communities, and changing consciousness toward social and political transformation. As Anzaldúa (1981) says:

> *With This Bridge*...hemos comenzado a salir de las sombras; hemos comenzado a reventar rutina y costumbres opresivas y a aventar los tabues; hemos comenzado a acarrear con orgullo la tarea de deshelar corazones y cambiar conciencias *(We have begun to break with routines and oppressive customs and to discard taboos; we have commenced to carry with pride the task of thawing hearts and changing consciousness)* [emphasis added] (p. v).

In response to Anzaldúa's call, the anthology is multi-voiced, multilingual, and multi-genre—the individual trajectories of the educators, scholars, and activists from multiple disciplines inform the collective political project of breaking silences across history, building coalitions among groups, and changing how knowledge about identity and difference is constructed. Anzaldúa's theories and methodologies for teaching about social issues are rooted in critical analysis of individual and collective oppression, therefore, grounded in identity, lived experience, and subjective agency on the one hand, and embedded in collective history and alliances across differences, on the other. As Anzaldúa (1981) reflects, "I believe that by changing ourselves we change the world...going deep into the self and expanding out into the world, a simultaneous recreation of the self and a reconstruction of society" (p. 208).

As an educator, Anzaldúa repositions herself as a teacher-writer-activist whose writing is an emancipatory project aimed at social and political transformation. Anzaldúa's emancipatory project calls on educators to teach about social issues and effect change beginning with self-analysis—identity/ies, history/ies, embodiment, experiences, and actions—the very paradigm of individual existence, and moves across difference toward a collective consciousness in response to an inclusionary vision. Anzaldúa's seminal single authored collection *Borderlands/La Frontera*, published in 1987, code-switches between English, Spanish, Tex-Mex, and Nahuatl, the language of the Aztecs, and marks a historical moment in the development of Chicana feminist theories and academic practices. Thereafter, Anzaldúa's concepts of Borderlands, mestiza consciousness, and autohistoria, to name a few, have been used as theories and methodologies to teach about social issues across multiple disciplines that go beyond Chicana feminist studies and queer theory to cultural, ethnic, gender and women's studies, and American, border/frontier and transnational studies.

In what follows, this chapter draws from the primary works of Gloria Anzaldúa, published between 1981 and 2002, with support from secondary sources, to delineate three key aspects of her writings, offering possibilities for teaching about social issues. First, an overview of key concepts and theories from Anzaldúa's academic writings are presented with a focus on the following interrelated concepts: borderlands as a relational theory for teaching about identity and difference; new mestiza consciousness as feminist epistemologies validating lived experiences; conocimiento as the path to changing consciousness toward self and other; and, El Mundo Zurdos, a vision for social and political transformation. The next section examines Anzaldúa's autohistoria-teoria as a methodology for teaching, learning, and activism that combines autobiography and history using language as a critical practice for deconstructing dominant knowledge and constructing transformative epistemologies. Third, this chapter discusses the enduring legacy of Anzaldúa's vision reflected in the ways educators, scholars, and activists across disciplines have mobilized her theories and methodologies to engage in emancipatory projects in their commitments to teaching about social issues. In order to capture the contested terrain of Anzaldúa's complex theorizing, this chapter situates her writing within critical academic debates that problematize her work, ascribing to them a new meaning, opening a range of teaching possibilities for a wider audience of educators to continue the political struggle for social justice from new contexts and positions.

KEY CONCEPTS AND THEORIES

Borderlands: Relational Theory for Teaching Difference

This section focuses on Anzaldúa's concepts and theories—Borderlands, mestiza consciousness, conocimiento, and El Mundo Zurdos—new visions and strategies for teaching about social issues such as identity, difference, and inclusion through breaking boundaries, building bridges, and changing consciousness toward social justice. For Anzaldúa, Borderlands is a theoretical framework that serves several purposes: First, Borderlands is a geographical, historical, and cultural experience in the production of identity/ies and difference/s. Second, the conceptualization of Borderlands as an ideological and political space intervenes in hegemonic discourses of power, knowledge and domination that perpetuate oppressive systems to systematically exploit, marginalize and exclude the cultural other. Third, Borderlands is a hybrid place and space of possibilities for reclaiming history/ies, creating emancipatory knowledge, and continuing the project of creating possibilities for changing consciousness toward social justice.

Borderlands is not a new concept in education; however, Anzaldúa's theory of difference is relational as it puts lived experience at the center, not essentialized identities, categories, binaries, or hierarchies (Yarbro-Nejarano, 1994). Writing out of Iberian and Latin American Cultures to examine the cultural (re)production of Chicanas/os and Latinas/os, Yarbro-Nejarano

(1994) describes Anzaldúa's theorizing as embodied theory emerging from oppressions suffered by women-of-color, and not something that is simply limited to Chicana or Latina. It is this relationality across a network of differences that, according to Yarbro-Nejarano, makes Anzaldúa relevant to teaching as it relates to all forms of "miscegenation" and "border crossing" (p. 7). Rather than view the border as stable in terms of geography (Perez, 1999), as specific discourses from margin and center (Castillo, 1995), or "consciousness in opposition" (Sandoval 2000, p. 54), Anzaldúa's theorizing is a relational "theory in the flesh" (Moraga & Anzaldúa 1981, p. 23), situated within a new paradigm for engaging with difference (Yarbro-Nejarano, 1994). As Anzaldúa (1994–1995) notes, "When I capitalize Borderlands, it means that it's not the actual Southwest or the Canada–U.S. border, but that it's an emotional Borderlands which can be found anywhere there are different kinds of people coming together" (p. 77). Thus, Borderlands, as a relational theory for teaching difference, offers educators a critique of identity politics that assumes a coherent, unified, and stable identity, rejects essentialism and universality of human experience and identity, and prompts educators to shift the dominant singular homogenous discourse in education toward perceiving identity as hybrid, multiple, and changing.

Borderlands is a complex theory grounded in the concrete experience of violent "otherization" of Mexican Americans in U.S. society and the border experience of marginality. Anzaldúa's critique of otherization of cultural difference is aimed not only against Anglo domination of Mexican Americans but also against a sexist, gendered, and homophobic Chicano culture that subjects women to an inferior status. In a chapter from *Borderlands/La Frontera* (1987), aptly titled, "Movimientos de Rebeldía y Las Culturas que Traicionan" ("Movements of Rebellion and the Cultures that Betray"), Anzaldúa confronts sexism and homophobia in Chicano culture, and questions the norms defined by the Catholic Church that labels homosexuality as sinful—as cultural constructions of Chicana woman and lesbian as the "other" within her own culture and religion. Grounding her writing in "woman's history of resistance" (p. 43), Anzaldúa's teaching, theorizing, and activism transgresses boundaries imposed on her by culture, religion, and politics to claim that "I, like other queer people, am two in one body, both male and female. I am the embodiment of hieros gamos: the coming together of opposite qualities within" (p. 19).

Anzaldúa's conceptualization is brought to bear on American and Canadian Studies as Feghali (2011) compares Anzaldúa's notion of negotiating in-between-ness with Homi Bhabha's (1994) notion of hybridity and Third Space as spaces at the "emergence of the interstices—the overlap and displacement of domains of difference . . . collective experiences of nationness, community interest, or cultural value are negotiated" (p. 2). Sociologist Mohammad Tamdgidi (2011) compares the emancipatory discourses and practices of Anzaldúa's theory of borderlands with Edward Said's (1979) critique of colonialism and the construction of the other. While Anzaldúa's theory of Borderlands resonates with Bhabha's Third Space and Said's anticolonial stand, Borderlands goes beyond critique and resistance inscribed within the binary of colonizer/colonized to offer an emancipatory path toward teaching social issues for effecting social and political transformation.

Bringing multiple oppressions of racism, classism, sexism and homophobia into the border experience, Anzaldúa's theory of Borderlands offers educators a language for complicating essentialized categories of identity and simultaneously creating spaces for building bridges across different forms of oppression in the fight for social justice. Her analysis of homophobia as a form of violence and oppression within the border experience serves as an example to educators in redefining and repositioning their knowledge of social issues and the fight against oppressions on many registers. First, Anzaldúa rejects received definitions of identity such as "lesbian" and "homosexual" and opts for the term, "mita y mita" (half and half), a term outside the English language, to subvert conventional sexual and gender categories. Second, by identifying her sexuality in non-English terms, as "mita y mita," Anzaldúa challenges the commonly accepted Chicano belief that homosexuality reflects identifying with Anglo-American culture. Third, for Anzaldúa (1987), occupying this space in-between genders and sexualities is liberating as it offers emancipatory possibilities away from an "absolute despot duality that says that we are able to be only one or the other" (p. 41). Anzaldúa emphasizes that everyone is mita y mita or of mixed identities and hybrid subjectivities. Fourth, Anzaldúa claims borderlands exist wherever there is dialectical tension between power and knowledge, therefore, the source and workings of power must be analyzed and contested. Fifth, writing in multiple genres of prose, poetry and essays, and moving effortlessly between multiple languages, Anzaldúa constructs Borderlands as a place and space—a relational theory for teaching difference by breaking conventional boundaries of categorical and binary thinking, building bridges across disparate communities, and changing consciousness.

Anzaldúa's multiple strategies for reconstructing Borderlands reminds educators that the intersection of race, ethnicity, language, class, gender, sexuality and oppression plays out at the U.S.–Mexico border and across several international sites (Bosnia, Armenia, Sudan, Rwanda) as a matrix of power relations, including legally sanctioned violence and intensive policing leading to cultural genocide for specific peoples and individuals affected by these dynamics of power. The above discourses of power, privilege and domination, the construction of social identities, and movements of resistance and oppression demand classroom analysis and reflection as they have consequences for students and teachers, and are, therefore, critical to how educators think about identity and engage in teaching as an act of social justice.

MESTIZA CONSCIOUSNESS: VALIDATING WOMEN'S LIVED EXPERIENCE AND KNOWLEDGE

Borderlands as a relational theory for teaching difference embodies multiplicity while *mestiza* (mixed racial ancestry, namely, European and indigenous) is the process of validating lived experience of the self and other, breaking boundaries, and bridging differences, aiming towards an inclusive consciousness. Anzaldúa (1987) introduces the concept of "a new mestiza consciousness, una conciencia de mujer" (p. 99), a consciousness of the Borderlands where cultures, races, and languages come together in a new awareness of the self as relational to difference. The mestiza consciousness represents a feminist epistemology denoting a shift "from convergent thinking, analytical reasoning that tends to use rationality to move toward a single goal (a Western mode), to divergent thinking, characterized by movement away from set patterns and goals toward a more whole perspective, one that includes rather than excludes" (Anzaldúa 1987, p. 101). Rejecting ontological categories and dualities such as woman/man, and Mexican/American, Anzaldúa reinvents the mestiza as collective Chicana identity/ies—mestiza, tejana, Aztec, Mexican and Mexican American. The concept of multiple identities of the new mestiza create spaces for educators to build bridges between diverse cultures, races, genders, and languages so that teaching and learning are acts of inclusion.

Anzaldúa's concepts align with, as well as subvert, existing forms of knowledge. She acknowledges the concept of mestiza is borrowed from Mexican philosopher and writer, José Vasconcelos (1997), whose writings offer indigenous and aesthetic knowledge in opposition to the privileged place of rationality in positivist Eurocentric epistemology. Vasconcelos' notion of a cosmic race, *la raza cosmica*, is a critique of racial essentialization in white America and promotes a cosmic identity as the solution to racial intolerance. Anzaldúa's new mestiza has also been compared to Françoise Lionnet's (1998) Métissage as a theory of mixed identities. Lionnet (1998), a Comparative Literature and African Studies scholar, explains that the Métissage allows women to "articulate new visions of ourselves, new concepts that allow us to think otherwise, to bypass the symmetries and dichotomies that have governed the ground and the very condition of the possibility of thought" (p. 326). According to Lionnet, Métissage is a reading practice, a poststructural construct exemplifying hybridity and multiplicity that transcends boundaries and confirms solidarity across differences when reading a text.

Although conceptually similar in many ways to Vasconcelos' cosmic race theory, and Lionnet's Métissage, Anzaldúa's mestiza is more than either a rejection of racial categories or a reading practice. The mestiza is a theoretical concept and a practice; it is a call and a collective space for political action against hegemonic and patriarchal discourses that construct women as the other. As Anzaldúa says (1987), it is time for educators to collectively challenge "dominant paradigms, predefined concepts that exist as unquestionable, unchallengeable" (p. 38). This transformative praxis of inclusivity is evidenced in Anzaldúa's edited collection of prose, essays and poems, *Making Face, Making Soul/ Haciendo Caras* (1990) that brings together diverse communities of women—new mestizas—whose teaching and writing is a form of undoing history, subverting the canon, and reclaiming the life stories of those who have been historically marginalized or excluded. As Anzaldúa (1990) says,

> In our mestizaje theories we create new categories for those of us left out or pushed out of the existing ones. We recover and examine nonwestern aesthetics while critiquing western aesthetics; recover and examine nonrational modes and blanked out realities while critiquing rational consensual reality; recover and examine indigenous languages while critiquing the languages of the dominant cultures (p. xxvi).

CONOCIMIENTO: THE PATH TO CHANGING CONSCIOUSNESS

Calling on all new mestizas, women, teachers, writers, students, and activists to fight against oppression, Anzaldúa (2002) says, "now let us shift [from personal change to collective transformation]...the path of conocimiento...inner work, public acts" (p. 571). Anzaldúa makes it clear that conocimiento is more than an intellectual concept; it offers educators a theory of spiritual activism achieved through aesthetic creativity and healing. As Anzaldúa (2002) explains, "writing, art-making, dancing, healing, teaching, meditation, and spiritual activism...Breaking out of your mental and emotional prison and deepening the range of perception enables you to link inner reflection and vision...with social, political and lived experiences to generate subversive knowledge" (pp. 541–542). Accordingly, the path to teaching about social issues by raising consciousness is the connection between the self-and other—personal awareness and a collective consciousness—a form of activism leading to social and political transformation.

As a theory for teaching about social issues such as domination and oppression and changing consciousness, conocimiento resembles Paulo Freire's (1970) "conscientization" as the process of developing critical awareness of teachers' social reality through reflection and collective action. According to Anzaldúa's longtime friend and coauthor, Women's Studies scholar Ana Louise Keating (2005), most of Anzaldúa's concepts lead to conocimiento, an epistemology for all educators that combines reflection, imagination, lived experience, political action, and social justice. According to Keating, conocimiento as a theory is relevant to scholars, teachers, students, writers, and activists involved in the critical work of changing consciousness toward social justice. Together, Borderlands, mestiza consciousness, and conocimiento are transformative in disrupting the status quo in contemporary educational practices.

EL MUNDO ZURDOS: SPIRITUAL ACTIVISM FOR PERSONAL, SOCIAL, AND POLITICAL CHANGE

Conocimiento is the bridge between the personal struggles of teachers and students and collective awareness across differences that leads to El Mundo Zurdos, a form of spiritual activism for social and political transformation. For Anzaldúa, self-change and teaching about social change are two sides of the same coin and she carefully constructs the teacher's position as reciprocal. As cited earlier, according to Anzaldúa (2002), "by changing ourselves we change the world, that traveling El Mundo Zurdos path is the path of a two-way movement—a going deep into the self and an expanding out into the world, a simultaneous recreation of the self and a reconstruction of society" (p. 208). El Mundo Zurdos offers educators an inclusive vision that seeks to dismantle the epistemic hierarchies embedded in Eurocentric epistemologies and supports the production of knowledge from the grassroots level, that is, knowledge produced by subalternized and marginalized communities. Not only does this approach call for inclusion of excluded knowledge from the border experience of marginality but calls for epistemic plurality in the classroom in contrast to the singular white hegemonic narrative embedded as the educational norm. Rather than accept essentialized and universalized approaches to identity and difference, El Mundo Zurdos, as a radical vision, combines spirituality and reflection with political commitment supporting diverse educational knowledge, histories, and experiences that are multilingual, multivoiced and multigender.

Thus, the power of Borderlands, mestizo, and conocimiento, and El Mundo Zurdos as teaching concepts for engendering changing consciousness about social issues stems from the ability of teachers and students to transform exclusions into bridges between the self and other, and from other to self. The move toward changing consciousness provokes teachers and students to reflect on the spaces they occupy in the matrix of power, knowledge, and/or oppression, and cautions against essentializing, universalizing and ranking categories of oppression. In addition, changing consciousness is empowering as it offers teachers and students opportunities for emancipatory praxis by shifting the dominant discourse from essentialism, universalization, and marginalization, to hybridity, multiplicity and inclusivity.

METHODOLOGY FOR BUILDING BRIDGES, CHANGING CONSCIOUSNESS

Autohistoria-Teoria: Writing As a Critical Practice

Combining auto/self with collective/historia, Anzaldúa (2002) describes her methodology as "autohistoria...a genre of writing about one's personal and collective history using fictive elements, a sort of fictionalized autobiography or memoir; an autohistoria—teoría is a personal essay that theorizes" (p. 578). As a counter narrative to the history of the U.S. American side of the border written from a Eurocentric perspective, Anzaldúa writes her own autohistoria-teoria, the simultaneous theorizing of personal autobiography and collective history through the critical lenses of Chicana, queer, and feminist, in a mixture of languages that draws extensively from Aztec and Mexican cultural myths. An effective teaching tool, Autohistoria—teoría promotes transformative change on many levels. In form and content autohistoria—teoría offers educators a methodology for challenging dominant discourses in education and society, disrupting Eurocentric perspectives and norms; critiquing the privileged place of English in academic settings; fighting against patriarchal silencing of women's ways of knowing; and using language as a critical practice for constructing identities that are multiple and hybrid.

Autohistoria-teoria renegotiates the traditional autobiographical "I" that has excluded the voices of women-of-color from autobiographical theories and practices. While the autobiographical "I" has been part of the emancipatory project reflected in women's writing in the 1980s (Gilmore, 1994), Anzaldúa rejects this universal female subject to call into question the exclusion of women-of-color from autobiographical writing; challenges the historical silencing of women in a male-dominated Chicano culture; and addresses the absence of Chicana writers in academic publishing in the United States. Anzaldúa invites women across the color line to explore alternative modes of self-writing for articulating their experience of exclusion and reclaiming their personal and collective presence in history and culture.

Drawing from her indigenous history, language and culture, Anzaldúa's methodology affirms the transformative use of language as a critical teaching tool for redefining the fight for social justice, disrupting normative functions of language steeped in labels that categorize and exclude through dualisms and hierarchies, recovering knowledge that has been silenced or erased, and creating hybrid knowledge in the classroom—knowledge that is multiple and inclusive. Offering educators an emancipatory methodology for theorizing and recovering history, Anzaldúa uses the term mestiza to address women's silence in history and culture. The language of the mestiza gives new meaning to women's experiences in ways that break the conventions of writing by reinventing symbols, metaphors, and styles that represent a new feminist consciousness. When educators see themselves as mestizas in the process of changing consciousness, they develop the ability to perceive the "meaning of deeper realities to see the deep structure below the surface . . . that communicates in images and symbols which are the faces of feelings" (Anzaldúa 1987, p. 60).

Mestizas' bridge-work is an opportunity for educators to build coalitions across different oppressed groups and a form of activism that uses diverse forms of resistance and multiple methods in the fight for social justice. Images and symbols that represent border crossing, bridging, and assembling are at the heart of the mestiza's bridge-work. According to Anzaldúa (1987), "[a]n image is a bridge between evoked emotion and conscious knowledge; words are the cables that hold up the bridge" (p. 90). As part of the bridge-work, Anzaldúa's use of indigenous concepts such as nepantla (in-between state), Coatlique (transitional state between oppression and liberation), and conocimiento—markers of changing consciousness, offer educators classroom strategies for validating students' lived experiences and cultural knowledge.

Anzaldúa's concepts engender a double consciousness in the act of teaching and learning about social issues such as identity and difference, and deconstruct the dynamics of power, knowledge and oppression. On one level of consciousness, drawing concepts from indigenous history and cultural knowledge is transformative as it gives educators a complex understanding of power relations and the historical and political act of recovery as a significant part of changing consciousness.

Contemporary Chicana Studies scholar Chela Sandoval (2000), who has written extensively on the connections between Third Space feminism and production of oppositional consciousness, argues that traditional forms of activism against historical oppression and conventional categories of analysis such as victim and oppressor do not work under present conditions of systematic exclusion of Chicana writing from academic and feminist knowledge. According to Sandoval (2000), Anzaldúa's teaching and writing reflects a "methodology of the oppressed" that plays out as a *"topography* of consciousness in opposition" (p. 54), a talking back to academic elitism, around which changing consciousness is organized. When classroom *topography* deconstructs power and knowledge by remapping excluded histories and cultures and reconstructing the social and political imagination, teachers and students utilize the new language of the mestiza as a form of empowerment for effecting social change.

On another level of consciousness, Anzaldúa's concepts offer educators new reading practices that are constantly being transformed, a condition necessary for teaching about social issues and the transformations that are made possible.

Anzaldúa expanded her theory of Borderlands to develop the concept of nepantla as an in-between space of transition that is not limited to geographical, state, or national lines of domination and exploitation. Rather, nepantla is a site for transformation where teachers and students question received knowledge from family, culture, and beliefs, and from the ensuing conflict, perspectives change. Thus, language becomes a critical tool for teaching about social issues, validating lived experience and diverse autobiographical knowledge, and documenting the process of social and political change.

Legacy of Borderlands, The New Mestiza, Bridgework, and Social Transformation Anzaldúa's epistemological, theoretical and methodological contribution to teaching about social issues is evident in the ways educators, scholars, and activists continue to expand, question, and complicate the range of her knowledge forms and reading practices to mobilize social justice. Anzaldúa's (1981) first coedited anthology, *This Bridge Called My Back*, called on feminist educators and lesbian women-of color to envision new forms of communities and practices and was one of the first anthologies in the United States to reflect a new kind of feminism from women-of-color, ranging from Latina, Black, Native American, and Asian American. Crossing epistemic and methodological boundaries, *Borderlands/La Frontera* (1987) was transformative in disrupting male dominated Chicana writing, challenging oppression by Anglos and Chicano men, and rupturing the politics of language and representation by articulating the new consciousness of border crossers, hybrid identities and multiple differences. This was followed by *Making Face, Making Soul* (1990), a provocative anthology celebrating emancipatory knowledge production by women-of-color largely ignored by white feminists and hitherto excluded from academic publishing. A complement to the first coedited anthology, *This Bridge We Call Home* (2002) revisits identity politics to offer a radical vision for teaching about social issues aimed at promoting social and political transformation in the twenty first century bringing together a plurality of differences, races, sexes, genders, classes, peoples, groups, and cultures.

In recognition of her teaching, scholarship and raising consciousness, Anzaldúa was honored with the Before Columbus Foundation American Book Award (1986), Lesbian Rights Award (1991), Sappho Award of Distinction (1992), National Endowment for the Arts Fiction Award (1991), Lambda Lesbian Small Press Book Award (1991), American Studies Association Lifetime Achievement Award (2001), and was posthumously awarded a doctor of philosophy in Literature by University of California, Santa Cruz. Among Anzaldúa's many honors is an archive containing her published and unpublished works housed at the Nettie Lee Benson Latin American Collection at The University of Texas, Austin. Equally significant to her legacy is The Society for the Study of Gloria Anzaldúa, established in 2005 by The University of Texas, San Antonio where an international conference was held in Anzaldúa's honor in 2012, under the title, "*El Mundo Zurdo: An International Conference. Transformations.*"

The enduring legacy of Anzaldúa's teaching, scholarship and activism is invaluable to educators invested in social justice. While Black and Latina feminists and lesbian and queer theorists have captured the complexity of lived experiences using multiple epistemologies and methodologies, Anzaldúa's works refocuses educators toward analyzing the ways in which multiple movements such as Chicano/a, feminist, queer, and lesbian have informed teaching and learning as a complex emancipatory and resistance project for rethinking identity and changing consciousness toward inclusion. Since the 1980s, Latina feminists have contributed to autobiographical theorizing and the politics of identity along a spectrum of positionalities ranging from de-colonial fictionalized narratives (Perez, 1999), methodology of the oppressed, (Sandoval, 2000), critical Latina race theory, (Hurtado, 1996; Castillo, 1995), and identity and difference, (Alarcón, 1990). Similarly, critical race theorists such as hooks (1989), poet-activist, Lorde (1984), and McKay (1998) have questioned the rejection of Black women's autobiography from academic writing, while postcolonial feminist Mohanty (1991) challenges the exclusion of third world feminists from the narratives of white feminism. In comparison, Anzaldúa articulates a range of new theoretical approaches, contexts, and conversations that opens spaces for educators to contribute toward shifting conventional boundaries of thought in education, history, geography, art and literature; Chicana, feminist, and queer movements; Chicana, ethnic, cultural, American, border and transnational studies for teaching about social issues and change consciousness toward social and political transformation.

When educators are aware of intersectionality, that is, the relationship of categories defining identities and of the ways in which meaning is assigned to and between categories, they are able to reconceptualize a transformative vision of education based on multiplicities of shifting identities and coalitions across race, class, gender, language, sexuality and other differences. According to Davalos (2008), when compared with Black and Latina scholars theorizing difference, Anzaldúa's prominence in feminist theory is based on the gap her work addresses in theorizing multiple subject positions—race, class, gender, and sexuality along with the day-to-day reality of social issues that impact education such as immigration, language, religion, and nationality. Davalos (2008) notes that Anzaldúa's multiply situated and multi-genre writing was largely ignored by ethnic studies, postmodern analysis, and mainstream feminist scholarship under claims that her writing was "poetic but not theoretical, and, worse, divisive or irrelevant" (p. 152), and while other fields such as cultural studies used her work they did not acknowledge the influence of her contribution to theory or methodology. Davalos views Anzaldúa's methodology as a major landmark for opening possibilities for Chicana feminism while Acosta-Belén and Bose (2000) credit Anzaldúa with introducing gender into ethnic studies, racial issues into women's studies, and fostering a dialogue on international issues such as human rights, peace, immigration, and the environment.

Anzaldúa's methodology, autohistoria-teoria, offers educators a form of critical inquiry reflecting a search for emancipatory knowledge that is disruptive, unconventional, and nonlinear and offers transformative possibilities for knowing identity/ies, experiences and the world otherwise. Tara Lockhart (2006), a professor of English, speaks of Anzaldúa's multigenre, multivoiced writing as a process of negotiation and inclusion that expands the possibilities of how classroom knowledge is constructed. According to Lockhart, Anzaldúa's writing is in the lineage of radical feminists such as Wollstonecraft, Woolf, de Beauvoir, and hooks', reflecting a privileging of marginalized experiences as opposed to canonical knowledge, disrupting arbitrary categories and hierarchies that divide academic disciplines and scholarly writing, and championing the cause of social justice.

While the above scholars support Anzaldúa's works and perceive its ongoing educational and transformative value, her work has also generated criticism for many reasons. For example, Maria Lugones (2005) argues that when theorizing the mestiza consciousness, Anzaldúa fails to speak to the psychology of oppression and resistance in relation to collective resistance, weakening the solidarity that Anzaldúa herself documents. For Lugones (2005), "[u]nless resistance is a social activity, the resistor is doomed to failure in the creation of a new universe of meaning, a new identity, a *rata mestiza*" (mixed race) (Lugones 2005, p. 97). Similarly, Pablo Vila (2003) finds Anzaldúa's mestiza theory abstract and utopian while Benjamin Alire Saenz (1997) views Anzaldúa's indigenous references as a case of romantic longing of little value to contemporary education. Castillo (2006) argues that Anzaldúa's personal experience as a Chicana lesbian feminist from the southwest of the United States essentializes identity and excludes other forms of border experiences thus limiting the teaching potential of her writing.

Both sides of the debate, however, agree that even though the notion of Borderlands and the new mestiza consciousness are problematic, they have transformative potential for education as they not only offer theories and methodologies for teaching about social issues but also call teachers and students to political action. A major contributor in keeping Anzaldúa's legacy alive, Keating (2005) maintains that most of Anzaldúa's concepts and their epistemological and emancipatory potential remain undertheorized and underexplored. Keating addresses this gap by bringing together a multidisciplinary group of teachers and scholars in an edited collection, *Entre Mundo/Among Worlds* (2005), to reflect critically on their own lived experiences in relation to Anzaldúa's concepts, theories, and methodologies. Accordingly, educators, scholars and activists explore Anzaldúa's theoretical and methodological contributions to Chicana, Latina and Xican, feminist, LGBTQ, emancipatory, and peace studies as well as critical and cultural theory using autohistoria-teoria for teaching about social issues and bringing political change.

Contributing to existing frameworks of critical theory and its emancipatory commitment to social issues aimed at promoting social justice, at the core of Anzaldúa's legacy is the opening of alternative knowledge forms, validating lived experiences and possibilities of existence, hitherto unacknowledged in teaching and learning. Anzaldúa's writing suggests that ongoing critique and resistance are preconditions for teaching about social issues aimed at emancipation from oppression, that emancipation rests on the ability of educators, scholars and activists to theorize difference using language as a critical practice in the construction of emancipatory knowledge, and that concepts such as Borderlands, mestiza consciousness, and autohistoria are theoretical and methodological tools for transformative praxis. Anzaldúa's theories and methodologies are not meant to override the importance of differences in race, ethnicity, gender, class, language or sexuality in envisioning a transformative political project of emancipation from oppression, rather, they underscore the significance of teachers and students working across differences and recognizing diversity and plurality. Anzaldúa's life-work is an emancipatory project of critiquing social issues in mainstream U.S. society and within the academic tradition to deconstruct ideological and institutional power differentials, reaching across communities to act against intolerance and oppression, and teaching about social issues by breaking boundaries, building bridges, and changing consciousness toward social justice.

HOW MIGHT TEACHERS TRANSFORM TEACHING AND LEARNING THROUGH ANZALDÚAN PEDAGOGY?

This section offers a pedagogical framework for teaching and learning that draws from five key components of Anzaldúa's scholarship. These five interrelated components, aligned with the major tenets of critical theory are: (a) dialogue and discussion as democratic practices; (b) critique as inquiry; (c) counter-narratives as production of knowledge; (d) critical self-reflection for personal change; and, (e) activism for social and political transformation. In a traditional classroom, teaching is grounded in the teacher as the central authority in the classroom where standardized content knowledge reflects dominant cultural values and learning is measured by assimilation into dominant social, cultural, and educational norms. In contrast, Anzaldúan pedagogy is based on teaching as a political act. Subsequently, the desired goal of education is liberation from imposed social, cultural, and educational norms that categorize and exclude, and in favor of the transformation of students from passive recipients of dominant knowledge to agents of personal and social change, as well as student empowerment through an ongoing commitment to social justice.

Dialogue and Discussion

A radical pedagogy committed to social change centered on dialogue and discussion implies active participation of teachers and students in the class-room. Rather than invest authority in the central figure of the teacher in the classroom and attempt to teach students as passive listeners, Anzaldúan pedagogy grounded is in dialogue and discussion is interactive, directing teachers and students toward discussing and examining their own experiences, all the while developing a critical social consciousness by validating the voices of all students in the classroom. One way to structure such a classroom is to place classroom desks and chairs in a Freirian circle, and have students lead class-room discussion so that the focus of learning is not the teacher or content knowledge but the validation of experiential knowledge. Students are the "experts" and learning is a collaborative and democratic process where no single source of knowledge is privileged over others.

In order to initiate discussion, short films, current news clips, YouTube videos, and local, national and international events are presented for elicit-ing student response and opening students' to sharing their own perspec-tives as well as recognizing multiple perspectives in the classroom. Discus-sion and dialogue break the culture of silence in traditional classrooms and present all students with opportunities for speaking, thus creating a climate for students—including those who have been historically outside the dominant culture of schooling—to participate fully in the learning pro-cess. When students listen to multiple perspectives they are able to recog-nize differences in race, class, gender, language, and sexuality. Thus, teach-ing begins with student knowledge, while multiple ways of knowing diffuse centralized power in the classroom thus counteracting domination, hierar-chies, and exclusion by generating students' cultural knowledge and cocre-ating a curriculum in which experience is a source of academic knowledge.

Critique as Inquiry

Anzaldúan pedagogy of critique as inquiry refers to a systematic analysis of social, cultural, political, and educational issues with the spotlight fo-cused on understanding the roots of inequality, exploitation, and oppres-sion, and resisting all forms of domination that maintain or reproduce the status quo in school and society. Classroom activities focus on examining race, ethnicity, gender, and language based domination and oppression. The aim of critique as inquiry is to transform student consciousness, which goes beyond a shift in attitude toward developing critical thinkers capable of delving deeper into issues and problems in order to analyze the politi-cal nature of questions such as, "What knowledge is of most worth? Who decides? Who is rendered silent or invisible in the process? Who is excluded? Who benefits? How am I implicated in these processes? How is language implicated in this process of knowledge formation and organization? What other ways might knowledge be constructed?"

For example, in a social studies course, students might raise the aforementioned critical questions when comparing three different types of readings: (a) the history textbook suggested by the school district, (b) *The Making of Americans: Democracy and Our Schools* by E. D. Hirsch Jr. (2010), and (c) *A People's History of the United States* by Howard Zinn (2001). By developing critical reading skills for critique and analysis, students go beyond dominant forms of knowledge to using a radical and democratic approach to identifying, analyzing and transforming knowledge through critique as inquiry. In addition, Anzaldúan pedagogy of critique as inquiry can be used by teachers to create more empowering learning environments for students, where students are able to explore various intersections of gender, race, power, and privilege, and begin to see how school subjects, institutional structures, culture of schooling, and cultural diversity and differences are interrelated in complex ways.

Counter-Narratives as Knowledge That Counts

The term "counter-narratives" is a political position in opposition to the dominant narrative. The dominant narrative refers to the domination of Western philosophical tradition in social, cultural, and educational knowledge that is based on universalization, and is articulated through categories, binaries and hierarchies that marginalize and exclude. Therefore, anyone who is outside the dominant narrative is excluded based on cultural or academic difference, such as race, nationality, ethnicity, language, sex, gender, language or ability. In simplistic terms, the norm as suggested by the dominant narrative represents white, middle class, heterosexual males, while counter-narratives emerge from marginalized groups such as girls, students of color, gay, lesbian, bisexual, transgender students, and students who speak English as a second language. When including counter-narratives in their pedagogy, teachers might design curriculum aimed at deconstructing the dominant narrative, and offer alternatives to the dominant discourse in school and society.

For example, students might study identity development and the production of knowledge in relation to the dominant and counter-narratives by working on an interdisciplinary class assignment inquiring into various aspects of hip-hop as pedagogy. Students might investigate the historical, geographical and cultural origins of hip-hop; the different trajectories of thought within hip-hop; how hip-hop has been received by the dominant

narrative; how it challenges dominant narratives of African-American stereotypes and generalizations in society; how youth navigate the space of hip
hop music in relation to race, class, gender, embodiment, inequality, and
privilege, race relations in society, urban gentrification, civil rights; and hip
hop as a social and cultural emancipatory movement. In this sense, counter-
narratives as pedagogy transforms how students think about and transform
knowledge in and outside the classroom.

Critical Self-reflection for Personal Change

The goal of Anzaldúan pedagogy is student emancipation that begins
with critical reflection. Such a pedagogical approach provides students with
the space for dialogue and discussion, a language of critique, recognition of
multiple narratives, and opportunities to question their own roles in sustaining various forms of domination, subordination, hierarchies, and exclusion.
Ideally, when reflecting, students analyze their own assumptions, beliefs, and
practices vis-à-vis self and others, and question their role in sustaining practices
such as sexism, racism, homophobia and class exploitation. In the process of
self-examination, students have a heightened awareness of the self and other
worldviews, especially in terms of racism, sexism, oppression, and domination.

In the classroom, teachers who support self-reflection as a measure of
student learning offer students opportunities to reflect in different ways,
such as journal writing, blogging, and digital storytelling on a regular basis.
When mentoring students, teachers might provide guiding questions or
introductory sentences to provoke thinking, and help them move from description of events to deeper analysis, and critical self-reflection. According
to Anzaldúan pedagogy, language reproduces dominant power relationships, but transformative teachers use language to critique and dismantle
oppressive structures of society. As a point of reflection, students use language as a critical teaching tool for fighting oppression by analyzing their
own language practices and disrupting the traditional language of the classrooms structured within binaries, such as success and failure and categories
such as Low English Proficiency learners (LEPs) and advancement placement grouping. The new language of the classroom validates multiplicities
of identities, experiences, histories, and languages without privileging any
single identity or narrative.

Activism for Social and Political Transformation

According to Anzaldúan pedagogy, social and political transformation
is a reflective and collaborative process referring to the application of

knowledge that goes beyond critiquing systems of power and privilege to addressing injustices and inequality in school and society. Such transformations combine theory and practice, encompass social justice ideals and envision hope for the future. This pedagogical approach attempts to create new forms of knowledge grounded in emancipatory practices articulating the narratives of the oppressed, and combines critical knowledge with social and political action.

As agents of change, students and teachers produce transformative knowledge from their own lived experiences and oppressions. Through democratic dialogue and discussion that reflect the principles of nondiscrimination and nonrepression students are given opportunities to develop, formulate, and present their viewpoints and listen to diverse views. Teachers and students make a conscious effort to engage in debates on controversial social and political issues such as gun control, immigration and civil rights, equal pay for equal work, which raise students' consciousness about social injustices and incite them to engage in political actions for bringing change. Anzaldúan pedagogy is a set of classroom practices, teaching strategies, approaches to content, and relationships to people and community that is aimed at social and political transformation and committed to social justice.

NOTES

1. A particularly important issue for Anzaldúa was the un-kept promise of the Guadalupe-Hidalgo treaty of 1848 between the United States and Mexico, which left Mexicans on the U.S. side of the border dispossessed of land and their civil rights undermined by Anglo domination. According to Anzaldúa, (1987) this exploitation is reflected in the current historical patterns of criminalization, incarceration, and marginalization of Chicano/a border communities and their continued otherization. Anzaldúa (1987) asserted that she was always conscious of her marginalized status within U.S. American society, which fueled her resistance against different forms of oppression, and brought her closer to Mexican-Aztlán cultural narratives, aesthetics, and spirituality.

REFERENCES

Acosta-Belén, E. & Bose, C. E., (2000). U.S. Latina and Latin American feminisms: Hemispheric encounters. *Signs, 25(4)*, 113–1119.

Alarcón, N. (1990). The Theoretical subject(s) of This bridge called my back and Anglo- American feminism. In Cherri Moraga & Gloria Anzaldúa (Eds.), *Making face/Making soul Haciendo Caras* (pp. 356–359). San Francisco, CA: Aunt Lute Books.

Anzaldúa, G. E. (1981). El Mundo Zurdo: The vision. In Cherrie Moraga and Gloria Anzaldúa (Eds.). *This bridge called my back: Writings by radical women-of-color*, (pp. 195–96). New York, NY: Kitchen Table: Women-of-color Press.

Anzaldúa, G. (1987). *Borderlands/La frontera: The new mestiza*. San Francisco: Spinsters/Aunt Lute Books.

Anzaldúa, G. (1990). Haciendo caras, una entrada. In Gloria Anzaldúa (Ed.), *Making face, Making soul/Haciendo caras: Creative and critical perspectives by women-of-color* (p. xv–xxviii), San Francisco, CA: Aunt Lute Foundation.

Anzaldúa, G. (1994–95). Working the borderlands, becoming mestiza: An interview with Gloria Anzaldúa, *disClosure: A Journal of Social Theory*, Vol. 4, 75–96.

Anzaldúa, G. E. (2000). Now let us shift... the path of conocimiento...inner work, public acts. In G. E. Anzaldúa & A. L. Keating (Eds.), *This bridge we call home: radical visions for transformation.* (pp. 540–578). New York, NY: Routledge, 540–78.

Anzaldúa, G. E. (2005). *Gloria Evangelina Anzaldúa Papers, 1942–2004.* English and Spanish Repository Benson Latin American Collection. Austin, TX: The University of Texas at Austin.

Anzaldúa, G. (2009). To(o) Queer the Writer-Loca, escritoria y chicana. In Ana Louise Keating (Ed.), *The Gloria Anzaldúa reader.* (pp. 163–175). Durham, NC: Duke University Press.

Anzaldúa, G., & Keating, A. (2002). (Un)natural bridges, (Un)safe spaces. In G. E. Anzaldua & A. L. Keating (Eds.). *This bridge we call home: Radical visions for transformations.* New York, NY: Routledge.

Bhabha, H. (1994). *The location of culture.* NY, NY: Routledge.

Castillo, A. (1995). *Massacre of the dreamers: Essays on Xicanisma.* Albuquerque, NM: University of New Mexico Press.

Castillo, D. A. (2006). Anzaldúa and transnational American Studies. *PMLA, 121(1),* 260–265.

Davalos, K. M. (2008). Sin Vergüenza: Chicana feminist theorizing. *Feminist Studies, 34(1/2),* 151–171.

Feghali, Z. (2011). Re-articulating the New Mestiza. *Journal of International Women's Studies. Special Issue, 12(2),* 61–74.

Freire, P. (1970). *Pedagogy of the oppressed.* NY, NY: Continuum.

Gilmore, L. (1994). *Autobiographics: A feminist theory of women's self-representation.* Ithaca, NY: Cornell University Press.

Hirsch, E. D. (2010). *The making of Americans: Democracy and our schools.* New haven, CT: Yale University Press.

Hurtado, A. (1989). Reflections of White Feminism: A Perspective from a woman of color. In S. Chan (Ed.), *Social and gender boundaries in the United States* (pp. 155–186). Lewiston, NY: Edwin Mellen Press.

hooks, b. (1989). Writing Autobiography. In S. Smith & J. Watson (Eds.), *Women, autobiography, theory* (pp. 429–432). Ithaca: Cornell University Press.

Keating, A. (2005). Shifting Worlds, una entrada. In A. L. Keating (Ed.), *EntreMundos/Among worlds: New perspectives on Gloria E. Anzaldúa* (pp. 1–12). NY, NY: Palgrave Macmillan.

Lionnet, Françoise. (1998). The Politics and Aesthetics of Métissage. In S. Smith & J. Watson (Eds.), *Women, autobiography, theory* (pp. 325–336). Ithaca, NY: Cornell University Press.

Lockhart, T. (2006). Writing the self: Gloria Anzaldúa, textual form, and feminist epistemology. *Michigan Feminist Studies*, Vol. 20, http://hdl.handle.net/2027/spo.ark5583.0020.002

Lorde, A. (1984). *Sister outsider: Essays and speeches.* Berkeley, CA: The Crossing Press.

Lugones, M. (2005). From within terminative stasis: Creating active subjectivity, resistant agency. In A. L. Keating (Ed.), *Entre mundos/among worlds: New perspectives on Gloria E. Anzaldúa.* (pp. 85–99). New York, NY: Palgrave Macmillan.

Lunsford, A. A. (1997). Toward a Mestiza Rhetoric: Gloria Anzaldúa on Composition and Postcoloniality. *JAC A Journal of Rhetoric, Culture, & Politics, 18*(1), 1–27.

McKay, N. Y. (1995). The narrative self: Race, politics, and culture in Black American women's autobiography. In D. C. Stanton & A. J. Stewart (Eds.), *Feminisms in the academy* (pp. 74–94). Ann Arbor, MI: University of Michigan Press.

Mohanty, C. T. (1991). Introduction: Cartographies of struggle. In C. Mohanty, A. Russo, & L. Torres. (Eds.), *Third world women and the politics of feminism* (pp. 1–47). Bloomington, IN: Indiana University Press.

Moraga, C. & Anzaldúa, G. (1981). Entering the lives of other: Theory in the flesh. In C. Moraga and G. Anzaldúa (Eds.), *This bridge called my back: Writings by radical women-of-color,* (p. 23). New York, NY: Kitchen Table: Women-of-color Press.

Perez, E. (1999). *The decolonial imaginary: Writing Chicanas into history.* Bloomington, IN: Indiana University Press.

Said, E. W. (1979). *Orientalism.* New York, NY: Random House.

Saenz, B. A. (1997). In the Borderlands of Chicano identity. In S. Michaelson & D. E. Johnson (Eds.), *Border theory: The limits of cultural politics* (pp. 68–96). Minneapolis: University of Minnesota Press.

Sandoval, C. (2000). *Methodology of the oppressed.* Minneapolis, MN: University of Minnesota Press.

Tamdgidi, M. (2011). The simultaneity of self- and global transformations: Bridging with Anzaldúa's liberating vision. In A. L. Keating & G. González-López (Eds.), *Bridging: How Gloria Anzaldúa's Life and Work Transformed Our Own* (pp. 218–225). Austin, TX: University of Texas Press.

Torres, H. A. (1992). Gloria Anzaldúa. (Editor). In *Dictionary of Literary Biography.* Francisco A Lumeli and Carl R. Shirley Vol.122. (pp. 1–17). Detroit, MI: Gale Research.

Vasconcelos, J. (1997). *The cosmic race: A bilingual edition.* 1925. Trans. Didier Jaen. Baltimore, MA: Johns Hopkins University Press.

Vila, P. (2003). The limits of American Border Theory. In Pablo Vila (Ed.), *Ethnography at the border* (pp. 306–341). Minneapolis, MN: University of Minnesota Press.

Yarbro-Bejarano, Y. (1994). Gloria Anzaldúa's Borderlands/La frontera: Cultural Studies, "Difference," and the non-unitary subject. *Cultural Critique, 28,* 5–28.

Zinn, H. (2001). *A people's history of the United States.* New York, NY: Harper Perennial Classics.

ANNOTATED BIBLIOGRAPHY

Anzaldúa, G. (1987). *Borderlands/La Frontera: The new mestiza.* San Francisco, CA: Aunt Lute Books.

This is a groundbreaking anthology of essays and poems, useful for teaching about identity and difference, challenging the politics of representation, and re-conceptualizing identity and difference as hybrid and multiple. Born out the border experience of marginality as a Chicana, lesbian, activist, and writer, the anthology remaps the meaning of border experience as a historical, ideological, and emotional site of resistance against raced, classed, gendered, and homophobic oppressions faced by peoples and cultures inhabiting different kinds of borders. *Borderlands* continues to influence educators from a range of disciplines such as Chicana, Latina, queer, feminist, American, literary, and border studies.

Anzaldúa, G. (1993). *Friends from the other side/Amigos del otro lado.* Ill. Consuela Mendez. San Francisco, CA: Children's Book Press.

Anzaldúa, G. (1995). *Prietita and the ghost woman/Prietita y la llorona.* Ill. Maya Christina Gonzalez. San Francisco, CA: Children's Book Press.

These two children's' bilingual books add an interesting dimension to Anzaldúa's writing as many of her ideas such as borderlands and conocimiento are introduced in them. These are narrative accounts of border crossings and friendships made during the process of crossing different kinds of borders beginning with the U.S.–Mexico border. Anzaldúa identified with the name Prieta as it represented mestizo identity that is Mexican American and Indian. Saying that although the books are fictionalized, parts of her life are embedded in the stories.

Anzaldúa G., (1990). (Ed.). *Making face, making soul/Haciendo caras: Creative and critical perspectives by women-of-color.* San Francisco, CA: Aunt Lute Foundation.

This book is interesting as it brings together women-of-color educators, writers, and activists from academia as well as outside academia. In regard to teaching about social issues, the chapters offer educators counter discourses to dominant discourses in society and traditional theorizing in academic writing. The authors analyze the complexity of internalized oppression and offer ways in which women-of-color are able to find their voice inventing by new theories and methodologies for reclaiming their history and experiences. The anthology is divided into seven sections that articulate the narratives of women-of-color on the theme of silencing, resistance, racism to love, humor and hope, and most importantly, about building coalitions across different communities.

Anzaldúa, G. & Keating, A. (2002). (Editors). *This bridge we call home: Radical visions for transformations.* New York, NY: Routledge.

This anthology is a sequel to *This Bridge Called my Back* and examines, expands, and critiques social and political issues that perpetuate privilege and oppression. Unlike the first anthology, this includes chapters by women-of-color as well as men on their experience with marginality based on race, gender, class, ethnicity, sexuality, nationality, religion, age, geographical location, and disability. This sequel focuses on building bridges across people, groups, and cultures and advocates integrating theory with practice and presents theorizing, critique, and interpretation as forms of praxis that lead to social change.

Anzaldúa, G. & Keating, A. (2000). *Interviews/Entrevistas*. Eds. Gloria Anzaldúa & Ana Louise Keating. New York, NY: Routledge.

These interviews with Gloria Anzaldúa span two decades, and are useful for readers as they open up her personal and professional world and provide a complex understanding of Anzaldúa's spiritual writing mind and an insight into her changing identity vis-à-vis social movements such as Chicana and feminist. *Interviews/Entrevistas* includes some intensely personal interviews elaborating on Anzaldúa's life and family, people she worked with, the complicated realities of her life, her beliefs about performativity and sexual identities, the politics of desire, the body, and spirituality.

Barnard, I. (1997). Gloria Anzaldúa queer *mestisaje. MELUS 22*, 35–53.

While there is considerable scholarship that explores Gloria Anzaldúa's contribution to Chicana feminism and Chicano/a studies, her contribution to queer theory remains unrecognized. Ian Bernard takes on the task of addressing this gap by examining Anzaldúa's uses of queerness in her book *Borderlands/La Frontera* published in 1987. According to Bernard, before the term "queer" was recognized as an academic concept, Anzaldúa was writing about the meaning of queer and queerness but seldom got credit for her contribution toward politicizing identity as an empowering state of queer-ness.

Cantú, Norma E. (2011). Doing work that matters: Gloria Anzaldúa in the international arena. *Signs, Vol. 37*(1), 1–5.

In this brief introduction to the Signs Comparative Perspectives Symposium on Gloria Anzaldúa, Norma Cantu maps Gloria Anzaldúa's work as part of the international legacy of Anzaldúa's theories and methodologies in academic circles around the world. The collection consists of writing by scholars from around the world, and includes such topics as the struggles of educators teaching about social issues, women fighting for social justice, and reflections on border experiences from Poland, Egypt, Japan, Spain, Italy, and Austria among others.

Contreras, S. M. (2008). *Blood lines: Myth, indigenism, and Chicana/o literature*. Austin, TX: The University of Texas Press.

An interesting book that looks at a broad range of authors, including Gloria Anzaldúa, focused on indigenous knowledge, theories and methods in Chicano cultural politics. Contreras brings a new understanding to Anzaldúa's writing by situating her within other scholars of her time and bringing out the contradictory and ambiguous relationship of the writers to the project of European modernism, on the one hand, and the postrevolutionary Mexican state, on the other. By highlighting intertextualities such as those between Anzaldúa and D. H. Lawrence, Contreras deconstructs the notion of indigenous, native, and primitive claiming that in the process of renouncing modernism it actually reinforces it.

Delgadillo, T. (2011). *Spiritual mestizaje religion, gender, race, and nation in contemporary Chicana narrative.* Durham, NC: Duke University Press.

Exploring Gloria Anzaldúa's mestiza consciousness as a theory of spiritual mestizaje, Delgadillo adds another layer of interpretation to Anzaldúa's theory previously unexplored to this extent. Delgadillo argues that the theory of the spiritual *mestizaje* is one of Anzaldúa's greatest legacies in terms of defining queer feminist Chicana theory, and providing Chicana feminists with a space to write their own autobiographies. Delgadillo analyzes the role of spiritual *mestizaje* in Anzaldúa's work and in relation to existing theories of spirituality that offer resistance to historical oppression.

Keating, A. (2005). (Ed.). *EntreMundos/AmongWorlds: New perspectives on Gloria Anzaldúa.* New York, NY: Palgrave MacMillan.

This collection of diverse writings is representative of Anzaldúa's influence in empowering 21st century classrooms as authors expand Anzaldúa's theories and methodologies in their own commitment to social change arguing for coalition building through interdisciplinary writing, multiplicities of identities, and social, political and spiritual activism. Authors expand concepts such as *nepantla* as spaces of opportunities, *auto-historia* for validating funds of knowledge, *nos/otras* as the bridge between self and other, and *conocimiento* as deep perception leading to change for teaching about social issues and practicing inclusion.

Keating, A. (2009). (Ed.). *The Gloria Anzaldúa reader.* Durham, NC: Duke University Press.

This collection is a must for readers as it contains several previously unpublished pieces that offer critical insights into Gloria Anzaldúa's life and career, her childhood, education, her writing process, teaching experiences, health issues, and her spiritual activism. The collection also provides evidence of the role Anzaldúa's writing played in shaping contemporary Chicano/a studies, queer theory, the challenges facing gay and lesbian writers, and coalition-building as part of teaching and learning. The book is considered critical to understanding identity and difference in light of current U.S.–Mexico border tensions and its relation to immigration, incarceration, and border policing.

Keating, A. (Ed.) (1996). *Women reading, women writing: Self-invention in Paula Gunn Allen, Gloria Anzaldúa, and Audre Lorde.* Philadelphia, PA: Temple University Press.

In this book, Ana Louise Keating adds another theoretical dimension to Anzaldúa's works by juxtaposing her with Paula Gunn Allen and Audre Lorde. Keating compares Allen's liminality and Native American consciousness, Lorde's sister/outsider and African American consciousness, and Anzaldúa's *mestiza* experience as Chicano/a border consciousness to argue for their empowering and transformative potential in teaching about social issues. Keating provokes readers to reflect on their own border experiences, insider/outsider positions, and subjectivities and to reposition their identity as multiple, hybrid and always-in-the-making.

Keating, A. L., & González-López, G. (2011). (Eds.). *Bridging: how Gloria Anzaldúa's life and work transformed our own.* Austin, TX: The University of Texas Press.

A unique tribute to the intellectual legacy of Gloria Anzaldúa, this collection offers teachers and students a window into the wider international significance of Anzaldúa's theories and methodologies. The five sections in the collection are examples of how Anzaldúa's writing has influenced educators and scholars around the world. The authors examine the influence of Anzaldúa's concepts in relation to their own lives, further expanding her theories and methodologies such as Borderlands, the new *mestiza, nepantla,* and *autohistoria* as the sites for resistance and possibilities.

Lioi, A. (2008). The best-loved bones: Spirit and history in Anzaldúa's "Entering into the Serpent." *Feminist Studies, The Chicana Studies Issue, 34*(1/2), 73–98.

In this provocative article, Anthony Lioi examine Gloria Anzaldúa's writing from a new perspective – that as a Catholic writer. According to Lioi, while readers might not view Anzaldúa as following any particular catholic tradition, Anzaldúa's writing is replete with symbols, images, and narratives from Catholicism. Lioi notes Anzaldúa's *mestizaje* is a theological concept combining Mexican, Mexican American, Chicana, Aztec, Nahua, Catholic, and Neopagan forms of spiritualities and evidences a profound humanism and universalism.

Moraga, C. & Anzaldúa, G. (Eds.) (1981). *This bridge called my back: Writings by radical women-of-color.* New York, NY: Kitchen Table Press.

This book coedited by Anzaldúa and Cherrie Moraga is a must for educators invested in teaching about social issues such as the marginalization of women-of-color from mainstream U.S. society, white feminism, and academic publication. A revolutionary collection of poems, essays, letters, public statements, journal entries, and interviews written by women-of-color, the collection continues to influence Chicana feminism, Chicana lesbian writers, as well as feminist and queer theory. Autobiographical in content, selections illustrate how Third World radical feminist thought can bring change in the lives of the oppressed.

CHAPTER 21

EXPANDING NOTIONS OF PEDAGOGY

The Works of Carmen Luke

Lisa Edstrom and Rachel Roegman[1]

BEGINNINGS

Carmen Luke was born in Germany and immigrated with her family to Canada when she was six years old, where she completed her schooling, including receiving her BA and MA, from Simon Fraser University in British Columbia. While at Simon Fraser, Luke had an opportunity to work with Professor Kieran Egan (Faculty of Education), a curriculum theorist who expresses an interest in "the way cognitive tools shape our learning and understanding." In addition, Luke worked with Professor Paul Delany, of the English Department, whose publications shortly after Luke's graduation reflect an interest in technology, specifically computers, and literacy. Also in the English Department at Simon Fraser University was Professor Sheila Delany, whose research interests include the roles of women in medieval and modern literature. In addition to these faculty members, Professor Michael E. Manley-Casimir had a direct impact on Luke's developing career

Educating About Social Issues in the 20th and 21st Centuries, pages 433–457
Copyright © 2014 by Information Age Publishing
All rights of reproduction in any form reserved.

as the chairperson of her thesis committee and coeditor of *Children and Television: A Challenge for Education* (1987).

Luke took her first academic position in 1984 in the Department of Social and Cultural Studies at James Cook University in Queensland, Australia, where she earned her PhD and eventually received tenure. During her time there, she founded a women's study center and began publishing feminist scholarship. She also received funding through a James Cook University Merit Research Grant, which partially supported *Feminisms and Critical Pedagogies*, which she coedited with Jennifer Gore (Newcastle University). In 1996, she took a position at University of Queensland in the Graduate School of Education. Her teaching has expanded to include international students on her campus as well as teaching abroad throughout Southeast Asia.

Across her career, Luke has collaborated with a number of different scholars and curriculum theorists, including her husband Allan Luke (University of Queensland), Suzanne de Castell (Simon Fraser University), Vicki Carrington (University of Tasmania), her daughter Haida Luke (Queensland Medical Education Centre), and Diane Mayer (Deakin University).

The historical, gendered, and racialized cultural dynamics of Luke's experiences have worked to influence her academic interests. As she writes in her 1994 article, "White Women in Interracial Families," her own history provides the impetus for much of her work. Important experiences in her life include being in an interracial relationship as a White woman married to a Chinese American man living in Canada and Australia. Additionally, Luke notes the experience as a child of emigrating from Germany to rural Canada after the Second World War and its associated discourses of anti-Semitic and anti-German sentiments. Also of note is that in Luke's early career she was only given short-term teaching contracts to prevent her from being on a tenure track, amidst slights such as colleagues not calling her by her title or even by her name. She ascribes this sexist treatment to gendered dynamics in the university, which constrained her desire to engage in feminist scholarship. After receiving tenure, Luke began to publish more feminist scholarship as she had greater academic freedom.

Luke's first book, *Pedagogy, Printing and Protestantism: The Discourse on Childhood*, examines the relationship between the invention of the printing press, the rise of Protestantism, and the evolution of discourses on childhood. Based on her master's thesis, this book ranges from the connections between the spread of Martin Luther's religious teachings and the use of the printing press as a way of disseminating information, to the ways that Luther's conceptions of childhood changed the popular discourses on children, parenting and education during the sixteenth century. Utilizing Foucauldian discourse analysis (Foucault, 1972, 1981), Luke examines what she calls "the history of an idea" (p. 1) by exploring the discourse of childhood through an analysis of historical texts and studies. In this book, Luke outlines how Luther's teachings, as well as his beliefs about family and God, led to more faith practices in the home that shifted popular conceptions of the role of school and family in childrearing as well as a basic understanding of what childhood and adolescence means. In this shift, schools came under control of the state, instead of under control of local churches representing a variety of Christian faiths. Formal education became mandated so that children were guided along a pathway to salvation following Lutheran doctrine. Children were viewed not only as future citizens, but also as the foundation of a new German country.

She describes the emergence of discourses still valued by today's western society (such as the need for accountability, grouping and sorting of students, and teacher credentialing) as well as the foundations for modern western schooling and curricular approaches. This first work provides the basis for Luke's research and teachings throughout her career. In this book we see the emergence of Luke's interest in ways that technology helps shape the discourses on childhood and feminism, themes she continues to address in her later works. We also see the beginning of an ongoing exploration of who has a voice and whose voices are heard. Luke also employs Foucauldian discourse analysis methodology (Foucault, 1972, 1981), which she has made use of throughout her career when analyzing text from a postrstructuralist feminist standpoint.

SCHOLARSHIP

Luke's early writings on emergent communications technology, literacy, and systems of education are recurrent themes across her scholarship. While she has been involved in research and writing across several lines of inquiry, among the most significant foci across her career are the influences of globalization, hybridization of identity, new literacies, and discourses of childhood. Regardless of the focus or line of inquiry, her standpoint as a poststructural feminist underlies her body of work.

NEW LITERACIES

From the invention of the printing press through texting and tweeting to a call for integrating multiliteracies in the curriculum, the relationships between communications technology and literacy have been central to Luke's work. New technologies and new literacies offer places for education systems to engage students not just in learning higher order skills, but in developing their capacities as critical readers. She argues that new technologies will shape "coming generations' understanding of self and other, local and global politics, social and communicative practices" (2007, p. 54).

Instead of being neutral, technologies can be used as tools to reproduce hegemonic forces or to enable users to challenge hegemonic discourses. Thus it is imperative for students to be aware of the ways that ideologies and their reproduction rely on media technologies—and imperative for schools to engage students in critical analysis of this reliance.

Further demonstrating the need for critical literacy skills, Luke argues that media, whether print-based such as books and magazines, or electronic such as television, the internet, or tweeting, is not something passively absorbed by users. Instead, she asserts that users bring their prior knowledge or schemata to what they see and place this new information into frameworks that already exist. Luke shares data from her research with preservice teachers to show that coursework focusing on the use of multiple literacies can enable future teachers to develop their skills in a way that they may then engage their students in critical ways around multiple literacies.

New literacies offer multiple pedagogical possibilities for preservice teachers (as well as experienced teachers, of course) and youth alike. In addition to introducing preservice teachers to instructional approaches involving new literacies, Luke uses multiple forms of media to introduce preservice teachers to theory and cultural studies. The use of media builds on students' prior knowledge and familiarity with technological literacies, engaging them in ways that traditional texts do not, thus enabling them to develop more complex ideas and analysis. Concomitantly, Luke notes how contemporary youth have greater access to and knowledge of several newer literacies and argues that schools should build on this knowledge base in developing curricula and engaging youth. Instead of being wary of youth who know more about new literacies, this knowledge and expertise is an opportunity to re-engage in formal education.

Across genres, whether print magazines or cybertechnology, Luke raises questions of representation, gender, and race. In regards to gender, Luke and her coauthor H. Luke (1997) argue that that "we need to pay more attention to the way women produce and read themselves into cultural texts and practices, and to pay attention to the generational differences among women so that we don't reproduce a fixed and generalized feminine other —one who no longer matches the multiple realities of many women's lives today" (p. 57).

The focus on multiple realities in relation to gender echoes Luke's work on hybridization of identity as well as her attention to the local standpoint (local standpoint refers to the perspectives of individuals from specific, localized contexts). For Luke, gender, race, culture, and other components of identity do not work as homogenizing forces with one-dimensional subjects.

This focus on new technologies and pedagogy led to Luke's participation with the New London Group. This collective of scholars including Courtney Cazden, James Gee, Norman Fairclough, and eight other educators concerned with literacy pedagogy, began working together in 1994. Their "main concern was the question of life chances as it relates to the broader moral and cultural order of literacy pedagogy" (Cazden, et al., 1996, p. 62). This group produced what they called a manifesto, calling for two things: first, the recognition of the fact that schools increasingly serve multilingual populations, and second, that new technologies are changing the very notions of what it means to be literate in society. Therefore, they focused on "multiliteracies." Whether from her participation in the New London Group, her historical analysis of the Reformation, or her discussions of technology, Luke highlights intersections of identity, questions of power, and tensions in pedagogies.

DISCOURSES OF CHILDHOOD

Beginning with her historical study of Luther, analyses of discourses of childhood have permeated Luke's work. Beginning with the politics and social change taking place in Germany during the sixteenth century she explores shifting notions of childhood up through today, examining the impact that changing technologies and media have on discourses of childhood and family. Throughout, Luke problematizes normalizing discourses that assume a natural state of childhood, noting how different notions of childhood become part of mainstream discourses and how they are then used in different contexts. She takes a critical eye to the ways that educational systems talk about youth, particularly in relation to literacy. For example, she challenges assumptions that early intervention reading strategies can "cure" adolescent disengagement. In an essay coauthored with A. Luke, she argues that "the history of literacy is fraught with a tendency to turn history into nature, when in fact its formation, its practices, and its social distribution are the artifacts of the very material and discourse conditions" (2001, p. 117) of the contexts in which they take place. In other words, literacy is not a "natural" concept, but something socially constructed across time and place.

Within a year of releasing her first book, Luke released *Constructing the Child Viewer: A History of the American Discourse on Television and Children, 1950–1980* (1990). Similar to her first book, Luke uses Foucauldian discourse analysis (Foucault, 1972, 1981) to analyze the influences of technology on children, focusing on television. Luke once again examines the discourses of childhood and family in *Feminisms and Pedagogies of Everyday Life* (1996). In a chapter in this collection of works, she explores the content of parenting magazines from Australia, England, and the United States. Luke writes, "Parenting, then, is a seductive but disciplining discourse embedded in fantasies of idealized normative femininity, exclusively white, middle-class, and heterosexual" (p. 17). Across these texts, Luke questions the idea of "normal," showing how media, policy, and politics attempt to create discourses of childhood—and parenting—that are in fact social constructions that privilege certain groups over others.

INFLUENCES OF GLOBALIZATION

Much of Luke's later work has focused on ways that globalization forces have affected or are likely to affect institutions of higher education, with a particular emphasis on women's experiences in higher education management in Southeast Asia as well as the flow of capital, resources, and people between/across countries. Across this work, Luke makes two key points about globalization, drawing from Appadurai's (1996a, 1996b) notions of the local. First, Luke demonstrates that local standpoints mediate people's experiences of globalization. While globalization is often discussed as a totalizing force in mainstream discourse, Luke's case studies of women's experiences in higher education management in Southeast Asian countries show that "politics of place"—the local sites, cultural histories, and specific sociopolitical and economic factors—allow for women in different contexts to have different experiences of seemingly similar global forces. Luke acknowledges the isomorphic nature of universities across the globe while at the same time showing how women in her studies experience different cultural expectations, requiring analyses at the local level to truly understand the impact of globalization across different sites. For example, in *Globalization and Women in Southeast Asian Higher Education Management* (2002), Luke writes of the Western one-dimensional concept of the glass ceiling that focuses only on patriarchal structures and male actions that prevent women from achieving promotions:

> [Western] women's complicity in glass ceiling politics seems to be a taboo subject. On this issue, however, the women in this study were candid and forthright, explaining why women self-select out at more junior ranks and how senior women can misuse power and be just as diverse and unsupportive of women as men. Patriarchy isn't just about men—the politicians, generals, mullahs, academics, captains of industry, or media—but is powerfully embodied in and enacted by hegemonized women. Patriarchy is indeed a global form but locally inflicted, encoded and enacted. Relatedly, the Asian values of Islamic values resurrection is unquestionably the work of ruling patriarchs across the region. But women are as much its coauthors and supporters as its critics. (p. 655)

Second, Luke questions the idea of center/periphery in discourses of globalization. Western discourses, for example, frequently position people from certain countries, such as those in Southeast Asia where she conducted her research, as peripheral to globalization forces—as places where globalization happens *to* the people and society. In contrast, building off of the idea of local experiences of globalization and based on data from her research, Luke emphasizes how women from so-called peripheral countries actually see themselves as having agency, centering their experiences as part of the impacts and influences of globalization.

HYBRIDIZATION OF IDENTITY AND RACE

A smaller, though no less important, body of Luke's work addresses the hybridization of identity and the role that race plays in societal discourses. In part based on her own experiences in an interracial family, Luke writes about the racialized experiences and ensuing hybridized identities of couples and children in interracial families. Drawing on post-colonial, feminist, and critical race theories, this work demonstrates the need for the social sciences to continue to use the category of "race" in research and policy because of the racialized practices that people experience. In her 2000 article ("Race Matters") with Vicki Carrington, Luke argues, "Racisms exist only insofar as people act upon ideologies of race differentiation; hence prejudice, exclusion, discrimination, racial slurs, or feelings of alienation dislocation or estrangement, are the consequences of socially embedded and legitimated practices that racialize others and that suggest to us that 'race matters.'" (p. 7)

These racialized practices may be particularly evident to people in interracial relationships because the union of two people across different races opens up possibilities for multiple, mixed, and/or shifting identities. In addition, they "may not experience the sense of connectedness or belonging that is typically theorized in the politics of racial identity" (p. 7). Instead, they may experience different treatment, including estrangement, from their families, friends, or workplace as a result of their relationship. Luke's writing encourages readers to consider the specificity of situations in which race is lived, recognizing that for interracial couples there may be additional complexities due to the combination of "lived experiences" and discourses of cultures and races and the hybridization of identity.

POST-STRUCTURAL FEMINISM

While her standpoint is not as clearly stated in her earliest publications, there is no denying that feminism weaves throughout all of Luke's work. From her first book, where she identifies the missing voices of women and children and the implications of this in historical documents as she analyzes the discourses on childhood, to more recent pieces on globalization and new literacies, Luke positions herself as a researcher for whom gender is significant. And, in fact, over the course of her career, Luke has become a champion of poststructural feminist thought. Tackling issues like women's voices in the academy or women's relationships with new technologies, she explores multiple discourses that evolve within male-dominated fields, challenging masculine discourses as well as critical feminist discourses that take a limited view of women's roles and potential.

In 1992, Luke, along with coeditor Jennifer Gore, published *Feminisms and Critical Pedagogy.* In this volume, Luke and Gore compiled a collection of pieces that had been recently published or presented that they believed to be "part of an ongoing provisional debate that challenges the assumptions and political effects generated by critical pedagogy" (p. 8). The editors take a poststructuralist feminist stance in bringing together essays that reject the notion of "single-strategy pedagogies of empowerment, emancipation, and liberation" (p. 7). Luke followed with another volume, which she edited alone, *Feminisms and Pedagogies of Everyday Life* (1996). In this book, the focus is on theorizing feminisms across multiple identities, including gender, race and class. The essays explore ways in which identities are learned, and how popular culture as well as legal and academic discourses shape the ways that individuals are situated and experience the world. Luke writes,

> This anthology is part of the feminist project of revealing the powerfully insistent hegemony of public discourse in maintaining hierarchy and inequality, and of contesting identities of the same and rewriting difference, albeit from the old institutional ground of "the book-system, publishing." Insofar as the teaching machine of institutionalized scholarship is still the primary venue for differentiating, qualifying and authorizing speakers to speak authoritatively within and of a discourse, this book—this unit of discourse—is part of the "habit-change" or ways of thinking things differently within established ground. It emerges from those gaps, endemic to all discourse which are neither stable, constant, nor absolute. (p. 26)

Throughout her works, Luke looks for those gaps that allow opportunities for questioning hegemonic public discourses. In *Globalization and Women in Academia: North/West–South/East* (2001), Luke discusses the challenges of working as a woman at James Cook University, where she eventually established The Centre for Women's Studies. The interdisciplinary center, which collaborates with other universities and local organizations, has as its stated purpose, to "facilitate a critical exploration of women's experiences and achievements through research and teaching" (http://www.jcu.edu.au/sass/swcw/JCUPRD_021265.html, para. 2).

RESEARCH PROJECTS AND ACCOMPLISHMENTS

More recently (2012), Luke has initiated two research projects both funded by the Australian Research Council, that bring together her interests in technology and pedagogy. One project focuses more on globalization and the broader influences of technology, while the other focuses more specifically on school libraries. *Multi-literacies, Libraries and Cybraries: Comparative Case Studies of Australia and the United States* (2002–2003), coinvestigated with Bertram C. Bruce of the University of Illinois at Urbana-Champaign, College of Education, examines the transitions of school libraries into cyber libraries, what the investigators call "cybraries." As a comparative study, this project examines the ways that online information technologies impact school libraries in Australia and the United States. Considering that "new forms of text, knowledge and literacy [are] enabled by networked cybraries," this research explores the ways and documents how educational systems enable and impede such developments" (http://www.uq.edu.au/uqresearchers/researcher/lukec.html?uv_category=prj&prj= 1902388, para. 1).

Luke's other project, *Globalisation: New Media, New Literacies, and Identities* (2002–2004), is comprised of three related investigations. This project looks at: (i) the social effects of new information technologies on literacy and identity, (ii) the impact of globalisation on education, and (iii) new forms of social identity among multiracial families and children. Out of this work Luke hopes to generate new knowledge about, (i) shifts from print to digital literacies and identities among Australian youth, (ii) the role, responsibility, and futures orientation of education systems, and (iii) changing family structures and identities in new socio-demographic contexts (http://www.uq.edu.au/uqresearchers/researcher/lukec.html?uv_category=prj&prj=1902376 para. 1).

In addition to her teaching and research, Luke was awarded a Professorial Research Fellowship at the Centre for Critical and Cultural Studies, University of Queensland, for 2005–2007. She retired from the University and academics in 2007. Over the years, she has sat on many journal and book series editorial boards, and since 1999, remains a coeditor of *Teaching Education*, a quarterly peer reviewed journal published by Taylor & Francis. She is also on the editorial board of *Digital Culture & Education* (DCE), an interactive, open-access, web-published, international interdisciplinary, peer-reviewed journal, devoted to analyzing the impact of digital culture on society.

CONCLUDING THOUGHTS

Carmen Luke has demonstrated through her academic work that she deserves recognition as a scholar who asks questions and explores the ways in which discourses emerge, evolve, and persist in the face of ever changing technology and globalization. From a poststructural feminist standpoint, Luke has explored the positioning of women in the academy in both Western and Asian communities, questioning whose voices are heard and when, as well as the impact that local cultural values have on the experiences and tensions within the discourses about women in academia. Luke expands the discussion of women's roles in academia by moving away from Western centric notions and investigating the experiences of women in Southeast Asia. Moving beyond the academic world, Luke also explores the ways in which popular culture through media and technology creates and shapes discourses of women and childhood. As a feminist scholar, Carmen Luke has contributed to an ongoing conversation about education by expanding notions of pedagogy to include effects of new technologies, globalization, and everyday discourses.

NOTES

1. Special thanks to Carmen Luke for her insights and feedback on this chapter.

REFERENCES

Appadurai, A (1996a) Disjuncture and difference in the global cultural economy. In *Modernity at large: Cultural dimensions of globalization* (pp. 24–47). Minneapolis, MN: University of Minnesota Press.

Appadurai, A (1996b) *Modernity at large: Cultural dimensions of globalization.* Minneapolis, MN: University of Minnesota Press.

Cazden, C., Cope, B., Fairclough, N., Gee, J., & et al. (1996). A pedagogy of multiliteracies: Designing social futures. *Harvard Educational Review, 66*(1), 60–92.

Foucault, M. (1972). *The archeology of knowledge.* New York: Harper and Row.

Foucault, M. (1981). Questions of method: An interview. *Ideology and Consciousness, 8,* 3–14.

Luke, C. (1990). *Constructing the child viewer: A history of the American discourse on television and children, 1950–1980.* New York: Praeger.

Luke, C. (1994). White women in interracial families: Reflections on hybridization, feminine identities, and racialized othering. *Feminist Issues, 14*(2), 49–72.

Luke, C. (Ed.). (1996). *Feminisms and pedagogies of everyday life.* Albany, NY: State University of New York Press.

Luke, C. (2001). *Globalization and women in academia: North/West-South/East.* Mahwah, NJ: Lawrence Erlbaum Associates, Inc.

Luke, C. (2002). Globalization and women in Southeast Asian higher education management. *Teachers College Record, 104*(3), 625–662.

Luke, C. (2007). As seen on TV or was that my phone? New media literacy. *Policy Futures in Education, 5*(1), 50–58.

Luke, C., & Carrington, V. (2000). Race Matters. *Journal of intercultural studies, 21*(1), 5–24.

Luke, C., & Gore, J., (Eds.). (1992). *Feminisms and critical pedagogy*. New York: Routledge, Chapman and Hall, Inc.

Luke, A., & Luke, C. (2001). Adolescence lost/childhood regained: On early intervention and the emergence of the techno-subject. *Journal of Early Childhood Literacy, 1*(1), 91–120.

Luke, C., & Luke, H. (1997). Techno-textuality: Representations of femininity & sexuality. *Media International Australia, 84*(1), 46–58.

Manley-Casimir, M. E., & Luke, C. (Eds.). (1987). *Children and television: A challenge for education*. Westport, CT: Praeger Publishers.

UQ Researchers (n.d.). *Carmen Luke Research: Multi-literacies, libraries and cybraries: Comparative case studies of Australia and the United States (2002–2003)*. Retrieved from: http://www.uq.edu.au/uqresearchers/researcher/lukec.html?uv_category=prj&prj=1902388

UQ Researchers (n.d.). *Carmen Luke Research: Globalisation: New media, new literacies, and identities (2002–2004)*. Retrieved from: http://www.uq.edu.au/uqresearchers/researcher/lukec.html?uv_category=prj&prj=1902376

ANNOTATED BIBLIOGRAPHY OF SELECTED WORKS

Luke, C. (2007). As seen on TV or was that my phone? *New media* literacy. *Policy Futures in Education, 5*(1), 50–58.

In this essay, Luke argues that information literacy, media literacy, technology literacy, computer literacy, and other newer forms of literacies need to be taught in interdisciplinary and interconnected ways, beyond being independent classes. Additionally, she argues that in learning about these literacies, students need to develop and draw on their critical and analytic skills, and not merely learn about them for instrumental purposes. This critical media literacy should encourage students to analyze the politics of representation, such as stereotyping and exclusions, as well as linguistic changes, including new words, acronyms, and old words with new meanings (e.g., emoticon, PDF, or scroll). Luke describes media responses to several recent world events, including 9–11 and the 2004 Boxing Day tsunami in the Indian Ocean, to demonstrate the intersections between politics and the media as places for students to engage in critical analysis.

Luke, C. (2006). Eduscapes: Knowledge capital and cultures. *Studies in Language & Capitalism, 1(1)*, 97–120.

In this conceptual essay, Luke explores the push-pull dynamics of the effects of globalization in higher education. Three dynamics that she highlights are ways that local and global interests work together, the flows of capital and people between countries, and the politics of knowledge capital in relation to research, libraries, and publishing. Luke applies Appadurai's metaphor of scapes (info, techno, finance, media and ideo-scapes) to the disjunctive flows of ideas and knowledge across the globe, in contrast to neoliberal notions of a one-way flow from the West to the "periphery." She writes that "Appadurai's analytic allows us to see the flows of consumer and symbolic goods, people, ideas or knowledge, as multi-hued, as tide pools or swirling eddies – much like oil on water – that constitute 'scape' formations" (pp. 100–101). As the role of the university across the globe changes to an entrepreneurial industry and it becomes less tied to national educational frameworks, space opens up for higher education to be transformed to become a site for genuine international education across cultures. At the same time, if education is no longer a public good but a tradable commodity, then Luke argues the need for global consumer protections and quality assurance measures.

Luke, C. (2006). Cyberpedagogy. In J. Weiss, et al. (Eds.) *The international handbook of virtual learning environment.* pp. 269–277. Dordrecht, NL: Springer.

In this essay, Luke provides commentary on a developing notion of cyberpedagogy for students growing up with new technologies. Situating this essay in the context of a wired and wireless world, where online teaching is becoming more prevalent, she explores the compatibility of digital technologies and constructivist theories of teaching. Luke posits that these technologies lend themselves to collaborative and constructivist approaches to pedagogy. Calling for a balance between online learning options and traditional face-to-face teaching, Luke suggests the role of the teacher becomes the craft expert who inducts learners into communities of practice through guidance and consultation. Luke concludes that further research remains crucial to understanding cyberpedagogy, as the challenge is to create innovative analytic tools for understanding learning in digital contexts.

Luke, C. (2005). Capital and knowledge flows: Global higher education markets. *Asia Pacific Journal of Education, 25*(2), 159–174.

This conceptual piece considers the impact of globalization on higher education, acknowledging how higher education across the world has become more standardized and uniform while at the same time showing how people's experiences of higher education at the local level are more heterogeneous than the globalization discourse allows. Drawing on Appadurai's notion of scapes (info, techno, finance, media, and ideoscapes), Luke analyzes the flow of knowledge and goods as complex and overlapping. Instead of a model of globalization based on an idea of a center and a periphery, Luke sees globalization as always situated within a localized experience based on the overlapping scapes of each context. The role of the nation state, for example, is still significant in terms of policies and funding of higher education. Luke concludes by raising a critical question—if the role of the nation state is diminishing as a result of globalization, what will happen to state-supported education, especially for a democratic society? The capitalist and consumerist trends currently in higher education threaten the role of education as a potential democratic lever.

Luke, C. (2003). Pedagogy, connectivity, multimodality, and interdisciplinarity. *Reading Research Quarterly, 38*(3), 397–403.

In this essay, Luke calls for a reconceptualization of pedagogy, particularly around literacy, in light of "technologically mediated access to and relations with knowledge" (p. 398). This new pedagogy embraces collaboration, problem-solving, and multi-literacies. Luke also calls for the use of new technologies in research methodologies, such as electronic transcript analysis, and literacy research that goes outside of the classroom. While she advocates the integration of technology into school-based pedagogy, Luke also advances research questions around issues of equity and access to new technologies.

Luke, C. (2003). Glocal mobilities: Crafting identities in interracial families. *International Journal of Cultural Studies, 6*(4), 379–401.

This qualitative study of 60 interracial Australian families focuses on identity formation and coping strategies in relation to racializing experiences. Each couple had one parent of Indo-Asian descent and one of Anglo-European Australian descent. Luke found that several participants had a shift in identity from their identification with their cultural or ethnic group of birth to the cultural group of their partner. Multiple or mixed identifications were common across participants as well, in relation to language, child-rearing, nationality, and even self-classification of race. Luke concludes by making the argument that "race" should continue to be a category within Australian social science research, because race mediates people's lived experiences, which is particularly evident in the experiences of interracial families.

Luke, C. (2002). Globalization and women in Southeast Asian higher education management. *Teachers College Record, 104*(3), 625–662.

Using concepts of globalization and "glocalization" (meaning, how global actions affect local sites and vice versa) to frame this case study of women in higher education management positions, Luke investigates how cultural differences impact career opportunities, aspirations, and experiences. The study focused on 44 women from Hong Kong, Singapore, Malaysia, and Thailand who held management level positions in education, including dean, department head, or research center director, across a range of fields, including humanities, natural sciences, and medicine. Luke explores the concept of patriarchy and the Western notion of a "glass ceiling," finding that when cultural specificity is taken into account, there is no one universal barrier to women's achievement. Luke acknowledges that women in this study, as well as women in Western and other non-Western societies claim the "double-day" of professional and household responsibilities, and that childbearing and rearing early in a woman's career can impede research productivity, impacting their careers. Additionally, there is the claim that the academy is centered around male values and ways of operating. For the women in this study, cultural expectations of what it means to be feminine shape their experiences, as they operate both within the cultural norms and push against it in their careers. Thus, Luke concludes that despite the global nature of the university, a more local and situated analysis is required to understand global patterns and the changing nature of women's status in higher education.

Luke, A., & Luke, C., (2002). A new toolkit for understanding early intervention: A dialogue with Stuart McNaughton and Douglas Kellner. *Journal of Early Childhood Literacy, 2*(1), 113–116.

McNaughton, S. (2002). On making early interventions problematic: A comment on Luke and Luke (2001). *Journal of Early Childhood Literacy, 2*(1), 97–103.

Kellner, D. (2002). New life conditions, subjectivities, and literacies: Some comments on Luke and Luke's reconstructive project. *Journal of Early Childhood Literacy, 2*(1), 105–112.

In their brief essay, Luke and Luke respond to McNaugton's and Kellner's thoughts regarding early intervention strategies and the construction of adolescence in their article, "Adolescence Lost/Childhood Regained" (2001). McNaugton's central concern is their claim that the focus of early intervention is an inoculation model of development and the reification of print. McNaughton also problematizes Lukes' privileging of new literacies over traditional literacies, which carries a risk of marginalized populations not having access to print literacies.

In Kellner's response, he highlights three points from the article that he sees as Luke and Luke's contribution to contemporary philosophy of education. Firstly, they articulate the need to reframe schooling based on new life conditions and experiences of youth. Secondly, Luke and Luke focus on the need for schools to support the development of multiple literacies. Finally, he discusses Luke and Luke's proposal to restructure and democratize education.

In Luke and Luke's response to these two pieces, they note recent work by educational psychologists that draws on social and cultural theories and frameworks, while arguing that much of this work does not use a Hegelian or poststructural analysis, as Kellner advocates. Luke and Luke highlight the need to engage in analyses related to power, race, and class, leading them to ask: "What versions of sociocultural theory and analyses of literacy development actually reach early childhood literacy teachers, teacher educators, apprentice researchers, and policy makers?" (p. 115). Luke and Luke conclude by confirming the need for print literacy, but not necessarily as a prerequisite to engaging with new literacies.

Milojevic, I., Luke, A., Luke, C., Mills, M., & Land, R. (2002). *Moving forward: Students and teachers against racism.* Melbourne, AU: Eleanor Curtain Publishing.

This book relates the stories of faculty members, students and community members in eleven schools taking positive steps to combat racism. The schools in this study are a mixture of governmental and nongovernmental schools in Queensland, Australia. The book emphasizes the need for solutions to be local and culturally relevant to specific communities. It becomes evident that there is no single right way, but that through strategies that promote respect and fairness, students, faculty and communities can change school culture in ways that improve educational outcomes for students of diverse backgrounds.

Luke, A., & Luke, C. (2001). Adolescence lost/childhood regained: On early intervention and the emergence of the techno-subject. *Journal of Early Childhood
Literacy, 1*(1), 91–120.

In this essay, Luke and Luke argue that education systems use discourses
about literacy as part of their rhetorical/political strategy. In general, the
authors see literacy crises, which arise during times of upheaval or change,
such as the current trend toward globalization, as reasons given to restructure
institutions. By claiming a current crisis in print literacy and focusing their
attentions on early childhood reading skills, the authors argue that education systems avoid addressing the actual problem of disengaged adolescents.
These youth, developing new identities in relation to new technologies, are
seen as unruly or subversive because of their mastery of new literacies, including the internet and video games that their families and teachers cannot sur-
veil and often cannot comprehend. Thus adolescents' competence with new
technologies is reframed as incompetence with print literacy, and education
systems delay the inclusion of new literacies within the curriculum by focusing
on remediation and early literacy skills that are purported to have the ability
to prevent these youngsters from becoming unruly adolescents.

Luke, C. (2001). *Globalization and women in academia: North/West-South/East.* Mahwah, NJ: Lawrence Erlbaum Associates, Inc.

Luke presents four case studies of women in higher education management
from Southeast Asian countries of Thailand, Singapore, Hong Kong, and Malaysia. In so doing, she considers the forces of globalization, especially within
academia, from a western feminist perspective, and aims to build the knowledge
base around the experiences of women academics in nonwestern contexts. After
outlining trends around women in academia in western countries and analyzing how globalization is affecting higher education across the globe, the four
case studies demonstrate the intersections of globalization and local standpoints
through the experiences of urban, upper middle class, educated women in senior
management positions. The western concept of the "glass ceiling" and a generic
patriarchy that similarly impacts all women are shown to be limited analytic tools
for understanding these women's experiences. Instead the politics of place—the
local sites, cultural histories, and specific sociopolitical and economic factors—
are required to understand these women's career trajectories and opportunities,
such as values of filial responsibility or social norms that expect women to work
behind the scenes. To accomplish that involves highlighting intersections of localized gender ideologies and global discourses, in contrast to a view of globalizing forces as fundamentally changing local practices.

Luke, C. (2000). New literacies in teacher education. *Journal of Adolescent & Adult
Literacy, 43*(5), 424–435.

In this paper, Luke describes a semester-long teacher education course at the
University of Queensland that combines media-cultural studies and information technology, and offers this combination as a new approach to literacy
education. This combination merges the critical deconstruction of text from

the discipline of media studies with the skills-based focus of computer literacy courses, leading the professors of the course to ask students to critically view websites, identify software and internet genres, and consider how e-mail has changed communication practices. Feedback from the 300 students who took the course demonstrated students' belief in the need for critical technology literacy in addition to computer skills as well as their ability to use mutliliteracies in their coursework.

Luke, A., Luke, C. & Mayer, D. (2000). Redesigning Teacher Education. *Teaching Education, 11*(1), 5–11.

This article is an introduction to a volume of *Teaching Education* devoted to reforming teacher education. The authors briefly identify some of the forces driving teacher education practice and teacher education reform in various locations around the globe. Considering the institutionalization of teacher education, they challenge the reader to consider the following questions:

- What kinds of students and future citizens do we want teachers and school practices to shape?
- What are the tools and practices, and calculated social fields of new times where these teachers and their students will work? (p. 9)

They further ask one to consider how the current teacher education practices are complicit in the reproduction of school practices that many find problematic, such as discipline and knowledge segregation, suggesting that radical reform is needed. Admitting that such reform may not be appealing to those working in teacher preparation, they suggest that we start by considering new tools needed to prepare teachers and students to be critically oriented knowledge producers.

Luke, C. (2000). Cyber-schooling and technological change: Multiliteracies for new times. In Cope, B. & Kalantzis, M. (Eds.), *Multiliteracies: Literacy learning and the design of social futures* (pp. 69–91). South Yarra, Victoria, Australia: Macmillan.

In this chapter, Luke considers the role of new information and communication technologies (ICT) for education. She argues that educators need to be involved in developing ICT pedagogies that engage students in critical literacies, instead of allowing corporations to determine what is taught. Critical ICT literacies include developing an understanding of how knowledge and information are structured across contexts, mastering both functional and analytic skills, and developing an understanding of how skills are taken up in social relations and across institutions.

Luke, C., & Carrington, V. (2000). Race Matters. *Journal of intercultural studies, 21*(1), 5–24.

This paper draws on a study involving interviews with 50 interracial families. The authors discuss couples' detachments and critical change events in life histories and then examine "experiences of estrangement from family, friends and workplace" (p. 6). Luke and Carrington argue that race matters for interracial families in ways that transcend traditional ways of theorizing race, as well as identity, color, culture, and notions of us/them and /insider/outsider. The authors find that at the localized site of interracial family's discourses of race signify complex social and cultural dynamics which transcend postcolonial theorizings of race. Warning not to discard race as an analytic category, the authors suggest that researchers should be aware of "how race discourses and racializing practices are re-articulated within and across diasporic cultural groups and cross-generationally" (p. 22). In addition, they stress the significance of locality and politics within that locality, in the ways individuals experience race. They conclude by discussing how most of the participants in their study have renegotiated their identities in a space, referred to as a third space that lies outside the norms of either partner's culture.

Luke, C. (1999). What next? Toddler netizens, playstation thumb, techno-literacies. *Contemporary Issues in Early Childhood, 1*(1), 95–100.

In this short conceptual article, Luke raises four critical issues related to changing technologies, conceptions of literacy, and youth. Firstly, she notes that young children's access to and interactions with multiple technologies, challenge more traditional developmental or linear theories around literacy. Secondly, the abundance of software options for children under the age of six makes it difficult for adults, especially parents and teachers, to determine what is of high quality and what may be problematic, such as role-playing games that reproduce gender stereotypes. Connected to the question of quality is the question of critical media skills and how these skills need to evolve to take into account new types of media. Finally, Luke raises the issue that not all families have equal access to the range of new technologies. What could be a democratizing force, such as the internet, could also reproduce or increase socioeconomic disparities, and thus demands that schools have a role in providing access to youth of all ages.

Luke, C. (1999). Media and cultural studies in Australia. *Journal of Adolescent & Adult Literacy, 42*(8), 622–626.

In this essay, Luke describes the current state of critical literacy in K–12 schools in Australia as well as a brief historical overview of media studies in that country. She discovered that the basic tenets of critical literacy that guided pedagogical decisions are: coding practice (How does this text work?), text-meaning practice (What different readings does this text enable?), pragmatic practice (How does this text work in different contexts?) and critical practice (How does this text attempt to position me?). Luke argues that media literacy studies need to be guided by principles of social justice and equity so that students learn how media and mass cultural texts, which may be oppressive, are always socially constructed and thus re-constructable. She also argues that "[t]he task for teachers is to balance critical analyses of media representations of culture and society with the diversity of student readings and productions, backgrounds, abilities, and creativity" (p. 625).

Luke, C., & Luke, A. (1999). Theorizing interracial families and hybrid identity: An Australian perspective. *Educational Theory, 49*(2), 223–249.

This theoretical essay draws on interview data from the first phase of a three year study on interethnic families in Australia, exploring how interracial families are sites where identity becomes hybridized. Situating this piece within the context of a current debate over immigration and multiculturalism in Australia, the authors explore the complexities of identity formation believing that the situatedness of place, locality, and racializing practices are significant. The authors work from postcolonial and feminist frameworks, arguing that interracial families are local sites that add a complex challenge for social and educational researchers trying to comprehend discourses of identity and family in which hybrid cultures come together and in conflict and are reinterpreted anew by the interracial family. The authors conclude with implications from their study for multicultural and antiracist educational practice and research.

Luke, C. (1998). Cultural politics and women in Singapore higher education management. *Gender and Education, 10*(3), 245–263).

In this article, Luke presents findings from a case study of nine women who work in senior positions in higher education across three universities in Singapore. Considering the local policy context of Singapore, including policies related to family planning (especially around increasing the national birth rate) and housing (such as subsidies for living with one's parents), Luke explores the ways that cultural practices mediate women's experiences, including their perceptions of gender in higher education. The women reported cultural expectations around traditional notions of femininity, filial responsibility, and saving face (avoiding disgrace or humiliation of one's self or the organization one is affiliated with). To be successful in their careers, women had to negotiate these notions by being loyal to their superiors and working invisibly behind the scenes, for example, by proposing new ideas to their superiors privately, instead of publicly, which could be interpreted as negative or contrary. Luke also found that the women participants frequently spoke about tensions and lack of support between women, often related to gossiping, competition for promotions, or fear of being seen as weak. She concludes by discussing the idea that "culturally specific expectations of women's conduct mediate women's workplace and public conduct and relationships" (p. 261).

Luke, C. (1998). "I got to where I am by my own strength": Women in Hong Kong higher education management. *Education Journal, 26*(1), 31–58.

Luke reports on case studies of eleven ethnic Chinese women in senior positions in higher education management at four Hong Kong universities and their perceptions and experiences of career advancement. In so doing, Luke considers how the Western concept of the "glass ceiling" is not directly applicable to the sociohistorical context of these women's experiences. This study emerged from Luke's questioning of the disparity between women's representation in higher education versus in higher education management. Hong Kong's unique identity as a "cultural hybrid" as a result of 150 years of British rule intersecting with Chinese cultural traditions is part of the specific set of historical, political, social, and cultural factors that shape women's experiences in educational institutions. In her findings, Luke reports that structural constraints within universities are not as great as ideological or cultural restraints around expectations for women within the family. She also found that her participants' experienced a lack of support from other women in senior positions, and she noted different experiences across generations as women experienced different cultural and patriarchal attitudes in different eras.

Luke, C., & Luke, A. (1998). Interracial families: Difference within difference. *Ethnic and Racial Studies, 21*(4), 728–754.

In this study, Luke and Luke draw on post-colonial, feminist, and critical race theories to analyze identity formations within 20 interracial families of Anglo-Australian and Indo-Asian descent in two different cities in Australia. They explore ways that gender, class, and location mediate the experiences of interracial families, as opposed to assuming homogeneity of experience. The authors identify four themes. First, a person's geographic and temporal location affords specific narratives of what "race" means, as they noted different racial discourses in the two different cities. Second, participants viewed their social class as mediating their racialized experiences in different ways, enabling different types of career opportunities and treatment by society in general. Third, each partner's family and subsequent cultural practices strongly influenced the married couple, at first as a source of tension or disapproval and then, for some couples, the partner's reconsideration of their ethnic or cultural identities. Finally, traditional gendered roles were destabilized, especially for heterosexual couples in which the male was a recent arrival to Australia. The Indo-Asian men were more likely to participate in cooking, and White women were more likely to take on the role of public negotiator for the household. Further, some of the Asian women in the study reported being interested in marrying Anglo-Australian men because they believed these men would take on more of a role in household work. The article concludes that being in an interracial relationship enables individuals to develop new, hybridized identities and practices as neither individual's cultural understandings are assumed by the other.

Luke, C., & Luke, H. (1997). Techno-textuality: Representations of femininity & sexuality. *Media International Australia, 84*(1), 46–58.

In this article, the authors explore how femininity and sexuality are textually mediated and culturally recorded into new discourses about cyberspaces and IT in popular print magazines. The authors used a "cyberfeminist" lens to analyze advertisements that depicted only women and portrayed women as users of technology. They found a range of representations, ranging from what they consider to be the traditional, offensive stereotypes to those offering counter-discourses about women and technology. The authors raise the concern that critical political and research agendas may actually silence women by writing them into "victim narratives" as uniform discourses that ideologically subjugate women. Therefore, the authors argue for attending to the multiple ways in which women produce and read themselves into cultural texts and practices so that they avoid reproducing a "fixed and generalized feminine other."

Luke, C. (1997). Quality assurance and women in higher education. *Higher Education,* June, 3(4), 433–451.

In this study, Luke examines, via a Foucaldian perspective, one Australian university's response to quality assurance (QA) initiatives. In contrast to critiques of QA initiatives as repressive, Luke demonstrates how a QA initiative actually created more open accountability and performance targets, particularly related to gender equity, that had been absent in the previous governmental structure. Foucault's idea of governmentality as making things visible is thus seen as a positive—making visible practices that had previously been used to maintain a patriarchal system. Luke concludes by calling on women who have benefited from these types of initiatives to use their "power and influence to move in direction that are consistent with feminist agendas of socially just and inclusive democratic and feminist principles" (p. 448).

Luke, C. (1996). Feminist pedagogy theory: Reflections on power and authority. *Educational theory, 46*(3), 283–302.

In this essay, Luke explores notions of power and authority in relation to women in the academy working within a feminist pedagogical framework. Tensions arise from the idea that a feminist approach to pedagogy rejects male notions of authority and teacher dominance in the classroom, in favor of a more equitable distribution of power, while in actuality, a feminist pedagogue cannot escape "institutionally granted power" or "intellectual authority" (p. 285). Luke situates the piece in relation to Jane Gallop's concept of "good girl" feminism, which she sees as claiming to empower women students through the absence of teacher power. Luke raises questions about normativity and the theoretical validity of feminisms.

Luke, C., Ed. (1996). *Feminisms and pedagogies of everyday life.* Albany, NY: State University of New York Press.

This collection of essays envisions pedagogy as much more than what happens within formal schooling, with a focus on learning and teaching in day-to-day life, particularly around how individuals were taught to become girls, then women, then academics. The authors in this collection write about power/knowledge relations that make up all pedagogical encounters, focusing on identity formation, pedagogy in popular culture, and academic and legal discourses around pedagogy.

Cazden, C., Cope, B., Fairclough, N., Gee, J., & et al. (1996). A pedagogy of multi-literacies: Designing social futures. *Harvard Educational Review, 66*(1), 60–92.

This article, generally known as the New London Group's manifesto, was written by a group of scholars (including C. Luke) responding to what they identified as a need for a shift in literacy teaching and learning to address both the changing technologies of the time, as well as an increase in globalization, resulting in multilingualism and changes to the uses of the English language. At the time this was written, when portable computers were new to the market and the internet was not world-wide, the New London Group was seeing shifts in the way in which people communicated in the workplace and the community, and thus developed a multilitieracies approach to pedagogy that they hoped would support students in achieving access to language, engaging critically in designing their social futures and, ultimately, becoming successfully employed.

Luke, C. (1996). Childhood and parenting in children's popular culture and child-care magazines. In Luke, C. (Ed.), *Feminisms and pedagogies of everyday life* (167–187). Albany, NY: State University of New York Press.

In this chapter, Luke analyzes Australian, American, and British parenting magazines from 1992 for gendered and racialized messages. She found that the articles, advertisements, and illustrations clearly reproduced traditional gender roles, with few images of people of color, gays and lesbians, or men in active parent roles. Further, the construct of motherhood in these magazines carried the expectation that mothers consume specific toys, clothes, and other products to be seen as good mothers. Luke notes that the images of motherhood and gender portrayed in these magazines is in contrast to other visions of family and parenting in other media, such as movies or television sitcoms that celebrate varied family make-ups.

Luke, C. (1994). Childhood and parenting in popular culture. *Journal of Sociology, 30*(3), 289–302.

Drawing from Foucault's sense of discourse, this article examines the pedagogical impact of popular culture texts and artifacts, namely toys and media for children and parenting magazines, on the social construction of childhood and parenthood. Through an analysis of toys and chain stores worldwide, Luke presents the argument that the toy industry's gendered discourse of childhood is a pedagogy. A textual analysis of parenting magazines over a six-month period shows both gendered and racialized constructs of childhood and parenting. Luke concludes that these texts and artifacts lead parents to accept a normalized discourse of childhood and parenthood that is white, middle-class, heterosexual and gender segregated.

Luke, C. (1994). White women in interracial families: Reflections on hybridization, feminine identities, and racialized othering. *Feminist Issues, 14*(2), 49–72.

In this essay, Luke considers issues of identity for white women in interracial relationships and white mothers of biracial children. Her analysis challenges identity theories that see race as static, instead arguing that white women in these relationships are positioned as "outsider within" as they experience racism because of their partner's or children's (perceived) race, though they do not carry racial markers of women of color themselves. A tentative conclusion from this study is that white women with Black partners see themselves as positioned to be "less white" as a result. Further, Luke considers the multiple, and at times contradictory, identity positions of members of interracial families. Luke finds that schooling is the greatest source of challenge for white mothers of interracial children, primarily because of the school staff's assumptions about them and their children's identities, and finds that fathers of color often choose to not attend school functions in the belief that their absence will benefit the children's relationships with their teachers.

Luke, C. (1994). Women in the academy: The politics of speech and silence. *Journal of Sociology of Education, 15*(2). 211–230.

Situated in feminist sociology, but drawing widely on feminist research in other disciplines, including education and sociolinguistics, this article examines women's voices and silences in the academy. Luke maps out spaces in the academy where women's voices are enabled, constrained and/or silenced. She suggests that recognizing, identifying and attempting to counter masculine power structures by creating spaces for women's voices can result in the silencing of women, despite the intent. Luke explores the notion of silence for women and men of color in the classroom and the idea that silence becomes a survival strategy. She then provides some concrete ways that a feminist pedagogy might be introduced through teacher education to alter women's and men's understandings from a young age about participation in discourse. Finally, Luke discusses the shift in feminist theoretical focus from "we" to "I" and the impact it has had on feminist unity. She concludes that "women are tired of researching and politicizing their marginality. Women of all colours, it seems to me, want to take charge of the rules and of those discourses that define centre and margin, insider and outsider, ruler and ruled" (p. 227).

Luke, C. (1993). Media and popular culture in education and society: An introduction to education studies. *Teaching Education, 5*(2), 41–56.

This article outlines how Carmen Luke uses media to introduce cultural studies and feminist theory to undergraduate education students who traditionally are resistant to learning theory. In some detail, she introduces a curriculum of a five-week media studies unit in which feminist poststructuralist theories are used in the analysis of popular media as part of a set of compulsory courses designed to articulate equity issues focused on class, gender, and race/ethnicity as they relate to the politics of schooling. In the unit, students are encouraged to explore the ways in which cultural texts are implicated in our lives, including our various identity formations and how we think about and interact with others. Luke argues that this unit's success and accessibility for students is due to the fact that it builds on knowledges they already have and engages them in ways that theoretical textbooks cannot. Students are able to develop critical and political perspectives in their own educational epistemologies as they consider children's culture, their own identities, positioning, classroom discourses, and pedagogies.

Luke, C., & Gore, J., Eds. (1992). *Feminisms and critical pedagogy.* New York, NY: Routledge, Chapman and Hall, Inc.

In this collection of essays, feminist educators discuss their personal experiences with and theoretical thinking about critical pedagogy and its emphasis on empowerment and emancipation. The authors discuss challenges they face in their readings of emancipatory texts, students' reactions to emancipatory pedagogy, and the connections between feminism and male-authored critical pedagogy. Luke and Gore see this collection as a revisioning of what pedagogy can be, as opposed to a break from critical pedagogy. They see their poststructuralist feminist task as examining where and how the feminine is positioned in emancipatory discourses.

Luke, C. (1992). Feminist politics in radical pedagogy. In Luke, C., & Gore, J., (Eds.), *Feminisms and critical pedagogy* (pp. 25–53). New York: Routledge, Chapman and Hall, Inc.

In this chapter, Luke delineates the concept of the subject in critical pedagogy, arguing that it is an Anglo-European and male subject, a public citizen participating in a liberal democracy. As such, feminism and attention to feminist standpoints is only possible in critical pedagogies if there is a rethinking of who the subject is. When this does not occur, Luke argues that critical pedagogies are actually reproducing patriarchal narratives. Instead of one pedagogy, Luke envisions pedagogies that privilege undecidability and partiality, which are based on a foundation of difference, and that do not claim to know what empowerment means for others.

Luke, C. (1990). *Constructing the Child Viewer: A History of the American Discourse on Television and Children, 1950–1980.* New York, NY: Praeger.

Luke uses discourse analysis to analyze the influences of technology on children, with the focus on television. She begins by looking back and providing an overview of the influences that earlier technologies and media, specifically film, radio, and comics, were believed to have on the discourse of childhood. From there, Luke shifts to television, taking a chronological approach, from the "televiewing child" to the "behavioral subject" to the "cognitive subject." Luke's poststructualist stance stresses the importance of situating the documents she uses as data in both time and place as she analyzes the ways in which children's television viewing is understood.

Luke, C. (1989). *Pedagogy, printing, and Protestantism: The discourse on childhood.* Albany, NY: State University of New York Press.

Luke, C. (1989). Luther and the foundations of literacy, secular schooling and educational administration. *The Journal of Educational Thought, 23*(2), 120–140.

In this book and article, Luke explores the history of the discourse on childhood as it evolved in sixteenth century Germany, along with the Protestant Reformation and the spread of the printed word. Using Foucauldian discourse analysis Luke considers conceptions of childhood by examining adult notions about children as they are depicted in literature, art, and relics such as children's toys and dress, locating shifting discourses of childhood within the politics and social change taking place in Germany during the sixteenth century. Finding significant connections between the spread of Martin Luther's influence and the printing press, and the impact it had on evolving conceptions of childhood, family and public schools, Luke weaves together a story of the emergence of distinct periods of childhood and adolescence in response to peasant uprisings and the need to educate a populous that is prepared for civic duty in the new Protestant order. Church control gave way to state control, and education became mandated so that children were guided along a pathway to salvation, as they developed into the citizens for a new social order.

Luke, C. (1985). Television discourse processing: A schema theoretic approach. *Communication Education, 34*(2), 91–105.

In this essay, Luke argues that research on the effects of television on children that sees children as passive viewers who are entirely manipulable is too limited, and research instead requires an understanding of children as active viewers whose background knowledge and experience mediate their television viewing. Drawing on schema theory, Luke details how children's vastly different background knowledge, their schemata, leads them to respond to a television program in different ways as they place the new data from the program into their already constructed schematic categories as they make meaning of it. Reconceptualizing the child television viewer as active leads Luke to highlight the need for educators and families to develop critical television literacy skills in children to broaden their schemata and use television as a learning tool.

Luke, C., de Castell, S., & Luke, A. (1989). Beyond criticism: The authority of the school text. In S. de Ccastell, A. Luke, & C. Luke, (Eds.), *Language, authority and criticism: Readings on the school textbook* (pp. 245–260). New York, NY: The Falmer Press.
Luke, C., de Castell, S., & Luke, A. (1983). Beyond criticism: The authority of the school text. *Curriculum Inquiry, 13*(2), 111–127.

This chapter and article attempt to critically explore the school text as laid forth by David R. Olson in the 1970's and in his 1980 book *On the Language and Authority of Textbooks*, which posits that textbooks embody what society authorizes as valid knowledge, drawing on Foucault for their theoretical framing of text as discursive. The claim is that school texts put meanings into print to make them more explicit, and those meanings become "above criticism." The authors tackle the question of whether meaning is in the texts, exploring the constraints of what can count as authorized content. Exploring notions of author, authority and authorization, Luke, de Castell and Luke find that students are not within the social group sanctioned to critically analyze or critique the texts, and the authorization the school administration places on texts puts them in the position of being above criticism, yet they acknowledge the importance of the institutional context in determining the treatment of the texts. The article/chapter then explores the text as an icon, teacher and text identity, and finally concludes with the idea that the text is not the curriculum, but rather one component that students respond to in a localized context to which they bring their own prior knowledge and experiences.

CHAPTER 22

PATTI LATHER

Laura A. Valdiviezo and Jennifer Lee O'Donnell

[Patti Lather] has moved critical pedagogy to a more contingent epistemological stance, as she problematizes any facile closure in relation to questions of truth and the effort to represent reality. (Kincheloe 2008, pp. 96–97, Critical Pedagogy Primer)

Liberatory practices of scholars are particularly susceptible to reproducing sites of domination, especially within the primarily Marxist, male dominated theoretical sphere of critical pedagogy. Patti Lather writes that Marxist theory has always taken feminism as the "handmaiden" or "wife," neglecting women and women's issues as sites of resistance in the movement. Lather suggests poststructural feminism—a theory of impermanence, of partiality, of transformation—as a means to disrupt the high theory of Marxism. She proposes that there are no innocent libratory discourses; however, as such, she feels differences between theoretical positioning can be fruitful places to develop a more critically reflexive pedagogy.

Lather's major critique of neo-Marxist theory is that it ignores women and women's efforts relevant to a true revolutionary praxis. Through the politicization of lived experiences, her work highlights the ways in which women's studies programs have been instrumental in bringing about new, anti-patriarchal, anticapitalistic forms of politics that put women at the center of concerns for social transformation. Lather emphasizes the important role such programs play in raising people's consciousness to social

Educating About Social Issues in the 20th and 21st Centuries, pages 459–480
Copyright © 2014 by Information Age Publishing
459

inequalities, providing critical spaces to explore issues of power, knowledge production, and injustices.

Lather contributes a further analysis on the "gender blindness" of neo-Marxist scholarship in respect to education. Calling it an issue of "and women, of course," she discusses the ways in which neo-Marxist movements have only recently added on an analysis of the subordination of women and work to their project of class-based social reform, ignoring the realities and necessities of a complete paradigm upheaval if they are to actually include gender based oppressions into their analysis of life under capitalist regimes.

Contextualizing her analysis on a debate that is not new but that nonetheless remains current, Lather continues to critique critical pedagogy as a "boy thing," not for its proliferation of male scholars but for its universal, abstract sense of righteous superiority. In her view, universal attempts to transform education within the larger social structure through Marx-based attention to class and material struggle, visions of utopia and new social alternatives, are regurgitative of an outdated critical method. She does agree, however, that it is necessary to rethink critical pedagogy in contemporary historical contexts, preferring to let go of the security of grand Marxist theory in favor of a tentative, incomplete not knowing praxis.

PLACE IN HISTORY

As a feminist methodologist and educator of education researchers, Patti Lather's work on research and research pedagogy has provided significant contributions to educating about social issues. For almost three decades, Lather has been an important voice in questioning assumptions about truth, the universality of knowledge, and inquiry approaches that impact how we know and what we know about schools and society. While the present moment in qualitative research seeks to blur the boundaries between the social sciences and humanities, experimenting with various forms of representing research through literature, poetry, autobiography, multivocal dialogues, visuals and performance (Denzin & Lincoln 2005), the work of Patti Lather aims at troubling any assumed accomplishment in this respect, calling attention also to present trends that risk bringing educational research and pedagogy into a more restrictive and marginalizing state (Lather 2010). With work particularly concerned with empowering participants and raising consciousness through the research process, Lather (1986, 1993) has been a leading voice in postmodern and poststructural feminist paradigms that disturb the notion of validity itself, opening space for a more balanced, politically oriented, and emancipatory investigative process of knowledge production.

Lather's work explores the intersections of varying critical, feminist and poststructural theories, with the purpose of making the qualitative research process more valid, reliable, authentic, and democratic. In problematizing both positivist and postpositivistic paradigms and the grand narratives of science, Lather critiques the traditional collection and analysis of data, questioning research itself as a method of truth-formation. She aims at troubling tidy binaries and considers the nature of knowledge production whereby the researcher surrenders—"gets lost" "gets messy" "gets transgressive"—in order to know what's beyond what's known, opening unexplored space where "new imaginings are possible and where, while being lost, one moves on, perhaps forward" (Lather, 2006; Rachel, 2009, p. 205).

Lather's work reminds us that though early postpositivist inquiry was qualitative in intent, it still relied upon conventional scientific methods—observation, hypothesis, experimentation, data collecting, coding and classifying—to prove theories of truth. Through the study of culturally diverse people of the world, such research was primarily concerned with formulating theories about history, culture, and civilization based on in-depth studies of human behavior. The early forms of qualitative inquiry traditionally granted agency to the social scientist to observe and analyze the lives of those in positions of less power, particularly in their attempts to discovering and classifying the ethnic "other."

While taking place decades later, Lather's work can be traced to social movements of the 1960s and 1970s, a time when important issues regarding voice and ways of representing subjects that inquiry situated as "other" were being reconceptualized. Native American, Latino, Asian American, and African American scholars began actively contesting earlier theories of qualitative inquiry based on essentialist notions of "otherness," developing ethnic studies programs where they could take control over research impacting their communities. The decades that followed ushered in postmodern and poststructural challenges to qualitative inquiry, changing the way researchers represent themselves and their own influence in the investigative process.

Along with the development of ethnic studies departments in public universities, which grew as a result of the civil rights movement in the United States, an increase in underrepresented bodies began entering academia in the 1960s and 1970s. The 1980s brought with it a "crisis of representation" that emerged in qualitative scholarship, seeking to revise how subjects were being studied, represented, and talked about in public life. Illuminated by poststructuralism, debates surrounding qualitative inquiry have challenged the foundations and structure of qualitative research practices where power dynamics concerning the researcher and the participant and the role of the researcher as subject of interpretation are problematized (Keene & Colligan, 2004; Pillow, 2003). Born of critical theorists and cultural critics, scholars began struggling with the political tensions endogenous to the research process. Qualitative research became more reflexive, calling into question taken for granted assumptions about race, gender, and class. Anthropo-logical, colonial projects (which were government-sponsored projects that studied Indigenous peoples in the service of colonial expansion) based in scientific objectivity, linearity (characteristic of scientific process that in-cludes sequential hypothesis, prediction, test, analysis, replication and gen-eralizability), and essentialist truths (knowledge recognized as necessarily generalizable and universal), were challenged by new interpretive, critical inquiry that confronted meaning making and validity. Such is the era where we encounter Patti Lather's first intellectual production.

Growing out of this turn of events, qualitative researchers, such as Lather, realize that culture cannot be "captured" on the page, that any inquiry is filtered and otherwise created by the researcher based on his or her biases, perspectives, and interpretations. That is, inquiry is being reconceptualized through the participatory body of the researcher speaking and listening, rather than seeing, surveying, and writing. Validity, generalizability, and reli-ability are contested terminology, giving way to more performative (popular theater, dance, poetry, etc.), interpretive (ethnographic novel, ethnographic film, documentary, etc.), and critical methods of understanding society. De-scribing the changes that have emerged in qualitative inquiry, which Lather has been championing since the 1980s, Denzin and Lincoln (2005) com-ment that epistemologies from previously underrepresented groups have now emerged to directly address these challenges. Without letting scholar-ship simply indulge in such "accomplishments" (meaning, being satisfied with new ways of conceptualizing epistemology and inquiry that countered long held, until then undisputed, authority of positivistic science), Lather's ideas emphasize the centrality of inquiry that fosters actual spaces for the un-derrepresented to speak up and to engage in knowledge production.

Lather's work at the turn of the century (moving from the twentieth to the twenty-first) carefully takes the pulse of not only what academia is saying about research but also what institutional processes are set in place to define the conversations that researchers and organizations are having about education. In this sense, Lather finds the new federal efforts "to legislate proper scientific method" extremely problematic (Lather, 2006, p. 10). During a gallery talk at the University of South Carolina Museum of Education (JSNCRG, 2009), Lather asserted that federal legislation as of late, beginning with the Bush administration's No Child Left Behind act, has initiated an intrusive, undemocratic environment that can adversely impact the education of future educational researchers. In doing so, Lather pointed to the grave economic and political consequences of the narrow-ing and submission of research agendas in line with such policy regula-tions. Additionally, acknowledging the pervasiveness of such trends and the risks of letting them go unchallenged, Lather (2010) asked "Why are we so easily convinced that what happens in classrooms is best understood as objective, transparent, measurable, that mechanistic promises that all students can learn to the same standard make democratic sense, that the inner life of teachers is disposable in the quest for quality schools?" (p. 63) In her search for and sense of urgency to see more nuanced and sophisticated ways to know the realities of schools, teaching and learning, Lather clarifies that in this moment that calls for socially useful social science research it is important to know that "the key is that what is contested in not science or rigor or even evidence-based practice but, rather, orthodox views of such matters" through which one-size fits all models are imposed (Lather, 2010, p. 67). Her aim is to find possibilities of where researchers and all actors have the capacity to negotiate across "standard procedures from many paradigms to engage with the uncertainties of knowledge towards more nuanced thinking" and thus towards a less imperialistic social science (67). Calling particularly on those committed to critical pedagogy, Lather adds that improved policy and practice is an important aim in this quest.

MAJOR THEORIES

Lather (1992) identifies herself as a feminist methodologist, "a person who does research on research" (p. 87). As such, her major theories regarding teaching about social issues involve teaching educational research students more socially just means of being knowledge producers. She encourages her students to think about how their lives are mediated by systems of inequality vis-à-vis racism, sexism, classism, etc., and to find ways of incorporating an understanding of this into their own inquiry.

From primarily qualitative and feminist perspectives, Lather's work contributes to a postpositivist educational inquiry that moves away from measurable, quantifiable units toward inquiries of interpretive, "uneasy" social theory. She teaches graduate students learning to be educational researchers that validity is essential to knowledge production. Believing that there is no such thing as interest free knowledge, she advocates educational researchers to be emancipatory, interactive, and action inspiring, in which they produce work that improves upon the social conditions for those being researched.

To achieve this, Lather asserts, it is essential to develop methods or "self-corrective techniques" that check and recheck the truth claims of the research process to ensure biases are not overlooked, further preventing misrepresentation or potential harm to vulnerable communities. These processes involve the researcher in paying attention to places in their research where data possibly converges with or counters established or developing theories, as well as continuously reflecting upon their own positionality and its effect on the research outcome. It involves having members of the community being researched check the accuracy or conclusions of the process and product to ensure the research is not misrepresenting community members. Finally, it involves reflecting upon how the research has affected the researcher and participants for the better, and/or if it has led to activism or change for social justice.

Lather (2006) believes that ethical educational research requires moving outside of predefined, competitive paradigms and methodological influence toward efforts which contemplate problems within knowledge production itself. She asks that her graduate students embark on cross-disciplinary inquiries that question what is possible in the way of promoting a socially just inquiry, situating themselves theoretically and methodologically in the tensions that characterize various fields of knowledge production. Lather advocates moving toward a messiness that interrupts and exceeds predetermined categories by "perverting" theoretical paradigms in an effort to open new space for what is possible.

Finding places of impasse where paradigms rub up against one another and metaphorically get stuck, Lather's theories about teaching social issues focus on helping students resist technical thought and method and moving toward more playful sites of resistance within theoretical frameworks. She encourages students to engage in objectivity debates, fostering an understanding of how politics, desires, and beliefs influence the nature of epistemology. She encourages students to challenge the fixed categories of paradigms themselves, considering them as something to think with rather than "a master narrative." This is done through the use of intersectional frameworks that complicate rigid categories, shifting possibilities for how we may interpret our methodologies. This requires a fierce attention to the processes and power arrangements inherent to paradigms and the research effort itself.

Lather (2006) believes students should constantly question the unethical aspects of all research, exceeding the precipice that "qualitative is good" and "quantitative is bad," toward reflecting upon the invasive nature of surveillance in any scientific field. Rather than simply presenting numerical facts or honoring voice, students should develop an interpretive sense of the ways people make sense of their lives and order their thoughts. She feels it is important that the researcher locate themselves within the context of the research, disrupting subjective/objective binaries in their work.

Lather encourages students to think hard about validity, questioning who has the rights and authority to construct knowledge claims, recognizing validity is often influenced by political factors. She champions rigorous training for education researchers that incorporates foundational courses in history, philosophy, sociology, and ethnic studies, with critical work of feminist, indigenous, and race-specific movements, so that they may gain an understanding of truth as something more than a technical issue solved by adjusting methodological approaches and that its truth is tied to power and political dimensions within all fields of research, their own and others.

MAJOR ACCOMPLISHMENTS

With numerous published books and journal articles, Lather is a leading academic, researcher and author in feminist theory, educational policy, and qualitative inquiry. The research she has conducted is cross disciplinary in nature, covering such issues as women living with HIV/AIDS, auto-ethnography and performance studies, theoretical topics that provoke feminist methodologies, critical policy studies, critical pedagogy, and poststructural theory. A brief look into her trajectory provides an idea of the persona behind the big ideas. Lather graduated from South Dakota State University with a Bachelor of Arts degree in English in 1970, after which she pursued a Master's degree in American Studies at Purdue. In 1983 she received her PhD in Curriculum and Instruction from Indiana University. Lather has been a professor of Education in the School of Educational Policy and Leadership at Ohio State University since 1988, where she has taught courses on qualitative research, gender in education, and feminist methodology.

Lather has lectured widely and held a number of distinguished visiting lecture positions, including positions at the University of British Columbia, Goteborg University, York University, the Danish Pedagogy Institute, and the Humanities Research Institute at the University of California–Irvine. In 1989 she received a Fulbright Scholarship to study in New Zealand. In addition, her published work continuously receives critical praise including several recognized academic awards. *Getting Smart: Feminist Research and Pedagogy With/in the Postmodern* won the 1991 Critics Choice Award; *Troubling the Angels: Women Living with HIV/AIDS* was the winner of the 1998 Choice Outstanding Academic Title; and *Getting Lost: Feminist Efforts Toward a Double(d) Science* won 2008's Critics Choice Award. Lather was also honored with The American Educational Research Association's 2010 Lifetime Achievement Award. As someone who prolifically, critically and reflexively engages in knowledge production, Lather asserts that such endeavor involves research that enables oppressed members of society to understand their conditions and potentially change them. Her activist work in communities where she researches (particularly communities of women living in marginalized conditions because of HIV/AIDS), encourages the same efforts in graduate students who are learning to be education researchers. One of Lather's key contributions to teaching about social issues involves representing the voice of marginalized women, in order to expose the unequal power relations of the gender binary system. She does not intend to be the "expert" regarding the lives of the women she researches, but rather seeks to have her research be a venue for the lived experiences of those involved in the research process—this includes both those being researched and the researcher.

Lather's work has inspired many researchers in diverse investigative fields to create new ways of representing research in more accessible, socially just and democratic ways. She has done this not only by challenging traditional ways of doing research, but by also challenging the structural, text-based norms that represent inquiry into social issues. The composition of her texts attempt to disrupt the traditional research format by juxtaposing the narratives of research participants with those of the researcher's. She does this by placing the researcher's interpretations in nonauthoritative positions, perhaps at the bottom of the page, while the participants' voices, stories and perspectives are made focal. She often boxes sections of text, scattering background information or footnotes here or there, in order to provide multiple layers to her studies. These spaces can often function as a guide to navigating the text, and also allows the reader to contemplate the narratives that are presented across the page in nonlinear ways. Lather's multivocal discourses serve to de-center the researcher, allowing participants a presence over the authorial rights of the research.

More recently, Lather's contributions speak directly to the ways research and policy, particularly education policy, intersect. She examines present federal efforts to regulate research and their implications not only for the nature of knowledge production, but also the overall impact of these efforts in the lives of the children, teachers and communities who research and policy are supposed to serve. Lather's current work makes an important call to pay attention to what happens beyond the lens of accountability, particularly when including ethics and responsibility in the research agenda.

Given the current political climate, Lather's contribution to teaching about social issues promises to continue being prolific and responsive to the sign of the times. But far from being merely reactionary, Lather's work challenges common assumptions and top-down policy decisions in education while creatively and rigorously developing ways to make research and knowledge more democratic and socially responsive. Her thinking remains particularly alert to contextual and historical epistemology as well as current political trends which she analyzes in depth. In this sense, we consider that a chronological presentation of her work, as presented in this annotated bibliography, allows a fair understanding of the trajectory and context of her major contributions to the field.

CONCLUSIONS

Patti Lather has been influential in the conceptualization and reconceptualization of knowledge, inquiry and pedagogy. Through her publications and work as educator of education researchers, she addresses key issues that continue to challenge social scientists today—power relations with subjects in the field, the crisis of representation, praxis, ethics, responsibility, subjectivity/objectivity, narrative strategy, reflexivity, and situatedness. Her encouragement to find the stuck places, false starts, and dead ends in the research process has influenced a more ethical, contemplative research approach where being messy gives way to nuance, and uncertainty uncovers the possibility of the nature of inquiry itself.

In this light, Lather's more recent work points at relevant and costly new tendencies in the relation between research and policy. She problematizes intentions to regulate and standardize educational research and thus challenges claims concerning validity and evidence-based practice. The current debate which Lather keeps fueling in this respect is of central importance for educational researchers and particularly for those who teach about social issues. Lather stands by the belief that challenges are not only about the quality of knowledge but also about our own role and responsibility in relation to this knowledge—how we engage with communities in more or less democratic, nonauthoritarian constructions of knowledge and whether our participation as educators and researchers can foster a platform for multiple voices and social change.

REFERENCES

Denzin, N. K., & Lincoln, Y. S. (2005). Introduction: The discipline and practice of qualitative research. In N. K. Denzin & Y. S. Lincoln (Eds.), *The SAGE handbook of qualitative research* (pp. 1–32). Thousand Oaks, CA: Sage Publications.

JSNCRG. (2009). *Performing feminist poststructural research by Patti Lather*. Retrieved July 2012, from http://www.youtube.com/watch?v=YMUOOGYsCrU

Keene, A., & Colligan, S. (2004). Service-learning and anthropology. *Michigan Journal of Community Service Learning*, Summer, 5–15.

Kincheloe, J. (2008). *Critical pedagogy primer* (2nd Edition). New York, NY: Peter Lang.

Lather, P. (1986). Issues of validity in openly ideological research: Between a rock and a soft place. *Interchange, 17*(4), 63–84.

Lather, P. (1992). Critical frames in educational research: Feminist and poststructural perspectives. *Theory into Practice, 31*(1), 87–99.

Lather, P. (1993). Fertile obsession: Validity after poststructuralism. *The Sociological Quarterly, 34*(4), 673–693.

Lather, P. (2006). Paradigm proliferation as a good thing to think with: Teaching research in education as a wild profusion. *International Journal of Qualitative Studies in Education, 19*(1), 35–57.

Lather, P. (2010). *Engaging science policy: From the side of the messy*. New York, NY: Peter Lang.

Pillow, W. (2003). Confession, catharsis, or cure? Rethinking the uses of reflexivity as methodological power in qualitative research. *Qualitative Studies in Education, 16*(2), 175–196.

Rachel, J. F. (2009). Deconstruction and the problematics of social engagement: Fertile tensions. *Frontiers: A Journal of Women Studies, 30*(1), 204–211.

ANNOTATED BIBLIOGRAPHY

The following annotated bibliography of Lather's work presents articles and books she has published since the 1980s until her most recent book in 2010. It also includes work she has co-authored as part of research and or dialogues with other scholars in the field.

Lather, P. (1984). Critical theory, curricular transformation and feminist main-streaming. *Journal of Education, 166*(1), 49–62.

As part of Lather's early work, this article discusses how critical inquiry probes at the structural, hegemonic forces that both constrain and sustain unequal power relations. Lather believes women's studies programs serve as "laboratories" where such counter-hegemonic efforts emerge. She states however that theoretical work done in the name of critical neo-Marx based pedagogy often ignores the lived experiences of women in favor of larger social theories, pushing issues pertinent to women to the margins of economic concerns. This article is useful in presenting Lather's major critique of neo-Marxist theory, which she feels ignores women and women's efforts relevant to a true revolutionary praxis. Through the politicization of lived experiences, this work further shows how women's studies programs have been instrumental in bringing about new, anti-patriarchal, anti-capitalistic forms of politics that put women at the center of concerns for social transformation. Lather emphasizes the important role women's studies programs play in raising people's consciousness to social inequalities, providing critical spaces to explore issues of power, knowledge production, and injustices.

Lather, P. (1986). Research as praxis. *Harvard Educational Review, 56*(3), 257–278.

This article explores what it means to have an emancipatory approach to research in the human sciences, a Gramscian based "praxis of the present," in the context of an unjust world. This piece allows us to identify Lather's earlier references in her work about the present time as a postpositivistic period of the human sciences. An approach of research as praxis, Lather asserts, will allow us to understand and help change inequality—what she calls a mal-distribution of power—in the world. In order to develop her argument, Lather presents two assumptions: (a) we are in a postpositivistic period of the human sciences where there has been little exploration on methodologies of emancipatory research, and (b) such research explicitly committed to social justice can offer an important contribution to this debate and context. In addition, Lather's exploration of postpositivistic praxis-oriented research is based on what she calls three programs: feminist research, neo-Marxist critical ethnography and Freirean "empowering" or participatory research. Lather argues that they are important postpositivistic research approaches as they oppose prevailing scientific norms that justify the status quo. Moreover, each approach is premised with a transformative agenda for social structures as well as research methods, in other words, with research as praxis.

Overall, this article problematizes the claimed neutrality of scientific research, stressing that there is no value-neutral approach to knowing, and thus challenging what is presented as the truth by positivistic stances in this respect. Such ideas will be recurrent in Lather's later publications. Here, she already warns against the risk of paralleling positivistic hyper-objectivity. Thus the task of praxis-oriented researchers is the confrontation with issues of empirical accountability. She also indicates that critical inquiry as such differs from the "rape model of research" (using Reinharz terms); a model which, following the researchers top-down agenda, often opts for participant-exploitive forms of inquiry. With these considerations, two questions arise from praxis-oriented research: what is the relationship between data and theory in emancipatory research? And how does one avoid reducing explanations to the intentions of social actors,—by taking into account the deep structures—both social and psychological (conscious and unconscious) that shape human experience and perceptions, without committing theoretical imposition?

False consciousness is the denial of how our commonsense ways of looking at the world are permeated with meanings that sustain our disempowerment. Lather suggests an interactive approach to research that requires reciprocal reflexivity and critique. In efforts to liberate vulnerable communities, the neo-Marxist approach to research claims that the role of the researcher is "interpreter of the world." In their move toward recognizing marginalized groups, their approach often results in an imposition of claims which repress and dominate as they seek to identify and emancipate. In this context, critical inquiry constitutes a response to less democratic ways of knowing and becomes both a process that is fundamentally dialogic and mutually educative.

Lather, P. (1986). Issues of validity in openly ideological research: Between a rock and a soft place. *Interchange, 17*(4), 63–84.

This article begins with a discussion of the postpositive break with positivism's methods of objectivity and neutrality, presenting one of Lather's most compelling arguments that all research is ideologically driven. Lather argues that postpositivistic methodological intentions are as ideologically laden as positivistic inquiry, however much empowering and emancipatory in nature they aim to be. Moving beyond the objective/subjective binary, she discusses how validity can be re-conceptualized in openly ideological Marxist, feminist, and Freirean research paradigms.

Lather recommends an inquiry which is more self-aware of its claims to truth through methods of (a) triangulation, (b) construct validity, (c) face validity, and (d) catalytic validity. Triangulation involves the checking of various methods of verification to establish if consistent results emerge. Construct validity using "systemized reflexivity" checks to ensure that the methods used to construct truth are adequately able to do so. Face validity checks in with research members to verify their reactions to developing theoretical claims and makes appropriate changes in response. Catalytic validity looks at how the research has impacted the community members being researched as well as the researcher, potentially leading to a transformation of society.

Lather, P. (1987). The absent presence: Patriarchy, capitalism and the nature of teacher work. *Teacher Education Quarterly, 14*(2), 25–38.

Lather further contributes to analyze the "gender blindness" of neo-Marxist scholarship in respect to education. Calling it an issue of "and women, of course," she discusses the ways in which neo-Marxist movements have only recently added on an analysis of the subordination of women and work to their project of class-based social reform, ignoring the realities and necessities of a complete paradigm upheaval if they are to actually include gender based oppressions into their analysis of life under capitalist regimes.

Lather believes to truly understand the conditions of the teaching profession, issues of gender are essential. Under the capitalist system, teaching has been historically constructed as an extended functional role of motherhood, one which women are expected to perform in addition to work within the family. As such, teaching patriarchal values to children ensures that the subordinate role of "women as caretakers" continues to future generations both inside the family unit and in the classroom.

Lather believes capitalism and Marxism have historically ignored the work women do both inside and outside of the home—in addition to being caretakers or not. She puts forth that women can benefit from the extensive theoretical body of knowledge within Marxist theory, but must resist becoming perpetuators of another male dominated discourse. This requires a praxis which moves beyond grand social theories toward empirical research which places women's issues at the forefront of concerns for social equality.

Lather, P. (1988). Feminist perspectives on empowering research methodologies. *Women's Studies International Forum, 11*(6), 569–581.

This piece is useful in presenting Lather's major ideas concerning feminism and emancipatory, praxis-based inquiry. Feminist researchers highlight gender and gendered perspectives in order to foster an understanding of women's positionality in the world. For feminist researchers, this process involves interactive, interpretive meaning-making rather than predictable, controlled knowledge production. Instead of concentrating on results, Lather's work as exemplar of poststructural feminist research uses the investigative process as an empowering method through dialogue, consciousness raising, and data generated and analyzed by research participants.

In this work, later expanded upon in *Getting Smart,* Lather puts forth a better understanding of how poststructural feminism de-centers totalizing discourses that often fall into theoretical, universalist traps. She says that to be "essence-less," to lack foundational grounds, requires practices of critique and self-reflexivity, further accepting the often biased, intersectional and transitory nature of knowledge construction itself.

Lather, P. (1991). *Getting smart: Feminist research and pedagogy with/in the postmodern.* New York, NY: Routledge.

Lather's take on critical social science in *Getting Smart: Feminist Research and Pedagogy with/in the Postmodern* focuses on the ways in which postmodernism problematizes subjectivity, agency, and how power saturates the construction of knowledge production. In discussing her own research into students' resistance in a women's studies program at the Ohio State University, Lather challenges the authoritative voice in qualitative research by presenting a multivocal work that displaces the "expert researcher" in foundational based academic inquiry.

Writing from within the discourses she also critiques, this piece questions what is to be done to salvage emancipatory praxis within theoretically established, often incongruous paradigms. She believes it is necessary to remain open-ended and self-reflective, recognizing that no research or theory is without ideology. In order to enact emancipatory action within established frames, Lather finds it is necessary to deconstruct the politics of the research agenda itself, including neo-Marxist, feminist, or others which may replicate domination within the libratory discourses they propose.

This book contributes to a better understanding of how meaning is constructed within different discourses of inquiry particularly relevant to the study of pedagogical spaces. Lather sees pedagogy residing at the intersection of the teacher, the learner, and the knowledge they produce together. She concludes however that "transmissive" rather than "interactive" pedagogy has often failed the emancipatory educational project and that more open, transparent methods should be practiced in order to sustain more responsible critical work. This book broadens Lather's major concerns with authority in qualitative, postmodern research in the construction of knowledge and truth.

Lather, P. (1991). Post-critical pedagogies: A feminist reading. In C. Luke & J. Gore (Eds.), *Feminisms and critical pedagogy* (pp. 120–137). New York, NY: Routledge.

Lather defines deconstruction as the continual displacement to safeguard against dogmatism. As a researcher's tool, it continuously problematizes wholeness and resolutions, unsettling established theories and paradigms. For Lather, deconstruction keeps the critical conversation going by revealing the components that make up the "noninnocence" of truth claims. This article continues Lather's work in probing at emancipatory frames of inquiry which can also serve to perpetuate relations of domination. Its further purpose explores whether the salvaging of praxis itself, a discussion she developed in earlier writings (1986), is possible in the current antifoundational era.

Liberatory practices of scholars are particularly susceptible to reproducing sites of domination, especially within the primarily Marxist, male dominated theoretical sphere of critical pedagogy. Lather writes that Marxist theory has always taken feminist practices as the "handmaiden" or "wife," neglecting women and women's issues as sites of resistance in the movement. Lather suggests post structural feminism—a theory of impermanence, of partiality, of transformation—as a means to disrupt the high theory of Marxism. She proposes that there are no innocent libratory discourses however, as such, she feels differences between theoretical positioning can be fruitful places to develop a more critically reflexive pedagogy.

Lather, P. (1992). Critical frames in educational research: Feminist and post-structural perspectives. *Theory into Practice, 31*(2), 87–99.

Seeking to move away from positivistic methodology and quantitative methods applied to the study of human beings, Lather mentions a "paradigm shift" in qualitative inquiry, a shift that moves away from calculable, value-free measures toward an "uneasy social science" of the postmodern era. Educational research has traditionally resided in the behavioralist, psychological strand of positivistic inquiry. Born of interpretive methods in anthropology, however, poststructural feminist research in education is seeking to undergo a paradigm shift, and has since turned toward more participatory, contextualized meaning making methods to inquire into the social sciences. Such research not only contests positivistic methodology, but further explores and seeks to rectify the power imbalances endogenous to the research process.

To contend with these power imbalances, feminists doing research in education, amongst other fields, situate gender as a social construct. First wave feminism worked within positivistic frames, however, it wasn't until the second wave, when feminists began questioning power, the right to do research and make knowledge possible, and the objective/subjective divide, that the movement began to document a new understanding of what it means to do social inquiry. Lather believes these frames will lead way to more constructivist, participatory practices for researchers serving anti-racist, anti-classist, anti-sexist agendas within pedagogy and society at large.

Lather, P. (1993). Fertile obsession: Validity after poststructuralism. *Sociological Quarterly, 34*(4), 673–693.

This article intends to help researchers rethink validity in antifoundational discourse theory. Lather calls for validity grounded in theorizing practice itself, one which begins by questioning our obsessions with truth, in order to displace hegemonic belief systems and potentially open space for what is possible outside the normative frames of social science.

Such spaces offer counter-practices to traditional forms of scientific method and deconstructs the political nature of validity and its claims to exact categorization. These structural counter-practices seek truth through acknowledging biases, preconceptions, and influence upon the investigative method. Lather defines four ways in which validity can be reconceptualized to create a more socially just knowledge production. These include reconceptualizing a poststructural validity as (a) ironic, (b) neo-pragmatic, (c) rhizomatic, and (d) situated.

Lather sees such poststructural validity as "transgressive," however much working within the established discourses of traditional scientific methods. Within such systems of power, poststructural validity has the ability to deconstruct ideological problematics, opening new spaces for social science. Such validity questions the inability of research to make truth claims and challenges academic inquiry as an authority to develop such claims. It does not rely upon metanarratives or paradigm codes but rather instabilities, multimodalities, nonlinearities, and indeterminacies to provide space for new forms knowledge development. Such forms of validity rely upon participants being given space to provide voice and input to the researcher and in the research process, thus displacing the privilege of the academic as the all powerful administer of truth.

Lather, P. (1996). Troubling clarity: The politics of accessible language. *Harvard Educational Review, 66*(3), 525–545.

Referencing Giroux's "politics of clarity," the quest for intelligibility is a pressing issue in educational research that is concerned with the relationship between theory-practice. As Lather states in this important article, the debate at hand transcends the binary of plain speaking and complex writing. She responds to critiques of inaccessible language specifically targeting language use featured through feminist writing, and to the claim that writing ought to be intelligible and realistic. Through her response, she advocates for multivoiced texts which express the complexity of understandings and sense making of the world, moving textual representations from realist to interrogative.

Using the work on *Troubling Angels,* Lather depicts how inter-textual, multivocal texts, instead of simple realistic tales, pay justice to the stories of the participants and researchers in the study. This move towards multiple texts and voices also points to the question of what types of knowledge are considered "worthy" in struggles for social justice. Thus, Lather furthers the discussion by turning the attention of her analysis to ethnographic representation in the Western feminist traditions which, she finds, tends to be preoccupied with fieldwork and rhetorical strategies. She questions the romantic aspirations of "giving voice" to the disempowered when plain representation encourages "manipulation, violation and betrayal" (539).

Lather, P. & Smithies, C. (1997). *Troubling the angels: Women living with HIV/AIDS.* Boulder, CO: Westview Press.

In this award winning book, Lather and Smithies' qualitative study of HIV positive women primarily deals with the emotional aspects of living with HIV/AIDS and how this condition affects their lives. Featuring a collection of voices from conversations held during support groups and one-on-one meetings, this book is useful in exemplifying Lather's major ideas concerning poststructural feminist approaches to representing research.

Keeping reflexive notes on the bottom of each page that provide a type of commentary on the researchers' emotional experiences during the research process, as well as through the course of developing intimate relationships with the participants in the study, Lather and Smithies present themselves as fully as their participants in their study. They further provide readers with statistical data and facts that assist in a better, intersectional understanding of the context within which these women living with HIV/AIDS, as well as those conducting the research, find themselves.

By seeking to contest the researcher/researched binary, Lather and Smithies' work draws attention to the power differentials intrinsic to the investigative process, as well as to the potential influence this has on the women's stories and readers' reactions to them. This demonstrates Lather's belief that qualitative research needs to become openly ideological and reflexive for a more participatory and emancipatory social science, one which presents multiple access points to understanding how those being studied make sense of their lives.

Lather, P. (1998). Critical pedagogy and its complicities. *Educational Theory, 48*(4), 487–497.

This article broadens Lather's major concerns with the abstract and universal nature of critical pedagogy as a male-centered theory. In this work she seeks to reimagine critical pedagogy as a more open praxis of "not being so sure." Lather particularly critiques the libratory mission of McLaren's and Gur-Ze'ev's work which takes up class struggles and utopia, believing "the new" revolutionary pedagogy they propose is still situated in an already rationalist form of democracy that is too closed, too "stiff," too homogenizing. Instead, she proposes a more incomplete, tentative critical pedagogy that is more praxis-based and subject-centered. She suggests a method which works through problems or "aporias" in order to learn from the "stuck places" and failures of a critical approach to education.

Lather, P. (2000). Reading the image of Rigoberta Menchu. *Qualitative Studies in Education, 13*(2), 153–162.

Because language is unreliable, often influenced by informants' "desire to persuade, protect, and preserve," Lather suggests interpreting the performance of language itself, looking to how a story is told rather than what is being told, what's being left out as much as what is offered (p. 154). Rather than interpreting the words of participants, Lather finds an understanding of the performative aspects of giving an account of oneself is a much more graspable means of understanding an event than defining words as truth. This piece serves as an introduction to Lather's inquiry into performance studies and auto-ethnography.

Lather discusses the popular means of storytelling in Latin America known as "testimonio"—accounts not only of the storyteller but of people within a historical context. Focusing on the acclaimed testimonio of Rigoberta Menchu, an indigenous Guatemalan woman who provides an account of her and her community's experiences during her country's massacre of Indian-ladino peasants, Lather deconstructs the "undecidability" of her narrative, citing that the words Menchu doesn't provide is just as important as what she does.

Lather believes there are no innocent testimonios left untouched by colonial, academic, scientific, or other paradigmatic sensibilities, and instead looks "to the ruins" of what remains once testimonio has undergone such translation. She believes translation as dissemination through mimesis or imitation, and not containment, can shift and change constantly, producing rather than reflecting truths.

Lather, P. (2001). Ten years later, yet again: Critical pedagogy and its complicities. In K. Weiler (Ed.), *Feminist engagements: Reading, resisting, and revisioning male theorists in education and cultural studies* (pp. 183–195). New York, NY: Routledge.

Contextualizing her analysis on a debate that is not new but that nonetheless remains current, Lather continues to critique critical pedagogy as a "boy thing," not for its proliferation of male scholars but for its universal, abstract sense of righteous superiority. Viewing critical pedagogy as undisciplined, occurring most potently between "the ruins" of divergent notions of what the field should be, Lather again takes issue with the McLaren School's revolutionary approach to pedagogy. She suggests the discipline should recognize the heterogeneous, open and indefinable characteristics of critical work.

In this piece Lather takes particular issue with the limited use of poststructuralist critique in McLaren's essay *Revolutionary Pedagogy in Post-revolutionary Time: Rethinking the Political Economy of Critical Education*. In her view, McLaren's universal attempts to transform education within the larger social structure through Marx-based attention to class and material struggle, his visions of utopia and new social alternatives, are regurgitative of an outdated critical method.

Though she does agree with McLaren that it is necessary to rethink critical pedagogy in contemporary historical contexts, Lather prefers letting go of the security of grand Marxist theory in favor of a tentative, incomplete, not knowing praxis.

Lather, P. (2004). Foucauldian 'indiscipline' as a sort of policy application. In B. Baker & K. Heyning (Eds.), *Dangerous coagulations? The uses of Foucault in the study of education* (pp. 279–304). New York, NY: Peter Lang Publishers.

Despite the increase of postparadigm shifts in critical knowledge production in the last decade, positivism and evidence-based research seem to dominate policy made decisions, particularly in education. As part of Lather's latest concerns, this article is useful in presenting her critique of policy-regulated qualitative education research. Here she relates science based-policy making as applied to education as a form of Foucauldian bio-politics, and offers insights into the ways in which policy can be reconceived as a counter-science.

Using Foucault's notion of "positivities," Lather sees counter-science as a new era of blurred paradigms and disciplines, accompanied by movements of social change by the marginalized. She envisions a Nietzschean "gay science," one which critiques modern nineteenth-centuries' positivistic approach to measuring and cataloguing in the name of science, in favor of knowledge production that is life-affirming, courageous, and enraptured in possibility. Conceived in such a way, this approach does not reject the potential of modern science, but rather envisions a turn toward politics of culture rather than quantifiable numerical values. This work helps revision inquiry from a queer theoretical perspective, one which relishes upon error, the unresolved, and looks to the problems as a way of producing new forms of knowledge.

Lather, P. (2004). Scientific research in education: A critical perspective. *British Educational Research Journal*, *30*(6), 759–772.

One of the important assertions Lather includes in this article is that in fact little evidence is available that shows that evidence-based practice works (763). Lather identifies issues surrounding the claims of scientific research as a question of politics more than of quality of work. Formulas to satisfy the claim for transparent accountability construct objectivity with intentions of balance across multiple methods, however, such intentions only translate into the displacement of description, interpretation and discovery that can be offered through qualitative perspectives. Moreover, Lather sees the push for transferring a medical model of research to education as an assault on multiculturalism. She advocates for the kind of science that embraces rich ambiguities and stays close to complexities and contradictions of existence, fostering "understanding, reflection and action instead of a narrow translation of research into practice" (p. 767).

Lather argues further for the inclusion of critical qualitative perspectives in the education of program evaluators and policy analysts. The purpose of such preparation is to make these actors capable of "fuzzying the lines between both research and evaluation" as well as "between empirical research, politics, and the philosophical renewal of public deliberation" (p. 767). Lather warns readers of the consequences of applying scientific research to education following a golden standard. She asserts that trying to do so is far from allowing gains in the research and practice endeavor, and even more so when the loss of messiness and complexity have grave consequences on the lives of children and adults who are part of our schools.

Lather, P. (2004). Critical inquiry in qualitative research: Feminist and poststructural perspectives: Science after truth. In K. DeMarrais & S. Lapan (Eds.) *Foundations for research; Methods of inquiry in education and the social sciences* (pp. 203–216). Mawah, NJ: Lawrence Erlbaum Associates.

In this chapter, Lather discusses postpositivism as the present moment in paradigm proliferation, a moment which claims that there is no one way to do scientific inquiry. It is a time of contending paradigms where legitimacy and authority are questioned given the displacement of the orthodox consensus of what it means to do science. Thus, advocacy vs. neutrality and disclosure vs. prescription are characteristic of debates concerning this time. In this sense, Lather positions critical inquiry within the social sciences that deal with what are multi-voiced, messy, and uneasy approaches to knowing. The focus of Lather's analysis is on poststructuralism and what it offers to critical empirical inquiry in the social sciences. One important question she poses for her analysis is how to bring together scholarship and advocacy in order to generate ways of knowing that disrupt power inequalities. The latter is an important question in that it destabilizes the position of the researcher as, what Foucault would term, "The Great Liberator"—one who speaks for, rather than to/with those struggling for social justice.

Lather presents several examples of research methods that address feminist methods, including her own and coauthor Smithies' reflexive approach during the research and writing of *Troubling the Angels*. Lather's honest questioning of her role as researcher, and the overall purpose of her project, proves instructive to those engaged in qualitative approaches, particularly to those concerned with the ethical implications of such undertakings. More than bringing closure to the urgency of rethinking inquiry work, Lather acknowledges the challenge "of being left to work from traditions of research that appear no longer adequate to the task. Between the no-longer and the not-yet lies the possibility of what was impossible under traditional regimes of truth in the social sciences" (p. 214). Being one committed to work with uneasy social science, she embraces this dilemma as her main task.

Lather, P. (2006). Paradigm proliferation as a good thing to think with: Teaching research in education as a wild profusion. *International Journal of Qualitative Studies in Education, 19*(1), 35–57.

As a good continuation of the publication presented above ("Critical Inquiry in Qualitative Research: Feminist and Poststructural Perspectives: Science After Truth"), this article discusses ways in which theories and approaches to inquiry are mapped and compared through a process of "coloring epistemologies," which represent a permanent effort, never a finished state, in the quest for knowing. Lather calls her approach a "paradigm proliferation." She presents a series of charts that not only show ways in which she teaches her students, but also analyzes the affordances and limitations of utilizing this means to develop student thinking towards unpacking discursive formations and embracing the multiplicity of knowledge as education researchers. Lather's methods here aim at directly addressing present movements towards top-down government imposition of the experimental design as the standard to follow in research methods.

One of the relevant questions Lather poses is what it means to claim the status of "knowledge producer" when academic work becomes juxtaposed to counter knowledge from different communities, some of them traditionally situated as the studied ones, the receivers, if not consumers, of produced knowledge. The proliferation of such knowledge is also the object of attention in Lather's analysis. She advocates for praxis that disrupts the construct of transformative intellectuals who are on a quest to liberate others, thus becoming a praxis that fosters diverse practices or what she calls "practices of excess, affect, speed and complexity" (p. 45).

Lather proceeds to situate what this all means for the teaching of research in education and, moreover, she calls attention to the present institutionalization of limited definitions of educational research. From the National Research Council's report of 2002 to the Carnegie Initiative, these attempts aim at impacting doctoral preparation of educational researchers as well as the very ways in which research is focused and implemented.

Lather, P. (2007). *Getting lost: Feminist efforts toward a double(d) science.* Albany, NY: State University of New York Press.

As it is characteristic of Lather's publications, the reader can see a continuation of her ideas throughout her writing. Lather revisits these ideas through analyzing research from students and recognized scholars in order to discuss theory and research approaches, including issues of validity in the field. This important book constitutes the further development of her ideas concerning feminist epistemologies and methodologies as another way of knowing that counters hegemonic pretensions of positivistic science. Lather provides clear definitions of commonly utilized notions important to her work—postmodernism, poststructuralism and deconstruction, for example—notions that have not previously conveyed agreed upon definitions in the field of qualitative inquiry.

Lather provides useful clarification by outlining the differences between postmodernism and poststructuralism. Postmodernism, Lather argues, constitutes the material and historical shifts of "the global uprising of the marginalized, the revolution in communication technology, and the fissures of global-multinational hyper-capitalism," while poststructuralism "refers more narrowly to a sense of the limits of Enlightenment rationality" (p. 5) and the problematization of totalizing universalistic intends in positivistic trends. Based on Derrida's seminal work on deconstruction, Lather provides a method to disrupt universal and binary intends. She further illustrates an anti-method for making ontological claims.

Through this book, Lather aims at challenging the "social imaginary" concerning research in times when claims about the death of high theory are being made. Lather asserts that this is neither a beginning nor an end but an in-between. A central claim is that such a state of suspension, or aporias, is an ethical practice in disenchanted times. This ethical practice does not close the debate but in fact opens the door for something else to come about. It is a direct response to what she calls the neoliberal audit culture and its demands for inquiry and knowledge of quantifiable value.

Lather, P. (2008). Getting lost: Critiquing across differences as a methodological practice. In K. Gallagher (Ed.), *The methodological dilemma: Creative, critical and collaborative approaches to qualitative research* (pp. 219–231). New York, NY: Routledge.

Lather looks at cultural epistemologies as places from which to speak about race and racial categories—how they are created, inhabited, changed, and destroyed. Within these spaces, the ways in which race is talked about is dynamic and, as such, have the ability to enhance a decolonizing project.

Doing a queer theoretical reading of Hill-Collins' "working the ruins" as a political practice, Lather questions the role of identity and its ability to strategically operate within and transform dominant paradigms. One radical idea that Lather suggests in this piece is an encouragement of "not-knowing," an "ambivalence" strategy for transforming spaces where the dominant culture tries to appropriate differences. For example, mis- or dis-identifications done by researchers has the potential to become sights of critical production in emancipatory discourses.

Rather than neglecting intersectionality in favor of ambivalent identity construction, Lather suggests blowing the categories up to whole new levels of multiplicities. She believes multiple "othernesses" will contribute to resistance against dogmatic reductionism inherent in identity politics. Her views on "getting lost" recognize the limitlessness of epistemology, where what we don't know becomes fertile, ethical grounds for understanding the racial, gendered, classed complexities of society.

Lather, P. (2009). Against empathy, voice and authenticity. In A. Youngblood Jackson & L. Mazzei (Eds.), *Voice in qualitative inquiry: Challenging conventional, interpretive, and critical conceptions in qualitative research* (pp. 17–26). New York, NY: Routledge.

To come out of the crisis of representation was an ethnography that privileged the voice and authenticity of all participants involved in the research process. Confessions, researcher reflections, multivocalities, and personal narratives have been a way for ethnography to move away from scientific methods toward more humanities based approaches.

Lather, however, encourages researchers to resist the notion that a poststructural feminist inquiry must be based on empathy toward one's subjects of study. She compellingly suggests moving away from a desire of mutual, shared experience and "touristic" intimacy, instead emphasizing a Nietzschean "gay science" that splinters with established scientific methods of control and results, moving beyond fixed categories and immobilizing paradigms even within qualitative inquiry.

She also cautions that too much empathy can be a violation which—because we assume to know, to relate, and to understand—prevents us from actually listening and paying attention to what is being said by others. In considering empathy as a liberal attempt to know and to, at the very least, understand "the other" in social science inquiry, Lather suggests that researchers deconstruct their own assumptions regarding the rights they assume they have in knowing "the other." In doing such reflexive work, researchers will begin to realize the inevitable inability to ever know their participants at all, to ever capture their voice or experience, except through their own interpretive frames. This article is useful in presenting Lather's ideas concerning the authority of qualitative feminist poststructuralist and postmodernist research in its claims to knowledge construction.

Lather, P. (2010). *Engaging science policy: From the side of the messy.* New York, NY: Peter Lang.

Lather's latest book continues to emphasize the urgency to trouble the imperialistic aims of positivistic trends in educational research. Voicing ideas already developed in her various publications after the year 2000, Lather stresses what she finds to be a new movement towards federal regulation of educational research. Such movement has been invigorated in Washington through the No Child Left Behind act. The book points directly at this movement as patriarchal government intrusion, thus situating the discussion in similar terms to those of her earlier contributions in the debates over feminist research, poststructural epistemologies and critical pedagogy. The book discussion centers then on problematizing the trends in educational research that attempt to impose a one-size fits all model to inquiry, dangerously disguising knowledge as "objective" and "neutral." Resonating with her ideas in earlier publications, the book also points at how these models are undemocratic and how they directly exclude other ways of knowing about schools and education.

Moss, P. A., Phillips, D. C., Erickson, F., Floden, R., Lather, P., & Schneider, B. (2009). Learning from our differences: A dialogue across perspectives on quality in education research. *Educational Researcher, 38*(7), 501–517.

In company with *Engaging Science Policy: From the Side of the Messy*, this publication presents Lather's current concerns about education research. Based on a forum that took place at the Annual Conference of the American Education Research Association, which brought together education researchers such as Pamela Moss, Denis Phillips, Frederick Erickson, Robert Floden, Patti Lather, and Barbara Schneider, this article is the publication form of a dialogue between scholars who represent different perspectives concerning the timely issue of quality in research education. Interestingly, the central question that occupies this discussion is one that Lather has been addressing throughout her own publications: whether "social sciences should approach the study of social phenomena in the same ways natural sciences have approached the study of natural phenomena" (502)?

In the discussion presented in this article, Lather reaffirms the ideas she has established quite emphatically throughout her work while also expressing their relevance as she shares her main fear: "one-best-way thinking, especially as endorsed by governmental force, will continue to enact the management, containment and marginalization of both, qualitative research and, more important, research that can make a difference in improving our schools" (p. 506).

As shown across her publications, from her individually authored publications to her collaborative works, Lather consistently brings perspectives together, as well as scholars together, in dialogue that has a substantial impact on our understandings about our own perspectives, the quality of research and the directions that research itself (as well as the teaching of it) takes to enhance knowledge about social issues. Lather points educators and researchers not only to the knowledge that has been produced thus far, but most importantly, to the historical and political processes underlying this production. She adds a necessary critical and ethical lens to education research and its praxis aimed at disrupting inequality, constructing democratic ways of knowing, and impacting society at large.

ABOUT THE EDITORS

Samuel Totten is Professor Emeritus, University of Arkansas (U of A), Fayetteville, College of Education and Health Professors, Department of Curriculum and Instruction. Prior to his 25 years at the U of A, Totten taught English and social studies in Australia (1976–1978), California (1978–1979 and 1980–1981); Israel (1979–1980); and the U.S. House of Representatives Page School (1984–1985). He also served as principal of Esparto K–8 School in California from 1985 to 1987.

He earned a MEd and EdD at Teachers College, Columbia University, where he studied under Dr. Maxine Greene, Dr. Dwayne Huebner, Dr. Lawrence Cremin, and Dr. Ann Lieberman, among others.

From 2003 to 2013, Totten served as the managing editor of a series entitled *Genocide: A Critical Bibliographic Review* (New Brunswick, NJ: Transaction Publishers). The last four volumes in the series under his editorship were: *Plight and Fate of Women During and Following Genocide* (2009), *The Genocide of Indigenous Peoples* (with Robert Hitchcock) (2011), *Impediments to the Prevention and Intervention of Genocide* (2012); and *The Plight and Fate of Children During and Following Genocide* (2014).

From 2005 to 2012 he served as founding coeditor of *Genocide Studies and Prevention: An International Journal,* the official journal of the International Association of Genocide Scholars (University of Toronto Press).

In 2008 Totten served as a Fulbright Scholar at the Centre for Conflict Management at the National University of Rwanda.

For the past twenty years, Totten's primary field of study was Genocide Studies. Among the books he has written, coauthored and coedited on

Educating About Social Issues in the 20th and 21st Centuries, pages 481–482
Copyright © 2014 by Information Age Publishing

genocide are: *Genocide in Darfur: Investigating Atrocities in the Sudan* (New York: Routledge, 2006); *Dictionary of Genocide* (Westport, CT: Greenwood Publishers, 2008); *An Oral and Documentary History of the Darfur Genocide* (Santa Barbara, CA: Praeger Security International, 2010); *We Cannot Forget: Interviews with Survivors of the 1994 Genocide in Rwanda* (New Brunswick, NJ: Rutgers University Press, 2011); *Genocide by Attrition: The Nuba Mountains, Sudan* (New Brunswick, NJ: Transaction Publishers, 2012); and *Centuries of Genocide.* Fourth Edition (New York: Routledge, 2012).

One of his specialties in the field of education was teaching and learning about social issues. Beginning in 1994, he teamed up with Dr. Jon Pedersen and over the next eighteen years they edited eight books related to addressing social issues in the secondary classroom.

Jon E. Pedersen is currently the Associate Dean for Research in the College of Education and Human Sciences at the University of Nebraska–Lincoln. He has long been involved in scholarly work about social issues and science education. He has coedited a number of books with Samuel Totten, including: *Researching and Teaching Social Issues: The Personal Stories and Pedagogical Efforts of Professors of Education* (Lanham, MD: Lexington Books, 2005); *Addressing Social Issues Across the Curriculum: The Pedagogical Efforts of Pioneers in the Field* (Charlotte, NC: Information Age, 2007); *Social Issues and Community Service/Service Learning at the Middle Level* (Information Age, 2007); *Teaching and Studying Social Issues: Major Programs and Approaches* (Information Age, 2011); and *Educating About Social Issues in the 20th and 21st Centuries: An Annotated Bibliography, Volumes 1–4* (Information Age, 2012, 2013, and 2014). Pedersen has also published numerous articles related to social issues in science including, "The Effects of Cooperative Controversies, Presented as STS Issues, on Anxiety and Achievement in Secondary Science Classrooms in *School Science and Mathematics Journal*); "An Indoor Study of the Great Outdoors" in Science and Children; and with Samuel Totten "Strengthening Community Service Projects in Middle Schools by Under Girding Them with the Study of Pertinent Social Issues" (*Current Issues in Middle Level Education*); "Taking Action at the Local Level: The Study of Social Issues in the Middle School in *Inquiry in Social Studies*" (*Curriculum, Research, and Instruction*); and "Social Studies Students' Perceptions and Knowledge of Social Issues: A National Study" (*Inquiry in Social Studies: Curriculum, Research, and Instruction*).

ABOUT THE CONTRIBUTORS

Charlene Johnson Carter is an associate professor in the Department of Curriculum and Instruction at the University of Arkansas, Fayetteville. She has developed and taught courses on multicultural education and African American Studies. She is a member of the American Educational Research Association's Special Interest Group, Research Focus on Black Education. She was the co-author of "Racing into the Academy: Pedagogy and Black Faculty, Some Implications in *Race in the Classroom: Pedagogy and Politics* (New Brunswick, NJ: Rutgers University Press, 2002), and "Egalitarianism and Empowerment in Partnerships in the *Journal of Educational Research.* She coauthored the proposal that was instrumental in establishing an Arkansas state chapter of the National Association for Multicultural Education (N.A.M.E.), and is President-Elect of the organization, 2013–2014.

Michael W. Carter, PhD is an Assistant Teaching Professor of Finance at the University of Missouri, Columbia Missouri. As a high school student, Carter experienced segregation and desegregation in the public school system in Pine Bluff, Arkansas. Subsequently, he worked to garner voter support for minority city council candidates in Waco, Texas, and to support enforcement of court-ordered desegregation in Waco, Texas.

Todd Cherner is an Assistant Professor of Education at Coastal Carolina University. He teaches English Education and Literacy courses in the Spadoni College of Education's Middle Level, Literacy, and Masters of Arts in Teaching programs. He earned his PhD in Secondary Education (English)

Educating About Social Issues in the 20th and 21st Centuries, pages 483–493 from the University of Tennessee. His primary areas of research are school improvement policies and literacy initiatives. At the heart of his work, Todd believes deeply in literacy being an essential part of freedom and works to promote that notion in the classes he teaches and in his writing.

Tabitha Dell'Angelo earned her PhD from the University of Pennsylvania in 2009 and is currently an Assistant Professor at The College of New Jersey, in Ewing, New Jersey. She is the coordinator of the Urban Education Program and teaches courses in Child Development, Urban Education, Teacher Research, and Cultural Foundations. Dr. Dell'Angelo has also taught courses in Theatre of the Oppressed and lead improvisational acting programs in local urban public schools. She has also been working on bringing mindfulness and yoga to elementary school classrooms in order to support students' ability to cope adaptively with stressors and enhance self-regulation skills. Her current research is examining how preservice and in-service teachers understand social justice and how a social justice orientation is implemented into their pedagogical choices. Dr. Dell'Angelo is also writing about how teachers and students coconstruct their identities, especially when they are from disparate cultural backgrounds.

Deborah Donahue-Keegan, EdD, is a Lecturer in the Department of Education at Tufts University, as well as an Education Associate with the Teacher Education Program at Wellesley College. She received her Master of Social Work from Boston College, and her Master of Education and Doctor of Education degrees from Harvard Graduate School of Education.

Her dissertation was based on a qualitative study of ten public high school teachers' work to foster students' sociomoral and civic learning, specifically via constructive approaches to conflict. A recent article ("Fostering Social, Emotional, Ethical, Civic and Academic Learning Through Constructive Controversy: What are the Implications for the Professional Development of High School Teachers?" (*Factis Pax*, 2011) draws on her dissertation study.

Donahue-Keegan's research and teaching focus on social-emotional learning (SEL) and development, equity, and social justice, particularly in terms of teacher preparation. As a Steering Committee member of the Social and Emotional Learning Alliance of Massachusetts (S.A.M.), Donahue-Keegan coleads the Massachusetts SEL-Teacher Education Consortium. Additionally, she is an advisory board member of WhyWellness, an online SEL initiative, and a member of the advisory group for the CARE (Cultivating Awareness and Resiliency in Education) for Teachers program.

Lisa Edstrom is a doctoral student at Teachers College, Columbia University in the department of Curriculum & Teaching. She is also a lecturer and the certification officer for the Barnard Education Program at Barnard College, Columbia University. Her research interests include the role of parent activists in educational policy formation and enactment in schools as well as the situated experiences of families with public schooling more generally.

Kirsten T. Edwards is Assistant Professor of Adult and Higher Education at the University of Oklahoma in Norman, Oklahoma. Edwards' research is most concerned with issues of equity and access in education. Her research merges womanism and womanist theology, curriculum studies, and philosophies of higher education. More specifically, she is interested in the ways that faith, race, gender, class, and culture impact learning, teaching, and knowledge production in university settings. Her publications have additionally considered how identities impact pedagogical approaches in the study of equity, inclusion, and social justice along the educational pipeline.

Edwards' work has been published in various peer-reviewed venues such as the *Journal of Curriculum Theorizing*, the *International Journal of Leadership in Education*, and the *Journal of Curriculum and Pedagogy*. Additionally, she has been invited to deliver several addresses related to topics concerning the experiences of women of color on college campuses; feminism, identity politics and globalization; and college curriculum and Black women scholars.

Edwards' honors and awards include being a finalist in the 2012 *International Journal of Leadership in Education*'s Emergent Scholar Manuscript Competition, Louisiana State University Dissertation Year Fellowship recipient, the 2010 Louisiana State University Black Faculty and Staff Caucus Most Outstanding Graduate Student, and the National Council for Black Studies Summer Research Institute participant. She is also the recipient of the Louisiana State University School of Education's Outstanding Dissertation Award for her dissertation entitled *"She Speaks With Wisdom and Faithful Instruction": The Influence of a Religio-Spiritual Epistemology on the Academic Knowledge, Pedagogy, and Theorizing of Black Women University Teachers."*

Dr. Edwards received her PhD in Higher Education Administration with a specialization in Curriculum Theory in the Department of Educational Theory Policy and Practice at Louisiana State University in Baton Rouge (USA). She additionally holds a cognate in Women's and Gender Studies.

Ronald W. Evans is a leading authority on social studies and curriculum history. His book *The Social Studies Wars*(Teachers College Press, 2004) was named an Outstanding Academic Title for 2004 by *Choice* Magazine. His biography of controversial progressive educator Harold O. Rugg, *This Happened in America* (Information Age, 2007) won the 2008 Exemplary Research Award from the National Council for the Social Studies (NCSS). His book *The Hope for American School Reform* (Palgrave Macmillan, 2011), on the origins and development of the new social studies of the 1960s, also won the Exemplary Research Award from NCSS (2011). His most recent book, *The Tragedy of American School Reform* (Palgrave Macmillan, 2011), examines the turbulent period of school reform from the 1950s through the conservative restoration of the 1980s. He founded the Issues Centered Education Community of NCSS in 1988, and served as first editor of the *Handbook on Teaching Social Issues* (NCSS, 1996). Currently, he is a Professor in the School of Teacher Education at San Diego State University. He lives in the San Diego area with his wife, two children, and a cat.

Kenneth J. Fasching-Varner is the Shirley B. Barton Professor of Education in the College of Human Sciences and Education at Louisiana State University. Fasching-Varner has published two books as well as numerous articles and chapters related to social issues. Fasching-Varner's first book, *Occupying the Academy*, was coedited with Christine Clark and Mark Brimhall-Vargas and published in 2012 by Rowman and Littlefield, and addresses issues of diversity in higher education. His second book, *Working Through Whiteness*, was published in 2012 by Lexington Press and addresses issues of white racial identity among preservice teachers. Fasching-Varner has published articles in such journals as *Social Identities, Literacy and Social Justice, Midwestern Educational Researcher, and Think College Policy Briefs*.

Rachael Gabriel is an Assistant Professor of Reading Education in the Neag School of Education at the University of Connecticut. She is a former fellow of the Baker Center for Public Policy at the University of Tennessee and a current associate of the Center for Education Policy Analysis at the University of Connecticut. She currently teaches graduate courses in literacy education. As a researcher, she has focused on teacher preparation, development and evaluation with a specific interest in related policy and a continued interest in literacy instruction, and disability studies. Her research most often lies at the intersections of these fields with issues of equity, access and social justice.

Shaun Johnson is a former public elementary teacher in Washington, DC and currently a teacher educator (assistant professor of elementary education) at Towson University in Maryland. He also teaches elementary students each summer in a Washington, D.C. public charter school.

Shaun has published on social studies education, male teachers, and education reform for publications such as *Theory and Research in Social Education, Journal of Men's Studies*, and the *Journal of Education and Teaching*, respectively. More importantly, in the winter of 2010, Shaun founded a progressive education blog and radio show called *At the Chalk Face*. The website has expanded its authorship to include numerous education activists and the radio has expanded to broadcasts on mainstream airwaves out of Madison, Wisconsin. Shaun's advocacy for public education also includes contributions for *The Baltimore Sun, The Huffington Post, GOOD Magazine,* and *Inside Higher Education.*

After about a year of writing editorials and commentary online, Shaun joined a small group of educators from around the United States to form the public school activist organization, *United Opt Out National (UOO),* which focuses heavily on the destructive nature of scripted curricula, high-stakes standardized testing, and other hallmarks of neoliberal education reform. The group considers "opting out" of high-stakes testing to be the only strategy left to protest what it sees as the corruptible influences of privatization. With no sponsorship of any kind, UOO has created an extensive social media presence and organized the second of its *Occupy the US Department of Education* events for April 2013. A four-day event, *Occupy 2.0: The Battle for Public Schools* included guest speakers and teach-ins on the grounds of the USDE from public school activists nationwide, such as Diane Ravitch, Karen Lewis, Kevin Kumashiro, and Nancy Carlsson-Paige.

Lynda Kennedy is on the faculty of the Metropolitan College of New York as part of the Masters in Education program, and has served in leadership capacities in the education departments of many cultural organizations such as the Lower East Side Tenement Museum, the Museum of Moving Image and the New York Public Library. Her research interests have centered on collaborations between school, university and cultural institutions and teacher professional growth.

Cathy Leogrande has been a teacher educator for over twenty years at Le Moyne College in Syracuse, New York, one of 28 Jesuit colleges in the United States. A hallmark of Jesuit education is a focus on social justice, and Leogrande has promoted equity and opportunity throughout her career in the areas of teaching, service and scholarship. Her areas of interest include students with disabilities, adolescent development, and new literacies. She has been involved with a number of social action organizations in New York, including The Harry Potter Alliance, HOPE for Ariang, and The Q Center. In 2010, she received the Millennium Award from the Auburn-Cayuga branch of the NAACP. Her most recent work builds on the use of Web 2.0 technologies and social media to empower, provoke, critique and make the world a better place.

Jessica Nina Lester is an Assistant Professor in Educational Psychology at Washington State University. She holds a PhD in educational psychology and research from the University of Tennessee. Her research interests include qualitative methodologies, critical notions of human learning and development, and the educational experiences of targeted youth in educational settings.

Desiree R. Lindbom-Cho is a doctoral student at Louisiana State University. She has a BA in elementary education and English literature and a MEd in gifted education. She has taught general education and gifted education to elementary students in Minnesota and Louisiana in private and public school settings. She has also taught English at the middle and high school levels in an alternative setting in New Hampshire and in an urban school district in Louisiana. Her interests include critical issues in education and systems of education. Recently, he work was featured in *Parenting for High Potential* and *A Teacher's Guide to Working with Children and Families from Diverse Backgrounds*.

Timothy Lintner is Associate Professor of Social Studies Education at The University of South Carolina, Aiken.

Christine Brigid Malsbary received her PhD in Social Sciences and Comparative Education from the University of California at Los Angeles (UCLA) with a focus on Educational Anthropology. She holds a position as Assistant Professor in the College of Education at University of Hawaii, Manoa. She has worked in the field of Immigration and Education for over a decade as a high school teacher, teacher educator, and researcher. Most recently, Malsbary was the guest editor (with Carlos Alberto Torres) of a two-volume special issue entitled "International Migration and Social Justice Education" for *Encyclopaideia: Journal of Phenomenology and Education*, with contributions from Michael Apple, Marjorie Orellana, Stacey Lee and Robert Arnove, among others.

Malsbary's dissertation was on the sociocultural lives of recently arrived immigrant youth in a multiethnic high school. More specifically, in her dissertation she theorized "transcultural repertoires of practice," which developed out of her documentation of the comparative knowledges, resources and practices that immigrant youth from different cultures gained through the process of migration. Malsbary was recognized as making major contributions to the study of diversity by the University of Michigan's National Center for Institutional Diversity, and her dissertation was nominated for an outstanding dissertation award by the American Educational Research Association's Division G: Social Contexts and Education.

Malsbary maintains an active line of research and writing on issues of culture, identity, and power in ethnolinguistically diverse social landscapes. In addition to her scholarship, Malsbary established and directs a multiagency policy advisory group located in Hawaii. The group is currently working on university and state policy that supports more inclusive and compassionate education for immigrant children and youth, and language minorities in Hawaii's K–12 public schools.

Roland W. Mitchell is the Assistant Director of the School of Education in the College of Human Sciences and Education at Louisiana State University. He is an Associate Professor and CoDirector of the Curriculum Theory Project. He has a BA in History from Fisk University, a MEd in Higher Education from Vanderbilt University, and a PhD in Educational Research from The University of Alabama. His articles have appeared in *Urban Education, International Journal of Qualitative Studies in Education* and *The Review of Education Pedagogy and Cultural Studies.*

Jennifer Lee O'Donnell is a doctoral candidate in the Language, Literacy, and Culture concentration in the school of education at the University of Massachusetts, Amherst. Her dissertation research is an ethnographic study focusing on social movements in Buenos Aires, in which she is examining examples of critical pedagogies that emerge between teachers' activism practices and popular education classroom instruction. Her article, "The Indigenous, National, and International Language in Higher Education: Students' Academic Trajectories in Oaxaca, Mexico" was published in *The International Journal of Applied Linguistics* in 2010.

Laura Quaynor is an Assistant Professor of Curriculum and Instruction in the School of Education at the University of South Carolina–Aiken. She received her undergraduate and Master's degrees from the University of Virginia and completed a PhD in Educational Studies at Emory University. Her research interests include issues of equity and measurement in large-scale assessments as well as citizenship education for refugee students and students in transitional and postconflict states. Her work includes the following articles and chapters: "Citizenship Education in Postconflict Contexts: A Review of the Literature" in *Education, Citizenship, and Social Justice* (2012); "Becoming the Enemy? Schooling and Postcolonial Conceptions of Citizenship in the Akuapem region of Ghana" in *The African Symposium* (2012); "Providing a Global Education to Refugee Students" in *Social Studies and the Young Learner* (2012); and, "Gender and Civic Education" in the *SAGE Encyclopedia of Diversity and Education* (2012).

Karen Ragoonaden is a Senior Instructor, Professor of Teaching stream at the Faculty of Education of the University of British Columbia's Okanagan Campus. She has lived, studied and worked in North America, Europe and Africa. Her publications and research interests lie in the area of the Scholarship of Teaching and Learning, French Education, and Diversity Pedagogy. Her most recent articles focus on intercultural communication competence, critical pedagogy and self-study of teacher and teacher education practices. As a university teacher and researcher, her educational leadership has been recognized by virtue of her on campus and community work relating to equity, diversity and inclusion.

Rachel Roegman is a doctoral candidate at Teachers College, Columbia University in the Curriculum and Teaching Department. As a former middle school teacher in both traditional and alternative public schools, her research interests include educational equity and teacher education. She comes to education from a perspective of social justice and a desire to create public schools that serve all students well, regardless of race, gender, dis/ability, or ethnicity.

Gail Russell-Buffalo is a PhD student in English Education at Teachers College, Columbia University. She is a private consultant on cross-disciplinary literacy for secondary schools and an instructor of teacher research methods at City College of New York City.

Gregory D. Seaton serves as Associate Professor at the College of New Jersey in the Department of Education Administration and Secondary Education. He teaches courses for pre- and in-service teachers in educational psychology, adolescent learning and development, and research methods. His research is primarily focused on how teacher identity development impacts the development and academic achievement of minority youth, particularly black boys.

Seaton brings a unique blend of practical training experiences in urban schools and communities and a rigorous academic background. He has served as a youth outreach worker for the Orlando Housing Authority where he was responsible for job readiness and life skill training for public housing residents. Additionally, Seaton served as Executive Director for Teacher Education for America's Minorities (TEAM) at the University of Central Florida. As director, he recruited and trained minority teachers to provide high quality instruction in urban and poorly funded schools. Most recently, Seaton aided in the design, teaching, and evaluation of a four-year school-based health curriculum implemented throughout Philadelphia public high schools. Currently, Seaton is conducting a research-based intervention that examines the role of media in shaping the copping and emotional expression of boys.

Seaton has an EdM from Harvard University and a PhD in Educational Leadership and Human Development from the University of Pennsylvania.

Suniti Sharma is an Assistant Professor in the Department of Teacher Education at Saint Joseph's University, Philadelphia. She teaches literacy across the curriculum and methods courses for social studies and English language arts. Her research interests include literacy for at-risk youth and curriculum change, multicultural competencies for preservice teachers through international field experiences, and autoethnographic studies in identity, culture, and curriculum. She has published articles in *Race Ethnicity and Education, Issues in Teacher Education,* and *Teachers College Record.* She has co-authored chapters in *The Curriculum Studies Handbook—The Next Moment,* and *Handbook of Public Pedagogy: Education and Learning Beyond Schooling.* She is the author of *Girls Behind Bars: Reclaiming Education in Transformative Spaces.*

Nathaniel W. Smith earned his PhD from the University of Pennsylvania in 2000. He has since taught graduate education courses in a variety of areas for the University of Pennsylvania, Bryn Mawr, and The College of New Jersey. Most recently he left the university to teach high school full time in Taiwan. He continues to teach graduate education courses in a range of subjects for the College of New Jersey's Global Programs.

For well over a decade he dedicated himself to improving teacher education and education in the urban districts of Philadelphia. He participated in and conducted a host of professional development sessions for teachers there. In his current position, he has spearheaded an inquiry driven research project with fellow English teachers, looking specifically at modes of grammar instruction suited for ESL students abroad. He has also been involved in professional development sessions with local Taiwanese public school teachers regarding inquiry based pedagogies and assessments. He has published in *Anthropology and Education Quarterly, Radical Teacher,* and *Rethinking Schools.* Currently, he is working on a contribution to Greg Fried's *Mirror of Race* website, focused on teaching students about the social construction of race. Ultimately he will coauthor several pieces with fellow teachers engaging in their newly initiated inquiry project concerning the instruction of grammar for ESL students.

Nichole E. Stanford earned her doctorate from CUNY Graduate Center and is currently a writing consultant at CUNY Baruch College. She specializes in code meshing and translanguaging practices, focusing on the responsibilities of academics in "Publishing in the Contact Zone: Strategies from the Cajun Canaille" (2011). Stanford is currently writing from a critical pedagogical perspective about English composition education among Louisiana's speakers of Cajun Vernacular English.

Margaret-Mary Sulentic Dowell is Associate Professor of Literacy and Urban Education in the School of Education, College of Human Sciences and Education at Louisiana State University, Baton Rouge. Social issues figure prominently in her work as a scholar. In 2009, she was named editor of the *ejournal of Literacy and Social Responsibility*, the International Reading Association's, Literacy and Social Responsibility Special Interest Group publication. In 2007, she was awarded The Kenneth S. Goodman "In Defense of Good Teaching Award," which was established to honor professional educators who have stood up to laws, policies, and practices and recognizes an individual who has experienced economic or social consequences as a result of "standing up."

Sulentic Dowell is a member of the International Reading Association's Urban Diversity Committee (2010–2013) and served the association as a member of its Professional Standards and Ethics Committee (2008–2011); Intellectual Freedom Committee (1997–2000) and Gender Issues and Literacy Committee (1994–1995). She is also a member of the American Educational Research Association's Literacy and Social Processes SIG.

Sulentic Dowell's work related to social issues includes several book chapters: "Repositioning the Hook: (Re)committing to Equity Through Autoethnographic Exploration in *Unhooking from Whiteness: The Key to Dismantling Racism in the United States* (2013); "So What? Who Cares? And What's Our Point About Diversity?" In *Occupying The Academy: Just How Important is Diversity Work in Higher Education? Stories from the Frontlines* (2012); and "Preservice Teachers Explore Pedagogy & Service-Learning in a Place Called New Orleans East: Assumptions, Tensions, & Innovation in a Post-Katrina Charter School" in *Cultural Dynamics and Tensions within Service-learning* (2011). She is also author of several articles related to social issues: "Addressing the Complexities of Literacy and Urban Teaching in the United States: Strategic Professional Development as intervention in the *Teaching Education Journal* (2012); "Transformative Opportunities for Community Engagement within Teacher Education: Creating Opportunities for Preservice Teachers for Urban Environments in Post-Katrina New Orleans" in *Journal of Community Engagement and Higher Education* (2009); "Overcoming Overwhelmed and Reinventing Normal: A District Administrator's Account of Living in Hurricane Katrina's Aftermath" in *Journal of Education for Students Placed at Risk* (2008); and, "Academic-Service Learning as Pedagogy: An Approach to Preparing Preservice Teachers for Urban Environments" in *The Journal of Teaching and Learning* (2008).

Nancy Taber is an associate professor in the Faculty of Education at Brock University. Her research interests include an exploration of the ways in which gender and militarism are learned in daily life, women's experiences in western militaries, interconnections between military and academic discourses, and sociocultural issues in fiction and popular culture. A selection of her recent publications include: "Detectives, Bail Bond "Persons," and Fairy Tales: A Feminist Antimilitarist Analysis of Gender in *Grimm* and *Once Upon a Time*" (*Gender Forum: An Internet Journal for Gender Studies*, in press);

"A Composite Life History of a Mother in the Military: Storying Gendered Experiences" (*Women's Studies International Forum*, 2013); and "'You Better Not Get Pregnant While You're Here': Tensions Between Masculinities and Femininities in Military Communities of Practice" (*International Journal of Lifelong Education*, 2011). Taber's co-edited book, *Building on Critical Traditions: Adult Education and Learning in Canada* was published in 2013 by Thompson Publishing, and includes her chapter, "Learning War through Gender: Masculinities, Femininities, and Militarism."

Laura A. Valdiviezo is Assistant Professor of Language, Literacy and Culture at the University of Massachusetts–Amherst. She has published research on the ethnographic and multilevel analysis of policies of diversity (language diversity) in Peruvian Indigenous schools, among others. Some of her publications include: "'Don't You Want Your Child to Be Better Than You?': Enacting Ideologies and Contesting Intercultural Policy in Peru" in *Critical Approaches to Comparative Education: Vertical Case Studies from Africa, Europe, the Middle East, and the Americas* (Palgrave Macmillan, 2009); "Class-first Analysis in a Continuum: An Approach to the Complexities of Schools, Society, and Insurgent Science" in *Cultural Studies of Science Education* (2010). Valdiviezo has served as program chair and chair elect for the Bilingual Education Research Special Interest Group at the American Educational Research Association. Her work in public schools that serve culturally and linguistically diverse students involve issues of social justice and the reinterpretation of policy through pedagogy.

Winmar Way is a doctoral candidate in Social Sciences and Comparative Education at the University of California, Los Angeles (UCLA) Graduate School of Education and Information Studies. Her research undertakes a phenomenological study of citizenship, race and culture in formal and nonformal education, specifically investigating the experiences of students from refugee and immigrant backgrounds who have resettled in the United States. She is a member of the Paulo Freire Institute at UCLA.

Miguel Zavala is Assistant Professor in the Department of Secondary Education at California State University, Fullerton. His research centers on critical curriculum studies, decolonizing research methodologies, and grassroots organizing.

CPSIA information can be obtained
at www.ICGtesting.com
Printed in the USA
LVHW081509091221
705748LV00004B/100

9 781623 966287